Future Directions for the Demography of Aging

PROCEEDINGS OF A WORKSHOP

Mark D. Hayward and Malay K. Majmundar, *Editors*

Committee on Population

Division of Behavioral and Social Sciences and Education

The National Academies of
SCIENCES · ENGINEERING · MEDICINE

THE NATIONAL ACADEMIES PRESS
Washington, DC
www.nap.edu

THE NATIONAL ACADEMIES PRESS 500 Fifth Street, NW Washington, DC 20001

This activity was supported by contracts between the National Academy of Sciences and the National Institute on Aging of the National Institutes of Health (HHSN26300110). Any opinions, findings, conclusions, or recommendations expressed in this publication do not necessarily reflect the views of any organization or agency that provided support for the project.

International Standard Book Number-13: 978-0-309-47410-8
International Standard Book Number-10: 0-309-47410-8
Digital Object Identifier: https://doi.org/10.17226/25064

Additional copies of this publication are available for sale from the National Academies Press, 500 Fifth Street, NW, Keck 360, Washington, DC 20001; (800) 624-6242 or (202) 334-3313; http://www.nap.edu.

Suggested citation: National Academies of Sciences, Engineering, and Medicine. (2018). *Future Directions for the Demography of Aging: Proceedings of a Workshop.* Washington, DC: The National Academies Press. doi: https://doi.org/10.17226/25064.

Preface

Almost 25 years have passed since the *Demography of Aging* (1994) was published by the National Research Council. The volume was a major contribution that defined the contours of an emerging field. Nine major themes in the demography of aging were assessed by experts in the field. The themes were

1. Formal demography of population aging, transfers, and the economic cycle
2. Retirement and labor force behavior of the elderly
3. Income, wealth, and intergenerational economic relations of the aged
4. The elderly and their kin: patterns of availability and access
5. Care of the elderly: division of labor among the family, market, and state
6. Medical demography: interaction of disability dynamics and mortality
7. Socioeconomic differences in adult mortality and health status
8. Geographic concentration, migration, and population redistribution among the elderly
9. Research on the demography of aging in developing countries.

The original volume stimulated the interest of a new generation of population scientists. It provided the scientific foundations for new research collaborations and interdisciplinary approaches, the development of innovative data resources, and the forging of institutional partnerships—all of which contributed to rapid advancements in scientific knowledge and the scaling up of scientific questions.

The current volume is, in many ways, the successor to the original volume. The Division of Behavioral and Social Research at the National Institute on Aging (NIA) asked the National Academies of Sciences, Engineering, and Medicine, through its Committee on Population, to produce an authoritative guide to new directions in demography of aging. The Steering Committee for a Workshop on the Future Directions for the Demography of Aging was appointed by the National Academies to carry out this project. The papers published in this volume were originally presented and discussed at a public workshop held in Washington, D.C., August 17–18, 2017.

The workshop discussion made evident that major new advances had been made in the last two decades, but also that new trends and research directions have emerged that call for innovative conceptual, design, and measurement approaches. Changes in fertility, life expectancy, and population-age structure have had profound effects on the opportunities and constraints facing individuals, their families, and their communities. The older population has become more racially/ethnically diverse. Kin relationships have become more complex and fluid, and more people now approaching old age have been divorced and many have never been married. Population health now spans a web of health processes including biological risk, disability, cognition, and disease. The health and well-being of the older population are now seen as the consequences of long-run and cumulative effects of social, economic, and contextual factors over the entire life course.

The current volume reviews these recent trends and also discusses future directions for research on a range of topics that are central to current research in the demography of aging. For example, how is the older population changing in its racial/ethnic composition, and what is the role of nativity in shaping health and well-being? What are the major debates about how life course socioeconomic conditions influence health at older ages, and what are the major biological and behavioral pathways? What health problems are looming for future birth cohorts, and how is inequality in health shaping national trends? How are changes in life course exposures linked to cognitive aging and the future of dementia? How is disability associated with disease, the environment, and relationships? How does "place," defined at a variety of levels, influence health? How is the timing and nature of retirement changing, and how are changes in health interacting with retirement? How is the incorporation of new technologies and measures leading to a better understanding of aging? How is the growth of global data resources in aging changing our understanding of population aging both in developing and developed countries?

These questions represent only a subset of the rich array of issues taken up in this volume. Looking back over the past two decades of demography of aging research shows remarkable advances in our understanding of the health and well-being of the older population. Equally exciting is that this volume sets the stage for the next two decades of innovative research—a period of rapid growth in the older American population.

Many people have been responsible for the development and production of this volume. We gratefully acknowledge NIA for guidance and financial support. Special thanks also go to the members of the workshop steering committee: Vicki A. Freedman, Linda J. Waite, David R. Weir, and Rebeca Wong. They helped shape the contents of this volume by laying out the specific topics to be addressed; identifying leading scholars in the field to write papers on those topics; and providing valuable feedback to the paper authors before, during, and after the workshop.

Several staff members of the National Academies also made significant contributions to the volume. Mary Ghitelman ensured that the workshop ran smoothly, assisted in preparing the manuscript, and provided key logistical and administrative support throughout the project. Thanks are also due to Kirsten Sampson Snyder for managing the report review process, Yvonne Wise for managing the report production process, and Robert Katt for his skillful editing.

This Proceedings of a Workshop was reviewed in draft form by individuals chosen for their diverse perspectives and technical expertise. The purpose of this independent review is to provide candid and critical comments that will assist the National Academies in making each published proceedings as sound as possible and to ensure that it meets the institutional standards for quality, objectivity, evidence, and responsiveness to the charge. The review comments and draft manuscript remain confidential to protect the integrity of the process.

We thank the following individuals for their review of this proceedings: Jennifer Ailshire, Leonard Davis School of Gerontology, University of Southern California; Lisa F. Berkman, Harvard Center for Population and Development Studies, Harvard University; Gary Burtless, Economic Studies, Brookings Institution; William H. Dow, School of Public Health, University of California, Berkeley; Pamela Herd, Robert M. LaFollette School of Public Affairs, University of Wisconsin–Madison; Jennifer J. Manly, Gertrude H. Sergievsky Center and the Taub Institute for Research in Aging and Alzheimer's, Columbia University; Jennifer Karas Montez, Department of Sociology, Syracuse University; Fernando Riosmena, Population Program and Institute of Behavioral Science, University of Colorado Boulder; Robert F. Schoeni, Population Studies Center, Institute for Social Research, University of Michigan; Judith A. Seltzer, California Center for Population Research and Department of Sociology, University of California, Los Angeles; Cássio M. Turra, Demography Department, Universidade Federal de Minas Gerais; and Debra J. Umberson, Population Research Center, University of Texas at Austin.

Although the reviewers listed above provided many constructive comments and suggestions, they were not asked to endorse the content of the proceedings nor did they see the final draft before its release. The review of this proceedings was overseen by Kirsten Sampson Snyder, Reports Office, Division of Behavioral and Social Sciences and Education. She was responsible for making certain that an independent examination of this proceedings was carried out in accordance with standards of the National Academies and that all review comments were carefully considered. Responsibility for the final content rests entirely with the authors and the National Academies.

Mark D. Hayward, *Chair*
Malay K. Majmundar, *Study Director*
Steering Committee for a Workshop on the
Future Directions for the Demography of Aging

Contents

PART I

Health Trends and Disparities

1

Trends in Mortality, Disease, and Physiological Status in the Older Population

Eileen Crimmins

INTRODUCTION

Mortality and health trends in the last two to three decades relevant to the older population are the focus of this chapter. The emphasis is on research reporting trends relevant to the older population since 1980 in mortality, disease prevalence and incidence, and underlying physiological status. Trends in disability and functioning are treated in the chapter by V. Freedman.

In recent years there have been a number of disquieting trends, along with some positive changes, in mortality, life expectancy, disease presence, and physiological status in the United States. This chapter discusses those trends and how they might be explained both more narrowly in terms of proximate causes and more broadly by changes in American society. Most of the research on national trends reports trends in averages for the population or for significant subgroups of the population. In addition, this chapter highlights new theoretical approaches and data that are now becoming available for the study of mortality and health in aging individuals and that are likely to be increasingly incorporated into mortality and health outcome research in the coming decade. These approaches are aimed at explaining variability in individual aging at a more basic biological level; our belief is that future research on mortality risk and health change among aging individuals is likely to increasingly incorporate these mechanisms in the coming decades to explain differences among subgroups and changes over time.

RECENT TRENDS IN MORTALITY

Life expectancy continues to increase in the United States but at different rates for Black and White men and women (see Figure 1-1). Increases from 1980 to 2013 were relatively slow for White women, rising from 78.1 years to 81.4 years for an increase of 3.3 years over the 33-year period, or 1.2 months per year (Figure 1-1). For Black women, life expectancy increased from 72.5 years to 78.4 years, for an increase of 5.9 years over 33 years or 2.1 months per year. This was very similar to the increase among White men, from 70.7 years to 76.7, an increase of 6.0 years or 2.2 months per year. The greatest increase was experienced by Black men, rising from 63.8 years to 72.3 years, an increase of 8.5 years over the period or 3.1 months per year. So among these four population subgroups, White women have had the slowest increase in mortality over this period.

Whereas life expectancy for the general population had been increasing fairly steadily over recent decades, the last 2 years have seen a change. In December 2017, the Centers for Disease Control and Prevention reported a slight decline in life expectancy (0.1 year) for 2016, which followed a similar decline from 2014 to 2015 (Kochanek et al., 2017).

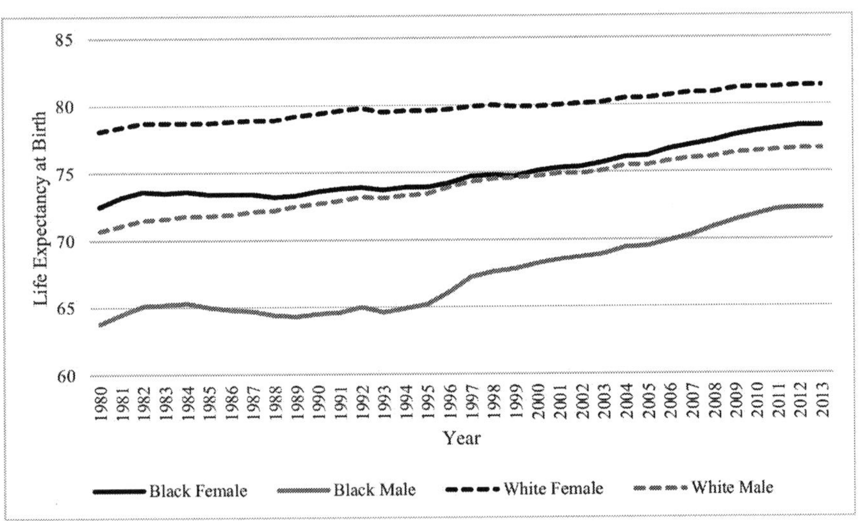

FIGURE 1-1 Mortality trends: U.S. life expectancy at birth, 1980–2013.
SOURCE: Chong et al. (2015).

Changing Differentials in Life Expectancy in the United States

Changes in mortality differentials between population subgroups have been substantial in recent years. The differential changes in life expectancy reported above result in narrower differences by gender and race at the end of the 33-year period shown in Figure 1-1. The difference in life expectancy at birth between White men and women declined from 7.4 years longer lives for women in 1980 to 4.7 years in 2013; for Black men and women, the greater life expectancy of females decreased from 8.7 to 6.1 years. As indicated above, life expectancy continued to increase for both Black and White women between 1980 and 2013, but for White women life expectancy increased only 1.2 months a year, while for Black men it increased 3.1 months a year. This resulted in reductions between 1980 and 2013 in life expectancy differentials by race at birth from 5.6 to 3.0 years for White versus Black women and from 6.9 to 4.4 years for White versus Black men—reductions over the 33 years of 46 percent for women and 36 percent for men. Results continue to confirm that Hispanic mortality is lower than African American mortality and fairly comparable to that of non-Hispanic Whites (Hummer and Hayward, 2015).

There is significant evidence that differentials in life expectancy by socioeconomic status (SES) have gotten wider in recent years (Olshansky et al., 2012). Meara et al. (2008) noted that the SES gap, as indicated by educational differentials, increased by about 30 percent between 1980 and 2001; this gap has continued to grow through 2010 (Sasson, 2016a, 2016b). Hayward and colleagues suggested that the shape of the association between educational attainment and U.S. adult life expectancy has changed over time, with mortality decline being concentrated among the most highly educated (Hayward et al., 2015; Montez et al., 2012).

Mortality trends by education have differed by gender. Mortality decline has occurred among men at almost all educational levels since 1980, but among women mortality has only declined for the highly educated. For women without a high school education, mortality actually increased during some periods (Montez et al., 2011; Sasson, 2016a). Figure 1-2 shows changes in life expectancy for four educational groups and four race-by-gender groups over a 20-year period. While a decrease in life expectancy only occurred among White women in the lowest educational group, in each of the other three educational groups White women experienced the smallest increases. On the other hand, the increases in life expectancy were substantial among all educational groups for Black men, although there was an increasing educational differential with increase in educational level even for Black men. Adding to the evidence of increasing life expectancy differentials by increasing SES, Chetty et al. (2016) have provided analysis by income levels that shows that higher income was associated with

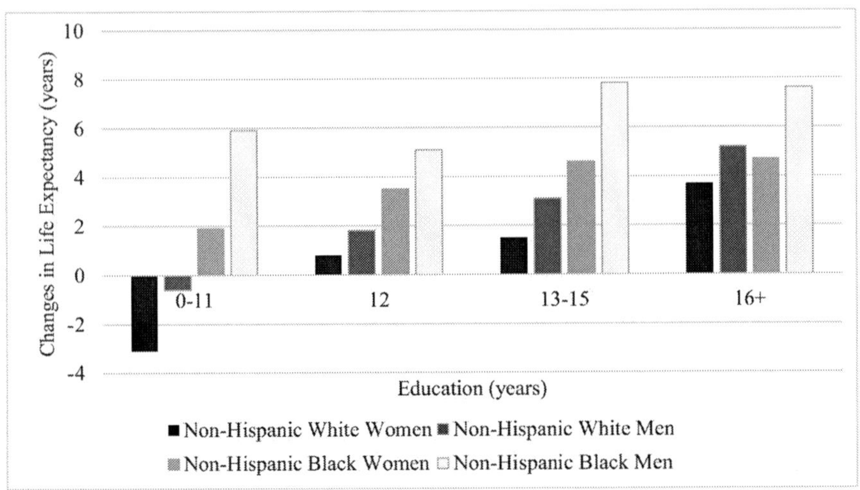

FIGURE 1-2 Change in life expectancy at age 25, by education, 1990–2010.
SOURCE: Data from Sasson (2016b).

greater longevity and that the differences in life expectancy across income groups increased from 2000 to 2014. Whereas different authors provide different estimates of the changes in life expectancy by SES group, there is no disagreement on the fact that life expectancy differentials by SES have increased in recent decades (Bound et al., 2015; Montez et al., 2016a).

Another recent focus of research on mortality in the United States has been on geographic differentials in life expectancy; this research has produced evidence of large spatial differentials across the country, as well as varying patterns of changes in these differentials. Murray et al. (2006) described life expectancy differentials in what they called "eight Americas": eight groups of counties divided by location, density, race, income, and homicide rate. They found life expectancy differences that ranged up to 35 years across these groups and reported that between 1982 and 2001, the ordering of life expectancy among the eight Americas and the absolute difference between the advantaged and disadvantaged groups remained largely unchanged (Murray et al., 2006). Ezzati et al. (2008) pointed out that in many counties mortality actually increased for some groups during the last two decades of the 20th century. Chetty et al. (2016) examined state differences and changes in life expectancy and reported that for individuals with low incomes, life expectancy was lowest in Indiana, Nevada, and Oklahoma and highest in California, New York, and Vermont. They also reported, "the gap in life expectancy between the lowest and highest income quartiles decreased in some areas, such as areas within New Jersey and Alabama, but increased by more than 3 years in other areas, such as areas within Florida" (Chetty et al., 2016, p. 20).

Explanations for Trends and Changing Differentials

Explanations for differences and trends in life expectancy can be done at many levels. There are proximate explanations in terms of composition, such as changing age patterns and causes of death—that is, which causes are increasing or decreasing. There are explanations in terms of changes or differences in risk factors for disease or death, such as smoking or obesity. Differences in health care availability and treatment offer another explanation. Then, there are larger-level policy-related factors and fundamental social causes, which may provide an even more upstream level of explanation (Woolf and Braveman, 2011).

Deaths from misuse of opioids have been noted as an increasingly important factor influencing the overall trend in life expectancy, especially for the White population (Case and Deaton, 2015; Ho, 2017). Ho (2017) has shown that mortality from drug overdose increased for men and women in all education groups, but more so for those with low education, and more so for non-Hispanic Whites. Her assessment is that mortality from drug overdose accounts for a sizable proportion of the increases in educational gradients in life expectancy, particularly at the prime adult ages (ages 30–60), where she estimates it accounts for 25 to 100 percent of the widening in educational gradients between 1992 and 2011 (Ho, 2017). The fact that opioid deaths occur at relatively young adult ages has been an important factor in overall life expectancy trends. The very recent decrease in life expectancy for the general population appears to reflect adverse changes in most of the major causes of mortality but with women experiencing more deterioration due to chronic diseases than men (Acciai and Firebaugh, 2017).

The decrease in the life expectancy differential by race can be attributed to the relative rate of decrease in mortality from homicide, HIV, unintentional injuries, diabetes, and heart disease (Harper et al., 2007, 2014). In recent years, the greater increase among Whites than Blacks in deaths from unintentional poisonings including drugs has reduced the race differential (Harper et al., 2012).

Meara et al. (2008) and Sasson (2016b) have emphasized a role for changes in smoking behavior as an explanation for the growing inequality by SES. Ho and Fenelon (2015) estimated that smoking accounts for half of the increase in the mortality gap by education between the 1980s and 2006 for White women but does not explain the increasing gap for White men. Smoking behavior is important in the relatively low mortality of Hispanics (Lariscy et al., 2015). Montez and Zajacova (2013a) have also associated smoking and other behaviors to the poor trends among low-education women.

Race differences in life expectancy and mortality are generally assumed to primarily reflect SES composition of the population. A recent estimate is that socioeconomic and demographic characteristics account for 80 percent of the gap in life expectancy between Black and White males and 70 percent of the gap between Black and White females (Geruso, 2012). Recent work has suggested that better specification of SES might result in even fuller explanation (Do et al., 2012). In the case of Hispanics, the relatively low mortality of Hispanics tends to be confined to those of lower SES (Turra and Goldman, 2007) and the important compositional factor is that a large number are foreign born (Lariscy et al., 2015).

Avendano and Kawachi (2014) have noted that life expectancy is particularly low for regions in the U.S. South and Midwest. Examination of county differences in death rates by cause has found that regions differ in the causes of relatively high mortality. Cardiovascular-related mortality is higher among counties that border the southern half of the Mississippi River. Mortality rates from self-harm and violence were higher in counties in the Southwest, and mortality rates from chronic respiratory disease were highest in counties in eastern Kentucky and western West Virginia (Dwyer-Lindgren et al., 2016). Chetty et al. (2016) reported that most of the variation in life expectancy across geographic areas was related to differences in health behaviors, including smoking, obesity, and exercise. In examining county-level changes in mortality up to 2000, Ezzati et al. (2008) ascribed increases in county-level female mortality to increases in chronic diseases related to smoking, overweight and obesity, and high blood pressure.

Researchers who have examined a variety of differentials and trends return to fundamental social causes as the underlying explanation for multiple differentials and trends (Phelan and Link, 2015). Montez and colleagues examined trends by gender and differences by state and concluded that these patterns resulted from more fundamental social issues such as the lack of good paying jobs for women with limited education and the lack of cohesion resulting from an adverse policy environment (Montez and Zajacova, 2013a, 2013b; Montez et al., 2016b). Murray et al. (2006) concluded that county-level differences in life expectancy are not fully explained by race, income, or basic health care access and utilization, and they suggested broader underlying causes. Phelan and Link (2015) suggested that racism is a fundamental cause of the persistent difference in life expectancy between Blacks and Whites.

Trends in U.S. Life Expectancy Relative to Other Countries

There has also been significant research in recent years on how mortality rates and life expectancies in the United States compare to those of other countries (Crimmins et al., 2010a; National Research Council, 2011). This stream of work has tried to gain perspective on why the United States has the levels and trends in mortality that have been observed. The poor performance of the United States relative to peer countries has been noted in two National Research Council and Institute of Medicine studies (National Research Council, 2011; Institute of Medicine and National Research Council, 2013). The focus of the first study was the population age 50 and older; the focus of the second was on younger ages. Figure 1-3 extends and expands the comparisons shown in those studies to show the relative trend in life expectancy at birth from 1980 to 2015 for the 40 countries in the world with the highest life expectancy in 2015. The dark dashed line in the figure shows the continued relative decline of life expectancy in the United States relative to the other 39 countries. The United States falls from ranking 20th in 1980 to ranking 40th in 2015. The countries ranking from 30 to 39 in 2015 included Bermuda, the Channel Islands, Cyprus, Lebanon, Costa Rica, Puerto Rico, Cuba, Czech Republic, Brunei, and

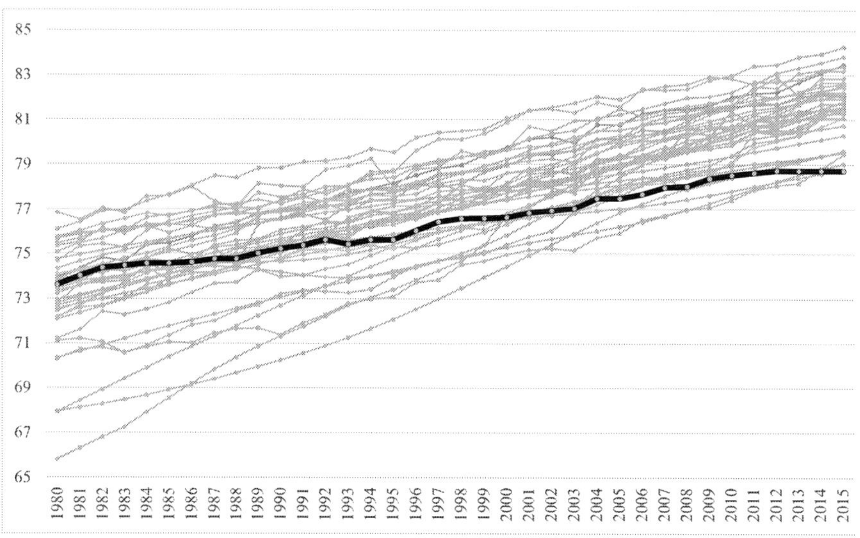

FIGURE 1-3 Life expectancy at birth between 1980 and 2015, by country; the United States ranked 20th in 1980 and 40th in 2015.
SOURCE: The World Bank Life Expectancy at Birth. Available: https://data.world-bank.org/indicator/SP.DYN.LE00.IN [April 2018].

Qatar. In 1980, most of these countries had lower life expectancies than the United States.

The poor performance of the United States in life expectancy is due to many conditions and diseases (Crimmins et al., 2010a; Glei et al., 2010; Institute of Medicine and National Research Council, 2013). It is worse at younger than older ages (Ho and Preston, 2010; Ho, 2013) and is not explained by racial/ethnic differences, as it characterizes the non-Hispanic White population as well as the general population (National Research Council, 2011). Potential explanations examined include individual behaviors, social integration and inequality, health care availability, environmental factors, policies, and social values (National Research Council, 2011; Institute of Medicine and National Research Council, 2013). Explanations differ markedly by age. For the older population, individual behaviors were a major contributor to the overall pattern and health care availability was not as important. Cohort patterns of both smoking and obesity play a major role in explaining the relative position of the U.S. older population (National Research Council, 2011; Preston and Stokes, 2011). For the population under age 50, the causes for the higher U.S. mortality are many, and they differ by age. They include infant and childhood conditions, accidents, chronic conditions, and violent deaths, particularly violent deaths related to firearms. At another level of explanation, causation is related to SES and the relatively large effect on mortality of low SES in the United States. Most analyses have concluded that the focus on immediate causes may not be appropriate for differentials that characterize most ages, many causes, and most social groups (Institute of Medicine and National Research Council, 2013; Avendano and Kawachi, 2014). Fundamental social and policy causes may be implicated (Link and Phelan, 1995).

RECENT TRENDS IN OTHER DIMENSIONS OF HEALTH

Changes in population health over the past century are more difficult to characterize succinctly than changes in life span. First of all, health has many dimensions, which do not necessarily change in the same way over time and which are not related to mortality change in the same way (Crimmins et al., 2010b). Crimmins and colleagues have characterized the morbidity process for populations as health change related to aging that begins with the physiological dysregulation indicated by a number of biological risk factors, which is followed by subsequent diagnosis of diseases, loss of functioning and disability, frailty, and death (Crimmins et al., 2010b). This section discusses recent trends in disease prevalence and incidence, as well as changes in physiological status associated with the beginning of the process of morbidity progression. These data are less available than those for mortality, and the varying availability of data results in differences in timing of the trends and ages considered. The chapter by Freedman in this volume discusses trends in disability, functioning, and frailty—the later stages in morbidity progression.

The prevalence of some diseases has declined in the older population in recent decades. For instance, fewer persons have bronchitis and emphysema; reductions in smoking are assumed to be the cause. On the other hand, the prevalence of diabetes has been increasing steadily since before the 1980s. This trend reflects improved survival among diabetics, as well as increased incidence due to increasing numbers of overweight persons. The prevalence of certain other chronic diseases—cancer, heart disease, and stroke—has also increased from the 1970s through the 1990s (Crimmins, 2015a). This may in part reflect improved diagnosis, but it certainly reflects increased survival among those who have the conditions (Crimmins and Saito, 2000). As we make progress in defeating mortality by delaying death among those who have disease, the prevalence of disease increases in the population. Trends in this century indicate that the prevalence of heart disease and stroke may have declined somewhat after 2000, whereas cancer and diabetes prevalences continue to increase (see Figure 1-4).

Trends in incidence are better indicators than prevalence trends of the current health changes in the population, but data on incidence of health change are not as available. Since 2000, incidence of heart disease and stroke may be beginning to decline, which would explain part of the change

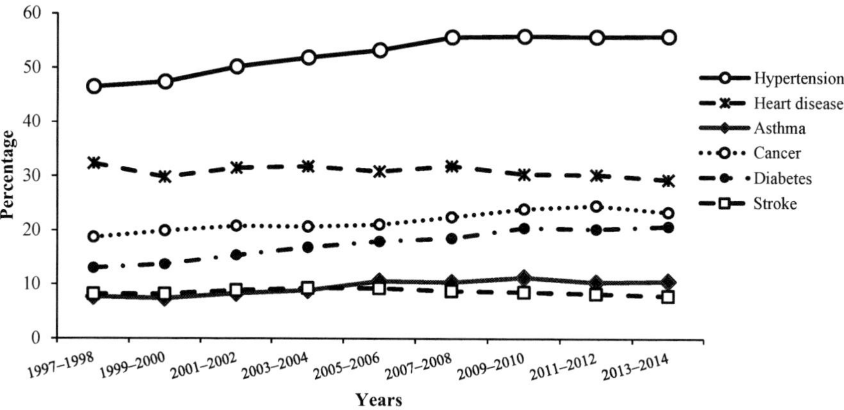

FIGURE 1-4 Percentage of people aged 65 and older who reported having selected chronic health conditions, 1997–1998 through 2013–2014.
SOURCE: Centers for Disease Control and Prevention. *Health, United States, 2015* (Tbl. 17b). Available: https://www.cdc.gov/nchs/data/hus/hus15.pdf [February 2018].

in prevalence. This has been reported from recent trends in incidence of acute myocardial infarction, which indicate that the increasing trend in incidence may have ended around 1990, followed by a period of stability up to 2000, after which there have been marked reductions of 20 to 40 percent (Chen et al., 2010; Rosamond et al., 2012; Talbott et al., 2013; Wang et al., 2012; Yeh et al., 2010). Stroke incidence, indicated by hospitalizations, is also reported to have peaked around 1997 for those age 65 and older and to have now declined somewhat (Fang et al., 2014). Examination of disease onset in two cohorts in the Health and Retirement Study (HRS) showed that those born from 1943 to 1953 experienced a lower rate of heart attack than those who were born in 1931–1941; however, the rates of overall heart disease and stroke did not appear to differ (Crimmins and Levine, 2015). It is possible that we are beginning to see the beginning of reductions in incidence in some conditions that could reflect improvement in innate health of older persons, but more data over a longer period and for the whole country are needed to make this a general conclusion.

The onset of a number of diseases important in old age increase exponentially with age, including the diseases discussed above (St. Sauver et al., 2015). Exponential increase is also a characteristic of loss of physical and cognitive functioning. This has led to growing recognition that aging is a process that often involves multimorbidity and to a belief that the explanations of disease increase and deterioration in functional aging may be common across outcomes (Kennedy et al., 2014). Two-thirds of older persons in the United States have two or more chronic diseases; for those over 85 the fraction is more than 80 percent (Espeland et al., 2017; Salive, 2013). Multimorbidity is more common among those of lower education, those who have experienced financial hardship as a child, and African Americans (Tucker-Seeley et al., 2011; St. Sauver et al., 2015). This might lead to an expectation of different outcomes for any one disease for these groups who differ in overall disease burden. Multimorbidity is also more prevalent in the United States than in other countries (Crimmins et al., 2010a). The incorporation of multimorbidity into research reflects advances in empirical clarity, theoretical developments, and interventional potentials.

TRENDS IN PHYSIOLOGICAL STATUS

Physiological deterioration and dysregulation is an upstream aspect of health that may precede disease diagnosis and mortality and may indicate a stage for initial medical or behavioral intervention in order to delay the progression to morbidity and mortality. Physiological dysregulation has been indicated by markers of the functioning of many systems and organs. Since cardiovascular diseases are among the most important sources of mortality and morbidity, we first examine trends in two markers of car-

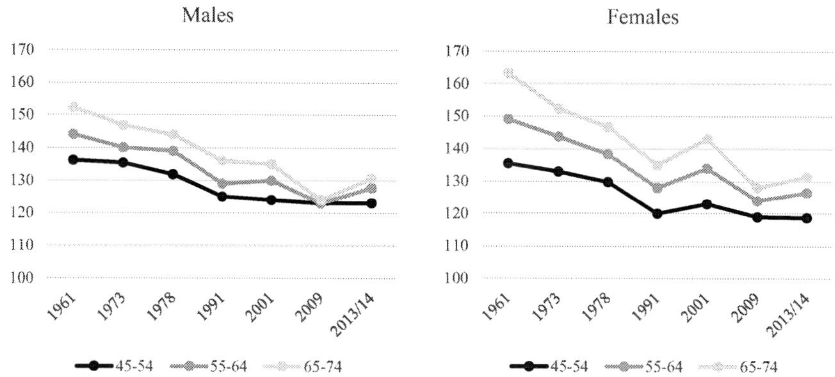

FIGURE 1-5 Mean systolic blood pressure for people ages 50 and older: 1961–2014. SOURCES: Kumanyika et al. (1998): 1960–1980; National Health and Nutrition Examination Survey: 1998–1994, 1999–2002, 2007–2010, 2013–2014.

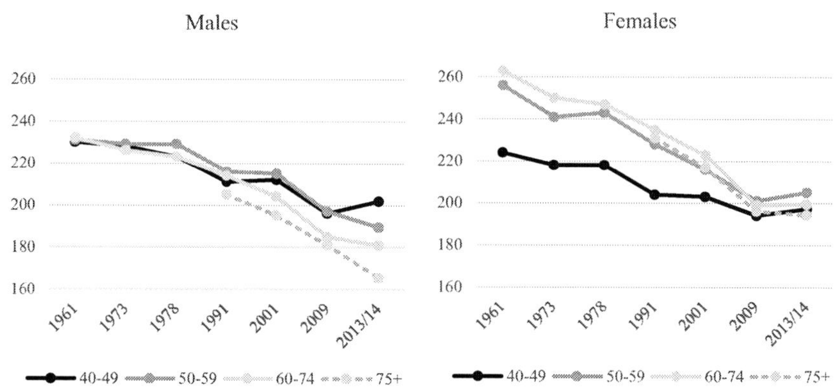

FIGURE 1-6 Mean total cholesterol for people ages 50 and older: 1961–2014. SOURCES: Carroll et al. (2005): 1960–1978; National Health and Nutrition Examination Survey: 1998–1994, 1999–2002, 2007–2010, 2013–2014.

diovascular health: blood pressure and cholesterol. We present trends over the longest period we can, more than 60 years, because the consistent pattern of change over this long period indicates that these are very long-term trends. As shown in Figures 1-5 and 1-6, for almost 60 years the United States has experienced remarkable declines in measured blood pressure and cholesterol (Crimmins et al., 2010a; Crimmins, 2015a; Ong et al., 2013). The use of effective antihypertensives and statins has reached high levels and is one of the major reasons for the current low levels of hypertension and high cholesterol (Crimmins, 2015a). However, dietary changes, reduced smoking, and perhaps improved early-life development and healthier lives may have also played a role in these declines (Finch and Crimmins, 2004).

While prevalences of high blood pressure and elevated cholesterol have become lower over time, obesity has increased (Alley et al., 2010). There is also some evidence of increase in adverse levels of biomarkers related to obesity and diabetes, such as plasma glucose (Beltrán-Sánchez et al., 2013).

In attempting to summarize change over time in physiological status, researchers have examined summary indicators. The change over time in the average number of cardiovascular-metabolic measures for three dates, spanning almost 20 years from about 1990 to 2010, shows that the average number of risk factors measured at clinically defined high-risk levels has been reduced in the past two decades for ages above 50 years (Crimmins, 2015a). Other researchers have reported small reductions in the prevalence of metabolic syndrome, which includes a set of biomarkers related to metabolism, in the most recent decade (Beltrán-Sánchez et al., 2013). In addition, a recent study of change from around 1990 to 2010 in "biological age" based on eight indicators of physiology has shown that at a given chronological age "biological age" has been reduced, with the largest reductions in the oldest age group (Levine and Crimmins, 2018).

NEW APPROACHES TO INCORPORATING PHYSIOLOGICAL STATUS AND EPIGENETIC MARKERS IN MODELS OF AGING HEALTH OUTCOMES

The discussion above of population health trends has demonstrated the use of population-level data to portray a picture of health differences and trends in the U.S. general population or in subgroups of that population. This work tends to focus on change in the mean or prevalence in the population. However, much of the research effort in recent years reflects a focus on individual "aging" or health changes with age, where the aim is to predict variability in who "ages" later and who "ages" at an earlier chronological age. This work follows individuals over time as they age and links prior risk factors and life circumstances thought to affect the process of aging health change with subsequent health outcomes. Over recent decades the empirical models of individual health change indicating the factors affecting the level of risk have incorporated variables from multiple domains, becoming increasingly multidisciplinary, with increasing explanatory power (Crimmins and Seeman, 2004; Institute of Medicine and National Research Council, 2013). Most of the population differentials discussed above would be included in a list of social and demographic variables that influence health, but a full explanatory model for most researchers would now also include economic, psychological, policy, and context variables as mediating or moderating variables. In addition, the last two decades have seen much greater incorporation of the biological pathways that explain how social variables "get under the skin" to affect age-related downstream health outcomes such as disease, disability and functioning loss, and death. Figure 1-7 is a heuristic model that includes a selection of the independent variables that represent social, economic, psychological, and policy influences and the growing biological mechanisms posited as being mechanisms that influence "aging." This model is presented to illustrate the typical multidisciplinary model that is tested in studies of individual aging. This section focuses on the growing interest in the biological mechanisms intervening between social factors and health outcomes, as these mediators are thought to clarify the biological pathways that explain why health changes with age.

An interest in summarizing biological risk, such as the measures mentioned above in summarizing recent change in physiological status, initially developed as a way of incorporating multiple physiological and sometimes behavioral risk factors into a succinct indicator of relative risk for spe-

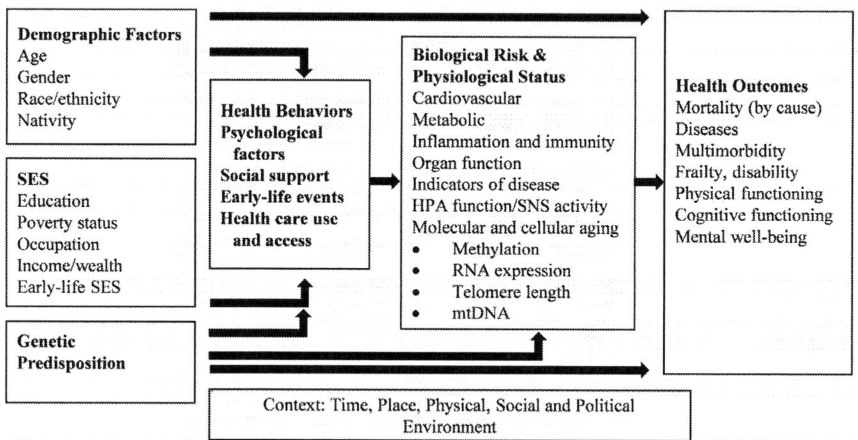

FIGURE 1-7 Multidisciplinary model for examining individual trajectories of health with aging.
NOTES: Demographic, socioeconomic status earlier in life, and genetic factors are determined prior to health behaviors, psychological factors, current social support, health care use and access. Biological risk and physiological status represent the biological pathways through which the prior variables affect health outcomes.

TABLE 1-1 Summary Indicators of Physiological Dysregulation and Molecular and Cellular Changes with Age

Multisystem-Variable Physiological Dysregulation with Age	Framingham risk score (Wilson et al., 1998)
	Allostatic load (Seeman et al., 1997)
	Biological age (Levine, 2013)
	Pace of aging (Belsky et al., 2015)
	Age-related homeostatic dysregulation (Cohen et al., 2015)
Molecular and Cellular Changes with Age	Telomere length (Blackburn et al., 2006)
	Biological clock–DNA methylation (Horvath, 2013; Hannum et al., 2013; Weidner et al., 2014)
	Gene expression–RNA (Holly et al., 2013; Peters et al., 2015)
	Proteomics (Menni et al., 2015)
	Metabolomics (Menni et al., 2015; Hertel et al., 2016)

cific health outcomes. This began with the Framingham risk score, which developed an indicator of the 10-year likelihood of having a cardiac event (Wilson et al., 1998) based on both behaviors and clinical indicators of cardiovascular risk (see Table 1-1). Expanding on this approach, Seeman et al. (1997) developed an indicator of allostatic load that reflected the growing belief that multiple systems contribute to the overall level of physiological dysregulation that characterizes aging; this indicator included cardiovascular, metabolic, neuroendocrine, and inflammatory markers of risk. The allostatic load concept emphasized that small changes in a number of systems could result in adverse health outcomes. It also recognized that the challenges to homeostasis increase with age and with deterioration of physiology. Allostatic load has been linked to a number of subsequent health outcomes including loss of functioning ability, cognitive loss, disease, and mortality (Seeman et al., 2001), as well as being associated with SES and race (Geronimus et al., 2006).

The last decade has seen exponential growth in the number of population studies including biological or physiological measures, as well growth in the type of markers included. Many studies now include the individual measures discussed above—for example, blood pressure, cholesterol, measured glucose levels, obesity, and/or inflammation. But a far greater number of indicators are now available in many national and population-representative studies. Recent research has compared the value of these measures in predicting health outcomes to the predictive value of more standard measures and to the value of behavioral and psychological measures (Cornman et al., 2017; Goldman et al., 2016; McClintock et al., 2016). Cross-national research has also demonstrated that biological measures are context specific and not universal across aging populations (Crimmins, 2015b; Rehkopf et al., 2016).

The increase in measures has encouraged continued refinement and development of summary indicators of physiological aging. Gruenewald et al. (2006) have used a more sophisticated recursive partitioning approach, along with novel markers of aging, in defining the risk of allostatic load. Levine (2013) introduced a measure of biological age based on values of a set of 10 markers of physiological regulation of multiple systems and organs. This measure, which has the desirable characteristic of being in units of age (years), has been shown to change over time (Levine and Crimmins, 2018), to be related to social and behavioral factors, and to partly explain race differences in mortality (Levine and Crimmins, 2014). Using a somewhat similar but expanded approach, Belsky et al. (2015) developed a measure they call "pace of aging," which has been related to relevant health outcomes and change in those outcomes—for a middle-aged population. Cohen et al. (2015) represent another approach; they combined 43 indicators into a measure they called "age-related homeostatic dysregulation." Belsky et al. (2015) compared "biological age," the "pace of aging," and "age-related homeostatic dysregulation" in the Dunedin, New Zealand, middle-aged population and found that these measures have a correlation of 0.4–0.6, which indicates they are related but not the same measure.

The last few years have brought the development of measures of biological aging at the molecular and cellular level (see lower half of Table 1-1). Telomere length has been suggested as a summary measure of biological aging and could reflect all of the types of systems in the physiological measures (Blackburn et al., 2006). In practice, telomere length has been inconsistently related to outcomes of aging (Blackburn et al., 2015; Glei et al., 2016; Mather et al., 2011). The National Institute on Aging and the National Institute of Environmental Health Sciences recently held a workshop to try to understand some of the confusion surrounding telomere work in populations (National Institutes of Health, 2017).

Summary measures built with molecular and cellular markers could reflect change that is prior to some of the physiological and clinical measures contained in the above physiological measures. This would include epigenetic markers of DNA methylation as well as RNA expression. To date, three "biological clocks" have been defined, based on DNA methylation (Horvath, 2013; Hannum et al., 2013; Weidner et al., 2014). These clocks are based on different numbers of largely overlapping markers, and their values are related to each other in the study of the middle-aged population in Dunedin, New Zealand (Belsky et al., 2017) and generally indicate whether someone is aging more rapidly or slowly than his/her chronological cohort. Belsky et al. (2017) compared these three measures and again found modest correlation. They also found low correlation between these measures and both the physiology-based measures and telomere length. In addition, the statistical correlations with health outcomes in middle age of all measures were relatively modest. Additional summary measures based on RNA expression, proteomics, and metabolomics have been proposed even more recently (Table 1-1). Jylhävä et al. (2017), in a review of existing literature, compared the links between mortality and the "biological age" measure, the "biological clock" measure, the measure based on metabolomics, and telomere length. They concluded that mortality appears best predicted by the "biological age" and "biological clock" constructs and was not well predicted by telomere length. Continued refinement of measures of this type, and development of data and links between health outcomes and DNA methylation, RNA expression, proteomics, and metabolomics, are likely to be extensive in the coming decade.

INTEGRATING GENETIC RISK INTO RESEARCH ON HEALTH AND AGING

Not mentioned as yet in this discussion is the recent expansion of research on the role of DNA in affecting health outcomes of older populations. This role is indicated in Figure 1-7 as "Genetic Predisposition." The growth of DNA-based data on large populations in this century offers new approaches to determining how innate genetic characteristics both directly affect aging health and interact with the environment and behaviors of individuals. The technological developments that have allowed large-scale throughput of DNA samples have resulted in data with information on millions of single-nucleotide polymorphisms for millions of people. While this progress builds on research over many years using twin and familial samples, it also offers a new approach to determining genetic effects on health and aging. Unlike the RNA-based measures and the DNA methylation measures discussed above, these genetic characteristics are fixed and not changed by environments.

Large population studies have been used to determine genetic markers for a number of risk factors for health outcomes such as body mass index (Locke et al., 2015) but also socioeconomic risk factors such as educational attainment (Rietveld et al., 2013; Okbay et al., 2016). Much work has used large agglomerations of data to produce megasamples, which can be used to discover genes related to health outcomes such as longevity (Broer et al., 2015), Alzheimer's disease (Lambert et al., 2013), and cognitive ability (Kirkpatrick et al., 2014). Social scientists have used the data to investigate how genetic characteristics might change over time in the population, how life cycle–social influences interact with time trends in behaviors as well as with the genome to affect health, and how genetic characteristics of social networks can influence health outcomes (Conley et al., 2016; Domingue et al., 2018; Liu and Guo, 2015). A significant amount of work is now ongoing to investigate heterogeneous genetic risk in populations that could be related to differential effects of adverse social events and circumstances (Domingue et al., 2017). The genomic links with the downstream biomarkers discussed above will increasingly be integrated into investigations of aging health and longevity (Deelen et al., 2013).

Social scientists have benefited from the development of polygenic risk scores (PRSs): scores built to reflect the influence of many individual genes that affect complex health outcomes (Belsky and Israel, 2014; Dudbridge, 2013). These scores are quite complex to define initially, as they tend to be based on large samples and investigate millions of genetic markers, but once determined, they provide a fairly easy way for social scientists to integrate genetics into analyses. Large population studies such as HRS are providing already-derived PRSs for complex traits to data users. These have the additional characteristic of not being highly restricted data, since they do not identify individuals as do the raw DNA data. As an example, we have used the PRSs provided by HRS to demonstrate that there are statistically significant relationships between the PRS for a number of outcomes and the gender, education, and age of individuals in the HRS sample (see Table 1-2).

TABLE 1-2 Significant Differences in Polygenic Risk Scores in White Health and Retirement Study Sample by Sex, Education, and Age

	Female/male	Education[a]	Age[b]
Alzheimer's Disease			
General Cognition		High	
Body Mass Index		Low	Younger
Waist Circumference		Low	
Waist-to-Hip Ratio			
Height		High	Older
Mean Arterial Pressure			
Educational Attainment		High	Older
Ever Smoker		Low	Younger
Depressive Symptoms		Low	
Major Depressive Disorder		Low	
Neuroticism		Low	
Schizophrenia	+Female	Low	
Subjective Well-being			

[a]High = education $\geq$ 12 years; Low = education $\leq$ 11 years.
[b]Younger = polygenic risk scores are higher for younger people; Older = polygenic risk scores are higher for older people.

These associations merely indicate that genetic risk is associated in a given direction with the characteristic; causation is not implied. There are almost no associations between the PRSs in HRS and gender; only the PRS for schizophrenia indicates a higher risk for females. The PRS associations with age shown in Table 1-2 probably reflect survival selection or possibly that smoking and obesity are correlated with earlier age at death, whereas the height and educational attainment PRSs are associated with later age at death. The large number of PRS associations with education may reflect many pathways. Our point here is that a relationship exists between educational attainment as a broadly used social variable and genetic risk for a large number of outcomes. If analyses want to control for related risks, this is a good use of the PRSs. The relatively new availability of genetic data should allow this influence on health outcomes to be better represented in future research. It should also help clarify who is most at risk from genetic factors that, at this point, are immutable.

SUMMARY AND IMPLICATIONS FOR FUTURE TRENDS IN MORTALITY AND FOR HEALTH AND RESEARCH ON LONGEVITY AND AGING HEALTH

Recent trends are a mixture, some favorable and some unfavorable, and one's classification of them into favorable or unfavorable may depend on whether the focus of one's interest is on relative or absolute differences. U.S. life expectancy has increased, albeit slowly, until the last couple of years. This could be viewed as a favorable trend, until one looks at the progress of other countries, and the U.S. trend seems relatively unfavorable by comparison. The prevalences of most diseases, with the exception of those clearly related to tobacco smoking, have been increasing for decades. This seems clearly to be an unfavorable trend, until one realizes that it is in large part due to the reduction of mortality. Long-term reductions in prevalence of hypertension and high cholesterol are a positive health trend, but they have been accompanied by an increase in obesity and metabolic dysregulation related to diabetes. So changes in physiological dysregulation consist of both positive and negative trends.

Could we have predicted the recently observed changing health differentials observed in recent years? That men and women would become more similar in longevity is not surprising, given that women and men are behaving more similarly. When women behave more like men, for instance by smoking more and taking illegal drugs, their health outcomes are likely to become more like those of men because this behavioral component of the mortality difference will be reduced. On the other hand, the extremely adverse trends among women of lower educational attainment might not have been predicted. As indicated above, numerous researchers have concluded that the policies and social fabric of American society have affected women's health more adversely than men's. This may be more characteristic of early adult life, when women are often single parents and sole supporters of children, but researchers have also increasingly clarified the lifelong health effects of early life hardships such as these. Increasing the relative rate of mortality decline for women may require social changes that are not on the immediate horizon.

The greater relative improvement of mortality and health among African Americans was somewhat surprising, given that it occurred in a period when socioeconomic differences in mortality, as well as in many other aspects of life, were widening in the general population. Whereas the relative size of the Black/White difference in life expectancy was affected by trends in deaths from violence and drugs, there also was some contribution from the reduction in deaths from chronic conditions. One factor that has not been considered in explaining the greater relative improvement in life expectancy for African Americans is cohort factors. It is possible that life circumstances of African Americans now reaching old age improved earlier in life with changes in civil rights, and these changed circumstances have resulted in improved mortality, relative to earlier cohorts of their peers or to Whites in the same cohort, in later life. If this is the explanation for the observed changes in life expectancy trends and differentials, the effect may play out in the future only as long as the relevant life circumstances improve over the life cycle.

Policies that are likely to reduce socioeconomic, racial, and geographic differentials in health and mortality in the United States seem unlikely to change in the near future. If anything, current policies such as rescinding the expansion of health insurance availability or having large geographic differentials in availability of support for health insurance for those of low SES may cause continued growth in the differentials in health and mortality between lower and higher socioeconomic groups. SES may thus become an even stronger predictor of health and longevity in the future.

For the U.S. population as a whole, the outlook for future morbidity and longevity depends on whether the onset and progression of the morbidity process are delayed and whether interventions at early points in the process are both feasible and implemented. One possibility is that the prevalence of disease could continue to increase but with reduced links to disability and death, as has occurred recently. Another possibility is that more and earlier intervention actions could be undertaken to attempt to prevent the changes in physiology that occur with aging. The reductions in cholesterol and blood pressure are a prototype for this alternative. The last few decades of work have shown that many biological factors, in addition to cholesterol and blood pressure, affect the rate of aging. The focus on "biological aging" and developing measures of aging that capture the process that begins with the beginning of life promises the best hope for eventually intervening in, and delaying, the process of health change with age. Certainly, better understanding of individual differences in susceptibility to poor health outcomes, as well as individual differences in genetic influences of behaviors and life circumstances, suggests that delaying aging health change may become more personalized and targeted in the future.

The integration of research on aging health across disciplines has been very promising in clarifying the complex pathways through which life circumstances operate. The multidisciplinary model of health and mortality outlined in Figure 1-7 has developed over the past four decades, with each decade expanding the model while improving understanding of observed differences in aging health. Numerous social and behavioral sciences were natural allies in building this model, but they have been increasingly joined by the biological sciences, so that the view of health and age is at once more similar across disciplines yet more complex than it was a decade ago. The coming decade will see much expansion in relevant research, as research clarifies how life circumstances "get under the skin" biologically. This will add important answers as we continue to address basic questions about how socioeconomic, gender, race, and geographic differences in health and mortality arise. The basic questions that are the point of social science investigation of health and mortality have been the same for more than a century, but the kinds of answers that can be provided have expanded steadily.

The rapid development of data and methods is likely to continue. A wealth of longitudinal cohorts has increased focus on health change with age, seeing it as a process with different timing across individuals and groups. The development of multivariable measures such as multimorbidity, frailty, polygenic risk scores, biological risk, pace of aging, and biological clocks have helped capture the complexity and the multisystem nature of the process. Much of the reward in improved understanding that can result from these developments is still promise; but the near future is likely to bring rapid increases in understanding. Results are only beginning to be integrated into health care so that outcomes for individuals are maximized. Optimizing health for aging populations may require social and policy changes that do not depend on scientific progress.

REFERENCES

Acciai, F., and Firebaugh, G. (2017). Why did life expectancy decline in the United States in 2015? A gender-specific analysis. *Social Science and Medicine, 190*, 174–180.

Alley, D.E., Lloyd, J., and Shardell, M. (2010). Can obesity account for cross-national differences in life expectancy trends? In National Research Council, *International Differences in Mortality at Older Ages: Dimensions and Sources* (pp. 164–192). E.M. Crimmins, S.H. Preston, and B. Cohen (Eds.). Panel on Understanding Cross-National Health Differences among High-Income Countries. Washington, DC: The National Academies Press.

Avendano, M., and Kawachi, I. (2014). Why do Americans have shorter life expectancy and worse health than do people in other high-income countries? *Annual Review of Public Health, 35*, 307–325.

Belsky, D.W., and Israel, S. (2014). Integrating genetics and social science: Genetic risk scores. *Biodemography and Social Biology, 60*(2), 137–155.

Belsky, D.W., Caspi, A., Houts, R., Cohen, H.J., Corcoran, D.L., Danese, A., Harrington, H., Israel, S., Levine, M.E., Schaefer, J.D., et al. (2015). Quantification of biological aging in young adults. *Proceedings of the National Academy of Sciences of the United States of America, 112*, E4104–E4110.

Belsky, D.W., Moffitt, T.E., Cohen, A.A., Corcoran, D.L., Levine, M.E., Prinz, J.A., Schaefer, J., Sugden, K., Williams, B., Poulton, R., et al. (2017). Eleven telomere, epigenetic clock, and biomarker-composite quantifications of biological aging: Do they measure the same thing? *American Journal of Epidemiology*, 1–11. doi: 10.1093/aje/kwx346.

Beltrán-Sánchez, H., Harhay, M.O., Harhay, M.M., and McElligott, S. (2013). Prevalence and trends of metabolic syndrome in the adult U.S. population, 1999–2010. *Journal of the American College of Cardiology, 62*, 697–703.

Blackburn, E.H., Greider, C.W., and Szostak, J.W. (2006). Telomeres and telomerase: The path from maize, *Tetrahymena* and yeast to human cancer and aging. *Nature Medicine, 2*(10), 1133–1138.

Blackburn, E.H., Epel, E.S., and Lin, J. (2015). Human telomere biology: A contributory and interactive factor in aging, disease risks, and protection. *Science, 350*, 1193–1198.

Bound, J., Geronimus, A.T., Rodriguez, J.M., and Waidmann, T.A. (2015). Measuring recent apparent declines in longevity: The role of increasing educational attainment. *Health Affairs, 34*(12), 2167–2173.

Broer, L., Buchman, A., Deelen, J., Evans, D., Faul, J., Lunetta, K., Sebastiani, P., Smith, J.A., Smith, A.V., Tanaka, T., et al. (2015). GWAS of longevity in CHARGE consortium confirms APOE and FOXO3 candidacy. *Journal of Gerontology Series A: Biological Sciences and Medical Sciences, 70*(1), 110–118.

Carroll, M., Lacher, D., Sorlie, P., Cleeman, J., Gordon, D., Wolz, M., Grundy, S., and Johnson, C. (2005). Trends in serum lipids and lipoproteins of adults, 1960–2002. *Journal of the American Medical Association, 294*, 1773–1781.

Case, A., and Deaton, A. (2015). Rising morbidity and mortality in midlife among white non-Hispanic Americans in the 21st century. *Proceedings of the National Academy of Sciences of the United States of America, 112*, 15078–15083.

Chen, J., Normand, S.L.T., Wang, Y., Drye, E.E., Schreiner, G.C., and Krumholz, H.M. (2010). Recent declines in hospitalizations for acute myocardial infarction for Medicare fee-for-service beneficiaries. *Circulation, 121*, 1322–1328.

Chetty, R., Stepner, M., Abraham, S., Lin, S., Scuderi, B., Turner, N., Bergeron, A., and Cutler, D. (2016). The association between income and life expectancy in the United States, 2001–2014. *Journal of the American Medical Association, 315*, 1750–1766.

Chong, Y., Tejada Vera, B., Lu, L., Anderson, R.N., Arias, E., and Sutton, P.D. (2015). *Deaths in the United States, 1900–2013.* Hyattsville, MD: National Center for Health Statistics.

Cohen, A.A., Milot, E., Li, Q., Bergeron, P., Poirier, R., Dusseault-Belanger, F., Fülöp, T., Leroux, M., Legault, V., Metter, J.E., et al. (2015). Detection of a novel, integrative aging process suggests complex physiological integration. *PLoS One, 10*(3), e0116489.

Conley, D., Laidley, T., Boardman, J., and Domingue, B. (2016). Changing polygenic penetrance on phenotypes in the 20th century among adults in the U.S. Population. *Scientific Reports, 6,* 30348. doi: 10.1038/srep30348.

Cornman, J.C., Glei, D.A·, Goldman, N·, and Weinstein, M. (2017). Physiological dysregulation, frailty, and risk of mortality among older adults. *Research on Aging, 39*(8), 911–933. doi: 10.1177/0164027516630794.

Crimmins, E. M. (2015a). Lifespan and healthspan: Past, present, and promise. *The Gerontologist, 55,* 901–911.

Crimmins, E.M. (2015b). Physiological differences across populations reflecting early life and later life nutritional status and later life risk for chronic disease. *Journal of Population Aging, 8,* 51–69.

Crimmins, E.M., and Levine, M. (2015). Current status of research on trends in morbidity, healthy life expectancy, and the compression of morbidity. In M. Kaeberlein and G. Martin (Eds), *Handbook of the Biology of Aging* (Ch. 18; pp. 495–505). St. Louis, MO: Elsevier Science.

Crimmins, E.M., and Saito, Y. (2000). Change in the prevalence of diseases among older Americans: 1984–1994. *Demographic Research, 3,* 1–20.

Crimmins, E.M., and Seeman, T.E. (2004). Integrating biology into the study of health disparities. *Population and Development Review, 30,* 89–107.

Crimmins, E.M., Garcia, K., and Kim, J.K. (2010a). Are international differences in health similar to international differences in life expectancy? In National Research Council, *International Differences in Mortality at Older Ages: Dimensions and Sources* (pp. 68–101). Washington, DC: The National Academies Press.

Crimmins, E.M., Kim, J.K., and Vasunilashorn, S. (2010b). Biodemography: New approaches to understanding trends and differences in population health and mortality. *Demography, 47,* S41–S64.

Deelen, J., Beekman, M., Capri, M., Franceschi, C., and Slagboom, P.E. (2013). Identifying the genomic determinants of aging and longevity in human population studies: Progress and challenges. *Bioessays, 35*(4), 386–396.

Do, D.P., Frank, R., and Finch, B.K. (2012). Does SES explain more of the black/white health gap than we thought? Revisiting our approach toward understanding racial disparities in health. *Social Science & Medicine, 74,* 1385–1393.

Domingue, B.W., Liu, H., Okbay, A., and Belsky, D.W. (2017). Genetic heterogeneity in depressive symptoms following the death of a spouse: Polygenic score analysis of the U.S. Health and Retirement Study. *American Journal of Psychiatry, 174*(10), 963–970.

Domingue, B.W., Belsky, D.W., Fletcher, J.M., Conley, D., Boardman, J.D., and Harris, K.M. (2018).The social genome of friends and schoolmates in the National Longitudinal Study of Adolescent to Adult Health. *Proceedings of the National Academy of Sciences of the United States of America, 115*(4), 702–707. doi: 10.1073/pnas.1711803115.

Dudbridge, F. (2013). Power and predictive accuracy of polygenic risk scores. *PLoS Genetics, 9*(3), e1003348. doi: https://doi.org/10.1371/journal.pgen.1003348.

Dwyer-Lindgren, L., Bertozzi-Villa, A., Stubbs, R.W., Morozoff, C., Kutz, M.J., Huynh, C., and Flaxman, A.D. (2016). U.S. county-level trends in mortality rates for major causes of death, 1980–2014. *Journal of the American Medical Association, 316,* 2385–2401.

Espeland, M.A., Crimmins, E.M., Grossardt, B.R., Crandall, J.P., Gelfond, J.A., Harris, T.B., Kritchevsky, S.B., Manson, J.E., Robinson, J.G., Rocca, W.A., et al. (2017). Clinical trials targeting aging and age-related multimorbidity. *Journals of Gerontology Series A: 72,* 355–361.

Ezzati, M., Friedman, A.B., Kulkarni, S.C., and Murray, C.J. (2008). The reversal of fortunes: Trends in county mortality and cross-county mortality disparities in the United States. *PLoS Medicine, 5,* 557–568.

Fang, M.C., Perraillon, M.C., Ghosh, K., Cutler, D.M., and Rosen, A.B. (2014). Trends in stroke rates, risk, and outcomes in the United States, 1988 to 2008. *The American Journal of Medicine, 127*, 608–615.

Finch, C.E., and Crimmins, E.M. (2004). Inflammatory exposure and historical changes in human life-spans. *Science, 305*, 1736–1739.

Geronimus, A.T., Hicken, M., Keene, D., and Bound, J. (2006). "Weathering" and age patterns of allostatic load scores among Blacks and Whites in the United States. *American Journal of Public Health, 96*(5), 826–833.

Geruso, M. (2012). Black-White disparities in life expectancy: How much can the standard SES variables explain? *Demography, 49*, 553–574.

Glei, D.A., Meslé, F., and Vallin, J. (2010). Diverging trends in life expectancy at age 50: A look at causes of death. In National Research Council, *International Differences in Mortality at Older Ages: Dimensions and Sources* (pp. 1–38). E.M. Crimmins, S.H. Preston, and B. Cohen (Eds.), Panel on Understanding Cross-National Health Differences Among High-Income Countries. Washington, DC: The National Academies Press.

Glei, D.A., Goldman, N., Risques, R.A., Rehkopf, D.H., Dow, W.H., Rosero-Bixby, L., and Weinstein, M. (2016). Predicting survival from telomere length versus conventional predictors: A multinational population-based cohort study. *PLoS One, 11*(4), 1–18. doi: 10.1371/journal.pone.0152486.

Goldman, N., Glei, D.A., and Weinstein, M. (2016). What matters most for predicting survival? A multinational population-based cohort study. *PLoS One, 11*(7), 1–11. doi: 10.1371/journal.pone.0159273.

Gruenewald, T.L., Seeman, T.E., Ryff, C.D., Karlamangla, A.S., and Singer, B.H. (2006). Combinations of biomarkers predictive of later life mortality. *Proceedings of the National Academy of Sciences of the United States of America, 103*(38), 14158–14163.

Hannum, G., Guinney, L., Zhao, L., Zhang, G., Hughes, S., Sadda, B., Klotzle, B., Bibikova, M., Fan, J., Gao, Y., et al. (2013). Genome-wide methylation profiles reveal quantitative views of human aging rates. *Molecular Cell, 49*, 359–367.

Harper, S., Lynch, J., Burris, S., and Smith, G.D. (2007). Trends in the Black-White life expectancy gap in the United States, 1983–2003. *Journal of the American Medical Association, 297*, 1224–1232.

Harper, S., Rushani, D., and Kaufman, J.S. (2012). Trends in the Black-White life expectancy gap, 2003–2008. *Journal of the American Medical Association, 307*, 2257–2259.

Harper, S., MacLehose, R.F., and Kaufman, J.S. (2014). Trends in the Black-White life expectancy gap among U.S. states, 1990–2009. *Health Affairs, 33*, 1375–1382.

Hayward, M.D., Hummer, R.A., and Sasson, I. (2015). Trends and group differences in the association between educational attainment and U.S. adult mortality: Implications for understanding education's causal influence. *Social Science & Medicine, 127*, 8–18.

Hertel, J., Friedrich, N., Wittfeld, K., Pietzner, M., Budde, K., van Der Auwera, S., Lohmann, T., Teumer, A., Völzke, H., Nauck, M., and Grabe, H.J. (2016). Measuring biological age via metabonomics: The metabolic age score. *Journal of Proteome Research, 15*, 400–410.

Ho, J.Y. (2013). Mortality under age 50 accounts for much of the fact that U.S. life expectancy lags that of other high-income countries. *Health Affairs, 32*, 459–467.

Ho, J.Y. (2017). The contribution of drug overdose to educational gradients in life expectancy in the United States, 1992–2011. *Demography, 54*, 1175–1202. doi: 10.1007/s13524-017-0565-3.

Ho, J.Y., and Fenelon, A. (2015). The contribution of smoking to educational gradients in U.S. life expectancy. *Journal of Health and Social Behavior, 56*, 307–322.

Ho, J.Y., and Preston, S.H. (2010). U.S. mortality in an international context: Age variations. *Population and Development Review, 36*, 749–773.

Holly, A.C., Melzer, C.D., Pilling, L.C., Henley, W., Hernandez, D.G., Singleton, A.B., Bandinelli, S., Guralnik, J.M., Ferrucci, L. and Harries, L.W. (2013). Towards a gene expression biomarker set for human biological age. *Aging Cell, 12*(2), 324-326.

Horvath, S. (2013). DNA methylation age of human tissues and cell types. *Genome Biology, 14*, 1-19.

Hummer, R.A., and Hayward, M.D. (2015). Hispanic older adult health and longevity in the United States: Current patterns and concerns for the future. *Daedalus, 144*, 20–30.

Institute of Medicine and National Research Council. (2013). *U.S. Health in International Perspective: Shorter Lives, Poorer Health.* S.H. Woolf and L. Aron (Eds.), Panel on Understanding Cross-National Health Differences Among High-Income Countries, Committee on Population. Washington, DC: The National Academies Press.

Jylhävä, J., Pedersen, N.L., and Hägg, S. (2017). Biological age predictors. *EBioMedicine, 21*, 29–36. doi: 10.1016/j.ebiom.2017.03.046.

Kennedy, B.K., Berger, S.L., Brunet, A., Campisi, J., Cuervo, A.M., Epel, E.S., Franceschi, C., Lithgow, G.J., Morimoto, R.I., Pessin, J.E., et al. (2014). Geroscience: linking aging to chronic disease. *Cell, 159*(4), 709–713. doi: 10.1016/j.cell.2014.10.039.

Kirkpatrick, R.M., McGue, M., Iacono, W.G., Miller, M.B., and Basu, S. (2014). Results of a "GWAS plus": General cognitive ability is substantially heritable and massively polygenic. *PLoS One, 9*(11), 1–13. doi: 10.1371/journal.pone.0112390.

Kochanek, D.K., Murphy, S.L., Xu, J., and Arias, E. (2017). *Mortality in the United States, 2016* (NCHS Data Brief. No. 293). Hyattsville, MD: National Center for Health Statistics.

Kumanyika, S.K., Landis, J.R., Matthews-Cook, Y.L., Almy, S.L., and Boehmer, S.J. (1998). Systolic blood pressure trends in U.S. adults between 1960 and 1980: Influence of antihypertensive drug therapy. *American Journal of Epidemiology, 148*, 528–538.

Lambert, J.C., Ibrahim-Verbaas, C.A., Harold, D., Naj, A.C., Sims, R., Bellenguez, C., Jun, G., DeStefano, A.L., Bis, J.C., Beecham, G.W., et al. (2013). Meta-analysis of 74,046 individuals identifies 11 new susceptibility loci for Alzheimer's disease. *Nature Genetics, 45*(12), 1452–1458. doi: 10.1038/ng.2802.

Lariscy, J.T., Hummer, R.A., and Hayward, M.D. (2015). Hispanic older adult mortality in the United States: New estimates and an assessment of factors shaping the Hispanic paradox. *Demography, 52*, 1–14.

Levine, M.E. (2013). Modeling the rate of senescence: Can estimated biological age predict mortality more accurately than chronological age? *The Journals of Gerontology Series A: Biological Science and Medical Science, 68*(6), 667–674.

Levine, M.E., and Crimmins, E.M. (2014). Evidence of accelerated aging among African Americans and its implications for mortality. *Social Science and Medicine, 118*, 27–32.

Levine, M.E., and Crimmins, E.M. (2018). Is 60 the new 50? Examining changes in biological age over the past two decades. *Demography, 55*(2), 387–402.

Link, B., and Phelan, J. (1995). Social conditions as fundamental causes of disease. *Journal of Health and Social Behavior*, (Special Issue), 80–94.

Liu, H., and Guo, G. (2015). Lifetime socioeconomic status, historical context, and genetic inheritance in shaping body mass in middle and late adulthood. *American Sociological Review, 80*, 705–737.

Locke, A.E., Kahali, B., Berndt, S.I., Justice, A.E., Pers, T.H., Day, F.R., Powell, C., Vedantam, S., Buchkovich, M.L., Yang, J., Croteau-Chonka, D.C., et al. (2015). Genetic studies of body mass index yield new insights for obesity biology. *Nature, 518*(7538), 197.

Mather, K.A., Jorm, A.F., Parslow, R.A., and Christensen, H. (2011). Is telomere length a biomarker of aging? A review. *The Journals of Gerontology Series A: Biological Science and Medical Science, 66*(2), 202–213.

McClintock, M.K., Dale, W., Laumann, E.O., and Waite, L. (2016). Empirical redefinition of comprehensive health and well-being in the older adults of the United States. *Proceedings of the National Academy of Sciences of the United States of America, 113*(22), E3071–E3080.

Meara, E.R., Richards, S., and Cutler, D.M. (2008). The gap gets bigger: Changes in mortality and life expectancy, by education, 1981–2000. *Health Affairs, 27*, 350–360. doi: 10.1377/hlthaff.27.2.350.

Menni, C., Kiddle, S.J., Mangino, M., Viñuela, A., Psatha, M., Steves, C., Sattlecker, M., Buil, A., Newhouse, S., Nelson, S., et al. (2015). Circulating proteomic signatures of chronological age. *The Journals of Gerontology Series A: Biological Science and Medical Science, 70*, 809–816.

Montez, J.K., and Zajacova, A. (2013a). Trends in mortality risk by education level and cause of death among U.S. White women from 1986 to 2006. *American Journal of Public Health, 103*(3), 473–479.

Montez, J.K., and Zajacova, A. (2013b). Explaining the widening education gap in mortality among U.S. White women. *Journal of Health and Social Behavior, 54*(2), 166–182.

Montez, J.K., Hummer, R.A., Hayward, M.D., Woo, H., and Rogers, R.G. (2011). Trends in the educational gradient of U.S. adult mortality from 1986 through 2006 by race, gender, and age group. *Research on Aging, 33*, 145–171.

Montez, J.K., Hummer, R.A., and Hayward, M.D. (2012). Educational attainment and adult mortality in the United States: A systematic analysis of functional form. *Demography, 49*, 315–336.

Montez, J.K., Sasson, I., and Hayward, M.D. (2016a). Declining U.S. life expectancy, 1990–2010. *Health Affairs, 35*, 550.

Montez, J.K., Zajacova, A., and Hayward, M.D. (2016b). Explaining inequalities in women's mortality in U.S. states. *SSM-Population Health, 2*, 561–571.

Murray, C.J., Kulkarni, S.C., Michaud, C., Tomijima, N., Bulzacchelli, M.T., Iandiorio, T.J., and Ezzati, M. (2006). Eight Americas: Investigating mortality disparities across races, counties, and race-counties in the United States. *PLoS Medicine, 3*, 1513–1524.

National Institutes of Health. (2017). *Telomeres as Sentinels for Environmental Exposures, Psychosocial Stress, and Disease Susceptibility.* A Workshop Co-sponsored by the National Institute of Environmental Health Sciences and the National Institute on Aging. Research Triangle Park, NC: National Institute on Aging.

National Research Council. (2011). *Explaining Divergent Trends in Longevity in High-Income Countries.* E. Crimmins, S.H. Preston, and B. Cohen (Eds.), Panel on Understanding Divergent Trends in Longevity in High-Income Countries, Committee on Population, Division of Behavioral and Social Sciences and Education. Washington, DC: The National Academies Press. doi: https://doi.org/10.17226/13089.

Okbay, A., Beauchamp, J.P., Fontana, M.A., Lee, J.J., Pers, T.H., Rietveld, C.A., Turley, P., Chen, G.B., Emilsson, V., Meddens, S.F.W., et al. (2016). Genome-wide association study identifies 74 loci associated with educational attainment. *Nature, 533*(7604), 539-542.

Olshansky, S.J., Antonucci, T., Berkman, L., Binstock, R.H., Boersch-Supan, A., Cacioppo, J.T., Carnes, B.A., Carstensen, L.L., Fried, L.P., Goldman, D.P., et al. (2012). Differences in life expectancy due to race and educational differences are widening, and many may not catch up. *Health Affairs, 31*, 1803–1813.

Ong, K.L., Allison, A., Cheung, B.M., Wu, B.J., Barter, P.J., and Rye, K.A. (2013). Trends in C-reactive protein levels in U.S. adults from 1999 to 2010. *American Journal of Epidemiology, 177*, 1430–1442. doi: http://dx.doi.org/10.1093/aje/kws443.

Peters, M.J., Joehanes, R., Pilling, L.C., Schurmann, C., Conneely, K.N., Powell, J., Reinmaa, E., Sutphin, G.L., Zhernakova, A., Schramm, K., et al. (2015). The transcriptional landscape of age in human peripheral blood. *Nature Communications, 6*, 8570.

Phelan, J.C., and Link, B.G. (2015). Is racism a fundamental cause of inequalities in health? *Annual Review of Sociology, 41,* 311–330. doi: https://doi.org/10.1146/annurev-soc-073014-112305.

Preston, S.H., and Stokes, A. (2011). Contribution of obesity to international differences in life expectancy. *American Journal of Public Health, 101,* 2137–2143. doi: 10.2105/AJPH.2011.300219.

Rehkopf, D.H., Rosero-Bixby, L., and Dow, W.H. (2016). A cross-national comparison of twelve biomarkers finds no universal biomarkers of aging among individuals aged 60 and older. *Vienna Yearbook of Population Research, 14,* 255–277.

Rietveld, C.A., Medland, S.E., Derringer, J., Yang, J., Esko, T., Martin, N.W., Westra, H.J., Shakhbazov, K., Abdellaoui, A., Agrawal, A., et al. (2013). GWAS of 126,559 individuals identifies genetic variants associated with educational attainment. *Science,* (2013), 1–11.

Rosamond, W.D., Chambless, L.E., Heiss, G., Mosley, T.H., Coresh, J., Whitsel, E., Wagenknecht, L., Hanyu, N., and Folsom, A.R. (2012). Twenty-two year trends in incidence of myocardial infarction, CHD mortality, and case-fatality in four U.S. communities, 1987 to 2008. *Circulation, 125,* 1848–1857.

Salive, M.E. (2013). Multimorbidity in older adults. *Epidemiologic Reviews, 35,* 75–83. doi: 10.1093/epirev/mxs009.

Sasson, I. (2016a). Diverging trends in cause-specific mortality and life years lost by educational attainment: Evidence from United States vital statistics data, 1990-2010. *PLoS One, 11,* 1–16.

Sasson, I. (2016b). Trends in life expectancy and lifespan variation by educational attainment: United States, 1990–2010. *Demography, 53,* 269–293.

Seeman, T.E., Singer, B.H., Rowe, J.W., Horwitz, R.I., and McEwen, B.S. (1997). Price of adaptation—Allostatic load and its health consequences. MacArthur studies of successful aging. *Archives of Internal Medicine, 157,* 2259–2268.

Seeman, T.E., McEwen, B.S., Rowe, J.W., and Singer, B.H. (2001). Allostatic load as a marker of cumulative biological risk: MacArthur studies of successful aging. *Proceedings of the National Academy of Sciences of the United States of America, 98*(8), 4770–4775.

St. Sauver, J.L., Boyd, C.M., Grossardt, B.R., Bobo, W.V., Rutten, L.J.F., Roger, V.L., Ebbert, J.O., Therneau, T.M., Yawn, B.P., and Rocca, W.A. (2015). Risk of developing multimorbidity across all ages in an historical cohort study: Differences by sex and ethnicity. *The BMJ, 5,* 1–13. doi: 10.1136/bmjopen-2014-006413.

Talbott, E.O., Rager, J.R., Brink, L.L., Benson, S.M., Bilonick, R.A., Wu, W.C., and Han, Y.Y. (2013). Trends in acute myocardial infarction hospitalization rates for U.S. states in the CDC tracking network. *PLoS One, 8,* 1–8.

Tucker-Seeley, R.D., Li, Y., Sorensen, G., and Subramanian, S.V. (2011). Lifecourse socioeconomic circumstances and multimorbidity among older adults. *BMC Public Health, 11,* 1–9.

Turra, C.M., and Goldman, N. (2007). Socioeconomic differences in mortality among U.S. adults: Insights into the Hispanic paradox. *The Journals of Gerontology Series B: Psychological Sciences and Social Sciences, 62,* S184–S192.

Wang, O.J., Wang, Y., Chen, J., and Krumholz, H.M. (2012). Recent trends in hospitalization for acute myocardial infarction. *The American Journal of Cardiology, 109,* 1589–1593.

Weidner, C.I., Lin, Q., Koch, C., Eisele, L., Beier, F., Ziegler, P., Bauerschlag, D., Jöckel, K., Erbel, R., Mühleisen, T.W., et al. (2014). Aging of blood can be tracked by DNA methylation changes at just three CpG sites. *Genome Biology, 15,* R24.

Wilson, P.W., D'Agostino, R.B., Levy, D., Belanger, A.M., Silbershatz, H., and Kannel, W.B. (1998). Prediction of coronary heart disease using risk factor categories. *Circulation, 97*(18), 1837–1847. doi: 10.1161/01.CIR.97.18.1837.

Woolf, S.H., and Braveman, P. (2011). Where health disparities begin: The role of social and economic determinants—and why current policies may make matters worse. *Health Affairs, 30,* 1852–1859.

Yeh, R.W., Sidney, S., Chandra, M., Sorel, M., Selby, J.V., and Go, A.S. (2010). Population trends in the incidence and outcomes of acute myocardial infarction. *New England Journal of Medicine, 362,* 2155–2165.

2

Racial/Ethnic and Nativity Disparities in the Health of Older U.S. Men and Women[1]

Robert A. Hummer[2]
and
Iliya Gutin

INTRODUCTION

Over the last couple of decades, demographers have documented an array of racial/ethnic health disparities. While the National Research Council's 1994 *Demography of Aging* volume did not include any chapters specifically devoted to racial/ethnic disparities, it later published two entire volumes focused on the topic (National Research Council, 1997, 2004). However, the racial/ethnic demography of the country has changed dramatically in the intervening years. Beyond changing population composition, it is also important to continually reassess racial/ethnic health disparities, given the fundamental importance of good health and long life to each group's overall well-being, especially in the context of a society that has long been stratified along racial/ethnic lines.

[1]This research was supported in part by grant R24 AG045061, The Network on Life Course Health Dynamics and Disparities in 21st Century America, funded by the National Institute on Aging. We also received support from the Population Research Training grant (T32 HD007168) and the Population Research Infrastructure Program (P2C HD050924) awarded to the Carolina Population Center at the University of North Carolina at Chapel Hill by the Eunice Kennedy Shriver National Institute of Child Health and Human Development. We are grateful to the National Center for Health Statistics and Minnesota Population Center for making the public-use data available for this paper. We also thank Daniel Powers for his expert statistical assistance.

[2]Department of Sociology and Carolina Population Center, University of North Carolina at Chapel Hill, Chapel Hill, NC, 27516. The authors share equal responsibility for this paper. Please contact Robert A. Hummer at rhummer@email.unc.edu for any questions or comments.

Demographers have also learned that it is insufficient to narrowly assess racial/ethnic health disparities; simultaneous consideration of nativity (i.e., whether individuals are U.S. or foreign born) and gender is paramount. Nativity is of critical concern because more than one in eight Americans is foreign born; further, the foreign-born proportions in each racial/ethnic group differ and are changing (Colby and Ortman, 2015). Moreover, a large body of research has demonstrated that foreign-born individuals in most racial/ethnic groups tend to have more favorable health patterns than their U.S.-born counterparts (Hummer et al., 2015). Furthermore, while it is very well documented that U.S. women live longer but less healthy lives than men (Case and Paxson, 2005), it is less well recognized that racial/ethnic disparities in health are generally wider among women than men (Brown et al., 2016; Richardson and Brown, 2016). Clearly, it is important to differentiate racial/ethnic health disparities by both nativity and gender to best understand which groups exhibit the largest and smallest disparities and why.

The goal of this chapter is to provide a contemporary portrait of U.S. racial/ethnic disparities in older adult (ages 65+) health, while simultaneously considering nativity- and gender-specific subpopulations. To provide insight into future racial/ethnic health disparities among the older population, we also estimate and briefly discuss middle-aged (ages 45–64) racial/ethnic health disparities. We consider a wide range of health measures, including those tapping dimensions of general health, morbidity, functioning and disability, health care, and mortality. Our chapter first provides brief overviews of some key theoretical and methodological considerations in the study of older adult health disparities. Doing so provides a context within which to interpret the disparities that we document. We close with a summary of the analysis and a forward-thinking agenda on which to push future research in this critical area of study.

THEORETICAL AND METHODOLOGICAL CONSIDERATIONS

A Context for Understanding Racial/Ethnic Health Disparities

It is very well recognized that Black Americans have been seriously discriminated against both institutionally and individually throughout the course of U.S. history, stemming from the earliest days of the Slave Trade, through the era of Jim Crow, to the mid- and late-20th-century decades of almost complete residential segregation from Whites, and into the present post–civil rights period (Gates et al., 2012). While the forms of discriminatory treatment have changed over the years, racism on the part of the White majority population continues to be the critical ideology underlying such discrimination, which contributes to both lower socioeconomic status

(SES) and poorer health profiles among Blacks relative to Whites (Williams et al., 2010). Each year, Blacks suffer between 60,000 and 100,000 excess deaths compared to Whites, a figure calculated by applying the annual death rate of Whites to the Black population (Satcher et al., 2005). The worse health and higher mortality of Blacks is due both to their lower level of SES resources (Hayward et al., 2000) and to the accumulated physiological stress of dealing with discrimination across the life course (Phelan and Link, 2015).

Fortunately, the gap in life expectancy between Blacks and Whites, which was about 14 years in 1900, is now smaller than ever before, at 3.5 years (Arias et al., 2017). This long-term narrowing reflects improved African American well-being due to both public health improvements (e.g., sanitation and vaccinations) and specific civil rights and health care legislation (Masters et al., 2014). However, the narrowing gap in life expectancy is also due to recent increases in mortality rates among Whites. Indeed, research has highlighted the dramatic surge in mortality affecting White adults, with the opioid epidemic being the driving force behind such adverse trends. Moreover, there has been a disproportionate impact on White adults with a high school education or less (Case and Deaton, 2015). In fact, the magnitude of increased mortality attributable to accidental poisonings almost entirely accounts for the recent decline in life expectancy among Whites and for the country as a whole (Kochanek et al., 2016). Clearly, then, Black–White health and mortality disparities have exhibited dynamic changes in recent years.

The Native American population has also experienced a tragic history of racism, resulting in their near genocide and continued social and economic marginalization. At present, the Native American population exhibits patterns of low SES and poor health that are similar to African Americans (Jones, 2006). Many Native American communities are geographically and socially isolated, resulting in limited opportunities for individual socioeconomic mobility (Smith-Kaprosy et al., 2012). Perhaps unsurprisingly, a recent analysis shows that counties with Native American reservations exhibit among the worst health profiles in the United States, with life expectancy figures often 10 years below the national average (Dwyer-Lindgren et al., 2017).

In recent decades, some Native American communities have experienced an influx of resources owing to the growth of the gambling industry. However, this influx has not uniformly resulted in positive health changes. On the one hand, some tribal economies have improved, leading to the greater availability of community health resources and social services, as well as increased individual financial stability. Conversely, this additional income may have a negative population health impact by enabling substance abuse, increasing the availability of unhealthy food, and, more broadly, disrupting traditional social value systems (Kodish et al., 2016). Studies have reached mixed conclusions regarding the effects of this influx (Bruckner et al., 2011; Costello et al., 2010; Jones-Smith et al., 2014; Wolfe et al., 2012). The continued assessment of Native American health is both necessary and important in the context of Native Americans' persistent social disadvantages and the changes in economic structure that some communities are experiencing.

While both the Asian American and Hispanic populations trace their American roots centuries into the past, the vast majority of individuals in both groups are either post-1960s immigrants or the descendants of those migrants. Together, Latinos and Asians have been instrumental in reshaping American diversity over the course of the late 20th and early 21st centuries (Lee and Bean, 2007), most notably among children and young adults but increasingly among older adults as well. Much work on the Latino and Asian populations has pointed to the importance of healthy immigrant selectivity in shaping the relatively favorable population health patterns of these rapidly growing groups (Akresh and Frank, 2008). However, at least some work finds that U.S.-born Hispanics and Asian Americans exhibit less favorable health and mortality patterns than their immigrant counterparts. Such a pattern of worsening health for the U.S.-born relative to the immigrant generation may vary across racial/ethnic groups, based on each group's experience with socioeconomic incorporation (Hummer et al., 2015).

Asian Americans exhibit substantial diversity, not only by immigrant status but also by national origin. Most national-level population health work, including the present effort, cannot address such heterogeneity, given relatively small sample sizes of specific groups within national datasets. Nonetheless, the Chinese, Japanese, and Korean national origin subgroups have been shown to exhibit more favorable health profiles when compared to the South and Southeast Asian origin subgroups (Frisbie et al., 2001). Overall, though, the strong health and educational selectivity of most Asian immigrant groups in the United States have led to a relatively positive context for favorable population health among Asian Americans as a whole.

The Hispanic population, which now comprises 18 percent of the U.S. population and a rapidly growing share of older adults (Flores, 2017), is also very diverse and includes individuals who trace their roots in the United States for centuries, along with recent immigrants who arrived from nations throughout Central and South America and the Caribbean. Much demographic work documents diversity in health patterns across Hispanic subgroups, with Puerto Ricans generally exhibiting the worst population health profile, Cubans the most positive, and the Mexican origin population in the middle (Cho et al., 2004). The Mexican origin population constitutes the largest subgroup, accounting for 63 percent of all Hispanics; about one-third of the Mexican origin population in the United States is foreign born (Flores, 2017). Given the large size of the Mexican origin population, our documentation examines them separately, along with a heterogeneous group of other Hispanics.

Although positive health and educational selectivity has long characterized Hispanic immigration and has helped to account for the favorable health patterns among the immigrant generation (Akresh and Frank, 2008), such patterns of positive selectivity may be waning, particularly for immigrants from Mexico (Feliciano, 2005). Notably, Mexico now has the highest obesity rate in the world and, as a result, Mexican immigrants to the United States also exhibit higher obesity rates than ever before (Hummer and Hayward, 2015). In the United States, Mexican immigrants also encounter an array of challenging social conditions, including high levels of stress, fear, and discrimination (particularly among undocumented immigrants); low wages and hazardous working conditions in manual-labor industries; and lack of access to health care (Hummer and Hayward, 2015). Given that the second and higher generations of Hispanics encounter multiple forms of discrimination and poor access to high-quality schooling and jobs (National Research Council, 2006), it is critical that researchers continue to carefully document population health patterns, trends, and heterogeneity among both the immigrant and U.S.-born segments of this rapidly growing group.

Health as a Multidimensional Concept

Given the multidimensionality of health, capturing only one or a few of its dimensions may lead to biased conclusions regarding racial/ethnic health disparities. As just one noteworthy example, older-age Hispanics exhibit substantially lower mortality rates than Whites but far higher rates of disability (Hayward et al., 2014). Consequently, an important goal of our chapter is to provide a *comprehensive* documentation of racial/ethnic differences in older adult health. Thus, we take a broad view in terms of conceptualizing and measuring health. Per the World Health Organization, physical, mental, and social well-being are equally relevant in developing a multifaceted understanding of health (World Health Organization, 2006). Therefore, we include indicators of "global" physical and mental health status, medical conditions/diseases and pain, functioning and activity limitations, access to and utilization of health care, and mortality. We also document differences in SES across groups, to better contextualize racial/ethnic health disparities.

Methodological Considerations in the Documentation of Racial/Ethnic Health Disparities

Documentation of racial/ethnic health disparities is not a straight-forward endeavor. First, there is the question of who identifies in which racial/ethnic groups in health surveys. Self-reported surveys provide respondents with the opportunity to choose groups they most closely identify with, which is an important strength of the empirical patterns we describe below. This also means that empirically derived health disparities are subject to shifting understandings and reporting patterns of race/ethnicity across time and space (Sandefur et al., 2004). Moreover, as discussed above, many specific subgroups (e.g., Native American tribes, national origin subgroups of racial/ethnic groups) are numerically too small to be identified in the datasets that we use. Given such limitations, it is important to note that the health disparity patterns described below are based on individuals who are identifying with internally heterogeneous groups at one specific point in historical time and in one national context.

Second, there is selectivity with regard to the individuals who are included or excluded in the datasets used to document disparities. Perhaps most important, individuals necessarily have survived long enough to be in the dataset(s) being used; moreover, mortality differentials prior to the age groups under study strongly influence subsequent age-specific health disparities (Hayward et al., 2000). This well-known demographic issue of selective survival results in relatively healthy subgroups of individuals in population-based datasets, which mutes racial/ethnic disparities in older ages, given the selective processes involved (Palloni and Ewbank, 2004). Other issues of selection in nationally representative datasets involve the inclusion/exclusion of institutionalized, homeless or transient, and undocumented residents. The datasets we use below are household-based surveys; consequently, they likely exclude institutionalized, homeless, and transient individuals. Thus, estimates of racial/ethnic disparities are systematically tilted toward a modestly healthier older adult population than is actually the case in the complete population. While undocumented residents living in U.S. households are eligible for such surveys, such individuals may be highly skeptical about actually participating in them.

DATA AND METHODS

Data come from the National Health Interview Survey (NHIS) and the National Health and Nutrition Examination Survey (NHANES). NHIS is the largest nationally representative survey of health, with tens of thousands of annual participants providing information on a range of topics (National Center for Health Statistics, 2016). NHANES is also nationally representative and is another valuable source of health data through its unique combination of interviews and physical examinations (National Center for Health Statistics, 2005). We use the smaller NHANES for anthropometric and biomarker data, while relying on the statistical power of NHIS for questionnaire-based measures of health and the assessment of mortality disparities. NHIS is especially useful for mortality documentation because of its large size and self-reported racial/ethnic data, which alleviates the well-known problems with racial/ethnic reporting in vital statistics data (Bilheimer and Klein, 2010).

Drawing on both surveys, we provide population-level estimates of over 50 different health measures, categorized into five broad domains. First, the *Global Health* domain includes subjective reports of individuals' overall physical and mental health status. We also include body mass index and waist circumference as proxies for weight-related health in this domain. In doing so, we distinguish survey-based definitions of obesity at the population level—which represent a summary measure of weight-related health status and risk (Gutin, 2017)—from clinical obesity at the individual level as a diagnosed condition (i.e., a "morbidity"). Measures of *Morbidity* are primarily based on individuals' reports of being diagnosed with various conditions or diseases, as well as their reports of pain. Importantly, we also include NHANES-based biomarker assessments of hypertension and diabetes in this domain. In the case of *Functioning and Disability*, we use respondent information on confusion and/or memory problems, functional limitations and their interference with work, and multiple measures of activity limitations. We also focus on survey reports related to *Health Care*, including possession of health insurance, assessments of access, and an overview of individuals' receipt of care in the past year. Finally, *Mortality* is documented as a rate per 100,000 person-years of exposure for each group, focusing both on all-cause mortality and underlying causes of death.

Limiting our analyses of both the NHIS and NHANES data to older (65+) and middle-aged (ages 45–64) adults, we pool survey data from 16 waves of NHIS between 2000 and 2015 and 8 waves of continuous 2-year NHANES between 1999 and 2014. For measures obtained from NHIS, we provide estimates for non-Hispanic Whites, non-Hispanic Blacks, Mexican Americans, other Hispanics, Asians or Pacific Islanders, and Native Americans. Due to the smaller sample sizes, we exclude Asians or Pacific Islanders and Native Americans from NHANES-based estimates. Given our stratification of racial/ethnic groups by both nativity and gender, there are nevertheless population subgroups for whom reliable estimates of certain health indicators are not possible because of small cell sizes. We thus exclude any estimates based on a group-specific prevalence of less than 10 cases. To account for differences in the age distribution of adults across groups, we standardized all proportions and means to the age distribution of adults in the 2000 decennial U.S. Census (as per National Center for Health Statistics [NCHS] recommendations). We applied appropriate survey weights to facilitate unbiased estimates and appropriate statistical significance levels when comparing across groups. Finally, we specified U.S.-born non-Hispanic Whites as the referent group in testing for racial/ethnic/nativity differences across measures of health included in our analyses; we note significant nativity differences within racial/ethnic groups as well.

RESULTS

The Socioeconomic Context for Racial/Ethnic Health Disparities

Table 2-1 uses NHIS data to examine the distribution of SES across racial/ethnic groups, focusing on individuals' educational attainment and a ratio of income to needs (adjusted for inflation and changing poverty guidelines across years). Non-Hispanic Whites and Asian Americans, both U.S. and foreign born, exhibit the most favorable socioeconomic profiles, while Native Americans, U.S.-born Blacks, foreign-born Mexican Americans, and other Hispanics exhibit the least favorable distributions. Turning first to education, foreign-born Mexican American men and women exhibit the lowest levels of high school completion (~17%), and less than 1 in 10 have any postsecondary education. Rates of high school completion and post-secondary schooling are higher among their U.S.-born counterparts, at ~50 percent and ~20 percent, respectively, though still far lower than all other racial/ethnic groups. For instance, non-Hispanic Black, other Hispanic, and Native American women and men have more than double the percentage of postsecondary educational attainment (~25–45%). Asian Americans and non-Hispanic Whites have by far the highest proportion of highly educated older adults; approximately 40 percent of women and 55 percent of men are in the "some college" or "college+" categories.

Table 2-1 also shows stark disparities in ratio of income to needs. Non-Hispanic White and Asian older men and women are also the most affluent: ~30 percent of White women, ~35 percent of Asian women, ~37 percent of White men, and ~40 percent of Asian men report an income at least four times greater than the poverty line. By contrast, U.S.-born Black, foreign-born Mexican American and other Hispanic, and Native American older adults have far less favorable distributions of income to needs relative to their non-Hispanic White and Asian counterparts. Strikingly, almost 70 percent of foreign-born Mexican Americans and ~60 percent of Native Americans and foreign-born other Hispanics have an income less than twice the poverty line. However, among other Hispanics, the U.S. born fare slightly better, with around ~50 percent in the same income-to-needs bracket. Conversely, foreign-born Blacks—especially women—exhibit a more favorable income distribution than their U.S.-born counterparts (52% versus 38% with an income-to-needs ratio of 2.00+).

Global Assessments of Health

Table 2-2 considers our global assessments of health. Non-Hispanic Whites fare much better on these measures compared to most of their minority counterparts. Under one-quarter of U.S.-born White adults report fair/poor health, compared to 30–45 percent of Blacks, Mexican Americans, other Hispanics, foreign-born Asians, and Native Americans. For both genders, foreign-born Mexican Americans report the highest levels of fair/poor health (~43%), while U.S.-born Asians compare favorably to Whites and other racial/ethnic groups. Nativity is a particularly important distinction for reports of poor health or declines in health over the last year. With the exception of Blacks, foreign-born men and women consistently report higher levels of poor health than their U.S.-born counterparts. Further, foreign-born Mexican Americans, other Hispanics, Asians, and non-Hispanic Whites all report higher levels of worsening health over the past year (15–20%) as compared to ~13 percent among U.S.-born Whites and ~8 percent of U.S.-born Asian Americans.

Although reports of poor self-rated health are comparable for women and men, women consistently report a higher average number of days of poor physical and mental health than their male counterparts. However, there are clear racial/ethnic differences within genders, as foreign-born Mexican American and other Hispanic women report nearly 8 days of poor physical health and 4–5 days of poor mental health in the last month, compared to only 4–5 days of poor physical health and 2–3 days of poor mental health for Blacks and non-Hispanic Whites. Among men, Mexican Americans again have the highest average number of days of poor physical health in the last month (~6), while foreign-born Blacks and Whites have a significantly lower number of poor mental health days (<1) than their U.S.-born White counterparts (1.62). Racial/ethnic disparities in mental health are also wide. While approximately one-quarter of U.S.-born Black, Mexican American, Other Hispanic, Native American, and foreign-born non-Hispanic White women (and 18% of men) report two or more severe mental health symptoms, only 18 percent of U.S.-born non-Hispanic White and 10 percent of U.S.-born Asian women (and 13% and 10%, respectively, of men) report the same problems.

With respect to overall weight-related health status, Black and Mexican American women have much higher prevalence of obesity and at-risk waist circumference than non-Hispanic Whites, other Hispanics, and Asians. Approximately 40 percent of U.S.-born Black women are obese based on self-reported height and weight (and more than 50% based on measured

TABLE 2-1 Racial/Ethnic Composition and Socioeconomic Status among U.S. Adults, by Gender, Ages 65+ (NHIS 2000–2015)

	N-H Black		Mexican American	
	F-B	US-B	F-B	US-B
FEMALE				
Overall	0.01	0.08	0.02	0.02
Education				
<HS	0.42	0.40	0.82	0.54
HS	0.29	0.29	0.10	0.28
Some College	0.15	0.19	0.05	0.13
College+	0.13	0.12	0.02	0.05
Income-to-Needs Ratio				
0–1.00	0.22	0.29	0.34	0.21
1.01–1.99	0.25	0.33	0.35	0.33
2.00–3.99	0.32	0.25	0.23	0.30
4.00+	0.20	0.13	0.08	0.16
MALE				
Overall	0.01	0.07	0.02	0.02
Education				
<HS	0.33	0.44	0.83	0.47
HS	0.29	0.28	0.08	0.27
Some College	0.15	0.17	0.05	0.17
College+	0.23	0.12	0.03	0.09
Income-to-Needs Ratio				
0–1.00	0.22	0.18	0.33	0.14
1.01–1.99	0.25	0.32	0.36	0.33
2.00–3.99	0.30	0.31	0.23	0.33
4.00+	0.23	0.19	0.08	0.20

NOTES: NHIS N(Overall) = 181,924; NHIS N(Female) = 102,971; NHIS N(Male) = 78,953. HS = high school completion, NH = non-Hispanic, PI = Pacific Islander, F-B = foreign born, US-B = U.S. born.

Percent/mean estimates based on nonmissing responses for given survey item or measure. Income-to-needs ratio of 1.00 represents income at the poverty line.

Other Hispanic		N-H Asian/PI		Native Amer.	N-H White	
F-B	US-B	F-B	US-B	US-B	F-B	US-B
0.03	0.01	0.03	0.01	0.00	0.05	0.75
						ref.
_0.53_	0.36	_0.37_	0.13	0.43	0.26	0.19
_0.23_	0.33	_0.24_	0.39	0.26	0.31	0.39
_0.12_	0.20	_0.11_	0.26	0.23	0.23	0.24
0.12	0.11	_0.28_	0.22	0.08	0.20	0.17
_0.30_	0.16	_0.21_	0.05	0.30	0.14	0.09
0.31	0.34	0.23	0.19	0.31	0.25	0.26
_0.24_	0.30	_0.26_	0.35	0.26	0.32	0.36
_0.14_	0.20	_0.30_	0.40	0.13	0.29	0.29
0.03	0.01	0.03	0.01	0.00	0.04	0.78
						ref.
_0.48_	0.29	_0.21_	0.12	0.39	0.23	0.19
0.23	0.27	_0.20_	0.30	0.28	0.23	0.30
_0.12_	0.23	_0.13_	0.26	0.21	0.18	0.22
_0.16_	0.21	_0.45_	0.32	0.12	0.36	0.28
_0.25_	0.10	_0.18_	0.03	0.17	0.11	0.05
_0.33_	0.26	_0.23_	0.14	0.37	0.22	0.19
_0.26_	0.35	_0.26_	0.34	0.27	0.31	0.38
_0.15_	0.30	_0.33_	0.48	0.20	0.36	0.38

All estimates age-standardized to 2000 U.S. Census and weighted based on NCHS-provided survey weights, to be representative of the U.S. population.

Bold indicates significantly different from U.S.-born non-Hispanic Whites at p<0.05.

Underline indicates significantly different from U.S.-born members of same racial/ethnic group at p<0.05.

TABLE 2-2 Global Health Indicators among U.S. Adults, Ages 65+ (NHIS 2000–2015, NHANES 1999–2015)

	N-H Black		Mexican American	
	F-B	US-B	F-B	US-B
FEMALE				
GLOBAL HEALTH				
Fair/poor health	0.35	0.39	0.44	0.36
Health status worse compared to last year	0.17	0.13	0.18	0.14
N days physical health not good last month	3.44	5.65	7.78	5.29
N days mental health not good last month	2.65	3.32	**5.49**	**4.52**
Two+ severe mental health symptoms[a]	**0.20**	**0.20**	**0.25**	**0.23**
Obese (self-report)[b]	0.29	0.39	0.34	0.30
Obese (measured)[b]	0.52	0.50	0.43	0.32
Risky waist circum.[c]	0.87	0.80	0.78	0.76
MALE				
GLOBAL HEALTH				
Fair/poor health	0.32	0.38	0.42	0.33
Health status worse compared to last year	0.12	0.11	0.13	0.14
N days physical health not good last month	3.28	4.91	5.89	5.95
N days mental health not good last month	0.34	2.12	1.20	2.25
Two+ severe mental health symptoms[a]	0.15	**0.16**	**0.18**	**0.18**
Obese (self-report)[b]	0.17	**0.25**	0.25	**0.27**
Obese (measured)[b]	0.17	0.32	0.26	0.30
Risky waist circum.[c]	0.39	0.47	0.42	0.50

NOTES: NHIS N(Overall) = 181,924; NHANES N(Overall) = 11,173; NHIS N(Female) = 102,971; NHANES N(Female) = 5,734; NHIS N(Male) = 78,953; NHANES N(Male) = 5,439.

HS = high school completion, N-H = non-Hispanic, PI = Pacific Islander, F-B = foreign born, US-B = U.S. born.

Percent/mean estimates based on nonmissing responses for given survey item or measure.

All estimates weighted based on NCHS-derived weights, and age-standardized to 2000 U.S. Census.

Cells with <10 incidences excluded.

Other Hispanic		N-H Asian/PI		Native Amer.	N-H White	
F-B	US-B	F-B	US-B	US-B	F-B	US-B
						ref.
0.39	0.32	0.32	0.18	0.37	0.25	0.22
0.17	0.15	0.19	0.10	0.19	0.16	0.13
7.63	4.06	—	—	—	5.00	5.07
4.88	2.79	—	—	—	2.24	3.39
0.27	0.21	0.18	0.10	0.27	0.21	0.18
0.25	0.28	0.08	0.13	0.33	0.21	0.23
0.33	0.24	—	—	—	0.26	0.32
0.76	0.67	—	—	—	0.69	0.73
						ref.
0.35	0.31	0.29	0.22	0.37	0.25	0.23
0.16	0.14	0.18	0.08	0.18	0.15	0.12
5.12	1.74	—	—	—	3.64	4.18
2.09	2.78	—	—	—	0.71	1.62
0.18	0.18	0.11	0.10	0.21	0.17	0.13
0.22	0.23	0.05	0.12	0.31	0.20	0.23
0.25	—	—	—	—	0.33	0.29
0.47	0.27	—	—	—	0.57	0.59

Bold indicates significantly different from U.S.-born non-Hispanic Whites at $p<0.05$.
Underline indicates significantly different from U.S.-born members of same racial/ethnic group at $p<0.05$.
[a]Severe mental health symptoms measured in NHIS include reports of feeling everything an effort; feelings interfering with life; hopelessness; nervousness; restlessness; sadness; and worthlessness sometimes or often in the past month.
[b]Obese defined as having body mass index $\geq$ 30.0.
[c]Risky waist circumference defined as $\geq$88 cm for women and $\geq$102 cm for men.

height and weight), while over 80 percent have a waist circumference considered "at risk" for poor health. These prevalence levels are the highest among the groups we examine, especially compared to Asian women (of whom ~11% are obese based on self-reports) and non-Hispanic White women (of whom 25–30% are obese based on both self-reports and measurements). As a group, older men have more favorable weight-related health than their female counterparts. Though non-Hispanic White men and women have similar obesity prevalence, approximately 25–30 percent of U.S.-born Black and Mexican American men are considered obese, based on self-reports and physical measurements, compared to 40–50 percent of their female counterparts. Men of any race/ethnicity also have a lower prevalence of risky waist circumference than women (~46% vs. 76%). Looking more closely, U.S.-born Black, Mexican American, and Native American men also have higher self-reported obesity than their non-Hispanic White counterparts; yet non-Hispanic White men have a 10–30 percent higher prevalence of risky waist circumference. Asian-American men have the lowest self-reported obesity (<15%), while foreign-born Blacks have the lowest measured obesity (17%).

Morbidity

Table 2-3 considers measures of morbidity among those aged 65 and older. Although non-Hispanic White adults show more favorable global health profiles than their minority counterparts, diagnoses of chronic conditions and diseases exhibit a much less consistent pattern of racial/ethnic disparities for both genders. For instance, hypertension is potentially underdiagnosed in this age group, as the combined undiagnosed or diagnosed/controlled rates observed in NHANES data are higher than the self-reports in NHIS (e.g., ~75% in NHANES compared to ~59% in NHIS for U.S.-born non-Hispanic White women; ~67% compared to ~57% for U.S.-born non-Hispanic White men). Nevertheless, across both measures of hypertension, Black, Mexican American, Native American, and foreign-born other Hispanic and Asian women have higher rates than non-Hispanic White women. Though Black, foreign-born Asian, and Native American men also have higher rates compared to non-Hispanic White men, foreign-born Mexican American and other Hispanic men instead have lower self-reported hypertension (~50% compared to 57% among non-Hispanic Whites), and comparable rates of undiagnosed/diagnosed or controlled hypertension (~66% compared to 67% among non-Hispanic Whites).

Looking at other measures of cardiovascular health, U.S.-born Black women report among the highest prevalence of coronary heart disease, congestive heart failure, and stroke, with approximately 12 percent reporting a diagnosis of one or more of these conditions. However, for heart attacks and any other heart condition, U.S.-born Whites report marginally higher rates than all other racial/ethnic/nativity groups (e.g., 17% report some other heart condition, compared to ~13% across other groups). This pattern holds for men as well, with significantly lower rates of reported coronary heart disease, congestive heart failure, other heart conditions, and heart attacks for Black, Mexican American, other Hispanic, Asian, and foreign-born non-Hispanic Whites relative to U.S.-born non-Hispanic Whites. Across both genders, foreign-born Blacks stand out as having a particularly low prevalence of heart problems, especially compared to their U.S.-born counterparts.

Also apparent is the lower prevalence of diabetes among non-Hispanic Whites compared to most other race/ethnic groups, regardless of nativity or gender. Black, Mexican American, and Native American women have the highest prevalence of reported diabetes (30–35%), followed closely by other Hispanic women (~24%) and foreign-born Asians (21%). Mexican American women also have the highest rates of diabetes based on diagnosis or measurement in NHANES (~55%), followed by U.S.-born Black women (52%). Older males exhibit a nearly identical racial/ethnic distribution of diabetes, though rates for all groups other than non-Hispanic Whites (with the exception of U.S.-born Asians) are closer in value, ranging from 25 percent for foreign-born Asians to 35 percent for U.S.-born Mexican Americans. However, when considering high blood glucose, these data show that U.S.-born Mexican American and foreign-born other Hispanic men have the highest rates of undiagnosed or diagnosed/controlled diabetes (61%), while prior racial/ethnic disparities on the basis of self-reported diabetes are less evident. Among the other common morbidities observed in this 65 and older age group, arthritis is significantly higher among U.S.-born Black compared to U.S.-born non-Hispanic White women, while foreign-born Black and non-Hispanic White women report lower rates. Diagnoses of cancer are significantly higher among U.S.-born non-Hispanic White women (23%) and men (29%) compared to all other groups, with foreign-born Mexican American and Asian adults having the lowest rates (8% for women, 10% for men). Generally speaking, cancer rates are lower for women (14%) as compared to men (~17%), and foreign born (~13%) as compared to U.S. born (~18%). However, we caution that cancer is a condition especially prone to under-diagnosis on the basis of racial/ethnic, nativity, and socioeconomic inequities in access to care (Ward et al., 2004).

Finally, across all four measures of pain (joints, lower back, neck, and severe migraines) and all racial/ethnic groups, women consistently report greater pain than their male counterparts. Among women, Native Americans stand out as having the highest reports of pain for three of the four measures, while U.S.-born Asians have the lowest reports in three of the four measures, as well. Older men show slightly different patterns of

TABLE 2-3 Measurements of Morbidity among U.S. Adults, Ages 65+ (NHIS 2000-2015; NHANES 1999–2014)

	N-H Black		Mexican American	
	F-B	US-B	F-B	US-B
FEMALE				
MORBIDITY				
Told you had:				
Coronary heart disease	0.09	0.14	0.15	0.17
Congestive heart failure	<u>0.02</u>	0.07	0.05	0.09
Heart condition	<u>0.09</u>	0.14	0.11	0.12
Heart attack	<u>0.07</u>	0.12	<u>0.09</u>	0.13
Stroke	<u>0.08</u>	0.12	0.08	0.11
Arthritis	<u>0.27</u>	0.45	**0.34**	0.42
Hypertension	**0.70**	**0.71**	**0.48**	**0.60**
Diabetes + taking medication	**0.33**	**0.28**	<u>0.28</u>	**0.36**
Undiagnosed or Diagnosed/Controlled[a]				
Hypertension[b]	0.75	**0.82**	0.63	0.69
Diabetes[c]	0.54	0.53	0.55	**0.61**
Experienced:				
Pain/aching joints, past mo.	0.46	0.45	0.39	0.41
Lower back pain, past 3 mo.	0.31	**0.25**	0.27	0.27
Neck pain, past 3 mo.	0.10	0.12	**0.16**	0.15
Severe migraine, past 3 mo.	0.08	**0.06**	0.06	0.05
MALE				
MORBIDITY				
Told you had:				
Coronary heart disease	0.09	0.14	0.15	0.17
Congestive heart failure	<u>0.02</u>	0.07	0.05	0.09
Heart condition	<u>0.09</u>	0.14	0.11	0.12
Heart attack	<u>0.07</u>	0.12	<u>0.09</u>	0.13
Stroke	<u>0.08</u>	0.12	0.08	0.11
Arthritis	<u>0.27</u>	0.45	**0.34**	0.42
Hypertension	**0.70**	**0.71**	**0.48**	**0.60**
Diabetes + taking medication	**0.33**	**0.28**	<u>0.28</u>	**0.36**
Undiagnosed or Diagnosed/Controlled[a]				
Hypertension[b]	0.75	**0.82**	0.63	0.69
Diabetes[c]	0.54	0.53	0.55	**0.61**
Experienced:				
Pain/aching joints, past mo.	0.46	0.45	0.39	0.41
Lower back pain, past 3 mo.	0.31	**0.25**	0.27	0.27
Neck pain, past 3 mo.	0.10	0.12	**0.16**	0.15
Severe migraine, past 3 mo.	0.08	**0.06**	0.06	0.05

NOTES: NHIS N(Overall) = 181,924; NHANES N(Overall) = 11,173; NHIS N(Female) = 102,971; NHANES N(Female) = 5,734; NHIS N(Male) = 78,953; NHANES N(Male) = 5,439.
HS = high school completion, N-H = non-Hispanic, PI = Pacific Islander, F-B = foreign born, US-B = U.S. born.
Percent/mean estimates based on nonmissing responses for given survey item or measure.
All estimates weighted based on NCHS-derived weights, and age-standardized to 2000 U.S. Census.
Cells with <10 incidences excluded.
Bold indicates significantly different from U.S.-born non-Hispanic Whites at p<0.05.

	Other Hispanic		N-H Asian/PI		Native Amer.	N-H White	
	F-B	US-B	F-B	US-B	US-B	F-B	US-B
							ref.
	0.15	0.21	0.15	0.20	0.21	0.21	0.22
	0.08	0.05	—	—	—	0.04	0.11
	0.11	0.19	0.14	0.18	0.17	0.19	0.21
	0.13	0.16	0.10	0.11	0.15	0.13	0.17
	0.09	0.10	0.10	0.09	0.13	0.09	0.09
	0.34	0.21	—	—	—	0.30	0.46
	0.53	0.60	0.61	0.60	0.65	0.51	0.57
	0.28	0.33	0.27	0.21	0.34	0.20	0.20
	0.69	0.60	—	—	—	0.72	0.67
	0.61	0.52	—	—	—	0.48	0.51
	0.34	0.52	0.28	0.35	0.54	0.37	0.46
	0.30	0.29	0.19	0.22	0.33	0.27	0.29
	0.19	0.19	0.09	0.06	0.16	0.12	0.13
	0.06	0.06	0.04	0.01	0.05	0.05	0.04
							ref.
	0.15	0.21	0.15	0.20	0.21	0.21	0.22
	0.08	0.05	—	—	—	0.04	0.11
	0.11	0.19	0.14	0.18	0.17	0.19	0.21
	0.13	0.16	0.10	0.11	0.15	0.13	0.17
	0.09	0.10	0.10	0.09	0.13	0.09	0.09
	0.34	0.21	—	—	—	0.30	0.46
	0.53	0.60	0.61	0.60	0.65	0.51	0.57
	0.28	0.33	0.27	0.21	0.34	0.20	0.20
	0.69	0.60	—	—	—	0.72	0.67
	0.61	0.52	—	—	—	0.48	0.51
	0.34	0.52	0.28	0.35	0.54	0.37	0.46
	0.30	0.29	0.19	0.22	0.33	0.27	0.29
	0.19	0.19	0.09	0.06	0.16	0.12	0.13
	0.06	0.06	0.04	0.01	0.05	0.05	0.04

Underline indicates significantly different from U.S.-born members of same racial/ethnic group at p<0.05.

[a]Controlled is defined as those individuals taking a medication, which accounts for a small percentage of adults who do not report hypertension and/or diabetes despite taking medication. Uncontrolled includes adults having either diagnosed or undiagnosed (on the basis of NHANES measures) hypertension and/or diabetes.

[b]Hypertension is defined as >140 mmHg for systolic BP OR >90 mmHg for diastolic.

[c]High blood glucose is defined as >100 mg/dL for blood glucose.

racial/ethnic variation in pain-related morbidity. Although Asian Americans report the lowest pain, no single racial/ethnic group emerges as consistently reporting the highest level.

Functioning and Disability

Table 2-4 turns to functioning and disability. Across all 15 measures, one can see the extent to which older Black, Mexican American, other Hispanic, and Native American adults experience significantly higher rates of functional, physical, and cognitive limitations as compared to non-Hispanic Whites, while Asian adults consistently exhibit the lowest rates. These racial/ethnic patterns are similar for both women and men, though women have a higher prevalence of functional limitations and disability, on average. Intriguingly, this racial/ethnic pattern of functional limitations would not be apparent solely based on adults reporting "any functional limitation." Across all groups, an average of 67 percent of women report any functional limitation, with U.S.-born Blacks and Native Americans having the highest rates (~75%) and Asians and foreign-born non-Hispanic Whites reporting the lowest (~60%). By comparison, ~57 percent of older men report having any functional limitation, with Native Americans having a far higher prevalence than any other group (72%) and Asians and foreign-born other Hispanics and non-Hispanic Whites experiencing significantly lower rates (~50%) than their U.S.-born non-Hispanic White counterparts (60%). However, when focusing on the more detailed assessments of functioning and disability, one observes clearer racial/ethnic gradients for both genders. For instance, U.S.-born Blacks, foreign-born Mexican Americans, and Other Hispanics are significantly more likely than U.S.-born non-Hispanic Whites to report limitations keeping them from working and/or impeding the amount of work they could do or report that they experienced confusion/memory problems. This was especially true of foreign-born Mexican Americans who, unlike their U.S.-born counterparts, reported ~10–20 percent higher rates across all three types of functional limitations.

Though functional limitations primarily relate to mental and cognitive health, we also observe many of the aforementioned patterns across multiple measures of disability. Approximately 13 percent of Native American, U.S.-born Black, and foreign-born Mexican American, other Hispanic, Asian, and non-Hispanic White women report 8 or more days of disability requiring bed rest in the past year; this is significantly higher than the 10 percent among U.S.-born non-Hispanic Whites. Based on NHIS estimates, U.S.-born Blacks, Mexican Americans, and Native Americans have the highest rates of any activity limitation (~42%), while foreign-born non-Hispanic Whites and Asians of any nativity report significantly lower rates (~28%), compared to ~34 percent of U.S.-born non-Hispanic

Whites. NHANES-based estimates of activity limitations are higher than those obtained from NHIS, yet we observe a similar pattern of disparities. Once again, a more fine-grained analysis of activity limitations helps to reveal the full extent of racial/ethnic differences in disability among older adults. Among individuals reporting 10 or more activity limitations, we continue to observe higher rates for U.S.-born Black, Mexican American, and other Hispanic women (~29%) compared to non-Hispanic White women (~17%), and higher rates for U.S.-born Black (15%) and foreign-born Mexican American (21%) men compared to U.S.-born non-Hispanic White men (12%).

Further subclassifying activity limitations based on physical or psychosocial health, older U.S.-born non-Hispanic White adults experience lower rates of disability than all other racial/ethnic groups (with the exception of U.S.-born Asians). Only ~6 percent of U.S.-born non-Hispanic White and Asian women and men report any activity of daily living limitations, compared to ~12 percent of women and ~8 percent of men across all other racial/ethnic groups. Similarly, ~12 percent of U.S.-born non-Hispanic White and Asian women and ~8 percent of men report any instrumental activity of daily living limitations, compared to ~19 percent of women and ~12 percent of men for all other racial/ethnic groups. These same patterns are replicated across measures of disability relating to limitations in leisure and social activities and general physical activities. Though women report higher average rates than men, for both genders U.S.-born Blacks and Mexican Americans (of any nativity) stand out as having the highest rates on these measures. That said, one can clearly see the critical role of nativity as a source of disparity in functional limitations and disability-related health among Mexican American and Asian women, as foreign-born adults have significantly worse health than their U.S.-born counterparts on nearly every measure.

Health Care

Given the importance of health care access and utilization as critical determinants of health among older adults, it is not surprising to find that many of the previously noted racial/ethnic patterns are reflected in health care measures as well (Table 2-5). Though the proportion of older adults reporting having no health insurance is low (owing to Medicare), Black, Mexican American, other Hispanic, Native American, and foreign-born Asian and non-Hispanic White men and women are significantly more likely to report not having health insurance compared to their U.S.-born non-Hispanic White counterparts. Nativity is particularly important, as foreign-born adults report the highest rates, especially Mexican American women (12%) and men (10%).

TABLE 2-4 Measures of Functioning and Disability among U.S. Adults, Ages 65+ (NHIS 2000–2015; NHANES 1999–2014)

	N-H Black		Mexican American	
	F-B	US-B	F-B	US-B
FEMALE				
FUNCTIONING				
Any functional limitation	0.64	**0.72**	**0.70**	**0.70**
Limitations keep you from working	0.15	**0.24**	<u>**0.39**</u>	**0.21**
Limited in amount of work you can do	<u>0.24</u>	**0.42**	<u>**0.47**</u>	**0.36**
Experience confusion/memory problems	0.14	**0.20**	<u>**0.34**</u>	**0.18**
DISABILITY				
Bed disabled 8+ days last year	0.10	**0.12**	<u>**0.13**</u>	0.10
Has any activity limitation (NHIS)	<u>0.34</u>	**0.47**	**0.41**	**0.40**
Has any activity limitation (NHANES)	0.72	**0.78**	<u>**0.87**</u>	**0.76**
N of activity limitations	4.86	**5.68**	<u>**6.70**</u>	**5.30**
Has 10+ activity limitations	0.21	**0.26**	<u>**0.35**</u>	**0.24**
Help w/ ADLs (NHIS)[a]	0.11	**0.13**	<u>**0.15**</u>	0.12
Any ADL limit (NHANES)	0.25	**0.36**	<u>**0.47**</u>	**0.33**
Help w/ IADLs (NHIS)[b]	<u>0.17</u>	**0.22**	0.21	0.19
Any IADL limit (NHANES)	0.37	**0.46**	<u>**0.56**</u>	**0.41**
Any limitation in leisure and social activities[c]	0.27	**0.39**	**0.49**	**0.40**
Any limitation in general physical activities[d]	<u>**0.61**</u>	**0.75**	<u>**0.82**</u>	**0.69**
MALE				
FUNCTIONING				
Any functional limitation	0.54	**0.60**	**0.59**	**0.56**
Limitations keep you from working	0.18	**0.22**	**0.35**	**0.26**
Limited in amount of work you can do	0.41	0.41	**0.44**	**0.42**
Experience confusion/memory problems	0.12	0.13	**0.23**	**0.18**
DISABILITY				
Bed disabled 8+ days last year	0.09	0.10	0.09	0.10
Has any activity limitation (NHIS)	<u>0.31</u>	**0.40**	**0.35**	**0.35**
Has any activity limitation (NHANES)	0.61	0.64	**0.72**	**0.72**
N of activity limitations	<u>2.96</u>	**3.94**	**4.77**	**4.27**
Has 10+ activity limitations	0.11	0.15	**0.21**	**0.15**
Help w/ ADLs (NHIS)[a]	0.08	0.08	0.08	0.08
Any ADL limit (NHANES)	0.16	**0.24**	**0.31**	**0.27**
Help w/ IADLs (NHIS)[b]	<u>0.09</u>	**0.14**	0.13	0.11
Any IADL limit (NHANES)	0.33	0.37	**0.40**	**0.42**
Any limitation in leisure and social activities[c]	<u>0.18</u>	**0.26**	<u>**0.39**</u>	**0.27**
Any limitation in general physical activities[d]	0.57	0.58	0.59	**0.64**

NOTES: NHIS N(Overall) = 181,924; NHANES N(Overall) = 11,173; NHIS N(Female) = 102,971; NHANES N(Female) = 5,734; NHIS N(Male) = 78,953; NHANES N(Male) = 5,439.

HS = high school completion, N-H = non-Hispanic, PI = Pacific Islander, F-B = foreign born, US-B = U.S. born.

Percent/mean estimates based on nonmissing responses for given survey item or measure.

All estimates weighted based on NCHS-derived weights, and age-standardized to 2000 U.S. Census.

Cells with <10 incidences excluded.

Bold indicates significantly different from U.S.-born non-Hispanic Whites at p<0.05.

Underline indicates significantly different from U.S.-born members of same racial/ethnic group at p<0.05.

Other Hispanic		N-H Asian/PI		Native Amer.	N-H White	
F-B	US-B	F-B	US-B	US-B	F-B	US-B
						ref.
0.66	0.68	0.63	0.54	0.79	0.62	0.69
0.26	0.35	—	—	—	0.16	0.17
0.42	0.51	—	—	—	0.36	0.39
0.22	0.30	—	—	—	0.15	0.14
0.14	0.11	0.12	0.05	0.16	0.12	0.10
0.35	0.41	0.33	0.24	0.53	0.32	0.35
0.69	0.81	—	—	—	0.65	0.75
5.18	6.62	—	—	—	4.13	4.40
0.25	0.34	—	—	—	0.18	0.16
0.12	0.10	0.12	0.05	0.13	0.08	0.06
0.34	0.41	—	—	—	0.26	0.25
0.17	0.18	0.17	0.10	0.25	0.15	0.14
0.42	0.50	—	—	—	0.37	0.37
0.34	0.45	—	—	—	0.25	0.27
0.34	0.73	—	—	—	0.59	0.72
						ref.
0.51	0.65	0.48	0.49	0.72	0.52	0.60
0.24	0.31	—	—	—	0.15	0.16
0.40	0.50	—	—	—	0.31	0.37
0.19	—	—	—	—	0.19	0.12
0.09	0.10	0.09	0.06	0.13	0.11	0.09
0.28	0.37	0.28	0.25	0.49	0.29	0.33
0.62	0.69	—	—	—	0.57	0.63
3.86	3.96	—	—	—	3.74	3.33
0.17	—	—	—	—	0.16	0.12
0.09	0.08	0.08	0.06	0.10	0.08	0.05
0.29	—	—	—	—	0.29	0.22
0.11	0.11	0.12	0.07	0.16	0.11	0.08
0.33	0.43	—	—	—	0.33	0.30
0.22	0.28	—	—	—	0.26	0.21
0.58	0.67	—	—	—	0.48	0.57

[a]ADLs: dressing oneself, eating and drinking, walking between rooms, getting in and out of bed.

[b]IADLs: managing money/finances; performing household chores; preparing meals.

[c]Leisure and social activities: going out for events/activities; attending social gatherings; performing leisure activities at home.

[d]General physical activities: pushing and pulling large objects; grasping/holding small objects; standing or sitting for long periods; reaching up over head; stooping, crouching, and kneeling; lifting or carrying; standing from an armless chair.

TABLE 2-5 Measures of Health Care Use and Access among U.S. Adults, Ages 65+ (NHIS 2000–2015)

	N-H Black		Mexican American	
	F-B	US-B	F-B	US-B
FEMALE				
HEALTH CARE				
Uninsured	<u>0.09</u>	0.01	<u>0.12</u>	0.01
During last year:				
Medical care delayed due to cost	0.06	0.06	0.07	0.06
Couldn't afford medical care	0.05	0.05	<u>0.06</u>	0.04
Had 10+ care visits	<u>0.18</u>	0.23	<u>0.23</u>	0.20
In hospital overnight	0.18	0.19	0.16	0.16
MALE				
HEALTH CARE				
Uninsured	<u>0.05</u>	0.01	<u>0.10</u>	0.01
During last year:				
Medical care delayed due to cost	<u>0.07</u>	0.04	0.06	0.04
Couldn't afford medical care	<u>0.06</u>	0.04	<u>0.04</u>	0.03
Had 10+ care visits	<u>0.17</u>	0.21	0.19	0.19
In hospital overnight	0.17	0.19	0.15	0.17

NOTES: NHIS N(Overall) = 181,924; NHANES N(Overall) = 11,173; NHIS N(Female) = 102,971; NHANES N(Female) = 5,734; NHIS N(Male) = 78,953; NHANES N(Male) = 5,439.

HS = high school completion, N-H = non-Hispanic, PI = Pacific Islander, F-B = foreign born, US-B = U.S. born.

Percent/mean estimates based on nonmissing responses for given survey item or measure.

All estimates weighted based on NCHS-derived weights, and age-standardized to 2000 U.S. Census.

| Other Hispanic | | N-H Asian/PI | | Native Amer. | N-H White | |
F-B	US-B	F-B	US-B	US-B	F-B	US-B
						ref.
<u>0.05</u>	0.01	<u>0.04</u>	0.00	0.03	0.02	0.00
0.05	0.06	<u>0.03</u>	0.02	0.07	0.04	0.04
0.03	0.04	<u>0.02</u>	0.01	0.05	0.03	0.02
<u>0.23</u>	0.19	<u>0.19</u>	0.15	0.29	0.19	0.20
0.16	0.16	0.11	0.11	0.23	0.15	0.17
						ref.
<u>0.03</u>	0.01	<u>0.04</u>	0.00	0.04	0.02	0.00
0.04	0.04	<u>0.03</u>	0.02	0.07	0.04	0.03
0.03	0.03	<u>0.02</u>	0.01	0.06	0.03	0.02
0.20	0.20	0.16	0.15	0.23	0.20	0.20
0.16	0.19	0.12	0.11	0.19	0.16	0.18

Cells with <10 incidences excluded.
Bold indicates significantly different from U.S.-born non-Hispanic Whites at p<0.05.
Underline indicates significantly different from U.S.-born members of same racial/ethnic group at p<0.05.

These patterns are similar with respect to health care during the last year. U.S.-born Black, foreign-born Mexican American and other Hispanic, and Native American women are more likely to report delaying medical care due to cost or not being able to afford medical care than are their U.S.-born non-Hispanic White and Asian counterparts. These racial/ethnic and nativity patterns are true of older men as well, with the addition of foreign-born Black, U.S.-born Mexican American, and foreign-born non-Hispanic White men also reporting more difficulties in receiving care than U.S.-born non-Hispanic White and Asian men. At the same time, non-Hispanic White and Asian women are less likely to have 10 or more health care visits in the last year (~17%), compared to U.S.-born Blacks, Native Americans, and foreign-born Mexican Americans and Other Hispanics (~24%). Similarly, U.S.-born Black and Native American women have the highest rate of overnight hospital stays (not related to surgery) at ~20 percent, while Asian women have the lowest at 11 percent. Asian American men also have the lowest rates of frequent care visits and overnight hospital stays compared to other groups.

Mortality

Table 2-6 highlights racial/ethnic and nativity differences in mortality among older adults. U.S.-born Blacks and Native Americans have higher all-cause mortality rates than do U.S.-born non-Hispanic Whites and other minority groups, while foreign-born non-Hispanic Whites and Asians have the lowest rates. These all-cause racial/ethnic patterns are replicated in the case of diseases of the heart, cancer, and mortality from all other causes. Cancer and all-other-cause mortality rates are particularly high among Native American men. Nativity is crucial in shaping mortality among older adults; foreign-born groups have lower all-cause and cause-specific mortality rates than do U.S.-born groups, across both genders (with the exception of Asian women).

Though many of the detailed causes of death have cell counts for specific groups that are too small to report reliably estimated rates, we note racial/ethnic variation across a number of cause-specific categories. Chronic lower respiratory disease is the only cause for which U.S.-born non-Hispanic White adults have higher mortality relative to U.S.-born Blacks, Mexican Americans, and foreign-born Hispanics and non-Hispanic Whites. Conversely, diabetes mortality is highest for those groups, and lowest among U.S.-born non-Hispanic White women (while second lowest among U.S.-born non-Hispanic White men). Cerebrovascular disease mortality is especially high among U.S.-born Black women and men, as is kidney-related disease, when compared to the other groups.

Racial/Ethnic Health Disparities among Middle-Aged Adults

Our main results above focused on racial/ethnic disparities among older U.S. adults. In this section, we briefly discuss disparities among middle-aged adults. Given the rapidly changing demographic composition of the United States, a multidimensional perspective on the health of younger adults provides valuable insight on the *future* of health disparities among rising cohorts of aging Americans. In a series of supplementary analyses, we examined racial/ethnic disparities in the same measures of health among adults aged 45–64 (tables available from the authors by request).

Though there is considerable and predictable age-based variation in the prevalence of certain health measures and conditions, our results nevertheless demonstrate that the above-described racial/ethnic health disparities in older adult health are largely evident among middle-aged adults as well. For example, though middle-aged adults report 20–30 percent less poor/fair health than older adults, Blacks, Mexican Americans, other Hispanics, and Native Americans report significantly higher levels than their non-Hispanic White counterparts. They are also more likely to indicate a recent decline in health and more days of poor health. Meanwhile, Asian adults and foreign-born non-Hispanic Whites continue to have the lowest rates of poor/fair or worsening health. In contrast to self-rated health, this younger age group has a 5–20 percent higher prevalence of obesity and risky waist circumference across all groups compared with older adults, with women continuing to have worse weight-related health than men. Black, Mexican American, and Native American women have the highest rates of self-reported and measured obesity (~40–60%) and risky waist circumference (~70–90%), while Asians have the lowest obesity rate among all groups at ~10–20 percent. In general, foreign-born men have the lowest rates of self-reported or measured obesity.

With respect to morbidity, though prevalence for most conditions and diseases is far lower than older adults, there is a remarkable degree of consistency in group differences when compared to their older counterparts. Self-reported hypertension follows similar racial/ethnic patterns for this age group as among older adults, with Black, Mexican American, and Native American women reporting the highest rates (37–55%). For both genders, foreign-born Asians and non-Hispanic Whites continue to have the lowest reports of hypertension. U.S.-born Black and Native American women have the highest reported diagnoses of heart-related conditions, while foreign-born Asian adults exhibit the best overall indicators of positive heart health. Foreign-born Black, Mexican American, other Hispanic, and non-Hispanic White men also compare favorably on these measures against U.S.-born non-Hispanic White men. Diabetes continues to be higher for non-White and Hispanic compared to non-Hispanic White adults, with

TABLE 2-6 Mortality among U.S. Adults, Ages 65+ (NHIS 2000–2015)

	N-H Black		Mexican American	
	F-B	US-B	F-B	US-B
FEMALE				
MORTALITY (rate per 100,000 person-years)				
All-cause	<u>2410</u>	4341	<u>2898</u>	3262
Disease of heart	<u>399</u>	964	<u>514</u>	573
Malignant neoplasms	<u>643</u>	910	<u>476</u>	530
Chronic lower respiratory diseases	—	139	<u>126</u>	115
Cerebrovascular diseases	—	323	<u>177</u>	242
Alzheimer's disease	—	146	—	233
Diabetes mellitus	—	232	<u>208</u>	244
Influenza/pneumonia	—	122	—	—
Kidney-related diseases	—	143	105	105
Accidents	—	40	—	86
All other causes	<u>627</u>	1298	1009	1046
MALE				
MORTALITY (rate per 100,000 person-years)				
All-cause	<u>3883</u>	5924	<u>3592</u>	4484
Disease of heart	<u>947</u>	1289	<u>784</u>	866
Malignant neoplasms	<u>1030</u>	1635	<u>856</u>	1047
Chronic lower respiratory diseases	—	275	<u>116</u>	254
Cerebrovascular diseases	—	296	<u>298</u>	216
Alzheimer's disease	—	120	—	132
Diabetes mellitus	—	198	256	—
Influenza/pneumonia	—	129	—	124
Kidney-related diseases	—	213	<u>107</u>	166
Accidents	—	105	105	—
All other causes	<u>855</u>	1636	<u>845</u>	1280

NOTES: NHIS N(Overall) = 181,924; NHANES N(Overall) = 11,173; NHIS N(Female) = 102,971; NHANES N(Female) = 5,734; NHIS N(Male) = 78,953; NHANES N(Male) = 5,439. HS = high school completion, N-H = non-Hispanic, PI = Pacific Islander, F-B = foreign born, US-B = U.S. born.

Public use NHIS data up to 2009 are linked to National Death Index records through December 31, 2011.

Percent/mean estimates based on nonmissing responses for given survey item or measure.

Other Hispanic		N-H Asian/PI		Native Amer.	N-H White	
F-B	US-B	F-B	US-B	US-B	F-B	US-B
						ref.
2407	2936	2334	1871	4533	2586	3568
536	676	352	460	627	503	639
580	624	603	274	—	601	787
85	—	—	77	—	160	279
164	—	303	—	—	206	246
80	—	—	—	—	—	148
127	—	139	—	—	—	92
—	—	—	—	—	—	90
77	—	—	—	—	—	76
—	—	—	—	—	80	78
672	1047	575	603	1520	785	1121
						ref.
4259	4662	3097	3295	6470	3674	5308
1167	847	549	576	—	828	1147
958	1315	883	790	1748	1068	1321
153	—	151	—	—	79	418
266	—	389	—	—	208	277
—	—	—	—	—	149	133
208	—	—	—	—	68	151
110	—	—	—	—	—	116
82	—	—	—	—	—	121
77	—	—	—	—	—	121
1085	1210	759	868	1709	1056	1488

All estimates weighted based on NCHS-derived weights, and age-standardized to 2000 U.S. Census.
Cells with <10 incidences excluded.
Bold indicates significantly different from U.S.-born non-Hispanic Whites at $p<0.05$.
Underline indicates significantly different from U.S.-born members of same racial/ethnic group at $p<0.05$.

Native American adults having the highest self-reported rates and Mexican Americans having among the highest measured or diagnosed rates. The most significant age differences are related to pain. Among middle-aged adults, reported pain is lower on average, and the gender gap among older adults is largely absent. For both genders, Native Americans report the most pain across all indicators, while Asians and foreign-born Blacks and non-Hispanic Whites report the least. Overall, middle-aged U.S.-born non-Hispanic White adults report higher levels of pain compared to all other groups except Native Americans, consistent with recent studies (Case and Deaton, 2015).

Compared to measures of global health and morbidity, functional limitations and disability are much less frequent among middle-aged adults. Nonetheless, again, many of the same racial/ethnic patterns noted for older adults are observed. U.S.-born Blacks have worse functioning- and disability-related health than their Asian and non-Hispanic White counterparts. As with older adults, Mexican Americans, other Hispanics, and U.S.-born Blacks have a greater prevalence of severe mental health symptoms compared to U.S.-born non-Hispanic Whites. However, nativity is particularly important in shaping racial/ethnic group differences: foreign-born Blacks, Mexican Americans, other Hispanics, and non-Hispanic Whites consistently exhibit more favorable functional health and disability rates than their U.S.-born racial/ethnic counterparts and, in some cases, than U.S.-born non-Hispanic Whites.

U.S.-born non-Hispanic White and Asian men and women also continue to report greater health care access and utilization than their racial/ethnic counterparts. Although more adults in this age range report not having health insurance (~20% across all groups), foreign-born Mexican Americans still have the highest rates (~44%) and U.S.-born Asians have the lowest (~6%), compared to ~10 percent for U.S.-born Whites. These middle-aged adults also report more issues with the cost or affordability of medical care in the last year, especially among U.S.-born Black, Mexican American, other Hispanic, and Native American women. Overall, foreign-born adults have the lowest levels of interaction with the health care system in this age range.

Finally, patterns of racial/ethnic disparities in mortality at these ages are entirely consistent with those among older adults. All-cause mortality is highest for U.S.-born Blacks and Native Americans among both genders. U.S.-born Asians have among the lowest mortality rates; foreign-born other Hispanic and non-Hispanic White adults have similarly low levels of mortality. Nativity remains a key stratifying variable, as mortality among foreign-born groups is lower than among their U.S.-born counterparts in every group. U.S.-born Black women have high rates of mortality due to diseases of the heart, cancer, and the all-other-causes category, while U.S.-

born Black men also have high rates of mortality from these causes, close to the rates observed among Native American men.

SUMMARY AND DISCUSSION

Summary of Disparities

Our results reveal five overarching patterns that best describe current racial/ethnic health disparities among older Americans. First, Asian American men and women, especially the U.S. born, consistently have the most favorable health profiles. Both U.S.- and foreign-born non-Hispanic White adults are comparable to Asians on some but not all measures of health; most important, U.S.-born Whites exhibit higher rates of obesity and smoking, a greater prevalence of heart-related conditions, and higher mortality rates than Asians. Second, there is a substantial gap in overall population health between, on the one hand, Asian Americans and non-Hispanic Whites, who exhibit the healthiest overall profiles in the country, and Blacks, Mexican Americans, and other Hispanics, who exhibit the least healthy overall profiles. Though the latter three groups are similar on a number of measures (e.g., self-rated health, heart-related morbidities, functioning and disability, health care access/use), U.S.-born Black adults typically report the poorest overall, physical, and mental health and well-being. By contrast, there are measures on which foreign-born Blacks compare favorably to their non-Hispanic White and Asian-American peers (e.g., low rates of obesity and smoking). Third, Native American older adults exhibit the worst overall health profile. For the majority of available measures, their rates of poor health are far higher than the elevated rates among U.S.-born Black adults. Fourth, we find that the above-described racial/ethnic disparities are typically more pronounced among women than men. For instance, a number of indicators of poor health—obesity, risky waist circumference, hypertension, pain, and most measures of impaired functioning and disability—exhibit similar patterns of racial/ethnic disparities by gender, but the disparities tend to be greater among women. Finally, nativity is an important moderator of racial/ethnic disparities in health, with the direction of its influence varying across groups. Foreign-born non-Hispanic White adults are typically healthier than their U.S.-born counterparts, although the former report higher rates of poor/fair health. Similarly, foreign-born Blacks often have better health than their U.S.-born Black counterparts, and in many cases better health than U.S.-born non-Hispanic Whites. Conversely, foreign-born Asian Americans tend to fare worse than their U.S.-born counterparts, though most of the disparities are small. Similarly, foreign-born Mexican Americans have worse functioning, disability-related health, and subjective health than U.S.-born Mexican

Americans, while only the latter is true among other Hispanics. Yet foreign-born members of both groups have lower mortality compared to U.S.-born adults. Notably, there is no uniform pattern of healthy immigrants relative to the U.S. born across racial/ethnic groups.

Clearly, these racial/ethnic disparities are vital to understanding overall population health in the United States. Yet, consistent with our objective of providing a *comprehensive* and *multidimensional* portrait of older adult health, we find that a narrow focus on specific health disparities is equally warranted, as reflected in the unique patterns observed for particular measures of health. For example, the subjective health of groups other than non-Hispanic Whites, with the exception of Asian Americans, is far worse in terms of physical, mental, and overall well-being than their U.S.-born non-Hispanic White counterparts (and for foreign-born adults relative to their U.S.-born co-racial/ethnic group members). Women generally fare worse than men, and foreign-born Mexican American women consistently have the worst subjective health across all groups. Weight-related health risk is also particularly high among Black women, especially compared to men. Only Native American men consistently exhibit poor health across all global health indicators.

Morbidity patterns are also nuanced. U.S.-born Black, Mexican American, and other Hispanics typically have higher levels of diabetes and hypertension, yet lower or similar rates of diagnosed cardiovascular conditions when compared to non-Hispanic Whites; this is perhaps attributable to racial/ethnic disparities in health care access. Nativity is particularly salient in comparing reports of diagnosed conditions, as foreign-born adults exhibit lower disease prevalence than their U.S.-born counterparts (especially among Black adults); again, access to health care may be playing a role. Native Americans again emerge as a group with consistently elevated disease prevalence. Pain, while on the rise among non-Hispanic White adults (Case and Deaton, 2015), is highest among foreign-born Mexican Americans and other Hispanics and among Native Americans, especially women.

Relatedly, functioning and disability represent other dimensions of health in which groups other than non-Hispanic Whites (with the exception of Asians) fare worse, as is especially evident for U.S.-born Blacks and foreign-born Mexican Americans. Older adults other than Asians and non-Hispanic Whites have much higher rates of physical and mental disability and impaired functioning, even at younger ages where these conditions are far less prevalent. Nativity is once again critical as, with the exception of Mexican Americans, U.S.-born adults often fare worse than their foreign-born counterparts. Yet again, Native American men and women exhibit the least favorable patterns of functional health, consistently reporting the highest rates among all groups of impaired functioning, poor mental health, and everyday disabilities or limitations.

Finally, mortality is especially high among U.S.-born Blacks for all-cause, disease of the heart, cancer, and residual causes of mortality—especially among men—whereas Asian Americans have the lowest rates. As with most of the health measures discussed above, we again emphasize the very high rates of mortality among Native Americans, comparable with U.S.-born Blacks. On the other hand, rates of mortality are particularly low among foreign-born Mexican Americans and Other Hispanics, as well as other foreign-born groups relative to the U.S. born, consistent with the well-documented immigrant mortality advantage (Hummer et al., 2015).

Future Directions

The U.S. older population is rapidly growing and diversifying (Ortman et al., 2014). At the same time, both the older adult and middle-aged populations exhibit very wide racial/ethnic and nativity disparities in educational attainment and family income. But with the important exceptions of Asian Americans (both foreign born and U.S. born), foreign-born Blacks, and foreign-born non-Hispanic Whites, most racial/ethnic and nativity groups exhibit worse health across a number of important domains relative to U.S.-born non-Hispanic Whites, who also (along with Asian Americans) exhibit the most favorable socioeconomic profile for health. Thus, as we look ahead to a larger and more diverse U.S. older adult population as the 21st century unfolds, there is substantial concern for the health of older Americans—especially Mexican Americans, other Hispanics, U.S.-born Blacks, and Native Americans—given the extent of the socioeconomic and health disparities we outlined above, both among older Americans and among middle-aged adults.

One key role of the demographic research community will be to continue to carefully document racial/ethnic and nativity disparities in health as the size and diversity of the older adult population changes. This documentation will not be straightforward, given changing immigration and emigration streams and shifts in racial/ethnic identities across time. Fortunately, the NHIS and NHANES data we used here, while imperfect, provide the research community with invaluable sources of information on the health of the U.S. population. Importantly, the continued production of these datasets relies on adequate federal government budget allocations to the National Center for Health Statistics. Thus, we urge researchers not only to use these datasets for continued documentation of disparities but to help provide justification to policy makers for the continued production of such data, without which researchers will not have the information necessary to produce detailed accounts of U.S. health disparities.

Given both racial/ethnic disparities in SES and wide racial/ethnic health disparities in middle age, we unfortunately expect that racial/ethnic health disparities in older adulthood will continue to be wide well into the future. As supported by decades of research, the higher levels of education and income observed among non-Hispanic White, Asian American, and foreign-born non-Hispanic White and Black middle- and older-aged adults coincided with their better health outcomes across a variety of outcomes. While SES disparities do not *perfectly* map onto health disparities (e.g., Mexican immigrants have the lowest educational attainment, yet do not consistently exhibit the worst health), they are strongly aligned with observed racial/ethnic variations in health. Even with rising overall educational attainment in the United States across all racial/ethnic and nativity groups (Everett et al., 2011), large educational and income disparities across groups persist. Future research efforts will need to focus on the extent to which socioeconomic differences across groups are responsible for observed health disparities. In turn, our nation's policy efforts will continue to need to emphasize the reduction of disparities in educational attainment, income, and other dimensions of SES if one wishes to reduce and/or eliminate racial/ethnic disparities in health.

Our documentation focused on health disparities, with socioeconomic disparities provided for context. This does not mean that other factors are not important for the understanding of racial/ethnic disparities in health. Consider, for example, cigarette smoking, which not only is responsible for over 500,000 adult deaths per year in the United States (Carter et al., 2015) but also undoubtedly contributes to some of the racial/ethnic disparities documented here. Historically higher patterns of smoking among U.S.-born Blacks, Native Americans, and non-Hispanic Whites relative to other groups are in part responsible for some of the higher rates of mortality for those groups exhibited above. In this case, policies and programs to eliminate cigarette smoking in the United States would have major influences not only on improving older adult population health but also on reducing some of the racial/ethnic and nativity disparities documented above.

Our chapter focused on national-level estimates, and consequently our future research suggestions and policy recommendations also focus on the national level. At the same time, racial/ethnic disparities in older adult health are not uniform across geographic areas. Recent research, for example, highlights important variations in social and policy environments across states—variations that may be particularly important in structuring access to resources that engender good health, especially for women (Montez et al., 2016, 2017), and may have important impacts on racial/ethnic disparities in health. Other research documents substantial geographic variation in the clustering of key health behaviors and conditions—such as smoking, alcohol and substance use, and obesity—that further contributes to the geographic patterning of morbidity and mortality (Fenelon, 2013; Patel et al., 2014; Tencza et al., 2014) and may impact racial/ethnic disparities. Looking ahead, a greater focus on both the individual level and on the contexts within which individuals are embedded will be important for the more complete understanding of racial/ethnic health disparities.

Perhaps most importantly, our analysis of the health of older adults reveals the need to look further "upstream" in the population age distribution to uncover the etiology of racial/ethnic disparities in health. In the present study, we also examined the group ages 45–64 to estimate disparities among contemporary middle-aged adults. The middle-aged group will soon become the next generation of older adults; consequently they provide an indication of America's future health patterns and needs. As evidenced by our results (available from the authors by request), the majority of disparities documented among older adults are mirrored among this younger generation, suggesting that the origins of many group health inequities can be traced back earlier in the life course. A more complete understanding of health disparities would benefit from the careful documentation of racial/ethnic differences in health among even younger-aged groups, including childhood.

In closing, we turn back to one of the key theoretical considerations with which we opened. Given the tragic history of racism that has been so influential in the social and economic life of African Americans and Native Americans, it is unfortunately no surprise that these two groups stood out for generally exhibiting the worst older-adult population health across nearly all measures, in comparison with the other groups we considered. The socioeconomic and health disparities we documented among middle-aged individuals, for which African Americans and Native Americans also exhibited substantial disadvantages on most measures relative to the other groups, further suggest that racial/ethnic health disparities will not disappear anytime soon. Such evidence strongly suggests that the national policy agenda must focus aggressive attention on promoting socioeconomic equity between African Americans, Native Americans, and non-Hispanic Whites— without which large disparities in population health will likely linger well into the future.

REFERENCES

Akresh, I.R., and Frank, R. (2008). Health selection among new immigrants. *American Journal of Public Health*, 98(11), 2058–2064.

Arias, E., Heron, M., and Xu, J. (2017). *United States Life Tables, 2013* (National Vital Statistics Reports, vol. 66 no. 3). Hyattsville, MD: National Center for Health Statistics.

Bilheimer, L.T., and Klein, R.J. (2010). Data and measurement issues in the analysis of health disparities. *Health Services Research*, 45(5), 1489–1507.

Brown, T.H., Richardson, L.J., Hargrove, T.W., and Thomas, C.S. (2016). Using multiple-hierarchy stratification approaches to understand health inequalities: The intersecting consequences of race, gender, SES and age. *Journal of Health and Social Behavior, 57*(2), 200–222.

Bruckner, T.A., Brown, R.A., and Margerison-Zilko, C. (2011). Positive income shocks and accidental deaths among Cherokee Indians: A natural experiment. *International Journal of Epidemiology, 40*(4), 1083–1090.

Carter, B.D., Abnet, C.C., Feskanich, D., Freedman, N.D., Hartge, P., Lewis, C.E., Ockene, J.K., Prentice, R.L., Speizer, F.E., Thun, M.J., and Jacobs, E.J. (2015). Smoking and mortality—beyond established causes. *New England Journal of Medicine, 372*(7), 631–640.

Case, A., and Deaton, A. (2015). Rising morbidity and mortality in midlife among White non-Hispanic Americans in the 21st century. *Proceedings of the National Academy of Sciences of the United States of America, 112*(49), 5078–5083.

Case, A., and Paxson, C.H. (2005). Sex differences in morbidity and mortality. *Demography, 42*(2), 189–214.

Cho, Y., Frisbie, W.P., Hummer, R.A., and Rogers, R.G. (2004). Nativity, duration of residence, and the health of Hispanic adults in the United States. *International Migration Review, 38*(1), 184–211.

Colby, S.L., and Ortman, J.M. (2015). *Projections of the Size and Composition of the U.S. Population: 2014 to 2060* (Current Population Reports P25-1143). Washington, DC: U.S. Census Bureau. Available: https://census.gov/content/dam/Census/library/publications/2015/demo/p25-1143.pdf [February 2018].

Costello, E.J., Erkanli, A., Copeland, W., and Angold, A. (2010). Association of family income supplements in adolescence with development of psychiatric and substance use disorders in adulthood among an American Indian population. *Journal of the American Medical Association, 303*(19), 1954–1960.

Dwyer-Lindgren, L., Bertozzi-Villa, A., Stubbs, R.W., Morozoff, C., Mackenbach, J.P., van Lenthe, F.J., Mokdad, A.H., and Murray, C.J. (2017). Inequalities in life expectancy among U.S. counties, 1980 to 2014: Temporal trends and key drivers. *JAMA Internal Medicine, 177*(7), 1003–1011.

Everett, B.G., Rogers, R.G., Krueger, P.M., and Hummer, R.A. (2011). Trends in educational attainment by race/ethnicity, nativity, and sex in the United States, 1989-2005. *Ethnic and Racial Studies, 34*(9), 1543–1566.

Feliciano, C. (2005). Educational selectivity in U.S. immigration: How do immigrants compare to those left behind? *Demography, 42*(1), 131–152.

Fenelon, A. (2013). Geographic divergence in mortality in the United States. *Population and Development Review, 39*(4), 611–634.

Flores, A. (2017). How the U.S. Hispanic population is changing. *Fact Tank: News in the Numbers.* Pew Research Center. Available: http://www.pewresearch.org/fact-tank/2017/09/18/how-the-u-s-hispanic-population-is-changing/ [March 2018].

Frisbie, W.P., Cho, Y., and Hummer, R.A. (2001). Immigration and the health of Asian and Pacific Islander adults in the U.S. *American Journal of Epidemiology, 153*(4), 372–380.

Gates, H.L., Steele, C., Bobo, L.D., Dawson, M., Jaynes, G., Crooms-Robinson, L., and Darling-Hammond, L. (Eds.). (2012). *The Oxford Handbook of African American Citizenship, 1865–Present.* New York: Oxford University Press.

Gutin, I. (2017). In BMI we trust: Reframing the body mass index as a measure of health. *Social Theory & Health,* 1–16. doi: https://doi.org/10.1057/s41285-017-0055-0.

Hayward, M.D., Miles, T.P., Crimmins, E.M., and Yang, Y. (2000). The significance of socioeconomic status in explaining the racial gap in chronic health conditions. *American Sociological Review, 65*(6), 910–930.

Hayward, M.D., Hummer, R.A., Chiu, C.T., González-González, C., and Wong, R. (2014). Does the Hispanic paradox in U.S. adult mortality extend to disability? *Population Research and Policy Review, 33*(1), 81–96.

Hummer, R.A., and Hayward, M.D. (2015). Hispanic older adult health and longevity in the United States: Current patterns and concerns for the future. *Daedalus, 144*(2), 20–30.

Hummer, R.A., Melvin, J.E., and He, M. (2015). Immigration, health, and mortality. In J.D. Wright (editor-in-chief), *International Encyclopedia of Social and Behavioral Sciences* (2nd ed., vol. 11, pp. 654–661). Oxford: Elsevier Press.

Jones, D.S. (2006). The persistence of American Indian health disparities. *American Journal of Public Health, 96*(12), 2122–2134.

Jones-Smith, J.C., Dow, W.H., and Chichlowska, K. (2014). Association between casino opening or expansion and risk of childhood overweight and obesity. *Journal of the American Medical Association, 311*(9), 929–936.

Kochanek, K.D., Arias, E., and Bastian, B.A. (2016). *The Effect of Changes in Selected Age-Specific Causes of Death on Non-Hispanic White Life Expectancy Between 2000 and 2014.* NCHS Data Brief 250, pp. 1–7. Hyattsville, MD: National Center for Health Statistics. Available: https://www.cdc.gov/nchs/data/databriefs/db250.pdf [February 2018].

Kodish, S.R., Gittelsohn, J., Oddo, V.M., and Jones-Smith, J.C. (2016). Impacts of casinos on key pathways to health: Qualitative findings from American Indian gaming communities in California. *BMC Public Health, 16*(1), 621–633.

Lee, J., and Bean, F.D. (2007). Reinventing the color line: Immigration and America's new racial/ethnic divide. *Social Forces, 86*(2), 561–586.

Masters, R.K., Hummer, R.A., Powers, D.A., Beck, A., Lin, S., and Finch, B.K. (2014). Long-term trends in adult mortality for U.S. Blacks and Whites: An examination of period- and cohort-based changes. *Demography, 51*(6), 2047–2073.

Montez, J.K., Zajacova, A., and Hayward, M.D. (2016). Explaining inequalities in women's mortality between U.S. states. *SSM Population Health, 2*, 561–571.

Montez, J.K., Hayward, M.D., and Wolf, D.A. (2017). Do U.S. states' socioeconomic and policy contexts shape adult disability? *Social Science & Medicine, 178*, 115–126.

National Center for Health Statistics. (2005). *National Health and Nutrition Examination Survey: Overview.* Available: https://www.cdc.gov/nchs/data/nhanes/nhanes_13_14/nhanes_overview_brochure.pdf [March 2018].

National Center for Health Statistics. (2016). *About the National Health Interview Survey.* Available: https://www.cdc.gov/nchs/nhis/about_nhis.htm [March 2018].

National Research Council. (1994). *Demography of Aging.* L.G. Martin and S.H. Preston, Eds. Committee on Population, Commission on Behavioral and Social Sciences and Education. Washington, DC: National Academy Press.

National Research Council. (1997). *Racial and Ethnic Differences in the Health of Older Americans.* L.G. Martin and B.J. Soldo, Eds. Committee on Population, Commission on Behavioral and Social Sciences and Education. Washington, DC: National Academy Press.

National Research Council. (2004). *Critical Perspectives on Racial and Ethnic Differences in Health in Late Life.* N.B. Anderson, R.A. Bulatao, and B. Cohen, Eds. Panel on Race, Ethnicity, and Health in Later Life. Committee on Population, Division of Behavioral and Social Sciences and Education. Washington, DC: The National Academies Press.

National Research Council. (2006). *Multiple Origins, Uncertain Destinies: Hispanics and the American Future.* Panel on Hispanics in the United States. M. Tienda and F. Mitchell (Eds.), Committee on Population. Division of Behavioral and Social Sciences and Education. Washington, DC: The National Academies Press.

Ortman, J.M., Velkoff, V.A., and Hogan, H. (2014). *An Aging Nation: The Older Population in the United States.* Current Population Reports P25-1140. Washington, DC: U.S. Census Bureau.

Palloni, A., and Ewbank, D.C. (2004). Selection processes in the study of racial and ethnic differentials in adult health and mortality. In N.B. Anderson, R.A. Bulatao, and B. Cohen, (Eds.), *Critical Perspectives on Racial and Ethnic Differences in Health in Late Life* (pp. 171–226). Committee on Population, Division of Behavioral and Social Sciences and Education. Washington, DC: The National Academies Press.

Patel, S.A., Narayan, K.V., Ali, M.K., and Mehta, N.K. (2014). Interstate variation in modifiable risk factors and cardiovascular mortality in the United States. *PLoS One, 9*(7), e101531.

Phelan, J.C., and Link, B.G. (2015). Is racism a fundamental cause of inequalities in health? *Annual Review of Sociology, 41*(1), 311–330.

Richardson, L.J., and Brown, T.H. (2016). (En)gendering racial disparities in health trajectories: A life course and intersectional analysis. *Social Science & Medicine: Population Health, 2*(1), 425–435.

Sandefur, G., Campbell, M.E., and Eggerling-Boeck, J. (2004). Racial and ethnic identification, official classifications, and health disparities. In N.B. Anderson, R.A. Bulatao, and B. Cohen (Eds.), *Critical Perspectives on Racial and Ethnic Differences in Health in Late Life* (pp. 25–52). Committee on Population, Division of Behavioral and Social Sciences and Education. Washington, DC: The National Academies Press.

Satcher, D., Fryer, G.E., Jr., McCann, J., Troutman, A., Woolf, S.H., and Rust, G. (2005). What if we were equal? A comparison of the Black-White mortality gap in 1960 and 2000. *Health Affairs, 24*(2), 459–464.

Smith-Kaprosy, N., Martin, P.P., and Whitman, K. (2012). An overview of American Indians and Alaska Natives in the context of Social Security and Supplemental Security Income. *Social Security Bulletin, 72*(4), 1.

Tencza, C., Stokes, A., and Preston, S. (2014). Factors responsible for mortality variation in the United States: A latent variable analysis. *Demographic Research, 21*(2), 27–70.

Ward, E., Jemal, A., Cokkinides, V., Singh, G.K., Cardinez, C., Ghafoor, A., and Thun, M. (2004). Cancer disparities by race/ethnicity and socioeconomic status. *CA: A Cancer Journal for Clinicians, 54*(2), 78–93.

Williams, D.R., Mohammed, S.A., Leavell, J., and Collins, C. (2010). Race, socioeconomic status, and health: Complexities, ongoing challenges, and research opportunities. *Annals of the New York Academy of Sciences, 1186*(1), 69–101.

Wolfe, B., Jakubowski, J., Haveman, R., and Courey, M. (2012). The income and health effects of tribal casino gaming on American Indians. *Demography, 49*(2), 499–524.

World Health Organization. (2006). *Constitution of the World Health Organization* (Basic Documents, 45th ed., Supplement). Available: http://www.who.int/governance/eb/who_constitution_en.pdf [March 2018].

3

Socioeconomic Status, Health, and Mortality in Aging Populations

Angela M. O'Rand and Scott M. Lynch
Duke University

INTRODUCTION

Nearly 25 years ago, Preston and Taubman (1994) summarized major observations from demographic research on socioeconomic differences in adult mortality and health in a National Research Council volume on the *Demography of Aging*. By then, the associations between socioeconomic status (SES) and health and mortality were widely reported, although the measurement of these phenomena was not firmly established nor were the causal relationships between them. Most notable among the findings they reported was the widening of educational differences in mortality for men over the previous three decades, evident especially in the magnitude of educational differences in heart-disease death rates among White men. Mortality caused by cardiovascular disease had declined overall, but the majority of educational differences in mortality were attributable to differentials in heart disease for all sex–racial/ethnic groupings. Similarly, educational differentials in disability, poor health, and chronic conditions were evident by midlife (ages 45–54), although differences appeared to diminish at later ages. Finally, their evaluation of the growing literature on the effects of numerous intervening, proximate variables such as health behaviors (including smoking), personality, social relationships, environmental factors, and access to medical care revealed the "persistent failure" of these variables to account fully for the relationship between education and health.

The authors considered alternative measures of SES and adopted the most commonly used measure in the literature, education (years of school-

67

ing), as the most reliable choice for their analyses because of its stability within individuals, its interval measurement scale, and its unique significant association at that time (based mainly on cross-sectional studies) with health behaviors and cardiovascular risk. Education's apparent effects were widely attributed to cognitive skills and greater access to information. Other measures of SES were considered to be limited by issues of endogeneity, including selectivity and reverse causation. Occupation, for example, excludes persons who do not work (the retired, housewives, the disabled), a status that may be determined by health. Income suffers from the same problem of endogeneity since health may limit hours worked. In addition, income can be measured in several ways (earnings, transfers, savings, other household members' incomes), each with different implications for health outcomes. They did acknowledge that education may also be affected by long-term disability and its effects on later morbidity and mortality, but they found reverse causation to be less of a problem in the general population.

The robust relationship between SES and health continues as a dominant theme in the demography of aging. Since the publication of the 1994 Preston and Taubman summary (referred to as *PT94* in the remainder of this essay), life course theory has emerged as a key organizing framework for examining the relationship between SES and health over longer periods of the life span, during which the onset, duration, co-occurrences, and sequential contingency (if not causal relationship) between SES and health-related events can be observed. The development of life course theory has been facilitated as longitudinal databases have matured and have incorporated increasingly precise measures of health and disease and as they have been augmented via linkages to administrative data such as Social Security, Medicare, and/or patient records. Linkages to administrative data have also improved the measurement of mortality and health costs (especially with access to Medicare records) relative to reported income and to the diverse geographical contexts of aging (using Decennial Census, health and vital statistics, and GPS data). Genomic databases have emerged most recently to add precision to the measurement of the etiology of diseases and may contribute to the resolution of questions regarding causality, especially as gene-by-environment interactions can be more readily modeled. Further, analytic statistical tools for dealing with endogeneity, in particular selectivity and other unobserved heterogeneity, have been developed to better assess causality, although the complexity of this relationship over time poses continuing challenges.

This chapter begins by examining the current relationship between SES, mortality, and health and the major advances in understanding this relationship since *PT94*. Then we review the contribution of the life course framework to understanding this relationship across the life span and the analytical challenges in doing so. We then summarize the biological and behavioral pathways in the SES-health-mortality association that are current foci of demographic research and conclude by considering the approaches and challenges of these foci for selected future directions in research.

SES, HEALTH, AND MORTALITY IN THE 21ST CENTURY

In this section we conduct analyses that update *PT94*. We use data from the Integrated Health Interview Survey (IHIS), a combined collection of the National Health Interview Survey (NHIS) (Minnesota Population Center and State Health Access Data Assistance Center, 2015). NHIS is a nationally representative, repeated cross-sectional survey of community-dwelling persons (National Center for Health Statistics, 2014). We use two major health outcomes in our analyses: all-cause mortality and self-rated health (SRH). Our main goal is to evaluate whether the broad patterns in the association between SES and health that *PT94* reported from 1960 through the mid-1980s have changed or have continued in recent decades. Because these are not entirely comparable data to those used in *PT94*, we cannot perfectly extend the results reported there.

Mortality Analyses

Mortality data have been incorporated into the IHIS from 1986 to 2009, with the survey tracking mortality to 2011 (National Center for Health Statistics, 2015). Using these data, we constructed a person-year dataset (with individuals limited to a 5-year follow-up period) and estimated a number of discrete time logistic regression models (Allison, 1984) predicting mortality by age group (30–44, 45–54, 55–64, 65–74, and 75+ years; measured with four dummy variables). We disaggregated the data and estimated models separately for two time periods (respondents interviewed between 1986 and 1995 and those interviewed between 1996 and 2005) for four different educational attainment groups (<12 years of schooling, 12 years, 13–15 years, 16+ years) and by sex and racial/ethnic group (non-Hispanic Whites and non-Hispanic Blacks; hereafter, just "Whites" and "Blacks"). The models are thus nonparametric. The models predict the 1-year mortality probability for a person in a given 15-year age group whose interview data are in the IHIS in the given period. The mortality probabilities are therefore age group–specific annual period probabilities. Greater detail on the methodology is available from the authors.

Figures 3-1 and 3-2 show the results of the mortality analysis for females and males, respectively. In each figure, the upper panel shows the results for both time periods for Whites, while the lower panel shows

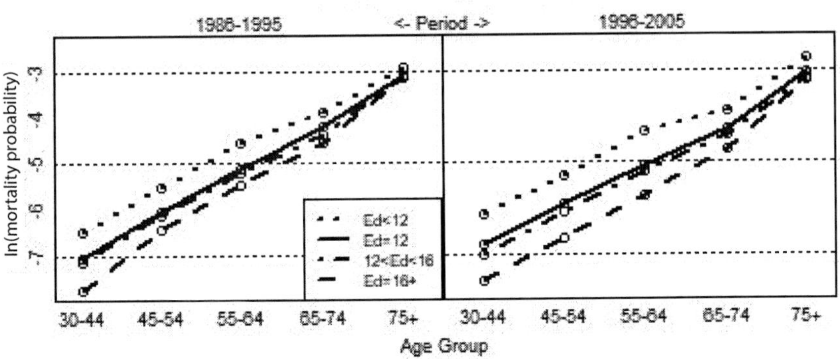

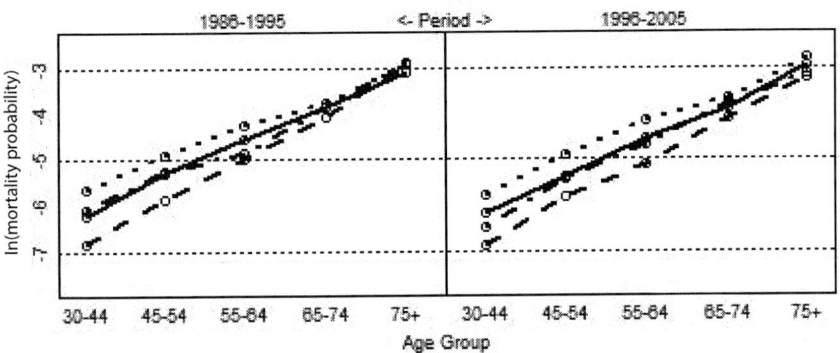

FIGURE 3-1 Log mortality probabilities by age and period for non-Hispanic White and non-Hispanic Black females.

results for Blacks. The figures report mortality probabilities in log scale. In general, log mortality probabilities increase fairly linearly with age. In all cases, there is a clear education gradient in mortality, with persons with a college degree or more (educational attainment ≥ 16 years) evidencing the lowest mortality rates and persons with less than a high school diploma (educational attainment < 12 years) evidencing the highest rates. In most cases, however, there is little difference in mortality risk for persons with a high school diploma (education = 12 years) compared to those with some college (12 < education < 16 years). The education gradient tends to shrink across age for all sex–racial/ethnic groups, so that the largest mortality risk differences are observed for persons aged 30–44. The gradient seems more

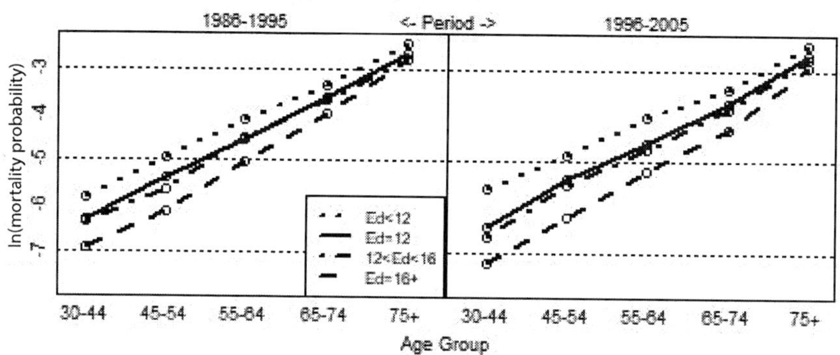

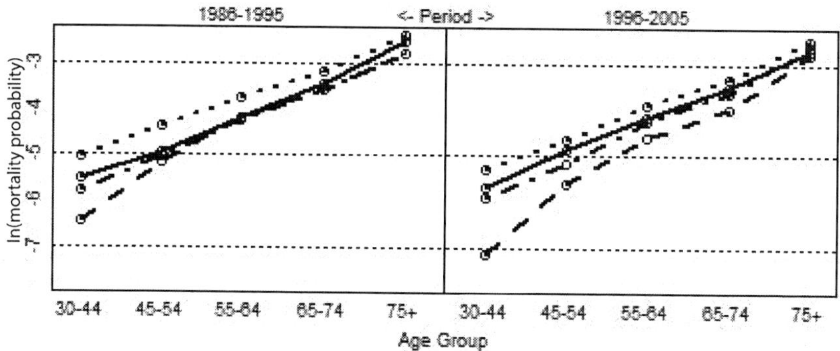

FIGURE 3-2 Log mortality probabilities by age and period for non-Hispanic White and non-Hispanic Black males.

pronounced for Whites than for Blacks, and this is especially so for females. Consistent with all prior research on mortality, White mortality risk is lower than Black mortality risk for both sexes for each education category and for almost all age groups. The Black-White disparity appears to shrink at the oldest ages, however. Finally, the gradient appears to be larger for all sex–racial/ethnic groups in the more recent period.

In summary, our mortality analysis shows that the broad patterns of socioeconomic differences in mortality found by *PT94* continue: Educational differentials are large, continue to become more pronounced over time, and disproportionately benefit those with the most schooling. These patterns are true for both Whites and Blacks but are more apparent for Whites.

SRH Analyses

SRH is a commonly used measure of general health, and SRH data have been collected in NHIS since 1972. We use data from 1986 forward to obviate the need to collapse the measure because of a change in outcome category measurement in 1982 and to keep consistent with the periods used in our mortality analyses. From 1982 forward, the survey asked respondents to rate their health as "excellent," "very good," "good," "fair," or "poor." We coded these outcomes sequentially with integers from 4 to 0, respectively, for our analyses.

We use SRH as our health measure for several reasons. First, SRH is the only health measure that has been collected in every wave of NHIS. Second, SRH is well known to be a reliable and valid measure of general health, and it does not suffer from selection problems that some other measures have, such as asking about health limiting the respondent's ability to work. That is, measures regarding work limitations are only relevant for persons who work, and limitations may depend on the kind of work one does. Third, we feel that a general measure is better than any specific one for assessing long-term trends because, in any period, specific health conditions may differentially increase or decrease in incidence and prevalence, thereby providing only a partial picture of health patterns.

Our analyses of SRH follow the same strategy used in our mortality analyses. We created five age groups and four education groups as before, but we separated the data into three periods: 1986–1995, 1996–2005, and 2006–2015. We estimated separate linear regression models for each sex-by-race-by-period-by-education group, with dummy variables for age groups in each model. We then computed predicted scores for all combinations. As with the mortality models, the models are nonparametric, given the extent of our disaggregation.

Figures 3-3 and 3-4 show the results. Figure 3-3 shows the results for females, while Figure 3-4 shows the results for males. In both figures, the upper plot shows results for Whites and the lower plot shows results for Blacks. The results show a strong educational gradient in health. Persons with educational attainment of a college degree or more have the best health, whereas those with less than a high school diploma have the worst health. Unlike the results from the mortality models, the models for health reveal a clear difference in health for persons with a high school diploma compared to those with some college for all subgroups, with the exception of Black males, ages 65–74, in the earliest period (1986–1995).

In all plots, the gradient in health appears to widen across age groups

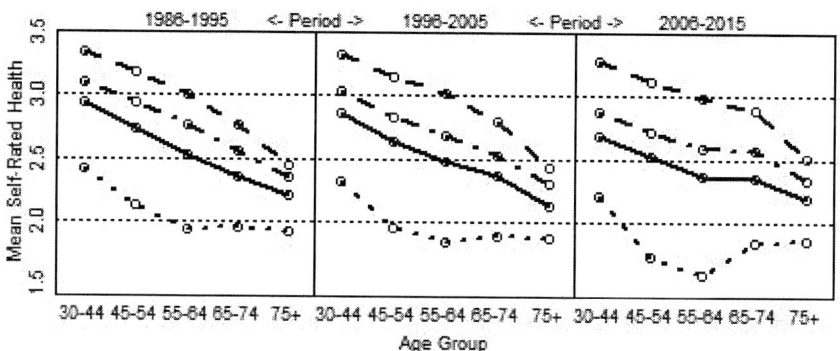

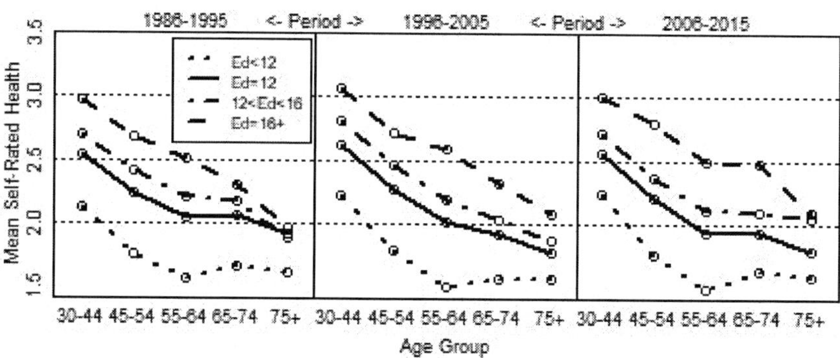

FIGURE 3-3 Mean self-rated health by age and period for non-Hispanic White and non-Hispanic Black females.

up to 55–64 before narrowing in subsequent age groups. This result is consistent with numerous studies published since the 1990s (e.g., House et al., 1994; Lynch, 2003) and appears to be the result of a more rapid decline in health in early adulthood for persons with less schooling than for persons with more schooling, coupled with a floor effect on the measure. That is, while health continues to decline across age for persons with higher levels of schooling, the health decline for persons with low levels of schooling begins to level off at ages beyond midlife, leading toward convergence in health across education groups in later life. The underlying cause of the leveling-off of health for the least educated could be selective survival of the most robust members of the least-educated population, or it could be that health ratings are increasingly made in reference to one's peers at older ages; both arguments have been made in the literature.

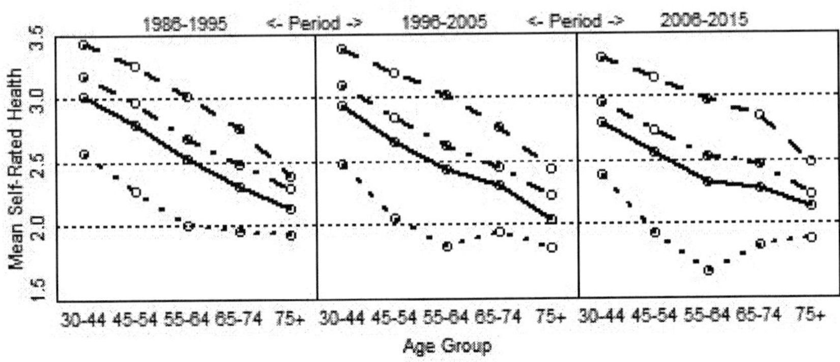

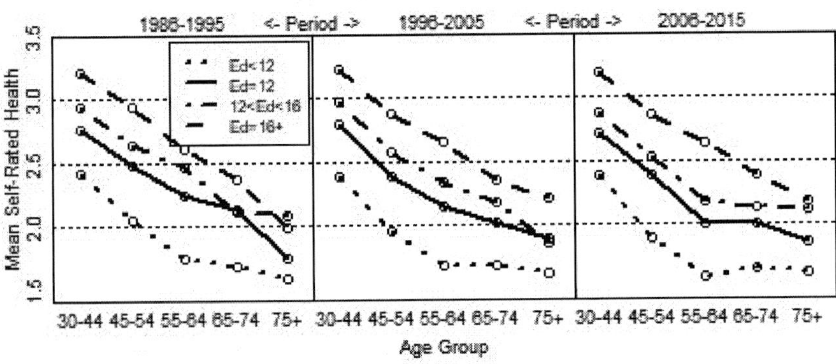

FIGURE 3-4 Mean self-rated health by age and period for non-Hispanic White and non-Hispanic Black males.

As with the results of the mortality model, the gradient tends to be stronger for Whites than for Blacks, for both men and women. Additionally, health for Whites is better than health for Blacks, with the exception that health for Blacks with less than a high school diploma is often better than health for Whites at the same level of schooling. Finally, health appears to have been fairly stable across the three periods within educational attainment groups, in some case even evidencing a slight decline. Given that overall population health has generally improved, increasing educational attainment has thus masked education-specific declines. That is, those with the most schooling have the best health, so that slight declines in health even at the highest levels of schooling are offset at the aggregate level by a greater percentage of persons obtaining more schooling. Further, large observed educational gains over the last several decades imply that the low-education groups are becoming increasingly negatively selective: those who do not obtain higher levels of schooling are increasingly a less healthy subset of the overall population.

Overall, our mortality and health analyses, as well as a large recent literature, show that the patterns and trends observed in *PT94* have continued. Most notably, the educational gradient in health and mortality is strong and growing, and Whites tend to have a stronger gradient than Blacks.

THE LIFE COURSE LENS ON SES, HEALTH, AND MORTALITY

Findings from the social, psychological, epidemiological, and biological sciences have converged regarding patterns in the associations among SES, health, and mortality. They have converged generally along two lines. First, they have independently observed that adult disparities in health and mortality are significantly correlated with childhood socioeconomic conditions and health (Schafer et al., 2011; McEwen and McEwen, 2017). Developmental and epidemiological studies hypothesize that the enduring impact of these early conditions may reflect "critical" or "sensitive" periods of biological and behavioral development that are highly responsive to environmental factors and that these changes tend to endure over the life course (Ben-Shlomo and Kuh, 2002; Shanahan and Hofer, 2011). The *critical period hypothesis* attempts to identify the limited time window during development in which an individual is subject to adverse or protective influences on structural development. The *Barker hypothesis* has identified the prenatal period as a critical period when nutritional or other environmental deprivation or damage produces lifelong consequences for health including gene transcription (Barker, 1995). The *sensitive period hypothesis* posits that an organism experiences more than one developmental period with an elevated vulnerability to disease risks. Exposure to persistent socioeconomic adversity and health risks in childhood, adolescence, or young adulthood can lead to the "biological embedding" of diverse behavioral and biological phenotypes that endure throughout adulthood (Hertzman and Boyce, 2010).

The second line of multidisciplinary convergence is that the differential accumulation of exposures to lower SES and to related successive health risks over time produces differential trajectories of health across adulthood. These independent observations of accumulation processes have yielded multiple terminologies across disciplines, resulting in some confusion. (Ferraro and Morton [2016] provide clarifications and guidelines.) Chains of risk, cumulative exposure, cumulative adversity, and weathering are terms, among others, that are intended to capture how one exposure increases the likelihood of subsequent exposures and how the chain of such exposures additively accumulate to produce poor health. Epidemiologists think of this as *cumulative exposure*, where risks accumulate within the body as one is exposed to adverse conditions over the life course. *Cumulative disadvantage* theory provides the dominant sociological framework for these observations of widening heterogeneity and inequality observed within aging cohorts experiencing differential opportunities and risks over time (Dannefer, 1987; DiPrete and Eirich, 2006). Early-life conditions matter in this theory, but broader institutional and environmental sources of inequality throughout the life course are also implicated. Institutional arrangements such as educational systems, institutional racism, health care policies, and labor market conditions can serve to reinforce, amplify, or reduce inequalities in the population. Linking cumulative exposure and disadvantage, some scholars identify the *biology of disadvantage* as the current frontier of aging research (Adler and Stewart, 2010; Wolfe et al., 2012). An integrative theory of *cumulative inequality* now proposes a deductive framework for hypothesis testing based on this biosocial linkage (Ferraro and Shippee, 2009). Cumulative inequality is depicted as a path-dependent biosocial pattern in the life course with persistent direct links between earlier and later socioeconomic and health conditions.

Despite considerable recent interdisciplinary agreement regarding divergence of health trajectories, *PT94* reported that educational health disparities peaked at ages 55–65 and then declined, a finding that replicated earlier results (Kitagawa and Hauser, 1973) and concurrent research (House et al., 1994), including ours above. Why disparities decline after midlife at older ages has been a focus of some debate since 1994. Almost every empirical study, especially those using cross-sectional data, has confirmed that health disparities narrow in later life. A common explanation for this pattern is that aging levels the playing field in health, both biologically and socially. And, with the exceptions of automobile accidents, sudden heart attacks, and other health shocks, biological processes dominate social processes and everyone's health eventually declines prior to death. Furthermore, social policies such as Medicare may equalize access to health care, effectively slowing health decline for older persons of lower SES (House et al., 1994). An alternative to this "age-as-leveler" view is *mortality selection*: persons of lower statuses who are particularly susceptible to the detriments of lower status are selected out of the population via mortality at a faster rate than persons who are less susceptible, leaving a robust subset of those with lower status (Dupre, 2007). The result is that aggregate health disparities appear to diminish at older ages, although the health trajectories for, say, any pair of low-versus-high status individuals continue to diverge, as expected by the cumulative disadvantage perspective (Lynch, 2003; Willson et al., 2007).

Numerous studies continue to support the cumulative disadvantage hypothesis through middle age by documenting the persistent effects of SES and childhood health conditions on mortality, disability, disease risk, and perceived well-being (e.g., Elo and Preston, 1992; Hayward and Gorman, 2004; Hamil-Luker and O'Rand, 2007). Many of these analyses draw on data from the Health and Retirement Study (HRS), which collects repeated, multiple measures of health and economic status but also depends on retrospective accounts of childhood conditions related to parental education, parental employment, financial strain, welfare receipt, and father's absence. The latter data pose potential challenges to validity based on biased or poor memories, diminished cognitive capacities, or depressive symptoms at the time of survey. Although some disagreements on the validity of these data persist, the recall of conditions of severe adversity and poor health appears to be largely valid after controlling for current cognitive level (see Haas, 2007; Vuolo et al., 2014).

THE CAUSALITY CONUNDRUM

Nearly as soon as the association between SES and health was discovered, scholars began questioning whether the relationship was causal. Early research questioned the causal direction of the relationship, whereas more recent research asks whether the association is causal in general. The *PT94* discussed the selection-causation problem in their original chapter, but research on the topic at the time was limited in two major ways. First, most research on the relationship between SES, health, and mortality involved cross-sectional data, so there were few avenues for resolving the dilemma. Second, most research was limited to adults and few surveys asked about early-life SES or health, both of which precede status and health in adulthood. Indeed, much of the research at that time in demography, epidemiology, and sociology assumed a causation perspective and sought to identify intervening mechanisms that explained the SES-health relationship. This assumption was often explicitly made as a justification for using educational attainment as the measure of SES. Research over the last two decades, however, has shown that, although early-life socioeconomic conditions affect later-life health, early-life health also affects cognitive development, thereby playing a major role in influencing educational attainment and therefore occupational status and earnings (Case et al., 2002). Thus, we consider the original selection-causation question to be overly simple: it is clear that the relationship between SES and health is reciprocal across the life course of individuals and is, in fact, intergenerational.

Contemporary research has turned to assessing more generally the extent to which the relationship between SES and health is causal. This growing attention has been enabled by the collection of several long-term panel datasets, such as the HRS and the National Longitudinal Survey of Youth, as well as by the development of methods and software for analyzing panel data. The most prevalent methods in use for analyzing panel data include fixed effects and random effects methods. The former are preferred in economics, and justifiably so.

Fixed effects methods control out all sources of time-invariant unobserved heterogeneity that may confound relationships between SES and health outcomes. However, there are some key limitations to applying these methods in this genre of research. First, fixed effects methods require measures to be time varying, and education is fixed by age 30 for more than 95 percent of the population. Studies that apply fixed effects methods to education data therefore may resolve endogeneity due to omitted variables at the expense of inducing sample selection–based endogeneity. Second, although income is also commonly used as a measure of SES, income is volatile. So sample selection issues are less problematic. However, treating income as a predictor of health in a fixed effects model begs the question of causal direction, and lagging income does not resolve the problem and may even exacerbate it (Vaisey and Miles, 2017).

Random effects methods are commonly used in research outside of economics, in part because of the requirement that variables must be time varying in fixed effects models. Over the last two decades, countless studies have been published using random effects methods, including studies using random intercept models, random coefficient (or [latent] growth) models, and latent class models. Although these studies have taught researchers much about how SES is associated with long-term patterns of health, random effects methods are not causal methods, despite common misconceptions. Random effects methods merely yield efficient measures of association, net of controlled variables. For example, growth models yield unique intercepts and slopes for individual health trajectories, but this simply resolves the violation of the non-independence of errors assumption of regression modeling by clustering a portion of the error term. In short, the random effects are part of the error term, and so the key assumption of these models is that the random effects are uncorrelated with other regressors. Thus, the "random effects assumption" does not address any endogeneity concerns due to omitted variable bias or reciprocality.

In economics, the use of *natural experiments* is becoming increasingly common in an attempt to establish the causality of the relationship between SES and health. Several studies have attempted to exploit policies, such as changes in compulsory schooling, in this effort (e.g., Lleras-Muney, 2005). The argument is that because individuals do not generally influence large-scale schooling laws, changes in the age at which students can drop out of school are exogenous shocks that differentiate attainment for younger birth cohorts over older birth cohorts. Thus, mortality (or health) differences between cohorts that cannot be explained by other, remaining factors must be a result of the change in educational attainment. In general, this strategy may resolve issues regarding both direction of causality and omitted variables.

Despite their celebration in economics, we are not sanguine regarding the usefulness of natural experiments in this genre of research for several reasons. A key problem with natural experiments is that they almost surely violate the stable-unit-treatment-value assumption (SUTVA) of causal modeling (Imbens and Rubin, 2015). The essence of SUTVA is that the effect of a treatment is not influenced by treatment of others. In the context of the relationship between education and health, SUTVA implies that one person's receipt of additional schooling has no implication for the effect of the receipt of another person. One of the key arguments for using educational attainment as a measure of SES is that it is strongly related to, and prior to, two other key measures: occupation and income. Yet employers make hiring decisions and wage determinations at least in part on the basis of educational attainment. If everyone entering the labor market gains additional schooling, especially at a relatively low level, such gains do not change the relative position of anyone in the labor market, and so the policy change is likely to have minimal observable effect on health through occupation and income, two major factors implicated in the education-health association.

Our more general criticism of natural experiments applies not just to them but also to all methods attempting to determine "the" causal effect of SES on health. We question whether the notion that there is *a* causal effect is reasonable for two main reasons. First, as *PT94* found, and Lynch (2003) also found, the association between SES and health has strengthened across birth cohorts born in the last century. Thus, the effect of SES on health is not a single, stable quantity: it is context dependent. Second, Link and Phelan (1995) argued that SES was a "fundamental cause" of disease: over time, status is ALWAYS related to health. However, the predominant health outcomes extant in a society, and the mechanisms that link SES to them, change over time.

This argument also suggests that there is no single causal effect of SES on health for two additional reasons. First, *how* education affects downstream measures of status such as occupation and income differs by birth cohorts. For example, although Mirowsky and Ross (2003) made a strong case for measuring educational attainment as years of schooling, for use in health disparities research, because education's primary effect is via cognitive development, Lynch (2006) showed that an increasing proportion of the association between education and health across birth cohorts is accounted for by education's association with income. Further, more-recent research by Hayward et al. (2015) showed that education's association with mortality is increasingly nonlinear and follows a stair-step (or "sheepskin") effect, indicating that education's key contribution to mortality reflects the importance of the acquisition of credentials (i.e., high school diplomas and college degrees). Changes in the importance of credentials (versus years of schooling) across birth cohorts for several other health outcomes, including SRH, obesity, and activity limitations, should probably be addressed further.

Second, how status relates to particular health outcomes changes over time. As *PT94* noted, death rates due to heart disease declined dramatically from 1960 to 1994 and persons in different educational categories experienced differential rates of decline. In contrast, cancer deaths did not evidence the same rates of decline at either the population level or the education subgroup level. Thus, a study examining "the causal effect" of a policy change affecting educational attainment (for example) on one health outcome may reach a very different conclusion from one investigating a different health outcome, especially if such studies involve different birth cohorts.

In summary, we think that some progress has been made and will continue to be made in resolving—or at least delimiting—the causality conundrum. However, despite the fact that long-term longitudinal data and clever methods are increasingly available, the increasing complexity of theory—reflecting our increasing awareness of the complexity of the SES-health association—will most likely limit our ability to resolve the conundrum fully.

THE BIOLOGY OF DISADVANTAGE: BIOLOGICAL AND BEHAVIORAL PATHWAYS LINKING SES AND HEALTH

Increasing integration of survey data with medical biomarkers and other biological data over the last two decades has broadened life course research to include more precise consideration of physiological, psychodynamic, and neurocognitive processes that unfold across different contexts of development and aging. However, the literature in this highly interdisciplinary area is vast and varied, often yielding either incomparable findings based on different study designs (e.g., nationally representative surveys versus clinical or community studies) or seemingly inconsistent results across studies with similar designs (e.g., health selection versus SES effects on midlife health outcomes using national surveys). Consequently, the field still has not yet fully explained the SES-health-mortality association.

Nationally representative longitudinal surveys of different cohorts have added and updated biomarker and genomic data since the mid-1990s (e.g., HRS, Wisconsin Longitudinal Study, the Midlife in the United States study, the National Social Life, Health, and Aging Project, and Add Health) and some researchers have linked these data to other information sources such as health records, death indices, and Medicare files to augment self-reported (or proxy-reported) data and enhance validity. But the addition of these data has come later in the lives of study participants than would be ideal for purposes of explanation, and typically only subsamples of participants have been involved. Long-running epidemiological databases (NHIS and the National Health and Nutrition Examination Survey) continue to add new samples and biomarkers of biological processes and new measures of acute and chronic health outcomes, although their demographic information remains relatively sparse, thus limiting the inclusion of potentially confounding variables. Smaller community and clinical studies abound, often focused on specific measures of biological processes such as inflammation and on health outcomes such as cardiovascular disease or hypertension, but their dependence on cross-sectional data and their sample selectivity limit their comparability. Taken as a whole by our assessment, what emerges from these widely varying efforts are the following empirical generalizations:

1. SES differentials vary by behavioral or biological process (e.g., on average, smoking is more influenced by SES than is obesity).
2. SES differentials vary for different health outcomes (e.g., on average, cardiovascular disease is more influenced by SES than is hypertension).
3. N-way interactions (e.g., SES × race × gender × region) make interpretations of SES differentials a challenge, especially across studies.

Hence, precise biosocial linkages are still not firmly established, and challenges in the collection of biomarker and genomic data and their integration with other life course data persist (Gruenewald, 2013). Nevertheless, the formative role of environments, including SES and other social factors across the life course, remains central to the agenda of the demography of aging. The major question that persists is, "How do socially graded environmental factors elicit biological and behavioral responses that are cumulative and have durable effects on health and longevity?" The answer to this question will enable the answer to the next: "How can social-medical interventions alter adverse health trajectories?"

Biological Pathways

Several biological pathways of dysregulation in major physiological systems have been identified as associated with SES (see Wolfe et al., 2012). These pathways consist of disease precursors measured by biomarkers related to stress, inflammation, and immunosenescence; metabolic syndrome; and neurocognitive function that develop over the life course, long before they are typically diagnosed. Dysregulation in one system can effect changes in other systems and probably follows "a progression from neuroendocrine hormonal dysregulation and chronic inflammation (primary mediators) to dysregulated cardiovascular and metabolic systems (secondary mediators) to organ system dysfunction and disease (tertiary outcomes)" (Wolfe et al., 2012, p. 45). Therefore, these pathways appear to follow different age trajectories, with some racial/ethnic and gender variations, ultimately influencing differential onsets of life-threatening diseases and death (Crimmins et al., 2006). They are also intertwined with the relative adaptive capacities of individuals to resist stress and to recover "normal" physiological states as a result of medical and social interventions (Yashin et al., 2016).

Because these physiological processes must be measured with samples from saliva or blood or by instrumental readings of vital processes (e.g., blood pressure), data collection is often limited to cross-sectional, non-representative samples—that is, clinical, community, and older populations after the onset of disease—or data are collected on national samples without demographically rich information on the life course (Wolfe et al., 2012). Data collection has become more cost-effective as a result of technologies that can garner more information from single collections; this is leading to greater incorporation of these measures in longitudinal social surveys even though data collection occurs later in the life courses of participants. The HRS has added these data recently on subsamples of recent waves, to improve precision of measurements of these processes across cohorts in the U.S. aging population (Crimmins, 2013).

Stress and Allostatic Load

The stress process tradition in the social sciences (Wheaton et al., 2013) has focused most on the roles of acute and chronic stress on allostatic load (Juster et al., 2010), which was once measured primarily via cortisol levels but is now usually measured as a composite of biomarkers from several physiological systems, such as C-reactive protein, glycated hemoglobin, diastolic and systolic blood pressure, total cholesterol, high-density lipoproteins, body mass index (BMI) and hip-to-waist ratios, and resting pulse rate. Allostatic load in older populations has been treated as an indicator of frailty: the depleted capacity to resist stress or to rebound to normal functioning (Crimmins et al., 2006).

Cumulative life stresses associated with lower SES and poverty have been a major focus in the demography of aging research that emphasizes the biology of disadvantage. Stress is treated as a predominant means by which the immediate and perceived environment "gets under the skin." Disadvantaged childhood conditions, including poor health, anchor lifetime trajectories of exposures to risks and behavioral and biological responses to them that persist and proliferate across physiological systems. The life course consequences among the disadvantaged include earlier aging and premature death (Belsky et al., 2017; Crimmins et al., 2009; Levine and Crimmins, 2014), earlier onset of disability and disease (Hamil-Luker and O'Rand, 2007), lower adult income associated with more rapid disease or disability progression (Herd et al., 2007), and greater disability and shorter life expectancy across U.S. contexts (Montez et al., 2017; Chetty et al., 2016).

Inflammation and Immunosenescence

Inflammation is a response at the cellular level to trauma or infection that, when sustained at chronic levels, leads to mitochondrial damage, a degradation of the immune and endocrine systems, and chronic disease. Biomarkers of inflammation include C-reactive protein, interleukin-6, insulin resistance, type 2 diabetes, and T-cell markers of aging, some of which are associated with other biological pathways such as allostatic load and metabolic syndrome. The inflammation response is initially protective: intended to destroy pathogens, repair the affected tissues, and return the organism to normal functioning. But chronic inflammatory levels (immunosenescence) associated with poverty and other disadvantaged environments appear to increase the pace of aging (Crimmins and Finch, 2006; Crimmins et al., 2009). For example, disadvantaged environments increase the exposure to infections and the susceptibility to chronic infections that are implicated later in life in the negative association between income and T-cell markers of aging (Aiello et al., 2016).

Metabolic Syndrome

This syndrome includes a group of risks that strongly predict heart disease, diabetes, and stroke. These risks include high fasting blood sugar and insulin resistance, abdominal obesity, high BMI, high blood pressure, high triglyceride levels, and low LDL cholesterol. The prevalence of this syndrome appears to be (a) spreading in the population globally (GBD Collaboration, 2014); (b) emerging at higher rates earlier in the life course among successive U.S. cohorts, especially among women (Reither et al., 2009); and (c) becoming a candidate to surpass smoking as a leading killer (GBD Collaboration, 2014).

Health behaviors (summarized below) are strongly implicated in this pathway. The effect of excessively high BMI (BMIs well into the obese range) on risks of disease and all-cause mortality has now been observed across gender and age groups in U.S. and other populations (Freedman et al., 2006). Lower SES in childhood, lower education, and lower income in adulthood are associated with high BMI, insulin resistance and diabetes, and death related to these causes (Wolfe et al., 2012), although a good deal of this research comes from small cross-sectional samples.

Neurocognitive Development and Decline

Neuroscientists are relying on additional metrics besides biomarkers (e.g., beta-amyloids) to assess the relationship between SES and cognitive development in the young and cognitive decline in the old. These metrics include electroencephalography, which measures electrical activity on the scalp and partially reflects activity of neurons and other brain cells, and magnetic resonance imaging, which produces images of the brain's anatomy and responses in the brain to sets of stimuli including tasks and/ or visual images. These techniques provide data on the development and organization of the brain and the dynamics associated with cognition (e.g., visual-spatial information, language and syntax, executive functioning) and emotion (e.g., fear), which develop in childhood and adolescence (e.g., Hanson and Hackman, 2012).

A large literature reports that SES is positively associated with children's cognitive and emotional development (e.g., McEwen and McEwan, 2017). This substantial literature also reports that SES is negatively associated with adverse physical and psychological environments to which children are exposed as they develop (Evans, 2004), including toxins, poor nutrition, stress, parental neglect, lack of cognitive stimulation and nurturance, and neighborhood violence. Issues of causality are now prime preoccupations of this literature, much as they are for most life course research.

In later life, SES has been associated with measures of cognition (e.g., positively with working memory and negatively with processing time), but its relationship to rates of cognitive decline, especially with dementia and Alzheimer's disease is less clear (Wilson et al., 2006). Some evidence exists that higher SES enables easier adaptation to and compensation strategies for normal cognitive decline (Alwin and Hofer, 2011). However, although Alzheimer's disease and related dementias increase with age into the eighth and ninth decades of life, SES differentials have not been clearly identified at the oldest ages. In the case of these diseases, some progress has been made in biological research identifying genetic and inflammatory (beta-amyloid) precursors (Hardy and Selkoe, 2002).

Social Genomics

The relationship between genetics and aging has been a decades-long interest pursued initially through twin-sibling studies and then via target or candidate gene approaches. Another long-running focus has been on telomere length as a biomarker of aging. Telomeres, nucleoprotein structures at the ends of eukaryotic chromosomes, have been observed to shorten during cellular aging. Associations between telomere attrition and several indicators of disease and of mortality have been observed across (mainly cross-sectional and clinical) human studies (Mather et al., 2011). Thus, this area demands more longitudinal research on representative populations. New approaches in social genetics have shifted to genome-wide association studies (GWASs) that leverage DNA sequence variations called single-nucleotide polymorphisms to detect variation in disease susceptibility, as in the well-known case of the apolipoprotein E mutation associated with higher risk for Alzheimer's disease. More recent discoveries of SES-related genomic variations include asthma in children (Chen et al., 2006) and depression and other complex phenotypes (Bulick-Sullivan et al., 2015). Multiple polymorphisms are now being used to construct polygenic scores to predict risks for complex mental and physical diseases (Domingue and Belsky, 2017), as well as major killers such as cancer and (currently) Alzheimer's.

Epigenetics has emerged as the most recent approach to studying the genetic bases of aging and disease and of gene-environment interactions that influence the rate of aging (Belsky et al., 2017). The principal focus of epigenetics is on how environmental conditions and factors, including stress exposure, affect methylation of DNA (and related processes that lead to the masking of DNA subsequences), thus influencing the transcription process in cellular replication. This process then affects phenotypic expression of genes, producing health disparities. Given that epigenetics involves the interaction of genes with environment, it presents a new approach to adjudicating the nature-nurture debate in favor of a gene-environment interaction paradigm.

Social genomics researchers are also exploring the controversial topic of the genetic bases of educational attainment itself, using GWAS methods. The first study of this kind claimed the identification of a range of alleles associated with educational attainment that fell on a continuum yielding a polygenic score (Rietveld et al., 2013). This approach has since been applied in other studies reporting findings that suggest that polygenic scores predict adult achievement beyond educational attainment (Belsky et al., 2016).

Behavioral Pathways

Social surveys have investigated the impact of diverse behaviors on health and mortality, but three sets of behavioral traits have emerged repeatedly as significantly correlated with SES: health behaviors, social connectedness, and cognitive and noncognitive behavioral traits. While social connectedness and cognitive and noncognitive traits may not be treated as "behavioral pathways" typically in the social sciences, we propose that they are observed patterns of behavior or performance that are repeatedly associated with SES and health outcomes.

Health Behaviors

The relationships between poor health behaviors—such as smoking, obesity, excess drug and alcohol consumption, and physical inactivity—and adult health and mortality risk have been widely studied, but with mixed results regarding the role of SES for each behavior. Reviews of studies of socioeconomic differences suggest that SES has uneven effects on different health behaviors—for example, generally large effects on smoking and physical inactivity and more moderate effects on obesity—and that different health behaviors influence health and mortality in ways that are difficult to isolate from other factors, measured or otherwise. The association between SES and alcohol use is complicated by the distinction between high alcohol use (at higher SES) and problem drinking (associated with lower SES) (see Pampel et al., 2010, for a general review).

Because these health behaviors appear to be most strongly associated with preventable or more socially graded diseases such as cardiovascular disease, educational attainment is the widely advocated explanation for these findings because it is a marker of better access to knowledge, more effective problem solving, and greater self-control, among other cognitive and noncognitive (or personality) traits (Mirowsky and Ross, 2005). Also, since these behaviors usually emerge early in the life course, often in adolescence when lifelong behavioral tendencies are established (Moffitt et al., 2011), they are considered cumulative stocks of health-damaging behaviors that are inextricably intertwined with day-to-day living.

Other factors that have been identified as contributors to damaging health behaviors include *deprivation and stress,* which motivate stress-relieving or comfort-seeking dependence on these behaviors (Eibner and Evans, 2005); *peer relationships,* usually consisting of individuals of similar SES backgrounds who encourage and reinforce these behaviors (Smith and Christakis, 2008); *geographic locations* (neighborhoods, communities, states, etc.) where the concentration of low SES and prevalence of different health behaviors varies for a wide range of factors related to lifestyles, social networks, safety, drug availability, recreational opportunities, health care resources, and access to healthier foods (Boardman et al., 2005; Christakis and Fowler, 2007), and where variations in the income gradient are correlated with smoking behavior but not with other environmental conditions (Chetty et al., 2016); and *cohort differences* observable in changing habits of daily physical activity (in work or recreation), diet, and exposure to alcohol and drugs (Case and Deaton, 2017). Recent observations of significant geographic and cohort variations among non-Hispanic Whites living outside of urban areas in increased death rates from self-destructive health behaviors (suicide, drug overdose, alcoholism) have raised serious concerns about the sustained despair experienced in economically depressed regions (Case and Deaton, 2017). All of the above factors interact in complex ways that call for further research.

Social Connectedness

The extent to which individuals (a) are socially integrated in, or isolated from, their families and communities, (b) perceive positive or negative support from family members and communities, and (c) experience social strain in their relationships has been found to have diverse influences on health across the life course. Social relationships constitute the day-to-day social capital available to individuals to enable problem solving, facilitate access to resources, and reinforce social identities and cultural values. Among disadvantaged groups, social connectedness can compensate for fewer economic resources and buffer against poor health. However, connectedness to networks of disadvantage can also limit access to resources and inhibit efforts to access resources, as a result of cultural values and community norms. The distrust with which socially disadvantaged groups view health institutions is one way that health-seeking behavior is constrained and poor health is reproduced in these communities (Cook and Stepanokova, 2007). Thus, social connectedness can have countervailing effects on health (Smith and Christakis, 2008).

Few studies have examined these relational patterns and their outcomes across the life course. Fewer still have linked them to physiological processes that influence health and life expectancy. One recent study draws on four national surveys (Add Health, the National Health and Nutrition Examination Survey, the Midlife in the United States study, and the National Social Life, Health, and Aging Project) with biomarker data that measure precursors of inflammation and metabolic dysregulation at successive life course phases in different samples (Yang et al., 2016). The principal findings are that higher levels of social integration are associated with lower levels of physiological dysregulation in adolescence and later life. Lower levels of social integration are concomitantly associated with elevated risks for dysregulation. In the older population, the effect of social isolation on hypertension exceeds that of clinical factors such as diabetes.

Social isolation is a growing risk for poor health and mortality in the general population (Hawkley and Cacioppo, 2010). Social isolation is often intertwined with poverty, social inequality, and life chances in rural and urban contexts across countries and across age groups (Wilkinson and Marmot, 2003). In the older population, the risk of social isolation grows as members experience the loss of spouses, siblings, and friends and as financial resources become depleted over time and limit social activities and interactions. The perception of isolation is accompanied by feelings of loneliness, which predict impaired mental health, including depression associated with physiological dysregulation and mortality (Luo et al., 2012; Lynch and George, 2002).

Cognitive and Noncognitive Traits

SES has been demonstrated to affect children's brain development, measured intelligence, language skills, and executive function (Wolfe et al., 2012). The relationship between SES and cognitive development and abilities, through its associations with educational attainment and later adult achievement, is also well established. Small but significant gaps in early skills in basic mathematics, reading, and problem solving associated with SES grow into wider disparities as children and adolescents move through the educational system, which sequentially rewards earlier achievement and, with time, amplifies initial SES differences through sorting and tracking structures. These disparities are reinforced by SES differences in resources for nonschool learning opportunities in summer camps, music lessons, tutoring, and the like (Crosnoe and Benner, 2016). This early, institutionalized widening of inequality has motivated economists to calculate the costs of investing in early childhood education as opposed to later educational programs and remedial job training; they have found investments in disadvantaged children to be the most cost-effective (Heckman, 2006).

At the other end of the life course, cognitive abilities such as word recall and counting backwards have been associated with SES in childhood (Case and Paxson 2008), but the rate of cognitive decline with age and the onset of dementias have not. Research in this area has identified considerable heterogeneity and plasticity in the age trajectories of numerous cognitive abilities over the life course (Alwin and Hofer, 2011). The influence of SES across the life course on these patterns has yet to be fully investigated.

Noncognitive traits and "soft skills" (Heckman and Kautz, 2012) have been implicated in explaining educational attainment and SES across the life course. These factors include diverse measured traits such as conscientiousness, self-control, and delayed gratification, as identified by developmental psychologists (Moffitt et al., 2011), and mastery, self-efficacy, personal control, and planful competence, as identified by sociologists (Hitlin and Kwon, 2016). Self-control and conscientiousness in childhood have been found to predict health and well-being in adulthood (Moffitt et al., 2011). The educational system also amplifies these noncognitive patterns of social behavior that endure into adulthood and predict damaging health behaviors that increase the risks for disease, influence patterns of achievement in the workplace, affect compliance with the health care system, and constrain patterns of well-being (Heckman et al., 2006).

NEW DIRECTIONS IN RESEARCH:
APPROACHES AND CHALLENGES

The SES-health-mortality association will continue to preoccupy the demography of aging. The results of our analyses, and others available in this large literature, indicate continued relationships among these variables. Educational differentials in mortality are significant and continue over time. Those with the least schooling are experiencing increases in mortality risk. While we know that some objective indicators of health (e.g., cardiovascular disease) have improved over time, probably in part as a result of increases in educational attainment in the population generally, educational differentials in SRH persist. The precise mechanisms by which this is occurring remain puzzles.

This essay has pointed throughout to new directions for research in the demography of aging. Biological data, linkages to administrative data that add information on geographical context, mortality, health records, analytic strategies to deal with causal relationships, and a life course framework all have emerged in the last two decades to enhance the demography of aging. We can nevertheless highlight major future directions in research that include the following:

Educational and other social status differentials will continue to demand attention as representative longitudinal survey datasets mature and become more enriched with the introduction of detailed health (biological) measures and administrative records *and* as epidemiological and medical datasets incorporate more demographically and socially rich data to augment their clinical records. More cooperation between these major data collection approaches is overdue. In the case of samples for nationally representative longitudinal surveys of aging, the introduction of biological data often comes late in the lives of participants (and usually on voluntary subsamples of the panel), after underlying biological processes have been set in motion. Longitudinal datasets collected on younger samples offer one long-term solution to this challenge. For instance, the National Longitudinal Study of Adolescent to Adult Health includes biomarker data along with rich, fine-grained demographic information on multiple life transitions. Dependence on voluntary subsamples for biomarker data is still a limitation of most surveys.

In the case of epidemiological and clinical data, the addition of demographically rich data is essential to assist in dealing with selectivity bias. For example, both the critical period and sensitive period hypotheses examined in these studies, which are often tested on limited samples, are difficult to assess empirically in the general population due to limited information on later-life outcomes in clinical studies. A promising approach is to link clinical data on these early periods to follow-up surveys and clinical data collections later in life to capture patterns over the life course. Similarly, these studies depend on selective approaches to solicit participation and subsequently on voluntary participation by subjects. Innovative data collection/analytic designs that seek to identify underlying selection processes for study participation are overdue.

The apparent tightening interdependence of SES and health over the life course will continue to present inferential challenges calling not only for statistical and experimental innovations but also for more interdisciplinary synthesis of research findings to establish "robust associations" that may not meet some criteria of causality but can still inform health and social policies. In this context, the SES construct itself will require some interrogation along at least two lines. First, as cohort differences in educational levels and in their consequences for occupational placement, earnings, and health outcomes shift, the explanation for education's effect will be problematic and require multilevel strategies. Some clues lie in recent research cited in this essay that identifies credential effects rather than years of schooling effects. What are the period or structural factors bearing on the effect of education? Second, if educational stratification becomes even more differentiated to the extent that, for example, even heretofore advantaged college-educated populations become more finely stratified in health in later life by selectivity of degree and marketability of college major, how will the effects of education be interpreted along cognitive or social dimensions? Along these lines, age-period-cohort analyses are more feasible than ever, with nearly a century of poolable cross-sectional surveys and over a quarter-century of panel datasets and new analytic strategies to analytically decompose the effects of these major life course variables.

The creative concatenation of multiple panel datasets from different cohorts may be a useful strategy to compensate for single-cohort studies with limited generalizability for the longer life course. Single cohort panels have moved demography a good distance toward understanding the aging process, but datasets start at different ages (adolescence, young adulthood, later life), in spite of their respective longitudinal designs, and are thus limited in their generalizability. We have cited one recent effort to compensate for this with the concatenation of multiple cohort-based datasets (Yang et al., 2016). This approach faces several challenges, including the linkage of different sampling designs that follow different individuals over successive phases of the life course and the harmonization of measures, among others. Yet, the successful integration of multiple datasets may move life course theory forward.

Reported in the most recent studies in the demography of aging summarized earlier are clear regional variations (both across states and rural-urban) in the SES-health-mortality relationship that have provoked new questions. Indeed, across locales in the United States, life expectancy at birth varies by more than 10 years, and health disparities are equally large. Thus, the geography of inequality is probably as important as the biology of inequality. Much remains to be investigated to understand the source of these disparities, but part of the explanation is surely to be attributable to both SES disparities and to differences in how SES influences health across regions as a result of economic restructuring, migration, and technological transformations that have accompanied globalization.

The association of SES with health and mortality is a complex, multivariate, interactive, and multilevel puzzle for the demography of aging. This review only touches upon the nuances of this complexity. It will require genuine interdisciplinary research going forward, research in which boundaries are crossed between different styles of research and conceptual formulations.

REFERENCES

Adler, N.E., and Stewart, J. (Eds.). (2010). *The Biology of Disadvantage: Socioeconomic Status and Health*. New York: Wiley-Blackwell.

Aiello, A.E., Feinstein, L., Dowd, J.B., Pawelec, G., Derhovanessian, E., Galea, S., Uddin, M., Wildman, D.E., and Simanek, A.M. (2016). Income and markers of immunological cellular aging. *Psychosomatic Medicine, 78*, 657–666.

Allison, P.D. (1984). *Event History Analysis: Regression for Longitudinal Event Data* (Sage University Paper Series: Quantitative Applications in the Social Sciences, No. 07-46). Beverly Hills, CA: Sage.

Alwin, D.F., and Hofer, S.M. (2011). Health and cognition in aging research. *Journals of Gerontology: Psychological and Social Sciences, 66B*(S1), 9–15.

Barker, D.J.P. (1995). The fetal origins of coronary heart disease. *British Medical Journal, 311*, 171–174.

Belsky, D.W., Moffitt, T.E., Corcoran, D.L., Domingue, B., Harrington, H., Hogan, S., Houts, R., et al. (2016). The genetics of success: How single nucleotide polymorphisms associated with educational attainment relate to life-course development. *Psychological Science, 27*(7), 957–972.

Belsky, D.W., Caspi, A., Cohen, H.V., Kraus, W.E., Ramrakha, S., Poulton. R., and Moffitt, T.E. (2017). Impact of early personal-history characteristics on the pace of aging: Implications for clinical trials of therapies to slow aging and extend healthspan. *Aging Cell, 16*, 644–651.

Ben-Shlomo, Y., and Kuh, D. (2002). A life course approach to chronic disease epidemiology: Conceptual models, empirical challenges, and interdisciplinary perspectives. *International Journal of Epidemiology, 31*, 285–293.

Boardman, J.D., Saint Onge, J.M., Rogers, R.G., and Denney, J.T. (2005). Race differentials in obesity: the impact of place. *Journal of Health and Social Behavior, 46*(3), 229–243.

Bulick-Sullivan, B., Finucane, H.K., Anttila, V., Gusev, A., Day, F.R., Loh, P.R., et al. (2015). *Nature Genetics, 47*(11), 1236–1241.

Case, A., and Deaton A. (2017). *Mortality and Morbidity in the 21st Century* (Brookings Papers on Economic Activity (BPEA) Conference Drafts, March 23-24). Washington, DC: Brookings Institution.

Case, A., and Paxson, C. (2008). Height, health and cognitive function at older ages. *American Economic Review: Papers and Proceedings, 98*(2), 463–467.

Case, A., Lubotsky, D., and Paxson, C. (2002). Socioeconomic status and health in childhood: The origins of the gradient. *American Economic Review, 92*, 1308–1344.

Chen, E., Hanson, M.D., Paterson, L.Q., Griffin, M.J., Walker, H.A., and Miller, G.E. (2006). Socioeconomic status and inflammatory processes in childhood asthma: The role of psychological stress. *Journal of Allergy and Clinical Immunology, 117*(5), 1014–1020.

Chetty, R., Stepner, M., Abraham, S., Lin, S., Scuderi, B., Turner, N., Bergeron, A., and Cutler, D. (2016). The association between income and life expectancy in the United States, 2001–2014. *Journal of the American Medical Association, 315*, 1750–1766.

Christakis, N.A., and Fowler, J.H. (2007). The spread of obesity in a large social network over 32 years. *New England Journal of Medicine, 357*, 370–379.

Cook, K.S., and Stepanikova, J. (2007). The health care outcome of trust: A review of empirical evidence. In J. Brownlie, A. Greene, and A. Howson (Eds.), *Researching Trust and Health* (pp. 194–214). New York: Routledge.

Crimmins, E.M. (2013). *HRS Documentation Report: Documentation of Biomarkers in the 2006 and 2008 Health and Retirement Study.* Available: http://hrsonline.isr.umich.edu/sitedocs/userg/Biomarker2006and2008.pdf [March 2018].

Crimmins, E.M., and Finch, C.E. (2006). Infection, inflammation, height and longevity. *Proceedings of the National Academy of Sciences of the United States of America, 103*(2), 498–503.

Crimmins, E.M., Johnson, M.L., Hayward, M., and Seeman, T. (2006). Age differences in allostatic load: An index of frailty. In Z. Yi, E.M. Crimmins, Y. Carriere, and J.-M. Robine (Eds.), *Longer Life and Healthy Aging* (pp. 111–140). New York: Springer.

Crimmins, E.M., Kim, J.K., and Seeman, T.E. (2009). Poverty and biological risk: The "earlier" aging of the poor. *Journals of Gerontology: Biological and Medical Science*s, 64A(92), 286–292.

Crosnoe, R., and Benner, A.D. (2016). Educational pathways. In M.J. Shanahan, J.T. Mortimer and M.K. Johnson (Eds.), *Handbook of the Life Course: Volume II* (pp. 179–200). New York: Springer.

Dannefer, D. (1987). Aging as intracohort differentiation: Accentuation, the Matthew effect, and the life course. *Sociological Forum, 2*, 211–236.

DiPrete, T.D., and Eirich, G.M. (2006). Cumulative advantage as a mechanism for inequality: A review of theoretical and empirical developments. *Annual Review of Sociology, 32*(1), 271–297.

Domingue, B.W., and Belsky, D.W. (2017). The social genome: Current findings and implications for the study of human genetics. *PLoS Genetics, 13*(3), e1006615.

Dupre, M.E. (2007). Educational differences in age-related patterns of disease: Reconsidering the cumulative advantage and age-as-leveler hypotheses. *Journal of Health and Social Behavior, 48*(1), 1–15.

Eibner, C., and Evans, W.N. (2005). Relative deprivations, poor health habits, and mortality. *Journal of Human Resources, 40*(3), 591–620.

Elo, I.T., and Preston, S.H. (1992). Effects of early life conditions on adult mortality: A review. *Population Index, 57*, 186–212.

Evans, G.W. (2004). The environment of childhood poverty. *American Psychologist, 59*(2), 77–92.

Ferraro, K.F., and Morton, P.M. (2016). What do we mean by accumulation? Advancing conceptual precision for a core idea in gerontology. *Journals of Gerontology: Psychological and Social Sciences, 73B*(2), 269–278.

Ferraro, K.F., and Shippee, T.P. (2009). Aging and cumulative inequality: How does inequality get under the skin? *The Gerontologist, 49*, 333–343.

Freedman, D.M., Ballard-Barbash, R., Doody, M.M., and Linet, M.S. (2006). Body mass index and all-cause mortality in a nationwide U.S. cohort. *International Journal of Obesity, 30*, 822–829.

GBD Collaboration. (2014). Global, regional and national prevalence of overweight and obesity in children and adults, 1980-2013. *Lancet, 384*(9945), 766–781.

Gruenewald, T.L. (2013). Opportunities and challenges in the study of biosocial dynamics in healthy aging. In National Research Council, *New Directions in the Sociology of Aging* (pp. 217–237). Washington, DC: The National Academies Press. doi: https://doi.org/10.17226/18508.

Haas, S.A. (2007). The long-term effects of poor childhood health: An assessment and application of retrospective reports. *Demography, 44*, 113–135.

Hamil-Luker, J., and O'Rand, A.M. (2007). Gender differences in the link between childhood socioeconomic conditions and heart attack risk in adulthood. *Demography, 44*(1), 137–158.

Hanson, J., and Hackman, D.A. (2012). Cognitive neuroscience and disparities in socioeconomic status. In B. Wolfe, W. Evans, and T.E. Seeman (Eds.), *The Biological Consequences of Socioeconomic Inequalities* (pp. 158–186). New York: Russell Sage.

Hardy, J., and Selkoe, D.J. (2002). The amyloid hypothesis of Alzheimer's disease: Progress and problems on the road to therapeutics. *Science, 297*, 353–356.

Hawkley, L.C., and Cacioppo, J.T. (2010). Loneliness matters: A theoretical and empirical review of consequences and mechanisms. *Annals of Behavioral Medicine, 40*(2), 218–227.

Hayward, M.D., and Gorman, B.K. (2004). The long arm of childhood: The influence of early-life social conditions on men's mortality. *Demography, 41*(1), 87–107.

Hayward, M.D., Hummer, R.A., and Sasson, I. (2015). Trends and group differences in the association between educational attainment and U.S. adult mortality: Implications for understanding education's causal influence. *Social Science & Medicine, 127*, 8–18.

Heckman, J.J. (2006). Skill formation and the economics of investing in disadvantaged children. *Science, 312*, 1990–1902.

Heckman, J.J., and Krautz, T.D. (2012). Hard evidence for soft skills. *Labor Economics, 19*, 451–464.

Heckman, J.J., Stixrud, J., and Urzua, S. (2006). The effects of cognitive and noncognitive abilities on labor market outcomes and social behavior. *Journal of Labor Economics, 24*(3), 411–482.

Herd, P., Goesling, B., and House, J.S. (2007). Socioeconomic position and health: The differentials effects of education versus income on the onset versus the progression of health problems. *Journal of Health and Social Behavior, 48*(3), 223–238.

Hertzman, C., and Boyce, T. (2010). How experience gets under the skin to create gradients in developmental health. *Annual Review of Public Health, 31*, 329–347.

Hitlin, S., and Kwon, H.W. (2016). Agency across the life course. In M.J. Shanahan, J.T. Mortimer, and M.K. Johnson (Eds.), *Handbook of the Life Course* (pp. 431–449). New York: Springer.

House, J.S., Lepkowski, J.M., Kinney, A.M., Mero, R.P., Kessler, R.C., and Herzog, A.R. (1994). The social stratification of aging and health. *Journal of Health and Social Behavior, 35*(3), 213–234.

Imbens, G.W., and Rubin, D.B. (2015). *Causal Inference for Statistics, Social, and Biomedical Sciences: An Introduction.* New York: Cambridge University Press.

Juster, R.P., McEwen, B.S., and Lupien, S.J. (2010). Allostatic load biomarkers of chronic stress and impact on health and cognition. *Neuroscience and Biobehavioral Reviews, 35*, 2–16.

Kitagawa, E.M., and Hauser, P.M. (1973). *Differential Mortality in the United States: A Study in Socioeconomic Epidemiology.* Cambridge, MA: Harvard University Press.

Levine, M.E., and Crimmins, E.M. (2014). Evidence of accelerated aging among African Americans and its implications for mortality. *Social Science and Medicine, 118*, 27–32.

Link, B.G., and Phelan, J. (1995). Social conditions as fundamental causes of disease. *Journal of Health and Social Behavior, 35, Extra Issue*, 80–94.

Lleras-Muney, A. (2005). The relation between education and adult mortality in the United States. *The Review of Economic Studies, 72*(1), 189–221.

Luo, Y., Hawkley, L.C., Waite, L.J., and Cacioppo, J.T. (2012). Loneliness, health, and mortality in old age: A national study. *Social Science and Medicine, 74*(6), 907–914.

Lynch, S.M. (2003). Cohort and life course patterns in the relationship between education and health: A hierarchical approach. *Demography, 40*(2), 309–331.

Lynch, S.M. (2006). Explaining life course and cohort variation in the relationship between education and health: The role of income. *Journal of Health and Social Behavior, 47*, 324–338.

Lynch, S.M., and George, L.K. (2002). Interlocking trajectories of loss-related events and depressive symptoms among elders. *Journals of Gerontology: Social Sciences, 57B*, S117–S125.

Mather, K.A., Jorm, A.F., Parslow, R.A., and Christensen, H. (2011). Is telomere length a biomarker of aging? A review. *Journals of Gerontology: Biomedical Sciences, 66A2*, 202–213.

McEwen, C.A., and McEwen, B.S. (2017). Social structure, adversity, toxic stress, and intergenerational poverty: An early childhood model. *Annual Review of Sociology, 43*, 445–472.

Minnesota Population Center and State Health Access Data Assistance Center. (2015). *Integrated Health Interview Series: Version 6.* Minneapolis: University of Minnesota.

Mirowsky, J., and Ross, C.E. (2003). *Education, Social Status, and Health.* New York: Aldine de Gruyter.

Mirowsky, J., and Ross, C.E. (2005). Education, learned effectiveness and health. *London Review of Education, 3*, 205–220.

Moffitt, T.E., Arseneault, L., Belsky, D.W., Dickson, N., Hancox, R.J., and Harrington, H. (2011). A gradient of childhood self-control predicts health, wealth, and public safety. *Proceedings of the National Academy of Sciences of the United States of America, 108*(7), 2693–2698. https://doi.org/10.1073/pnas.1010076108.

Montez, J.K., Zajacova, A., and Hayward, M.K. (2017). Contextualizing the social determinants of health: Disparities in disability by educational attainment across U.S. states. *American Journal of Public Health, 107*(7), 1101–1108.

National Center for Health Statistics. (2014). *Survey Description, National Health Interview Survey.* Hyattsville, MD: National Center for Health Statistics.

National Center for Health Statistics. (2015). *Office of Analysis and Epidemiology, Public-use Linked Mortality File*. Hyattsville, MD: National Center for Health Statistics.

Pampel, F.C., Krueger, P.M., and Denney, J.T. (2010). Socioeconomic disparities and health behaviors. *Annual Review of Sociology, 36*, 349–370.

Preston, S.H., and Taubman, P. (1994). Socioeconomic differences in adult mortality and health status. In National Research Council, *Demography of Aging* (pp. 279–318). Washington, DC: National Academy Press.

Reither, E.M., Hauser, R.M., and Yang, Y.C. (2009). Do cohorts matter? Age-period-cohort analyses of the obesity epidemic in the U.S. *Social Science and Medicine, 69*(10), 1439–1448.

Rietveld, C.A., Medland, S.E., Derringer, J., Yang, J., Esko, T., Martin, N.W., Westra, H.-J., et al. (2013). GWAS of 126,599 individuals identifies genetic variants associated with educational attainment. *Science, 340*, 1467–1471.

Schafer, M.H., Ferraro, K.F., and Mustillo, S.A. (2011). Children of misfortune: Early adversity and cumulative inequality in perceived life trajectories. *American Journal of Sociology, 116*, 1053–1091.

Shanahan, M.J., and Hofer, S.M. (2011). Molecular genetics, aging and the life course: Sensitive periods, accumulation, and pathways models. In R.H. Binstock and L.K. George (Eds.), *Handbook of Aging and the Social Sciences*. New York: Elsevier

Smith, K.P., and Christakis, N.S. (2008). Social networks and health. *Annual Review of Sociology, 34*, 405–429.

Vaisey, S., and Miles, A. (2017). What you can—and can't—do with three-wave panel data. *Sociological Methods & Research, 46*(1), 44–67.

Vuolo, M., Ferraro, K.F., and Morton, P.M. (2014). Why do older people change their ratings of childhood health? *Demography, 51*(6), 1999–2023.

Wheaton, B., Young, M., Montazer, S., and Stuart-Lahman, K. (2013). Social stress in the twenty-first century. In C.S. Aneshensel, J.C. Phelan, and A. Bierman (Eds.), *Handbook of the Sociology of Mental Health* (pp. 299–323). New York: Springer.

Wilkinson, R.G., and Marmot, M. (Eds.). (2003). *Social Determinants of Health: The Solid Facts*. Copenhagen: World Health Organization.

Willson, A.E., Shuey, K.M., and Elder, G.H. (2007). Cumulative advantage processes as mechanisms of inequality in life course health. *American Journal of Sociology, 112*(6), 1886–1924.

Wilson, R.S., Li, Y., Bienas, J.L., and Bennett, D.A. (2006). Cognitive decline in old age: Separating retest effects from the effects of growing older. *Psychology and Aging, 21*(4), 774–789.

Wolfe, B., Evans, W., and Seeman, T.E. (Eds.). (2012). *The Biological Consequences of Socioeconomic Inequalities*. New York: Russell Sage.

Yang, Y., Boen C., Gerken, K., Li, T., Schorpp, K., and Harris, K.M. (2016). Social relationships and physiological determinants of longevity across the human life span. *Proceedings of the National Academy of Sciences of the United States of America, 113*(3), 578–583.

Yashin, A., Stallard, E., and Land, K.C. (Eds.). (2016). *The Biodemography of Aging* (Springer Series on Demographic Methods and Population Analysis). New York: Springer.

PART II

Social and Environmental Contexts Shaping Aging and Health

4

Social Well-Being and Health in the Older Population: Moving beyond Social Relationships

Linda J. Waite[1]

INTRODUCTION

In 1947, the World Health Organization (WHO) defined health as ". . . a state of complete physical, mental and *social* well-being and not merely the absence of disease or infirmity" (Glenn and Weaver, 1979). In 1977, psychiatrist George Engel built on this definition, calling for a new, biopsychosocial model (Engel, 1977). It integrated traditional medicine with psychosocial factors, which stimulated the field of psychosomatic medicine. Since then others have called for conceptualizations of health expanded to include positive health (Ryff and Singer, 1988) or successful aging (Rowe and Kahn, 1997), although these more inclusive definitions have rarely been applied to understanding the health of individuals or populations.

This chapter addresses the theoretical and conceptual underpinnings of various definitions of "social health." It presents commonly used measures of social well-being, rarely referred to as social health, and briefly reviews the relationship between these measures and other dimensions of health. It suggests ways that assessments of the health of individuals, groups, or populations could be expanded to include social health, and it discusses future directions for research on the demography of social well-being at older ages. Although the WHO definition of health, promulgated over half a century ago, includes social health as equal in importance to physical and psychological health, and some researchers have incorporated the social in

---

[1] University of Chicago and NORC.

their conceptual frameworks (e.g., Rowe and Kahn, 1997; Ryff and Singer, 1988), it has rarely been incorporated analytically in describing population health or in causal models of population health. Addressing this lack is an important future direction for the demography of aging, but it means that reviews of recent research have little to say on social well-being as a component of health and much more to say on social factors as causes of other dimensions of health. That lack shapes the discussion below on our understanding of the links between social well-being and health.

When WHO added "social well-being" to its definition of health, what did it have in mind? No generally accepted definition of social well-being exists. Obviously, it should include adequate and well-functioning social relationships, adequate social support, little or no social strain, some social participation, social inclusion in one's society, strong and well-functioning social networks, and, perhaps, sexuality as one desires. Some definitions might include more dimensions or types of social behaviors or activities, but we can start here. We begin with theoretical and conceptual approaches to social well-being as a component of health.

THEORETICAL AND CONCEPTUAL APPROACHES TO SOCIAL WELL-BEING AS A COMPONENT OF HEALTH

The standard Medical Model of Health, sometimes called the biomedical model, had its origins in the 1910 Flexner Report (Flexner, 1910), which codified medical education through a focus on diseases, specifically their pathology, biochemistry, and physiology (Stevens, 1971; Starr, 1982; Beck, 2004; Annandale, 2014). In this model, health is the absence of disease, dysfunction, or injury. Engel's (1977) biopsychosocial model integrated traditional medicine with psychosocial factors, which stimulated the field of psychosomatic medicine.

A focus on physical health and the avoidance of disease defined "successful aging" as conceptualized by Jack Rowe, a physician, and Robert Kahn, a psychologist. Successful aging was distinguished from normal aging, which might include health declines and chronic disease (Rowe and Kahn, 1997). Rowe (1990) defined "staying healthy" as not diseased, not disabled, with a hallmark of successful aging being a low risk of developing chronic disease. Later, Rowe and Kahn (1997) expanded the definition of success to include a low probability of disease and disease-related disability, high cognitive and physical functional capacity, and active engagement with life; one ages successfully if one achieves all three of these goals. No mention is made of good mental health. Subsequent research showed that very few people are able to maintain the high levels of functioning required to be classified as "successful" (Martin et al., 2015). Note that this definition of health includes one measure that may reflect social well-being: active engagement with life, defined as maintenance of personal relationships and engagement in paid or unpaid activities that produce goods or services of economic value (Rowe and Kahn, 1997).

The related ideas of "positive health" and "successful aging" incorporate the presence or absence of disease, cognitive and functional capacity (Ryff and Singer, 1998), and active engagement with life (Rowe and Kahn, 1997, 1998). Ryff and Singer (1998) pointed to the importance of *both* mind and body in positive health and focused on the effect of each on the other, but they ignored the social. Rowe and Kahn (1997) privileged cognitive function and ignored psychological well-being. Recent work has moved little beyond this point. Lowsky et al. (2014) defined "healthy aging," using self-reported health, as getting no help with activities of daily living or instrumental activities of daily living, having no work limitations due to health, not having been diagnosed with any major chronic disease, and having a perfect score on the health-related quality-of-life scale.

Recent research has focused on markers of physiological aging in young adults (Belsky et al., 2015), including physical functioning, cognitive function, and appearance. Social functioning is not included. And a sizable body of research has focused on the effect of social relationships on longevity (Yang et al., 2013, 2016), and the biological mechanisms through which these occur (Yang et al., 2013). These models are based on the assumption that social relationships affect health. But WHO includes social well-being as a component of health.

Lindau et al. (2003) proposed an "interactive biopsychosocial model" in which three components, the psychocognitive, biophysical, and social health of each social partner, affect and are affected by each other within a social environment (see Figure 4-1).

Theories Linking Social Well-being to Health

It is generally accepted that the social world "gets under the skin" to affect physical, functional, psychological, and cognitive health and that each of these other dimensions of health affects social well-being. The mechanisms by which this takes place are the focus of various theories linking social well-being to other domains of health. We outline here some of the most well known, beginning with *Stress Process Theory* (Thoits, 2011; Pearlin et al., 2005). This theory focuses on the body's physiological responses to stress, which is defined as demands on an organism that it may not have the resources to meet. For humans, this means demands that the person *feels* that she or he may not have the resources to meet. Stress leads to the stress response—activation of the hippocampal-pituitary-adrenal axis, with resultant increases in blood pressure and heart rate, dumping of cortisol into the blood stream, and increased vigilance. Robert Sapolsky

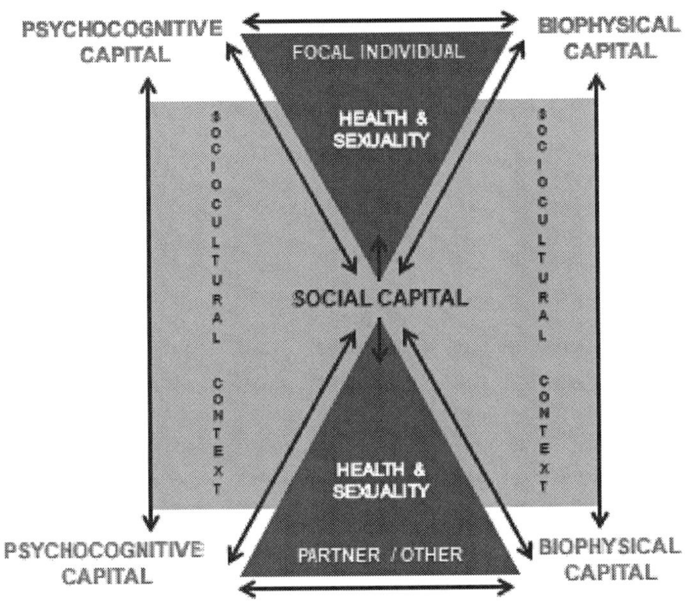

FIGURE 4-1 A model for the interaction among the biophysical, psychocognitive, and social aspects of overall health and well-being.
SOURCE: Lindau et al. (2003). Reprinted with permission of the Johns Hopkins University Press. From Lindau, S.T., Laumann, E.O., Levinson, W., and Waite, L.J. (2003). Synthesis of scientific disciplines in pursuit of health: The Interactive Biopyschosocial Model. *Perspectives in Biology and Medicine*, 46(3 Suppl), S74-S86. Permission conveyed through Copyright Clearance Center, Inc.

(2004) has detailed the various and manifold consequences of stress and the stress response in such works as *Why Zebras Don't Get Ulcers.*

For modern humans, stress is more often social or psychological than physical, given the nature of our lives, but social stress causes the same physiological responses, which can cause wear and tear on the body over time, leading to hypertension, cardiovascular disease, impaired immune function, and even stress-related eating and weight gain. Social relationships, if supportive, can reduce exposure to stress, mute the response to stress, and speed recovery from stress (Thoits, 2011), thereby improving health. Of course, social relationships can also be a source of stress if they are negative, demanding, difficult, or draining (Offer and Fischer, 2017).

Loneliness and Social Isolation

Loneliness and social isolation, important indicators of social health, are related, often confused with each other, but not the same thing. They are siblings rather than identical twins. Loneliness is the subjective assessment that one's social relationships are lacking, perhaps profoundly so. Lonely people feel that they lack companionship, don't have a circle of friends, and often feel left out. Socially isolated people may not have many close connections but may feel just fine about it. Theories of the effects of loneliness and social isolation point to different mechanisms through which each operates to put other dimensions of health at risk. Recent research suggests that loneliness is a factor in evolutionary fitness across the life span (Hawkley and Capitanio, 2015). Lonely people feel left out and isolated, that no one has their back. Thus they tend to surveil their social surrounding for risk and to perceive social threats in ambiguous situations. The constant checking for threats uses up cognitive capacity that could be put to other uses, which may contribute to the increased likelihood of developing Alzheimer's disease faced by lonely people (Wilson et al., 2007). Loneliness is a major source of stress, which puts chronically lonely people at risk of chronic inflammation, hypertension, cardiovascular disease, and stroke. Lonely people sleep more poorly, less often wake up rested, and have more trouble staying asleep. They are at risk for depression, poor executive function, accelerated cognitive decline, and impaired immune function (Hawkley and Capitanio, 2015). Loneliness is a candidate for an indicator of poor social health.

Social isolation works to affect other domains of health through mechanisms other than stress. The socially isolated are more likely than others to live alone, to be unmarried, to have small social networks, to participate in few groups, to have few friends, and to socialize infrequently (York Cornwell and Waite, 2009a). Social isolation may mean few sources of emotional or instrumental support. With fewer resources at their disposal, the socially isolated may face more sources of stress than others and have fewer means to alleviate that stress. Those with relatively little contact with others have fewer sources of information and influence to aid in decision making, potentially affecting health behaviors, health care usage, and socially contagious behaviors such as alcohol use, smoking, diet, exercise, and obesity (Smith and Christakis, 2008; Yang et al., 2013). Steptoe et al. (2013) suggested that social isolation may increase the risk of adverse events during acute illness episodes by reducing the availability of help and care. These authors found that social isolation increases risk of mortality, even when loneliness is taken into account, making both candidates as indicators of poor social health.

Social Capital Theory

Social capital is often thought of as the resources that reside within social relationships, especially networks of relationships, and as the information, influence, and even goods and services that flow through these networks. Theoretical development of this concept began with seminal work by Pierre Bourdieu (1986) and James Coleman (1988), who worked separately and developed different approaches, both highly influential. This work was built upon by Robert Putnam (2000), who tended toward a narrow definition of social capital as the nature and extent of networks and the norms of reciprocity they embody. Social capital, in this formulation, allows people to have *expectations of* access to resources from others in the network. These resources include instrumental and emotional help, advice, information, connection to those outside the network, surveillance of behavior within the network, and other products of relationships. Social capital resides strictly within relationships between individuals within the group of which they are members. Some network scholars argue, in contrast, that social capital consists of the flows of resources through networks, not the networks themselves (Lin, 2001).

Social capital theories all point to features of the social networks of individuals as sources of resources and by this means as indicators of social well-being. Social networks can have many different characteristics, ranging from their size to their configuration and their composition (Cornwell et al., 2009). We discuss these below in the section on dimensions of social well-being.

KEY DIMENSIONS OF SOCIAL WELL-BEING

The next section looks to theoretical perspectives and the research literature to determine the most important and most commonly assessed dimensions of social well-being. These are described briefly. We then discuss ways to measure each of these dimensions.

Presence and Quality of Social Relationships Including Social Dyads

By *social relationships* we mean any ongoing connection between two or more people. The most fundamental of these are the parent-child relationship and the intimate partner relationship. Together they comprise the family, the foundational social institution in human society (Coontz, 2008; Waite, 2005). The consequences of strong and positive bonds between parents and children have widely recognized consequences for the physical, psychological, cognitive, and financial well-being of both generations across the life course (Maccoby, 1980). Finding and keeping a mate in an intimate partnership is one of the key developmental tasks of adulthood (Kaufman, 2018), and a successful partnership, some argue, leads to better health of both members of the dyad across all dimensions of health (Waite and Gallagher, 2000). So we list happy childhood as a candidate measure of social health, along with being married or partnered. We might want to specify that a marriage or partnership must be of at least decent quality to count as an indicator of good social health. A poor-quality marriage or partnership, or none at all, would go in the negative social-health column of our measure.

Other social relationships we should consider include family, friends, colleagues, and other types of connections. These relationships serve different roles at various stages of the life course, and one need not have some of each to have good social health. Although there are few older adults who claim to have no friends or who claim to have no family, many have social networks that contain no or few family members and many have networks that contain no or few friends (Litwin and Shiovitz-Ezra, 2010).

Social Networks

People are connected to others in a variety of ways, from kin relationships to socializing to exchanges. Social networks are created by webs of connections among groups of people, so the social network of an individual includes that person's connections to others *and* the connections of those other people to each other (Cornwell et al., 2009). Berkman et al. (2000) developed an elegant conceptual model of the links between macro-level social forces, social networks, psychosocial factors, and pathways to health.

There are many ways to define social networks and many ways to measure them. The National Social Life, Health, and Aging Project (NSHAP) pioneered collection of social network data in older adults by focusing on their discussion networks: the people with whom they talk about things that are important to them.[2] The respondent names these people, called "alters," and then the relationship of each of them to the respondent (called "ego" in network research) is ascertained. Are they related and how? How old are they? Do they live with ego? And does ego talk to them about health? Then the respondent is asked in detail about the connection, if any, between each of the pairs of alters named. Did they know each other? Were they related? How often were they in contact? How close was their relationship? This innovation allows researchers to look closely at the links between all those in the network, including flows of information and affection (Cornwell et al., 2009).

---

[2]Table 4-1 in this chapter lists the measures derived from Waves 1 and 2 of NSHAP, together with the mean value of each measure.

TABLE 4-1 Measures Estimated from Waves 1 and 2 of NSHAP

NSHAP Measure	Mean (Wave #)
1. PRESENCE/QUALITY OF SOCIAL RELATIONSHIPS	
Happy childhood (1-disagree → 6-agree)	4.49 (W2)
(a) Relationship quality	
Quality of marriage/relationship (1-unhappy → 7-very happy)	6.33[f]/6.35[g] (W2)
Thinking that relationship is going well (1-never → 6-all the time)	5.01[f] (W2)
Quality of relationship, in general (1-not very close→ 4-extremely close)	3.59[f] (W2)
Spend time together/separately (1-separate; 2-some together, some separate; 3-together)	2.34[f] (W2)
Frequency of sleeping in same bed (1-never → 6-all the time)	4.09[f] (W2)
Number of friends (0-none → 5-twenty or more friends)	3.41 (W2)
Number of children (range: 0–18 children)	2.77 (W2)
Number of grandchildren (range: 0–30 grandchildren)	4.60 (W2)
2. SOCIAL NETWORKS	
Network size (0–5 people)	3.80[c] (W2)
Proportion living in respondent's household/coresident (0–1)	0.20[c] (W2)
Proportion kin (0–1)	0.66[c] (W2)
Relationship between alters/network density (0–1)	0.77[c] (W2)
Frequency of contact with alters (1-less than once a year → 8-every day)	6.76[c] (W2)
Emotional closeness to alters (1- not very close → 4-very close)	3.09[c] (W2)
Likelihood of discussing health with alters (1-not likely → 3-very likely)	2.56[c] (W2)
Frequency of contact among alters (0-have never spoken to each other → 9-every day)	4.13[c] (W2)
Closeness to alters (1-not very close → 4-extremely close)	3.16[a] (W1)
3. SOCIAL PARTICIPATION	
Attend religious services (0-never → 6-several times/week)	3.27[b] (W1)
Attend organized groups (1-never → 7-several times a week)	2.66[b] (W1)
Get together with friends, family (1-never → 7-several times a week)	4.39[b] (W1)
Socialize with neighbors (1-hardly ever → 5-daily or almost every day)	1.35[b] (W1)
Volunteer (1-never → 7-several times a week)	2.20[b] (W1)

TABLE 4-1 Continued

NSHAP Measure	Mean (Wave #)
4. SOCIAL ISOLATION/LONELINESS	
Felt left out (1-often→ 3-hardly ever/never)	1.32[b] (W1)
Felt isolated (1-often→ 3-hardly ever/never)	1.26[b] (W1)
Lacked companionship (1-often→ 3-hardly ever/never)	1.419[b] (W1)
Social disconnectedness (-0.1.30 → 2.34; low→ high disconnectedness)	-0.02[b] (W1)
Perceived isolation (-0.98 → 3.63; low→ high isolation)	-0.01[b] (W1)
5. SEXUALITY	
(a) Sexual Interest	
How often respondent thinks about sex (0-never → 5-several times a day)	2.06 (W2)
How often respondent masturbates (0-never → 9-more than once/day)	1.47 (W2)
Frequency of sex with spouse/partner (1-none → 6-once a day or more)	2.29[f] (W2)
(b) Sexual Attitudes	
Importance of sex in own lives (1-not at all important → 5-extremely important)	2.44 (W2)
Sex necessary for relationship (1-strongly disagree → 4-strongly agree)	2.98 (W1)
Feeling sex life as lacking in quality (1-strongly disagree → 4-strongly agree)	1.2[e] (W2)
Ability to have sex decreases with age (1-strongly disagree → 4-strongly agree)	2.92 (W1)
Love necessary for sex (1-strongly disagree → 4-strongly agree)	3.20 (W1)
Religious beliefs guided sexual behavior (1-strongly disagree → 4-strongly agree)	3.00 (W1)
Attitude toward marital infidelity (1-aways wrong → 4-not wrong at all)	1.25 (W1)
Attitude toward marital infidelity in case of dementia (1-always wrong → 4-not wrong at all)	1.60 (W1)
Attitude toward marital infidelity in case of long-term illness (1-always wrong → 4-not wrong at all)	1.61 (W1)
Find someone they don't know attractive (0-never → 5-more than once a day)	1.7[e] (W2)
Amount of effort put in to make themselves attractive to partner (0-no effort → 4-a great deal of effort)	2.2[e] (W2)
Amount of effort put in to make themselves attractive to someone they found attractive (0-no effort → 4-a great deal of effort)	1.3[e] (W2)
How often agree to sex when partner asks (0-never→ 4-always)	3.35 (W2)

continued

TABLE 4-1 Continued

NSHAP Measure	Mean (Wave #)
How often they had sex in past year compared to how often they preferred to have sex (1-much less often → 5-much more often)	2.05 (W1)
Extent to which they feel their sex life is lacking in quality (0-never → 5 always)	3.4[e] (W2)
How physically pleasurable they find sex with partner (0-not at all → 4-extremely)	2.97 (W2)
How emotionally satisfying they find sex with partner (0-not at all → 4-extremely)	3.00 (W2)
(c) Sexual/Intimate Activity	
Frequency of nonsexual acts before sex (1-much less often than prefer → 5-much more often than prefer)	2.4[e] (W2)
Frequency of kissing, hugging, touching before vaginal intercourse (1-much less often than prefer → 5-much more often than prefer)	2.7[e] (W2)
Appeal of being touched lightly (1-not at all appealing→ 4-very appealing)	3.2[e] (W2)
Appeal of hugging (1-not at all appealing→ 4-very appealing)	3.4[e] (W2)
Appeal of cuddling (1-not at all appealing→ 4-very appealing)	3.0[e] (W2)
Appeal of sexual touching (1-not at all appealing→ 4-very appealing)	2.7[e] (W2)
Frequency of caring touch (hug, cuddle, neck rub, holding hands) from partner (0-never → 6-many times/day)	3.6[e] (W2)
Frequency of caring touch (hug, cuddle, neck rub, holding hands) from non-partner (0-never → 6-many times/day)	2.6[e] (W2)
Frequency of touch with pet (0-never → 6-many times/day)	2.4[e] (W2)
(d) Sexual Functioning & Health (0-no, 1-yes)	
Pain during sex	0.06 (W2)
Lack of interest	0.48 (W2)
Lack of pleasure	0.14 (W2)
Anxiety about performance	0.17 (W2)
Early climax	0.12 (W2)
Failure to climax	0.33 (W2)
Erectile dysfunction	0.43 (W2)
Failure to lubricate	0.26 (W2)
Extent to which problems bothered respondent (0-not at all → 4-extremely)	1.00 (W2)

TABLE 4-1 Continued

NSHAP Measure	Mean (Wave #)
6. SOCIAL SUPPORT	
Opened up to family members (1=often → 3=hardly ever/never)	1.68[b] (W1)
Relied on family members (1=often → 3=hardly ever/never)	1.41[b] (W1)
Opened up to friends (1=often → 3=hardly ever/never)	1.97[b] (W1)
Relied on friends (1=often → 3=hardly ever/never)	1.68[b] (W1)
Opened up to spouse/partner (1=often → 3=hardly ever/never)	1.27[b] (W1)
Relied on spouse/partner (1=often → 3=hardly ever/never)	1.16[b] (W1)
Partner understands the way respondent feels about things (0-never → 3-often)	2.46 (W3)
Partner opens up to respondent if [he/she] needs to talk about [his/her] worries (0-never → 3-often)	2.40 (W3)
Partner relies on respondent for help if [she/he] has a problem (0-never → 3-often)	2.63 (W3)
7. SOCIAL STRAIN (0-never → 3-often)	
Partner makes too many demands	1.15[f] (W2)
Partner criticizes respondent	1.25[f] (W2)
Partner gets on respondent's nerves	1.42[f] (W2)
Partner lets respondent down when respondent is counting on [him/her]?	0.75 (W3)
Family makes too many demands	0.883 (W2)
Family criticizes respondent	0.802 (W2)
Friends make too many demands	0.532 (W2)
Friends criticize respondent	0.528 (W2)
8. ELDER MISTREATMENT (0-no, 1-yes)	
Anyone too controlling	0.11 (W1)
Anyone insults or puts respondent down	0.15 (W1)
Anyone who takes money or belongings	0.05 (W1)
Anyone who hits, kicks, or throws things at respondent	0.00 (W1)
Family conflict at home since respondent turned 60	0.21 (W3)
Respondent felt uncomfortable with anyone in family since respondent turned 60	0.21 (W3)
Respondent felt that nobody wanted them around since respondent turned 60	0.08 (W3)
Respondent told they gave others too much trouble since respondent turned 60	0.05 (W3)

continued

TABLE 4-1 Continued

NSHAP Measure	Mean (Wave #)
Respondent has been afraid of anyone in family since respondent turned 60	0.02 (W3)
Anyone close to respondent has tried to hurt or harm respondent since respondent turned 60	0.02 (W3)
Respondent has been made to stay in bed or go to bed by family since respondent turned 60	0.02 (W3)
Respondent has been called names or put down by someone close since respondent turned 60	0.13 (W3)
Respondent has been forced to do things respondent didn't want to do since respondent turned 60	0.04 (W3)
Respondent has had things taken without their OK since respondent turned 60	0.10 (W3)
Respondent has had money borrowed without it being paid back since respondent turned 60	0.21 (W3)
9. SOCIAL ENVIRONMENT (FI ratings)	
(a) Neighborhood Condition	
Density (1-buildings far apart → 5-buildings close together)	3.222^d (W2)
Neighborhood problems	
Litter (1 clean → 5 littered)	1.587^d (W2)
Noise (1 quiet → 5 noisy)	1.655^d (W2)
Traffic (1 no traffic → 5 heavy traffic)	1.985^d (W2)
Odor/polution (1 no smell → 5 strong smell)	1.319^d (W2)
Respondent's building (1 well-kept → 5 needs repairs)	1.567^d (W2)
Other buildings (1 well-kept → 5 very poorly kept)	1.652^d (W2)
Neighborhood social cohesion (1-strongly agree → 5-strongly disagree)	
Area is close-knit	3.16 (W2)
People around here willing to help their neighbors	3.78 (W2)
People in area generally don't get along with each other	2.34 (W2)
People in area don't share the same values	2.79 (W2)
People in area can be trusted	3.70 (W2)
Neighborhood social ties (0-never → 4-often)	
Frequency of people in area visit each other's homes	1.74 (W2)
Frequency of people doing favors for each other	1.93 (W2)
Frequency of people ask each other for advice about personal things	0.92 (W2)

TABLE 4-1 Continued

NSHAP Measure	Mean (Wave #)
Perceived neighborhood danger (1-strongly disagree → 5-strongly agree)	
People in area afraid to go out at night	2.44 (W2)
There are places in area where everyone knows "trouble" is expected	2.33 (W2)
Taking a big chance if walk alone in area after dark	2.35 (W2)
(b) Household Conditions	
Room temperature (1-cold → 5 hot)	3.05 (W2)
Room lighting (1-dark → 5 light)	3.57 (W2)
Room cleanliness (1-clean→ 5 dirty)	1.74 (W2)
Room tidiness (1-neat → 5 messy)	1.86 (W2)
Room noise (1-quiet → 5 noisy)	1.38 (W2)
Room odor (1-no smell → 5-strong smell)	1.49 (W2)

NOTES: The footnotes to the reported mean for a measure give the source for the measure and its mean, calculated from the indicated NSHAP wave (W1 = Wave 1, W2 = Wave 2). Means that are not footnoted are the means for responses to items in the NSHAP questionnaire for the wave indicated (i.e., the "measure" is an item in the questionnaire).
[a]Cornwell et al. (2009, Tbl. 3).
[b]York Cornwell and Waite (2009b, Tbl. 1).
[c]Cornwell et al. (2014, Tbl. 1).
[d]York Cornwell and Cagney (2014, Tbl. 1).
[e]Galinsky et al. (2014, Tbl. 2).
[f]Kim and Waite (2014, Tbl. 1).
[g]Kim and Waite (2014, Tbl. 2).
[h]York Cornwell and Waite (2009b, Tbl. 3).

The University of California Social Network Study (Offer and Fischer, 2017) took a different approach, asking each respondent about the people whom she or he was involved with in six spheres of activity, including socializing, confiding in, advice, practical help, emergency help, and providing support. The characteristics of the alter and relationship to ego were also obtained. This is a different type of social network than that based on discussion of important matters and does not obtain information about links between the alters.

Social networks are not cast in stone; they change as the situations of the people in them change. The second wave of NSHAP obtains the social network as described 5 years after the first time the social network was measured for respondents. The Wave 2 social network module asks specifically about losses and additions to the network and reasons for them (Cornwell et al., 2014). Social network characteristics have been linked, for example, to health and the management of chronic illness (York Cornwell and Waite, 2012), to erectile dysfunction (Cornwell and Laumann, 2011), and to medication use (Goldman and Cornwell, 2015). Network loss over 5 years has been found to be greater for older blacks and those of low socioeconomic status (Cornwell et al., 2014).

The study of social networks is poised to benefit from recent leaps in social connectivity and the technology that supports it and from the availability of data from these platforms. The ubiquity of smartphones also provides opportunities for passive collection of data on contacts and thus on networks.

Social Participation

The social participation dimension of social well-being is generally defined as attending organized groups or gatherings. These gatherings might include religious services or meetings of clubs, exercise groups or bowling leagues, playing on a sports team, singing in a choir, being a member of a book club, or being active in a local political or community organization. All involve participating in an organized group with others. One could participate in social events by getting together with family, going out with friends, or attending a neighborhood potluck. And volunteering in a soup kitchen, as a docent in a museum, or at the information desk in a hospital all involve organized groups of people doing things together. Social participation creates weak links between people, may link participants to sources of support—or provide support to others. It offers opportunities to display and act on shared values and beliefs with others and to spend time with others in useful and/or pleasant activities. Social participation is linked to better sleep among older adults (Chen et al., 2016), to better cognitive function (Bowling et al., 2016; Kotwal et al., 2016), to lower or higher levels of depression, depending on the type of organization in which one participates (Croezen et al., 2015), to health behaviors (Lindström et al., 2001), and to preservation of general competence. Social participation is almost always measured by asking respondents whether they participate in various social activities and if so, how often they participate. This could change with the application of tracking technology such as GPS on smartphone, tracking of movements of individuals using cell phone records, use of social media to track searches, and use of data from cameras or tracking devices in public places. Future research in the demography of aging will almost certainly take advantage of these tracking opportunities.

Social Isolation

The theories on social isolation described above point to the mechanisms linking both perceived social isolation, which psychologists call loneliness, and objective social isolation to other domains of health. And these links appear to be strong. To summarize briefly, the socially isolated face higher risks than the well-connected of poor sleep, unhealthy behaviors such as alcohol use and smoking, obesity, early cognitive decline and Alzheimer's disease, poor mental health including depression, poor self-rated health, and early mortality (Hawkley and Capitanio, 2015; York Cornwell and Waite, 2009a). Being lonely or objectively socially isolated is a source of stress, increases exposure to other stressors, and exacerbates their effects. The socially isolated are cut off from sources of instrumental, emotional, advisory, financial, or other support. They use up attention and executive function worrying about social threats and so have less of these resources for the rest of life. If they get sick, they are less likely than others to have people who will help them. This is a powerful case for the inclusion of assessments of loneliness and objective social isolation in any composite or global measure of social well-being.

Measuring Loneliness

Since loneliness is a feeling—the perception that one's social relationships are lacking or inadequate—one can measure loneliness by asking people how they feel. Measures range from a single question, included as part of the CES-D scale: "I felt lonely," asked about the last 2 weeks or the last month (Payne et al., 2014), with responses ranging from "never" to "often." A short scale, included in the Health and Retirement Study and in NSHAP, asks respondents how often over the past 2 weeks they have experienced feelings such as "I lacked companionship," "I felt left out," or "I felt isolated from others" (Hughes et al., 2004). And the longest version of the scale, the UCLA Loneliness Scale, contains 20 items (Russell et al., 1980). About one person in five is lonely at any given time, with about half of current feelings of loneliness due to situational factors such as a recent move, and about half being hereditary (Hawkley and Capitanio, 2015).

Measuring Objective Social Isolation

Since being objectively isolated means having relatively few people around one, a fairly vague concept, there are many ways to measure it. York Cornwell and Waite (2009a) created a factor score from number of friends, characteristics of one's social network, frequency of getting together with friends, family, neighbors, attending meetings of organized groups, and volunteering. Social isolation has also been measured as living alone, being unmarried/unpartnered, or having infrequent contact with others, small social networks, or perceptions of low social support (Berkman et al., 2000; House et al., 1988; Ertel et al., 2008). McPherson and colleagues

(2006) operationalized social isolation as not having a confidant: someone to talk to about matters that are important to one.

Sexuality

Sexuality is an important component of health and well-being throughout the life course. A 2001 report of the U.S. Surgeon General pointed to sexuality as essential to well-being, with calls to attend to sexual health (Office of the Surgeon General, 2001). But serious research consideration of sexual behavior and attitudes, especially among older adults, is relatively recent. Sexuality can be conceptualized as a component of well-being, as a social indicator, and as a predictor or consequence of other dimensions of health (Galinsky and Waite 2014; Liu et al., 2016; Lee et al., 2016; Waite et al., 2009; Galinsky et al., 2014). Because of the increasing recognition by researchers in the demography of aging of the importance of understanding sexuality, detailed measures of sexual behavior, attitudes, beliefs, functioning, and well-being have been included recently in important national surveys of health, including the English Longitudinal Study of Ageing (ELSA) and NSHAP, and new measures are appearing in other health surveys, including the National Health and Nutrition Examination Survey. The inclusion of both partners in some longitudinal surveys of older adults, together with questions on sexuality asked of each individually, have allowed researchers to study the contribution of each partner to the sexuality of the dyad (Waite et al., 2017; Galinsky and Waite, 2014; Kim and Waite, 2014). However, the development of theories of sexuality at older ages has lagged behind descriptions of this dimension of social well-being. We point to this as a fruitful potential future direction in the demography of aging. Sexuality has been linked to self-rated health, especially of the male partner (Lindau et al., 2007), to marital quality in the face of health decline (Galinsky and Waite, 2014), and to perceived subjective well-being (Lee et al., 2016). Sexual problems have been shown to be more likely among those with poor mental health (Laumann et al., 2008).

The study of sexuality at older ages encompasses multiple dimensions. In the section below we concentrate on *measures* of sexuality primarily because much more work has been done on measurement than on conceptualization. This is an area ripe for attention. These measures include sexual desire or interest, sexual activity or behavior, sexual functioning, and sexual health (Lee et al., 2016). *Sexual desire* consists of both proceptive and receptive behaviors and feelings; proceptive sexuality leads a person to seek out a sexual partner, whereas receptive sexuality increases willingness to have sex when asked (Galinsky et al., 2014). *Sexual interest* has been measured by asking a person any or all of the following questions: how often he or she thinks about sex, whether in the recent past he/she has lacked interest in sex

(Schafer et al., 2017), how often he or she masturbates, the importance of sex, sexual activity, and failing to have sex because of lack of interest (Iveniuk and Waite, forthcoming).

Sexual attitudes predict partnered sex and sexual interest; those who think about sex more often and those who rate sex as important or very important in their lives have sex more often (Waite et al., 2017). Respondents in the first wave of NSHAP were asked about their attitudes toward sex and sexuality in general and their attitudes about sex in their current or most recent partnership. They were asked about the importance of sex in their own lives and for maintaining a relationship. They were also asked a series of questions about the circumstances under which they would consider sex between a married person and someone other than their marriage partner. In addition, they were asked about their values toward sex, through the extent of their agreement or disagreement with the following statements: "I would not have sex with someone unless I was in love with them," "My religious beliefs have shaped and guided my sexual behavior," and "Satisfactory sexual relations are essential to the maintenance of a relationship." The ability to have sex decreases as a person grows older (Waite et al., 2009).

Respondents in surveys of older adults have been asked if in the recent past they have found someone they don't know attractive; for those with partners, the amount of effort they put into making themselves attractive to their spouse or partner (spoiler alert: men say "not much" and women say "quite a bit"); or, for those unmarried or unpartnered, how much effort they put into making themselves attractive to someone they find attractive (men say "quite a bit" and women say "not much") (Galinsky et al., 2014). These questions were included in Wave 2 of NSHAP. A new set of questions asked people to evaluate the quality of their sex life and their social behavior with their partner. These include questions about how often they agree to have sex when their partner asks them; how often they have had sex in the past year, compared to how often they would have preferred to have sex; the extent to which they feel that their sex life is lacking in quality; and how physically pleasurable and, separately, how emotionally satisfying do they find their (sexual) relationship with their spouse/partner to be?

Sexual activity includes sex with a partner and masturbation. Especially at older ages it is important to define sexual activity with a partner quite broadly, as the activities that couples engage in shift away from vaginal intercourse toward touching, cuddling, and kissing (Waite et al., 2009), and sexual inactivity among those with a partner increases with age (Lindau et al., 2007). Assessment of sexual activity might include the specific activities that the person engaged in the last time he or she had sex, such as sexual touching or oral sex (Waite et al., 2009).

Sexual functioning is generally assessed through a series of questions about whether the person experienced each of a set of symptoms for 3 months or more over the past year. These include pain during sex, lack of interest, lack of pleasure, anxiety about performance, early climax, failure to climax, erectile dysfunction (men), and failure to lubricate (women). Some studies ask the extent to which the problems bothered the person (Waite et al., 2009; Laumann et al., 2008; Lee et al., 2016).

Sexual health at older ages is defined by Lee et al. (2016) based on data from ELSA as continued sexual desire, activity, and functioning and is linked to positive subjective well-being with different patterns of these measures for men and women. Older men who have problems with sexual functioning were more likely to have low subjective well-being, whereas for women sexual desire and the frequency of partnered sexual activities predicted positive subjective well-being.

Social Support

The theoretical perspectives outlined above all include mention of social support as a mechanism or pathway through which social capital, social relationships, or social isolation affect health (Berkman et al., 2000). Social support is, quite broadly, any resource that flows between people. These resources can be exchanged within social dyads, such as between spouses or partners, and within social networks or larger social groups such as communities or neighborhoods. Anything that people can exchange can act as a social support resource, but we think most often of instrumental support (such as help with a home repair or picking something up at the store), emotional support, advice or information, financial support, provision of care (such as when one is sick), moral support in a crisis, and social connections to others (such as when a friend calls her sister, the doctor, to ask if she can be seen today for that odd symptom, as a favor to her). The research evidence to date suggests strongly that it is the perception that one has good social support that reduces stress, rather than the actual receipt of support (Thoits, 2011). This makes sense if we think of stress as the perception that one has inadequate resources for the challenges one faces. Knowing one has support *is* a resource, like money in the bank. It acts as a resource, even if one doesn't need to spend it now. Berkman et al. (2000) pointed to health behaviors, such as smoking and exercise; psychological pathways, such as depression and self-efficacy; and physiological pathways, such as allostatic load and immune function, as examples of pathways through which social support affects health and mortality.

Social Strain

We know quite a bit about the presence or absence of social ties but less about their quality. More research has been done, for example, on the impact of being married than on the quality of the marital relationship. This is especially true of the social "bad" or negatives in social well-being, but recent research points to their existence and effects. Strains in social dyads are a source of chronic stress and appear more often in relationships that are obligatory, as in the parent-child or sibling relationships. As people have more ability to shed or avoid relationships with a negative component, such as conflict, criticism, or demands, they do so; as a result, their negative relationships become rarer. Divorce or relationship dissolution can rid people of a poor-quality marriage or romantic partnership (Kalmijn and Monden, 2006), one can avoid a sibling or in-law with whom one doesn't get along, and friends are generally retained only if they provide greater benefits than costs (Offer and Fischer, 2017). Recent research suggests that mild strain, such as nagging or criticizing, may be a benefit in some close relationships. Warner and Adams (2016) found that for disabled married men, increases in negative marital quality, as indexed by criticism, making too many demands, and getting on one's nerves, reduced loneliness. These relatively mild negatives in the marriage seem to encourage men to persist in social activities that they might give up without the wife's pushing. In a study that asks directly about difficult people in social networks, Offer and Fischer (2017) found that these people tend to be in close and obligatory social roles with the alter, particularly women relatives and aging parents. One could measure good social health by the lack of negative relationships or poor social health by their presence.

Caregiver Burden

As people age, they face increasing risks of chronic disease, disability (see the chapter by V. Freedman in this volume), cognitive decline, and death. They also often face these challenges in their spouse or partner. Differences by race in the risk of these outcomes and in the age at which they occur have been documented (Umberson, 2017; also see the chapter by Hummer and Gutin in this volume). Poor health, disability, cognitive decline, and other changes with age increase the chances that an older adult will require help with activities of daily living or that his or her spouse or partner will. Having a life partner is generally the first line of defense against declines in functioning for older adults, with adult children, especially daughters, next in line as caregivers (Oldenkamp et al., 2016). Some caregivers experience stress, strain, and physical and emotional exhaustion as a result of the demands of care-giving for an older adult. This is especially the case when the caregiver is also old, perhaps with chronic disease or mobility limitations (Oldenkamp et al., 2016). Caregiving may lead to depression, physical stress, and mortality, although results are inconsistent (Fredman et al., 2015). The costs of care-giving for the caregiver may differ by the caregiver's gender, race, ethnicity, and relationship to the care recipient (Jessup et al., 2015), and so these costs are spread unequally across the population (Umberson, 2017). Changes in family relationships across cohorts now entering older ages may result in changes in risks of needing to provide care for others, widening gaps in the burden of care-giving.

Elder Mistreatment or Abuse

As people advance in age, they may become vulnerable to abuse, mistreatment, or neglect in a way that they were not earlier in life. Poor physical functioning, cognitive decline, social isolation, and the need for assistance that can follow frailty or functional limitations make older adults more dependent, and can strain close relationships, increasing the risk of physical and financial abuse and neglect (Dong et al., 2011a, 2011b). Financial abuse becomes more likely because cognitive declines may result in older adults having difficulty recognizing deception in others (Wong and Waite, 2017). Mistreatment puts older adults at risk of poor emotional health (Luo and Waite, 2011), injuries, and mortality (Dong et al., 2011b). This makes a report of abuse by an older adult a candidate for measuring poor social health.

Social Environment

In the same way that the physical environment affects health, through pollution or safe and pretty places to walk, the social environment can reflect and affect health. As one example, recent research (Cagney et al., 2014) found that older adults who lived in neighborhoods in which the rate of foreclosure was high during the Great Recession were more likely to experience incident depression than those in more stable neighborhoods, regardless of their own financial situation. A relatively new literature has focused on the conditions of the household itself, including the presence of dirt, clutter, smell, poor repair, and noise, which together suggest household disorder (York Cornwell, 2013). This research shows links in both directions between household disorder and health. For example, low-income and African American older adults live in more disordered conditions, as do those with poorer physical and mental health. Risk of living in a messy, dirty, noisy household in poor repair is lower for older adults who have a coresident partner, more nonresidential network ties, and more sources of instrumental support (York Cornwell, 2013). At the same time that household disorder reflects a lack of social support, over time it leads to more kin-centered networks and more strain within family relationships (York Cornwell, 2016).

Neighborhoods act as part of the local social context in which households and individuals are nested. A healthy neighborhood can be distinguished from one that is less salubrious, with measures of neighborhood characteristics obtained through the perceptions of respondents, observations by field interviewers, and linking to administrative and government data (York Cornwell and Cagney, 2014). Using measures included in Wave 2 of NSHAP, researchers have constructed scales of neighborhood problems, neighborhood social cohesion, neighborhood social ties, and perceived neighborhood danger and assessed their reliability and validity (York Cornwell and Cagney, 2014). This research shows that older women report greater neighborhood cohesion and more neighborhood ties than older men, but women also perceive more neighborhood danger. Black and Hispanic older adults reside in neighborhoods with more problems, lower cohesion, fewer social ties, and greater perceived danger. Neighborhood characteristics also vary across residential densities. Neighborhood problems and perceived danger increase with block-level density, but neighborhood social cohesion and social ties were lowest among residents of moderate-density blocks. Neighborhood characteristics have been linked to health conditions including asthma (Cagney and Browning, 2004), health behaviors such as walking (Mendes de Leon et al., 2009), emotional well-being (Cagney et al., 2014), and mortality (Browning et al., 2006).

It has become well established by recent literature that health and mortality vary dramatically across cities and regions and that the link between social and economic characteristics of individuals and households varies as well. Chetty et al. (2016) found, as others have, that life expectancy differs substantially across local areas, with especially dramatic variations for the poorest individuals. These differences were associated with health behaviors such as smoking and with characteristics of local areas such as expenditures. Although it is clear that where one lives has enormous consequences for health and is a candidate for inclusion in a global measure of social health, the most important characteristics of areas and the mechanisms through which they operate are not well understood.

DIFFERENTIALS IN SOCIAL WELL-BEING: GENDER, RACE, ETHNICITY, AND SOCIOECONOMIC STATUS

Describing and understanding differences in various dimensions of social well-being across groups is a key future direction in the demography of aging. How do social networks differ by race and ethnicity, for example? How do various measures of social well-being for men and women diverge with age? We know that at older ages men are much more likely to be married and thus much more likely to be sexually active than are women the same age (Lindau et al., 2007). Recent work by Umberson (2017) points to shockingly higher rates of death of close family members for blacks than for whites in the United States. Umberson points to the impact on social networks, social support, and successful social relationships that may follow from these losses, but little research addresses this and related issues. Gaps in social well-being may be widening. Raley et al. (2015) pointed to a growing racial and ethnic divide in U.S. marriage patterns, for example. And there is no reason to expect that these gaps are similar by gender, race, ethnicity, and socioeconomic status. This is an important area for future research in the demography of aging and key to understanding health disparities.

It is more important still to describe and understand differences in the *links* between various dimensions of social well-being and other components of health, for example by race and gender. Liu and Waite (2014) found that marital quality affected cardiovascular risk for older women but not for older men. And recent work by Uchino et al. (2016) found no link between social support and levels of C-reactive protein (CRP), a measure of systemic inflammation. However, social support moderated the effect of CRP in that Blacks (but not Whites), with higher levels of social support showed lower levels of CRP. And we know virtually nothing about variations in social well-being by socioeconomic status, or about differences in the effects of social well-being on health by education or income. Since it could well be the case that race, gender, ethnicity, and socioeconomic status *interact* in their effects on the link between social well-being and health, this intersectionality deserves attention in future research in the demography of aging.

HOW DO WE MEASURE SOCIAL WELL-BEING?

Social well-being is an essential component of health, according to WHO, so evaluating it is important. People can be healthy on some dimensions of social health if they *perceive* them to be good. We could put loneliness in this category; if one feels left out, excluded, or alone, then one is lonely. Relationship quality is similar in this respect; one's marriage is good if one feels that it is. For these dimensions of social well-being, we can just ask each person for her or his evaluation. For other dimensions of social well-being, researchers ask people to describe their social lives and then create measures from those descriptions. Social participation is evaluated by asking people how often they attend religious services; go to meetings of community groups; participate in organized groups like bowling leagues; and get together with family, friends, or neighbors. Various measures of social participation can be created from the answers to these questions, depending on the research question being asked. Social isolation is measured, generally, by asking people if they are married or have a romantic partner, who lives in their household, how often they participate in activities with other people, how often they are in contact with family members, and what their social networks are like. If they see lots of people often, they are socially connected. If they see few people infrequently, live alone, and so on, they are socially isolated. Social networks can be measured by asking people about those to whom they are connected. But they could also be measured by counting contacts of some type—for example, social media contacts, cell phone call records, or overlaps in activity space (Browning et al., 2017; Cagney and York Cornwell, 2017).

New technology has introduced "objective" measurement of some social activities, such as sleep and exercise. Fitness trackers fitted to research subjects can measure various components of sleep, including latency, the time it takes to fall asleep, sleep efficiency measured as the amount of time in bed spent in sleep, sleep duration, and sleep disturbances (Lauderdale et al., 2014). These same activity-tracking devices can measure day-time activity, from sedentary to vigorous (Huisingh-Scheetz et al., 2014). Activity trackers in homes can map location of and contact between residents.

Social well-being has long been assessed through vital records, administrative data, and business activity. These sources include Social Security earnings and disability income, employment records, mortality records, Medicare claims data, licenses, and legal proceedings such as those for marriage, adoption, and divorce. Mapping programs allow measurement of features of local areas such as parks and night clubs (Browning et al., 2006). The ability to measure dimensions of social health vastly exceeds existing theoretical perspectives from which to understand their actions and importance.

HOW IS SOCIAL WELL-BEING CONNECTED TO OTHER DIMENSIONS OF HEALTH?

Berkman et al. (2000, p. 843) developed a comprehensive conceptual model of the mechanisms through which social integration affects health in ". . . cascading causal process beginning with the macro-social to psychobiological processes that are dynamically linked together . . . ." Throughout, the authors used "social integration" and "social networks" interchangeably, although I would argue that they are quite distinct dimensions of social well-being.

In this model, the macro-structural forces that affect social integration through social networks include culture, socioeconomic factors, politics, and social change, each with subcomponents. These forces condition the extent, shape, and nature of social networks, which comprise the mezzo level. Berkman et al. focused on social network structure, such as size, density, and range and on characteristics of network ties, such as frequency of contact and intimacy. Here the authors sneak in a measure that many would consider social participation and not a characteristic of a social network. In fact, this measure is described as "frequency of organization participation (attendance)" (Berkman et al., 2000, Fig. 1, p. 847). Simply expanding the mezzo level to encompass "social capital" makes the model more general and more in line with current thinking.

Berkman and colleagues called the next level of their model "psychosocial mechanisms at the micro level." These mechanisms include social support, social influence, social engagement, person-to-person contact, and access to resources and material goods, all of which affect health through health behaviors and through psychological and physiological pathways.

To summarize this elegant model briefly, and to extend and expand it, social well-being affects and is affected by other dimensions of health through access to *resources*, such as time, advice, care-giving, housing, expertise, and money (York Cornwell and Waite, 2012); through *emotional support* (Warner and Kelley-Moore, 2012; Warner and Adams, 2016); through *stress reduction and management* (Thoits, 2011); through *shared social environments* such as shared social networks (Cornwell, 2012), households (Schafer et al., 2017), and neighborhoods; through *physiological processes* (Sbarra, 2009) that lead to chronic disease (Liu and Waite, 2014; Liu et al., 2016; Das, 2013); through physiological processes that lead to social outcomes (Das, 2017); through *gender display, power, and status* (Cornwell and Laumann, 2011; Liu et al., 2016); through *mistreatment and discrimination* (Wong and Waite, 2017; Das, 2013); and through *gene expression* (Cole et al., 2015).

FUTURE DIRECTIONS IN SOCIAL WELL-BEING AT OLDER AGES

The most exciting opportunities to understand social well-being over the next decade or so build on new sources of data, new research questions, new analytic techniques, and new theoretical and conceptual models. Here are some examples.

Genes and the Social

Recent research has shown the extraordinary complexity of links between the social world and our genes. One example comes from the body of work by Steven Cole, John Cacioppo, and their colleagues on the relationship between genes, gene expression, and loneliness (Cole et al., 2015). The mechanisms linking them are being unraveled with the help of new technology; the availability to the research community of banks of genotyped data; genotyping of respondents in large, longitudinal surveys like the Health and Retirement Study; new theoretical perspectives (Cacioppo et al., 2014); and interdisciplinary research teams.

Environments and the Social

Theoretical perspectives on activity space (Browning et al., 2017), combined with GPS and other mapping and tracking technologies, provide opportunities to understand the environments in which people spend their time and their interactions with others in the various spaces in which they conduct their lives (Cagney and York Cornwell, 2010). Linking of data from environmental sensors, for example, allows researchers to characterize particulate matter in the local environment and its association with various dimensions of health (Adams et al., 2016).

Physiological variation both affects and responds to social factors. For example, Das (2017) used data on salivary testosterone obtained from respondents in NSHAP to test hypotheses about social modulation of hormones and hormonal regulation of women's sociality and finds evidence for both. Social support and social strain predict inflammation later, with social support modestly protecting against inflammation and social strain substantially increasing the risks (Yang et al., 2014).

Direct observation gets personal. The popularity and ubiquity of fitness and health tracking devices has begun to change the way data on health and functioning are collected in survey research and will ultimately change clinical practice, too. These devices can now measure heart rate, blood pressure, sleep, exercise, and activity (now mostly in steps taken) over the day. They can identify location of the wearer. Nearness to other device wearers could track social contacts.

Creation of Global Measures of Social Well-being

Following on the example of measures of labor force participation, it should be possible to create measures of social well-being. These could be included, for example, in the Current Population Survey done by the U.S. Census Bureau or in the American Community Survey. Doing so would enable characterization of the social well-being of the population by subgroups and the use of these measures as social indicators. One approach is illustrated by an effort by the OECD, which has produced a conceptual framework for well-being indicators and is compiling these across countries (OECD, 2011). This global indicator of well-being includes "social contact with others" and "social network support" to compare measures of social connections across countries. Each indicator of well-being is characterized for each country as falling either in the top two deciles of OECD countries, in the bottom two deciles, or in the six intermediate deciles. These two social measures are based on the Gallup World Survey, which asks respondents about their frequency of getting together with others and whether a respondent agrees that during times of need he or she can count on someone to help.

Various dimensions of social well-being have strong links, generally reciprocal, with physical, physiological, functional, psychological, and cognitive dimensions of health. Understanding these connections and how they operate constitutes future directions in the demography of aging.

REFERENCES

Adams, D., Ajmani, G.S., Pun, V.C., Wroblewski, K.E., Kern, D.W., Schumm, L.P., McClintock, M.K., Suh, H.H., and Pinto, J.M. (2016). Nitrogen dioxide pollution exposure is associated with olfactory dysfunction in older U.S. adults. *International Forum of Allergy & Rhinology, 6*(12), 1245–1252. doi: 10.1002/alr.21829.

Annandale, E. (2014). *The Sociology of Health and Medicine: A Critical Introduction* (2nd ed.). Cambridge, UK: Polity Press.

Beck, A.H. (2004). The Flexner report and the standardization of American medical education. *Journal of the American Medical Association, 291*(17), 2139–2140.

Belsky, D.W., Caspi, A., Houts, R., Cohen, H.J., Corcoran, D.L., Danese, A., Harrington, H., Israel S., Levine, M.E., Schaefer, J.D., et al. (2015). Quantification of biological aging in young adults. *Proceedings of the National Academy of Sciences of the United States of America, 112*(30), E4104–E4110. doi: 10.1073/pnas.1506264112.

Berkman, L.F., Glass, T., Brissette, I., and Seeman, T.E. (2000). From social integration to health: Durkheim in the new millennium. *Social Science & Medicine, 51*, 843–857.

Bourdieu, P. (1986). The forms of capital. In: J. Richardson (Ed.), *Handbook of Theory and Research for the Sociology of Education* (pp. 241–258). Westport, CT: Greenwood Press.

Bowling, A., Pikhartova, J., and Dodgeon, B. (2016). Is mid-life social participation associated with cognitive function at age 50? Results from the British National Child Development Study (NCDS). *BMC Psychology, 4*, 58. doi: 10.1186/s40359-016-0164-x.

Browning, C.R., Wallace, D., Feinberg, S.L., and Cagney, K.A. (2006). Neighborhood social processes, physical conditions, and disaster-related mortality: The case of the 1995 Chicago heat wave. *American Sociological Review, 71*(4), 661–678.

Browning, C.R., Calder, C.A., Krivo, L.J., Smith, A.L., and Boettner, B. (2017). Socioeconomic segregation of activity spaces in urban neighborhoods: Does shared residence mean shared routines? *Russell Sage Foundation Journal of the Social Sciences, 3*(2), 210–231. doi: 10.7758/RSF.2017.3.2.09.

Cacioppo, J.T., Cacioppo, S., and Boomsma, D.I. (2014). Evolutionary mechanisms for loneliness. *Cognition & Emotion, 28*(1), 3–21. doi: 10.1080/02699931.2013.837379.

Cagney, K.A., and Browning, C.R. (2004). Exploring neighborhood-level variation in asthma and other respiratory diseases: The contribution of neighborhood social context. *Journal of General Internal Medicine, 19*(3), 229–236. doi: 10.1111/j.1525-1497.2004.30359.x.

Cagney, K.A., and York Cornwell, E. (2010). Neighborhoods and health in later life: The intersection of biology and community. *Annual Review of Gerontology and Geriatrics, 30*(1), 323–348. doi: 10.1891/0198-8794.30.323.

Cagney, K.A., and York Cornwell, E. (2017). Aging in activity space: Results of smart-phone based GPS tracking of urban seniors. *Journal of Gerontology Series B: Psychological and Social Sciences, 72*(5), 864–875.

Cagney, K.A., Browning, C.R., Iveniuk, J., and English, N. (2014). The onset of depression during the great recession: Foreclosure and older adult mental health. *American Journal of Public Health, 104*(3), 498–505. doi: 10.2105/AJPH.2013.301566.

Chen, J., Lauderdale, D.S., and Waite, L.J. (2016). Social participation and older adults' sleep. *Social Science & Medicine, 149*, 164–173. doi: 10.1016/j.socscimed.2015.11.045.

Chetty, R., Stepner, M., Abraham, S., Lin, S., Scuderi, B., Turner, N., Bergeron, A., and Cutler, D. (2016). The association between income and life expectancy in the United States, 2001–2014. *Journal of the American Medical Association, 315*(16), 1750–1766. doi: 10.1001/jama.2016.4226.

Cole, S.W., Capitanio, J.P., Chun, K., Arevalo, J.M.G., Ma, J., and Cacioppo, J.T. (2015). Myeloid differentiation architecture of leukocyte transcriptome dynamics in perceived social isolation. *Proceedings of the National Academy of Sciences of the United States of America, 112*(49), 15142–15147. doi: 10.1073/pnas.1514249112.

Coleman, J. (1988). Social capital in the creation of human capital. *American Journal of Sociology, 94*, S95–S120.

Coontz, S. (2008). *The Future of Marriage* (Cato Unbound, January 14, 2008). Washington, DC: Cato Institute. Available: www.cato-unbound.org/2008/01/14/stephanie-coontz/future-marriage [March 2018].

Cornwell, B. (2012). Spousal network overlap as a basis for spousal support. *Journal of Marriage and Family, 74*(2), 229–238.

Cornwell, B., and Laumann, E.O. (2011). Network position and sexual dysfunction: Implications of partner betweenness for men. *American Journal of Sociology, 117*(1), 172–208.

Cornwell, B., Schumm, L.P., Laumann, E.O., and Graber, J. (2009). Social networks in the NSHAP Study: Rationale, measurement, and preliminary findings. *Journal of Gerontology: Social Sciences, 64B*(S1), i47–i55.

Cornwell, B., Schumm, L.P., Laumann, E.O., Kim, J., and Kim, Y. (2014). Assessment of social network change in a national longitudinal survey. *Journals of Gerontology Series B: Psychological Sciences and Social Sciences, 69*(Suppl 2), S75–S82. doi: 10.1093/geronb/gbu037.

Croezen, S., Avendano, M., Burdorf, A., and van Lenthe, F.J. (2015). Social participation and depression in old age: A fixed-effects analysis in 10 European countries. *American Journal of Epidemiology, 182*(2), 168–176. doi:10.1093/aje/kwv015.

Das, A. (2013). How does race get "under the skin"?: Inflammation, weathering, and metabolic problems in late life. *Social Science & Medicine, 77*, 75–83.

Das, A. (2017). Network connections and salivary testosterone among older U.S. women: Social modulation or hormonal causation? *Journals of Gerontology: Series B*, gbx111. Epub prior to printing. doi: 10.1093/geronb/gbx111.

Dong, X.Q., Simon, M.A., Rajan, K., and Evans, D.A. (2011a). Association of cognitive function and risk for elder abuse in a community-dwelling population. *Dementia and Geriatric Cognitive Disorders, 32*(3), 209–215. doi: 10.1159/000334047.

Dong, X.Q., Simon, M.A., Beck, T.T., Farran, C., McCann, J.J., Mendes de Leon, C.F., Laumann, E.O., and Evans, D.A. (2011b). Elder abuse and mortality: The role of psychological and social wellbeing. *Gerontology, 57*(6), 549–558. doi: 10.1159/000321881.

Engel, G.L. (1977). The need for a new medical model: A challenge for biomedicine. *Science, 196*(4286), 129–136.

Ertel, K.A., Glymour, M.M., and Berkman, L.F. (2008). Effects of social integration on preserving memory function in a nationally representative U.S. elderly population. *American Journal of Public Health, 98*(7), 1215–1220.

Flexner, A. (1910). *Medical Education in the United States and Canada.* Washington, DC: Science and Health Publications.

Fredman, L., Lyons, J.G., Cauley, J.A., Hochberg, M., and Applebaum, K.M. (2015). The relationship between caregiving and mortality after accounting for time-varying caregiver status and addressing the healthy caregiver hypothesis. *Journals of Gerontology, Series A: Biological Sciences and Medical Sciences, 70*(9), 1163–1168. doi: 10.1093/gerona/glv009.

Galinksy, A, and Waite, L. (2014). Sexual activity and psychological health as mediators of the relationship between physical health and marital quality. *Journals of Gerontology, Series B: Psychological Sciences and Social Sciences, 69*(3), 482–492. doi: 10.1093/geronb/gbt165.

Galinsky, A., McClintock, M.K., and Waite, L.J.. (2014). Sexuality and physical contact in National Social Life, Health, and Aging Project Wave 2. *Journals of Gerontology: Series B, 69*(Suppl 2), S83–S98. doi: 10.1093/geronb/gbu072.

Glenn, N.D., and Weaver, C.N. (1979). A note on family situation and global happiness. *Social Forces, 57*, 960–967.

Goldman, A.W., and Cornwell, B. (2015). Social network bridging potential and the use of complementary and alternative medicine in later life. *Social Science & Medicine, 140*, 69–80. doi: 10.1016/j.socscimed.2015.07.003.

Hawkley, L.C., and Capitanio, J.P. (2015). Perceived social isolation, evolutionary fitness and health outcomes: A lifespan approach. *Philosophical Transactions of the Royal Society B: Biological Sciences, 370*(1669). doi.org/10.1098/rstb.2014.0114.

House, J.S., Landis, K.R., and Umberson, D. (1988). Social relationships and health. *Science, 241*(4865), 540–545.

Hughes, M.E., Waite, L.J., Hawkley, L.C., and Cacioppo, J.T. (2004). A short scale for measuring loneliness in large surveys: Results from two population-based studies. *Research on Aging, 26*(6), 655–672.

Huisingh-Scheetz, M., Kocherginsky, M., Schumm, L.P., Engelman, M., McClintock, M., Dale, W., Magett, E., Rush, P. and Waite, L. (2014). Measuring functional status in the National Social Life, Health, and Aging Project (NSHAP): Rationale, measurement, and preliminary findings. *Journals of Gerontology: Social Sciences, 69*(Suppl 2), S177–S190. doi: 10.1093/geronb/gbu091.

Iveniuk, J., and Waite, L. (forthcoming). The psychosocial sources of sexual interest in older couples. *Journal of Social and Personal Relationships.*

Jessup, N.M., Bakas, T., McLennon, S.M., and Weaver, M.T. (2015). Are there gender, racial, or relationship differences in caregiver task difficulty, depressive symptoms, and life changes among stroke family caregivers? *Brain Injury, 29*(1), 17–24. doi: 10.3109/02699052.2014.947631.

Kalmijn, M., and Monden, C.W.S. (2006). Are the negative effects of divorce on psychological well-being dependent on marital quality? *Journal of Marriage and Family, 68*(6), 1197–1213.

Kaufman, M. (2018). *Redefining Success in America: A New Theory of Happiness and Human Development.* Chicago: University of Chicago Press.

Kim, J., and Waite, L.J. (2014). Relationship quality and shared activity in marital and cohabiting dyads in the National Social Life, Health and Aging Project, Wave 2. *Journals of Gerontology: Social Sciences, 69*(Suppl 2), S64–S74. doi: 10.1093/geronb/gbu038.

Kotwal, A.A., Kim, J., Waite, L., and Dale, W. (2016). Social function and cognitive status: Results from a U.S. nationally representative survey of older adults. *Journal of General Internal Medicine, 31*(8), 854–862. doi: 10.1007/s11606-016-3696-0.

Lauderdale, D.S., Schumm, L.P., Kurina, L.M., McClintock, M.K., Thisted, R.A., Chen, J., and Waite, L. (2014). Assessment of sleep in the National Social Life, Health and Aging Project. *Journals of Gerontology: Social Sciences, 69*(Suppl 2), S125–S133. doi: 10.1093/geronb/gbu092.

Laumann, E.O., Waite, L.J., and Das, A. (2008). Sexual dysfunction among older adults: Prevalence and risk factors from a nationally representative U.S. probability sample of men and women 57 to 85 years of age. *Journal of Sexual Medicine, 5*(10), 2300–2312.

Lee, D.M., Vanhoutte, B., Nazroo, J., and Pendleton, N. (2016). Sexual health and positive subjective well-being in partnered older men and women. *Journals of Gerontology: Series B, 71*(4), 698–710. doi: 10.1093/geronb/gbw018.

Lin, N. (2001). *Social Capital: A Theory of Social Structure and Action.* New York: Cambridge University Press.

Lindau, S.T., Laumann, E.O., Levinson, W., and Waite, L.J. (2003). Synthesis of scientific disciplines in pursuit of health: The Interactive Biopyschosocial Model. *Perspectives in Biology and Medicine, 46*(3), S74–S86.

Lindau, S.T., Schumm, P., Laumann, E.O., Levinson, W., O'Muircheartaigh, C.A., and Waite, L.J. (2007). A national study of sexuality and health among older adults in the U.S. *New England Journal of Medicine, 357*(8), 762–774. doi: 10.1056/NEJMoa067423.

Lindström, M., Hanson, B.S., and Östergren, P.O. (2001). Socioeconomic differences in leisure-time physical activity: The role of social participation and social capital in shaping health related behaviour. *Social Science & Medicine, 52*(3), 441–451.

Litwin, H., and Shiovitz-Ezra, S. (2010). Social network type and subjective well-being in a national sample of older Americans. *Gerontologist, 51*(3), 379–388.

Liu, H., and Waite, L.J. (2014). Bad marriage, broken heart? Age and gender differences in the link between marital quality and cardiovascular risks among older adults. *Journal of Health and Social Behavior, 55*(4), 403–423.

Liu, H., Waite, L.J., and Shen, S. (2016). Diabetes risk and disease management in later life: A national longitudinal study of the role of marital quality. *Journals of Gerontology, Series B: Social Science, 71*(6), 1070–1080. doi: 10.1093/geronb/gbw061.

Lowsky, D.J., Olshansky, S.J., Bhattacharya, J., and Goldman, D.P. (2014). Heterogeneity in healthy aging. *Journals of Gerontology, Series A: Biological Sciences and Medical Sciences, 69*(6), 640–649. doi: 10.1093/Gerona/glt162.

Luo, Y., and Waite, L.J. (2011). Mistreatment and psychological well-being among the elderly: Exploring the role of psychosocial resources and deficits. *Journals of Gerontology: Social Sciences, 66B*(2), 217–229.

Maccoby, E.E. (1980). *Social Development: Psychological Growth and the Parent-Child Relationship.* New York: Harcourt Brace Jovanovich.

Martin, P., Kelly, N., Kahana, B., Kahana, E., Willcox, B.J., Willcox, D.C., and Poon, L.W. (2015). Defining successful aging: A tangible or elusive concept? *Gerontologist, 55*(1), 14–25.

McPherson, M., Smith-Lovin, L., and Brashears, M.E. (2006). Social isolation in America: Changes in core discussion networks over two decades. *American Sociological Review, 71*(3), 353–375.

Mendes de Leon, C.F., Cagney, K.A., Bienias, J.L., Barnes, L.L., Skarupski, K.A., Scherr, P.A., and Evans, D.A. (2009). Neighborhood social cohesion and disorder in relation to walking in community-dwelling older adults: A multi-level analysis. *Journal of Aging and Health, 21*(1), 155–171. doi: 10.1177/0898264308328650.

OECD. (2011). *Compendium of OECD Well-being Indicators.* OECD Better Life Initiative. Available: http://www.oecd.org/std/47917288.pdf [April 2018].

Oldenkamp, M., Hagedoorn, M., Slaets, J., Stolk, R., Wittek, R., and Smidt, N. (2016). Subjective burden among spousal and adult-child informal caregivers of older adults: Results from a longitudinal cohort study. *BMC Geriatrics, 16*, 208. doi: 10.1186/s12877-016-0387-y.

Offer, S., and Fischer, C.S. (2017). Difficult people: Who is perceived to be demanding in personal networks and why are they there? *American Sociological Review*. doi: 10.1177/0003122317737951.

Office of the Surgeon General. (2001). *The Surgeon General's Call to Action to Promote Sexual Health and Responsible Sexual Behavior*. Rockville, MD: Office of the Surgeon General.

Payne, C., Hedberg, E.C., Kozloski, M., Dale, W., and McClintock, M.K. (2014). Using and interpreting mental health measures in the National Social Life, Health, and Aging Project. *Journals of Gerontology: Series B, 69*(Suppl 2), 99–116. doi: 10.1093/geronb/gbu100.

Pearlin, L.I., Schieman, S., Fazio, E.M., and Meersman, S.C. (2005). Stress, health, and the life course: Some conceptual perspectives. *Journal of Health and Social Behavior, 46*(2), 205–219.

Putnam, R. (2000). *Bowling Alone: The Collapse and Revival of American Community*. New York: Simon and Schuster.

Raley, R.K., Sweeney, M.M., and Wondra, D. (2015). The growing racial and ethnic divide in U.S. marriage patterns. *The Future of Children/Center for the Future of Children, the David and Lucile Packard Foundation, 25*(2), 89–109.

Rowe, J.W. (1990). Toward successful aging: Limitation of the morbidity associated with "normal" aging. In W.R. Hazzard (Ed.), *Principles of Geriatric Medicine and Gerontology* (2nd ed., pp. 138–141). New York: McGraw-Hill.

Rowe, J.W., and Kahn, R.L. (1997). Successful aging. *Gerontologist, 37*(4), 433–440.

Rowe, J.W., and Kahn, R.L. (1998). Successful aging. *Aging (Milano), 10*(2), 142–144.

Russell, D., Peplau, L.A., and Cutrona, C.E. (1980). The Revised UCLA Loneliness Scale: Concurrent and discriminant validity evidence. *Journal of Personality and Social Psychology, 39*, 472–480.

Ryff, C., and Singer, B. (1998). The contours of positive health. *Psychological Inquiry, 9*, 1–28.

Sapolsky, R.M. (2004). *Why Zebras Don't Get Ulcers: The Acclaimed Guide to Stress, Stress-Related Diseases, and Coping—Now Revised and Updated*. New York: Holt.

Sbarra, D.A. (2009). Marriage protects men from clinically meaningful elevations in C-reactive protein: Results from the National Social Life, Health, and Aging Project (NSHAP). *Psychosomatic Medicine, 71*(8), 828.

Schafer, M.H., Upenieks, L., and Iveniuk, J. (2017). Putting sex into context in later life: Environmental disorder and sexual interest among partnered seniors. *Gerontologist*, Epub ahead of print. doi: 10.1093/geront/gnx043.

Smith, K.P., and Christakis, N.A. (2008). Social networks and health. *Annual Review of Sociology, 34*, 405–429. doi: 10.1146/annurev.soc.34.040507.134601.

Starr, P. (1982). *The Social Transformation of American Medicine: The Rise of a Sovereign Profession and the Making of a Vast Industry*. New York: Basic Books.

Steptoe, A., Shankar, A., Demakakos, P., and Wardle, J. (2013). Social isolation, loneliness, and all-cause mortality in older men and women. *Proceedings of the National Academy of Sciences of the United States of America, 110*(15), 5797–5801. doi: 10.1073/pnas.1219686110.

Stevens, R. (1971). *American Medicine and the Public Interest*. New Haven, CT: Yale University Press.

Thoits, P.A. (2011). Mechanisms linking social ties and support to physical and mental health. *Journal of Health and Social Behavior, 52*(2), 145–161.

Uchino, B.N., Ruiz, J.M., Smith, T.W., Smyth, J.M., Taylor, D.J., Allison, M., and Ahn, C. (2016). Ethnic/racial differences in the association between social support and levels of C-reactive proteins in the North Texas Heart Study. *Psychophysiology, 53*(1), 64–70. doi: 10.1111/psyp.12499.

Umberson, D. (2017). Black deaths matter: Race, relationship loss and effects on survivors. *Journal of Health and Social Behavior, 58*(4), 405–420.

Waite, L.J. (2005). Marriage and family. In D. Poston and M. Micklin (Eds.), *Handbook of Population* (pp. 87–108). Boston: Springer.

Waite, L.J., and Gallagher, M. (2000). *The Case for Marriage: Why Married People Are Happier, Healthier, and Better Off Financially.* New York: Doubleday.

Waite, L.J., Laumann, E.O., Das, A., and Schumm, L.P. (2009). Sexuality measures of partnerships, practices, attitudes, and problems in the National Social Life, Health, and Aging Project. *Journals of Gerontology: Social Sciences, 64B*(S1), i56–i66.

Waite, L.J., Iveniuk, J., Laumann, E.O., and McClintock, M.K. (2017). Sexuality in older couples: Individual and dyadic characteristics. *Archives of Sexual Behavior, 46*(2), 605–618.

Warner, D.F., and Adams, S.A. (2016). Physical disability and increased loneliness among married older adults: The role of changing social relations. *Society and Mental Health, 6(2)*, 106–128.

Warner, D.F., and Kelley-Moore, J. (2012). The social context of disablement among older adults: Does marital quality matter for loneliness? *Journal of Health and Social Behavior, 53*(1), 50–66. doi: 10.1177/0022146512439540.

Wilson, R.S., Krueger, K.R., Arnold, S.E., Schneider, J.A., Kelly, J.F., Barnes, L.L., Tang, Y., and Bennett, D.A. (2007). Loneliness and risk of Alzheimer's disease. *Archives of General Psychiatry, 64*(2), 234–240.

Wong, J.S., and Waite, L.J. (2017). Elder mistreatment predicts later physical and psychological health: Results from a national longitudinal study. *Journal of Elder Abuse and Neglect, 29*(1), 15–42. doi: 10.1080/08946566.2016.1235521.

Yang, Y.C., McClintock, M.K., Kozloski, M., and Li, T. (2013). Social isolation and adult mortality: The role of chronic inflammation and sex differences. *Journal of Health and Social Behavior, 54*(2), 183–203. doi: 10.1177/0022146513485244.

Yang, Y.C., Schorpp, K., and Harris, K.M. (2014). Social support, social strain and inflammation: Evidence from a national longitudinal study of U.S. adults. *Social Science & Medicine, 107*, 124–135.

Yang, Y.C., Boen, C., Gerken, K., Li, T., Schorpp, K., and Harris, K.M. (2016). Social relationships and physiological determinants of longevity across human life span. *Proceedings of the National Academy of Sciences of the United States of America, 113*(3), 578–583.

York Cornwell, E. (2013). Social resources and disordered living conditions: Evidence from a national sample of community-residing older adults. *Research on Aging, 36*(4), 399–430. doi: 10.1177/0164027513497369.

York Cornwell, E. (2016). Household disorder, network ties, and social support in later life. *Journal of Marriage and the Family, 78*(4), 871–889. doi: 10.1111/jomf.12299.

York Cornwell, E., and Cagney, K.A. (2014). Assessment of neighborhood context in a nationally representative study. *Journals of Gerontology Series B: Psychological Sciences and Social Sciences, 69*(Suppl 2), S51–S63. doi: 10.1093/geronb/gbu052.

York Cornwell, E., and Waite, L.J. (2009a). Social disconnectedness, perceived isolation, and health among older adults. *Journal of Health and Social Behavior, 50*(1), 31–48.

York Cornwell, E., and Waite, L.J. (2009b). Measuring social isolation among older adults using multiple indicators from the NSHAP study. *Journals of Gerontology Series B: Psychological Sciences and Social Sciences, 64B*(suppl. 1), ie34–ie46. doi: 10/1093/geronb/gbp037.

York Cornwell, E., and Waite, L.J. (2012). Social network resources and management of hypertension. *Journal of Health and Social Behavior, 53*, 215–231.

5

Place, Aging, and Health

Kathleen A. Cagney[1]
and
Erin York Cornwell[2]

INTRODUCTION

Aging in place suggests the goal of many older adults to age within the long-term residence or community where they have spent much of their adult lives. However, this concept also recognizes that aging is a process that occurs within a particular place. Whether older adults reside in their long-term communities or move to other locations, the characteristics of the places within which they experience the aging process—and the psychosocial and quality-of-life benefits potentially conferred by these places—likely have profound consequences for their abilities to adapt to changes such as bereavement, retirement, and deteriorating health, as well as their capacity to recover from illness (Latham et al., 2015) and maintain independent community residence.

What is place, and why does it matter for the lives of older adults? Place suggests a physical space with environmental conditions that may directly impact older adults' health. *Place* also encompasses a built environment that may promote or impede mobility and an organizational, institutional, municipal, or policy setting that determines access to resources such as health care, fresh foods, and social services. Importantly, these characteristics of places may also facilitate or impede social interaction and engagement (Hand and Howrey, 2017; Jacobs, 1961; Sampson, 2012). One may readily acknowledge that place likely structures the lives of older

---

[1]University of Chicago.
[2]Cornell University.

131

adults but an evidence-based understanding of its impact across age, time period, and context is relatively nascent.

In this chapter, we focus on the places that older adults inhabit and the implications of these places for their health. We ask what place means, and we conceive of place as both physical and social. We note that place and its influences may exist in multiple facets, at multiple levels (Andrews et al., 2013), so we focus on both formal and informal conceptions of place. This leads to an exploration of theory and how theory related to place may inform scientific investigations and interpretation of findings. We acknowledge that place can shape opportunity, so we examine how place might lead to such factors as structural inequality and restricted migration. Throughout the chapter, we draw on the extant literature addressing place and bring to bear relevant findings of this body of scholarship to aging and place. We close with new directions in research on place and discuss how potential insights from this work could lead to fundamental reconsiderations of place. This, in turn, may inform how best to exploit the aspects of place that are health enhancing, particularly for older adults.

THE STUDY OF AGING IN CONTEXT

The literature that speaks broadly to place, aging, and health employs various conceptions of place, including nested and overlapping spaces (e.g., states, cities, neighborhoods, locations of daily activities), with consequences for health operating at different scales. While some research takes the definition of place as a relatively straightforward concept, other work theorizes about place and its meaning. In this section, we outline three broad theoretical perspectives that inform much of the research examining place and health in later life: (1) environmental gerontology, (2) geographical gerontology, and (3) social scientific research on "neighborhood effects."

First, although context has been central to gerontological research since at least the late 1940s (Smith, 2014), the work of Lawton and colleagues was particularly influential in fostering a subdiscipline that acknowledged the influence of place. Lawton and Nahemow's (1973) Ecological Model of Aging provided a foundation for *environmental gerontology* by explicitly introducing environmental considerations into research on health and aging, rather than relying solely on a biological framework. Their Ecological Model of Aging "focused on the description, explanation, and modification or optimization of the relation between elderly persons and their sociospatial surroundings" (Wahl and Weisman, 2003, p. 616), elaborating the concept of person–environment fit. This work describes a dynamic relationship between older adults and their living environments: as older adults experience changes in functional capacities, they either adapt themselves or adapt their surroundings to achieve a balance between their abilities and the demands of their environment. Informed by this perspective, home modifications, nursing services, building design, and new technologies aim to reduce environmental press and thereby promote older adults' abilities to age in the community (Vasunilashorn et al., 2012).

Psychologists with a focus on aging have been particularly active in developing scholarship in environmental gerontology (e.g., Birren, 1999), drawing out responses to, and perceptions of, physical and social environments including the household. Canter and Craik (1981), in this tradition, later proposed the term "sociophysical environment" to capture the interrelationship between the physical and the social. Moore's more recent work (2014) proposes an Ecological Framework of Place that incorporates people, place, and activity related to that place, emphasizing the dynamic nature of each. See Wahl and Weisman's (2003) excellent review of environmental gerontology for a fuller treatment of its origins and contributions.

Second, and roughly over the same period, geography became more central to gerontological concerns (e.g., Golant, 1972; Rowles, 1981). The subfield of geographical gerontology, which has its roots in social geography, emphasizes the interconnectedness and interdependence of spaces and services and underscores the uniquely spatial concerns of older adults (Andrews et al., 2007, 2013). Theories, concepts, and methods of geography are brought to bear on questions related to aging and the life course. One key distinguishing feature is the focus on scale, whether it be within the space of a household, neighborhood, or nation; attention to scale both orients the work and informs the research questions. Some consensus exists, as Cutchin (2009) explicated, that geographical gerontology has not been as impactful as it might. A new text by Skinner and colleagues (2017) aims, in part, to address concerns that geographical gerontology is undertheorized by laying out the theory, analyses, and themes related to geography and its implications for aging. They emphasize the distinguishing features of "place, space, scale, landscape and territory" with the goal of differentiating this work from other research largely aimed at contextual considerations. That is, the conceptual and empirical focus rests with what is distinctly geographical in nature, rather than environmental (e.g., therapeutic landscapes see Winterton, 2017).

Third, a large body of social, scientific, and epidemiological research has been devoted to examining how social context affects health. Early ecological perspectives, associated with the Chicago School, argued that the density and unpredictability of urban environments leads to stress (Simmel, 1903) and erodes the close, personal ties with family members and friends that were presumed to be common in rural areas (Wirth, 1938). These ecological perspectives laid the groundwork for a significant "spatial turn" in later 21st century social scientific research, with the predominant perspective in this area focused on the assessment of "neighborhood effects." This work considers characteristics of the local built environment, as well as social factors such as neighborhood composition (e.g., age structure, racial/ethnic heterogeneity), collective properties such as the concentration of poverty or affluence, and contextual factors such as the neighborhood service environment (Subramanian et al., 2006) as well as social cohesion, informal control, and the combined notion of collective efficacy (Sampson, 2012; Sampson and Groves, 1989; Sampson et al., 1997). Sociological research has been particularly concerned with the implications of the neighborhood social context for the health and well-being of older adults who reside there. We describe this work in more detail below.

Research has identified neighborhood effects on individual outcomes across the life course, but some researchers argue that neighborhood conditions may be particularly salient for health and well-being in later life (Robert and Li, 2001). Consistent with the idea of person-environment fit (Lawton and Nahemow, 1973), work in environmental gerontology and sociology emphasizes how life changes such as bereavement, retirement, and the advent of health problems may make older adults especially dependent upon a neighborhood's physical and social context (Cagney and York Cornwell, 2010; Schieman, 2005). Older adults may also be more vulnerable than younger and middle-aged adults to local physical and environmental conditions (Cannuscio et al., 2003), and they may rely more heavily on opportunities for social integration and support through local institutions such as community-based senior centers and churches or informal interactions with neighbors (e.g., Shaw, 2005; Wethington and Kavey, 2000).

These three broad theoretical approaches—environmental gerontology, geographical gerontology, and neighborhood effects—provide a sense of the more general conceptualizations of the role of place in later life. We now turn to examining various spatial units in which contextual processes may have implications for older adults' health and well-being. We call attention to research that examines these conventional designations in a novel manner and that incorporates governance and political implications.

SPATIAL UNITS AND INDIVIDUAL HEALTH AND WELL-BEING

Urban, Suburban, and Rural Areas

The three designations of urban, suburban, and rural are a central organizing principle by which researchers have examined place and aging (Shiode et al., 2014; Singh and Siahpush, 2014). Nonmetropolitan or rural areas are defined by exclusion; the Census Bureau defines urbanized areas as those with 50,000 or more people and urban clusters as those with at least 2,500 and less than 50,000 people. Operational definitions employed at the community level are of course more fluid, as, for instance, traditional rural contexts give way to aspects of suburban development and some older suburbs feel more like a neighborhood of the central city (e.g., Oak Park in Chicago).

Of particular interest is the difference in the age distribution across these areas. The median age for adults in rural areas is 51, as compared to 45 in urban areas (U.S. Census Bureau, 2017). The data in Figure 5-1 indicate that the percentage of the population over age 65 varies across metropolitan, micropolitan, small town, and rural spaces. While all four types of place experienced some growth, the greater share of older adults, and the greatest growth, is in rural areas. Data compiled by the Urban Institute (Pendall et al., 2016) indicate that 15 percent of the rural population was older than 65 between 2000 and 2011, as compared to 13 percent in metropolitan regions. The gap is predicted to widen; estimates suggest that by 2040, 25 percent of rural households will be 65 or older, as compared to 20 percent of urban households. These changes are accompanied by stark differences in population growth as a whole. Between 2020 and 2030, rural population growth is predicted to hover around 1 percent; urban population growth is expected to be approximately 8 percent.

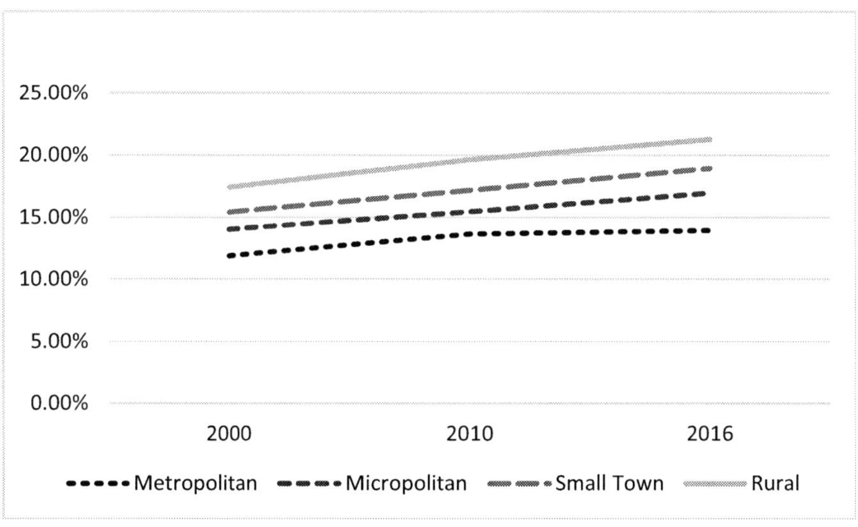

FIGURE 5-1 Percentage of population ages 65 and older, by type of place.
NOTES: Population composition: Metropolitan (50,000 or more), Micropolitan (at least 10,000 but fewer than 50,000), Small Town (at least 2,500 but fewer than 10,000), Rural (all other).
SOURCE: U.S. Census Bureau.

We note that within the broader category of urban spaces, suburban areas are aging more rapidly than comparatively more-urban spaces. Golant wrote, over 40 years ago, that the older population would be increasingly suburban, surmising that the move to the suburbs to begin a family would not result in a return (Golant, 1975). Now, approximately 8 in 10 of the age 65-plus population live in U.S. metropolitan areas, and nearly two-thirds of these metro dwellers live in the suburbs rather than its central cities (McCarthy and Kim, 2005). Nearly one-half (46%) of our current older suburban population is aged 75 or older, and a further increase in this proportion is expected (Golant, 2009). The structure of most suburban areas—car dependent, clustered commercial spaces, single-family two-story homes—makes aging in that physical environment especially challenging. Furthermore, architects have long argued that the single-family garage has eroded social capital because residents do not have a sight line on one another when entering or exiting a car and thus lack the opportunity to interact informally (e.g., Besel and Andreescu, 2013).

Central to the association of place and age is the ability of communities, particularly rural and suburban ones, to accommodate an aging population both physically and socially. Ecological research suggests that characteristics of urban, suburban, and rural places shape individuals' abilities to build social networks and access support. Consistent with the theory that densely populated urban areas erode close, personal ties (Wirth, 1938), some studies have found that urban residents have more segmented and smaller networks compared to rural residents (e.g., Hofferth and Iceland, 1998; Curtis White and Guest, 2003). But a recent study finds no difference in network size or the closeness of network ties across older adults living in metropolitan and nonmetropolitan areas (York Cornwell and Behler, 2015). Data are limited on the extent to which levels of social capital are lower in suburbs compared to cities, but if so, suburban older adults may lack proximal social support when faced with challenges related to navigating their areas and meeting routine needs.

Patterns of urban-rural migration may also contribute to the availability of social and instrumental support for older adults. In China, caregivers in rural areas are often brought in from the Philippines; children have left for job opportunities in urban centers and are not available for the forms of hands-on care needed (Fishman, 2010). A similar dynamic is at play in rural communities of the United States, where out-migration has meant that the pool of informal familial-based caregivers is smaller (Buckwalter and Davis, 2011). Formal long-term care, whether institutional or through home health, may also be more limited in rural areas (Glasgow and Brown, 2012). In the general case, access to health care and formal long-term care varies considerably by context. Residence in a rural location may mean fewer services and longer travel times to obtain needed care (Caldwell et al., 2016).

Nations, States, and Municipalities

Nation and state boundaries can be important not only for service provision but also for political identity and the political economy of place. In the United States, numerous safety net provisions vary by state, making some states more suitable for or attractive to individuals who are in need of support or assistance. States like Utah, Iowa, and South Carolina are often listed as optimal places to grow old, based on estimated cost of living, quality of life, and other factors such as the cost of home health care. Age-related policies and practices also may reflect state-based priorities. Jirik and Sanders (2014), for instance, found substantial variation across states in elder abuse statutes, and the AARP found considerable state-based differences in long-term services and supports, creating an annual scorecard for such measures (Reinhard et al., 2012).

Figure 5-2 indicates that counties and states differ substantially in median age and that this difference has grown dramatically since 2000. We also observe important regional differences in age structure, such that areas of the east coast and north (and some selected areas of the south) have substantially older age structures. Administrative and political boundaries shape governance and resource allocation and may reflect norms related to care of vulnerable populations, including the aged. They also may reflect norms and expectations about older adults in general. To examine the long-held belief that Eastern cultures, as compared to Western, hold the aged in higher esteem, North and Fiske (2015) conducted a meta-analysis (37 papers representing 23 countries) of cross-cultural attitudes toward the aged. They found the highest levels of senior derogation in East Asia and non-Anglophone Europe, and contrary to expectations, they found that cultural individualism, rather than collectivist traditions, predicted positivity toward the aged.

Attitudes toward the aged may also be informed by the psychological well-being that older adults report, and this may indeed be influenced by the structure of supports around them. Hogan et al. (2016) examined happiness as an outcome across key metropolitan areas. They found that the happiness of older residents is associated more with the provision of quality governmental services; these same variables also have an effect on health and social connections, which are then linked to happiness. Steptoe et al. (2015), in an analysis of subjective well-being, found that the U-shaped life evaluation documented in high-income English-speaking countries—that life evaluation dips in middle age and rises again in old age—did not hold in eastern Europe and the former Soviet Union, sub-Saharan Africa, and the Caribbean and Latin America (where life evaluation decreases with age). They further found that, outside high-income English-speaking countries, worry, lack of happiness, and physical pain increase with age; anger and

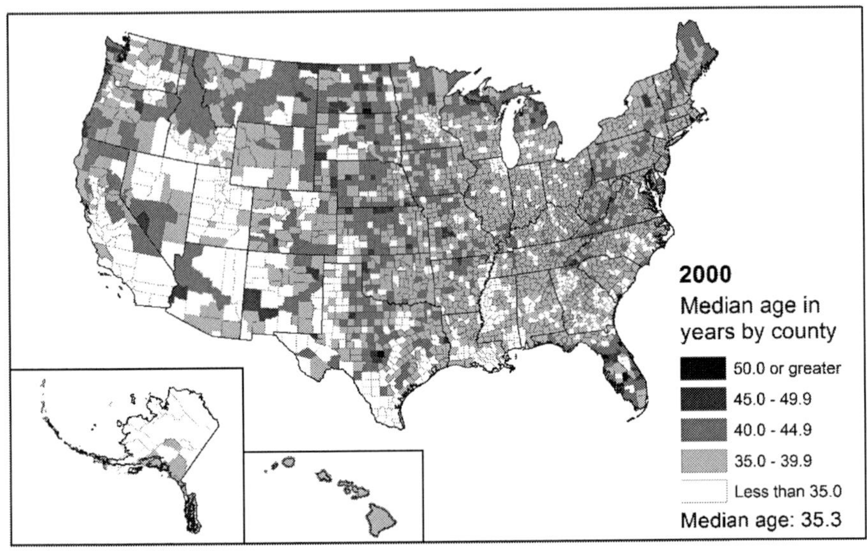

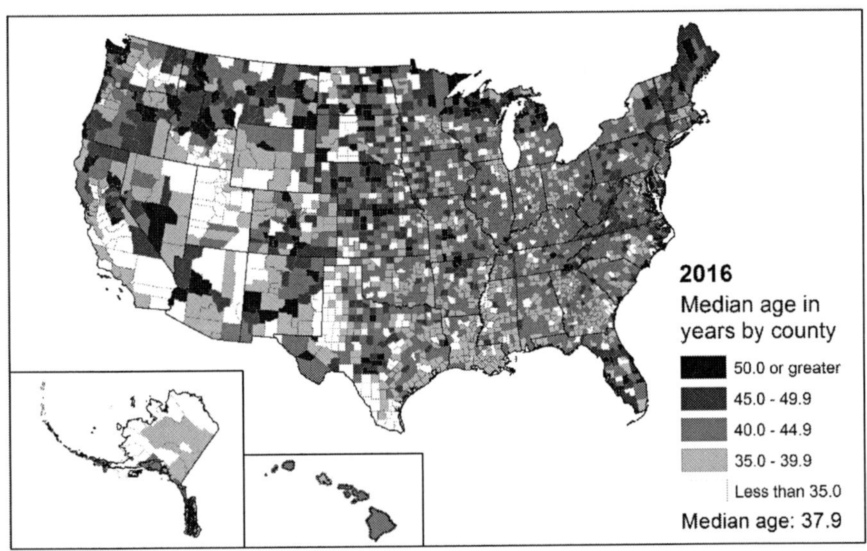

FIGURE 5-2 Median age across counties, 2010 and 2016.
SOURCE: U.S. Census Bureau.

stress decrease. Other indicators of emotional well-being also may differ by location and its characteristics. The vast literature on loneliness at older ages (Hawkley et al., 2010) suggests that living alone and social isolation are risk factors (Shaw et al., 2017); these, in turn, may vary by municipal area (e.g., 58% of persons in Stockholm live alone).

Compositional characteristics at the state level may also be consequential for older adult well-being. Novel research in this area illustrates that state-level analyses can be informative. For instance, Montez et al. (2017a) found that disparities in disability by education vary across states, primarily driven by differences in prevalence among those with fewer years of education. In related work, Montez et al. (2017b) found that disability was lower in states with better economic output, greater income equality, longer histories of tax credits for low-income workers, and higher cigarette taxes (for middle-age women). They argued that a state's socioeconomic and policy contexts appear particularly important for older adults.

Residential Neighborhoods

While the work on neighborhood context and health is too vast to summarize effectively in this chapter, we note that neighborhood influences on health have been documented for physical and mental health, with neighborhood conditions linked to outcomes such as asthma (Cagney and Browning, 2004), obesity (King et al., 2011), coronary heart disease (Diez-Roux et al., 2001), cognitive function (Wight et al., 2006), and mortality (Subramanian et al., 2005). Antecedents to much of this work can be found in early Chicago School research (Browning et al., 2014), with its attention to the structural and social process factors that affect individual- and neighborhood-level outcomes. Social disorganization theory, in particular, elaborates a process through which structural conditions such as concentrated poverty and residential instability (and, to some extent, racial/ethnic heterogeneity) weaken social bonds among neighbors and reduce community involvement. Low-income neighborhoods often lack the foundation for effective social organization, exchanges of support, and informal social control (Sampson, 2012; Wilson, 1987). Connectedness and trust among residents of cohesive neighborhoods may be important for older adults' health and well-being because they contribute to neighborhood-level collective efficacy, which enables the neighborhood to take action for the common good (Sampson, 2012). They may also enhance the diffusion of health-promoting information within the neighborhood (Cagney and Browning, 2004) and provide just-in-time support, such as assistance during a medical emergency (York Cornwell and Currit, 2016). Neighborhood-level social cohesion has also been associated with greater sense of purpose and meaning in life (Kawachi and Berkman, 2003), as well as fewer depressive symptoms among middle-aged and older adults (Echeverría et al., 2008; Kim, 2010).

An important strand of research in this area examines the extent to which the neighborhood context structures older adults' access to social relationships, social capital, and social support. Research on aging and the life course has drawn attention to aging-related changes in social connectedness, stemming in part from changes in daily experiences, capacities for maintaining ties, and the need for support, particularly due to bereavement or health decline (Charles and Carstensen, 2010; Wellman and Wortley, 1990). Social connections, services, and resources available in the neighborhood can help older adults compensate for network instability and loss. Differences in opportunities for social connectedness across neighborhoods may contribute to disparities in the ability to form and maintain social ties with family members and friends (York Cornwell and Behler, 2015). These, in turn, may be crucial determinants of independent living, life satisfaction, and health trajectories.

Coping with environmental challenges, particularly in a resource-poor environment, may sap time and energy, thereby depleting individuals' abilities to maintain social ties, which may negatively impact health. Indeed, older adults who reside in socioeconomically disadvantaged neighborhoods appear to have smaller social networks. And older men who reside in such neighborhoods have been found to have less frequent social interaction with their network members (York Cornwell and Behler, 2015). An important alternative theory is that concentrated socioeconomic disadvantage may lead to the cultivation of social ties, including those with family members, friends, neighbors, and fictive kin (Stack, 1974). Long-term residents and women tend to take particularly active roles in exchanging support with neighbors (Schieman, 2005; Stack, 1974), especially during later life (Newman, 2003). However, many empirical studies suggest that residents of disadvantaged neighborhoods have fewer local social ties, overall, than those who reside in more-advantaged neighborhoods (e.g., Tigges et al., 1998; Small, 2007). As a result, older adults who reside in more socio-economically disadvantaged neighborhoods may be less likely to benefit from localized social exchanges and support from neighbors, such as visiting, sharing advice, and doing favors, which can promote their physical health, mental health, and continued residence in the community (Mair et al., 2010; Shaw, 2005; Wethington and Kavey, 2000).

Local social integration may also be fostered by characteristics of the neighborhood and the presence of institutions. For example, buildings with front porches or stoops are associated with greater access to social support among older adults (Brown et al., 2009). Local institutions and venues may also provide opportunities to form and maintain social relationships. For older adults, local senior centers can be particularly critical sites for cultivating social ties (Glass and Balfour, 2003). Nearby welfare and social service offices, health care clinics, child care centers, retail establishments, recreational venues, and churches often promote socializing and exchanges of support with local others (e.g., Klinenberg, 2002; Small, 2009).

Neighborhood conditions may also determine whether an older adult is able to meet his or her daily needs, find satisfaction in daily life, and maintain independent residence in the community. Neighborhood context plays a critical role in the feasibility of everyday activities such as food shopping, household errands, or church attendance. In fact, physical activity is influenced by a variety of features of the neighborhood context, including the built environment, neighborhood-level social cohesion, and perceived safety (Tucker-Seeley et al., 2009). In a synthesis of over 120 articles, Yen et al. (2014) examined how place might shape physical mobility. They noted that three interrelated contexts—connectivity, land use, and aesthetics—are key drivers for whether older adults engage in outdoor space. Importantly, the key mechanism appears to be the perception of safety: not just a sense of whether the place seems safe but also more objective indicators such as speed limits, traffic lanes, and sidewalk quality.

To examine the role of perceived safety and associated characteristics of the neighborhood, we analyzed data from the National Social Life, Health, and Aging Project (NSHAP) Wave 2 (2010–2011). Figure 5-3 illustrates the bivariate associations between neighborhood structural disadvantage, social context, and one aspect of health: depressive symptoms. Although depres-

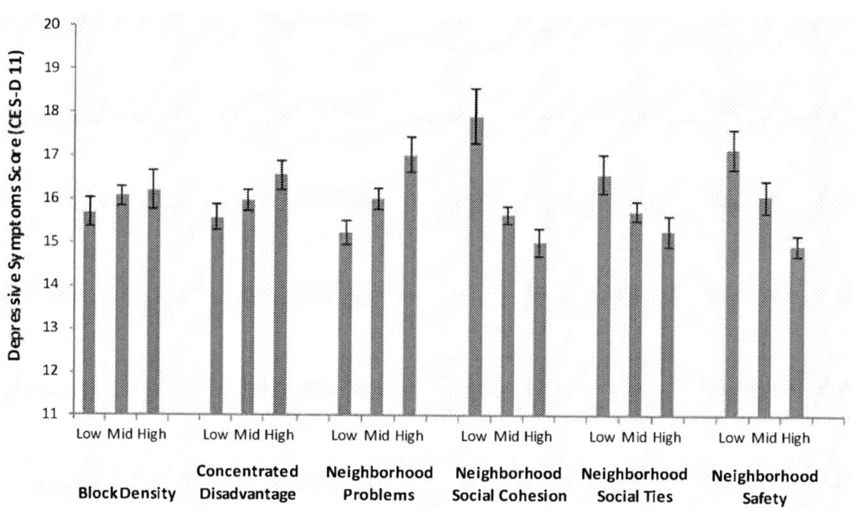

FIGURE 5-3 Neighborhood conditions and depressive symptoms.
SOURCE: Data from National Social Life, Health, and Aging Project, Wave 2.

sive symptoms do not markedly vary across levels of neighborhood density, respondents who reside in neighborhoods with greater concentrated socio-economic disadvantage and more neighborhood problems (e.g., buildings in disrepair, litter, odor, noise) had more depressive symptoms. Neighborhood social conditions, including cohesion, social ties, and safety, are negatively associated with depressive symptoms.

Activity Spaces

Research on neighborhood effects on health is primarily focused on the *residential* neighborhood, with little attention devoted to the other spaces that individuals encounter during their daily lives (Chaix, 2009; Diez-Roux, 2007; Matthews and Yang, 2013). Some scholars have suggested that focusing on the residential neighborhood is particularly appropriate when studying older adults, as age-related changes may reduce the geographic range of activities, increasingly anchoring daily life to the local, residential area (Inagami et al., 2007). But the assumption of shrinking turf in later life has not been empirically tested. Moreover, retirement may bring greater flexibility in structuring daily life, and older adults may move beyond their local neighborhood to access services, organizations, and amenities, as well as for social contact and participation in social activities (Cagney et al., 2013; York Cornwell and Cagney, 2017).

The notion of *activity spaces*—a concept stemming from research in geography—provides an alternative to the focus on residential neighborhoods (Golledge and Stimson, 1997). Activity spaces encompass the social environments that individuals encounter during their routine activities in everyday life (Browning and Soller, 2014; Cagney et al., 2013). Accordingly, activity spaces include, but are not limited to, residential neighborhoods.

The span and characteristics of activity spaces vary across individuals. For example, Figure 5-4 summarizes the activity spaces of three older adults from East Harlem in New York City, using data from a smartphone-based study that included location tracking in 5-minute intervals for 7 days (see York Cornwell and Cagney, 2017). Note that time spent outside of the residential census tract varies widely across individuals—from 36 to 65 percent. Respondents A and B stay relatively close to their residential tracts for their daily activities, as indicated by the small size of their standard deviation ellipses (i.e., a geographic measure of the space that encompasses about 68 percent of the respondents' observed locations) and the number of tracts they visited. Respondent C travels much further out into the city, encountering 86 different tracts during the course of the week. There is also heterogeneity in the characteristics of activity spaces where older adults spend their time. As shown here, Respondent A's exposure to poverty outside of her census tract is similar to that within her residential tract. However,

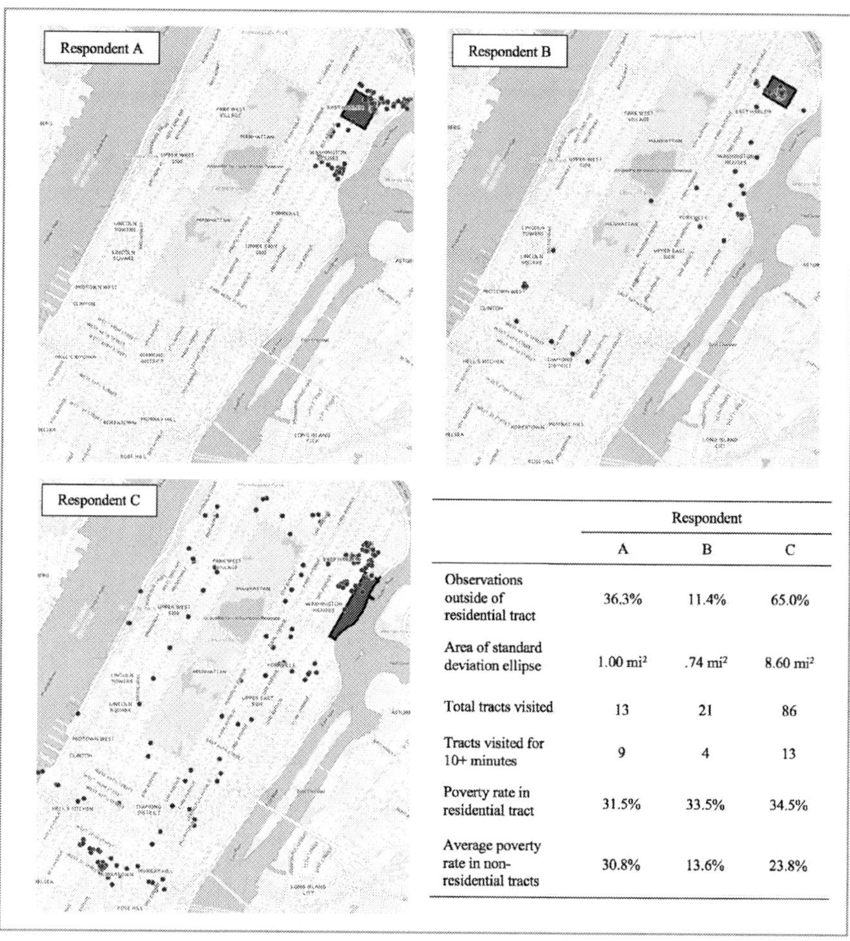

	Respondent		
	A	B	C
Observations outside of residential tract	36.3%	11.4%	65.0%
Area of standard deviation ellipse	1.00 mi^2	.74 mi^2	8.60 mi^2
Total tracts visited	13	21	86
Tracts visited for 10+ minutes	9	4	13
Poverty rate in residential tract	31.5%	33.5%	34.5%
Average poverty rate in non-residential tracts	30.8%	13.6%	23.8%

FIGURE 5-4 Activity space characteristics of three older adults from East Harlem in New York City.
NOTES: Dots represent respondents' locations captured during the study; residential tracts are shaded in dark gray.
SOURCE: Originally published in York Cornwell, E., and Cagney, K.A. (2017). Aging in activity space: Results from smartphone-based GPS-tracking of urban seniors. *Journal of Gerontology: Social Sciences, 72,* 864–875. Oxford University Press.

both Respondents B and C are exposed to lower poverty outside of their census tracts than within their census tracts. B tends to visit particularly low-poverty tracts, but he spends much less time in these tracts than A or C.

Residential neighborhood contexts, adjoining areas, and the availability of public transportation may also contribute to across-neighborhood differences in the extent to which individuals' daily lives are locally focused (Rainham et al., 2010). Even more important for research on place and health in later life is the possibility that variation in the space, span, and characteristics of activity spaces may contribute to within-neighborhood variation in older adults' health and well-being. That is, some older adults may be able to overcome limited local resources by accessing health care centers, pharmacies, and fresh food stores outside of their residential areas. Access to extra local resources may be influenced by individual characteristics, such as socioeconomic resources, social connectedness, health, and physical function (York Cornwell and Cagney, 2017; Kwan, 1999; Jones and Pebley, 2014). Or, access may be realized because such resources are located in areas that an individual frequently visits for other reasons, such as work, attending religious services, or making social visits (Kwan, 1999). Other older adults may be more tightly tethered to their residential areas, rendering physical and social features of the local residential context particularly salient.

MACRO-LEVEL EFFECTS OF AGING IN PLACE

Migration

Residential moves are not uncommon at later stages of the life course, and health status may be central to decisions about relocation. Older adults may migrate from another state, nation, or neighborhood; all such moves involve some form of relocation and all may be shaped by a variety of push and pull factors. Classical demographic theory suggests attention to migration patterns in any study of context (Longino, 1994), and this may be particularly salient for understanding the interplay of place, aging, and health. Although aging in place may reflect individual-level tastes to maintain residence in the community where one spent the bulk of his or her adult life, some communities might not be conducive to older adult needs, creating an incentive to relocate. As described earlier, housing structures typical to, for instance, suburban environments might not be suitable for older adults with mobility concerns or compromised health status.

At older ages, residential mobility is more prevalent among those who are retired, younger rather than older, with higher levels of income and wealth, poorer health, and urban dwelling (Sergeant and Ekerdt, 2008; Taylor et al., 2008; Walters, 2002). Poor weather and high tax rates may also be drivers of relocation (Walters, 2002). The literature on residential relocation related to children is sparse, but some evidence indicates that parents may make choices to move nearer adult children (Sergeant and Ekerdt, 2008).

In general, residential mobility drops after the age of 50; it continues to decline through the 1960s with a sharp uptick at approximately age 85.

Older adults who do make the choice to move disproportionately do so within their county or state. Approximately 14 percent move to another state, citing family reasons or retirement. Mobility rates for all age groups have fallen over the last two decades. Two-earner households and the long-term population shift to the south and west have reduced the later-life incentive to move (Harvard Joint Center for Housing Studies, 2014).

The structure of place shapes opportunity for movement. Recent research from the NSHAP suggests that when White older adults move, they move to communities at the same or a higher level of economic well-being. But when older African Americans move, they are more likely to relocate to communities at the same or lower economic levels (Riley et al., 2016). Consistent with this, Geronimus et al. (2014) found that African Americans are less likely to translate economic well-being into preferential moves. At the same time, patterns of residential mobility are themselves a structural property of place that may have consequences for community social context and individual outcomes. Residential instability may weaken neighborhood-level social cohesion (Sampson, 2012), but Cagney et al. (2005) found that when neighborhood-level affluence is low, residential stability is negatively related to individual health.

Our review of migration has focused primarily on voluntary moves, or moves that involve some agency on the part of the older adult. Involuntary moves are also a key component of migration patterns and are more prevalent among disadvantaged groups (Metzger et al., 2015). Residence in a disadvantaged neighborhood, for instance, increases mobility that stems from residential instability, such as eviction, or foreclosure, and poor housing conditions (Desmond and Shollenberger, 2015). Data suggest that such involuntary moves tend to be shorter in distance (Krysan and Crowder, 2017), but little is known about the consequences of involuntary moves for older adults' access to social support or for their health trajectories.

Attention to migration and its drivers will be all the more important as the Baby Boom generation actively engages in retirement and other later life transitions that might suggest or require relocation. It remains unknown how this generation will respond to such changes or whether the physical and social environment will innovate in ways that can keep pace with their needs and facilitate aging in place.

Inequality

We have described the spaces that older adults inhabit, the spaces they may traverse, and the theory that may assist us in interpreting relevant findings. To what extent do those spaces contribute to durable inequality among important population subgroups?

Racial/ethnic and socioeconomic disparities in later-life health outcomes, including chronic conditions, functional limitations, and mortality, are well documented in prior research and national health data (Pleis et al., 2010). However, individuals are embedded within communities, which expose them to sets of health-enhancing or heath-diminishing features that may exacerbate or ameliorate individual-level disparities. Cagney et al. (2005), for instance, found that neighborhood-level affluence attenuates the association between race and self-rated health. And Currie and Schwandt (2016), ranking counties by their poverty rates, found that among adults age 50 and over, mortality has declined more quickly in richer areas than in poorer ones; thus inequality in mortality has increased for older adults.

Metropolitan areas today are often characterized by deeply entrenched residential segregation, which generates differences in contextual exposure to health-related risks and resources (Sampson, 2012). As we noted above, physical and social characteristics of residential neighborhoods have been associated with a wide range of individual health outcomes. At the macro level, patterns of residential segregation may contribute to persistent disparities in health among older adults. Indeed, the spatial concentration of poverty or affluence is associated with health outcomes including mortality, even after adjusting for individuals' own socioeconomic status (Pickett and Pearl, 2001; Wen et al., 2003). This suggests that inequalities in place play an important role in generating and maintaining socioeconomic inequalities in later-life morbidity and mortality.

Williams and Collins (2001) noted that spatial separation of racial groups should be considered a "fundamental cause of racial disparities in health" because it generates disproportionate exposure to social and physical risks that adversely affect the health of African Americans. For example, racially segregated neighborhoods often suffer from disinvestment of economic and municipal resources, so that these areas are more likely to lack services, including high-quality medical care, and they are more likely to have poorly maintained infrastructure such as sidewalks and street lights, and low housing quality (Williams and Rucker, 2000). Residence in segregated neighborhoods may bring heightened exposure to acute and chronic stressors, including experiences of criminal victimization (Shihadeh and Flynn, 1996) and forms of institutional and interpersonal discrimination that both characterize and perpetuate such segregation (Williams and Collins, 2001). These stressors exact wear and tear on the body that contribute to a process of "weathering," leading to gradual health deterioration among Blacks. Exposure to segregated and discriminatory contexts over the life course is thought to result in racial disparities in chronic illness and disability that widen through middle age and into later life (Geronimus et al., 2006).

Exposure to green space, and the natural world more generally, varies not only by rural versus urban context but by microenvironments such as neighborhoods. Architects and urban planners have long considered the role of the natural world in the health and well-being of the population, but attention to it within the health literature is relatively recent. In the mid-1980s, Ulrich (1984) observed that hospital length of stay was shorter for patients who could see trees outside their windows, as compared to brick walls. This work seeded interest in the relationship between exposure to nature and health outcomes. Mitchell and Popham (2008), for instance, found that income-based health inequalities in both all-cause mortality and mortality related to circulatory diseases were lower in populations living in the greenest spaces. Berman et al. (2012) explored whether walking in nature may be beneficial for individuals with major depressive disorder, finding that participants exhibited significant increases in memory span after walking in nature as compared to an urban space. In related work, Berman and colleagues (Kardan et al., 2015) found that residents who live in areas with a greater number of trees report better health and fewer cardio-metabolic conditions as compared to those living in areas with lower numbers. Analyses of green space and its density suggest important differences by sociodemographic composition. Wen et al. (2013) found that poverty was negatively associated with distances to parks and percentages of green spaces in urban and suburban areas while positively associated in rural areas. In general, percentages of Blacks and Hispanics were negatively associated with distances to parks and green space coverage.

NEW DIRECTIONS

It is an exciting time in the social sciences, and in research on aging specifically, to attend to the role of place in health. As we have described, place—through its physical attributes, physical resources, and constraints and through its interplay with the social contact that may emerge—is critical to examine if we are to fully understand how health and disease manifest themselves in the lives of older adults. Individual characteristics are clearly predictive of health status in later life (Case and Deaton, 2015), but evidence suggests that the context in which individuals are situated shapes those influences. A focus on place may allow us to activate aspects of place that might be health enhancing, enabling individuals and communities to effectively engage resources that can help older adults flourish.

We laid out environmental and geographical gerontology as important contributors to the assessment of place, and we highlighted the role of historic and contemporary research in urban sociology and related disciplines that have had an impact on research related to age. While these all have different origins and emphases, they share a focus on the interplay between the person and his or her environmental context. We see these approaches as complementary rather than competing; they each bring novel insights to an examination of place, aging, and health.

We suggest five general considerations for advancing the field. First, exploration of place as a set of nested contexts is in keeping with a synthetic view of the background work we describe above. Urban and rural areas are nested within regional, state, and national contexts, which may have important implications for the extent to which services availability varies across the density of settlements. State-level policies and investments in the provision of home- and community-based services, for example, may reduce disadvantages faced by rural seniors (Coburn et al., 2017), while at the same time increasing rural seniors' engagement with their local contexts. We know very little about how residents perceive or experience "neighborhoods" outside of metropolitan areas, because research on neighborhood effects is primarily focused on urban areas (Burke et al., 2006; York Cornwell and Cagney, 2017). However, there is reason to believe that neighborhood effects on health and well-being vary across urban, suburban, and rural settings. For example, greater distance to health care and other services may make local social ties and support particularly important for nonmetropolitan older adults. The effects of local exposure to stressors may also be conditioned by one's location in urban, suburban, or rural settings. Recent work suggests that racial gaps in exposure to neighborhood problems are growing fastest outside of urban areas (York Cornwell and Hall, 2017) and that exposure to disorder may be particularly isolating for seniors who reside outside of the city (York Cornwell and Behler, 2015).

Second, we believe that new forms of data will allow for a better understanding of the role of place in the lives of older adults. New data (potentially described as "big data") allow for an unprecedented exploration of context (e.g., Gebru et al., 2017). We have already described "activity spaces" and the extent to which new technology facilitates their description in the moment and over time. Data such as these, and newly available sources that now can be readily linked to other data sources (e.g., crime, potholes, rat sightings) provide the opportunity to contextualize lives in a manner unknown just a few years ago. These novel data sources then allow us to husband social survey resources, since many of these data supplant respondent reports (e.g., hospital length of stay, procedures). We then can focus on what social surveys do best, which is to solicit opinions, preferences, and perspectives about the social world.

Third, we need to pay greater attention to how communities form and the barriers and inducements to residential sorting. One form of sorting is based on age, and evidence suggests that our communities are increasingly age segregated (Hagestad and Uhlenberg, 2005). What is the role of propinquity, and how might we theorize about the nature and extent of intergenerational exchange? Recent research suggests that the age composition of a community also may matter for health. Friedman et al. (2017) found that living in a neighborhood with a greater percentage of older adults is related to better individual cognition at baseline but is not associated with decline. Perceived cohesion and disorder may explain some of the association between age structure and cognition. We believe that greater attention to age structure and the extent to which it varies—by communities, states, and nation—will benefit our understanding of the role of place in health.

Fourth, we acknowledge that this chapter did not consider virtual places and the extent to which some forms of contact via technology may substitute for the forms of interaction typically provided in proximity. Recent evidence suggests that the use of communication technologies is positively associated with formal and informal social participation (Kim et al., 2017). However, devices (e.g., monitors) that facilitate independent living for many older adults may substitute for interpersonal interaction and reduce the need for local social support. Detailed consideration of this literature is beyond the scope of this chapter, but this area is particularly relevant for future research on aging in place.

Finally, we believe that foundational and well-developed theory matters. We have emphasized theory in urban sociology in part because it arguably has received the greatest vetting and engagement. It suggests that the relevant space to be considered should be based on theory. We encourage researchers to incorporate a model that describes the characteristics of the place they are examining and what they imagine that place confers physically and socially. Theory on context needs to be employed at all levels, and theory that may be invoked to describe implications of policy change at the state level, for instance, will likely be inadequate or poorly suited for smaller spaces such as the neighborhood. Moreover, neighborhood-based theory, rich in its sociological history, may fail to fully capture the political influences that manifest at various municipal levels. As Lawton and colleagues called for near the end of his career (e.g., Parmelee and Lawton, 1990), careful consideration of the role of place is critical for understanding the dynamic processes of health and aging. We suggest that our understanding of the role of place in aging is at a turning point, where new theory and new data can be brought to bear on important questions related to health, well-being, and longevity.

REFERENCES

Andrews, G.J., Cutchin, M., McCracken, K., Phillips, D.R., and Wiles, J. (2007). Geographical gerontology: The constitution of a discipline. *Social Science & Medicine, 65*(1), 151–168.

Andrews, G.J., Evans, J., and Wiles, J.L. (2013). Re-spacing and re-placing gerontology: Relationality and affect. *Aging and Society, 33*(8), 1339–1373.

Berman, M.G., Kross, E., Krpan, K.M., Askren, M.K., Burson, A., Deldin, P., Kaplan, S., Sherdell, L., Gotlib, I.H., and Jonides, J. (2012). Interacting with nature improves cognition and affect in depressed individuals. *Journal of Affective Disorders, 140*(3), 300–305.

Besel, K., and Andreescu, V. (2013). *Back to the Future: New Urbanism and the Rise of Neo-traditionalism in Urban Planning.* Lanham, MD: University Press of America.

Birren, J.E. (1999). Theories of aging: A personal perspective. In V.L. Bengtson and K. Warner Schaie (Eds.), *Handbook of Theories of Aging* (pp. 459-472). New York: Springer.

Brown, S.C., Mason, C.A., Lombard, J.L., Martinez, F., Plater-Zyberk, E., Spokane, A.R., Newman, F.L., Pantin, H., and Szapocznik, J. (2009). The relationship of built environment to perceived social support and psychological distress in Hispanic elders: The role of "eyes on the street." *Journals of Gerontology: Social Sciences, 64*(B), 234–246.

Browning, C.R., and Soller, B. (2014). Moving beyond neighborhood: Activity spaces and ecological networks as contexts for youth development. *Cityscape, 16,* 165–196.

Browning, C.R., Cagney, K.A., and Morris, K. (2014). Early Chicago School theory. In G. Bruinsma and D. Weisburd (Eds.), *Encyclopedia of Criminology and Criminal Justice* (pp. 1233–1242). New York: Springer.

Buckwalter, K.C., and Davis, L.L. (2011). Elder caregiving in rural communities. In R. Talley, K. Chwalisz, and K. Buckwalter (Eds.), *Rural Caregiving in the United States: Research, Practice, Policy* (pp. 33–46). New York: Springer.

Burke, J.G., O'Campo, P., and Peak, G.L. (2006). Neighborhood influences and intimate partner violence: Does geographic setting matter? *Journal of Urban Health, 83,* 182–194.

Cagney, K.A., and Browning, C.R. (2004). Exploring neighborhood-level variation in asthma and other respiratory diseases. *Journal of General Internal Medicine, 19,* 229–236.

Cagney, K.A., and York Cornwell, E. (2010). Neighborhoods and health in later life: The intersection of biology and community. *Annual Review of Gerontology and Geriatrics, 30,* 323–348.

Cagney, K.A., Browning, C.R., and Wen, M. (2005). Racial disparities in self-rated health at older ages: What difference does the neighborhood make? *Journals of Gerontology: Series B, 60*(4), S181–S190.

Cagney, K.A., Browning, C.R., Jackson, A.L., and Soller, B. (2013). Networks, neighborhoods, and institutions: An integrated "activity space" approach for research on aging. In L. Waite (Ed.), *New Directions in the Sociology of Aging* (pp. 151–174). Washington, DC: The National Academies Press.

Caldwell, J.T., Ford, C.L., Wallace, S.P., Wang, M.C., and Takahashi, L.M. (2016). Intersection of living in a rural versus urban area and race/ethnicity in explaining access to health care in the United States. *American Journal of Public Health, 106*(8), 1463–1469.

Cannuscio, C., Block, J., and Kawachi, I. (2003). Social capital and successful aging: The role of senior housing. *Annals of Internal Medicine, 139*(5 Part 2), 395–399.

Canter, D.V., and Craik, K.H. (1981). Environmental psychology. *Journal of Environmental Psychology, 1*(1), 1–11.

Case, A., and Deaton, A. (2015). Rising morbidity and mortality in midlife among White non-Hispanic Americans in the 21st century. *Proceedings of the National Academy of Sciences of the United States of America, 112,* 15078–15083.

Chaix, B. (2009). Geographic life environments and coronary heart disease: A literature review, theoretical contributions, methodological updates, and a research agenda. *Annual Review of Public Health, 30,* 81–105.

Charles, S.T., and Carstensen, L.L. (2010). Social and emotional aging. *Annual Review of Psychology, 61,* 383–409.

Coburn, A.F., Lundblad, J.P., and the RUPRI Health Panel. (2017). *Rural Long-Term Services and Supports: A Primer.* Iowa City: Rural Policy Research Institute.

Currie, J., and Schwandt, H. (2016). Inequality in mortality decreased among the young while increasing for older adults, 1990–2010. *Science, 352*(6286), 708–712.

Curtis White, K.J., and Guest, A.M. (2003). Community lost or transformed? Urbanization and social ties. *City & Community, 2,* 239–259.

Cutchin, M.P. (2009). Geographical gerontology: New contributions and spaces for development. *Gerontologist, 49*(3), 440–444.

Desmond, M., and Shollenberger, T. (2015). Forced displacement from rental housing: Prevalence and neighborhood consequences. *Demography, 52*(5), 1751–1772.

Diez-Roux, A.V. (2007). Neighborhoods and health: Where are we and where do we go from here? *Revue D'epidemiologie et de Sante Publique, 55*, 13–21.

Diez-Roux, A.V., Merkin, S.S., Arnett, D., Chambless, L., Massing, M., Nieto, F.J., Sorlie, P., Szklo, M., Tyroler, H.A., and Watson, R.L. (2001). Neighborhood of residence and incidence of coronary heart disease. *New England Journal of Medicine, 345*, 99–106.

Echeverría, S.E., Diez-Roux, A.V., Shea, S., Borell, L.N., and Jackson, S. (2008). Associations of neighborhood problems and neighborhood social cohesion with mental health and health behaviors: The multi-ethnic study of atherosclerosis. *Health & Place, 14*, 853–865.

Fishman, T.C. (2010). *Shock of Gray*. New York: Scribner.

Friedman, E.M., Shih, R.A., Slaughter, M.E., Weden, M.M., and Cagney, K.A. (2017). Neighborhood age structure and cognitive function in a nationally-representative sample of older adults in the U.S. *Social Science and Medicine,* (174), 149–158.

Gebru, T., Krause, J., Wang, Y., Chen. D., Deng, J., Aiden, E.L., and Fei-Fei, L. (2017). Using deep learning and Google Street View to estimate the demographic makeup of neighborhoods across the United States. *Proceedings of the National Academy of Sciences of the United States of America, 114*, 13108–13133.

Geronimus, A.T., Hicken, M., Keene, D., and Bound, J. (2006). "Weathering" and age patterns of allostatic load scores among blacks and whites in the United States. *American Journal of Public Health, 96*(5), 826–833.

Geronimus, A.T., Bound, J., and Ro, A. (2014). Residential mobility across local areas in the United States and the geographic distribution of the healthy population. *Demography, 51*(3), 777–809.

Glasgow, N., and Brown, D.L. (2012). Rural ageing in the United States: Trends and contexts. *Journal of Rural Studies, 28*(4), 422–431.

Glass, T.A., and Balfour, J.L. (2003). Neighborhoods, aging, and functional limitations. In I. Kawachi and L.F. Berkman (Eds.), *Neighborhoods and Health* (pp. 303–334). New York: Oxford University Press.

Golant, S.M. (1972). *The Residential Location and Spatial Behavior of the Elderly: A Canadian Example* (Research Paper No. 143). Chicago: University of Chicago, Department of Geography.

Golant, S.M. (1975). Residential concentrations of the future elderly. *Gerontologist, 15*(1 Part 2), 16–23.

Golant, S.M. (2009). Aging in place solutions for older Americans: Groupthink responses not always in their best interests. *Public Policy & Aging Report, 19*(1).

Golledge, R.G., and Stimson, R.J. (1997). *Spatial Behavior: A Geographic Perspective*. New York: Guilford Press.

Hagestad, G.O., and Uhlenberg, P. (2005). The social separation of old and young: A root of ageism. *Journal of Social Issues, 61*, 343–360.

Hand, C.L., and Howrey, B.T. (2017). Associations among neighborhood characteristics, mobility limitation, and social participation in late life. *Journals of Gerontology: Series B.* doi. 10.1093/geronb/gbw215. E-pub ahead of print.

Harvard Joint Center for Housing Studies. (2014). *Housing America's Older Adults: Meeting the Needs of an Aging Population*. Available: http://www.jchs.harvard.edu/research/publications/housing-americas-older-adults%E2%80%94meeting-needs-aging-population [April 2018].

Hawkley, L.C., Thisted, R.A., Masi, C.M., and Cacioppo, J.T. (2010). Loneliness predicts increased blood pressure: 5-year cross-lagged analyses in middle-aged and older adults. *Psychology and Aging, 25*(1), 132–141.

Hofferth, S.L., and Iceland, J. (1998). Social capital in rural and urban communities. *Rural Sociology, 63*(4), 574–598.

Hogan, M.J., Leyden, K.M., Conway, R., Goldberg, A., Walsh, D., and McKenna-Plumley, P.E. (2016). Happiness and health across the lifespan in five major cities: The impact of place and government performance. *Social Science & Medicine, 162*, 168–176.

Inagami, S., Cohen, D.A., and Finch, B.K. (2007). Non-residential neighborhood exposures suppress neighborhood effects on self-rated health. *Social Science & Medicine, 65*, 1779–1791.

Jacobs, J. (1961). *The Death and Life of Great American Cities.* New York: Vintage.

Jirik, S., and Sanders, S. (2014). Analysis of elder abuse statutes across the United States, 2011-2012. *Journal of Gerontological Social Work, 57*(5), 478–497.

Jones, M., and Pebley, A. (2014). Redefining neighborhoods using common destinations: Social characteristics of activity spaces and home census tracts compared. *Demography, 51*(3), 727–752.

Kardan, O., Gozdyra, P., Misic, B., Moola, F., Palmer, L.J., Paus, T., and Berman, M.G. (2015). Neighborhood greenspace and health in a large urban center. *Scientific Reports, 5*, 11610.

Kawachi, I., and Berkman, L.F. (2003). Social cohesion, social capital, and health. In L. Berkman and I. Kawachi (Eds.), *Social Epidemiology* (pp. 303–334). New York: Oxford University Press.

Kim, J. (2010). Neighborhood disadvantage and mental health: The role of neighborhood disorder and social relationships. *Social Science Research, 39*, 260–271.

Kim, J., Lee, H.Y., Christensen, M.C., and Merighi, J.R. (2017). Technology access and use, and their associations with social engagement among older adults: Do women and men differ? *Journals of Gerontology: Social Sciences, 72*, 836–845.

King, A.C., Sallis, J.F., Frank, L.D., Saelens, B.E., Cain, K., Conway, T.L., Chapman, J.E., Ahn, D.K., and Kerr, J. (2011). Aging in neighborhoods differing in walkability and income: Associations with physical activity and obesity in older adults. *Social Science & Medicine, 73*(10), 1525–1533.

Klinenberg, E. (2002). *Heat Wave: A Social Autopsy of Disaster in Chicago.* Chicago: University of Chicago Press.

Krysan, M., and Crowder, K. (2017). *The Cycle of Segregation: The Perpetuation of Residential Stratification in Metropolitan America.* New York: Russell Sage.

Kwan, M.-P. (1999). Gender and individual access to urban opportunities: A study using space-time measures. *Professional Geographer, 51*, 210–227.

Latham, K., Clarke, P., and Pavela, G. (2015). Social relationships, gender, and recovery from mobility limitation among older Americans. *Journals of Gerontology, Series B: Psychological and Social Sciences, 70*(5), 769–781.

Lawton, M.P., and Nahemow, L. (1973). Ecology and the aging process. In C. Eisdorfer and M.P. Lawton (Eds.), *The Psychology of Adult Development and Aging* (pp. 619–674). Washington, DC: American Psychological Association.

Longino, C.F. (1994). Where retirees prefer to live: The geographical distribution and migratory patterns of retirees. In A. Monk (Ed.), *The Handbook of Retirement* (pp. 405–416). New York: Columbia University Press.

Mair, C., Diez Roux, A.V., and Morenoff, J. (2010). Neighborhood stressors and social support as predictors of depressive symptoms in the Chicago Community Adult Health Study. *Health & Place, 116*, 811–819.

Matthews, S.A., and Yang, T.-C. (2013). Spatial Polygamy and Contextual Exposures (SPACEs): Promoting activity space approaches in research on place and health. *American Behavioral Scientist, 57*, 1057–1081.

McCarthy, L., and Kim, S. (2005). *The Aging Baby Boomers: Current and Future Metropolitan Distributions and Housing Policy Implications*. Office of Policy Development and Research. Washington, DC: U.S. Department of Housing and Urban Development.

Metzger, M.W., Fowler, P.J., Anderson, C.L., and Lindsay, C.A. (2015). Residential mobility during adolescence: Do even "upward" moves predict dropout risk? *Social Science Research, 53*, 218–223.

Mitchell, R., and Popham, F. (2008). Effect of exposure to natural environment on health inequalities: An observational population study. *Lancet, 372*(9650), 1655–1660.

Montez, J.K., Zajacova, A., and Hayward, M.D. (2017a). Disparities in disability by educational attainment across U.S. states. *American Journal of Public Health, 107*(7), 1101–1108.

Montez, J.K., Hayward, M.D., and Wolf, D.A. (2017b). Do U.S. states' socioeconomic and policy contexts shape adult disability? *Social Science & Medicine, 178*, 115–126.

Moore, K.D. (2014). An ecological framework of place: Situating environmental gerontology within a life course perspective. *International Journal of Aging and Human Development, 79*(3), 183–209.

Newman, K.S. (2003). *A Different Shade of Gray: Midlife and Beyond in the Inner City*. New York: The New Press.

North, M.S., and Fiske, S.T. (2015). Modern attitudes toward older adults in the aging world: A cross-cultural meta-analysis. *Psychological Bulletin, 141*(5), 993–1021.

Parmelee, P.A., and Lawton, M.P. (1990). Design of special environments for the elderly. In J.E. Birren and K.W. Schaie (Eds.), *Handbook of Psychology and Aging*, 3rd ed. (pp. 464–487). New York: Academic Press.

Pendall, R., Goodman, L., Zhu, J., and Gold, A. (2016). *The Future of Rural Housing*. Washington, DC: Urban Institute.

Pickett, K.E., and Pearl, M. (2001). Multilevel analysis of neighbourhood socioeconomic context and health outcomes: A critical review. *Journal of Epidemiology and Community Health, 55*, 111–122.

Pleis, J.R., Ward, B.W., and Lucas, J.W. (2010). Summary health statistics for U.S. adults: National Health Interview Survey, 2009. *Vital Health Statistics, 10*, 1–207.

Rainham, D., McDowell, I., Krewski, D., and Sawada, M. (2010). Conceptualizing the healthscape: Contributions from time geography, location technologies and spatial ecology to place and health research. *Social Science & Medicine, 70*, 668–676.

Reinhard, S., Kassner, E., Hendrickson, L., and Mollica, R. (2012). *State Long-Term Services and Supports Scorecard: What Distinguishes High- from Low-Ranking States? Overview of Three Case Studies*. Washington, DC: AARP.

Riley, A., Hawkley, L.C., and Cagney, K.A. (2016). Racial differences in the effects of neighborhood disadvantage on residential mobility in later life. *Journals of Gerontology Series B, 71*, 1131–1140.

Robert, S.A., and Li, L.W. (2001). Age variation in the relationship between community socioeconomic status and adult health. *Research on Aging, 23*, 233–258.

Rowles, G.D. (1981). The surveillance zone as meaningful space for the aged. *Gerontologist, 21*(3), 304–311.

Sampson, R.J. (2012). *Great American City: Chicago and the Enduring Neighborhood Effect*. Chicago: University of Chicago Press.

Sampson, R.J., and Groves, B.W. (1989). Community structure and crime: Testing social disorganization theory. *American Journal of Sociology, 94*, 774–802.

Sampson, R.J., Raudenbush, S.W., and Earls, F. (1997). Neighborhoods and violent crime: A multilevel study of collective efficacy. *Science, 227,* 918–923.

Schieman, S. (2005). Residential stability and the social impact of neighborhood disadvantage: A study of gender- and race-contingent effects. *Social Forces, 83,* 1031–1064.

Sergeant, J.F., and Ekerdt, D.J. (2008). Motives for residential mobility in later life: Post-move perspectives of elders and family members. *International Journal of Aging and Human Development, 66,* 131–154.

Shaw, B.A. (2005). Anticipated support from neighbors and physical functioning during later life. *Research on Aging, 27,* 503–525.

Shaw, J., Farid, M., and Noel-Miller, C. (2017). Social isolation and medicare spending: Among older adults, objective isolation increases expenditures while loneliness does not. *Journal of Aging and Health, 29,* 1119–1143.

Shihadeh, E.S. and Flynn, N. (1996). Segregation and crime: The effect of black social isolation on the rates of black urban violence, *Social Forces, 74*(4), 1325–1352.

Shiode, N., Morita, M., Shiode, S., and Okunuki, K. (2014). Urban and rural geographies of aging: A local spatial correlation analysis of aging population measures. *Urban Geography, 35*(4), 608–628.

Simmel, G. (1903). Metropolis and mental life. Reprinted in D.N. Levine (Ed.), *On Individuality and Social Forms* (1971, pp. 324–339). Chicago: University of Chicago Press.

Singh, G.K., and Siahpush, M. (2014). Widening rural–urban disparities in life expectancy, U.S., 1969–2009. *American Journal of Preventive Medicine, 46*(2), 19–29.

Skinner, M.W., Andrews, G.J., and Cutchin, M.P. (Eds.). (2017). *Geographical Gerontology: Perspectives, Concepts, Approaches.* Abington, UK: Routledge.

Small, M. (2007). Racial differences in networks: Do neighborhood conditions matter? *Social Science Quarterly, 88,* 320–343.

Small, M. (2009). *Unanticipated Gains: Origins of Network Inequality in Everyday Life.* New York: Oxford University Press.

Smith, P. (2014). A historical perspective in aging and gerontology. In H. Vakalahi, G. Simpson, and N. Giunta (Eds.), *The Collective Spirit of Aging Across Cultures (International Perspectives on Aging, 9,* pp. 7–27). Dordrecht: Springer.

Stack, C. (1974). *All Our Kin: Strategies for Survival in a Black Community.* New York: Basic Books.

Steptoe, A., Deaton, A., and Stone, A.A. (2015). Subjective well-being, health, and ageing. *Lancet, 385,* 640–648.

Subramanian, S.V., Chen, J.T., Rehkopf, D.H., Waterman, P.D., and Krieger, N. (2005). Racial disparities in context: A multilevel analysis of neighborhood variations in poverty and excess mortality among Black populations in Massachusetts. *American Journal of Public Health, 95*(2), 260–265.

Subramanian, S.V, Kubzansky, L., Berkman, L., Fay, M., and Kawachi, I. (2006). Neighborhood effects on the self-rated health of elders: Uncovering the relative importance of structural and service-related neighborhood environments. *Journals of Gerontology Series B, 61*(3), S153–S160.

Taylor, P., Morin, R., Cohn, D., and Wang, W. (2008). *American Mobility: Who Moves? Who Stays Put? Where's Home?* Washington, DC: Pew Research Center.

Tigges, L.M., Browne, I., and Green, G. (1998). Social isolation of the urban poor: Race, class, and neighborhood effects on social resources. *Sociological Quarterly, 39,* 53–77.

Tucker-Seeley, R., Subramanian, S.V., Li, Y., and Sorensen, G. (2009). Neighborhood safety, socioeconomic status, and physical activity in older adults. *American Journal of Preventive Medicine, 37*(3), 207–213.

Ulrich, R.S. (1984). View through a window may influence recovery from surgery. *Science, 224*(4647), 420–421.

U.S. Census Bureau. (2017). *The Nation's Older Population Is Still Growing* (Census Bureau Reports, Release No. CB17-100). Washington, DC: U.S. Census Bureau.

Vasunilashorn, S., Steinman, B.A., Liebig, P.S., and Pynoos, J. (2012). Aging in place: Evolution of a research topic whose time has come. *Journal of Aging Research, 2012*, 1–6. doi: 10.1155/2012/120952.

Wahl, H.-W., and Weisman, G.D. (2003). Environmental gerontology at the beginning of the new millennium: Reflections on its historical, empirical, and theoretical development. *Gerontologist, 43*(5), 616–627.

Walters, W.H. (2002). Later-life migration in the United States: A review of recent research. *Journal of Planning Literature, 17*(1), 38–66.

Wellman, B., and Wortley, S. (1990). Different strokes from different folks: Community ties and social support. *American Journal of Sociology, 96*(3), 558–588.

Wen, M., Browning, C.R., and Cagney, K.A. (2003). Poverty, affluence, and income inequality: Neighborhood economic structure and its implications for health. *Social Science & Medicine, 57*, 843–860.

Wen, M., Zhang, X., Harris. C.D., Holt, J.B., and Croft, J.B. (2013). Spatial disparities in the distribution of parks and green spaces in the U.S. *Annals of Behavioral Medicine, 45*(S1), 18–27.

Wethington, E., and Kavey, A. (2000). Neighboring as a form of social integration and support. In K. Pillemer, P. Moen, E. Wethington, and N. Glasgow (Eds.), *Social Integration in the Second Half of Life* (pp. 190–210). Baltimore, MD: Johns Hopkins University Press.

Wight, R.G., Aneshensel, C.S., Miller-Martinez, D., Botticello, A.L., Cummings, J.R., Karlamangla, A.S., and Seeman, T.E. (2006). Urban neighborhood context, educational attainment, and cognitive function among older adults. *American Journal of Epidemiology, 163*(12), 1071–1078.

Williams, D.R., and Collins, C. (2001). Racial residential segregation: A fundamental cause of racial disparities in health. *Public Health Reports, 116*, 404–416.

Williams, D.R., and Rucker, T.D. (2000). Understanding and addressing racial disparities in health care. *Health Care Financing Review, 21*, 75–90.

Wilson, W.J. (1987). *The Truly Disadvantaged: The Inner City, the Underclass, and Public Policy.* Chicago: University of Chicago Press.

Winterton, R. (2017). Therapeutic landscapes of ageing. In M.W. Skinner, M.P. Cutchin, and G.J. Andrews (Eds.), *Geographical Gerontology: Perspectives, Concepts, Approaches* (pp. 293–304). London: Routledge.

Wirth, L. (1938). Urbanism as a way of life. *American Journal of Sociology, 44*(1), 1–24.

Yen, I.H., Flood, J.F., Thompson, H., Anderson, L.A., and Wong, G. (2017). How design of places promotes or inhibits mobility of older adults: Realist synthesis of 20 years of research. *Journal of Aging and Health, 26*(8), 1340–1372.

York Cornwell, E., and Behler, R.L. (2015). Urbanism, neighborhood context, and social networks. *City & Community, 14*, 311–335.

York Cornwell, E., and Cagney, K.A. (2017). Aging in activity space: Results from smartphone-based GPS tracking of urban seniors. *Journals of Gerontology: Series B, 72*(5), 864–875.

York Cornwell, E., and Currit, A. (2016). Racial and social disparities in bystander support during medical emergencies on U.S. streets. *American Journal of Public Health, 106*, 1049–1051.

York Cornwell, E., and Hall, M. (2017). Neighborhood problems across the rural-urban continuum: Geographic trends and racial and ethnic disparities. *ANNALS of the American Academy of Political and Social Science, 672*, 238–256.

PART III

Families and Intergenerational Transfers

6

Demography of Aging and the Family

Emily M. Agree[1]

INTRODUCTION

Population aging is a marker of our success in both extending longevity and planning our reproduction. The demographic changes that result in the aging of the population also contribute to family change in aging societies. At the same time, changes in demographic behaviors, such as marriage and childbearing, have transformed the intergenerational structure of society. Each of these phenomena also has contributed to an increasing diversity of family forms, raising questions about societal and individual responsibility for well-being in old age. Countries vary in their approaches to social welfare, but even in the most generous ones, families remain the most tenacious and preferred sources of support when individuals need help. The role of the public-private divide in responding to the needs of aging populations has been as much at the center of demographic research on family change, living arrangements, and support as the changes in the family itself.

Demography also has contributed to methodological approaches that allow studies of families and intergenerational relations to be more complex and realistic. Demographers have developed and refined macrosimulation and microsimulation approaches to family change that enable the projection of distributions of family types for policy and planning purposes.

This chapter reviews the ways in which population aging has contributed to an increasingly complex set of family relationships in later life and

____

[1]Johns Hopkins University.

159

the implications for intergenerational support, care-giving, and new family forms.

DEMOGRAPHIC CHANGE AND FAMILY STRUCTURE

The process of population aging results from a confluence of trends, most notably declines in fertility and mortality and a shift in the timing of death to increasingly later ages. These trends have intersected with changes in the role of women, the decreasing size of family households, and the timing of family events to reshape families in later life.

Longevity

Population aging has been driven primarily by declines in fertility, but improvements in longevity since the latter part of the 20th century—especially survival at older ages—also have contributed to population aging. Increases in life expectancy allow for more years spent in family roles as a spouse, sibling, or parent but also for the possibility of occupying many family roles throughout one's lifetime—either concurrently or in succession—through divorce, remarriage, migration, changing living arrangements, and the acquisition and loss of other family relationships. As Bengtson (2001) noted, the importance of intergenerational relationships rises as the number of surviving generations increases.

Wiemers and Bianchi (2015) used the Panel Study of Income Dynamics (PSID) to show that almost two-thirds of American women in the Baby Boom cohort had at least one living parent when they were ages 45–64, substantially higher than women born during the 1920s and 1930s, about 38 percent of whom had a living parent at that age. Consistent with socioeconomic status (SES) differences in life expectancy, the likelihood of having a living parent is greater for those of higher social class. Henretta and colleagues (2002) analyzed Health and Retirement Study (HRS) data and found that the proportion of women ages 55–63 with a living parent was 5–7 percentage points higher among those with higher education, income, or occupations.

Improvements in old age survival also increase the likelihood of having a living spouse or ex-spouse. Joint survival of spouses has resulted both from the gains made by men in life expectancy in recent years and from enhanced survival among married individuals, especially married men (Rendall et al., 2011). These differentials may become exacerbated in future cohorts as they age, since newer marriages are becoming more educationally homogamous and marriages among those with higher education tend to be more stable (Schwartz and Mare, 2012; Cherlin, 2014). Siblings also are an important part of later-life family relationships, and most older persons have at least one living sibling, many with more than one—a legacy of the large families of the past (Agree and Hughes, 2012).

Fertility

Fertility has historically been the most powerful demographic factor contributing to population aging, eclipsing both mortality and migration in its impact on the age structure. Fertility is an important component of age structure change because it can change more rapidly than mortality and have an immediate effect. The most well-known example of this is the post–World War II Baby Boom, which slowed the aging of the U.S. population for some decades, with median age dropping from 30.2 in 1950 to 28.1 by 1970 (Hobbs and Stoops, 2002). The Baby Boom resulted from traditional preferences for larger families promoted by post-war economic growth and also from earlier marriages and less childlessness.

However, as women's roles evolved over the latter part of the last century, lower fertility intentions became more common and achievable, leading to declining family sizes. The mothers of the Baby Boom averaged 3.1 children ever born, and 36 percent had 4 or more children, whereas those born in the late 1960s averaged 1.9 children and only 11.6 percent had families of 4 or more. At the same time, a rising prevalence of childlessness in more recent cohorts increased the number of individuals reaching older ages with no children. Whereas only 10 percent of women born in the 1930s were childless at age 45, this statistic had risen to 17 percent for women born in the late 1960s (U.S. Census Bureau, 2017a).

Related trends in the timing of childbearing also took place over the past century. Two notable trends affecting kin availability at older ages are the decline in adolescent childbearing and the increasing age at first birth. Birth rates among those ages 15–19 rose steadily through the Baby Boom period from 54.1 per thousand in 1940 to 96.3 in 1957—the year with the peak volume of births (Lu et al., 2015). Since then, the rate has steadily declined, reaching an unprecedented low of 20.3 births per thousand teens in 2016 (Martin et al., 2017). The nature of teen births has changed as well. About 15 percent of teen births 80 years ago were premarital, compared with 75 percent of teen births today[2] (Bachu, 1999; Martin et al., 2017).

Equally significantly, birth rates at older ages have been increasing, with a substantial proportion of women having first births at ages 30 and older. Most of today's older women began childbearing by their early twenties, but since the mid-1970s the first-birth rate for older women has been rising.

---

[2]The proportion that was *either* conceived or born premaritally rose from 30 to 89 percent over this time period, and the proportion of teen premarital conceptions that led to marital births declined.

Only 2.5 percent of those born in the 1930s had a first birth after 35, versus 9–10 percent of cohorts born from 1956 to the 1960s (Matthews and Hamilton, 2014). Future cohorts are likely to have even later reproductive histories; in 2016, the fertility rate for 30–34-year-old women was higher than that of 25–29-year-olds for the first time (102.7 versus 102.1) and 30 percent of all first births were to women over 30 (Martin et al., 2017).

Increases in childlessness and later, shorter childbearing decreases the types and duration of family roles experienced by many adults and increases the average number of years separating generations. However, period trends in later childbearing intersect with the intergenerational transmission of fertility within families and the correlation between mothers and daughters in the timing of first birth (Kim, 2014). In those families where early parenthood is normative, the years between generations are small and family members occupy more roles for more years. Between 1998 and 2010, 40 percent of adults between ages 50 and 59 were part of families with four living generations. Even 11 percent of men and 5 percent of women in their seventies had a parent, children, and grandchildren alive (Margolis and Wright, 2017).

Nuptiality

The changes in fertility described above were a product of dramatic changes in the second half of the 20th century in women's roles, especially greater access to the labor force and to higher education. Employment and marriage were no longer seen as tradeoffs for women. All women, including married women and mothers, began working for pay in greater numbers; investments in women's education pushed marriage and childbearing to later ages, especially for those with a college education; and the stigma of nonmarital childbearing declined. Figure 6-1 shows the rise in median age at first marriage in the United States from about 20 for women and 22 for men in the 1960s to 27 for women and 30 for men in 2017. Older Americans today are just beginning to show evidence of these changes. The oldest old, born during the 1930s, married early (more than three-quarters of women married by age 25), compared to only one-half of the cohort born after 1956 (Kreider and Ellis, 2011).

Transformations in norms about sexuality and family life accompanied changes in women's roles. As more effective birth control became available, gender roles more fluid, and family responsibilities more volitional, alternatives to lifelong marriage commitments such as divorce, remarriage, and cohabitation became acceptable. Divorce rates began to rise, reaching a peak around 1980, and cohabitation in place of marriage became more common, first for those formerly married and then as a prelude or a substitute among those who had not yet married (Cherlin, 2010). Divorce rates have aged with the population; the divorce rate among adults ages 50 and

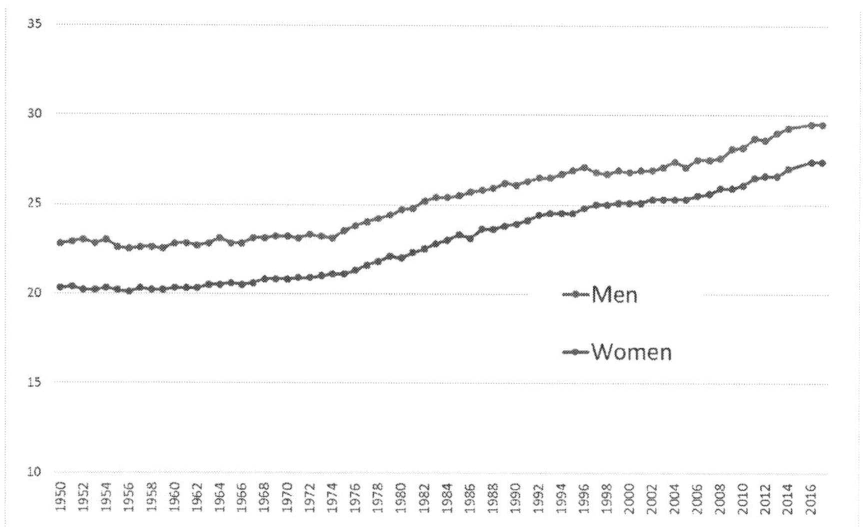

FIGURE 6-1 Age at first marriage among men and women in the United States, 1950–2017.
SOURCE: Data from U.S. Census Bureau, Current Population Survey, March and Annual Social and Economic Supplements.

older doubled between 1990 and 2010 (Brown and Lin, 2012). Despite these trends, marriage remains popular among both men and women. Almost all older adults married at least once, and remarriage rates after divorce or widowhood are high (Agree and Hughes, 2012).

Figure 6-2 shows the distribution by marital status of American men and women ages 65 and older in 2016. Fully 72 percent of men ages 65 and older are currently married, compared with 42 percent of women. Only about 5 percent of men and women never married, and far more women than men are widowed, in part because the female population is older and the loss of spouses rises substantially after age 85.

Cohort Succession

As Matilda White Riley pointed out years ago, the rapidity of demographic change can often lead to a lag in the compensating evolution of social structures (Riley et al., 1994). She was particularly concerned with the ways in which the growth in absolute numbers of older individuals would overtake their opportunities for roles in society. As social changes in family roles and expectations evolved, though, the opposite also has been

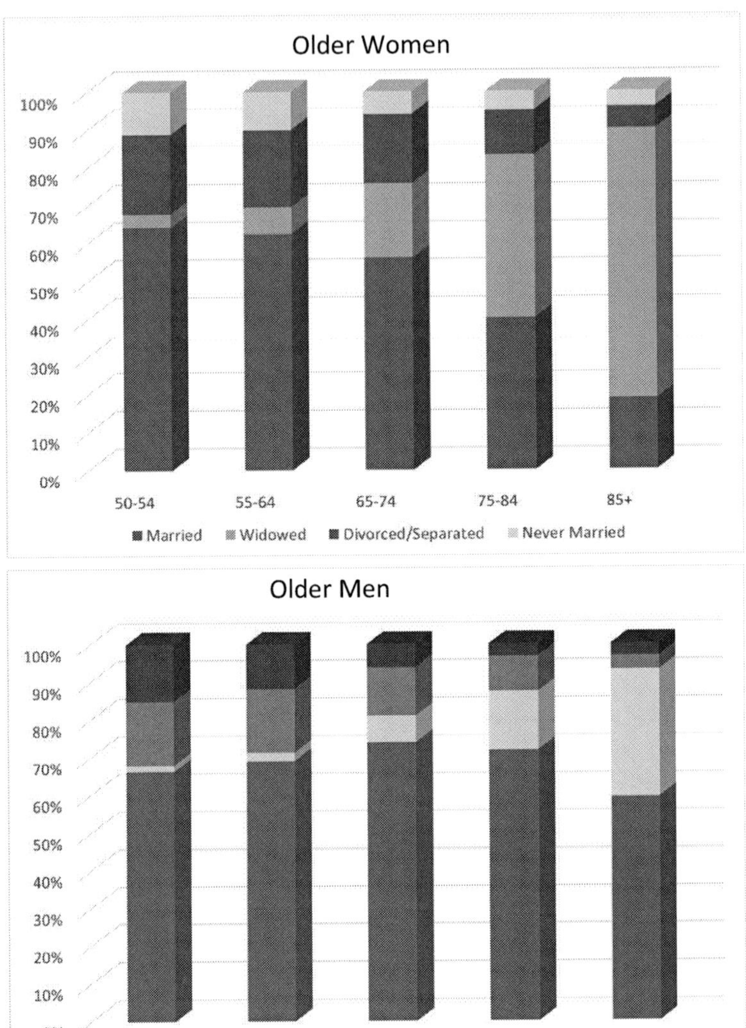

FIGURE 6-2 Marital status of older women and men in the United States in 2016. SOURCE: Data from tabulations from the 2016 U.S. Current Population Survey.

true: family roles have changed (and become more ambiguous), contributing to a poor fit for older people between their own lives and their roles within families (Dannefer et al., 2005).

One of the key contributions of demographic studies of aging and families is the study of cohort succession and its influence on family relationships. Family transitions in marriage and fertility behavior most often take place at younger ages and affect later-life families through the aging of generations with different norms and histories.

The cohort perspective is particularly important since new cohorts are entering old age with fewer traditional sources of support (spouses and biological children) but more ex-spouses, stepchildren, and surviving siblings. Whereas about 30 percent of ever-married women born in the 1930s divorced by age 60, almost 40 percent of those in the Baby Boom cohorts had divorced at least once (Kreider and Ellis, 2011). The postwar cohorts not only divorced at higher rates when they were younger, they are continuing to do so (Kennedy and Ruggles, 2014). They also were divorcing earlier than previous cohorts and remarrying earlier and more often. Over a quarter of Baby Boom men and women had married more than once by age 55, and almost 10 percent of men and 7 percent of the women had married three times (Lewis and Kreider, 2015).

Changes in childbearing for the cohorts that make up today's older population and the new cohorts that are aging are shown in Table 6-1. Almost 20 percent of women now in their 50s and 60s have never had children, and only 12 percent have had four or more living children. Coupled with the decline in teen births and the rise in delayed childbearing, new cohorts will reach old age with fewer biological children—and with children who are themselves younger and potentially less independent.

Table 6-1 also shows the detachment of childbearing from marriage.

TABLE 6-1 Cohort Changes in Childbearing among U.S. Women (in percentage)

Cohort	1926–1935	1936–1945	1946–1955	1956–1965	1966–1975
Childless	9	13	17	19	16
Four+ Children	37	24	12	11	12
Teen First Birth	23	29	19	18	19
30+ First Birth	8	8	19	25	24
Nonmarital First Birth	12	14	16	20	25

SOURCE: Author's calculations from the U.S. Census Integrated Public Use Microdata Series 1970; Survey of Income and Program Participation, various years; and the Current Population Survey, 2012–2016.

The proportion of women with a nonmarital first birth has risen across cohorts to 25 percent for those born in 1966 or later, and trends show this proportion increasing in younger generations. The popularity of cohabitation and selectivity of marriage have contributed to this trend, and future cohorts will reach old age with children born both in and out of traditional marriage. Much remains unknown about how bonds among family members will evolve in response to this trend. The propensity for and quality of family relationships will undoubtedly be different. As future cohorts age, we can expect to see not only more variation in family structures but also redefined relationships among family members.

Survival, Marriage, and Childbearing Create More Diverse Families

Demographers have shown that increased longevity, lower and later fertility, and serial marriage and partnership yield more-diverse networks of late-life family relationships than in the past. This degree of complexity is likely to grow in the near future. Projecting the distribution of these relationships is difficult. Though we have expanded data collection beyond nuclear families and household boundaries, accounting for family relationships that ended due to death or union dissolution is exceptionally difficult, even with some of our best data resources. Wolf (1994), in the previous publication under this title, and Wachter (1997, 1998) used microsimulation models to estimate the availability of kin under different hypothetical demographic regimes, including nonmarital fertility, divorce, and remarriage. Their studies were among the first to illustrate the expected decline in numbers of biological children available to older men and women and the anticipated increase in stepchildren—especially for men, who remarry more often and to younger women. More recently, Murphy (2010) showed that the proportion of younger adults with stepsiblings could increase from 7 percent in 1950 to 40 percent in 2050.

The understanding of what constitutes "family" within these augmented kin structures is itself undergoing transformation. Cohabitation, sequential partnerships, nonmarital childbearing, and stepparenting have become widespread in younger cohorts. However, these behaviors affect not only those generations but also their older relatives. For example, if an adult child divorces and remarries, one set of grandparents may involuntarily lose access to their grandchildren and the grandchildren may gain a new set of instant grandparents. The norms of these newly expanded families are still being negotiated. Grandparents can be stable relationships for children whose parents divorce, but those ties are also dependent on their relationship with the parent of that grandchild (Hagestad and Uhlenberg, 2007).

THE CONTINUUM OF PROXIMITY TO FAMILY

One of the most important areas of demographic research on aging has been the study of households, living arrangements, and proximity to family members, especially between older parents and their adult children. The first section of this chapter discussed the ways in which demographic changes have been accompanied by a general transition to families with smaller generations and how changes in women's roles and attitudes about cohabitation and divorce led to more complex extended families. Who lives with whom and the distance between family members is affected not only by these larger family changes but also by economic cycles, housing markets, and changes in the health and care needs of the older population.

Initially, interest in older adults' living arrangements arose out of concern to identify the most vulnerable elders and determine when family support was available to them. However, while living arrangements are important to understanding family relationships and provide opportunities for support, they are also a framework through which support is given and not necessarily an indicator of support itself. The determinants of co-residence can be complex and differ from decisions to live near family members.

Demographic studies of households were historically constrained by the nature of household surveys, which have difficulty capturing families that cross dwelling boundaries, households with more than one family, or families that live together but do not pool resources. This has particular relevance when looking at multigenerational households, where special arrangements such as "granny flats" may be made within homes but older household members function as a separate unit.

Multiple generations of families often live in close proximity but do not share homes, and nearby family members help with household tasks, such as shopping, housecleaning, cooking, or child care. This has led to much more robust data collection on family proximity, and several national U.S. surveys of aging now provide substantial longitudinal information about family location and characteristics, with especially detailed data on adult children.

It is important to note that though institutionalization rates among the older population are quite low (about 3% for the 65 and older population in the United States), a substantial number of older persons (more than 2 million in 2011) live either in nursing homes or in other residential care facilities (Freedman and Spillman, 2014b). Much research on later-life families commonly still focuses on the community-dwelling population and does not attempt to account for the role of institutionalization in family relations, which is especially important at the oldest ages and among those with cognitive impairment, for whom institutionalization rates are much higher.

Living Arrangements of the Older Population

Economic independence and improvements in health have contributed to the ability of older persons to live independently (McGarry and Schoeni, 2000). During the 20th century, there was a dramatic rise in the proportion of older people living alone or with a spouse. Many of them live nearby, but not with, their adult children and other family members. From 1960 to 2000 the proportion of older persons living alone rose from 18 to 28 percent. There is some evidence that living alone is declining among older women. From a peak of 38 percent in 1990, the proportion living alone declined to 32 percent in 2014, while for men the corresponding percentage rose slightly from 15 to 18 percent (Stepler, 2016). Older Americans are not the only adults who are increasingly living alone. In the United States, the proportion of all households occupied by single persons rose from 13 percent in 1960 to 28 percent in 2017 (U.S. Census Bureau, 2017b).

Table 6-2 shows the distribution of living arrangements for older men and women in the United States in 2015, stratified by marital status. For both men and women, around 80 percent of those with a partner are living independently with that partner and about 14 percent are also living with adult children (and possibly others) in multigenerational households. A very small percentage (< 1%) of married men and women are living alone, mainly because their spouse is institutionalized. Among those not currently married, about two-thirds of both men and women live alone, and the next most common arrangement is living with children. In this case, substantially more women than men (27.6 versus 14.8%) live with adult children, whereas more men live with other relatives or nonrelatives

TABLE 6-2 Living Arrangements of Men and Women, Ages 65 and Older, Living in Households in the Community, United States, 2015 (in percentage)

	Men		Women	
Living Arrangement	Unmarried	Married	Unmarried	Married
Alone	67.8	1.0	63.7	0.8
Spouse/Partner Only	—	79.5	—	82.2
Children and Others	16.4	14.8	27.6	13.4
Others Only	15.8	4.7	8.7	3.6

SOURCE: National Health and Aging Trends Study, weighted tabulations.

(15.8%, compared with 8.7% of women). The overall differences between men and women in living arrangements are largely driven by the differences in their marital status at older ages (shown in Figure 6-2), rather than differential propensities for co-residence.

Multigenerational Households

Declining fertility creates a demographic opportunity for the proportion of vertically extended households to increase (so long as fertility does not fall below replacement level) as the ratio of parents to children approaches unity (Yi, 1986). However, the demographic contributions of population aging to multigenerational households are not necessarily realized when better health and economic independence in later life promote separate living. Households with two or more adult generations have been declining in the United States, but they are more common among minority families and immigrants. In 2012, about 4.6 percent of households were multigenerational, but prevalence was almost twice as high among families with Black or Hispanic householders (8.3% and 8.6% respectively) (Vespa et al., 2013).

Families have been doubling up in part because of downward mobility among younger adult generations, a trend that was exacerbated by the recession in 2007 (Treas and Sanabria, 2016). Multigenerational households are often formed in response to needs for child care or to pool resources in the face of economic hardship (Harrington Meyer and Kandic, 2017). These households are as likely to have multiple families in the same generation (for instance, when adult siblings move in together) as to be multigenerational (Pilkauskas et al., 2014). Older immigrants in the United States are also far more likely to live in multigenerational households as a result of family reconstitution policies that allowed older family members to immigrate to join adult children and grandchildren (van Hook and Glick, 2007).

Geographic Proximity

There is a perception in the United States and many Western countries that occupational mobility and national job markets have increased internal migration, and thus families are more geographically dispersed than in the past, creating a potential threat to old age support if family members are not close enough to provide hands-on care. However, research beginning in the 1990s examined the dispersion of families and showed that over three-quarters of older parents live within 1 hour travel time of a child, and many live even closer (e.g., Clark and Wolf, 1992; Lin and Rogerson, 1995). This pattern has persisted over several decades; Raymo and colleagues (2017) used recent HRS data to show that 45 percent of men and women ages

65 and older lived within 10 miles of an adult child. Similar findings from the Survey of Health, Ageing and Retirement in Europe surveys show 85 percent of older parents in Europe had a child living within 25 km in 2004 (Hank, 2007). These levels of close proximity are borne out in studies from the adult children's perspective. Compton and Pollak (2013), using 1996 data, found that 40 percent of married couples, ages 25 and older, live within 30 miles of *both* the husband and wife's parents. Chan and Ermisch (2015) found similar levels of proximity in the United Kingdom in 2010, with almost two-thirds of couples living less than an hour travel time to an older parent. High rates of close proximity between older parents and their children do not reflect moves to become closer at later ages, as one would suspect in highly mobile societies. Rather, Wolf and Longino (2005) showed that the majority of job-related moves among children take place long before parents need care, and most people do not move far from their place of birth. Most older people therefore also stay in close proximity to at least one sibling (Miner and Uhlenberg, 1997; White, 2001).

Although data on proximity is substantially better than two decades ago, we are still limited in our ability to understand the geography of later-life families, especially the location of children and other relatives in relation to each other, since survey data are collected with measures relative to a focal individual. We also have difficulty identifying short-distance moves (e.g., within the closest category of noncoresidential proximity), and we know little about the *reasons* that older adults or their children move.

Determinants of Family Co-residence and Proximity

A key contribution of demographers to understanding family geography is that proximity and co-residence are necessarily conditioned on the demographic availability of kin (Wolf, 1984). The spatial distribution of families therefore must be based on propensities for persons who have the option of living near or with a particular category of relative (e.g., Ruggles, 1987; Martin, 1989; Wolf, 1994). Living arrangements and family distance are the product of decisions made across many different life stages and thus can be difficult to model. Demographic research has examined the characteristics of family members that are associated with different living arrangements. Beginning with Wolf and Soldo in 1988, the availability and characteristics of both older parents and their children were explicitly included in household and care models. Pezzin and Schone (1999) used game theory models to incorporate different preferences for co-residence between parents and multiple children, and many others have followed.

Proximity and co-residence with children is often assumed to be sensitive to the needs of older adults, especially health events. However, evidence has been conflicting. Cross-sectional studies consistently report a higher prevalence of co-residence with children among older adults in ill health (e.g., Wolf and Soldo, 1988; Silverstein, 1995; Compton and Pollak, 2013). Choi et al. (2015) found cardiovascular events related to decreases in distance between parents and children, but others found no relationship between parents' needs and proximity (Rogerson et al., 1993). Later timing of parenthood means some older adults are living with children who have never left home for reasons unrelated to health (Clark and Wolf, 1992; Wiemers et al., 2017a).

A small number of studies have looked at parent-child proximity from a dynamic perspective, examining moves or changes in proximity relative to various determinants. Painter and Lee (2009) found that older parents in the United States were more likely to remain in their home if they had children living in the same state. Zhang et al. (2013) showed that adult children were more likely than their parents to make a proximity-enhancing move, especially in response to a parent's illness or their own economic needs. In the United States and Germany, older parents' moves are associated with good health and young grandchildren (Zhang et al., 2013; Winke, 2017). Evidence in all these cases is quite indirect, and more needs to be done to understand the motivations underlying family mobility

CARE-GIVING

As other chapters in this volume discuss in more detail, increased longevity has been accompanied by improvements in health and functioning at later ages, leading to longer lives lived independently. Despite this, many older individuals eventually need assistance with day-to-day activities, and family members are the most common and consistent source of care (National Academies of Sciences, Engineering, and Medicine, 2016). Care-givers help with chronic disease management, basic self-care, and household tasks; they also provide emotional support.

Despite the dominance of family care-givers in informal care networks, relatively few efforts have been made to collect data about the family members who provide help (Wolff and Kasper, 2006). In part, identifying the universe of caregivers has been problematic (Giovanetti and Wolff, 2010). Family members who provide help to older members do not always identify themselves as care-givers, and measuring assistance in families can be challenging. Family members help each other, doing household tasks unrelated to health and from which everyone in the family may benefit. Freedman et al. (2014) addressed some of these issues for spousal care-giving with time-use diary data from the PSID. They found that both husbands and wives engaged in care activities for their spouse but that wives did household chores two to three times more often than husbands.

A long and robust literature has established that spouses and adult children are the most common family members to provide care and that the proportion of informal caregivers that are children has been rising since the 1990s (for reviews, see Silverstein and Giarrusso, 2010; Spillman and Pezzin, 2000; Wolff and Kasper, 2006). According to the U.S. National Health and Aging Trends Study, in 2011 spouses represented 21 percent of informal care-givers, 29 percent were daughters, and 18 percent were sons (Freedman et al., 2014). These figures are not additive since care can be provided by a combination of care-givers, but most older persons receive help from only one or two informal helpers at any given time (Freedman and Spillman, 2014a). Wives are more likely to provide assistance, spend more time, and help with more tasks than husbands (Stoller and Miklowski, 2008). However, in 2015 husbands represented about 45 percent of spousal care-givers and committed substantial amounts of time to care-giving (Wolff et al., 2017). Other family members, such as siblings and grandchildren, play a lesser role but may be called upon when the mainstays of the care arrangements are not available. Siblings can be important care-givers for older persons who are childless, and they play a role in deferring institutionalization (Freedman, 1996).

As health has improved and mortality has declined, the age at which care is needed has been delayed until quite late in life. Given that today's oldest old had children relatively young, not only are spouse care-givers quite elderly but adult children also may be near or in old age when they are called upon to help their parents. Almost 13 percent of care-givers were age 65 or older during the 1990s (Wolff and Kasper, 2006); since 1999, the proportion of care-givers ages 65–74 has grown slightly from 24 to 32 percent (Wolff et al., 2017).

Older adults are not merely recipients of family help; they also provide help to children and grandchildren. Financial support generally flows downward across generations until quite late in life, and parents are highly responsive to adult children's needs for financial assistance (Schoeni, 1997; McGarry, 2016). In addition, most grandparents are engaged with their grandchildren, providing emotional support and child care, with a small but important proportion acting as primary care-givers to grandchildren in the absence of parents (Casper et al., 2016).

"Sandwich" Care-giving

Later childbearing and longer survival also increase the potential for "sandwiched" generations. The term was coined to describe the potential for middle-aged adults to be engaged in care-giving for generations above and below them. The most important demographic predictors of dual care-giving are the timing of care needs among older parents and the length of generations in families. Most adults providing care to parents have children who are independent adults. A minority of women (between 10% and 30%) are estimated to be providing support simultaneously to parents and children (Soldo, 1996; Agree et al., 2003; Grundy and Henretta, 2006; Friedman et al., 2016). While this pattern is not dominant, women with college educations tend to marry and begin childbearing later, extending the length of generations in these families and putting them at greater risk of having a child at home when they need to care for an older parent (Agree et al., 2003). As the older population becomes more educated, there is likely to be some increase in such dual-support responsibilities.

Role of Kin Availability

Since care-givers to older persons are almost always spouses or adult children (or both), past fertility and marriage patterns play a large role in establishing the demographic availability of these types of close kin. As much as 90 percent of older men and women who are married depend on their spouses, and unmarried older persons most likely have a child (usually a daughter) on the front lines of care (Spillman and Pezzin, 2000; Freedman et al., 2004). Larger families have a greater choice among siblings, and studies show that care is shared and negotiated within families (e.g., Wolf et al., 1997; Pezzin and Schone, 1999; Checkovich and Stern, 2002). Pezzin and colleagues (2014) illustrated the complexities of care negotiations among siblings, showing that when a parent co-resides with one child it reduces the care received from non-co-resident siblings.

The high divorce rates and low fertility that characterize the aging Baby Boom cohorts are likely to bring with them differences in support and care-giving (Ryan et al., 2012). Most research on family care-giving has focused on spouses, sons, and daughters, but the role of siblings, friends, and more distant relatives may grow.

COMPLEX FAMILIES AND LATER-LIFE SUPPORT

Union formation and dissolution and childbearing occur at younger ages and affect late-life families through complex marital and fertility histories that create large, diffuse sets of kin relationships with ill-defined norms about support. Concerns persist that the rising numbers of nontraditional family relationships will contribute to a deterioration in family support for older persons and jeopardize the well-being of future cohorts as they age. The underlying assumption is that nontraditional family roles and structures are associated with rejection of traditional norms of family support. Alternately, as cohabitation and divorce become more acceptable, the tolerance for a variety of family forms could increase, and changing gender roles may strengthen family bonds as *both* men and women invest more time with their children (Bianchi et al., 2006). The same changes contributing to the rise in divorce and family instability in past decades could thus improve the ability of families to care for older generations in the future (Goldscheider et al., 2015).

There is a growing literature examining the consequences for support of parents, but it may take some time before empirical evidence accumulates of family adaptation at older ages; even today the proportion of older persons who have remarried and have stepchildren is quite low. Furthermore, surveys rarely collect information on past relationships, so limited information is available on ex-spouses and stepchildren in studies of health and aging. Estimates from a 2013 PSID special module that collected extensive family information showed about 2 percent of those ages 55 and older with a living stepparent, but about 13 percent of women and 18 percent of men had stepchildren[3] (Wiemers et al., 2016).

Studies most commonly show that divorce and remarriage are associated with less intergenerational contact, support, and relationship quality in comparison to those in long-term intact marriages (e.g., Furstenberg et al., 1995; Grundy and Shelton, 2001; Kalmijn, 2007; Noël-Miller, 2013; Pezzin and Schone, 1999; Shapiro, 2012). Divorced fathers are particularly vulnerable; they co-reside with adult children less often and receive fewer hours of informal care from them. Divorced grandfathers also have less contact with grandchildren and live further from their grandchildren than divorced grandmothers (King, 2003).

Transfers of support within families can be a function of need as well as preferences. Family members who are separated or divorced have more needs for financial support and care than those with a partner, and they receive more help (Glaser et al., 2008; Kalmijn, 2016). This is consistent with studies showing that remarried parents have weaker ties with children from prior relationships. Kalmijn (2013, 2015) found that adult children had less contact, less support, and poorer quality relationships with repartnered fathers than with fathers who remained divorced and lived alone.

Not surprisingly, just as interest in aging families has often focused on the availability of children for care-giving, research on the impact of divorce and remarriage has focused on the relationship between stepchildren and stepparents. Stepchildren are less likely to live near or with stepparents in later life, they provide less support (of all kinds) than biological children,

---

[3]Unfortunately, while it is an improvement over previous data collection, the PSID sample only collects stepparent information for respondents with living biological parents and only collects stepchild information for those currently in a union, so these figures likely underestimate the prevalence of stepkin.

and they receive less from stepparents (Seltzer et al., 2012). The greater numbers of kin added to families by stepparents and stepchildren does not appear to make up for the lower amount of support provided in these families (Wiemers et al., 2017b). Health outcomes for older stepparents may be worse as well. Both men and women with only stepchildren experienced greater disability and higher mortality than those with biological children alone. Interestingly, stepchildren appear beneficial for older women's health when biological children are present (Pezzin et al., 2013).

Family members in complex families are often linked through other individuals. For example, stepchildren are tied to a stepparent because of that person's relationship to their biological parent. Their relationship can differ depending on whether the biological parent is present and the closeness of that relationship. When an adult child's biological parent is alive, more care is given to the stepparent. Correspondingly, the presence of children (biological or step) increases the hours of care provided by spouses (Pezzin et al., 2009).

Support between parents and stepchildren also depends on the *quality* of the relationships in the family. We generally view these ties as more volitional and less obligatory than traditional nuclear family ties, but we have few tools to understand the variation within these families in their support. Current research is limited both by gaps in information about the extensive set of quasi-kin in complex families, and because we know little about the early-life antecedents that shape relationships with stepparents or half-siblings.

A few studies have examined differences in the quality of stepchild and stepparent relations. While biological children begin their relationships with parents at birth, stepchildren meet their stepparents at the time their parents marry. Research on younger adults has shown that the closeness between adolescents and their stepparents in adulthood is related to the quality of the biological parent's relationship to that parent's new spouse (King and Lindstrom, 2016). Some late-life studies show that stepchildren who lived during their childhood with the stepparent receive levels of support equivalent to that received by biological children (Pezzin and Schone, 1999; Kalmijn, 2013). Other evidence suggests that stepchildren who were older at the time their parents married were more likely to receive financial support in adulthood (Henretta et al., 2014). Reconciling these conflicting findings will require more data on complex families, with information about marital histories and these diverse sets of kin.

NEW FORMS OF FAMILY

Most family dynamics take place at young ages, when unions are being formed for independence and reproduction. Yet divorce, remarriage, cohabitation, and other forms of partnering have been rising among mid-life and older adults. Additionally, recent changes in U.S. law recognize same-sex marriage nationally, with consequences for older couples across the United States.

Late-Life Cohabitation

Cohabitation has been increasing at all ages in the United States, including among older adults. Just as the Baby Boom cohorts were more accepting of divorce earlier in life, they also are more open to cohabiting than earlier generations, and the proportions in these unions are expected to increase (Brown and Wright, 2015). The proportion of those ages 55 and older cohabiting with an opposite-sex partner rose from 8 percent of men and 6 percent of women in 2000 to 14 and 12 percent, respectively, in 2012 (Vespa et al., 2013). The majority of older cohabiters are previously divorced (85% in 2015), and many have children (Stepler, 2017; Brown and Wright, 2017). Unlike youthful cohabitations, late-life cohabitations are longer and more stable, which is consistent with the latter being less of a stepping-stone to marriage and more of an alternative to legal union (Brown et al., 2012).

The reasons older cohabiters choose not to marry are less well known. Some may not want to take the financial risks involved in legal marriage at a time when many are living on pension income or savings but prefer the companionship and cost effectiveness of living with a romantic partner. About a third of cohabiters in one study reported planning bequests to family members unrelated to their partner, and cohabitation may be a way of protecting these bequests (Vespa, 2012). As marriage becomes more selective for education, cohabitation has been growing primarily among those of lower SES, especially among those with less than a high school education. Older cohabiters appear to be similar in their profile: 49 percent of older cohabiters had a high school education or less (compared with 40% of those who remarried) and 21 percent were in poverty (versus only 4% of those who remarried) (Brown and Wright, 2017; U.S. Census Bureau, 2016).

Living Apart Together

An alternative to cohabitation, called "living apart together" or LAT, is defined as a committed romantic relationship in which both partners maintain separate households. It is more established in Europe than in the United States. The age distribution of LAT relationships is highly skewed toward younger ages. In the United Kingdom, over one-half were under the age of 25, but 8 percent of women ages 50–59 reported a regular partner-ship with someone they did not live with (Haskey, 2005). In France, older men were less likely than women to be in LAT relationships and more likely to cohabit (Régnier-Loilier et al., 2009).

As one would expect, given the expense of maintaining separate households in a committed relationship, individuals in LAT relationships tend to be better educated, more egalitarian, have higher incomes, and value autonomy (Strohm et al., 2009). Women report LAT as a way to maintain independence in a relationship, rather than conforming to gendered expectations (Haskey and Lewis, 2006). Older adults may enter into LAT relationships to avoid financial entanglements, especially when they have children, and to limit the impact if and when the relationship ends. Having been divorced, number of past unions, and presence of adult children were characteristics positively associated with LAT relationships at older ages in the Netherlands and France (de Jong Gierveld, 2004; de Jong Gierveld and Merz, 2013; Régnier-Loilier et al., 2009). In the United States, studying LAT relationships is hampered by lack of data on couple relationships and on same-sex partnerships (Strohm et al., 2009). It is also difficult to define LAT couples as distinct from a less-committed form of "dating" (de Jong Gierveld and Merz, 2013).

Same-Sex Relationships

With the *Obergfell* decision by the U.S. Supreme Court in June 2015, same-sex marriage became legal across the United States. Although it had been legal in a number of states before that, it was now possible for same-sex couples to receive the protections of legal marriage across the country. Same-sex spouses gain access to health insurance and other legal benefits in marriage. They have rights to more fully participate in medical decisions for a spouse. They also can be more secure in obtaining retirement or survivor benefits under Social Security in cases of divorce or death.

Obergfell was the culmination of a rapid change in popular attitudes about same-sex relationships and gender identity. In 2001, only 35 percent of American adults approved of same-sex marriage. By 2017, this proportion had risen to 62 percent, and 56 percent of Baby Boomers were in favor (Pew Research Center, 2017). As same-sex relationships became more widely accepted, the numbers of same-sex couples reported in surveys quintupled from 145,000 in 1990 to 1.1 million in 2016 (Romero, 2017). In the latter half of 2015, the percentage of new marriages that were same-sex unions rose from 6 percent pre-decision to 11 percent post-decision (Gates and Brown, 2015). According to the Williams Institute, the number of married same-sex couples has risen from about 390,000 in 2015 to 547,000 in 2017 (Romero, 2017). That legal marriage was now an option implies that a substantial number of older, established same-sex couples may be marrying. Statistics on older same-sex couples are limited, but the American Community Survey estimated that in 2016, 26 percent of unmarried and 42 percent of married same-sex couple households had a partner ages 55 and older.[4]

DIVERSITY

Socioeconomic inequality is central to understanding the present and especially the future of family change. The demographic trends described in this chapter are quite different for various segments of the population. Those without a college education and engaged in "blue-collar" work are more likely to have earlier, multipartner fertility. Couples with less education are also more likely to cohabit instead of marrying and to have a nonmarital first birth. Traditional marriage is increasingly becoming the province of the college educated (Carlson and England, 2011; Furstenberg, 2014). Educational differences are already being seen in the generational structure of families. The proportion of adults ages 75 and older with four sets of grandchildren was twice as great among those without a high school degree (38%) as for the college educated (19%) (Seltzer and Yahirun, 2014).

Social class differences affect multiple generations in families through many pathways. Older adults with a college education are more likely to give financial support to adult children—probably because they are financially better off—and children with a college education or more provide greater assistance to aging parents (McGarry and Schoeni, 1995). Grandparents who are primary care-givers for grandchildren are more likely to be in or near poverty, and poor areas with high multigenerational co-residence rates have more pneumonia and influenza hospitalizations at older ages (Cohen et al., 2011). There is also evidence that poor grandparental education is associated with low birth weight among grandchildren (McFarland et al., 2017).

Another important source of stratification among late-life families in the United States is race/ethnicity. While today's older population is less diverse than upcoming cohorts, minority families tend to be younger, have higher fertility, and live in multigenerational family households (Seltzer and Yahirun, 2014). Grandparents who live in these multigenerational households are often providing the household chores and child care for single parents or couples with two jobs (Treas and Marcum, 2011). African American elders who live with others tend to be among the poor-

---

[4]Statistics derived by author from the 2016 American Community Survey detailed tables, "Table 2. Household Characteristics of Same-Sex Couple Households by Relationship Type." Available: https://www.census.gov/data/tables/time-series/demo/same-sex-couples/ssc-house-characteristics.html [April 2018].

est and more often live with children out of economic necessity (Seltzer and Yahirum, 2014).

Older immigrants face unique challenges. While many came to the United States when they were younger, a substantial number are joining adult children through family reunification programs. They face unfamiliar new cultures and language problems, and they are often ignored by younger family members, who are busy and whose lifestyles are often quite different (Treas and Mazumdar, 2002). In some cases, policies that reduce benefit eligibility for noncitizens make immigrant elders completely dependent on children (Treas and Gubernskaya, 2015). Older immigrants who become naturalized are more likely to live on their own (Lee and Angel, 2002).

CONCLUDING THOUGHTS

Demographic change is both predictable and completely unknown. In the case of population aging, the slow increases in longevity over the past century were observable and well documented. The inevitable growth in the size and share of the population at older ages was clear. Yet, the implications of these age structure changes have been broadly debated and far less well understood. In particular, the aging of the population is interwoven with the process of family change. The gender revolution began 50 years ago, and yet its corresponding effects on fertility, marriage, and the quality of family relationships are still being evaluated. Studies that focus solely on the older population have to some extent been able to sidestep these questions for many years because gender role transformations largely affected men and women at younger ages. Now, as the cohorts at the forefront of these revolutions are themselves entering old age, there is a surge in interest about the implications of changing family structure and relationships for well-being in later life.

In this chapter, the demographic components of family change and the implications for family structure, co-residence, and support have been reviewed. One of the reasons this research is possible is the availability of family roster data and marital histories in surveys of aging. Many of the studies cited here use data from the HRS family of surveys, the PSID roster on generations and transfers, or the National Health and Aging Trends Study. Each of these sources has extended our knowledge about aging families and their relationships. Yet gaps in knowledge remain with regard to past (dissolved) relationships and early-life family circumstances. Projects that connect information about individuals' childhood circumstances and their reproductive and marital histories will be helpful in filling in some of the remaining gaps.

Another less-well-understood trend is the bifurcation of family lives by social class and by race/ethnicity. Overall trends in family change obscure substantial differences in marriage and fertility experienced by those in different social and economic positions, especially between those with different levels of education. These differences create unique vulnerabilities for those at the lower end of the SES distribution, since they tend to form families through less stable and more varied partnerships. More needs to be understood about these differences, but oversampling is rarely done in surveys on aging for minority elders or those in poverty or low income, and studying these families relies on specialized datasets and on small-scale or qualitative research.

Demographic changes in families are not only a function of normative social changes but also respond to economic policy and technological change. There is a growing set of studies that have examined the way in which national- and state-level policies, the availability of formal care services, and new technologies may affect the ways in which families live and care for each other, but these topics were beyond the scope of the chapter for this volume.

Finally, the emerging forms of families, such as large sets of quasi-kin, nonmarital partnerships, or same-sex marriages (many now with their own children), provide a fruitful area for further research. The transformation of gender and family roles that has led to this explosion of variety in family types and relationships, and the erosion of stereotypes about what families are and "should" be, allows researchers to develop new models and theoretical understanding of how kinship networks function and what old age means in these new and evolving families.

REFERENCES

Agree, E., Bissett, B., and Rendall, M.S. (2003). Simultaneous care for parents and care for children among mid-life British women and men. *Population Trends, 112,* 29–35.

Agree, E.M., and Hughes, M.E. (2012). Demographic trends and later life families in the 21st century. In R. Blieszner and V.H. Bedford (Eds.), *Handbook of Families and Aging,* 2nd ed. (pp. 9–33). Santa Barbara, CA: Praeger.

Bachu, A. (1999). Trends in premarital childbearing: 1930–1994. In *Current Population Reports* (pp. 23–197). Washington, DC: U.S. Census Bureau.

Bengtson, V.L. (2001). Beyond the nuclear family: The increasing importance of multigenerational bonds. *Journal of Marriage and Family, 63,* 1–16.

Bianchi, S.M., Robinson, J.P., and Milke, M.A. (2006). *The Changing Rhythms of American Family Life.* New York: Russell Sage Foundation.

Brown, S.L., and Lin, I.F. (2012). The gray divorce revolution: Rising divorce among middle-aged and older adults, 1990–2010. *Journals of Gerontology Series B: Psychological Sciences and Social Sciences, 67*(6), 731–741.

Brown, S.L., and Wright, M.R. (2015). Older adults' attitudes toward cohabitation: Two decades of change. *Journals of Gerontology Series B: Psychological Sciences and Social Sciences, 71*(4), 755–764.

Brown, S.L., and Wright, M.R. (2017). Marriage, cohabitation, and divorce in later life. *Innovation in Aging, 1*(2). doi: 10.1093/geroni/igx015.

Brown, S.L., Bulanda, J.R., and Lee, G.R. (2012). Transitions into and out of cohabitation in later life. *Journal of Marriage and Family, 74*(4), 774–793.

Carlson, M., and England, P. (2011). *Social Class and Changing Families in an Unequal America.* Stanford, CA: Stanford University Press.

Casper, L.M., Florian, S., Potts, C., and Brandon, P.D. (2016). Portrait of American grandparent families. In H. Meyer (Ed.), *Grandparenting in the United States* (pp. 109–132). Amityville, NY: Baywood.

Chan, T.W., and Ermisch, J. (2015). Proximity of couples to parents: Influences of gender, labor market, and family. *Demography, 52*(2), 379–399.

Checkovich, T.J., and Stern, S. (2002). Shared caregiving responsibilities of adult siblings with elderly parents. *Journal of Human Resources, 37*(3), 441–478.

Cherlin, A.J. (2010). *The Marriage-Go-Round: The State of Marriage and the Family in America Today.* New York: Vintage.

Cherlin, A.J. (2014). *Labor's Love Lost: The Rise and Fall of the Working-Class Family in America.* New York: Russell Sage Foundation.

Choi, H., Schoeni, R.F., Langa, K.M., and Heisler, M.M. (2015). Older adults' residential proximity to their children: Changes after cardiovascular events. *Journals of Gerontology Series B: Psychological Sciences and Social Sciences, 70*(6), 995–1004.

Clark, R., and Wolf, D. (1992). Proximity of children and elderly migration. In A. Rogers (Ed.), *Elderly Migration and Population Redistribution: A Comparative Perspective* (pp. 77–96). London: Belhaven Press.

Cohen, S.A., Agree, E.M., Ahmed, S., and Naumova, E.N. (2011). Grandparental caregiving, income inequality and respiratory infections in elderly U.S. individuals. *Journal of Epidemiology & Community Health, 65*(3), 246–253.

Compton, J., and Pollak, R.A. (2013). *Proximity and Coresidence of Adult Children and their Parents in the United States: Description and Correlates* (IZA Discussion Paper #7431). Bonn, Germany: Institute for the Study of Labor.

Dannefer, D., Uhlenberg, P., Foner, A., and Abeles, R.P. (2005). On the shoulders of a giant: The legacy of Matilda White Riley, *Journals of Gerontology Series B: Psychological Sciences and Social Sciences, 60*(6), S296–S304.

de Jong Gierveld, J. (2004). Remarriage, unmarried cohabitation, living apart together: Partner relationships following bereavement or divorce. *Journal of Marriage and Family, 66*(1), 236–243.

de Jong Gierveld, J., and Merz, E.M. (2013). Parents' partnership decision making after divorce or widowhood: The role of (step) children. *Journal of Marriage and Family, 75*(5), 1098–1113.

Freedman, V.A. (1996). Family structure and the risk of nursing home admission. *Journal of Gerontology: Social Sciences 51B* (2), S61–S69.

Freedman, V.A., and Spillman, B.C. (2014a). Disability and care needs among older Americans. *Milbank Quarterly, 92*(3), 509–541.

Freedman, V.A., and Spillman, B.C. (2014b). The residential continuum from home to nursing home. *Journal of Gerontology: Social Sciences, 69*(7), S42–S50.

Freedman, V.A., Aykan, H., Wolf, D.A., and Marcotte, J.E. (2004). Disability and home care dynamics among older unmarried Americans. *Journal of Gerontology: Social Sciences, 59*, S25–S33.

Freedman, V.A., Cornman, J.C., and Carr, D. (2014). Is spousal caregiving associated with enhanced well-being? New evidence from the PSID. *Journals of Gerontology Series B: Psychological Sciences and Social Sciences, 69*(6), 861–869.

Friedman, E.M., Park, S.S., and Wiemers, E.E. (2016). New estimates of the sandwich generation in the 2013 PSID. *Gerontologist, 57*(2), 191–196.

Furstenberg, F. (2014). Fifty years of family change: From consensus to complexity. *Annals of the American Academy of Political and Social Science, 654*(1), 12–30.

Furstenberg, F., Hoffman, S., and Shrestha, L. (1995). The effect of divorce on intergenerational transfers: New evidence. *Demography, 32*(3), 319–333.

Gates, G., and Brown, T.N. (2015). *Marriage and Same-Sex Couples after Obergefell*. Los Angeles: The Williams Institute.

Giovannetti, E.R., and Wolff, J.L. (2010). Cross-survey differences in national estimates of numbers of caregivers of disabled older adults. *Milbank Quarterly, 88*(3), 310–349.

Glaser, K., Stuchbury, R., Tomassini, C., and Askham, J. (2008). Long-term consequences of partner-ship dissolution for support in late life in the United Kingdom. *Ageing & Society, 28*(3), 329–351.

Goldscheider, F., Bernhardt, E., and Lappegård, T. (2015). The gender revolution: A framework for understanding family demographic behavior. *Population & Development Review, 41*(2), 207–239.

Grundy, E., and Henretta, J.C. (2006). Between elderly parents and adult children: A new look at the intergenerational care provided by the "sandwich generation." *Ageing & Society, 26*(5), 707–722.

Grundy, E., and Shelton, N. (2001). Contact between adult children and their parents in Great Britain 1986–99. *Environment and Planning A, 33*(4), 685–697.

Hagestad, G.O., and Uhlenberg, P. (2007). The impact of demographic changes on relations between age groups and generations. In K. Schale and P. Uhlenberg (Eds.), *Social Structures: Demographic Changes and the Well-Being of Older Persons* (pp. 239–261). New York: Springer.

Hank, K. (2007). Proximity and contacts between older parents and their children: A European comparison. *Journal of Marriage and Family, 69*(1), 157–173.

Harrington Meyer, M., and Kandic, A. (2017). Grandparents in the United States. *Innovation in Aging, 1*(2), 1–10.

Haskey, J. (2005). Living arrangements in contemporary Britain: Having a partner who usually lives elsewhere and living apart together (LAT). *Population Trends, 122*, 35–45.

Haskey, J., and Lewis, J. (2006). Living-apart-together in Britain: Context and meaning. *International Journal of Law in Context, 2*(1), 37–48.

Henretta, J.C., Grundy, E., and Harris, S. (2002). The influence of socioeconomic and health differences on parents' provision of help to adult children: British–United States comparison. *Ageing & Society, 22*(4), 441–458.

Henretta, J.C., Van Voorhis, M.F., and Soldo, B.J. (2014). Parental money help to children and stepchildren. *Journal of Family Issues, 35*(9), 1131–1153.

Hobbs, F., and Stoops, N. (2002). *Demographic Trends in the 20th Century* (Census 2000 Special Reports, Series CENSR-4). Washington, DC: U.S. Government Printing Office.

Kalmijn, M. (2007). Gender differences in the effects of divorce, widowhood and remarriage on intergenerational support: Does marriage protect fathers? *Social Forces, 85*(3), 1079–1104.

Kalmijn, M. (2013). Adult children's relationships with married parents, divorced parents, and stepparents: Biology, marriage, or residence? *Journal of Marriage and Family, 75*(5), 1181–1193.

Kalmijn, M. (2015). Relationships between fathers and adult children: The cumulative effects of divorce and repartnering. *Journal of Family Issues, 36*(6), 737–759.

Kalmijn, M. (2016). Children's divorce and parent–child contact: Within-family analysis of older European parents. *Journals of Gerontology: Social Sciences, 71*(2), 332–343.

Kennedy, S., and Ruggles, S. (2014). Breaking up is hard to count: The rise of divorce in the United States, 1980–2010. *Demography, 51*(2), 587–598.

Kim, K. (2014). Intergenerational transmission of age at first birth in the United States: Evidence from multiple surveys. *Population Research and Policy Review, 33*(5), 649–671.

King, V. (2003). The legacy of a grandparent's divorce: Consequences for ties between grandparents and grandchildren. *Journal of Marriage and Family, 65*(1), 170–183.

King, V., and Lindstrom, R. (2016). Continuity and change in stepfather–stepchild closeness between adolescence and early adulthood. *Journal of Marriage and Family, 78*(3), 730-743.

Kreider, R.M., and Ellis, R. (2011). *Living Arrangements of Children: 2009.* (Household Economic Studies). Washington, DC: U.S. Census Bureau.

Lee, G.Y., and Angel, R.J. (2002). Living arrangements and SSI among elderly Asians and Hispanics in the United States: Nativity and citizenship. *Journal of Ethnic Migration Studies, 28*(3), 553–563.

Lewis, J.M., and Kreider, R.M. (2015). *Remarriage in the United States* (American Community Survey Reports, ACS-30). Washington, DC: U.S. Census Bureau.

Lin, G., and Rogerson, P. A. (1995). Elderly parents and the geographic availability of their adult children. *Research on Aging, 17*(3), 303-331.

Lu, L., Chong, Y., Hamilton, B.E., Curtin, S.C., Martin, J.A., Tejada-Vera, B., and Sutton, P.D. (2015). *Natality Trends in the United States, 1909–2013.* Washington, DC: National Center for Health Statistics.

Margolis, R., and Wright, L. (2017). Older adults with three generations of kin: Prevalence, correlates, and transfers. *Journals of Gerontology, Series B: Psychological and Social Sciences, 72*(6), 1067–1072.

Martin, J.A., Hamilton, B.E., and Osterman, M.J.K. (2017). *Births in the United States, 2016* (NCHS Data Brief #287). Hyattsville, MD: National Center for Health Statistics.

Martin, L.G. (1989). Living arrangements of the elderly in Fiji, Korea, Malaysia, and the Philippines. *Demography, 26*(4), 627–643.

Matthews, T.J., and Hamilton, B.E. (2014). *First Births to Older Women Continue to Rise* (NCHS Data Brief #52). Hyattsville, MD: National Center for Health Statistics.

McFarland, M.J., McLanahan, S.S., Goosby, B.J., and Reichman, N.E. (2017). Grandparents' education and infant health: Pathways across generations. *Journal of Marriage and Family, 79*(3), 784–800.

McGarry, K. (2016). Dynamic aspects of family transfers. *Journal of Public Economics, 137,* 1–13.

McGarry, K., and Schoeni, R.F. (1995). Transfer behavior in the Health and Retirement Study: Measurement and the redistribution of resources within the family. *Journal of Human resources, 30,* S184–S226.

McGarry, K., and Schoeni, R.F. (2000). Social Security, economic growth, and the rise in elderly widows' independence in the twentieth century. *Demography, 37,* 221–236.

Miner, S., and Uhlenberg, P. (1997). Intragenerational proximity and the social role of sibling neighbors after midlife. *Family Relations, 46,* 145–153.

Murphy, M. (2010). Family and kinship networks in the context of ageing societies. In S. Tuljapurkar, N. Ogawa, and A.H. Gauthier (Eds.), *Ageing in Advanced Industrial States: Riding the Age Waves* (vol. 3, pp. 263–285). Dordrecht, Netherlands: Springer.

National Academies of Sciences, Engineering, and Medicine. (2016). *Families Caring for an Aging America.* Washington, DC: The National Academies Press.

Noël-Miller, C.M. (2013). Repartnering following divorce: Implications for older fathers' relations with their adult children. *Journal of Marriage and Family, 75*(3), 697–712.

Painter, G., and Lee, K. (2009). Housing tenure transitions of older households: Life cycle, demographic, and familial factors. *Regional Science and Urban Economics, 39*(6), 749–760.

Pew Research Center. (2017). *Support for Same-Sex Marriage Grows, Even Among Groups That Had Been Skeptical.* Washington, DC: Pew Research Center.

Pezzin, L.E., and Schone, B.S. (1999). Intergenerational household formation, female labor supply and informal caregiving: A bargaining approach. *Journal of Human Resources, 34*, 475–503.

Pezzin, L.E., Pollak, R.A., and Schone, B.S. (2009). Long-term care of the disabled elderly: Do children increase caregiving by spouses? *Review of Economics of the Household, 7*(3), 323–339.

Pezzin, L.E., Pollak, R.A., and Schone, B.S. (2013). Complex families and late life among elderly persons: Disability, institutionalization, and longevity. *Journal of Marriage and Family, 75*(5), 1084–1097.

Pezzin, L.E., Pollak, R.A., and Schone, B.S. (2014). Bargaining power, parental care, and intergenerational coresidence. *Journals of Gerontology, Series B: Psychological and Social Sciences, 70*(6), 969–980.

Pilkauskas, N.V., Garfinkel, I., and McLanahan, S.S. (2014). The prevalence and economic value of doubling up. *Demography, 51*(5), 1667–1676.

Raymo, J., Pike, I., and Liang, J. (2017). *A New Look at the Living Arrangements of Older Americans Using Multistate Life Tables* (CDE Working Paper #2017-03). Madison: University of Wisconsin.

Régnier-Loilier, A., Beaujouan, É., and Villeneuve-Gokalp, C. (2009). Neither single, nor in a couple. A study of living apart together in France. *Demographic Research, 21*, 75–108.

Rendall, M., Weden, M., Favreault, M., and Waldron, H. (2011). The protective effect of marriage for survival: A review and update. *Demography, 48*(2), 481–506.

Riley, M.W., Kahn, R.L., and Foner, A. (Eds.). (1994). *Age and Structural Lag: Society's Failure to Provide Meaningful Opportunities in Work, Family, and Leisure.* New York: Wiley.

Rogerson, P.A., Weng, R.H., and Lin, G. (1993). The spatial separation of parents and their adult children. *Annals of the Association of American Geographers, 83*(4), 656–671.

Romero, A.P. (2017). *1.1 Million LGBT Adults Are Married to Someone of the Same Sex at the Two-year Anniversary of Obergefell V. Hodges.* Los Angeles: Williams Institute, UCLA School of Law.

Ruggles, S. (1987). *Prolonged Connections: The Rise of the Extended Family in Nineteenth-Century England and America.* Madison: University of Wisconsin Press.

Ryan, L.H., Smith, J., Antonucci, T.C., and Jackson, J.S. (2012). Cohort differences in the availability of informal caregivers: Are the Boomers at risk? *Gerontologist, 52*(2), 177–188.

Schoeni, R.F. (1997). Private interhousehold transfers of money and time: New empirical evidence. *Review of Income and Wealth, 43*, 423–448.

Schwartz, C., and Mare, R. (2012). The proximate determinants of educational homogamy: First marriage, dissolution, remarriage, and educational upgrading. *Demography, 49*(2), 629–650.

Seltzer, J.A., and Yahirun, J.J. (2014). *Diversity in Old Age: The Elderly in Changing Economic and Family Contexts* (UCLA CCPR Population Working Paper). Los Angeles: California Center for Population Research.

Seltzer, J.A., Yahirun, J.J., and Bianchi, S.M. (2012). Doubling up when times are tough: Obligations to share a home in response to economic hardship. *Journal of Marriage and Family, 75*(5), 1164–1180.

Shapiro, A. (2012). Rethinking marital status: Partnership history and intergenerational relationships in American families. *Advances in Life Course Research, 17*(3), 168–176.

Silverstein, M. (1995). Stability and change in temporal distance between the elderly and their children. *Demography, 32*(1), 29–45.

Silverstein, M., and Giarrusso, R. (2010). Aging and family life: A decade review. *Journal of Marriage and Family, 72*(5), 1039–1058.

Soldo, B.J. (1996). Cross pressures on middle-aged adults: A broader view. *Journals of Gerontology, Series B, 51*(6), S271–S273.

Spillman, B.C., and Pezzin, L.E. (2000). Potential and active family caregivers: Changing networks and the "sandwich generation." *Milbank Quarterly, 78*(3), 347–374.

Stepler, R. (2016). *Smaller Share of Women Ages 65 and Older Are Living Alone: More Are Living with Spouse or Children*. Washington, DC: Pew Research Center.

Stepler, R. (2017). *Number of U.S. Adults Cohabiting with a Partner Continues to Rise, Especially Among Those 50 and Older*. Washington, DC: Pew Research Center.

Stoller, E.P., and Miklowski, C.S. (2008). Spouses caring for spouses: Untangling the influences of relationship and gender. In M. Szinovacz and A. Davey (Eds.), *Caregiving Contexts: Cultural, Familial, and Societal Implications* (pp. 115–131). New York: Springer.

Strohm, C.Q., Seltzer, J.A., Cochran, S.D., and Mays, V.M. (2009). "Living apart together" relationships in the United States. *Demographic Research, 21*, 177–214.

Treas, J., and Gubernskaya, Z. (2015). Policy contradictions and immigrant families. *Public Policy & Aging Report, 25*(3), 107–112.

Treas, J., and Marcum, C.S. (2011). Diversity and family relations in an aging society. In R.A. Settersten and J.L. Angel (Eds.), *Handbook of Sociology of Aging* (pp. 131–141). New York: Springer.

Treas, J., and Mazumdar, S. (2002). Older people in America's immigrant families: Dilemmas of dependence, integration, and isolation. *Journal of Aging Studies, 16*(3), 243–258.

Treas, J., and Sanabria, T. (2016). Marital status and living arrangements over the life course. In M.H. Meyer and E.A. Daniele (Eds.), *Gerontology: Changes, Challenges, and Solutions* (pp. 247–270). Santa Barbara, CA: Praeger

U.S. Census Bureau. (2016). *Current Population Survey, Annual Social and Economic Supplement*. Washington, DC: U.S. Census Bureau.

U.S. Census Bureau. (2017a). *Current Population Survey, June 1976-2016. Historical Tables*. Available: https://www2.census.gov/programs-surveys/demo/tables/fertility/time-series/his-cps [November 2017].

U.S. Census Bureau. (2017b). *Current Population Survey, Annual Social and Economic Supplements, 1960 to 2017*. Available: https://www.census.gov/data/tables/time-series/demo/families/households.html [November 2017].

van Hook, J., and Glick, J.E. (2007). Immigration and living arrangements: Moving beyond economic need versus acculturation. *Demography, 44*(2), 225–249.

Vespa, J. (2012). Union formation in later life: Economic determinants of cohabitation and remarriage among older adults. *Demography, 49*(3), 1103–1125.

Vespa, J., Lewis, J.M., and Kreider, R.M. (2013). America's families and living arrangements: 2012. *Current Population Reports, 20*, P570.

Wachter, K.W. (1997). Kinship resources for the elderly. *Philosophical Transactions of the Royal Society of London B: Biological Sciences, 352*(1363), 1811–1817.

Wachter, K.W. (1998). *Kinship Resources for the Elderly: An Update*. Berkeley: University of California.

White, L. (2001). Sibling relationships over the life course: A panel analysis. *Journal of Marriage and Family, 63*(2), 555–568.

Wiemers, E.E., and Bianchi, S.M. (2015). Competing demands from aging parents and adult children in two cohorts of American women. *Population and Development Review, 41*(1), 127–146.

Wiemers, E.E., Seltzer, J.A., Schoeni, R.F., Hotz, V.J., and Bianchi, S.M. (2016). *The Generational Structure of U.S. Families and their Intergenerational Transfers* (UCLA CCPR Population Working Paper). Los Angeles: California Center for Population Research.

Wiemers, E.E., Slanchev, V., McGarry, K., and Hotz, V.J. (2017a). Living arrangements of mothers and their adult children over the life course. *Research on Aging, 39*(1), 111–134.

Wiemers, E.E., Seltzer, J.A., Schoeni, R.F., Hotz, V.J., and Bianchi, S.M. (2017b). *Stepfamily Structure and Transfers between Generations in the United States.* Available: http://public.econ.duke.edu/~vjh3/working_papers/StepkinTransfers.pdf [April 2018].

Winke, T. (2017). Later life moves and movers in Germany: An expanded typology. *Comparative Population Studies, 42,* 3–24.

Wolf, D.A. (1984). Kin availability and the living arrangements of older women. *Social Science Research, 13*(1), 72–89.

Wolf, D.A. (1994). The elderly and their kin: Patterns of availability and access. In National Research Council, *Demography of Aging* (pp. 146–194). Washington, DC: National Academy Press.

Wolf, D.A., and Longino, C.F., Jr. (2005). Our "increasingly mobile society"? The curious persistence of a false belief. *Gerontologist, 45*(1), 5–11.

Wolf, D.A., and Soldo, B.J. (1988). Household composition choices of older unmarried women. *Demography, 25*(3), 387–403.

Wolf, D.A., Freedman, V., and Soldo, B.J. (1997). The division of family labor: Care for elderly parents. *Journals of Gerontology: Social Sciences, 52*(Spec. Issue), 102–109.

Wolff, J.L., and Kasper, J. (2006). Caregivers of frail elders: Updating a national profile. *Gerontologist, 46*(3), 344–356.

Wolff, J.L., Mulcahy, J., Huang, J., Roth, D.L., Covinsky, K., and Kasper, J.D. (2017). Family caregivers of older adults, 1999–2015: Trends in characteristics, circumstances, and role-related appraisal. *Gerontologist.* doi: 0.1093/geront/gnx093.

Yi, Z. (1986). Changes in family structure in China: A simulation study. *Population and Development Review, 12*(4), 675–703.

Zhang, Y., Engelman, M., and Agree, E.M. (2013). Moving considerations: A longitudinal analysis of parent-child residential proximity for older Americans. *Research on Aging, 35*(6), 663–687.

7

Intergenerational Transfers and the Older Population

Andrew Mason[1,2] and Ronald Lee

INTRODUCTION

Economic behavior varies in fundamental and important ways over the life cycle. Early, and again late in life, people consume more than they produce through their labor. In between these two phases of the life cycle, people produce more through their labor than they consume. The life cycle gives rise to institutions and economic systems that facilitate the reallocation of resources from one age to another. Intergenerational transfers constitute an essential part of the reallocation system, with governments and families playing distinctive roles. Families play a central role in child rearing with large intergenerational transfers of money and time from parents, and to some extent grandparents, to children. In some societies, intergenerational family transfers are also an important part of the old-age support system. Governments also are heavily involved in intergenerational transfers through public programs for education, health care, and pensions. Assets, in their varied forms including debt, provide another mechanism by which resources can be shifted from one age group to another. Young people can consume more than they produce by relying on credit—student loans or credit card debt, for example. Seniors can rely on wealth acquired

[1]Corresponding author.

[2]The authors' research for this paper was funded by the National Institutes of Health, NIA R24 AG045055. We are grateful to Michael Abrigo, Gretchen Donehower, and other members of the NTA network whose estimates we used. The researchers are identified and more detailed information is provided on the NTA Website: www.ntaccounts.org. See also Lee and Mason (2011) and United Nations Population Division (2013).

when younger, through bequests or life-cycle saving, to support themselves in old age.

People are deeply altruistic. They care about the well-being of others, particularly family members but even strangers. Intergenerational transfers are an important manifestation of altruism that serves multiple, essential functions in all contemporary economies. Achieving distributional objectives—for example, that children and the elderly do not live in poverty—depends on intergenerational transfers. Achieving economic growth and ensuring the welfare of future generations depend on parents and taxpayers investing heavily in the upbringing of children.

Systems of intergenerational transfers will experience considerable stress due to the unprecedented changes in population age structure discussed briefly in the next section. These effects will depend in part on why intergenerational transfers occur. So in the next sections we discuss the determinants and then economic consequences of intergenerational transfers from a theoretical perspective. Then we consider empirical patterns and projections of public and private intergenerational transfers around the world, drawing on National Transfer Accounts (NTA) estimates (Lee and Mason, 2011; United Nations Population Division, 2013). We conclude with a discussion of policy responses.

THE CHANGING DEMOGRAPHIC AND ECONOMIC SETTING

Demographic forces are important for any system of intergenerational transfers because they determine the numbers of those giving transfers and those receiving them. Transfers given must always equal transfers received; hence, changing population age distributions require adjustments in the per capita donations or receipts. Economic forces are important because they influence the resources of those giving transfers and the needs of those receiving them. The future of intergenerational transfer systems will ultimately depend on the interplay between demographic and economic forces. If they are mutually reinforcing, many countries will experience population aging and slowing economic growth with profound implications.

Although population growth and age distributions are affected by fluctuations in fertility and mortality, such as the U.S. Baby Boom, the big story is the demographic transition: the shift in mortality and fertility from high to low values. The demographic transition has been under way at the global level for about two centuries, but with very different timing and extent at the level of regions and nations. The transition leads first to rapid population growth and young populations. Next comes an era with rapid growth in the working-age population, often referred to as the demographic dividend. Population aging is the last stage of this process. Before the transition, roughly 4 percent of the total global population was age 65 or older (Lee,

2003, p. 168). In 2015 the share in Japan, the country with the oldest population, was 26 percent and is projected to rise to 37 percent in 2055 (United Nations Population Division, 2017, henceforth *UN 2017*). For the high-income countries as a group, the share will still be rising in 2100 (from 17.0% in 2015 to 31% in 2100; *UN 2017*). The rapid population growth that occurs during the transition has been replaced by decline in some high-income countries. Japan is already experiencing population decline, as are Eastern and Southern regions of Europe, and many other countries are expected to follow, with Eastern Asia projected to begin to decline in 2030–2035 and the more developed regions as a whole in 2045–2049 (*UN 2017*). The United States is somewhat exceptional among high-income countries, with slow population growth expected to persist for many decades.

Standard measures of population aging, including those used above, are based on chronological age. With improving health and vitality at older ages, alternative measures of aging are being explored. Measures based on mortality, disability, self-assessed health, or time until death (Sanderson and Scherbov, 2010; Coile et al., 2017) suggest that functional population aging is barely occurring at all. After an extended period of decline, the observed age at retirement has also been rising in most OECD countries since the mid-1990s. However, a countervailing trend in many countries is an increase in consumption at old age that often exceeds the additional resources produced by the elderly.

Responding to any increase in the number or needs of the elderly will prove to be much easier if economic growth is robust. Nondemographic factors will play a critical role here, but population change is also likely to prove important. Labor supply, saving, and asset-holding vary by age, so the number of people at each age influences the aggregate supply of labor and capital—and over time, the growth rates and levels of aggregate output, wages, and interest rates (rates of return on assets). Because the working-age population is growing more slowly or declining in many countries, in the absence of higher rates of labor force participation labor supply will grow more slowly or decline and total output growth will slow. Because assets are disproportionately held by older adults, capital is likely to rise relative to the number of workers. As capital increases relative to labor, wages will likely rise and interest rates decline (or remain at currently low levels). The increase in physical capital per worker may be reinforced by growth in human capital because lower fertility facilitates greatly increased human capital investments per child (Becker and Barro, 1988; Mason et al., 2016). Thus, demographic change likely will lead to slower growth in total output but more rapid growth in output per worker.

The effect of population on output per worker is not the entire story, however. First, the number of workers relative to the number of people (the support ratio) varies over the demographic transition. During the aging phase the support ratio is declining and, hence, output per capita grows more slowly than output per worker.

Second, the division of output between consumption (meeting current needs) and saving and investment (meeting future needs) varies. Higher saving rates are often proposed in preparation for population aging because they would spur more rapid economic growth and allow the elderly to depend less on old-age transfers. However, as Cutler et al. (1990) pointed out, if saving rates are high enough, saving more sacrifices current living standards with little or no benefit in the future. Moreover, the saving rate that maximizes per capita consumption is lower when the labor force grows more slowly. For this reason, aging societies can devote more of their resources to current standards of living and less to future needs. One possibility, then, is that lower saving would benefit the economy, whereas higher saving is needed to meet retirement needs. Under these conditions, expanding public transfer programs could eliminate the conflict by reducing the saving needed for retirement needs. Another possibility, and one that is quite likely, is that current saving rates are less than needed by the economy. Under these circumstances, policies that encourage higher saving by workers would both ease pressures on transfer systems and move economies closer to a desirable level of capital intensity.

A comprehensive analysis by Elmendorf and Sheiner (2017) concludes that changing demography will lead to slower growth in per capita consumption. Except for countries with very low fertility, higher birth rates do not offer a way out. Lee et al. (2014) show that moderately low fertility, a total fertility rate of 1.7 or so, and current mortality rates support the highest levels of sustainable per capita consumption.

THEORETICAL FOUNDATIONS FOR INTERGENERATIONAL TRANSFERS

The elderly depend heavily on intergenerational transfers and, in their absence, many would face lives of insecurity and impoverishment. The elderly are also an important source of intergenerational transfers, supporting their own descendants and, through their taxes, non–family members of younger generations. What explains the large flows of economic resources across generations? Do intergenerational transfers realize their goals? Do they have unintended consequences for better or for worse?

No single, unified theory explains what leads to intergenerational transfers (Arrondel and Masson, 2006). Altruism may motivate both public and private transfers to children (Becker, 1960, 1991; Willis, 1973) and to the elderly (Altonji et al., 1992, 2000; Lindert, 2004). Alternatively, economic flows that appear to be pure transfers may actually be a form of nonmarket exchange. Parents may view children as an investment (Leibenstein, 1972;

Caldwell, 1982) or as a form of insurance (Kotlikoff and Spivak, 1981), with flows from parents to children at one stage of the life cycle balanced by flows from adult children to parents later in life. In his seminal paper on the exchange motive, Cox (1987) hypothesized that transfers from parents to adult children were compensation for care-giving or attention. Adults also may leave bequests out of altruism or in exchange for attention and care-giving from adult children. And because of uncertainty about the age of death, incomplete annuitization, and precautionary saving, a substantial portion of bequests may be accidental.

Research often treats public transfers as exogenous or as a consequence of an essentially mechanical interaction between exogenous policy and changes in age structure. This approach is particularly favored in research on how public policy should respond to population aging (Feldstein and Liebman, 2002; Diamond, 2004; Feldstein, 2006; Elmendorf and Sheiner, 2017). But why public transfers vary across countries and over time is an important and interesting question. Public transfers may be a consequence of altruism, an entirely selfish outcome of self-serving political behavior (Lindert, 2004), or a mechanism for responding to incomplete markets or market failure. Public transfers arise through social insurance schemes that respond to health and long-term care needs, disability, and unexpected longevity, for example.

Influential research by Becker and Murphy (1988) combines altruism, investment motives, and market failure in a theory of intergenerational transfers. Parents care about the present and future well-being of their children, and they allocate their resources accordingly, providing for their children's current consumption and investing in their human capital to raise their future income. But parents also care about their own current and future consumption. Given their limited resources, many parents may invest less in their children's human capital than would be optimal, given the interest rate or rate of return to regular capital. In this case, the child might wish to borrow to fund further investment but be thwarted by credit market imperfections. Parents might then step in to loan their children the funds to invest further in their human capital, with the understanding that the children are expected to repay the loan when the parents are old. Then children's education would be funded partly by altruistic transfers from the parents and partly by a family credit market, or exchange. If adult children assist their parents, this could either reflect altruistic feelings toward them or it could be a repayment of an earlier loan.

If cultural values or institutional mechanisms are not in place to enforce repayment of this kind of parental loan, then children—and society—may be stuck with a lower level of education than would otherwise be desirable and efficient. This situation provides a rationale for introducing a public transfer system in which children receive public education, funded by taxing their parents' generations, while the adults who were compelled to pay for this education through taxes are themselves repaid through a public pension program, funded by taxing the children's generation. This is an elegant story about how private and public systems might interact to provide a better outcome, when public transfers improve on what is possible through the family alone.

Samuelson (1958) provided a different theoretical perspective on why public transfer programs may enhance welfare by responding to incomplete markets. He showed that in an economy with no capital or other durable goods, a credit market (intertemporal exchange) could not achieve an efficient pattern of life-cycle consumption. Achieving a desirable consumption trajectory requires saving during the working years to accumulate assets that can then be used to pay for consumption in old-age retirement. But in this model of society, every generation is a creditor, with larger or smaller stocks of assets, and no one is a debtor. In a credit market, however, one person's credit must be matched by another person's debt. Credit markets cannot be relied on to meet life-cycle needs. Samuelson showed that the life-cycle problem can be addressed through a social contract under which current elderly receive support from current workers, who receive support when old from the next generation of workers—and so on, forever.

Samuelson's approach is much like a Pay As You Go public pension system such as the U.S. Social Security system. For such a system, Samuelson showed that the rate of return earned by the contributions of workers, compared to their eventual benefits, would be equal to the rate of growth of aggregate income. This same insight applies equally to a familial system of support for the elderly. This feature of intergenerational transfer systems makes them highly vulnerable to slowing labor force growth and population aging. In a rapidly growing population there are many workers to support each elder, so contributions can be small relative to eventual benefits and the rate of return high. But in a declining population the opposite is true. Enter population aging: with slowing population growth rates and increasing numbers of elderly per worker, transfer programs for the elderly appear to be in trouble.

An alternative to relying on intergenerational transfers is to invest in productive capital, yielding a rate of return determined by markets and the underlying health of the economy. However, the desire to hold assets at each age, aggregated across the population, might be so large—particularly in an aging population—that the rate of return on capital could be driven below the rate of return on transfers (the population growth rate plus the productivity growth rate). In this case it would be efficient to satisfy some of the asset demand through transfer systems to the elderly, reducing asset holdings until their rate of return rises to equal that on transfers. This possibility, that population aging could raise the demand for assets to a point where interest rates drop toward zero, is one aspect of "secular stagnation" (Summers, 2014), and indeed proposed policies for ameliorating secular stagnation include increasing public transfers to the elderly and raising the retirement age (Teuligs and Baldwin, 2014). Government debt is another form of transfer to the elderly, and raising it has also been proposed.

There are many other ways in which public and private transfers interact with one another and with other aspects of economic behavior. Any transfer system alters economic incentives, influencing labor supply, saving, investment in human capital, and health care usage. In this way, public transfers may reduce economic growth further. Private transfers may be less subject to this side effect than public ones because of altruistic linkages and family monitoring of behavior. Public transfers also alter the private incentives for childbearing. Public pensions may reduce a parental motive to have children to provide old-age support, and the future contributions of children to public pension systems are now a societal benefit that does not accrue to their parents, resulting in lower fertility. In other settings, public provision of education and health care for children may encourage higher fertility.

Yet another possibility is that the government tries to raise the welfare of the elderly by giving them a larger pension, financed by taxing their children's generations. If the balance between their own consumption and their children's was already what the parents wanted, then they might offset increased public transfers by making private transfers to their children, as suggested by Barro (1974). This would undermine the public policy and would also effectively raise the cost to parents per child, further distorting the parental fertility incentives (Becker, 1993). This kind of private response would depend on the extent to which the motivation for private transfer behavior is altruistic and keyed to the well-being of each generation. If instead, the observed private flows of funds and care across generations are motivated by exchange, then these flows would not change in response to public policy.

ANATOMY OF THE U.S. GENERATIONAL ECONOMY

In 2011, Americans produced more through their labor than they consumed for a relatively short age span: from ages 28 to 59 inclusive. Those who were 28 and younger or 60 and older consumed more than they produced through their labor. Labor income was important for older Americans, funding 57 percent of consumption at age 65 and 27 percent at age 70. However, the gap between consumption and labor income was large at older ages. The per capita deficit was $50,000 at age 77 and exceeded $70,000 for those 88 and older. This compares with a peak deficit for children, realized at age 18, of just under $40,000. Spending on health care was the main reason that the very old in the United States have such a large life-cycle deficit (see Figure 7-1).

The elderly can fund their life-cycle deficit in only two ways. First, they can rely on assets, either the income generated by their assets or by spending down their wealth (borrowing is just another way of spending down their wealth). Second, they can rely on intergenerational transfers from family

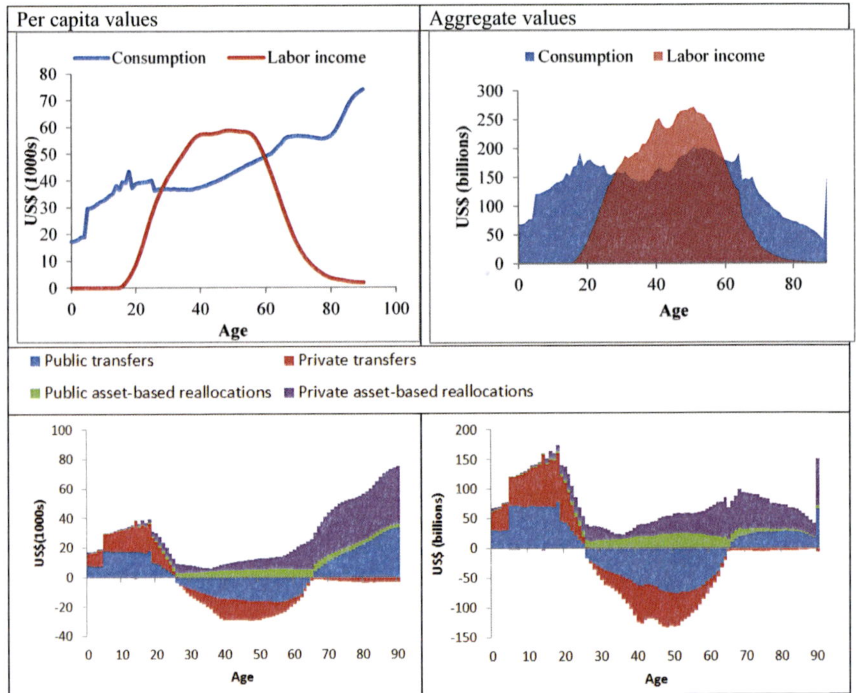

FIGURE 7-1 National Transfer Account, United States, 2011.
NOTES: Per capita values in the left-hand panels are in US$ thousands; aggregate values in the right-hand panels are in US$ billions. Life-cycle variables are in the upper panels; age reallocations are in the lower panels. *Consumption* includes all private and public consumption classified by the age of individuals, not the age of the household head or some other household marker. *Labor income* includes all compensation, including benefits, of employees and estimates of the value of labor by the self-employed and unpaid family workers. Both consumption and labor income are adjusted to match aggregate totals based on the U.S. National Income and Product Accounts. All transfers are net values defined as transfers received less transfers given. Asset-based reallocations are equal to asset income less saving.
SOURCE: Data from U.N. Population Division (2013), updated from Lee et al. (2011).

members or other private sources and through public programs such as Social Security, Medicare, Medicaid, disability insurance, and so forth.

Young seniors in the United States rely heavily on assets. The asset income they devoted to consumption, and not saving, was about $20,000 per year at age 60. By age 87, asset income devoted to consumption reached $40,000 per year, but it funded a much smaller share of the old-age deficit. Older Americans on average continued to save until their late 80s. They funded old-age consumption by relying on income from assets, but not by dis-saving.

Net transfers (public plus private) to young elderly, those between the ages of 60 and 65, were negative even though they were consuming more than they earned. Only after age 65 did they begin to look to inter-generational transfers as a resource. By age 75, net transfers to the elderly amounted to about $14,000 per year, increasing steadily to reach $30,000 for those 90 and older. At no age in the United States are net transfers to the elderly as large as asset-based reallocations.

However, net private transfers to the elderly are negative at every age. Even those 90 and older are giving about $3,000 more per year—not including bequests—to their children than they are receiving. Thus, the elderly are relying on net public transfers, which rise to $33,400 for those 90 and older.

How do public transfers to seniors compare to transfers to children? Per capita transfers depend on age. Public transfers to preschool children in the United States were between $7,000 and $8,000, and such transfers were between $17,000 and $18,000 for school-age children (ages 5–18). Net public transfers to the elderly were $16,900 at age 75 and $29,300 by age 85. On a per capita basis, then, net public transfers to older seniors exceeded net public transfers to school-age children—more for health than for education.

The aggregate features of the generational economy depend on popula-tion age structure in addition to the per capita values. The 0–24-year-old population was about two and half times the 65 and older population in 2011: 101 million versus 41 million. The total U.S. life-cycle deficit for children and the elderly combined was almost $5 trillion in 2011, more than 53 percent of total labor income (see Table 7-1). The child/youth defi-cit was about 60 percent of the total, while the deficit for older adults was 40 percent of the total. The life-cycle surplus of those between the ages of 25 and 64 was insufficient to fund the deficits of the young and the old. The shortfall was $3.4 trillion, equal to 37 percent of total U.S. labor income (Table 7-1). That portion of the deficit was funded by asset-based realloca-tions—asset income less saving.

TABLE 7-1 Summary National Transfer Account, United States, 2011

| | Life-Cycle Components | | | Reallocations | | | | |
| | | | | Net Transfers | | Asset-based Reallocations | | |
	Consumption	Labor Income	Life-Cycle Deficit	Public	Private	Public	Private	Total
Per Capita Flows (US$ 1000s)								
0–24	34.1	4.0	30.1	13.4	14.1	0.7	1.9	30.1
25–64	40.7	49.8	–9.1	–12.2	–8.4	4.7	6.7	–9.1
65+	58.7	12.0	46.7	15.9	–2.6	3.8	29.6	46.7
All ages	40.8	29.7	11.0	–0.2	–0.3	3.3	8.2	11.0
Aggregate Flows (US$ billions)								
0–24	3433	403	3030	1346	1417	74	193	3030
25–64	6842	8373	–1531	–2055	–1406	797	1133	–1531
65+	2429	497	1933	658	–108	159	1224	1933
All ages	12705	9273	3432	–52	–97	1030	2550	3432
Aggregate Flows (percentage of total labor income)								
0–24	37.0	4.3	32.7	14.5	15.3	0.8	2.1	32.7
25–64	73.8	90.3	–16.5	–22.2	–15.2	8.6	12.2	–16.5
65+	26.2	5.4	20.8	7.1	–1.2	1.7	13.2	20.8
All ages	137.0	100.0	37.0	–0.6	–1.0	11.1	27.5	37.0

NOTES: See Figure 7-1. Aggregate net transfers to the young deficit ages were much larger than aggregate net transfers to old deficit ages. Net transfers to those 0 to 24 years of age totaled $2.8 trillion (30% of total labor income), as compared with net transfers to the old deficit ages totaling only $0.6 trillion (5.9% of total labor income). Net public transfers to these young totaled $1.3 trillion (14.5% of total labor income) as compared with $0.7 trillion (7.1% of total labor income) to the 65 and older group.

COMPARATIVE FINDINGS

Aging is a global phenomenon, with every country in the world except Niger and Equatorial Guinea expected to have an older population in 2020 than in 2015 (*UN 2017*). However, the extent and pace of aging vary enormously by country, particularly when account is taken of variation across countries in the economic roles of older adults. In countries where the gaps between per capita labor income and per capita consumption are low among seniors, aging will be much less disruptive than in countries where the gaps are large. Moreover, countries vary greatly in the extent to which they rely on intergenerational transfers to fill those gaps. For those that rely heavily on intergenerational transfers, aging will be much more disruptive than in countries where seniors are relying on assets to fund their old-age needs.

Aging from an Economic Perspective: The Old-Age Gap

Many measures of aging, such as the old-age dependency ratio (OADR), rely on a stylized representation of the life cycle that ignores labor income of older adults and ignores the substantial variation in consumption with age. In the analysis presented here, the old-age deficit relative to labor income, denoted "GAP ratio," is used to capture the resource needs of the elderly, those 65 and older, relative to the resources available from all who work irrespective of their age. The GAP ratio is not a measure of dependency because old-age needs are met by relying on age reallocations: intergenerational transfers and asset-based reallocations. In the simple consumption loan economy of Samuelson, the life-cycle deficit would equal the net transfers required to support older adults. In the simple life-cycle saving economy of Modigliani and colleagues, the life-cycle deficit would equal the flows required to fund old-age needs relying exclusively on assets (asset income and dis-saving; see, for example, Modigliani and Brumberg, 1954).

The GAP ratio is calculated as follows:

$$GAP = \frac{\sum_{x=65}^{\omega}\left(c(x)-y^{l}(x)\right)N(x)}{\sum_{x=0}^{\omega}y^{l}(x)N(x)}$$

(1)

$c(x)$ = per capita consumption at age x

$y^{l}(x)$ = per capita labor income at age x

$N(x)$ = population of age x

GAP is constructed using population by age (*UN 2017*) and per capita consumption and labor income profiles based on NTA estimates available for 119 countries (Mason et al., 2016).

In 2015 the estimated GAP ratio for all countries combined was 11.5 percent of total labor income.[3]

The GAP ratio is closely related to the OADR. For the sake of illustration, suppose that (a) only those 20 to 64 had labor income and (b) the average consumption of those 65 and older was equal to the average labor income of those 20 to 64. In this instance, the GAP ratio would equal the OADR. In general, neither of these conditions hold because seniors contribute to labor income and seniors consume less than the average labor income of those 20 to 64. Thus, the OADR for 2015 of 16.3 percent was substantially overstated as compared with the GAP ratio of 11.5 percent. From an economic perspective, aging was a less disruptive force in 2015 than implied by the OADR.

The GAP ratio is very small in low-income countries because seniors have relatively high labor income and relatively low consumption. In 2015, the GAP ratio for these countries was only about one-third of the OADR: 3.0 percent as a compared with 8.7 percent. For middle-income countries, the GAP ratio was a little more than half of the OADR. For high-income countries, the GAP ratio was about three-quarters of the OADR: 19.7 percent versus 25.6 percent. From an economic perspective, rather than a purely demographic perspective, aging is an even more severe effect in high-income countries than it is in low-income countries.

Recently, labor income has increased at older ages in many high-income countries. But old-age consumption in the United States has increased even more than labor income, and hence the GAP ratio has continued to rise relative to the OADR.

The life-cycle patterns in high-income countries are reinforcing the effects of aging.

The GAP ratio varies considerably among the high-income countries. In 2 countries, Japan and Greece, the GAP ratio was more than one-third of total labor income; in 16 countries it was less than 20 percent of total labor income (see Figure 7-2). Except for Japan, the highest ratios are found in Europe. Lower GAP ratios are found in the Americas, Australia and New Zealand, and East Asia.

----

[3]Simple average based on 119 countries.

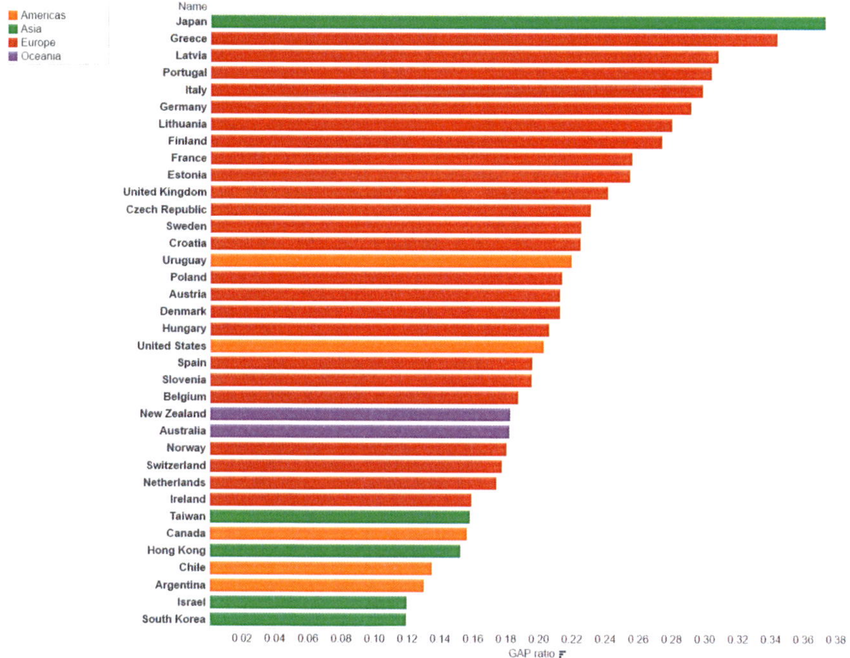

FIGURE 7-2 GAP ratio, 2015, selected high-income countries.
NOTES: A few small countries have not been included.

Intergenerational Transfers

A large GAP ratio represents a high potential demand for intergenerational transfers to seniors. However, as explained above, the old-age deficit may be funded by relying on assets. Moreover, countries may differ considerably in the extent to which they rely on public transfers rather than private, familial-based transfers. Using the most recently available data for 29 countries, we see extraordinary diversity in how countries are currently meeting the needs of their older populations.

Figure 7-3 shows the shares of the life-cycle deficit funded by public transfers, private transfers, and asset-based reallocations, based on the most recent estimate for each country. Before turning to the results, however, a word about interpreting the triangle graph might be helpful. A country located at any of the three vertices is relying exclusively on that source of funding. The Philippines (PH) and India (IN), for example, are relying almost entirely on asset-based reallocations while Hungary (HU) is relying almost exclusively on public transfers. No country in our dataset

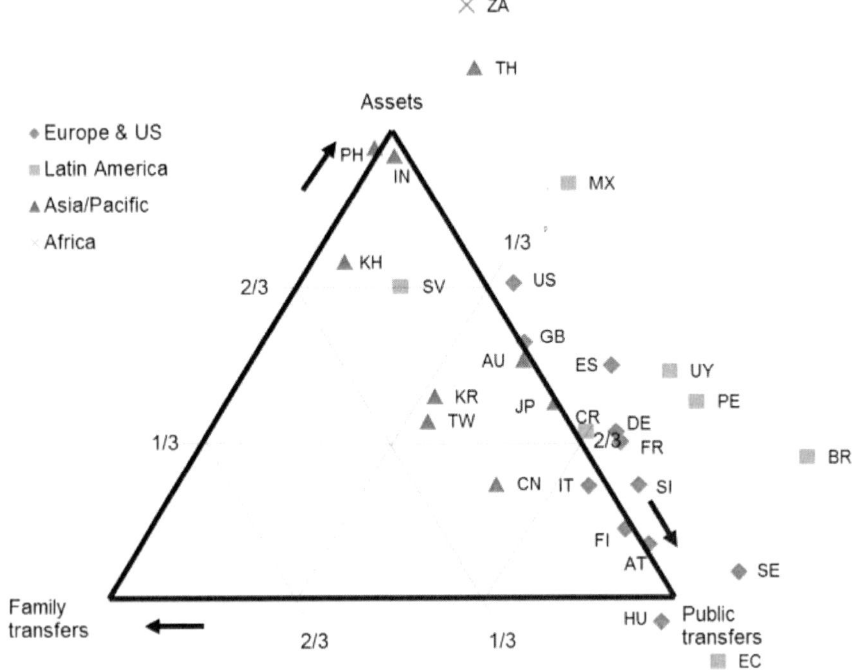

FIGURE 7-3 Funding the life-cycle deficit for those 65 and older. Asset-based reallocations, net public transfers, and net private transfers as a proportion of the life-cycle deficit.

NOTES: Country codes and values for the three sources of funding are shown in Table 7-2. Values for Indonesia (not shown): asset-based reallocations are 146 percent of the life-cycle deficit, net public transfers are 2 percent, and net private transfers are 48 percent.

is relying exclusively on private transfers. Countries located along any of the triangle's sides are relying exclusively on two sources of funding and not a third. For example, net private transfers to the elderly are zero in the United Kingdom (GB); they rely on a combination of public transfers and asset-based reallocations. At the intersection of the "1/3 gridlines" at the center of the triangle, the life-cycle deficit is funded equally from the three potential sources. Only South Korea (KR) and Taiwan (TW) have support systems that are relatively balanced in this way. There are many countries where net private transfers to older adults are negative, in other words the elderly are giving more to their children than they are receiving. Values can be read by extending gridlines beyond the triangle. In Mexico (MX), for example, public transfers are about one-third of the life-cycle deficit of the elderly. Values and country codes are shown in Table 7-2, which provides estimates of the age reallocations that funded the life-cycle deficit of those 60 and older and 65 and older. The latter estimates were used for Figure 7-3.

The importance of public transfers in the old-age support system varies greatly around the world. The key tradeoff is between asset-based reallocations and net public transfers. In countries where the elderly are relying more on net public transfers to fund their life-cycle deficit, they are relying less on asset-based reallocations. An increase in the public transfer share by one percentage point is associated with a 0.9 percentage point decline in the share funded by asset-based reallocations.

Three groups can be distinguished along the public transfer–asset-based reallocation axis in Figure 7-3. Public transfers dominate in most continental European and Latin American countries. Except for Spain and El Salvador, net public transfers fund at least two-thirds of the life-cycle deficit in this group. In four of these countries—Brazil, Ecuador, Hungary, and Sweden—net public transfers to the elderly exceed the life-cycle deficit.

Public transfers play a significant but more moderate role in East Asia (China, South Korea, Taiwan, and Japan), in Anglo-American countries (Australia, the United States, and the United Kingdom), and in Spain and Mexico. For elderly in these countries, asset-based reallocations also play an important role, funding between one-third and two-thirds of the life-cycle deficit. Mexico, with much heavier reliance on assets and less on the family, and China, with much less reliance on assets and more on family, are exceptions to this generalization.

In a third group, consisting mostly of middle- or low-income countries, the elderly depend heavily on asset-based reallocations and lightly on net public transfers. In most of these countries, the elderly are paying as much in taxes as they are receiving in benefits. Net public transfers are close to zero in Cambodia, India, Indonesia, the Philippines, South Africa, and Thailand.

Net public transfers to the elderly fund 65 percent or more of their life-cycle deficit in 8 of 10 European countries and 6 of 8 countries in Latin America.

Net public transfers fund between one-third and two-thirds of the life-cycle deficit in Anglo-American and East-Asian countries.

Net public transfers to the elderly are very low in lower-income countries—less than one-third of the life-cycle deficit and often close to zero.

TABLE 7-2 Reallocations as a Share of the Life-Cycle Deficit, Ages 60 and Older and 65 and Older

Country	Code	Year	60 and Older			65 and Older		
			Public Transfers	Private Transfers	Asset-Based Reallocations	Public Transfers	Private Transfers	Asset-Based Reallocations
Low Transfer Group			0.01	−0.24	1.23	0.05	−0.07	1.02
Cambodia	KH	2009	0.06	0.22	0.71	0.06	0.22	0.72
El Salvador	SV	2010	0.16	0.04	0.79	0.18	0.15	0.67
India	IN	2004	0.02	−0.14	1.11	0.03	0.02	0.95
Indonesia	ID	2005	0.00	−0.79	1.79	0.02	−0.48	1.46
Philippines	PH	1999	−0.09	−0.27	1.36	−0.01	0.05	0.96
South Africa	ZA	2005	−0.13	−0.40	1.53	0.00	−0.26	1.27
Thailand	TH	2011	0.03	−0.34	1.31	0.08	−0.22	1.13
Balanced Group			0.43	0.13	0.44	0.46	0.17	0.37
China	CN	2007	0.57	0.17	0.26	0.56	0.20	0.25
Japan	JP	2004	0.52	−0.03	0.51	0.57	0.01	0.42
South Korea	KR	2000	0.36	0.08	0.56	0.36	0.21	0.43
Taiwan	TW	2010	0.27	0.29	0.44	0.35	0.28	0.38
Partially Balanced Group			0.40	−0.12	0.72	0.46	−0.08	0.62
Australia	AU	2010	0.40	−0.01	0.61	0.47	0.02	0.51
Mexico	MX	2004	0.33	−0.41	1.08	0.37	−0.25	0.89
Spain	ES	2000	0.59	−0.10	0.51	0.63	−0.13	0.50
United Kingdom	GB	2007	0.38	0.00	0.61	0.46	0.00	0.55
United States	US	2011	0.28	−0.07	0.80	0.37	−0.05	0.68

High Public Transfer Group			0.84	−0.13	0.28	0.86	−0.08	0.22
Austria	AT	2010	0.85	0.00	0.15	0.89	−0.01	0.12
Brazil	BR	1996	1.06	−0.52	0.46	1.08	−0.38	0.30
Costa Rica	CR	2004	0.66	−0.12	0.46	0.66	−0.02	0.36
Ecuador	EC	2011	1.18	−0.16	−0.02	1.14	0.00	−0.13
Finland	FI	2006	0.77	0.02	0.21	0.83	0.02	0.15
France	FR	2011	0.70	−0.09	0.39	0.73	−0.07	0.34
Germany	DE	2003	0.66	−0.07	0.42	0.71	−0.07	0.36
Hungary	HU	2005	1.04	0.07	−0.11	0.99	0.05	−0.05
Italy	IT	2008	0.75	−0.06	0.30	0.81	−0.05	0.24
Peru	PE	2007	0.83	−0.37	0.54	0.82	−0.24	0.42
Slovenia	SI	2010	0.70	0.04	0.26	0.72	0.04	0.24
Sweden	SE	2006	1.08	−0.20	0.11	1.08	−0.13	0.06
Uruguay	UY	2006	0.62	−0.30	0.51	0.66	−0.21	0.49

NOTE: Group values are simple averages of group members.
SOURCES: Data from National Transfer Accounts; see www.ntaccounts.org. Also see Lee and Mason (2011), United Nations Population Division (2013).

Private/familial transfers play a secondary role in the old-age support system. In no case are net private transfers to those 65 and older more than one-third of their life-cycle deficit. To the extent that the elderly do rely on private transfers, region rather than country income appears to play a significant role. The countries with net private transfers to the elderly are found in East and Southeast Asia (Cambodia, China, South Korea, and Taiwan). The exception to this generalization is El Salvador.

In a number of Latin American countries, those 65 and older have net negative private transfers. They are contributing more to their children than they are receiving. In three of the countries, net public transfers to the elderly are very substantial: more than two-thirds of the life-cycle deficit in Uruguay and Peru, and more than the life-cycle deficit in Brazil. So this Latin American pattern may reflect an altruistic response of the elderly to the large public transfers they receive. This behavior is in line with the idea that heads of dynastic families formulate an idea of appropriate income sharing across the generations, and use private transfers to offset government taxes and transfers that distort that distribution (this is one interpretation of "Ricardian equivalence"; see Barro, 1974).

In four other countries, the elderly make relatively large downward transfers to younger generations in the absence of substantial net public transfers: Indonesia, Mexico, South Africa, and Thailand. The situation in Thailand is a very recent phenomenon. In the early 2000s, net public transfers to the elderly were very modest, while net private transfers to the elderly were equal to about one-third of the life-cycle deficit.

For many countries, net private transfers to the elderly are small. This includes Western countries (Australia, Europe, and the United States), some Latin American countries (Costa Rica and Ecuador), and several Asian countries (India, Japan, and Philippines). In Japan and many other countries, net private transfers do vary with age, turning positive for the oldest old.

Only in Asia, with minor exception, do the elderly rely on net private transfers to meet their old-age needs. Even there, net private transfers are less than one-third of the old-age deficit.

In three of the six Latin American countries where net public transfers to the elderly are very large, downward familial transfers are substantial.

The evidence for a tradeoff between public and private transfers is limited. In three Latin America countries (Brazil, Peru, and Uruguay), very substantial net public transfers to the elderly are offset by substantial downward transfers. Likewise, in four Asian countries (Cambodia, China, South Korea, and Taiwan), lower public transfers are accompanied by higher private transfers, suggesting the possibility of a tradeoff between the two. However, in many countries at varying levels of economic development and in different regions of the world, familial transfers are small, with no apparent connection to public transfers.

FUTURE TRENDS AND POLICY RESPONSES

We cannot be sure how the NTA age profiles will change in the future. In many OECD countries, the age at retirement has been rising over the last two decades, and public pension systems are being reformed in various ways. Meanwhile, cultural values and expectations related to familial support of the elderly are also changing. However, if current age patterns of consumption and labor income were to remain unchanged, population aging over the next 50 years would lead to a very substantial increase in the old-age deficit—particularly, but by no means exclusively, in high-income countries. The first round of effects of higher deficits would be on the old-age support systems comprised of public and private transfers and asset-based reallocations. Given the prevailing nature of old-age support systems, public transfer programs would experience the greatest pressures. This would particularly be true in continental Europe and Latin America, where net public transfers to the elderly as a share of total labor income are projected to double from already high levels. In another important group of aging societies, Anglo-American countries and East Asian countries, net public transfers would increase substantially but would not approach the levels found in Europe and Latin America.

In principle, private transfer systems could come under the same kind of pressure as public transfer systems. But only in East Asia do we see a substantial increase in net private transfers to the elderly. Even there, net public transfers are projected to be more than twice as important as net private transfers over the coming decades. However, it should be kept in mind that the public transfer burden is shared across all taxpayers, whereas the private transfer burden is not and may be quite substantial for those who have surviving, needy aging parents.

Aging has very little projected effect on asset-based reallocations in European and Latin American countries because they currently depend so little on assets to fund their retirement. In other countries—Anglo-American countries and East Asian countries—aging would lead to a substantial increase in asset-based reallocations.

Old-Age Deficit

Aging will be quite substantial, as measured by the projected GAP ratio, over the next 50 years in both high- and medium-income countries (see Figure 7-4). The GAP ratio is projected to rise in high-income countries from about 20 percent of total labor income in 2017 to 42 percent in 2065. The pace of aging is particularly rapid during the next two decades. The average GAP ratio is lower in upper-middle-income countries, but the increase is very substantial, rising from 8 percent of total labor income in 2017 to 24 percent in 2065. The change is similar in the lower-middle-income countries, but we see no increase for several decades in the low-income country group. The GAP ratio there is under 4 percent until 2049 and then rises slowly to reach 6 percent of total labor income in 2065.

Aging and the Old-Age Support System

The projected trend in public and private transfers to the elderly, along with asset-based reallocations, depends on the extent of aging as captured by the GAP ratio and the support system that prevails in each country. As shown in Figure 7-3, above, the most important variation across countries is in the extent to which they rely on public transfers versus asset-based reallocations. The projections distinguish four groups: (1) countries, mostly low-income countries, that rely lightly on intergenerational transfers and heavily on asset-based reallocations; (2) countries, mostly East Asian, relying on a full complement of mechanisms: public transfers, asset-based

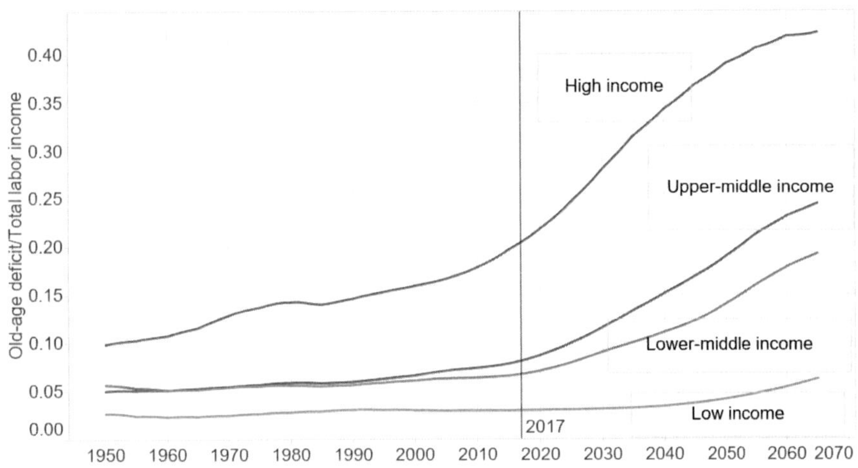

FIGURE 7-4 Projected GAP ratio, 1950 to 2065, by country income group.
NOTES: Countries are classified based on income group in 2016, using the World Bank classification scheme.
SOURCE: Based on medium variant population projection from *UN 2017* and fixed NTA age profiles of consumption and labor income for 188 countries.

reallocations, and family transfers; (3) countries, mostly Anglo-American, with a more balanced reliance on public transfers and asset-based reallocations but little reliance on private transfers; and (4) countries, mostly in the Caribbean, Europe, and Latin America, that rely heavily on public transfers (see Figure 7-5).

For the low-transfer countries, aging has had little impact in the past and only asset-based reallocations are projected to increase in the future, rising from roughly 5 percent of total labor income currently to 20 percent

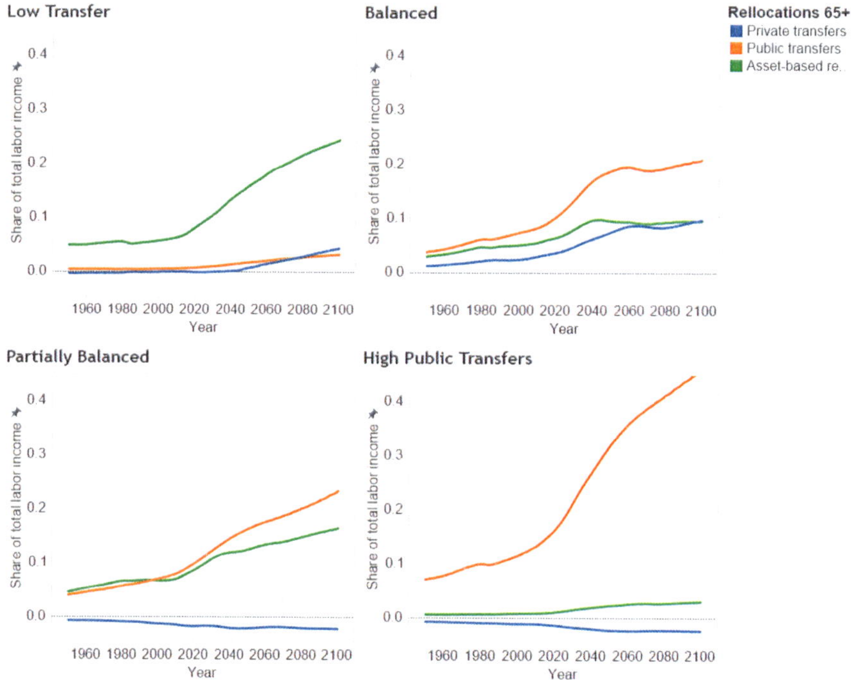

FIGURE 7-5 Projected reallocations to adults 65 and older as a share of total labor income, four reallocation groups (see Figure 7-3 and accompanying text).
NOTES: Low-transfer group consists of Cambodia, El Salvador, India, Indonesia, Philippines, South Africa, and Thailand. Balanced group consists of China, Japan, South Korea, and Taiwan. Partially balanced group consists of Australia, Mexico, Spain, the United Kingdom, and the United States. High-public-transfers group consists of Austria, Brazil, Costa Rica, Ecuador, Finland, France, Germany, Hungary, Italy, Peru, Slovenia, Sweden, and Uruguay.
SOURCE: Calculations (by the authors) use the medium variant of the population projections from *UN 2017* and NTA age profiles of public transfers, private transfers, and asset-based reallocations.

of total labor income in 2065. The share of asset-based reallocations is substantially higher than in other country groups, even though the extent of aging is much less in the low-transfer countries.

The balanced country group is projected to experience a substantial increase in net public transfers to those 65 and older, with public transfers as a share of total labor income increasing from about 5 percent in 1950 to over 20 percent in 2065. A distinctive feature of the balanced group is that private transfers rise substantially between now, at 1.6 percent of total labor income, and 2065, at 9.1 percent of total labor income. This occurs because the oldest old are much more dependent on familial transfers than the youngest old. Asset-based reallocations also increase in their importance in the balanced countries but do not quite reach 10 percent of total labor income in 2065.

The projected trends in public transfers and asset-based reallocations in the partially balanced group are similar to the trends for the balanced group, although by 2065 public transfers are lower by about 3 percentage points and asset-based reallocations higher by about 5 percentage points in the partially balanced group. Private transfers to the elderly remain negative throughout the projection period but trend slightly downward.

For the high-public-transfer countries, net public transfers to the elderly are projected to increase sharply, doubling from 19 percent of total labor income in 2017 to 39 percent of total labor income in 2065. For this country group, the projected increase in asset-based reallocations is small, rising from 1.8 to 3.0 percent of total income between 2017 and 2065. Net private transfers are projected to remain negative, trending downward in a fashion very similar to that found in the partially balanced group.

Fiscal Effects and Public Policy

If current age-specific benefit levels were to continue, public spending on old-age needs would grow quite rapidly, particularly over the next few decades, in both high- and middle-income countries. The share of national income devoted to old-age transfers in many European and Latin American countries would reach especially high levels. These undeniable realities have led to a broad consensus that current programs are not sustainable and that public-sector reform is critical (De Nardi et al., 1999; Feldstein, 2006). Adding further to the difficulties is the precarious state of public finances in many countries owing, in part, to the 2008 financial crisis (Holzmann, 2014).

The severity of a coming fiscal crisis will depend in large part on the overall health of the economy under the influence of aging, slowing labor force growth, and other factors that are not heavily influenced by demographic change (National Research Council, 2012). The specter of secular stagnation represents a pessimistic perspective on long-term prospects, but there is considerable disagreement on key issues (Keynes, 1937; Hansen, 1939; Gordon, 2015; Summers, 2015; Ito, 2016). The impact of age structure on job growth could be offset to some extent by expansive macroeconomic policy leading to higher job growth, higher female participation, and greater participation among young and old workers. Productivity gains, including those attributable to greater human capital investment, could offset the decline in the number of workers. These factors could boost revenue growth and support a larger public-sector role in the old-age support system. Trends in interest rates will have a more mixed impact. Low interest rates, if they continue, will benefit governments with high public debt but will hurt seniors expected to fund a larger share of their old-age needs relying on pensions and other private assets (National Research Council, 2012).

The economic hallmarks of aging at the individual level are the sharp decline in labor income and the rise in health care spending. These features of the life cycle figure prominently in policy formulations directed at curtailing the growth of public transfers to the elderly. A source of optimism is that improvements in health will alter the life cycle by reducing growth in health care spending and facilitating a longer work life (Milligan and Wise, 2012; Coile et al., 2017). This gives rise to two important issues. The first is that improvements in health status are far from certain. In the United States, for example, gains in health status appear to have stalled in recent years and the obesity epidemic raises alarms about the future (Martin et al., 2010; Freedman et al., 2013; see also the chapter by V. Freedman in this volume).

Second, history suggests that improvements in health status cannot be counted on to produce marked changes in the life cycle in the absence of effective policy. Recently, age at retirement in the United States and many other OECD countries has trended upward (see the article by C. Coile in this volume). Before this recent reversal, however, the retirement age was trending downward for a long period (Costa, 1998; De Nardi et al., 1999) and health care spending trended upward (European Policy Committee and European Commission, 2006; Feldstein, 2006; Ogawa et al., 2007), despite steady declines in mortality rates and improvements in health.

The way forward is clearest on the labor side. Improvements in health mean that people can work longer. If older workers remain in the labor force, evidence strongly suggests that young workers will not be adversely affected. Relatively straightforward policies, raising or eliminating the retirement age and reducing the incentives for early retirement created by high effective tax on labor income for older workers, will be effective (Gruber and Wise, 1999).

Health reform is exceedingly complex and contentious and cannot be addressed in any detail here.

Four important considerations are critical in efforts to moderate the growth of public transfers to the elderly. First, public transfers have profound distributional effects. They have helped to reduce poverty among the elderly, overall and relative to other age groups. However, public pension programs in the United States and possibly other countries are regressive because low-income individuals have much shorter life spans (National Academies of Sciences, Engineering, and Medicine, 2015). Second, public programs play an essential role in mediating the high risks faced by the elderly. Market-based alternatives such as lifetime annuities and long-term care insurance have not been adequate alternatives to public programs. Third, many individuals are not prepared to shoulder greater responsibility for the complex challenges of providing for old-age needs (Mitchell and Moore, 1998; Scholz et al., 2006). Finally, political uncertainty in some countries damages efforts by individuals and firms to play an essential role in meeting old-age needs.

Future Needs

In the past, analysis of the linkages between demographic changes and the macroeconomy has been constrained by a gap in national statistical systems. Demographic data are organized around the individual, whereas national accounts are organized around firms, households, and governments. This mismatch between demographic and economic data undermines efforts to analyze the economic effects of the most important demographic changes occurring in countries at all levels of development and at different stages of the demographic transition. Some of the most basic economic data about the elderly are not available.

National Transfer Accounts, used extensively in this paper, were developed to improve the linkages between demographic and macroeconomic data. The value of this approach is demonstrated by the widespread interest in constructing NTA. Currently, NTA are being constructed for more than 90 countries.

The construction of NTA is being carried out by country teams based in universities, think tanks, or government agencies, with coordination provided by an informal network supported through competitive research grants. However, the construction and dissemination of national statistical information is properly the responsibility of national and regional statistical agencies. Some national statistical agencies are exploring the possibility of incorporating NTA into their national statistical systems. Several U.N. agencies, notably the U.N. Population Fund, the U.N. Population Division, and the U.N. Development Program, have been actively involved in the development and dissemination of NTA. However, it is essential that the construction of NTA be incorporated into official statistical systems at the national, regional, or global level to ensure that this important source of information is broadly available on an ongoing basis.

CONCLUSIONS

Intergenerational transfer systems are critical to the functioning of all societies. They channel resources to children, providing for their material needs and, with a lag, influencing their productivity as adults. And they channel resources to the elderly, with profound implications for their health, their economic security, and other essential features of their lives.

As population aging occurs, old-age intergenerational transfer systems will become both more important and more difficult to sustain. Aging, however, is not a one-size-fits-all problem. Many countries in East and Southeast Asia and Southern and Eastern Europe can expect very rapid aging due to their low rates of fertility. Many countries in Europe and Latin America will face much greater imbalances in their old-age support systems because those public systems are so large. Elsewhere in the world, the United States included, aging is expected to be more moderate with more slowly shifting intergenerational transfer systems.

Public transfers are much more important to the elderly than familial transfers except in a few countries, mostly in East Asia. Consequently it is usually the public transfer systems that are particularly vulnerable to population aging. Even outside Europe and Latin America, the share of national resources needed to support old-age systems would grow substantially in the absence of significant reform.

A critical issue is whether aging will lead to economic stagnation. There is widespread agreement that demographic change will represent a significant headwind for high-income economies for some time. Slower growth of the working-age population will almost surely translate into slower growth in gross domestic product (GDP). It is possible, of course, that other factors could outweigh demographic ones. The impact of aging on per capita income and per capita consumption, in particular, is less certain because of the effects of population aging on human and physical capital accumulation.

The policy responses are likely to prove critical. Labor market and pension reforms are particularly appealing. If people have longer, healthier lives, they can surely work longer. And if people delay retirement, tax revenues can rise and spending on public pensions can be curtailed. Policy with regard to health care is also critical, particularly in the United States where health spending is such a high share of GDP and health policy is in such disarray.

It seems unlikely that private transfers will play a much greater role in the future, given their limited role today. Moving to a sustainable old-age support system will unquestionably require great reliance on other sources of support besides public or private transfers, notably increased labor at older ages and increased reliance by the elderly on asset income. Funded pensions and other forms of assets are likely to become increasingly important. Such a shift could have favorable growth effects by increasing capital accumulation and reducing tax rates, but it could also lead to other serious challenges, including declining rates of return, increased exposure to new sets of risks, and ignorance and vulnerability on the part of many elderly.

REFERENCES

Altonji, J.G., Hayashi, F., and Kotlikoff, L. (1992). Is the extended family altruistically linked? Direct evidence using micro data. *American Economic Review, 82*(5), 1177–1198.

Altonji, J.G., Hayashi F., and Kotlikoff, L. (2000). The effects of income and wealth on time and money transfers between parents and children. In A. Mason and G.Tapinos (Eds.), *Sharing the Wealth: Demographic Change and Economic Transfers between Generations* (pp. 306–357). Oxford, UK: Oxford University Press.

Arrondel, L., and Masson, A. (2006). Altruism, exchange or indirect reciprocity: What do the data on family transfers show? In S.-C. Kolm and J. M. Ythier (Eds.), *Handbook of the Economics of Giving, Altruism, and Reciprocity* (vol. 2, pp. 971–1053). Amsterdam: Elsevier.

Barro, R.J. (1974). Are government bonds net worth? *Journal of Political Economy, 82*(6), 1095–1117.

Becker, G. (1960). An economic analysis of fertility. In National Bureau of Economic Research, *Demographic and Economic Change in Developed Countries* (pp. 209–240). Princeton, NJ: Princeton University Press.

Becker, G. (1991). *A Treatise on the Family* (enlarged edition). Cambridge, MA: Harvard University Press.

Becker, G. (1993). Nobel lecture: The economic way of looking at behavior. *Journal of Political Economy, 101*(3), 385–403.

Becker, G.S., and Barro, R.J. (1988). A reformulation of the economic theory of fertility. *Quarterly Journal of Economics, 103*(1), 1–25.

Becker, G.S., and Murphy, K.M. (1988). The family and the state. *Journal of Law & Economics, 31*(April), 1–18.

Caldwell, J. (1982). The wealth flows theory of fertility decline. In C. Hohn and R. Mackensen (Eds.), *Determinants of Fertility Trends: Theories Re-examined* (pp. 169–188). Liege, Belgium: Ordina Editions.

Coile, C.C., Milligan, K.S., and Wise, D.A. (2017). Introduction. In D.A. Wise (Ed.), *The Capacity to Work at Older Ages* (pp. 1–33). Chicago and London: University of Chicago Press.

Costa, D.L. (1998). *The Evolution of Retirement: An American Economic History, 1880–1990*. Chicago: University of Chicago Press.

Cox, D. (1987). Motives for private income transfers. *Journal of Political Economy, 95*, 508–546.

Cutler, D.M., Poterba, J.M., Sheiner, L.M., and Summers, L.H. (1990). An aging society: Opportunity or challenge? *Brookings Papers on Economic Activity, 1990*(1), 1–56.

De Nardi, M., Imrohoroglu, S., and Sargent, T.J. (1999). Projected U.S. demographics and Social Security. *Review of Economic Dynamics, 2*(3), 575–615.

Diamond, P. (2004). Social Security. *American Economic Review, 94*(1), 1–24.

Elmendorf, D.W., and Sheiner, L.M. (2017). Federal budget policy with an aging population and persistently low interest rates. *Journal of Economic Perspectives, 31*(3), 175–194.

European Policy Committee and European Commission. (2006). *The Impact of Ageing on Public Expenditure: Projections for the EU25 Member States on Pensions, Health Care, Long-Term Care, Education and Unemployment Transfers (2004-2050).* Brussels: European Commission Directorate-General for Economic and Financial Affairs.

Feldstein, M. (2006). *The Effects of the Ageing European Population on Economic Growth and Budgets: Implications for Immigration and other Policies* (NBER Working Paper 12736). Cambridge, MA: National Bureau of Economic Research.

Feldstein, M., and Liebman, J.B. (2002). Social Security reform. In A. Auerbach and M. Feldstein (Eds.), *Handbook of Public Economics* (pp. 2245–2324). Amsterdam: Elsevier.

Freedman, V.A., Spillman, B.C., Andreski, P.M., Cornman, J.C., Crimmins, E.M., Kramarow, E., Lubitz, J., Martin, L.G., Merkin, S.S., Schoeni, R.F., et al. (2013). Trends in late-life activity limitations in the United States: An update from five national surveys. *Demography, 50*(2), 661–671.

Gordon, R.J. (2015). Secular stagnation: A supply-side view. *American Economic Review, Papers and Proceedings, 105*(5), 54–59.

Gruber, J., and Wise, D.A. (1999). *Social Security and Retirement around the World.* Chicago: University of Chicago Press.

Hansen, A.H. (1939). Economic progress and declining population growth. *American Economic Review, 29*(1), 1–15.

Holzmann, R. (2014). Global pension systems. In S. Harper and K. Hamblin (Eds.), *International Handbook on Ageing and Public Policy* (pp. 87–107). Cheltenham, UK, and Narthampton, MA: Edward Elgar.

Ito, T. (2016). *Japanization: Is it Endemic or Epidemic?* (NBER Working Paper 21954). Cambridge, MA: National Bureau of Economic Research.

Keynes, J.M. (1937). Some economic consequences of a declining population. *Eugenics Review, 29*(1), 13–17.

Kotlikoff, L.J., and Spivak, A. (1981). The family as an incomplete annuities market. *Journal of Political Economy, 89*(2), 372–391.

Lee, R. (2003). Demographic change, welfare, and intergenerational transfers: A global perspective. *Genus, 59*(3–4), 43–70.

Lee, R., and Mason, A. (Eds. and principal authors). (2011). *Population Aging and the Generational Economy: A Global Perspective.* Cheltenham, UK: Edward Elgar.

Lee, R., Donehower, G., and Miller, T. (2011). The changing shape of the economic lifecycle in the United States, 1960 to 2003. In R. Lee and A. Mason (Eds.), *Population Aging and the Generational Economy: A Global Perspective* (pp. 313–326). Cheltenham, UK, and Northampton, MA: Edward Elgar.

Lee, R., Mason, A., and Members of the NTA Network. (2014). Is low fertility really a problem? Population aging, dependency, and consumption. *Science 346*(6206): 229–234.

Leibenstein, H. (1972). An interpretation of the economic theory of fertility: Promising path or blind alley? *Journal of Economic Literature, 12*(2), 457–479.

Lindert, P. (2004). *Growing Public: Social Spending and Economic Growth Since the Eighteenth Century.* Cambridge, UK: Cambridge University Press.

Martin, L.G., Schoeni, R.F., and Andreski, P.M. (2010). Trends in health of older adults in the United States: Past, present, future. *Demography, 47*(Supplement), S17–S40.

Mason, A., Lee, R., and Jiang, J.X. (2016). Demographic dividend, human capital, and saving: Take it now or enjoy it later? *Journal of the Economics of Ageing, 7,* 106–122.

Milligan, K.S., and Wise, D.A. (2012). Introduction and summary. In D.A. Wise (Ed.), *Social Security Programs and Retirement Around the World: Historical Trends in Mortality and Health, Emloyment, and Disability Insurance Participation and Reforms* (pp. 1–39). Chicago: University of Chicago Press.

Mitchell, O.S., and Moore, J.F. (1998). Can Americans afford to retire? New evidence on retirement saving adequacy. *Journal of Risk and Insurance, 65*(3), 371–400.

Modigliani, F., and Brumberg, R. (1954). Utility analysis and the consumption function: An interpretation of cross-section data. In K.K. Kurihara (Ed.), *Post-Keynesian Economics.* New Brunswick, NJ: Rutgers University Press.

National Academies of Sciences, Engineering, and Medicine. (2015). *The Growing Gap in Life Expectancy by Income: Implications for Federal Programs and Policy Responses*: Washington, DC: The National Academies Press. doi: 10.17226/19015.

National Research Council. (2012). *Aging and the Macroeconomy: Longer-term Implications of an Older Population.* Washington, DC: The National Academies Press.

Ogawa, N., Mason, A., Maliki, Matsakura, R., and Nemoto K. (2007). Population aging and health care spending in Japan: Public and private sector responses. In R. Clark, A. Mason, and N. Ogawa (Eds.), *Population Aging, Intergenerational Transfers and the Macroeconomy* (pp. 192–223). Cheltenham, UK: Elgar Press.

Samuelson, P. (1958). An exact consumption loan model of interest with or without the social contrivance of money. *Journal of Political Economy, 66,* 467–482.

Sanderson, W., and Scherbov, S. (2010). Remeasuring aging. *Science, 329,* 1287–1288.

Scholz, J.K., Seshadri, A., and Khitatrakun, S. (2006). Are Americans Saving "optimally" for retirement? *Journal of Political Economy, 144*(4), 607–643.

Summers, L.H. (2014). Reflections on the "new secular stagnation hypothesis." In C. Teuligs and R. Baldwin (Eds.), *Secular Stagnation: Facts, Causes and Cures* (pp. 60–65). London: Centre for Economic Policy Research.

Summers, L.H. (2015). Demand side secular stagnation. *American Economic Review, Papers and Proceedings, 105*(5), 60–65.

Teuligs, C., and Baldwin, R. (Eds.). (2014). *Secular Stagnation: Facts, Causes and Cure.* London: Centre for Economic Policy Research.

United Nations Population Division. (2013). *National Transfer Accounts Manual: Measuring and Analysing the Generational Economy.* New York: United Nations.

United Nations Population Division. (2017). *World Population Prospects: The 2017 Revision.* New York: United Nations.

Willis, R.J. (1973). A new approcah to the economic theory of fertility behavior. *Journal of Political Economy, 81*(2 Part 2), S14–S64.

PART IV

Work and Retirement in the Older Population

8

The Demography of Retirement

Courtney Coile, Wellesley College

INTRODUCTION

Retirement refers both to the act of withdrawing from the workforce and to the period of life that follows this action. By either definition, retirement is central to any discussion of aging. Yet retirement only emerged as a distinct chapter of life during the 20th century—a "third act" that follows the childhood years during which education is acquired and the prime adult years during which people work and accumulate assets.

Longevity increases played a key role in this development. Life expectancy at age 65 in the United States, for example, rose from 11.9 years for men and 13.2 years for women in 1935, the year that Social Security was established, to 17.0 and 19.6 years in 2018, an increase of 5.1 and 6.4 years, respectively (Bell and Miller, 2005). The probability of living to age 65 rose substantially over this period as well.

The age of labor force withdrawal is the other factor that determines the length of retirement, and this too changed dramatically. In the past, it was typical to work at even the oldest ages; the labor force participation rate of U.S. men ages 65 and older exceeded 75 percent in 1880 (Costa, 1998). This rate declined continuously over the next century, falling to below 20 percent by 1990, a pattern also seen in France, Germany, and the United Kingdom. This trend, combined with longer lives, means that most workers today can expect to spend two decades in retirement, and those who end up being long-lived may be retired for three to four decades.

The retirement decision has long been of interest to analysts and policy makers alike. First, it is central to well-being; by working longer, an individual can accumulate more assets and has fewer years of retirement consumption to finance but also enjoys fewer years of leisure. For society as a whole, changes in the age of retirement affect taxes paid and transfers received, as well as the size of the labor force and the economy. As longevity increases tend to increase the share of societal resources going to the elderly, increases in the age of retirement can serve to counteract this trend.

In fact, there has been a strong trend toward later retirement for both men and women in the United States and around the world over the past several decades. Many factors may have contributed to this trend, including improvements in longevity and health, increases in education and sector shifts in the economy, and increasing labor force participation by women, which may induce husbands to work longer, due to the complementarity of leisure. Public and private pensions are also likely to have played a central role. Much as the increasing availability and generosity of public and private pensions helped to make earlier retirement possible over the course of the 20th century, changes to pensions in the past few decades that have raised retirement age and strengthened the financial incentives for work at older ages have encouraged people to work longer.

Not only is life's third act longer than in the past but the line between work and retirement is not always as distinct as suggested by this analogy. Workers often spend a period of time working part time, in self-employment, or at another job after leaving their career employer, or they may retire but subsequently re-enter the labor force. While analysts often abstract from this reality for simplicity and focus on labor force participation or employment, understanding the more complex realities of the retirement transition is necessary for designing retirement policy.

The trends of increasing longevity and longer work lives are in contrast with another trend in the United States, the rising frequency of labor force exit via the disability route before the standard age of retirement. While it may seem puzzling that these trends could coexist, one explanation is that disability insurance (DI) policy parameters, such as the stringency of medical screening, are critical determinants of the use of the disability route and may indeed be more important than health in explaining differences in the receipt of disability benefits across countries or over time. It may also be useful to look beyond population averages at trends in health and work by socioeconomic status (SES), to understand whether there are groups experiencing worsening health and economic opportunities that may be reflected in rising DI use. As public pensions continue to evolve in a way that both encourages and incorporates an expectation of longer work lives, it is important to assess the ability of different segments of the population to respond.

In this chapter, I first highlight key aspects of retirement behavior, including the trends in labor force participation, the complexity of the retirement transition, and the relationship between trends in disability and work. I then discuss findings from the retirement literature that help one to understand retirement decisions and to explain these trends. I conclude with some thoughts about the frontier of the retirement literature, including directions for future research. The analysis focuses on the United States but also offers some international context on these issues.

RETIREMENT PATTERNS AND TRENDS

Labor Force Participation

In the predecessor to this volume, Quinn and Burkhauser (1994) suggested that the trend toward earlier retirement for men in the United States may have stopped or even reversed. As seen in Figure 8-1, this analysis was prescient. For men ages 60 to 64, participation reached a trough of 53 percent in 1994 and has subsequently risen by 9 points, to 62 percent in 2016. For men ages 65 to 69, the trough occurred about a decade earlier, and participation has since risen by 13 points, to 37 percent. For men ages 55 to 59, participation fell by 4 points over this period, reaching a low of 77 percent in 2016.[1] This drop reflects a different labor market trend: declining participation among prime-age men.[2]

The trends for women, seen in Figure 8-2, show even larger increases in participation. From 1980 to 2016, participation rose by 17 points for women ages 55 to 59 and 60 to 64, reaching 66 and 50 percent, respectively. Participation among women ages 65 to 69 rose by 13 points, to 28 percent in 2016. Unlike the U shape in participation for older men, women's participation rose continuously over this period, reflecting rising participation by women of all ages. Goldin and Katz (2018) showed that the cohorts of women who are working longer at older ages had higher rates of participation throughout their life cycle; they found that cohort differences in work at older ages are largely a function of earlier changes in human capital accumulation, such as higher educational attainment and greater employment continuity.

The patterns in other developed economies are similar to those in the United States and are often larger in magnitude. Figure 8-3 displays

---

[1] The participation rate by age group may be affected by variation in the size of individual birth cohorts. For example, when there is a large cohort of 60-year-olds, the participation rate at ages 60 to 64 may rise because 60-year-olds work more than 64-year-olds. This concern is mitigated by focusing on the long-term trend in participation rather than short-term fluctuations.

[2] The Council of Economic Advisors (2016) documented this trend and explored supply- and demand-side factors that may have contributed to this decline. The authors concluded that the decline in real wages of less skilled workers is an important factor.

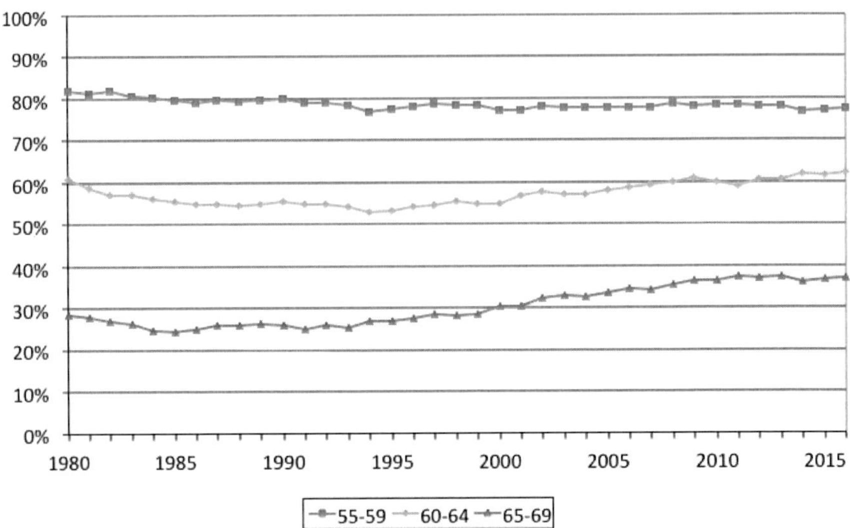

FIGURE 8-1 U.S. male labor force participation rate by age, 1980–2016.
SOURCE: Bureau of Labor Statistics series LNU01300189, LNU01300197, and LNU01300203.

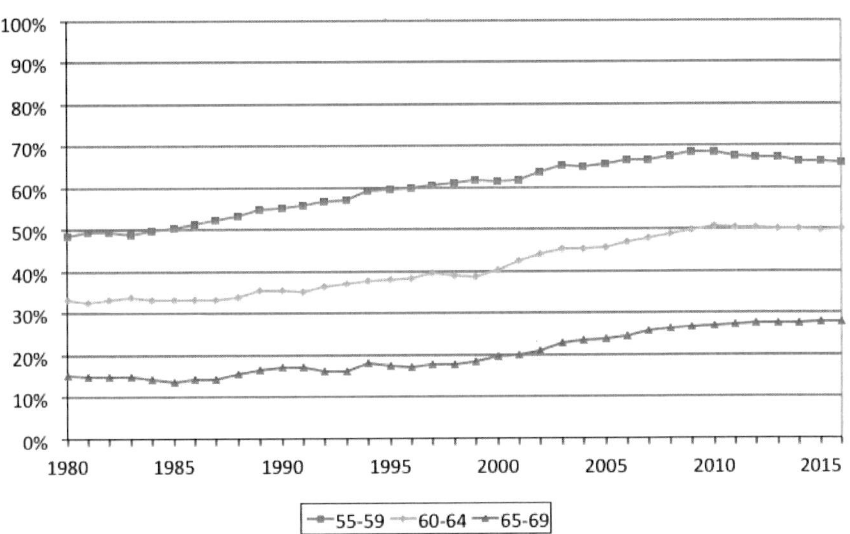

FIGURE 8-2 U.S. female labor force participation rate by age, 1980–2016.
SOURCE: Bureau of Labor Statistics Series LNU01300346, LNU01300352, and LNU01300358.

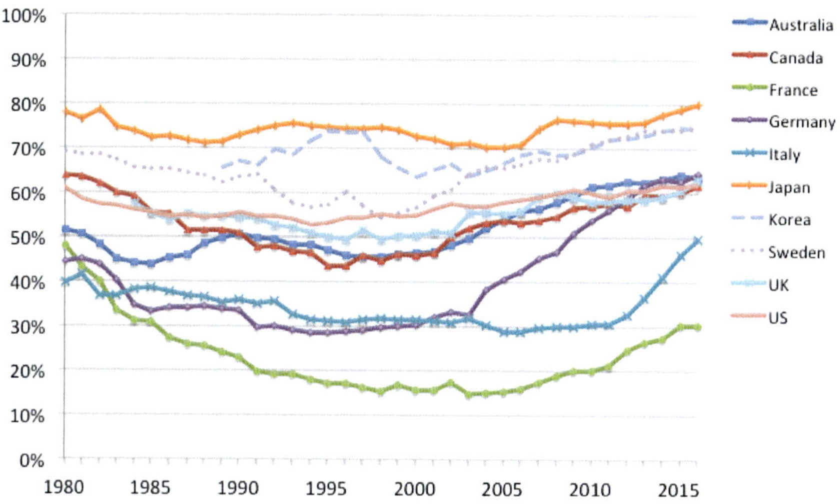

FIGURE 8-3 Labor force participation rate, men ages 60 to 64, by country and year.
SOURCE: OECD statistics, labor force status, by sex and age. Available: https://stats.oecd.org [April 2018].

the labor force participation rate for men ages 60 to 64 in selected countries from 1980 to the present. In all of the European countries (France, Germany, Italy, Sweden, and the United Kingdom) and in Australia and Canada as well, there is a U-shaped pattern in men's participation, with an increase of 14 to 21 percentage points from the trough to the 2016 value; Japan and Korea experienced an increase of 10 to 11 points. Despite similarities in trends, participation levels can vary substantially across similar countries. For instance, only 30 percent of men ages 60 to 64 in France were in the labor force in 2016, versus 65 percent in Germany and 75 percent in Sweden. Participation was highest in Japan, at 80 percent.

For older women, there have been large increases in participation in most countries, as seen in Figure 8-4. Many of the countries with the biggest changes are those where men's participation also rose substantially. Women's participation increased by 21 to 27 points in Canada, Italy, Sweden, and the United Kingdom, by 38 points in Australia, and by 44 points in Germany. Increases in the other developed economies have been smaller, at 8 to 17 points. Participation levels for women ages 60 to 64 in 2016 varied widely, from about 30 percent in France and Italy to 68 percent in Sweden. The gap in participation between men and women also varies across country, with older men being no more likely to work

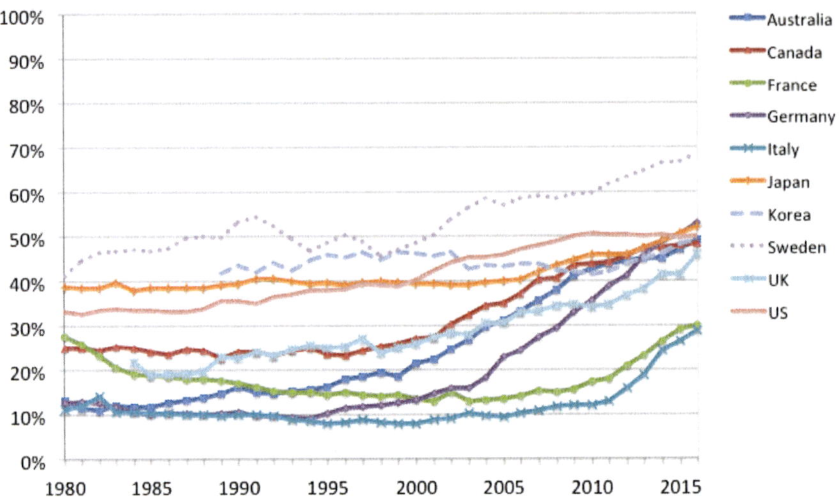

FIGURE 8-4 Labor force participation rate, women ages 60 to 64, by country and year.
SOURCE: OECD statistics, labor force status, by sex and age. Available: https://stats.oecd.org [April 2018].

than older women in France but about 15 percentage points more likely in most developed countries and more than 25 percentage points more likely in Japan and Korea.

The age pattern in retirement is also of interest. Most U.S. workers retire in their 60s; of those still working at age 60, about two-thirds of both men and women withdraw from the labor force by age 70. Retirement accelerates starting at age 60, with spikes in the retirement hazard (or probability of labor force exit at a given age, conditional on remaining in the labor force until that age) at ages 62 and 65. These spikes correspond to the traditional early and full retirement ages for Social Security and the Medicare eligibility age. Evidence suggests that these programs do contribute to the spikes. Burtless and Moffitt (1986) noted that the age-62 peak in retirement only emerged after the option of claiming benefits at 62 was introduced, and Mastrobuoni (2009) found that the rise in the Social Security full retirement age (FRA) has led to an increase in the average age of retirement that is half as large as that in the FRA. Gruber and Wise (1999) documented that the share of remaining workers who exit at the pension full retirement age is 60 percent or above in Belgium, France, Italy, the Netherlands, Spain, and the United Kingdom, far larger than the spike in the United States.

Labor force participation and retirement patterns differ substantially by education and race. Coile and Levine (2010) reported that the annual probability of retiring at ages 55 to 69 in the United States was a third or more lower for college graduates than for high school dropouts, leading to lower labor force participation rates at ages older than 55 for the less-educated. Flippen and Tienda (2000) noted that the employment rates for Black and Hispanic men ages 51 to 61 in 1992 were 15 and 8 points lower, respectively, than the rate for White men, while the rates for Black and Hispanic women were 2 and 10 points lower, respectively, than the rate for White women. Differences in labor supply of these groups at older ages could be driven by differences in longevity or in the enjoyment derived from work, among other factors. Bound et al. (1995) concluded that differences in health status can explain much of the Black versus White differences in labor force attachment and essentially all of the differences by education. Hayward et al. (1996) concurred that Blacks' lower participation rates are a function of disability but noted that due to their shorter life expectancy, Blacks spend more of their lives in the labor force than do Whites. They concluded that "retirement is more a White experience than a Black experience."

Indeed, a focus on labor force participation rates by chronological age ignores differences in life expectancy across racial and education groups and across birth cohorts. Groups that have a longer life expectancy at a given age, say age 65, may be expected to have higher labor force participation rates, reflecting the additional years of retirement consumption to be financed, as well as social norms about the share of adult life spent in work and retirement. Steuerle and Spiro (1999) calculated the labor force participation rate over time for a man with a constant life expectancy (as opposed to a constant chronological age). They found that the decline in their measure between 1940 and 1997 is about 15 percentage points greater than the decline in the traditional age-based measure.

In summary, labor force participation rates have risen for men and women over the past two decades, both in the United States and other developed economies. The pattern for men is a U shape, with the recent increase coming after a century of decline, whereas for women, participation rates have only increased. In the United States, most workers retire during their 60s, and the probability of retirement spikes at ages associated with Social Security and Medicare eligibility. Blacks, Hispanics, and those with less education have lower labor force participation at older ages than do their White and more-educated counterparts. Finally, focusing on participation at a given life expectancy rather than chronological age may alter perceptions of differences in participation over time or across demographic groups.

The Retirement Transition

Whereas researchers often focus on the labor force participation rate due to its ease of measurement, simplicity of interpretation, and longevity in survey data (Hayward et al., 1996), this measure does not capture the complexity of many retirement transitions. The traditional retirement transition is one in which a worker moves from full-time work for a career (or long-term) employer directly to full retirement. Yet many other paths are possible. First, workers may reduce hours but remain with the same employer, a practice known as "phased retirement." Second, workers may leave their career job for a transitional "bridge job" that may offer the opportunity to perform a different kind of work or to work fewer hours. Third, workers may switch from working for others to self-employment. Finally, an initial labor force exit may subsequently be followed by labor force re-entry or "unretirement."[3]

Collectively, the use of these other exit routes is quite high. Cahill et al. (2015) reported that among U.S. workers ages 51 to 56 who were working for a career employer in 1992, 4 in 10 had used a bridge job by 2010. About half of these bridge jobs were part-time jobs. Johnson et al. (2009) found that two-thirds of workers in their early 50s who moved to a new job before retiring also changed occupations. The most common career switch is from a managerial job into a sales or operator position. For those who change jobs, the new job typically features a lower hourly wage and is less likely to offer health insurance benefits, but it is also rated as having less stressful working conditions and higher worker satisfaction when compared to the old job.

Relative to the prevalence of bridge jobs, use of phased retirement is less common in the United States, with Cahill et al. (2015) finding that only 2 to 3 percent of workers reduced the hours on their career job by at least 20 percent over an 18-year period. Lack of access to phased retirement is one potential reason for the low utilization of this route. Hutchens (2010) found that while most white collar employers say that they permit phased retirement, employers are selective in providing employees with the opportunity to enter this arrangement, with older, high-performing workers more likely to be granted access.

---

[3]Other terms have also been used to describe these transitions. "Gradual retirement" is a generic term that refers to a gradual withdrawal from the labor force by any means that results in reduced work effort (Kantarci and Van Soest, 2008); this term could encompass phased retirement, bridge jobs, and transitions to self-employment. In a characterization related to the idea of unretirement, Mutchler et al. (1997, p. S4) distinguished between unidirectional "crisp" exits from the labor force and "blurred" transition patterns that "may include repeated moves in and out of the workforce, and may even include periods during which the roles of worker and retiree are held simultaneously;" they find that the latter is more common than the former.

Table 8-1 details the frequency of part-time work among older individuals in the United States. These values include part-time work on both career and bridge jobs. To allow for some comparison over time, averages are shown for the years 1980 to 1994 and 1995 to 2016, corresponding to the periods in which male labor force participation was falling and rising. For men, part-time work rises with age, with 5 percent of men ages 55 to 59 working part time in the more recent period, versus 10 percent of men ages 65 to 69. Values for women are higher, especially at younger ages: 13 percent of women ages 55 to 59 work part time.

It is also useful to consider the share of workers who are engaged in part-time work. This rises even more dramatically with age, with one-third of male workers and nearly half of female workers ages 65 to 69 working part time. There is no clear pattern of differences across the two time periods, as the share of individuals working part time rises while the share of workers doing so declines over time.

Comparable data for Europe are available from Kantarci and Van Soest (2008). In 2001, the share of workers ages 51 to 65 working part time averaged 9 percent for men and 42 percent for women in their sample of 14

TABLE 8-1 Part-Time Work and Self-Employment in the United States, 1980–2016 (in percentage)

	Part-Time Work			Part-Time Work as Share of All Work		
	55–59	60–64	65–69	55–59	60–64	65–69
Men, 1980–1994	4.3	6.2	10.0	5.7	11.7	39.2
Men, 1995–2016	5.4	7.5	9.9	7.2	13.4	31.5
Women, 1980–1994	13.0	10.5	8.0	25.7	31.5	53.8
Women, 1995–2016	12.7	12.3	10.3	20.3	27.5	44.8
	Self-Employment			Self-Employment as Share of All Work		
	55–59	60–64	65–69	55–59	60–64	65–69
Men, 1980–1994	13.8	11.6	8.1	18.3	22.0	31.8
Men, 1995–2016	14.6	12.9	9.6	19.7	23.1	30.3
Women, 1980–1994	4.9	3.4	2.2	9.7	10.3	14.8
Women, 1995–2016	6.8	5.8	3.9	10.9	13.0	16.9

NOTE: Part-time work is defined as working less than 35 hours per week.
SOURCE: Author's calculations from March Current Population Survey, 1980–2016. Data are weighed using person weights.

countries, with considerable variation across countries. This average value is the same as that for U.S. men and more than twice that for U.S. women. As in the United States, there is no clear trend over time. Partial retirement in Europe may be facilitated by the existence of partial pension schemes, which allow individuals to reduce work hours and draw a share of the full pension. Denmark, Finland, France, Germany, Spain, and Sweden all have, or have had, such schemes, and many other European countries make it possible for workers to combine work and pension receipt in some way (Reday-Mulvey, 2000). Kantarci and Van Soest (2008) noted that the relative lack of mobility in European labor markets, as compared to the U.S. market, may increase the appeal of phased retirement rather than a bridge job for those seeking part-time work.

For some, self-employment may offer yet another option for reducing labor force activity. Self-employment provides greater flexibility in hours, as well as greater autonomy and the potential to work a nonstandard schedule. Zissimopoulos and Karoly (2007) showed that the share of workers who are self-employed rises with age and estimated that this is primarily driven by net switching into self-employment at older ages, rather than by later retirement among the self-employed. Ramnath et al. (2017) found that the self-employment hazard rises at key Social Security eligibility ages and that transitions to self-employment are associated with declines in income (particularly at older ages) and hours worked, supporting the notion that self-employment can serve as a means of gradual retirement.

Table 8-1 reports the prevalence of self-employment by age and sex in the United States. In a reversal of the pattern for part-time work, self-employment is more common among men than women, with 15 percent of men and 7 percent of women ages 55 to 59 engaged in such work. The share of individuals who are self-employed falls with age, while the share of workers rises, reaching 30 percent of male workers and 17 percent of female workers at ages 65 to 69. There is a slight increase over time in the share of workers who are self-employed.

While treating labor force withdrawal as unidirectional may be convenient for analysts, it is fairly common for workers to re-enter the labor force after an initial exit. Maestas (2010) found that 24 percent of those who are not working for pay return to either part-time or full-time work within 6 years, while an additional 16 percent transition from part-time to full-time work. Interestingly, about four-fifths of those who unretire had anticipated making this transition; there is little evidence that people return to work due to negative financial shocks, but some indication that changes in leisure preferences may play a role. As with bridge jobs, the new jobs of those who re-enter often feature lower wages, fewer benefits, and a change of occupation, particularly from manufacturing and managerial or professional work into services, sales, and administrative support positions.

Overall, it is evident that many workers retire gradually, either by reducing hours on their current job, moving to a bridge job, or switching to self-employment; many also return to the labor force after an initial exit. Across all of these paths, it is typical for those who are still working at older ages to be in a different occupation, working fewer hours, and receiving lower pay and benefits as compared to their career job.

Disability and Work

The long-term trends toward increasing longevity and longer work lives run counter to another significant trend in health and work in the United States: the increasing prevalence of workers exiting the labor force due to disability. Disability and the receipt of DI benefits are distinct yet related concepts, both of which are relevant to this discussion.

While there is no universal definition of disability, it is generally understood to refer to having a physical or mental health condition that limits an individual's ability to work for pay. Given this broad definition, it is not surprising that identifying an ideal measure of disability prevalence is challenging. A self-report of a work-limiting disability is directly relevant to labor supply decisions and available in many surveys. However, responses may not be comparable across individuals and may be influenced by the availability of DI benefits or by the individual's work decision (Waidmann et al., 1995). This criticism is levied at self-reported measures more broadly, including health status, a widely used measure. Objective health measures, such as diagnoses of chronic diseases, skirt these issues but may be only imperfectly correlated with work ability (Bound, 1991). Comparisons over time may be complicated by changes in reported versus true prevalence or changes in the efficacy of treatment. Measures of functioning include self-reports of the ability to perform *activities of daily living* such as bathing and dressing, *instrumental activities of daily living* such as housework and cooking, and *physical tasks* such as walking and climbing stairs. These measures of functioning, as well as reports of pain and measurements of physical ability (for example, grip strength), complement other measures of disability but may be subject to some of the same concerns.

Early work on disability proposed several competing hypotheses about the implications of falling mortality rates for disability at older ages. The "compression of morbidity" theory posits that the age of disability onset will continue to rise as mortality declines reach a natural limit, leading the period of disability to be compressed into a shorter number of years at the end of life (Fries, 1980). By contrast, the "failure of success" view suggests that mortality rates will decline while the incidence of chronic diseases remains constant, resulting in individuals being disabled for a longer period of time (Gruenberg, 1977).[4] In the former scenario, workers who are living longer would have more years free of disability and might work longer as a result. In the latter, advances in life expectancy would not translate into increased capacity to work at older ages; indeed, the share of the cohort in poor health could be rising over time, if additional survivors are disproportionately drawn from the least healthy in the cohort.

The literature has not reached a consensus as to which view prevails. One reason for this uncertainty is the multiplicity of measures of disability and health, as discussed above. As Crimmins (2004) noted, measures do not necessarily all move in the same direction, at the same time, and equally for all age groups. Focusing on disease and mobility functioning, Crimmins and Beltrán-Sánchez (2010) found that the length of life with disease and mobility functioning loss increased between 1998 and 2008. By contrast, Cutler et al. (2014) defined disability in terms of impairments in activities of daily living and instrumental activities of daily living and concluded that disabled life expectancy shrank and disability-free life expectancy rose between 1991 and 2009. Crimmins (2004) reported that the health of older people improved along most dimensions in the preceding two decades.[5]

Relative to disability, DI receipt is easier to define and measure. Individuals who are disabled may be eligible to receive DI benefits. DI applicants typically must pass a medical screening to verify that their disability meets the established criteria. For example, the U.S. Social Security Act defines disability as "the inability to engage in any substantial gainful activity by reason of any medically determinable physical or mental impairment(s) which can be expected to result in death or which has lasted or can be expected to last for a continuous period of not less than 12 months." In the United States and many other countries, individuals must have worked and made payroll tax contributions to the DI program for some period before disability onset in order to be eligible for DI benefits (Wise, 2016).

The share of the population ages 60 to 64 that is receiving DI benefits provides a fair approximation of the use of the DI exit route from the labor force (as individuals can only claim DI until the Social Security FRA, now age 66 for those born from 1943 to 1954). In 2016, 14 percent of men and 12 percent of women ages 60 to 64 were receiving DI benefits, reflecting an increase of about 3 percentage points for both groups since the late 1980s. DI participation among the working-age population as a whole dipped briefly in the early 1980s, following a tightening of medical eligibility,

---

[4]An intermediate view is that both mortality and morbidity will continue to decline, with indeterminate effects on the relative length of disabled and disability-free life at older ages (Manton, 1982).

[5]See Cutler and Wise (2008) for additional analyses of health trends at older ages. More recently, evidence of rising morbidity and mortality in midlife for U.S. Whites (Case and Deaton, 2015) raises the concern that the heath of the elderly could decline in the future.

but has grown steadily over the past 25 years. Autor and Duggan (2006) attributed this growth to three factors: a 1984 law that loosened medical eligibility, the rise in women's labor force participation and DI eligibility, and the rise in DI benefits relative to income for low-income workers. Liebman (2015) estimated that DI growth in the 1980s was primarily driven by higher DI incidence rates after the 1984 law, whereas program growth since the early 1990s is largely the result of population aging and rising eligibility and incidence rates among women.[6]

The rate of DI receipt in the United States today is similar to that in many developed countries. Coile et al. (2016) found that the share of men ages 60 to 64 on the DI rolls is between 12 and 17 percent in nearly all (9 of 11) countries they studied. However, the time trend in the United States is quite different, with the United States being virtually alone in seeing a rise in participation over time. DI participation fell by 40 percent or more from its mid-1990s peak in six of the countries, with smaller decreases in three others. Wise (2012) found that these declines typically followed DI reforms, such as eliminating the ability to enroll in DI for nonhealth reasons and increasing reviews of DI recipients to verify medical eligibility. Koning and Lindeboom (2015) detailed how DI reforms ended the "Dutch disease" of high disability rates, while Banks et al. (2015) provided a similar analysis for the United Kingdom.

To recap, U.S. workers are increasingly likely to exit the labor force via the disability route, with about one in seven now receiving DI benefits before they reach Social Security eligibility. This trend runs counter to the trend in most other countries, where use of DI peaked in the mid-1990s but has fallen since then as a result of DI reforms, although current levels of DI use in the United States are similar to those in other countries. There is no clear evidence that the U.S. trend is driven by an increase in disability. Rather, changes in medical screening and demographic and economic factors may play a larger role.

EXPLAINING RETIREMENT BEHAVIOR AND TRENDS

Data and Methods

Before exploring explanations for recent trends in work at older ages, it is useful to survey what is known about the determinants of retirement,

---

[6]Pattison and Waldron (2013) also stressed the role of population aging and rising eligibility for women. Note that while population aging is important for explaining trends in DI receipt for the working-age population as a whole, it explains little to none of the increase in DI receipt among those ages 60 to 64.

beginning with a brief overview of the data and methods central to this work.

The retirement decision has been studied extensively over the past several decades. When the predecessor to this essay was written (Quinn and Burkhauser, 1994), much of the existing work on retirement relied on longitudinal surveys from the 1970s, including the Retirement History Survey and National Longitudinal Survey of Older Men. Although these surveys were critical for the research of that era, they lacked data on women and on more recent cohorts of older workers. A new longitudinal study, the Health and Retirement Study (HRS), had just been launched to fill the gap.

A quarter-century later, the retirement literature has been refreshed with a new series of studies, many of which use HRS. HRS is a nationally representative, longitudinal survey of the U.S. population, ages 50 and older. Respondents have been interviewed biennially since 1992, and the sample is refreshed regularly with new cohorts. The core survey collects extensive information on work, income, wealth, pensions, health, health care, family transfers, and more. This core is supplemented by links to administrative data including Social Security records, private pension data, and Medicare claims data and by the collection of health data such as biomarkers and venous blood.[7] HRS is the model for a growing international network of longitudinal aging studies (see the chapter by Lee and Smith in this volume). For example, the Survey of Health, Ageing, and Retirement in Europe (SHARE) includes data for 14 countries, and there are separate studies in China, Costa Rica, England, India, Ireland, Japan, Korea, and Mexico. These studies collect much of the same data as the core HRS, enabling international comparisons as well as within-country studies.[8]

A second data advance during the past quarter-century is the increase in researcher access to administrative datasets, such as Social Security earnings and benefits records and income tax records. These data offer larger sample sizes than traditional surveys, in some cases covering the full population, and greater accuracy in measuring income and benefits. However, they typically lack information on demographics and other variables of interest,

---

[7]To facilitate use of this extraordinarily rich and complex dataset, the RAND HRS provides researchers with a version of the data in which variables are defined consistently over time and named intuitively. For more information on RAND HRS and related data products, see https://www.rand.org/labor/aging/dataprod.html [April 2018].

[8]The current list of these studies (with start dates) includes SHARE (2004), the English Longitudinal Study of Aging (ELSA, 2002), the Irish Longitudinal Study on Aging (TILDA, 2010), the China Health and Retirement Longitudinal Study (CHARLS, 2011), the Japanese Study on Aging and Retirement (JSTAR, 2007), the Korean Longitudinal Study of Aging (KLoSA, 2008), the Longitudinal Aging Study in India (LASI, pilot), the Costa Rican Longevity and Healthy Aging Study (CRELES, 2005), and the Mexican Health and Aging Study (MHAS, 2001). For harmonized data from these studies, see https://g2aging.org/ [April 2018].

except where they have been linked to survey data or other administrative records.

There have also been significant advances in the empirical methods used in retirement research over the past quarter-century. First, empirical microeconomics has experienced a "credibility revolution" (Angrist and Pischke, 2010). Many studies in the 1970s and 1980s relied on "naïve" regression analysis using cross-sectional variation that did not adequately address perennial challenges such as omitted variable bias or did not produce results robust to assumptions. By contrast, researchers today realize that identifying a research design that will allow them to estimate a plausibly causal effect of X on Y is paramount. Obtaining experimental evidence through a randomized controlled trial is one means to this end; however, such trials can be expensive and may be difficult to adapt to some questions. A second option is to identify quasi-experimental variation in the key independent variable. Such variation might arise, for example, when a policy changes over time or applies only once people reach a certain age. Empirical techniques including instrumental variables, regression discontinuity design (RDD), and others allow the researcher to exploit this variation effectively. Many of the best recent papers in the retirement literature use such techniques.

Second, structural models have continued to evolve and to be an important part of the retirement literature. Structural models posit that individuals make work decisions so as to maximize lifetime utility (or happiness) as expressed in a specified function. Relative to the literature using cross-sectional or quasi-experimental variation, structural models have the advantage of being able to estimate parameters such as the discount rate (which reflects the strength of the preference for receiving money now rather than in the future) or degree of risk aversion, which can then be used to simulate the effect of policies outside the scope of real-world experience. However, key assumptions are less transparent than in the empirical methods listed above, and the validity of these models relies on specifying the correct form for the utility function. Over time, structural models of retirement have become more complex, incorporating features such as uncertainty in asset returns or in out-of-pocket medical expenses.

Third, advances in behavioral economics have begun to make their way into the retirement literature. While this is most notable in the literature on retirement savings decisions (Choi et al., 2004), insights from this field are beginning to influence the analysis of other questions in the retirement sphere, such as the Social Security claiming decision (Brown et al., 2016).

In short, the retirement research of the past 25 years has relied heavily on HRS but is increasingly making use of "sister studies" from other countries and of large administrative datasets. The empirical literature has come to be dominated by studies that use new techniques aimed at generating causal estimates, even as structural modeling continues to be used. The new data and methods are highly complementary. For example, using the RDD approach may require administrative data on the full population, in order to compare people in the immediate vicinity of an arbitrary cut-off (such as a January 1 birthdate) who are subject to different policy regimes but are otherwise similar. Calculating financial incentives from Social Security and pensions, whether to be used in a structural model or quasi-experimental estimation, relies on having individual earnings records and detailed information on private pensions. The richness of the current retirement literature is due in no small part to the availability of excellent data.

Determinants of Retirement: Labor Supply

Many factors may influence whether individuals continue to work at older ages. These factors may be divided into those that affect the individual's decision of whether to supply labor and those that relate to the demand for older workers. While a full examination of this large literature is beyond the scope of this chapter, I briefly review some key findings on labor supply and demand; see Coile (2015) for a longer discussion.

The effect of public and private pensions on retirement has been the subject of much research. One reason for the strong interest is that the long-term decline in labor force participation of older men occurred over the same period that public and private pensions expanded dramatically in the share of covered workers and in generosity. In theory, public and private pensions may influence work by creating income effects if individuals receive benefits in excess of their own contributions. They may also generate substitution effects if work at older ages raises or lowers the expected present value of pension wealth. Further, pensions can create liquidity constraints if individuals would like to retire earlier but are unable to access their pension wealth until the eligibility age. The spikes in the retirement hazard noted above at the early retirement age and FRA for Social Security benefits is consistent with this scenario.

Modeling the financial incentives from public and private pensions properly and convincingly identifying their effect have been an important focus of recent work. Much of the most compelling evidence of income effects comes from historical analyses. Costa (1995) found large effects of Union Army pensions on male labor force participation around 1900. Fetter and Lockwood (forthcoming) also found large income effects, using variation in the state-run Old Age Assistance program of the 1930s. They project that the growth of Social Security can explain more than half of the decline in men's participation from 1940 to 1960. The "Social Security Notch," in which benefits were cut sharply for those born in 1917 relative to earlier cohorts, provides a useful natural experiment. Krueger and

Pischke (1992) found that the cut did little to halt the long-term decline in labor force participation, whereas Gelber et al. (2016) obtained larger effects by comparing those born immediately on either side of the Notch. The latter used their estimates to project that growth in Social Security can account for at least half of the decline in older men's employment from 1950 to 1985.

In modeling substitution effects, it is important to focus not only on the "accrual," or change in pension wealth, from working one more year but also on forward-looking measures that capture the change in pension wealth from work in future years. Several measures have been proposed, including *tax force* (Gruber and Wise, 1999), which is the gain or loss in pension wealth from working to a specific age, relative to earnings; *peak value* (Coile and Gruber, 2007), which is the financial gain from working to the age when pension wealth is maximized; and *option value* (Stock and Wise, 1990), which is the increase in utility arising from retiring at the optimal future year.

Many studies find that these measures are related to retirement. Gruber and Wise (1999) estimated that 80 to 90 percent of the differences across a dozen countries in the share of men out of the labor force at ages 55 to 69 can be explained by differences in tax force. Friedberg and Webb (2005), Gruber and Wise (2004), and Samwick (1998) found that individuals with a larger incentive to work (PV or OV) retire later. Liebman et al. (2009) showed that Social Security incentives affect work on the intensive margin, using quasi-experimental variation arising from nuances of the Social Security benefit formula. Finally, early studies featuring structural retirement models (Gustman and Steinmeier, 1986; Stock and Wise, 1990) established the value of this approach for evaluating the effect of public and private pensions on retirement, while several recent studies have found that past or proposed future reforms may have large effects (Gustman and Steinmeier, 2009, 2015).

The DI program may affect labor force participation at older ages if medical screening is imperfect and access to the program is not limited to those who are unable to work. Maestas et al. (2013) used variation in DI awards generated by random assignment of DI applicants to disability examiners, as two similar applicants may receive different outcomes depending on the leniency of their examiner. They found that for the one-quarter of DI applicants on the margin of program entry, employment would be about 30 percentage points higher in the absence of the DI program, although additional earnings are fairly modest. French and Song (2014) similarly used random assignment of appeals of rejected DI applicants to judges and obtained comparable results, as did Chen and Van der Klaauw (2008), who used age-based differences in eligibility standards.

The retirement decision is likely to depend on an individual's total wealth, not on pensions alone. However, estimating the effect of wealth on retirement is difficult, since individuals decide how much to save and those who are high savers may have other characteristics that affect their retirement decision. Unanticipated shocks to wealth offer one fruitful means to explore this question. Imbens et al. (2001) documented that winning the lottery leads to reductions in labor supply for older workers, while Brown et al. (2010) showed that the receipt of an inheritance increases the probability of retirement, especially when unexpected. Stock market fluctuations also serve as a source of windfall wealth gains and losses, but the evidence for their effect on retirement is more mixed (Hurd et al., 2009; Coile and Levine, 2011a). In structural models, individuals make both work and savings decisions, and thus these models can be used to simulate the effect of wealth changes and borrowing constraints on retirement (French, 2005; Gustman and Steinmeier, 2005).

The role of health and health insurance has long been another focus of the retirement literature. The earlier discussion of disability measures hinted at some of the challenges in estimating the effect of health on retirement, such as the potential for self-reported health measures to be influenced by the work decision and the concern that objective measures only imperfectly capture work ability. Like wealth shocks, negative health events may provide compelling evidence of health's effect on retirement if the shocks are unanticipated and unrelated to other factors. McClellan (1998) found that workers who experience a heart attack, stroke, or new cancer diagnosis are much more likely to retire, especially when the shock is accompanied by a loss in functioning; Disney et al. (2006) had similar findings for the United Kingdom, while Bound et al. (1999) showed that changes in health are strongly associated with labor force exit.

A related question that has arisen more recently is the effect of retirement on health. This effect is of interest to policy makers, as policies that encourage later retirement could have unintended negative consequences for health, if health effects are negative. The empirical landscape is complex, but overall seems to suggest that retirement is good for physical health (Bound and Waidmann, 2007) and mental health (Charles, 2004; Johnston and Lee, 2009), but retirement is also associated with cognitive decline (Rohwedder and Willis, 2010) and an increased risk of mortality (Fitzpatrick and Moore, 2017). Notably, many of these studies use the increase in retirement at public pension eligibility ages to identify these effects.

Health insurance access is likely to be more important in the United States than in other countries, given that most U.S. workers obtain insurance coverage for themselves and their families through their employer, while coverage is typically not dependent on employment in other developed countries. Employees who are offered retiree health insurance by their employer may more easily be able to retire before age 65, when Medicare becomes available. Using data from firms with varying benefits, Nyce et al. (2013) showed that there is a large increase in retirement at ages 62 and 63 for employees who have such coverage, particularly when employers cover more of the premiums. A literature review on this topic concluded that health insurance is a "central determinant of retirement decisions" (Gruber and Madrian, 2004). However, the 2010 Affordable Care Act may reduce the importance of this factor by providing ways to obtain insurance outside the employment relationship.

Among the most important advances in the retirement literature over the past 25 years is the increasing attention paid to women's retirement decisions and to family issues. As noted above, the longitudinal datasets of the 1970s focused primarily on male workers, complicating the effort to study women's retirement. In addition, analysts often treated the husband's retirement status as an exogenous explanatory variable in studies of women's retirement, while excluding the wife's retirement status in studies of men's retirement (see Weaver, 1994, for a review of the early literature on women).

With the rise of two-career older couples, the lack of research on women and asymmetric treatment of husbands and wives in retirement models became increasingly anachronistic. The fact that both spouses retire within one year of each other in one-third of working couples (Coile, 2004) suggests that many couples approach retirement as a joint decision. The coordination in retirement timing could reflect several factors, including similarity of preferences, shared financial resources, and complementarity of leisure. Several authors estimated structural models of joint retirement and found complementarity of leisure to be a key driver of joint retirement (Gustman and Steinmeier, 2000; Maestas, 2001). Other authors (Baker, 2002; Coile, 2004) illustrated the presence of joint decision making by showing that the financial incentives facing one spouse have "spillover" effects on the other's retirement decision. On a different note, with women more likely to serve as caregivers for elderly family members, studies on the effect of caregiving on retirement (Fahle and McGarry, 2018) are another welcome addition to the literature.

Determinants of Retirement: Labor Demand

Although analysts have focused much of their attention on factors that affect the decision to supply labor at older ages, it is critical to also examine the demand for older workers. One important consideration is how productivity and wages change with age. Standard economic theory suggests that workers will be paid according to their contribution to the firm's output. Yet Skirbekk (2004) concluded from a review of the literature that productivity peaks in mid-career whereas earnings rise until late in the work life. One explanation for this divergence comes from Lazear (1983), who posited that firms offer a steep age-earnings profile, paying workers less than their value when young, with the promise of high wages when old in order to encourage them to put forth effort on the job. A defined benefit (DB) pension is part of the worker's deferred compensation and also provides an incentive for workers to retire (despite high wages) by having negative accruals in pension wealth after the plan's retirement age, which effectively reduces pay.

A mismatch between wages and productivity is one reason why older workers might experience age discrimination. Testing for age discrimination is challenging, as it is difficult to know whether age is the reason that a worker was not hired. The best evidence comes from field experiments, in which fictitious resumes are created for workers who vary in age but are otherwise comparable. Neumark et al. (2015) reported that there is age discrimination against older women, but less evidence of discrimination against men. Lahey (2008a) also found age discrimination against women and concluded that it is likely statistical discrimination, in which employers use the average characteristics of a group as a proxy for the unknown characteristics of the applicant.

Analysts have explored the effectiveness of laws to protect older workers, such as the Age Discrimination in Employment Act, obtaining mixed results. Neumark and Stock (1999) found the law boosted the employment of those ages 60 and older, while Lahey (2008b) concluded that employment of older workers is lower when there is also a state age discrimination law.

The business cycle may affect the demand for older workers, resulting in more transitions to retirement when the labor market is weak. Coile and Levine (2007) found this to be true for U.S. workers, particularly once they reach the age of eligibility for Social Security. Dorn and Sousa-Poza (2010) reported that involuntary retirement due to economic conditions is widespread in Europe, especially in countries with strict employment protections. Late-career job loss has many detrimental effects, including reduced employment and earnings (Chan and Stevens, 2001), lower retiree income (Coile and Levine, 2011b), and higher mortality (Sullivan and von Wachter, 2009).

Longer Work Lives

The preceding discussion points to several factors that may have contributed to the rise in work at older ages. A first candidate is improving longevity and health. The known association between poor health and early retirement lends credence to this possibility. However, for most workers, health is not the main cause of retirement. Most workers retire between ages 60 and 70, as discussed earlier, while health declines only slowly over this range. Moreover, comparing how much older individuals today work relative either to those in the past or to slightly younger individuals in similar health suggests that there is significant health capacity to work at older ages (Coile et al., 2017). Further, as the decline in mortality rates over time has been continuous, it seems unlikely to have precipitated the sudden reversal of the decline in men's participation (see Figure 8-1). Thus, while better health may have supported longer work lives, there is little evidence that it is a primary driver.

Another plausible candidate is the rise in education and shift away from physically demanding jobs. As noted above, those with more education have higher labor force participation at older ages. Yet, as with health, the educational attainment of the near-elderly population has improved continuously over time. Moreover, the male labor force participation rate for each education group has followed the same U-shaped trend as the overall rate, pointing to a need to look beyond the composition shift in education.[9]

Another potential factor is rising participation among women, which might encourage men to work longer due to complementarity of leisure between the spouses. Isolating this effect is challenging because both men and women's participation may rise over time due to other factors. Schirle (2008) overcame this constraint by using women's labor force participation at age 40 to predict their participation at older ages. She estimated that the rise in women's participation can explain one-quarter of the rise in men's participation in the United States, one-half in Canada, and one-third in the United Kingdom. Changes in U.S. men's education and age were estimated to explain about one-third of the rise, leaving 40 percent unexplained.

Changes in employer-provided benefits, including a shift from DB to defined contribution (DC) pensions and a reduction in retiree health insurance, also may have played a role. In DB plans, pension wealth typically grows until the plan's early or normal retirement age and declines thereafter. DC plans, by contrast, lack age-specific retirement incentives. Friedberg and Webb (2005) estimated that the absence of those incentives leads workers

---

[9]This statement reflects the author's calculations from the March Current Population Survey, not shown due to space constraints. Although the series are somewhat variable due to small sample sizes, among men ages 60 to 64 there is an increase in participation between 1995 and 2016 of 5 percentage points for high school dropouts, 6 percentage points for high school graduates, and 9 percentage points for male college graduates. The equivalent statistics for women are gains of 3, 7, and 9 percentage points, respectively. Thus, although college graduates have the largest increases, participation has risen substantially in other groups as well. In terms of the shift in educational attainment over time, there is a 20 percentage point increase in the share of men ages 60 to 64 who are college graduates between 1980 and 2016 and a 35 point decrease in the share that are high school dropouts. The analogous changes for women are very similar in magnitude.

with a DC plan to retire nearly 2 years later. A simple calculation suggests that the 25-point drop in the share of private-sector workers with a DB plan from 1980 to 2014[10] could have led to a roughly 6-month increase in the average retirement age, one-quarter of the total increase reported by Munnell (2015).

Public pension reforms in the United States and other developed countries also may have led to later retirement. The most significant changes in the United States are an increase in the FRA from 65 to 66, an increase in the benefit of delaying claiming after the FRA, and the elimination of the Social Security earnings test after the FRA. Mastrobuoni (2009) estimated that the FRA increase led to a 6-month increase in the mean retirement age. Most studies of the earnings test find its removal had little effect on retirement, though Gelber et al. (2017) concluded that it affects employment at ages 63 to 64. Many other developed countries have made reforms to their public pensions, raising eligibility ages and reducing benefits due to fiscal concerns. In Italy, Japan, and the United Kingdom, increases in eligibility ages were followed by sharp increases in employment at the affected ages (Banks et al., 2017; Brugiavini et al., 2016; Oshio et al., 2016).

While it is difficult to apportion precise shares to the various factors, available evidence suggests that changes in education, women's growing role in the economy, the shift from DB to DC pensions, and changes to public pensions all likely played some role in the trend of longer work lives. Although there have been considerable advances in mortality and health over time, the evidence of their contribution is less clear.

Reconciling Trends in Health and Work

The rise in prevalence of DI receipt in the United States runs counter to the trends of longer work lives, rising life expectancy, and (arguably) improving health at older ages. Research on the DI program helps to explain this discordance. Changes in population health have not been identified as a major driver of rising DI receipt. Rather, the 1984 law liberalizing medical eligibility is a key contributor, particularly for men during the late 1980s. Rising women's participation and population aging contributed to a rise in the share of nonelderly adults on DI but do not explain increases for men within a narrow age range.

The 1984 law was followed by significant shifts in the composition of the DI population. Awards rose sharply for musculosketal and mental conditions, which are often viewed as more difficult to verify, but were flat or declining for cancer and heart disease (Autor and Duggan, 2006). This pat-

---

[10]Employment Benefit Research Institute, see https://www.ebri.org/publications/benfaq/index.cfm?fa=retfaqt14fig1 [April 2018].

tern is consistent with greater leniency in the evaluation of applicants with the former conditions, even as population health held steady or improved. Alternatively, it could reflect an increase over time in the incidence of musculosketal and mental conditions or that labor market conditions for low-skill workers have changed so as to make it more attractive for those who have these conditions to apply (Liebman, 2015). Consistent with the latter theory, Autor and Duggan (2003) found that low-skill workers facing a negative shock to labor demand were more likely to exit the labor force to DI after the 1984 law liberalizing eligibility.

Overall, research from the United States and other countries suggests that reforms to the medical screening process and other program parameters have substantial effects on DI participation. These reforms interact with health and work, in that they may facilitate entry onto the program for those who have certain medical conditions or those with poor employment prospects. Thus, trends over time in health or work can magnify or diminish the initial effect of a reform.

DISCUSSION AND DIRECTIONS FOR FUTURE RESEARCH

The past few decades have been marked by large increases in labor force participation at older ages and an associated rise in the age of retirement. This trend is occurring against a backdrop of increasing life expectancy, yet improving health does not appear to be the primary driver of the trend. Rather, increasing education, women's greater participation in the economy, the shift from DB to DC pensions, and reforms to public pensions all appear to play a role. There is an increasing use of the DI route to exit the labor force, which also seems to be primarily explained not by changes in population health but by changing medical eligibility criteria and economic factors.

The retirement literature has advanced considerably over this period, making use of new data and benefiting from the "credibility revolution" in empirical economics to bolster knowledge on topics of longstanding interest, such as the effect of Social Security on retirement, as well as to explore new topics, such as joint retirement decision making by couples. Yet while much has been learned, important unanswered questions remain.

One critical question is whether there are forces that could impede the current trend toward longer work lives. Age discrimination is a potential factor, as older workers will be challenged to extend their working lives if employers are reluctant to hire them or if they are treated differently in pay and promotion decisions. The existing literature on this topic provides compelling evidence that older women are less likely to receive a call-back for a job interview. It has proven more difficult to examine how this translates into differences in actual hires and wage offers and also to see if older workers on the job are treated differently than younger workers, in part because interactions between employers and employees are often not empirically observable. New data and methods (such as the use of "big data") may provide an opportunity to push further in investigating this topic.

A related research issue is that while the retirement literature has long focused largely on supply-side factors that may affect retirement decisions, labor-demand-side topics merit more attention. Past work has sought to understand age profiles in wages and productivity, including how DB pensions may be part of an informal long-term employment contract; more recently, research has focused on how the business cycle affects retirement. At present, there is a pressing need to explore labor demand in the context of ongoing shifts in the economy. Trends such as sector shifts, technological change and automation, and the rise of alternative work arrangements (such as use of temporary and contract workers) may change the relationship between age and productivity, posing new challenges or opportunities for older workers.

A topic at the intersection of labor supply and demand that also merits further attention is the conditions of work. A job is defined not only by the tasks a worker performs in exchange for a wage and benefits package but also by many nonmonetary attributes. These might include, for example, whether the worker is able to set his or her own hours, shift to a part-time schedule, work remotely, receive training and opportunities for professional growth, or enjoy paid time off. Job attributes such as these (or their lack) may influence workers' decisions to remain on the job at older ages. Those attributes that contribute to a worker's ability to manage health problems could be more important for workers in poor health. Historically there has been little information on the conditions of work in the United States, but the 2015 American Working Conditions Survey provides such data and is just beginning to be used by researchers (Maestas et al., 2017). More work is needed to understand how job attributes are valued by older workers and affect their labor supply and whether firms are adapting jobs to match these preferences.

Finally, there is an increasing awareness of the importance of looking beyond population averages at the experience of groups of different SES. Those with less education are known to retire earlier, have shorter life expectancies, and be more likely to use DI. Trends over time by SES within the older population are sometimes more difficult to discern, but with respect to life expectancy, there is a clear trend toward rising inequality (National Academies of Sciences, Engineering, and Medicine, 2017). More research on trends in health and work at older ages by SES is needed, as well as research examining whether workers' responsiveness to labor supply factors such as pension incentives varies by SES and whether labor demand differs by SES. Given the long-run fiscal challenges facing public pensions and other programs for the elderly, such programs are likely to continue to evolve in a way that both encourages and includes an expectation of longer work lives. If various segments of the population are less able to respond to incentives to work longer, reforms may have unanticipated impacts on the well-being of older individuals.

REFERENCES

Angrist, J.D., and Pischke, J.-S. (2010). The credibility revolution in empirical economics: How better research design is taking the con out of econometrics. *Journal of Economic Perspectives, 24*(2), 3–30.

Autor, D.H., and Duggan, M.G. (2003). The rise in the disability rolls and the decline in unemployment. *Quarterly Journal of Economics, 118*(1), 157–206.

Autor, D.H., and Duggan, M.G. (2006). Disability rolls: A fiscal crisis unfolding. *Journal of Economic Perspectives, 20*(3), 71–96.

Baker, M. (2002). The retirement behavior of married couples: Evidence from the spouse's allowance. *Journal of Human Resources, 37*(Winter), 1–34.

Banks, J., Blundell, R., and Emmerson, C. (2015). Disability benefit receipt and reform: Reconciling trends in the United Kingdom. *Journal of Economic Perspectives, 29*(2), 173–190.

Banks, J., Emmerson, C., and Tetlow, G. (2017). Long-run trends in the economic activity of older people in the UK. Unpublished paper. Available: http://www.nber.org/chapters/c14051.pdf [April 2018].

Bell, F.C., and Miller, M.L. (2005). *Life Tables for the United States Social Security Area, 1900–2100* (Social Security Administration Actuarial Study No. 120, SSA Publication No. 11-11536, August). Washington, DC: Social Security Administration.

Bound, J. (1991). Self-reported objective measures of health in retirement models. *Journal of Human Resources, 26*, 103–138.

Bound, J., and Waidmann, T. (2007). *Estimating the Health Effects of Retirement* (Michigan Retirement Research Center Working Paper No. 2007-168). Ann Arbor: Michigan Retirement Research Center.

Bound, J., Schoenbaum, M., and Waidmann, T. (1995). Race and education differences in disability status and labor force attachment in the Health and Retirement Study. *Journal of Human Resources, 30*(Supp.), S227–S267.

Bound, J., Schoenbaum, M., Stinebrickner, T.R., and Waidmann, T. (1999). The dynamic effects of health on the labor force transitions of older workers. *Labour Economics, 6*(2), 179–202.

Brown, J.R., Coile, C.C., and Weisbenner, S.J. (2010). The effect of inheritance receipt on retirement. *Review of Economics and Statistics, 92*(2), 425–434.

Brown, J.R., Kapteyn, A., and Mitchell, O.S. (2016). Framing and claiming: How information-framing affects expected Social Security claiming behavior. *Journal of Risk and Insurance, 83*(1), 139–162.

Brugiavini, A., Pasini, G., and Weber, G. (2016). *Employment at Older Ages: Evidence from Italy.* Unpublished paper. Available: http://www.nber.org/chapters/c14046.pdf [April 2018].

Burtless, G., and Moffitt, R. (1986). Social Security, earnings tests, and age at retirement. *Public Finance Quarterly, 14*, 3–27.

Cahill, K.E., Giandrea, M.G., and Quinn, J.F. (2015). Retirement patterns and the macroeconomy, 1992–2010: The prevalence and determinants of bridge jobs, phased retirement, and reentry among three recent cohorts of older Americans. *Gerontologist, 55*(3), 384–403.

Case, A., and Deaton, A. (2015). Rising morbidity and mortality in midlife among White non-Hispanic Americans in the 21st century. *Proceedings of the National Academy of Sciences of the United States of America, 112*(49), 15078–15083.

Chan, S., and Stevens, A.H. (2001). Job loss and employment patterns of older workers. *Journal of Labor Economics, 19*(2), 484–521.

Charles, K. (2004). Is retirement depressing? Labor force inactivity and psychological well-being in later life. *Research in Labor Economics, 23,* 269–299.

Chen, S., and van der Klaauw, W. (2008). The work disincentive effects of the Disability Insurance Program in the 1990s. *Journal of Econometrics, 142*(2), 757–784.

Choi, J.J., Laibson, D., Madrian, B.C., and Metrick, A. (2004). For better or for worse: Default effects and 401(k) savings behavior. In D.A. Wise (Ed.), *Perspectives on the Economics of Aging* (pp. 81–126). Chicago: University of Chicago Press.

Coile, C.C. (2004). Retirement incentives and couples' retirement decisions. *B.E. Press Journal of Economic Analysis & Policy, 4*(1), 1–30.

Coile, C.C. (2015). Economic determinants of workers' retirement decisions. *Journal of Economic Surveys, 29*(4), 830–853.

Coile, C.C., and Gruber, J. (2007). Future Social Security entitlements and the retirement decision. *Review of Economics and Statistics, 89*(2), 234–246.

Coile, C.C., and Levine, P.B. (2007). Labor market shocks and retirement: Do government programs matter? *Journal of Public Economics, 91*(10), 1902–1919.

Coile, C.C., and Levine, P.B. (2010). *Reconsidering Retirement: How Losses and Layoffs Affect Older Workers.* Washington, DC: Brookings Institution Press.

Coile, C.C., and Levine. P.B. (2011a). The market crash and mass layoffs: How the current economic crisis may affect retirement. *The B.E. Press Journal of Economic Analysis & Policy, 11*(1), 1–22.

Coile, C.C., and Levine, P.B. (2011b). Recessions, retirement, and Social Security. *American Economic Review, 101*(3), 23–28.

Coile, C., Milligan, K.S., and Wise, D.A. (2016). Introduction and summary. In D.A. Wise (Ed.), *Social Security Programs and Retirement Around the World: Disability Insurance Programs and Retirement* (pp. 1–44). Chicago: University of Chicago Press.

Coile, C., Milligan, K.S., and Wise, D.A. (2017). Health capacity to work at older ages: Evidence from the U.S. In D.A. Wise (Ed.), *Social Security Programs and Retirement Around the World: The Capacity to Work at Older Ages* (pp. 359–394). Chicago: University of Chicago Press.

Council of Economic Advisors. (2016). *The Long-Term Decline in Prime-Age Male Labor Force Participation.* Washington, DC: Executive Office of the President of the United States. Available: https://obamawhitehouse.archives.gov/sites/default/files/page/files/20160620_cea_primeage_male_lfp.pdf [March 2018].

Costa, D. (1995). Pensions and retirement: Evidence from Union Army veteran. *Quarterly Journal of Economics, 110*(2), 297–319.

Costa, D. (1998). *The Evolution of Retirement: An American Economic History, 1880–1990.* Chicago: University of Chicago Press.

Crimmins, E.M. (2004). Trends in the health of the elderly. *Annual Review of Public Health, 25,* 79–98.

Crimmins, E.M., and Beltrán-Sánchez, H. (2010). Mortality and morbidity trends: Is there compression of morbidity? *Journals of Gerontology, Series B: Social Sciences 66B*(1), 75–86.

Cutler, D.M., and Wise, D.A. (2008). *Health at Older Ages: The Causes and Consequences of Declining Disability Among the Elderly.* Chicago: University of Chicago Press.

Cutler, D.M., Ghosh, K., and Landrum, M.B. (2014). Evidence for significant compression of morbidity in the elderly U.S. population. In D.A. Wise (Ed.), *Discoveries in the Economics of Aging* (pp. 21–51). Chicago: University of Chicago Press.

Disney, R., Emmerson, C., and Wakefield, M. (2006). Ill health and retirement in Britain: A panel data-based analysis. *Journal of Health Economics, 25*(4), 621–649.

Dorn, D., and Sousa-Poza, A. (2010). "Voluntary" and "involuntary" early retirement: An international analysis. *Applied Economics, 42*(4), 427–438.

Fahle, S., and McGarry, K. (2018). Women working longer: Labor market implications of providing family care. In C. Goldin and L.F. Katz (Eds.), *Women Working Longer: Increased Employment at Older Ages* (pp. 157–181). Chicago: University of Chicago Press.

Fetter, D.K., and Lockwood, L.M. (forthcoming). Government old-age support and labor supply: Evidence from the Old Age Assistance Program. Submitted to *American Economic Review*.

Fitzpatrick, M., and Moore, T. (2017). *The Mortality Effects of Retirement: Evidence from Social Security Eligibility at Age 62* (NBER Working Paper 24127). Cambridge, MA: National Bureau of Economic Research.

Flippen, C., and Tienda, M. (2000). Pathways to retirement: Patterns of labor force participation and labor market exit among the pre-retirement population by race, Hispanic origin, and sex. *Journals of Gerontology Series B: Social Sciences, 55B*(1), S14–S27.

French, E. (2005). The effects of health, wealth, and wages on labor supply and retirement behavior. *Review of Economic Studies, 72*(2), 395–427.

French, E., and Song, J. (2014). The effect of disability insurance receipt on labor supply. *American Economic Journal: Economic Policy, 6*(2), 291–337.

Friedberg, L., and Webb, A. (2005). Retirement and evolution of the pension structure. *Journal of Human Resources, 40*(2), 281–308.

Fries, J.F. (1980). Aging, natural death, and the compression of morbidity. *New England Journal of Medicine, 303*, 130–135.

Gelber, A.M., Isen, A., and Song, J. (2016). *The Effect of Pension Income on Elderly Earnings: Evidence form Social Security and Full Population Data* (NBER Working Paper). Unpublished manuscript. Available: https://gspp.berkeley.edu/assets/uploads/research/pdf/gelberisensong051716.pdf [April 2018].

Gelber, A.M., Jones, D., Sacks, D.W., and Song, J. (2017). *Using Kinked Budget Sets to Estimate Extensive Margin Responses: Method and Evidence from the Social Security Retirement Earnings Test* (NBER Working Paper 23362). Cambridge, MA: National Bureau of Economic Research.

Goldin, C., and Katz, L.F. (2018). Women working longer: Facts and some explanations. In C. Goldin and L.F. Katz (Eds.), *Women Working Longer: Increased Employment at Older Ages* (pp. 11–53). Chicago: University of Chicago Press.

Gruber, J., and Madrian, B.C. (2004). Health insurance, labor supply, and job mobility: A critical review of the literature. In C. McLaughlin, (Ed.), *Health Policy and the Uninsured* (pp. 97–178). Washington, DC: Urban Institute Press.

Gruber, J., and Wise, D.A. (1999). *Social Security and Retirement Around the World*. Chicago: University of Chicago Press.

Gruber, J., and Wise, D.A. (2004). *Social Security Programs and Retirement Around the World: Microestimation*. Chicago: University of Chicago Press.

Gruenberg, E.M. (1977). The failures of success. *Milbank Memorial Fund Quarterly: Health and Society, 1977*, 3–24.

Gustman, A.L., and Steinmeier, T.L. (1986). A structural retirement model. *Econometrica, 54*(3), 555–584.

Gustman, A.L., and Steinmeier, T.L. (2000). Retirement in dual-career families: A structural model. *Journal of Labor Economics, 18*(3), 503–545.

Gustman, A.L., and Steinmeier, T.L. (2005). The Social Security early entitlement age in a structural model of retirement and wealth. *Journal of Public Economics, 89*(2–3), 441–463.

Gustman, A.L., and Steinmeier, T.L. (2009). How changes in Social Security affect recent retirement trends. *Research on Aging, 31*(2), 261–290.

Gustman, A.L., and Steinmeier, T.L. (2015). Effects of Social Security policies on benefit claiming, retirement, and saving. *Journal of Public Economics, 129*(C), 51–62.

Hayward, M.D., Friedman, S., and Chen, H. (1996). Race inequities in men's retirement. *Journals of Gerontology: Social Sciences, 51B*(1), S1–S10.

Hurd, M.D., Reti, M., and Rohwedder, S. (2009). The effect of large capital gains or losses on retirement. In D.A. Wise (Ed.), *Developments in the Economics of Aging* (pp. 127–163). Chicago: University of Chicago Press.

Hutchens, R. (2010). Worker characteristics, job characteristics, and opportunities for phased retirement. *Labour Economics, 17*(6), 1010–1021.

Imbens, G.W., Rubin, D.B., and Sacerdote, B. (2001). Estimating the effect of unearned income on labor earnings, savings, and consumption: Evidence from a survey of lottery players. *American Economic Review, 91*(4), 778–794.

Johnson, R.W., Kawachi, J., and Lewis, E.K. (2009). *Older Workers on the Move: Re-careering in Later Life* (AARP Public Policy Institute No. 2009-09, April). Washington, DC: AARP Public Policy Institute.

Johnston, D.W., and Lee, W.-S. (2009). Retiring to the good life? The short-term effects of retirement on health. *Economic Letters, 103*(1), 8–11.

Kantarci, T., and Van Soest, A. (2008). Gradual retirement: Preferences and limitations. *De Economist, 156*(2), 113–144.

Koning, P., and Lindeboom, M. (2015). The rise and fall of disability insurance enrollment in the Netherlands. *Journal of Economic Perspectives, 29*(2), 151–172.

Krueger, A.B., and Pischke, J.-S. (1992). The effect of Social Security on labor supply: A cohort analysis of the notch generation. *Journal of Labor Economics, 10*(4), 412–437.

Lahey, J.N. (2008a). Age, women, and hiring: An experimental study. *Journal of Human Resources, 43*(1), 30–56.

Lahey, J.N. (2008b). State age protection laws and the age discrimination in employment act. *Journal of Law and Economics, 51*(3), 433–460.

Lazear, E.P. (1983). Pensions as severance pay. In Z. Brodie and J.B. Shoven (Eds.), *Financial Aspects of the United States Pension System* (pp. 57–90). Chicago: University of Chicago Press.

Liebman, J.B. (2015). Understanding the increase in disability insurance receipt in the United States. *Journal of Economic Perspectives, 29*(2), 123–150.

Liebman, J.B., Luttmer, E., and Seif, D. (2009). Labor supply responses to marginal social security benefits: Evidence from discontinuities. *Journal of Public Economics, 93*(11–12), 1208–1223.

Maestas, N. (2001). *Labor, Love, and Leisure: Complementarity and the Timing of Retirement by Working Couples.* Berkeley, CA: University of California, Berkeley.

Maestas, N. (2010). Back to work: Expectations and realizations of work after retirement. *Journal of Human Resources, 45*(3), 718–748.

Maestas, N., Mullen, K.J., and Strand, A. (2013). Does Disability Insurance receipt discourage work? Using examiner assignment to estimate causal effects of SSDI receipt. *American Economic Review, 103*(5), 1797–1829.

Maestas, N., Mullen, K.J., Powell, D., von Wachter, T., and Wenger, J.B. (2017). *The Value of Working Conditions in the United States.* Unpublished paper. Available: http://crr.bc.edu/wp-content/uploads/2017/08/7b.-Kathleen-Mullen.pdf [April 2018].

Manton, K.G. (1982). Changing concepts of morbidity and mortality in the elderly population. *Milbank Memorial Fund Quarterly: Health and Society, 60,* 183–244.

Mastrobuoni, G. (2009). Labor supply effects of the recent Social Security benefit cuts: Empirical estimates using cohort discontinuities. *Journal of Public Economics, 93*(11–12), 1224–1233.

McClellan, M.B. (1998). Health events, health insurance, and labor supply: Evidence from the Health and Retirement Survey. In D.A. Wise (Ed.), *Frontiers in the Economics of Aging* (pp. 301–350). Chicago: University of Chicago Press.

Munnell, A.H. (2015). *The Average Retirement Age: An Update* (Issue Brief No. 15-4). Boston: Center for Retirement Research, Boston College.

Mutchler, J.E., Burr, J.A., Pienta, A.M., and Massagli, M.P. (1997). Pathways to labor force exit: Work transitions and work instability. *Journals of Gerontology, Series B: Social Sciences, 52B*(1), S4–S12.

National Academies of Sciences, Engineering, and Medicine. (2017). *The Growing Gap in Life Expectancy by Income: Implications for Federal Programs and Policy Responses.* Washington, DC: The National Academies Press.

Neumark, D., and Stock, W.A. (1999). Age discrimination laws and labor market efficiency. *Journal of Political Economy, 107,* 1081–1125.

Neumark, D., Burn, I., and Button, P. (2015). *Is It Harder for Older Workers to Find Jobs? New and Improved Evidence from a Field Experiment* (NBER Working Paper 21669), Cambridge, MA: National Bureau of Economic Research.

Nyce, S., Schieber, S., Shoven, J.B., Slavov, S., and Wise, D.A. (2013). Does retiree health insurance encourage early retirement? *Journal of Public Economics, 104*(C), 40–51.

Pattison, D., and Waldron, H. (2013). Growth in new disabled-worker entitlements, 1970–2008. *Social Security Bulletin, 73*(4).

Oshio, T., Usui, E., and Shimizutani, S. (2016). *Labor Force Participation of the Elderly in Japan.* Unpublished paper. Available: http://www.nber.org/chapters/c14047.pdf [April 2018].

Quinn, J.F., and Burkhauser, R.V. (1994). Retirement and labor force behavior of the elderly. In L.G. Martin and S.H. Preston (Eds.), *Demography of Aging* (pp. 50–101). Washington, DC: National Academy Press.

Ramnath, S., Shoven, J.B., and Slavov, S.N. (2017). *Pathways to Retirement through Self-Employment* (NBER Working Paper 23551, June). Cambridge, MA: National Bureau of Economic Research.

Reday-Mulvay, G. (2000). Gradual retirement in Europe. *Journal of Aging & Social Policy, 11*(2–3), 49–60.

Rohwedder, S., and Willis, R.J. (2010). Mental retirement. *Journal of Economic Perspectives, 24*(1), 119–138.

Samwick, A.A. (1998). New evidence on pensions, Social Security, and the timing of retirement. *Journal of Public Economics, 70,* 207–236.

Schirle, T. (2008). Why have the labor force participation rates of older men increased since the mid-1990s? *Journal of Labor Economics, 26*(4), 549–594.

Skirbekk, V. (2004). Age and individual productivity: A literature survey. *Vienna Yearbook of Population Research, 2,* 133–153.

Steuerle, E., and Spiro, C. (1999). *Adjusting for Life Expectancy in Measures of Labor Force Participation* (Urban Institute Straight Talk on Social Security and Retirement Policy Brief No. 10). Washington, DC: The Urban Institute.

Stock, J., and Wise, D. (1990). Pensions, the option value of work, and retirement. *Econometrica, 58,* 1151–1180.

Sullivan, D., and von Wachter, T. (2009). Job displacement and mortality: An analysis using administrative data. *Quarterly Journal of Economics, 124*(3), 1265–1306.

Waidmann, T., Bound, J., and Schoenbaum, M. (1995). The illusion of failure: Trends in the self-reported health of the U.S. elderly. *Milbank Quarterly, 73*(2), 253–288.

Weaver, D.A. (1994). The work and retirement decisions of older women: A literature review. *Social Security Bulletin, 57*(1), 3–24.

Wise, D.A. (2012). *Social Security Programs and Retirement Around the World: Historical Trends in Mortality and Health, Employment, and Disability Insurance Participation and Reforms.* Chicago: University of Chicago Press.

Wise, D.A. (2016). *Social Security Programs and Retirement Around the World: Disability Insurance Programs and Retirement.* Chicago: University of Chicago Press.

Zissimopoulos, J.M., and Karoly, L.A. (2007). Transitions to self-employment at older ages: The role of wealth, health, health insurance, and other factors. *Labour Economics, 14,* 269–295.

PART V

Disability and Cognitive Health of the Older Population

9

Cognitive Aging, Dementia, and the Future of an Aging Population

Kenneth M. Langa[1]

INTRODUCTION

Dementia, a decline in memory and other cognitive functions leading to disability in daily function, is a common and feared geriatric condition. Over the past two decades, Alzheimer's disease (AD) and Alzheimer's disease–related dementias (ADRD) have been the focus of increasing attention from researchers, clinicians, and policy makers due to the projected significant increase in the number of dementia cases—and the associated burdens to patients, families, and government support programs—that is expected to result from the worldwide growth in the elderly population. However, a growing number of population-based studies have reported that the age-specific incidence and prevalence of dementia in a number of high-income countries may have declined over the past 25 years, suggesting that trends in some combination of demographic, behavioral, medical, and environmental factors have led to a decrease in dementia risk among older adults in these countries.

A better understanding of the potential causes for the decline in past decades in dementia risk, and whether there will be continued decline, leveling off, or an increase in lifetime dementia risk in future decades, has huge implications for individual and public health and for public policy. Dementia is unique in the extent to which its impact often ripples out across family members, affecting the lives of multiple generations due to the daily care-giving typically required. When families are unable or unwilling to

---

[1]M.D., Ph.D., University of Michigan and Veterans Affairs Ann Arbor Healthcare System, Ann Arbor.

249

provide the care needed, institutional long-term care is often required—at high financial costs to both families and public programs.

In addition to the optimistic and welcome trend of declining risk for dementia in a number of countries over the past few decades, an increasing number of studies point to a troubling trend in the United States: namely, growing disparities across socioeconomic status (SES) and race/ethnicity in dementia risk, general health status, and life expectancy. The nature and causes of these disparities, how they have grown in past decades, and how they might be mitigated in the future are also extremely important issues for demographers, policy makers, and other researchers to address in the coming decades.

Finally, there have been important advances in understanding the biology and pathophysiology of cognitive decline and dementia in recent decades, including the importance of cardiovascular risk factors (CRFs) that increase the risk for AD and dementia, as well as new technologies for identifying biomarkers that may aid in the early diagnosis, prevention, and treatment of cognitive decline. These new technologies bring with them important questions for the future of an aging population regarding their costs and cost effectiveness and regarding equitable access to their use among those at risk for cognitive decline and dementia.

GROWING IMPORTANCE OF COGNITIVE DECLINE AND DEMENTIA IN AGING POPULATIONS

Cognitive function plays a central role in determining the well-being and quality of life of adults as they pass from midlife to older ages, including their decisions to work, retire, and spend or save their money. Dementia due to AD or ADRD is characterized by a decline in cognitive function severe enough to cause the loss of independence in daily function (McKhann et al., 2011). Dementia has wide-ranging, direct and indirect effects on the well-being of older adults, their families, and the costs imposed on public programs, such as Social Security, Medicare, and Medicaid.

There were approximately 4.2 million adults living with dementia in the United States in 2010 and more than 135 million worldwide (Hurd et al., 2013; Prince et al., 2013). The economic impact of dementia has been estimated at $200 billion per year in the United States (Hurd et al., 2013) and $600 billion worldwide (Wimo et al., 2013), including a significant burden of unpaid family care-giving. Because the incidence of dementia rises sharply at ages greater than 75, the expected growth in the worldwide elderly population in the decades ahead has been projected to lead to a tripling of dementia cases by 2050, absent new interventions to prevent or slow the trajectory of cognitive decline (Prince et al., 2013; Langa, 2015).

As noted above, tempering the projections of large increases in dementia cases as the older population grows are recent studies suggesting a decline in dementia incidence and prevalence in high-income countries over the past 25 years, perhaps attributable to higher levels of educational attainment and more intensive treatment of CRFs (e.g., hypertension, diabetes, smoking, and hyperlipidemia) that increase the risk for cognitive decline (Schrijvers et al., 2012; Matthews et al., 2013, 2016; Satizabal et al., 2016; Langa et al., 2017; Leggett et al., 2017; Wu et al., 2017). However, it is unclear whether this positive trend in high-income countries will continue, as the prevalence of obesity and diabetes have grown (Larson et al., 2013; Langa, 2015), and it is also unclear whether there has been a similar or opposite trend in low- and middle-income countries (Chan et al., 2013; Wu et al., 2013, 2014).

The relationship of education to lifetime risk for cognitive decline and dementia is especially important to consider for a number of reasons. First, more years of education has consistently been associated with a lower dementia risk in a wide range of studies across different countries over the past two decades (Valenzuela and Sachdev, 2005; Meng and D'arcy, 2012). Second, low educational attainment has been identified as likely the largest contributor to preventable dementia risk worldwide, with an esti- mated population-attributable risk of nearly 20 percent of dementia cases in 2010 (Norton et al., 2014). Third, SES and racial/ethnic disparities in educational attainment, as well as the quality of education received, have been identified as potential causes for the SES and racial/ethnic disparities in dementia incidence and prevalence in the United States and other coun- tries around the world (Glymour and Manly, 2008). And finally, as noted above, increases in average levels of educational attainment in high-income countries over the past few decades have been associated with declines in dementia incidence and prevalence (Larson et al., 2013; Langa et al., 2017; Wu et al., 2017), suggesting that expanding access to education may help decrease population dementia risk.

How might more years of education decrease one's risk for dementia? Education-related increases in "cognitive reserve" is a widely cited theory for how education may decrease dementia risk. The cognitive reserve hypothesis posits that the cognitive challenges and stimulation associated with education lead to changes in brain structure (e.g., more neurons and more connections among the neurons) that allow one to better compensate when pathologies accumulate in the aging brain (Stern, 2012; Meng and D'arcy, 2012). Individuals with high cognitive reserve can continue thinking normally with significantly greater levels of neuropathology than those with low cognitive reserve, so they are less likely to experience the significant cognitive decline leading to dementia. Although years of formal education is the variable most often used as an indicator of cognitive reserve (likely because it is routinely collected in many epidemiological studies), other studies suggest that level of cognitive stimulation and cognitive challenge throughout life, including the characteristics of one's occupation, how one spends her leisure time, whether one partakes in "cognitive training" exercises, and the extent of social interactions may all play a role in building or maintaining cognitive reserve and decreasing lifetime dementia risk (Vemuri et al., 2014). The optimistic and increasing evidence that aging brains retain their plasticity to grow new neurons and compensate for age-related pathologies through "life long learning" and cognitive stimulation will likely be an important focus of both future research and potential preventive interventions in the decades ahead (Lindenberger, 2014; Gutchess, 2014).

Of course, there are likely many additional pathways besides a direct biological impact of education on the brain by which one's level of education is associated with better later-life health, cognition, and life expectancy. Hayward and colleagues (2015), in reviewing the literature on the relationship of education to life expectancy, provide a useful conceptual model that highlights the multiple positive health benefits of education, including information regarding the benefits of certain health behaviors and health care services, better jobs and lifetime income, larger and more supportive social networks, and cognitive skills that promote a greater sense of control and agency. Each of these pathways is likely important in promoting brain health, as well as a longer life.

While there has been a general trend toward increasing levels of education around the world in both high-income and low-income countries (Becker et al., 2010), there are significant international differences in the timing and magnitude of those increases, which will likely lead to differences in dementia trends across countries. For instance, while there has been a significant increase in the level of educational attainment among older adults in the United States over the past few decades, there will not be further significant increase in the next few decades, since education levels among those ages 65 to 69 now are similar to the education levels of those ages 25–29 (Lutz et al., 2014). However, educational attainment among China's older population, for example, will continue to increase in the decades ahead because the education level of those ages 25–29 now is significantly higher than those ages 65–69 now (Lutz et al., 2014). Tracking dementia trends across countries with differing time trends in educational attainment may provide opportunities for a better understanding of the causal pathways leading from early-life education to late-life dementia risk (Langa et al., 2018).

Recent large-scale studies incorporating genetic data from genome-wide association studies (GWASs) have raised some additional complexities for sorting out the life course impact of education on brain health and late-life dementia risk. A number of studies have found genetic loci (single-nucleotide polymorphisms, or SNPs) that are associated with the level of educational attainment, possibly through pathways that affect brain biology or structure, suggesting that there may be a component of genetically determined brain biology that might lead to both greater educational attainment and to lower risk for later-life dementia (Rietveld et al., 2013; Okbay et al., 2016). Other GWASs have shown a number of SNPs related to general cognitive function in mid- and late life (Davies et al., 2015), cognitive decline in later life (Deary et al., 2012), and the size of the hippocampus (the brain region associated with short-term memory typically affected by Alzheimer's disease) (Hibar et al., 2017). Future genetic epidemiological research on cognitive decline may help us better understand the complexity of how genetics and one's lifelong social and environmental exposures interact and combine to increase or decrease the risk for late-life dementia.

THE OVERLAP AND INTERACTION OF ALZHEIMER'S DISEASE, VASCULAR DISEASE, AND OTHER BRAIN PATHOLOGIES

Zlokovic (2011) has proposed a "two-hit vascular hypothesis" for AD, which highlights the likely overlap and interaction of vascular pathways and the classic AD amyloid-beta pathway in the onset of neurodegeneration and subsequent dementia (see Figure 9-1). In this model, vascular disease resulting from known risk factors, such as hypertension and diabetes, leads to decreased blood flow to brain cells as well as disruption of the "blood-brain barrier," both of which may lead to increased production or decreased clearance of amyloid-beta, resulting in neurodegeneration, loss of synapses and neurons, and eventual cognitive decline and dementia (Snyder et al., 2015). A key implication of this two-hit hypothesis is that prevention or adequate treatment of known CRFs may decrease the risk for AD and other dementias, both by decreasing vascular-related injury to the brain (including strokes) and by decreasing amyloid-beta-related injury to the brain (Zlokovic, 2011). In other words, the prevention or control of CRFs may also act as a "disease-modifying" treatment for AD by preventing or slowing the build-up of cerebral amyloid-beta.

For instance, recent studies show that having more CRFs in midlife is not only associated with a greater risk of cognitive decline in later life (Gottesman et al., 2014) but also associated with higher levels of amyloid-beta in the brain, consistent with the two-hit vascular hypothesis that CRFs may directly influence the development of AD pathology (Gottesman et al., 2017). Yaffe and colleagues (2014) showed that a life course perspective regarding the impact of CRFs on cognitive decline is important, as the cumulative exposure to elevated levels of CRFs over 25 years of follow-up in individuals who were 18 to 30 years old at baseline was associated with significantly worse cognitive function in middle age. As discussed in more detail below, the importance of CRFs, especially in early and midlife, as

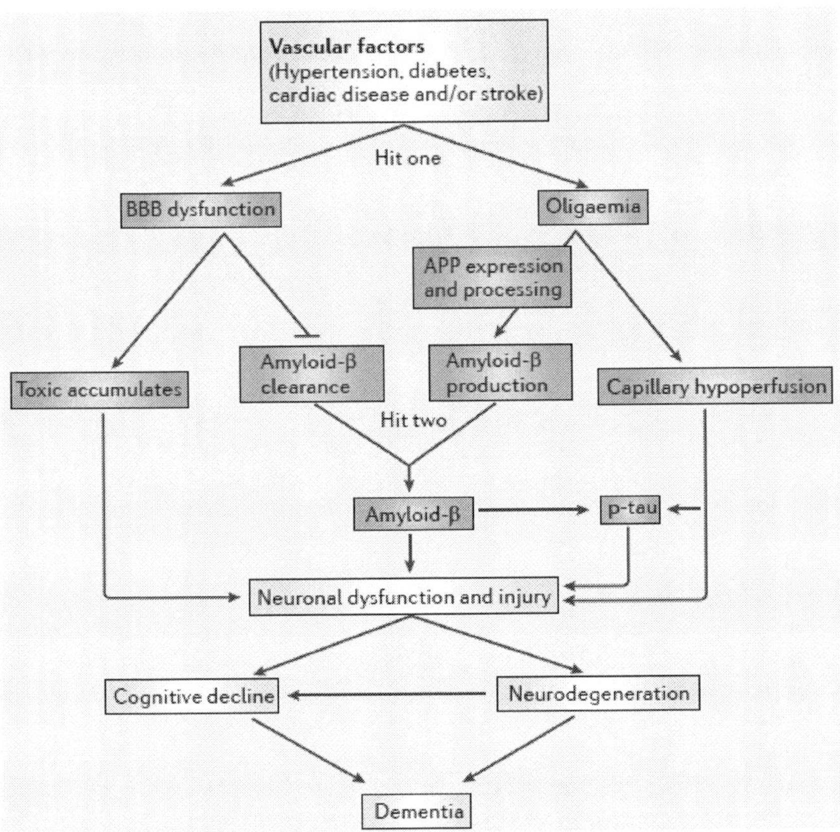

FIGURE 9-1 The two-hit vascular hypothesis for Alzheimer's disease.
SOURCE: Reprinted with permission from Springer Nature: Springer. Zlokovic, B.V. (2011, Box 1, p. 733). *Nature Reviews Neuroscience,* ©2011.

potential causes for late-life dementia may be one reason for the clear SES disparities in brain health and dementia risk, since CRFs are more prevalent in individuals from low-SES groups and the SES disparities in the prevalence of those risk factors has been increasing in recent decades.

An important issue regarding the relationship of CRFs to late-life dementia risk is whether better prevention or treatment of CRFs will not only reduce age-specific dementia risk later in life but will also lead to an extension of life expectancy that will, in turn, lead to a greater number of dementia cases due to people living to much older ages, when dementia risk increases sharply. Norton and colleagues (2014) concluded that a significant reduction of mid-life CRFs would lead to a significant decline in future dementia incidence and prevalence, but their analysis did not account for a possible increase in life expectancy due to the decline in CRFs. A more recent paper by Zissimopolous and colleagues (2018) used a microsimulation model that accounted for the expected increase in life expectancy associated with better prevention and treatment of hypertension and diabetes, along with the decrease in future age-specific dementia risk. They concluded that dementia cases would actually increase in future years, due to more individuals living to older ages when dementia risk is high. The different conclusions from these two analyses hinge on the relative magnitude of the decrease in dementia incidence associated with a decline in CRFs compared to the decrease in future mortality risk; this relative magnitude is currently uncertain. Future research to more clearly define how prevention and treatment of CRFs throughout the life course are related to both future dementia risk and mortality at older ages will be especially important to determine the public health implications of population-level trends in CRFs and their treatment and to determine whether additional years of life are more likely to be spent with good or poor cognitive function (Schoeni et al., 2018).

In addition to AD and vascular disease as causes for dementia, there are likely additional important disease processes and pathological pathways leading to cognitive decline and dementia that are not yet well understood. Boyle and colleagues (2013) showed that, surprisingly, only about 40 percent of late-life cognitive decline could be explained by the known common neuropathologies of AD, vascular disease, and Lewy body disease, a result that strongly suggests that other factors and causal pathways need to be identified and better understood to develop successful preventive interventions and treatments that address the multiple and mixed pathologies that are typically found in the brains of older adults (Neuropathology Group of the Medical Research Council Cognitive Function and Aging Study, 2001; Langa et al., 2004; Schneider et al., 2007; Sonnen et al., 2007). For instance, recent evidence suggests that hyperphosphorylated transactive response DNA-binding protein 43 (TDP-43), a pathological protein first identified in the brains of patients with frontotemporal dementia and amyotrophic lateral sclerosis, is also often present in those diagnosed with AD, and when present it significantly increases the risk for dementia (James et al., 2016).

Overall, the evidence gathered during the past 20 years from population-based studies, especially those that have included brain autopsies, has led to a much better understanding that cognitive decline and dementia are typically caused by a mix of neuropathologies that result from a complex interaction of risk factors (both social and biological) across the life course, likely including pathologies that are yet to be fully understood. As discussed in more detail below, an additional complexity identified with new neuroimaging techniques is that the neuropathologies leading to cognitive decline and dementia are often present decades prior to the onset of cognitive symptoms, further supporting the importance of a full life course perspective when identifying the causes and the potential preventive interventions for late-life dementia.

DISPARITIES IN LIFE EXPECTANCY, GENERAL HEALTH, AND BRAIN HEALTH IN THE UNITED STATES

An increasing number of studies show that health status has become significantly more unequal in the United States over the past few decades. Perhaps the clearest evidence of this growing disparity is the trends in life expectancy across rich and poor over the past 30 years. A recent National Academies report (National Academies of Sciences, Engineering, and Medicine, 2015), using data from the Health and Retirement Study, found that life expectancy at age 50 for women in the lowest income quintile and born in 1930 was 32.3 years, but life expectancy at age 50 has actually declined to 28.3 years for low-income women born in 1960. In contrast, life expectancy at age 50 for women in the highest income quintile born in 1930 was 36.2 years, but it had increased to 41.9 years for those in the same income quintile born in 1960. So the gap in life expectancy between rich and poor women in the United States has grown by nearly 10 years, from 3.9 to 13.6, in recent decades. The gap in life expectancy between rich and poor men also increased but by a slightly smaller amount (8 years) than for women.

A recent study by Chetty and colleagues (2016) used tax records to examine income and life expectancy across time and region in the United States between 2001 and 2014. Similar to the National Academies analysis, those with high income had significantly longer life expectancies, and the income gap in life expectancy increased significantly during the 13-year period. Life expectancy for those with low income also varied significantly across geographic regions and was correlated with smoking rates in those regions.

Disparities in general health status among older U.S. adults have also widened in recent years. For instance, the (age- and sex-adjusted) proportion of older U.S. adults who reported being in excellent or very good health (in the nationally representative Medical Expenditure Panel Survey) increased significantly between 2000 and 2014 among those who were white, well educated, or in the highest income quartile. But this proportion decreased significantly during this same time period for those who were Black, Hispanic, had a high school degree or less, or were in the lowest income quartile, thereby widening already significant differences across these groups (Davis et al., 2017).

As noted above, the presence and severity of CRFs in middle-aged and older adults are closely linked to the risk for subsequent cognitive decline and dementia, so trends in the presence of CRFs and their treatment may be especially important for understanding trends and growing disparities in dementia risk in recent decades. Using data from the National Health and Nutrition Examination Survey, Odutayo and colleagues (2017) found that mean systolic blood pressure and current smoking declined significantly between 1999 and 2014 among those with high income but did not decline among those at or below the poverty level. As a result, the proportion of individuals with high cardiovascular disease risk (i.e., $\geq$ 20% 10-year risk) widened significantly between those at low- and high-income levels in recent years.

SES and racial/ethnic disparities in dementia risk have been well documented in the United States. For instance, a recent study of older adults in California found significant differences in age-adjusted dementia incidence between 2000 and 2013, with African Americans having the highest risk (26.6 cases per 1,000 person-years), Latinos and Whites having intermediate risk (19.6 and 19.3 cases, respectively), and Asian Americans having the lowest risk (15.2 cases) (Mayeda et al., 2016). These differences were found for both men and women and across the entire age range. Differences across racial/ethnic groups in the presence of CRFs explained some of the difference in dementia incidence but not all of it. A similar pattern of racial/ethnic differences in overall cognitive function was found for a nationally representative sample of 19,000 U.S. adults ages 51 and older in 2010 (Díaz-Venegas et al., 2016).

Another community-based prospective cohort study of older adults in two U.S. locations (Pittsburgh and Memphis; the Health, Aging, and Body Composition Study) found a similar disparity in dementia incidence for African Americans compared to Whites over 12 years of follow-up, with African Americans having a greater risk (unadjusted hazard ratio 1.44) of dementia incidence (Yaffe et al., 2013). Most of the racial disparity was explained by socioeconomic factors (household income, education level, and literacy level), leading the authors to conclude that education's impact on the building of cognitive reserve throughout the life course, and chronic stress that may result from low SES, are likely important pathways leading to SES and racial/ethnic disparities in late-life dementia risk. Many other studies support the value of using a life course perspective to better understand and identify the complex and overlapping factors that have led to the large and growing SES and racial/ethnic disparities in dementia risk in the United States (for a review, see Glymour and Manly, 2008).

The potential importance of geography as a contributor to SES and racial/ethnic disparities in cognitive function and dementia risk has been an increasing focus of recent research. A study by Gilsanz and colleagues (2017) found that being born in a state that has a high stroke mortality rate (e.g., the "stroke belt" states in the southeastern United States, such as Alabama, Arkansas, Louisiana, and Mississippi) was associated with a significantly increased risk of dementia, even among individuals who moved away from those states during their life. The authors noted that "place of birth may reflect a host of social and environmental conditions in early life that could be some of the primary drivers of racial inequalities in rates of dementia," including access to and quality of education, poverty, poor nutrition, chronic stress, and the establishment of health behaviors that may increase cardiovascular risk later in life (e.g., smoking and physical inactivity) (Gilsanz et al., 2017, p. 1061).

Place of residence throughout life may also have an impact on dementia risk and on SES disparities in dementia risk, due to exposures to environmental toxins that affect brain development and health. For instance, individuals living closer to major roadways in Ontario, Canada, were found to have a significantly increased risk for dementia over 12 years of follow-up, possibly related to greater exposure to traffic-related air pollution (Chen et al., 2017). A growing number of other studies have also found a relationship between air pollution levels in one's region of residence and increased risk for dementia (Cacciottolo et al., 2017) or poor cognitive function (Ailshire et al., 2017).

Other characteristics of one's neighborhood, separate from potential toxins in the physical environment, have also been shown to be related to cognitive function and dementia risk. For instance, rural residence in the United States was associated with an increased risk for cognitive impairment and dementia compared to urban residence, although that gap decreased somewhat in recent years, possibly related to greater gains in educational attainment among those in rural areas (Weden et al., 2017). Other studies have shown that living in a neighborhood with institutional resources that may help promote cognitive reserve (e.g., community centers, libraries, and recreational facilities) was associated with better cognitive function, independent of individual risk factors for cognitive decline (Clarke et al., 2012).

THE IMPLICATIONS OF DIAGNOSING AND TREATING "PRECLINICAL ALZHEIMER'S DISEASE"

Over the past 20 years, there have been important advances in understanding the natural history of the brain pathologies leading to AD and ADRD, as well as the development of new diagnostic tests and technologies to identify those pathologies. The identification of biomarkers in the blood and cerebrospinal fluid that accompany the development of AD-related brain pathologies, as well as new neuroimaging technologies that can identify changes in brain structure (e.g., AD-related shrinkage of the hippocampus) and the extent of amyloid-beta protein deposition in the brains of individuals who do not yet show symptoms of cognitive decline, will have important and wide-ranging implications for prevention, treatment, and even the definition of who has AD and dementia. Karlawish and colleagues (2017, p. 379) called this the "Next Frontier" in understanding and management of AD and proposed that in the future, AD may no longer be "a disease leading to irrevocable cognitive and functional decline and death, but rather a chronic condition like cardiovascular disease, AIDS, or some cancers that can often be managed with early intervention."

One especially important new insight is that the brain pathologies and changes leading to AD and dementia are often present for decades prior to the onset of any cognitive decline. Jack and colleagues (2013) have proposed a hypothetical model (see Figure 9-2) based on the increasing number of biomarker and neuroimaging studies in older adults with and without dementia that found that a significant proportion of individuals had amyloid-beta protein in their brains but were still cognitively "normal." New diagnostic criteria proposed in 2011 by the National Institute on Aging and the Alzheimer's Association identify these individuals as having "Preclinical Alzheimer's Disease." In other words, they have the typical biomarker and neuroimaging findings of AD, but they do not yet show the typical cognitive decline associated with AD (Sperling et al., 2011). In addition, a descriptive classification system—the "A/T/N" classification scheme—has been proposed to synthesize, and more clearly organize, the presence or absence of key currently known biomarkers of AD, so they can be combined systematically to classify all individuals in both clinical and population-based research (Jack et al., 2016). In this proposed scheme, the "A" denotes biomarkers of amyloid protein accumulation in the brain; the "T" denotes biomarkers of tau protein accumulation; and the "N" denotes biomarkers of neurodegeneration or neuronal injury.

The hope is that targeting future AD treatments at individuals with preclinical AD will successfully prevent or delay the onset of cognitive decline, in much the same way that statin treatment for those with atherosclerosis and CRFs can prevent or delay future myocardial infarctions. There are currently multiple clinical trials testing potential AD-preventive treatments, such as the Anti-Amyloid Treatment in Asymptomatic Alzheimer (A4) Study (Sperling et al., 2014). The A4 Study is testing whether 4 years of treatment with solanezumab, a drug designed to decrease brain amyloid-beta deposition, slows the rate of cognitive decline in older adults with preclinical AD.

While the potential to prevent AD and dementia through new treatments such as solanezumab is understandably creating significant interest and optimism, a number of key issues and uncertainties regarding preventive treatments for those with preclinical AD should be considered (Karlawish and Langa, 2016). Perhaps most important is the danger of "overdiagnosis"

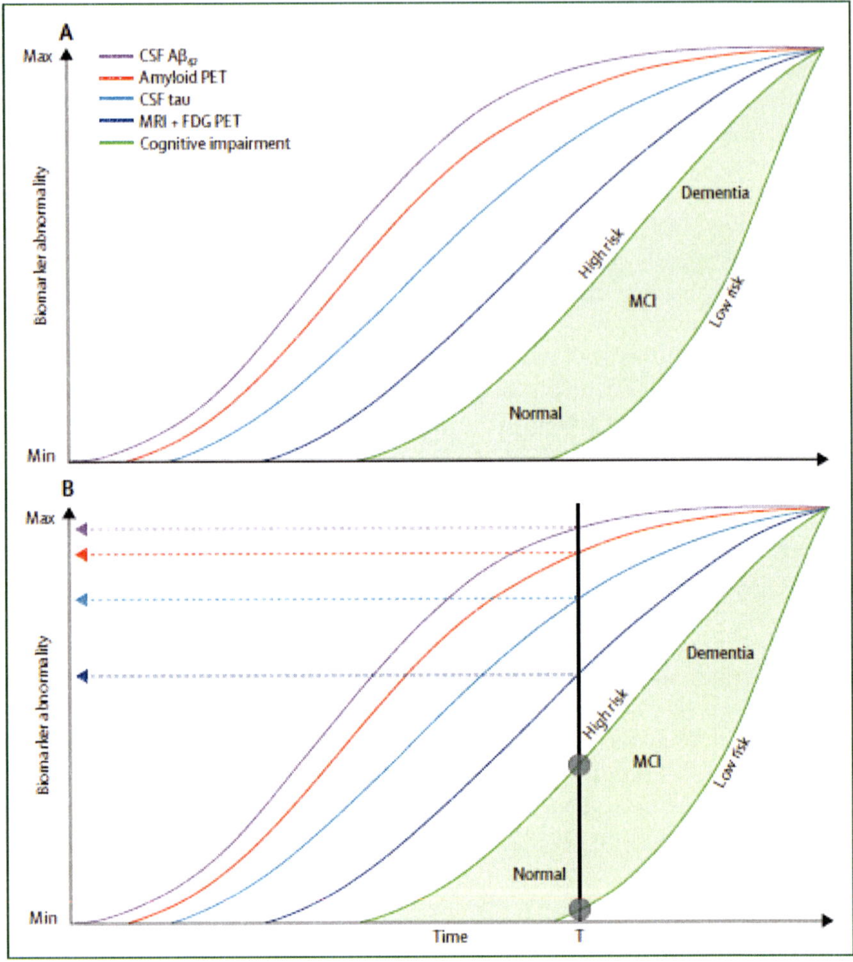

FIGURE 9-2 Dynamic biomarkers of the Alzheimer's disease pathological cascade.
SOURCE: Reprinted with permission from Elsevier. Jack et al. (2013, Fig. 5, p. 211). *The Lancet Neurology,* ©2013.

(Welch et al., 2011)—in other words, identifying a pathological change in the brain based on a biomarker abnormality that will not ultimately lead to dementia, prior to an individual dying from other causes. Overdiagnosis exposes individuals to the potential negative side effects, complications, and costs of treatment, without providing benefits in terms of actual prevention of a future disease. This important possible downside of "early diagnosis" for chronic diseases of aging has gained wider attention related to negative outcomes of screening for conditions such as prostate cancer, breast cancer, and osteoporosis (Welch et al., 2011). It could be especially prominent in screening for AD in middle-aged and older adults because the onset of AD or ADRD might not be expected for up to 25 years in the future and there will typically be significant competing risks for mortality from other causes during that time, especially cardiovascular disease (Langa and Levine, 2014).

Other important questions raised by screening for and treating pre-clinical AD include the costs and cost effectiveness of potential treatments, as well as the capacity of the health care financing and delivery systems to safely provide those treatments in an equitable way. For instance, solanezumab, the medication being tested in the A4 Study, is administered as an intravenous infusion requiring a monthly visit to an infusion site staffed by trained health care personnel. While the maker of solanezumab (Eli Lilly) has not announced what the target price of solanezumab would be for treatment of preclinical AD, similar monoclonal antibody drugs recently introduced for treatment of high cholesterol (evolocumab and alirocumab) currently cost about $14,000 per year (Kazi et al., 2016). A recent study estimated that at least 35 million adults in the United States likely have preclinical AD characterized by amyloid-beta deposition in the brain (Brookmeyer et al., 2017). Assuming a cost per person of $10,000 per year for solanezumab and assuming that only 30 percent of the esti-mated 35 million adults with preclinical AD obtain treatment, the total cost would be a staggering $105 billion per year (which was approximately one-third of the *total* expenditures for prescription medications in the United States in 2016) (Hartman et al., 2017). And since AD preventive treatments might be used for decades in someone who starts treatment at age 60 to 65 years, preclinical AD treatment would add a large and ongo-ing expenditure to the U.S. health care system. Given the likely high costs for the current preclinical AD treatments being studied, future analyses of the cost effectiveness of these interventions, as well as the distributional implications of the financing and delivery of these treatments, will be extremely important.

Finally, given the significant SES and racial/ethnic disparities in dementia risk noted above, one other key issue regarding the generalizability of current data is important to consider regarding potential treatments for preclinical AD. Since nearly all of the data on biomarker and neuroimaging testing to identify preclinical AD have thus far come from volunteer samples, with very limited representation of less-educated and minority individuals, there is still significant uncertainty regarding the generalizability of those studies to low-SES and minority populations. Future studies of biomarkers, neuro-imaging, and treatments in more representative populations will be especially important, given the higher risk for dementia in these populations (Falk et al., 2013; Karlawish et al., 2017).

CONCLUSIONS AND PRIORITIES FOR FUTURE RESEARCH

As the elderly population grows in the decades ahead, a better understanding of the life course factors that increase or decrease the risk for cognitive decline and dementia will be increasingly important, given the wide-ranging effects that cognitive decline has on older individuals, their families, and public expenditures. This review of recent developments in cognitive aging and dementia research points to a number of opportunities and challenges for future research and for potential interventions to prevent or delay the incidence of dementia.

As the brain is the most complex organ in the body, highly sensitive to any interruption in blood flow, it seems appropriate that the recent genetic, biological, and epidemiological evidence reviewed in this chapter highlight the complexity of identifying the causes for cognitive decline and dementia. One obvious theme is the growing evidence that dementia is best understood as a late-life condition that is influenced by a complex set of factors from across the entire life course: from genetics and early-life environment and education to mid- and late-life CRFs, to multiple factors in later life (e.g., cognitive stimulation and social networks) that will hopefully preserve and maintain cognitive reserve and the plasticity of the aging brain. Given the prominent role of education's association with dementia risk, future research that helps unpack the "black box" of how early-life education decreases later-life dementia risk would be extremely important for helping to develop and target useful public health and public policy initiatives. What are the "active ingredients" of education, and how can they be delivered efficiently to children across the SES spectrum? Is online education a lower-cost option that will provide similar benefits for building cognitive reserve?

The growing evidence that Alzheimer's disease and vascular disease are closely linked and may even be "two hits" of the same pathological process provides an important potential target for decreasing dementia risk, given the very high prevalence of CRFs among middle-aged and older adults and the known behavioral and pharmacologic interventions to prevent or treat them. However, the challenge of designing individual and population-level interventions for CRFs that address the large and growing SES and racial/ethnic disparities in those risks should be given especially high priority. Multifactorial interventions for life-style and CRF improvements, such as the FINGER study, have shown benefits for lowering dementia risk in clinical trials (Ngandu et al., 2015). Can those interventions be translated to successful implementation in low-SES populations that have the highest prevalence of CRFs and the greatest risk for dementia?

A recent National Academies report that comprehensively reviewed studies regarding risk factors for dementia recommended a number of areas that would be most useful to target for future research (National Academies of Sciences, Engineering, and Medicine, 2017). In line with the issues covered in this chapter, that report recommended future research on how treatments and behavioral interventions can better address CRFs (including hypertension, diabetes, high cholesterol, physical activity, and diet). It also recommended additional research on cognitive training interventions for older adults that have shown some benefit in randomized controlled trials for preventing cognitive decline and disability (Willis et al., 2006). Other promising avenues identified for research investment included interventions to improve sleep quality, treat depression, and facilitate social engagement at older ages. Additional pharmaceutical research on potential preventive medications, as discussed above, was also recommended.

It seems clear that given the complexity of the brain and the multiple factors that affect the brain's health across the life course, it is unlikely that a single "magic bullet" will be found that prevents dementia in the growing population of older adults (Larson, 2017). Given the centrality of good cognitive function to living with independence and intention, making good decisions and planning for the future, and contributing productively to the labor force and one's family and neighbors, the large and growing SES and racial/ethnic disparities for cognitive decline and dementia in the United States are especially pernicious and threatening to an aging society that hopes to provide some equity of access to the resources and environments that allow people to live long and well. Addressing these growing disparities in both dementia risk and life expectancy should be the main focus of public health and public policy in the decades ahead.

REFERENCES

Ailshire, J., Karraker, A., and Clarke, P. (2017). Neighborhood social stressors, fine particulate matter air pollution, and cognitive function among older U.S. adults. *Social Science & Medicine, 172,* 56–63.

Becker, G.S., Hubbard, W.H.J., and Murphy, K.M. (2010). Explaining the worldwide boom in higher education of women. *Journal of Human Capital, 4*(3), 203–241.

Boyle, P.A., Wilson, R.S., Yu, L., Barr, A.M., Honer, W.G., Schneider, J.A., and Bennett, D.A. (2013). Much of late-life cognitive decline is not due to common neurodegenerative pathologies. *Annals of Neurology, 74*(3), 478–489.

Brookmeyer, R., Abdalla, N., Kawas, C.H., and Corrada, M.M. (2017). Forecasting the prevalence of preclinical and clinical Alzheimer's disease in the United States. *Alzheimer's & Dementia, 14*(2), 121–129. doi: 10.1016/j.jalz.2017.10.009.

Cacciottolo, M., Wang, X., Driscoll, I., Woodward, N., Saffari, A., Reyes, J., Serre, M.L., Vizuete, W., Sioutas, C., Morgan, T.E., et al. (2017). Particulate air pollutants, APOE alleles and their contributions to cognitive impairment in older women and to amyloidogenesis in experimental models. *Translational Psychiatry, 7*(1), e1022.

Chan, K.Y., Wang, W., Wu, J.J., Liu, L., Theodoratou, E., Car, J., Middleton, L., Russ, T.C., Deary, I.J., Campbell, H., et al. (2013). Epidemiology of Alzheimer's disease and other forms of dementia in China, 1990–2010: A systematic review and analysis. *Lancet, 381*, 2016–2023.

Chen, H., Kwong, J.C., Copes, R., Tu, K., Villeneuve, P.J., van Donkelaar, A., Hystad, P., Martin, R.V., Murray, B.J., Jessiman, B., et al. (2017). Living near major roads and the incidence of dementia, Parkinson's disease, and multiple sclerosis: A population-based cohort study. *Lancet, 389*(10070), 718–726.

Chetty, R., Stepner, M., Abraham, S., Lin, S., Scuderi, B., Turner, N., Bergeron, A., and Cutler, D. (2016). The association between income and life expectancy in the United States, 2001-2014. *Journal of the American Medical Association, 315*(16), 1750–1766.

Clarke, P.J., Ailshire, J.A., House, J.S., Morenoff, J.D., King, K., Melendez, R., and Langa, K.M. (2012). Cognitive function in the community setting: The neighbourhood as a source of "cognitive reserve"? *Journal of Epidemiologic Community Health, 66*(8), 730–736.

Davies, G., Armstrong, N., Bis, J.C., Bressler, J., Chouraki, V., Giddaluru, S., Hofer, E., Ibrahim-Verbaas, C.A., Kirin, M., Lahti, J., et al. (2015). Genetic contributions to variation in general cognitive function: A meta-analysis of genome-wide association studies in the CHARGE consortium (N = 53949). *Molecular Psychiatry, 20*(2), 183–192.

Davis, M.A., Guo, C., Sol, K., Langa, K.M., and Nallamothu, B.K. (2017). Trends and disparities in the number of self-reported health of older adults in the United States, 2000 to 2014. *Journal of the American Medical Association Internal Medicine, 177*(11), 1683–1684.

Deary, I.J., Yang, J., Davies, G., Harris, S.E., Tenesa, A., Liewald, D., Luciano, M., Lopez, L.M., Gow, A.J., Corley, J., et al. (2012). Genetic contributions to stability and change in intelligence from childhood to old age. *Nature, 482*(7384), 212–215.

Díaz-Venegas, C., Downer, B., Langa, K.M., and Wong, R. (2016). Racial and ethnic differences in cognitive function among older adults in the USA. *International Journal of Geriatric Psychiatry, 31*(9), 1004–1012.

Falk, E.B., Hyde, L.W., Mitchell, C., Faul, J., Gonzalez, R., Heitzeg, M.M., Keating, D.P., Langa, K.M., Martz, M.E., Maslowsky, J., et al. (2013). What is a representative brain? Neuroscience meets population science. *Proceedings of the National Academy of Sciences of the United States of America, 110*(44), 17615–17622.

Gilsanz, P., Mayeda, E.R., Glymour, M.M., Quesenberry, C.P., and Whitmer, R.A. (2017). Association between birth in a high stroke mortality state, race, and risk of dementia. *Journal of the American Medical Association Neurology, 74*(9), 1056–1062.

Glymour, M.M., and Manly, J.J. (2008). Lifecourse social conditions and racial and ethnic patterns of cognitive aging. *Neuropsychology Review, 18*, 223–254.

Gottesman, R.F., Schneider, A.L., Albert, M., Alonso, A., Bandeen-Roche, K., Coker, L., Coresh, J., Knopman, D., Power, M.C., Rawlings, A., et al. (2014). Midlife hypertension and 20-year cognitive change: The atherosclerosis risk in the Communities Neurocognitive Study. *Journal of the American Medical Association Neurology, 71*(10), 1218–1227.

Gottesman, R.F., Schneider, A.L., Zhou, Y., Coresh, J., Green, E., Gupta, N., Knopman, D.S., Mintz, A., Rahmim, A., Sharrett, A.R., et al. (2017). Association between midlife vascular risk factors and estimated brain amyloid deposition. *Journal of the American Medical Association, 317*(14), 1443–1450.

Gutchess, A. (2014). Plasticity of the aging brain: New directions in cognitive neuroscience. *Science, 346*(6209), 579–582.

Hartman, M., Martin, A.B., Espinosa, N., Catlin, A., and the National Health Expenditure Accounts Team. (2017). National health care spending in 2016: Spending and enrollment growth slow after initial coverage expansions. *Health Affairs, 37*(1), 150–160. doi: 10.1377/hlthaff.2017.1299. E-pub online Dec. 6.

Hayward, M.D., Hummer, R.A., and Sasson, I. (2015). Trends and group differences in the association of educational attainment and U.S. adult mortality: Implications for understanding education's causal influence. *Social Science & Medicine, 127*, 8–18.

Hibar, D.P., Adams, H.H.H., Jahanshad, N., Chauhan, G., Stein, J.L., Hofer, E., Renteria, M.E., Bis, J.C., Arias-Vasquez, A., Ikram, M.K., et al. (2017). Novel genetic loci associated with hippocampal volume. *Nature Communications, 8*, 13624.

Hurd, M., Martorell, F., Delevande, A., Mullen, K., and Langa, K.M. (2013). The monetary costs of dementia in the United States. *New England Journal of Medicine, 368*, 1326–1334.

Jack, C.R., Jr., Knopman, D.S., Jagust, W.J., Petersen, R.C., Weiner, M.W., Aisen, P.S., Shaw, L.M., Vemuri, P., Wiste, H.J., Weigand, S.D., et al. (2013). Tracking pathophysiological processes in Alzheimer's disease: An updated hypothetical model of dynamic biomarkers. *Lancet Neurology, 12*(2), 207–216.

Jack, C.R., Bennett, D.A., Blennow, K., Carrillo, M.C., Feldman, H.H., Frisoni, G.B., Hampel, H., Jagust, W.J., Johnson, K.A., Knopman, D.S., et al. (2016). An unbiased descriptive classification scheme for Alzheimer disease biomarkers. *Neurology, 87*(5), 539–547.

James, B.D., Wilson, R.S., Boyle, P.A., Trojanowski, J.Q., Bennett, D.A., and Schneider, J.A. (2016). TDP-43 stage, mixed pathologies, and clinical Alzheimer's-type dementia. *Brain, 139*(11), 2983–2993.

Karlawish, J., and Langa, K.M. (2016). Unfinished business in preventing Alzheimer disease. *Journal of the American Medical Association Internal Medicine, 176*(12), 1739–1740.

Karlawish, J., Jack, C.R., Jr., Rocca, W.A., Snyder, H.M., and Carrillo, M.C. (2017). Alzheimer's disease: The next frontier. *Alzheimer's & Dementia, 13*(4), 374–380.

Kazi, D.S., Moran, A.E., Coxson, P.G., Penko, J., Ollendorf, D.A., Pearson, S.D., Tice, J.A., Guzman, D., and Bibbins-Domingo, K. (2016). Cost-effectiveness of PCSK9 inhibitor therapy in patients with heterozygous familial hypercholesterolemia or atherosclerotic cardiovascular disease. *Journal of the American Medical Association, 316*(7), 743–753.

Langa, K.M. (2015). Is the risk of Alzheimer's disease and dementia declining? *Alzheimer's Research & Therapy, 7*(1), 34.

Langa, K.M., and Levine, D. (2014). The diagnosis and management of mild cognitive impairment: A clinical review. *Journal of the American Medical Association, 312*(23), 2551–2561.

Langa, K.M., Foster, N., and Larson, E.B. (2004). Mixed dementia: Emerging concepts and therapeutic implications. *Journal of the American Medical Association, 292*(23), 2901–2908.

Langa, K.M., Larson, E., Crimmins, E., Faul, J., Levine, D., Kabeto, M., and Weir, D. (2017). A comparison of the prevalence of dementia in the United States in 2000 and 2012. *Journal of the American Medical Association Internal Medicine, 177*(1), 51–58.

Langa, K.M., Crimmins, E., and Hayward, M.D. (2018). Examining trends in dementia incidence and prevalence using an Age-Period-Cohort framework. In *Oxford Textbook of Neurological and Neuropsychiatric Epidemiology* (in press). Oxford, UK: Oxford University Press.

Larson, E. (2017). Prevention of late-life dementia: No magic bullet. *Annals of Internal Medicine, 68*(1), 77–79. doi: 10.7326/M17-3026. Epub Dec 19.

Larson, E., Yaffe, K., and Langa, K.M. (2013). New insights into the dementia epidemic. *New England Journal of Medicine, 369*(24), 2275–2277.

Leggett, A., Clarke, P., Zivin, K., McCammon, R.J., Elliott, M.R., and Langa, K.M. (2017). Recent improvements in cognitive functioning among older U.S. adults: How much does increasing educational attainment explain? *Journals of Gerontology, Series B: Psychological Sciences and Social Sciences*, published online, January 28.

Lindenberger, U. (2014). Human cognitive aging: Corriger la fortune? *Science, 346*(6209), 572–578.

Lutz, W., Butz, W., and Samir, K.C. (2014). *World Population and Human Capital in the Twenty-First Century*. Oxford, UK: Oxford University Press.

Matthews, F.E., Arthur, A., Barnes, L.E., Bond, J., Jagger, C., Robinson, L., Brayne, C., on behalf of the Medical Research Council Cognitive Function and Ageing Collaboration. (2013). A two-decade comparison of prevalence of dementia in individuals aged 65 years and older from three geographical areas of England: Results of the Cognitive Function and Ageing Study I and II. *Lancet, 382*(9902), 1405–1412.

Matthews, F.E., Stephan, B., Robinson, L., Jagger, C., Barnes, L., Arthur, A., and Brayne, C. (2016). Cognitive Function and Ageing Studies (CFAS) Collaboration. A two-decade dementia incidence comparison from the Cognitive Function and Ageing Studies I and II. *Nature Communications, 7*, 11398.

Mayeda, E.R., Glymour, M.M., Quesenberry, C.P., and Whitmer, R.A. (2016). Inequalities in dementia incidence between six racial and ethnic groups over 14 years. *Alzheimer's & Dementia, 12*(3), 216–224.

McKhann, G.M., Knopman, D.S., Chertkow, H., Hyman, B.T., Jack, C.R., Kawas, C.H., Klunk, W.E., Koroshetz, W.J., Manly, J.J., Mayeux, R., et al. (2011). The diagnosis of dementia due to Alzheimer's disease: Recommendations from the National Institute on Aging–Alzheimer's Association workgroups on diagnostic guidelines for Alzheimer's disease. *Alzheimer's & Dementia, 7*(3), 263–269.

Meng, X., and D'Arcy, C. (2012). Education and dementia in the context of the cognitive reserve hypothesis: A systematic review with meta-analyses and qualitative analyses. *PLoS One, 7*(6), e38268.

National Academies of Sciences, Engineering, and Medicine. (2015). *The Growing Gap in Life Expectancy by Income: Implications for Federal Programs and Policy Responses*. Washington, DC: The National Academies Press.

National Academies of Sciences, Engineering, and Medicine. (2017). *Preventing Dementia: A Way Forward*. Washington, DC: The National Academies Press.

Neuropathology Group of the Medical Research Council Cognitive Function and Aging Study. (2001). Pathologic correlates of late onset dementia in a multicentre, community based population in England and Wales. *Lancet, 357*, 169–175.

Ngandu, T., Lehtisalo, J., Solomon, A., Levälahti, E., Ahtiluoto, S., Antikainen, R., Bäckman, L., Hänninen, T., Jula, A., Laatikainen, T., et al. (2015). A 2-year multidomain intervention of diet, exercise, cognitive training, and vascular risk monitoring versus control to prevent cognitive decline in at-risk elderly people (FINGER): A randomised controlled trial. *Lancet, 385*(9984), 2255–2263.

Norton, S., Matthews, F.E., Barnes, D.E., Yaffe, K., and Brayne, C. (2014). Potential for primary prevention of Alzheimer's disease: An analysis of population-based data. *Lancet Neurology, 13*, 788–794.

Odutayo, A., Gill, P., Shepherd, S., Akingbade, A., Hopewell, S., Tennankore, K., Hunn, B.H., and Emdin, C.A. (2017). Income disparities in absolute cardiovascular risk and cardiovascular risk factors in the United States, 1999–2014. *Journal of the American Medical Association Cardiology, 2*(7), 782–790.

Okbay, A., Beauchamp, J.P., Fontana, M.A., Lee, J.J., Pers, T.H., Rietveld, C.A., Turley, P., Chen, G.B., Emilsson, V., Meddens, S.F., et al. (2016). Genome-wide association study identifies 74 loci associated with educational attainment. *Nature, 533*(7604), 539–542.

Prince, M., Guerchet, M., and Prina, M. (2013). *Alzheimer's Disease International. Policy Brief for Heads of Government: The Global Impact of Dementia 2013–2050.* London: Alzheimer's Disease International.

Rietveld, C.A., Medland, S.E., Derringer, J., Yang, J., Esko, T., Martin, N.W., Westra H.-J., Shakhbazov, K., Abdellaoui, A., Agrawal, A., et al. (2013). GWAS of 126,559 individuals identifies genetic variants associated with educational attainment. *Science, 340*(6139), 1467–1471.

Satizabal, C.L., Beiser, A.S., Chouraki, V., Chene, G., Dufouil, C., and Seshadri, S. (2016). Incidence of dementia over three decades in the Framingham Heart Study. *New England Journal of Medicine, 374*(6), 523–532.

Schneider, J.A., Arvanitakis, Z., Bang, W., and Bennett, D.A. (2007). Mixed brain pathologies account for most dementia cases in community-dwelling older persons. *Neurology, 69,* 2197–2204.

Schoeni, R., Freedman, V., and Langa, K.M. (2018). Introduction to a supplement on population level trends in dementia: Causes, disparities, and projections. *Journals of Geronotology: Social Sciences,* in press.

Schrijvers, E.M., Verhaaren, B.F., Koudstaal, P.J., Hofman, A., Ikram, M.A., and Breteler, M.M. (2012). Is dementia incidence declining? Trends in dementia incidence since 1990 in the Rotterdam Study. *Neurology, 78*(19), 1456–1463.

Snyder, H.M., Corriveau, R.A., Craft, S., Faber, J.E., Greenberg, S.M., Knopman, D., Lamb, B.T., Montine, T.J., Nedergaard, M., Schaffer, C.B., et al. (2015). Vascular contributions to cognitive impairment and dementia including Alzheimer's disease. *Alzheimer's & Dementia, 11*(6), 710–717.

Sonnen, J.A., Larson, E.B., Crane, P.K., Haneuse, S., Li, G., Schellenberg, G.D., Craft, S., Leverenz, J.B., and Montine, T.J. (2007). Pathological correlates of dementia in a longitudinal, population-based sample of aging. *Annals of Neurology, 62,* 406–413.

Sperling, R.A., Aisen, P.S., Beckett, L.A., Bennett, D.A., Craft, S., Fagan, A.M., Iwatsubo, T., Jack, C.R., Jr., Kaye, J., Montine, T.J., et al. (2011). Toward defining the preclinical stages of Alzheimer's disease: Recommendations from the National Institute on Aging–Alzheimer's Association workgroups on diagnostic guidelines for Alzheimer's disease. *Alzheimer's & Dementia, 7*(3), 280–292.

Sperling, R.A., Rentz, D.M., Johnson, K.A., Karlawish, J., Donohue, M., Salmon, D.P., and Aisen, P. (2014). The A4 study: Stopping AD before symptoms begin? *Science Translational Medicine, 6*(228), 228fs13.

Stern, Y. (2012). Cognitive reserve in ageing and Alzheimer's disease. *Lancet Neurology, 11*(11), 1006–1012.

Valenzuela, M.J., and Sachdev, P. (2005). Brain reserve and dementia: A systematic review. *Psychological Medicine, 35,* 1–14.

Vemuri, P., Lesnick, T.G., Przybelski, S.A., Machulda, M., Knopman, D.S., Mielke, M.M., Roberts, R.O., Geda, Y.E., Rocca, W.A., Petersen, R.C., et al. (2014). Association of lifetime intellectual enrichment with cognitive decline in the older population. *Journal of the American Medical Association Neurology, 71*(8), 1017–1024.

Weden, M.M., Shih, R.A., Kabeto, M.U., and Langa, K.M. (2017). Secular trends in dementia and cognitive impairment of U.S. rural and urban older adults. *American Journal of Preventive Medicine,* published online, December 6.

Welch, G., Schwartz, L., and Woloshin, S. (2011). *Overdiagnosed: Making People Sick in Pursuit of Health.* Boston: Beacon Press.

Willis, S.L., Tennstedt, S.L., Marsiske, M., Ball, K., Elias, J., Koepke, K.M., Morris, J.N., Rebok, G.W., Unverzagt, F.W., Stoddard, A.M., et al. (2006). Long-term effects of cognitive training on everyday functional outcomes in older adults. *Journal of the American Medical Association, 296*(23), 2805–2814.

Wimo, A., Jönsson, L., Bond, J., Prince, M., and Winblad, B. (2013). Alzheimer Disease International. The worldwide economic impact of dementia 2010. *Alzheimer's & Dementia*, 9, 1–11.

Wu, Y.T., Lee, H.Y., Norton, S., Chen, C., Chen, H., He, C., Fleming, J., Matthews, F.E., and Brayne, C. (2013). Prevalence studies of dementia in mainland China, Hong Kong and Taiwan: A systematic review and meta-analysis. *PLoS One, 8*, e66252.

Wu, Y.T., Lee, H.Y., Norton, S., Prina, A.M., Fleming, J., Matthews, F.E., and Brayne, C. (2014). Period, birth cohort and prevalence of dementia in mainland China, Hong Kong and Taiwan: A meta-analysis. *International Journal of Geriatric Psychiatry, 29*(12), 1212–1220.

Wu, Y.T., Beiser, A.S., Breteler, M.M.B., Fratiglioni, L., Helmer, C., Hendrie, H.C., Honda, H., Ikram, M.A., Langa, K.M., Lobo, A., et al. (2017). The changing prevalence and incidence of dementia over time—current evidence. *Nature Reviews Neurology, 13*(6), 327–339.

Yaffe, K., Falvey, C., Harris, T.B., Newman, A., Satterfield, S., Koster, A., Ayonayon, H., Simonsick, E., and Health ABC Study. (2013). Effect of socioeconomic disparities on incidence of dementia among biracial older adults: Prospective study. *BMJ, 19*, 347.

Yaffe, K., Vittinghoff, E., Pletcher, M.J., Hoang, T.D., Launer, L.J., Whitmer, R., Coker, L.H., and Sidney, S. (2014). Early adult to midlife cardiovascular risk factors and cognitive function. *Circulation, 129*(15), 1560–1567.

Zissimopoulos, J., Crimmins, E., and St. Clair, P. (2018). The impact of changes in population health and mortality on future prevalence of Alzheimer's disease and other dementias in the United States. *Journal of Geronotology: Social Sciences*, in press.

Zlokovic, B.V. (2011). Neurovascular pathways to neurodegeneration in Alzheimer's disease and other disorders. *Nature Reviews Neuroscience, 12*(12), 723–738.

10

The Demography of Late-Life Disability

Vicki A. Freedman[1,2]

INTRODUCTION

Worldwide, the number of people living with disability and the average number of years lived with disability is increasing (GBD 2015 Disease and Injury Incidence and Prevalence Collaborators, 2016). In the United States, 16 million adults ages 65 and older live in the community with a disability—defined broadly as a sensory, cognitive, mobility, self-care, or independent living limitation (Erikson et al., 2017); another 1 million older adults with severe limitations live in nursing home settings (Freedman and Spillman, 2014a). One in four older adults successfully accommodates losses in physical capacity and continues to carry out daily activities without difficulty or assistance (Freedman and Spillman, 2014b). Yet for others, late-life disability may result in undesirable outcomes including the loss of one's ability to live independently, the need for family members to provide care, and reduced well-being. Given the aging of the continued Baby Boom population, the number of older Americans living with disability is projected to increase dramatically in the near future (Institute of Medicine, 2007). Long-term services and supports for this population are also projected to increase sharply between now and 2050 (Congressional Budget Office, 2013).

[1]Institute for Social Research, University of Michigan.

[2]Prepared for the Committee on Population Conference on Future Directions of the Demography of Aging, August 17–18, 2017, Washington, DC. Funding was provided through a grant from the National Institute on Aging (U01-AG032947). The views presented are those of the author alone and do not represent those of the University of Michigan or the funding agency.

Understanding the population-level implications of late-life disability in the context of an aging population was once considered the purview of a subfield of demography referred to as medical demography (Manton and Stallard, 1994). Rooted in classical demography and bioactuarial sciences, medical demography involved estimating biologically plausible models of chronic disease, disability, and mortality. Early research on this topic focused on the shifting age distributions of mortality and implications of interactions between mortality and disability processes for the size and health of the older population (Land and Yang, 2006). The field has also given rise to a substantial literature on disability trends, including the seminal finding that the prevalence of activity limitations in the United States declined during the 1980s (Manton et al., 1993) and 1990s (Manton et al., 1997; Manton and Gu, 2001). More recent studies have documented that such declines did not continue into the first and second decades of the 21st century (Freedman et al., 2013) and the percentage of nonelderly adults reaching late life with limitations in place appears to be increasing (Martin and Schoeni, 2014).

Much of the literature to date has focused narrowly on disability defined as activity limitations. As conceptual frameworks and measures of disablement have evolved, a better understanding is emerging of the constructs that constitute late-life disablement; its physiological, environmental, and behavioral underpinnings; its progression with age and relation to mortality; and consequences for individuals and their families. Advances in modeling individual trajectories have opened up new avenues for estimating biologically and environmentally plausible models that recognize compensatory strategies adopted by older adults as they age. Trend analyses can now distinguish changes in underlying capacity from how older adults accommodate such declines.

Given these developments, late-life disablement is a topic central to the growing field of the demography of aging. The next section reviews conceptual and empirical issues, including definitions of disability and corresponding measurement advances. Although the centrality of cognition to the disablement process is recognized here, another chapter in this volume covers measurement issues related to cognitive impairment and dementia in more detail. The third section provides a broad portrait of late-life disability, drawing upon the 2015 round of the National Health and Aging Trends Study (NHATS), an annual study of U.S. older adults that began in 2011 and has an explicit focus on late-life disability trends and trajectories (Kasper and Freedman, 2014). Section four focuses on advances in modeling individual-level disability trajectories and in tracking population-level trends in the United States. The final section provides an overview of future directions.

THE LANGUAGE AND MEASUREMENT OF DISABILITY

The literature on late-life disability is characterized by a history of competing conceptualizations, inconsistent terminology, and ambiguous measurement. Over a dozen definitions of disability are in use by U.S. federal government programs, complicating the task of monitoring disability at the population level (Gregory, 2004). In this chapter, the term "disability" is used broadly to include four domains: impairments in body functions or structures; reduced physical, sensory, or cognitive functioning; difficulty carrying out self-care or household activities by oneself, receipt of help, or use of compensatory strategies that signal the need for help; and restrictions in participation in productive, social, or community life. As described below, other approaches persist that define disability more narrowly as activity limitations.

The Language of Disability

Background

Historically, two distinct models—the medical model and the social model—governed society's approach to addressing disability (Iezzoni and Freedman, 2008). For the 19th and most of the 20th century, the medical conceptualization of disability dominated. Disability was viewed as solely caused by disease, trauma, or other health conditions and was therefore under the purview of physicians. Their aim was to cure the underlying disease or adjust the individual's behavior to compensate for loss of functioning. The medical model's emphasis on the underlying medical cause of disability is evident in several U.S. programs (e.g., worker's compensation, disability insurance), which classify applicants by the condition causing their disability. The medical model is limited for studying late-life disability because there is no explicit recognition of the social and environmental context of disability. In contrast, the social model of disability, which gained prominence in the 1970s and 1980s, views disability as a socially created problem and has as its aim the full integration of individuals into society. The social model emphasizes that disability is not an attribute of an individual but created by environmental barriers. Consequently, this model's focus is on the removal of barriers to participation.

The Nagi Model

Recognizing both perspectives, a disablement model was suggested by Nagi (1965), adopted by the Institute of Medicine (1991), and advanced by Verbrugge and Jette (1994) and others. The Nagi model distinguishes an individual's underlying capacity to carry out tasks from socially defined role limitations. Disablement in this framework consists of four stages: ***pathology, impairment, functional limitations, and disability.*** *Pathology* is defined at the organ level and refers to compromised function as the result of a chronic or acute condition or an injury. *Impairment* is defined at the system level and refers to loss of system function. *Functional limitation* is defined at the level of the whole person and refers to limitations in physical or mental actions. Finally, *disability* refers to the final stage in the process: the inability to carry out a socially defined role, such as work or self-care or household activities.

The Nagi model was the dominant model used in gerontological research for many decades. Researchers who drew upon the framework benefited from the availability of well-developed measures for each stage (Guralnik and Ferrucci, 2009). They were able to accumulate a body of evidence demonstrating, for example, the importance of mobility limitations for the onset of disability and mortality (Guralnik et al., 1995). In addition, geriatricians expanded upon the Nagi framework to make the clinically relevant distinction between experiencing difficulty with an activity versus receiving help from another person (Gill et al., 1998).

Although not explicit, the Nagi model also provided a framework for studying environmental influences on disability (Verbrugge and Jette, 1994). In particular, building on Lawton's original competence-environment press theory (Lawton, 1986), Verbrugge and Jette theorized that disability occurs when there is a gap between an individual's capabilities and environmental demands. In this context, assistive devices (e.g., a cane) may alter an individual's capabilities and environmental modifications (e.g., a grab bar) may reduce corresponding environmental demands. For some activities, individuals may reduce the frequency of such tasks or fundamentally change how a task is carried out, for instance, washing up at the sink instead of climbing in and out of a bathtub. Fried and colleagues (Fried et al., 2001; Weiss et al., 2007) refer to such compensatory strategies as "preclinical" disability, in which changes in behavior (e.g., the frequency or way in which an activity is carried out), not detected with conventional self-reported difficulty, signals an increased risk for needing assistance.

The ICF Framework

Over the last decade, the World Health Organization's disability model, the *International Classification of Functioning, Disability, and Health* (ICF; World Health Organization, 2002), has gained prominence. Although initially somewhat slow to be embraced by the U.S. gerontological community (Jette, 2009), the ICF is recognized as providing an internationally agreed-upon terminology for understanding the consequences of health conditions for participation in society (Institute of Medicine, 2007). Like the Nagi model, the ICF integrates both medical and social perspectives into a framework that reflects biologic, individual, and social processes. Unlike the Nagi model, the ICF defines disability as an umbrella term encompassing multiple domains, rather than as a final stage in the disablement process.

In the ICF, there are four main domains: ***health conditions, body functions and structures, activities, and participation.*** The last three domains have negative analogues that constitute disability: impairments, activity limitations, and participation restrictions. *Health conditions* include diseases, disorders, and injuries. *Body functions and structures* include basic physiological functions and anatomical parts of the body such as organs and limbs, whereas *impairments* are considered a significant deviation or loss in body function or structures. *Activities* are the tasks of daily life, and *activity limitations* are difficulties an individual has in completing such activities. *Participation* includes involvement in productive activities such as work or volunteering, in social activities with friends or family, and in community and civic activities. *Participation restrictions* are defined as problems an individual may experience with these life situations. The framework also explicitly recognizes both personal (internal) and environmental (external) contextual factors. Personal factors include social, demographic, and other background characteristics of the individual, whereas environmental factors include social, physical, and legal environments. These contextual factors influence the entire disablement process.

The ICF approach offers several advantages over the Nagi framework. First, it applies to all individuals regardless of their level of functioning. Second, contextual factors are explicit rather than implied. Third, it recognizes the value of participation in activities that are central to people's lives beyond self-care and household activities. Finally, the framework recognizes that new ("secondary") health conditions may emerge as a consequence of the disablement process.

The NHATS Framework

Begun in 2011 with funding from the National Institute on Aging, NHATS is a national panel survey of Medicare beneficiaries ages 65 and older that is specifically designed to promote research to reduce disability, maximize independent functioning, and enhance quality of life at older ages. The sample is refreshed periodically to allow study of national-level disability trends as well as individual-level trajectories. Annual, in-person interviews provide detailed information on the disablement process and its consequences.

NHATS developed an enhanced framework for studying disablement—highlighted in Figure 10-1—that builds upon both the Nagi and

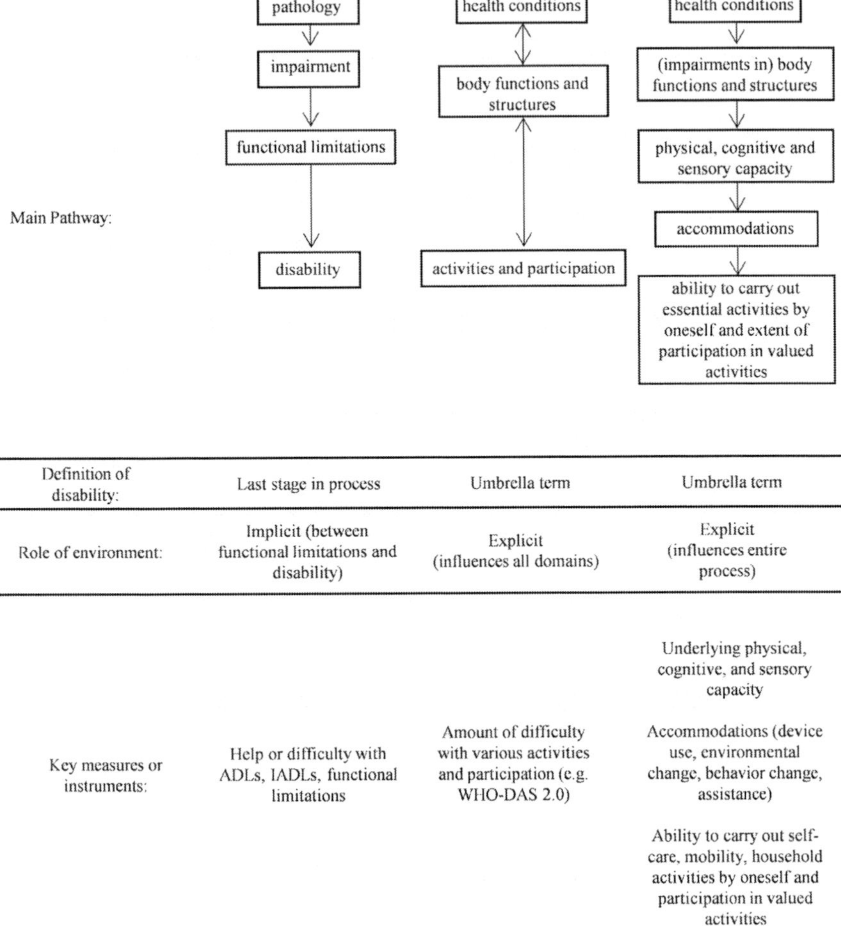

FIGURE 10-1 Comparison of three disablement frameworks.
SOURCE: Author-generated, see also Freedman (2009).

ICF approaches (Freedman, 2009). The main pathway recognizes that health conditions influence body functions and structures, which in turn influence activities and participation. However, the NHATS framework incorporates three distinct features, which open up new opportunities for research (Kasper and Freedman, 2014). First, the framework explicitly distinguishes between the underlying capacity of individuals and the accommodations that they make in order to carry out activities. *Capacity* refers to an individual's physiological, cognitive, and sensory capabilities that form the building blocks to carry out activities. *Accommodations* are identified in a separate domain that captures *how* activities are carried out. Common accommodations include using assistive technology, adapting the physical environment (e.g., adding a grab bar), changing the demands of the activity (e.g., cleaning up at the sink instead of bathing), reducing how often an activity is undertaken, and receiving help from another person. Second, the NHATS framework makes a distinction between the ability to carry out by oneself essential self-care, mobility, and household activities and the extent of participation in valued but elective activities. Third, the framework acknowledges that the physical, social, technological, and service-related environment of an older adult influences the entire process. As described in the next section, NHATS has re-engineered traditional measures of late-life disability to provide researchers with a new set of validated measures mapping to each of these domains.

The NHATS framework fosters testing of theories about disablement from multiple disciplinary perspectives. For instance, it can be used to test psychological and social theories linking compensatory strategies to quality-of-life outcomes such as continued participation in activities of value and maintenance of subjective well-being. It can also be used to test hypotheses about behavioral responses to declines in capacity—for instance, the circumstances under which preclinical disability occurs before reports of difficulty, or the pathways from intrinsic changes in activity performance (e.g., more slowly, less often) to extrinsic changes (modifications to the environment or use of devices). It can also be used to evaluate questions of particular interest to the geriatric research community, such as the link between specific conditions—for example, obesity, sarcopenia, chronic pain—and physical capacity or the biological underpinnings of physical capacity. For demographers, the approach is valuable because it allows fuller characterization of the disablement process and therefore supports estimation of models linking chronic disease, disability, and mortality that are physiologically, environmentally, and behaviorally plausible.

The Measurement of Disability

As the conceptual underpinnings of disablement have evolved, so too have the measures available to researchers. Initially researchers were restricted to activity limitation measures—most often, Katz's activities of daily living (ADLs) and Lawton and Brody's instrumental activities of daily living (IADLs) (Katz et al., 1963; Lawton and Brody, 1969)—and Nagi's functional limitation measures that assessed upper and lower body limitations (Nagi, 1965). Since that time, however, notable advances in the assessment of disability domains have occurred (National Research Council, 2009). Many have been incorporated into the comprehensive, validated NHATS disability protocol (Kasper and Freedman, 2014), making it possible for the first time to examine for a national sample annual changes in physical capacity, compensatory strategies, activity limitations, participation restrictions, and consequences such as unmet need. Both classical and modern approaches to test development have been used to evaluate the protocol (Freedman et al., 2011; Kasper et al., 2017).

Limitations in Self-Care and Household Activities

ADL and IADL measures were developed half a century ago for use by clinicians evaluating older patients. Difficulty with daily tasks (without help or special equipment) and receipt of help were typically ascertained. However, wording—and meaning—varied considerably across studies. Some protocols asked about whether the older adult needed help; others asked about receipt of help. Some protocols specified without help or special equipment, others were ambiguous. Although widely used for research and programmatic purposes, these items do not provide insight into the physiology of disablement or the role of environmental and compensatory strategies. Such distinctions are valuable for promoting independent functioning in later life (Freedman et al., 2014).

In NHATS, measures of activity limitations have been re-engineered to explicitly measure difficulty by oneself, with devices if used, and have been broadened to include various behavioral adaptations (e.g., assistive device use, environmental modification use, less frequent performance, and receipt of help). The measures have been used to develop a spectrum of accommodation that reflects a hierarchy of underlying physical and cognitive capacity and is more strongly related than age to well-being (Freedman et al., 2014). The spectrum includes four groups, those who either are fully able, have successfully accommodated using devices, remain a target for accommodation (because they have reduced their activity level or report difficulty despite current accommodations), or receive assistance from another person. Previous approaches to measurement in national studies did not allow identification of individuals who successfully accommodated or those who reduced their activity level. In their evaluation of this spectrum, Gill and Williams (2017) confirmed its monotonic gradient in risk of functional dependence and mortality and its success in identifying a very low-risk, fully able group. Their findings underscore that the various adaptive behaviors are unlikely to represent an orderly set of stages and that more research is needed on the complex pathways to dependence and death.

Physical Capacity

Nagi (1965) developed functional limitation measures to assess the rehabilitation potential of applicants for disability benefits to the federal Social Security program. A team of medical evaluators and the applicant both scored the applicant's maximum ability using a scale from 0 (no ability) to 7 (no restriction). The physical requirements of the applicant's job were also scored. The general approach of asking older adults to rate their physical restrictions has been widely implemented in national surveys. Protocols generally include questions about ability to carry out both upper (reaching up, reaching out, grasping) and lower (bending, lifting and carrying, climbing stairs) body movements. Most often respondents are asked about difficulty without help from another person or use of special equipment. Several shortcomings of these measures have been identified (Freedman et al., 2011). First, they cover a relatively narrow range of functioning (for an exception, see Simonsick et al., 2001). Second, some older adults may not carry out a particular activity without their devices (e.g., walking several blocks) and thus are not able to report on level of difficulty. Third, as with activity limitations, the Nagi items rely on subjective assessments of ability.

Increasingly common on surveys of older adults are standardized performance tests (Gill, 2010). Individuals are asked to carry out specific movements while trained observers make ratings using predetermined, objective criteria (Guralnik et al., 1989). One of the most common protocols to measure lower body functioning is the Short Physical Performance Battery (SPPB) (Guralnik et al., 1995). This set of standardized procedures includes a short walking test to evaluate usual gait speed, a series of progressively more difficult balance tests, and an assessment of the individual's ability to rise from a chair multiple times. The SPPB has been established as a strong predictor of subsequent disability and mortality (Guralnik et al., 1994, 1995) and is able to detect change within individuals (Ostir et al., 2002; LIFE Study Investigators, 2006). Additional performance batteries have been developed to measure upper body functioning, such as grip strength and lung function (Roberts et al., 2011; Fragoso et al., 2008).

NHATS measures physical capacity using an expanded set of self-reported measures adapted from Nagi (Freedman et al., 2011) and a standard battery of physical performance tests (Kasper et al., 2012). The self-reported items assess ability (yes/no) to carry out six pairs of more and less challenging tasks by oneself and without special equipment, if used. The pairs of tasks include walking three and six blocks, going up 10 and 20 stairs, lifting and carrying 10 and 20 pounds, bending over and kneeling down, reaching up and putting a heavy book on an overhead shelf, and grasping small objects and opening a sealed jar. For each pair, respondents were first asked about the more-challenging task; those who reported being unable or having no opportunity to carry out that task were then asked about the less-challenging task. Rather than use the phrase "special equipment," NHATS tailored the questions to name devices mentioned earlier in the interview (e.g., "without using your cane" rather than "without special equipment"). The NHATS physical-performance battery includes the full SPPB (usual walking speed, nested balance tests, chair stand tests), along with tests of grip strength and peak air flow. Item Response Theory analyses suggest the two sets of measures are complementary (Kasper et al., 2017). Specifically, the self-reported items discriminate at the lower end of the physical capacity range, whereas the performance tests distinguish across a broader range. A score drawing upon both self-reports and performance tests provides better measurement precision across the full spectrum and appears better suited than either approach alone for studying age-related changes in physical capacity.

The Physical, Service, and Technological Environments

For many years, measures of the home environment, developed primarily for clinical interventions (Gitlin, 2003), have been mostly absent from national health surveys, as have environmental measures related to mobility disability (Satariano et al., 2012). Surveys were also not well equipped to capture the expansion in different types of residential settings, in part because respondents were often not able to accurately report place type or available services. Measures of the technological environment in which tasks are conducted have also been lacking. With respect to the latter, the Internet is a potentially important tool for persons with limited mobility, since a number of household activities—shopping, banking, ordering prescriptions—can be carried out online. And, with the exception of items to measure equipment use, which often produce marked underestimates (Cornman et al., 2005), compensatory strategies have rarely been assessed in a national context.

The NHATS protocol measures the physical, service, and technological environments of older adults. For instance, there are measures of the physical structure of the living environment (e.g., multifloor homes, multiunit buildings) and the existence and addition of environmental features that support functioning (e.g., grab bars, raised toilets, stair glides). An additional questionnaire administered to a facility informant allows NHATS to distinguish the level of services available for the nearly 6 million older adults (15%) living in residential care settings (Freedman and Spillman, 2014a). The technological environment and use of the Internet to carry out social, household, and health-related activities is also assessed (Levine et al., 2016).

Participation Restrictions

Participation in valued activities and participation restrictions are now recognized as integral to disability models (World Health Organization, 2002), but measures in national U.S. studies of health and aging remained limited until recently. For eight activities, NHATS assessed whether the respondent participated in the last month, whether their health or functioning limited their participation, and how important it was to the respondent to be participating in the activity. Given the central role of transportation to participation in community activities, there are also follow-up items on whether a transportation problem limited the respondent's participation. Activities included socializing in person, attending religious services, attending organized club meetings, going out for enjoyment, caring for another person, working for pay, and volunteering. In addition, a favorite activity was assessed, along with participation in the last month and whether the respondent's health or functioning limited participation. Analyses confirm that the construct of participation restriction is reliable and distinct from limitations in self-care and household activities (Freedman et al., 2011).

Unmet Need and Adverse Consequences

Although not explicit in existing frameworks, the concept of unmet need has appeared in the social gerontological literature for many years. Earliest measures asked respondents directly whether they "needed more help" with daily activities, making it difficult to interpret findings. Allen and colleagues developed an alternative approach that asks directly about adverse consequences that are the result of unmet need (Allen and Mor, 1997). In NHATS, respondents who had difficulty or received assistance with a given activity were asked if a particular consequence occurred—for instance, not being able to get dressed, go out, or eat a hot meal—because no one was there to assist with the activity or because it was too difficult to perform the activity alone (Allen et al., 2014).

A PORTRAIT OF LATE-LIFE DISABLITY IN THE UNITED STATES

This section provides a snapshot of late-life disability in the United States for several major demographic groups and highlights the distinctive disadvantage of minority women. Although disablement is a fundamentally dynamic phenomenon, understanding cross-sectional differences in the domains that constitute the components of disablement is instructive. Drawing upon the 2015 round of NHATS, the tables provide a nuanced description of the activity limitations experienced by different groups of older adults, along with underlying physical, sensory, and cognitive capacity; the physical, service, and technological environments in which older adults carry out daily activities; and consequences of those limitations. There are many additional factors—such as regional and local variation, factors from early and midlife, and current behaviors—that influence late-life disablement, but they are beyond the scope of this portrait.

Portrait by Stage of Disablement

Activity Limitations

Focusing on limitations in daily activities, reflected in reports of help from another person or difficulty by oneself (with devices, if used), about 38 percent of older adults have a self-care or mobility activity limitation (see Table 10-1). In addition, about 6 percent of older adults do not report difficulty but carry out their self-care and mobility activities less often than a year ago. Another one in four older adults (28%) report no difficulty, assistance, or change in frequency but use assistive devices when carrying out self-care or mobility activities ("successful accommodation"). Finally, just under 30 percent of older adults are fully able to carry out their self-care and mobility activities. For household activities, 39 percent of older adults have a limitation (have difficulty or receive help related to their health or functioning), about 8 percent have reduced the frequency of their activities, and the remaining 54 percent are fully able.

Patterns for difficulty and assistance are consistent with past studies highlighting disparities in such outcomes (Stuck et al., 1999; Schoeni et al., 2005, 2009). Differences in behavioral accommodations are also apparent. For instance, the percentage performing activities less often is relatively low for all groups (ranging from 4.5% to just over 7%) but, like difficulty and assistance outcomes, is higher for women and those with fewer years of completed education. Successful accommodation, however, follows a distinctive pattern, increasing from ages 65–69 through ages 75–79 and then decreasing with each successive age group. Successful accommodation is also more common among women, among older adults who are White and those who live with a spouse or partner, and for those at higher levels of education. Other studies suggest that successful accommodation is more likely for those with more children and those living in homes with environmental features already installed and that those who successfully accommodate report well-being on par with, and participation restrictions only slightly below, those who are fully able to carry out activities (Freedman et al., 2014, 2017).

Physical, Sensory, and Cognitive Capacity

Underlying the patterns in activity limitations are important differences in older individuals' capacity to carry out daily activities. Focusing on a composite measure of physical capacity that blends self-reported items with performance tests, mean scores range from 23 (out of 32) for 65-to-69-year-olds to just 9.2 for those ages 90 and older (see Table 10-2). Men and older adults who are White, live with a spouse or partner, or have more years of education are more likely to have a high physical capacity score (≥27) than other groups.

The percentage of older adults with poor vision (either blind or unable to see far or near even when wearing glasses) and poor hearing (deaf or unable to use the telephone, hear conversation in a quiet room, or hear conversation with background noise) increases steadily with age, from a low of 7 percent and 10 percent for poor vision and poor hearing, respectively, among 65-to-69-year-olds, to a high of 24 percent and 34 percent among those ages 90 and older. The percentages with poor vision or poor hearing decrease as educational attainment increases. Poor vision is also higher for women and minorities, whereas poor hearing is lower for women and for Black older adults.

Table 10-2 also shows the percentage of older adults classified as having probable and possible dementia. The classification (see Kasper et al., 2013) is based on reported diagnosis of dementia, proxy reports from a validated informant instrument, and scores on domains of cognitive functioning (executive functioning, memory, orientation). For these estimates, individuals may not "recover" in the subsequent round and it is assumed that 72 percent of long-stay nursing home residents have dementia. Overall, more than 9 percent of older adults can be considered to have probable dementia and another 6 percent have possible dementia. The risks of having probable dementia are substantially higher for minority groups, those living alone or with someone other than a spouse or partner, and those with lower levels of educational attainment.

Age gradients for four of the measures (low physical capacity, poor vision, poor hearing, and probable dementia) and a summary measure of poor physical, sensory, or cognitive capacity are displayed in Figure 10-2. These age-specific prevalence estimates are the result of several distinct underlying forces: onset among those without poor capacity, recovery among those with poor capacity, and the history of mortality for each group. Just over 20 percent of adults ages 65–69 are considered to have poor capacity in any of the four domains; this figure increases to more than 80 percent by age 90. Low physical capacity (score of ≤ 14 out of 32) has the strongest age gradient whereas poor vision, poor hearing, and probable

TABLE 10-1 Activity Limitations among U.S. Adults, Ages 65 and Older, 2015

	Self-Care and Mobility Activities				
	Fully Able	Successful Accommo-dation	Less Often	Difficulty	Assistance
65–69	41.7	24.0	5.9	16.2	12.1
70–74	36.2	29.1	4.8	16.9	13.1
75–79	25.5	32.8	5.2	19.3	17.2
80–84	16.9	29.1	7.3	20.6	26.1
85–89	9.4	27.6	5.8	21.0	36.2
≥ 90	4.2	16.5	4.7	15.0	59.7
Male	36.6	25.5	4.5	18.2	15.2
Female	23.7	29.2	6.4	17.6	23.1
White	29.7	29.5	5.3	17.4	18.1
Black	25.4	22.1	6.9	21.0	24.6
Other	30.3	19.6	6.3	18.9	24.9
Alone	22.9	26.7	6.4	21.5	22.4
With spouse	36.2	30.1	5.0	15.0	13.7
With spouse/others	29.1	28.8	5.0	15.8	21.2
With others	22.5	20.1	6.0	20.3	31.1
< High school	23.8	19.8	7.3	22.0	27.2
High school	26.7	27.5	5.6	19.1	21.1
Some college	31.1	30.3	5.5	18.6	14.5
College graduate	34.1	33.6	4.9	15.1	12.3
> College	39.6	30.6	5.3	15.0	9.5
All	29.4	27.5	5.6	17.9	19.6

NOTES: $N = 7,859$; for education groups, nursing home residents are omitted and $N = 7,499$; p-values for F-tests are significant at $p \leq .001$.
SOURCE: Data from National Health and Aging Trends Study.

Household Activities			
Fully Able	Less Often	Difficulty by Oneself	Help for Health/ Functioning Reasons
62.2	8.5	16.1	13.2
62.8	6.6	15.5	15.1
55.2	8.7	15.0	21.2
43.0	8.6	13.2	35.2
32.0	7.0	12.8	48.2
15.7	3.3	8.1	73.0
62.2	5.4	14.7	17.7
46.9	9.4	14.6	29.1
55.7	7.5	14.8	22.0
43.3	9.7	14.6	32.4
48.4	7.5	13.7	30.4
42.1	9.9	16.1	31.9
65.3	5.9	14.2	14.6
56.1	7.6	13.2	23.1
40.8	8.2	13.8	37.3
43.1	6.7	13.7	36.6
49.2	9.6	14.7	26.6
59.0	7.8	14.7	18.5
62.8	6.4	14.8	16.0
63.5	6.9	17.8	11.8
53.7	7.6	14.7	24.0

TABLE 10-2 Physical, Sensory, and Cognitive Capacity among U.S. Adults, Ages 65 and Older, 2015

	Physical		
	Mean Score	% High Score	% Low Score
65–69	23.4	42.1	12.7
70–74	22.3	33.0	15.1
75–79	19.9	20.1	23.8
80–84	16.6	10.6	38.3
85–89	13.9	4.1	51.2
≥90	9.2	0.9	76.1
Male	22.8	41.6	16.4
Female	17.9	14.1	32.2
White	20.8	29.3	22.3
Black	17.3	14.9	35.9
Other	17.7	16.2	35.0
Alone	17.3	15.1	35.3
With spouse	23.1	38.8	13.6
With spouse/others	20.8	28.3	21.2
With others	16.1	10.1	42.3
< High school	16.3	10.5	41.3
High school	18.8	17.2	29.3
Some college	21.4	27.2	18.3
College grad	23.4	43.1	13.5
> College	24.7	50.4	8.6
All	20.1	26.3	25.2

NOTES: N = 7,859; nursing home residents are omitted for physical capacity by education groups and for poor vision, poor hearing (N = 7,499); p-values for F-tests are significant at p ≤ .001 except gender differences in dementia (p = .116).
SOURCE: Data from National Health and Aging Trends Study.

Sensory		Cognitive	
% Poor Vision	% Poor Hearing	% Probable Dementia	% Possible Dementia
6.5	9.5	2.6	3.5
6.4	8.7	3.9	3.4
8.3	10.1	8.0	5.3
9.1	16.3	15.9	7.9
15.5	20.0	23.3	11.9
23.8	33.4	36.3	15.1
7.0	13.8	8.4	5.3
10.0	10.9	9.7	6.0
7.3	11.7	8.1	4.6
12.1	6.6	12.3	10.0
14.2	18.1	13.1	9.4
9.7	12.5	13.2	7.8
5.6	10.2	4.5	3.4
10.0	15.9	8.3	4.9
15.3	15.5	15.4	8.6
17.9	20.7	15.9	11.4
9.7	13.4	9.3	6.0
6.4	10.0	4.1	3.3
4.9	9.7	4.9	2.3
3.7	6.5	2.9	3.1
8.7	12.2	9.1	5.7

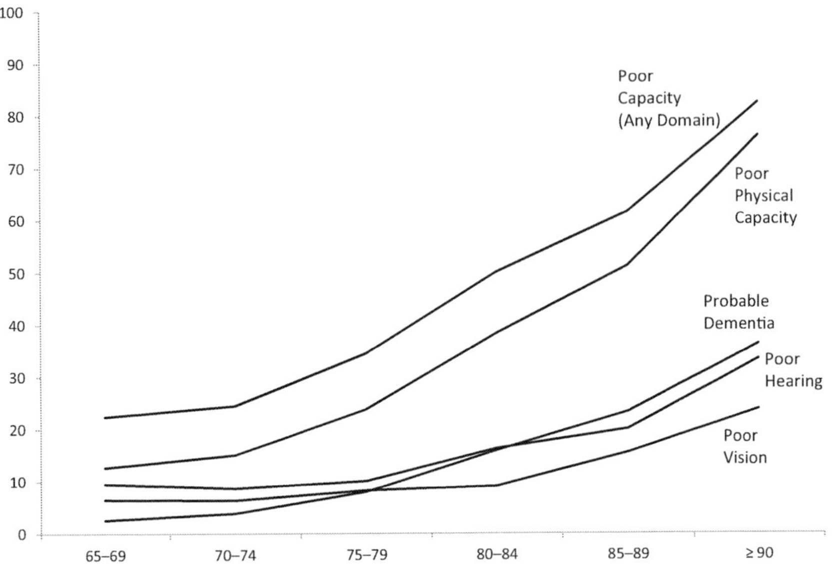

FIGURE 10-2 Age-specific estimates of poor physical, sensory, and cognitive capacity, adults ages 70 and older, 2015.
NOTES: *N* = 7,859; nursing home residents are omitted for poor hearing and poor vision and summary category of poor capacity (*N* = 7,499).
SOURCE: Data from National Health and Aging Trends Study.

dementia increase at more moderate slopes, reaching about 25–35 percent for those ages 90 and older, depending on the measure.

Physical, Service, and Technological Environment

The environments in which older adults carry out their daily activities also vary for older adults (see Tables 10-3 and 10-4). Overall, 10 percent live in a home without a bedroom, bathroom, and kitchen on one floor, just over 4 percent live in mobile homes, and 16 percent live in multiunit buildings such as apartments. The latter are more common at older ages and for women, minority groups, those who live alone, and those with less than a high school education. These differences can influence the types of environmental modifications that older adults have and can put into place. Modifications, such as grab bars, seats for the tub or shower, and raised toilet seats are less common among (non-Black) minorities. Others have demonstrated that among those with activity limitations, mobile home dwellers report fewer bathroom safety modifications (Al-rousan et al., 2015).

Also shown in Table 10-3 are the service environments in which older adults live. Overall, about 13 percent live in settings where services may be available, 2.5 percent live in nursing homes, 4.5 percent live in other residential care settings (e.g., assisted or independent living) and nearly 6 percent live in retirement or senior housing communities. These settings are more common with age; 42 percent of those ages 90 and older live in a setting that is not a traditional community setting, compared with only 6 percent of those ages 65–69. Such settings are more common for women and for individuals who live alone.

Differences in older adults' technological environments are illustrated in Table 10-4. Nearly two-thirds of older adults living in settings other than nursing homes in 2015 reported going online in the last month. Internet use was much higher at younger ages, for White respondents, for those living with a spouse or partner, and for those with more completed years of education. Going online for social activities was much more common than using the Internet for household or health-related activities. Nevertheless, more than one-third of older adults used the Internet to carry out basic household activities, such as shopping, ordering prescriptions, or banking, although racial and education-related differences were substantial.

Participation Restrictions and Unmet Need

The negative consequences of living with activity limitations can be substantial for some older adults (see Table 10-5, which focuses on older adults in settings other than nursing homes). More than one in four (27%) older adults report being unable to participate in a valued activity in the last month because of their health or functioning. Overall, nearly 11 percent of older adults report having an unmet need for mobility or self-care and 6 percent report an unmet need for household activities (and 14% report either type of unmet need, not shown in Table 10-5). These figures translate to 31 percent of older adults with activity limitations (difficulty or assistance) reporting at least one unmet need in the last month. Unmet needs and restrictions increase with age and decrease with education and are greater for minority groups and those living with people other than a spouse or partner.

The Distinctive Disadvantage of Minority Women

The distinctive disadvantage of older minority women in the United States is illustrated in Table 10-6. This analysis is limited to older adults ages 80–89 in order to partially control for differences in the age distributions across groups. The age group is also of substantive interest, since disability risks increase sharply in the eighth decade of life. Note that the table

TABLE 10-3 Physical and Service Environments in Which U.S. Adults Ages 65 and Older Live, 2015

	Type of Home			Environmental Modifications	
	2+ Floors	Mobile Home	Multiunit Building	Had Any Features	Added Any Features
65–69	12.6	3.8	10.9	57.7	10.6
70–74	11.7	5.5	11.8	65.3	13.5
75–79	8.7	4.1	13.9	72.1	16.8
80–84	7.6	3.4	21.1	80.3	19.0
85–89	6.6	3.6	27.4	86.7	19.0
≥90	4.8	3.0	41.8	92.1	19.1
Male	10.7	4.7	12.1	66.9	13.7
Female	9.6	3.9	19.1	71.1	15.5
White	10.5	4.7	14.4	71.5	15.0
Black	8.3	1.8	23.7	64.5	15.9
Other	8.9	3.1	20.5	59.2	12.3
Alone	5.8	5.1	34.6	72.6	14.2
With spouse	13.2	3.4	6.8	68.6	14.2
With spouse/others	12.7	3.5	3.7	66.6	14.1
With others	8.0	5.5	12.1	65.7	17.8
< High school	4.0	6.2	18.7	66.4	17.7
High school	7.9	5.5	12.9	71.2	15.6
Some college	10.6	4.6	11.1	69.2	15.2
College graduate	15.7	1.8	14.6	68.7	11.0
> College	17.3	1.8	14.5	68.9	11.9
All	10.1	4.2	16.0	69.2	14.7

NOTES: N = 7,859; nursing home residents are omitted for education groups and environmental features (N = 7,499); p-values for F-tests are significant at $p \leq .001$ except for education differences in having any features ($p = .292$); gender, racial, and living arrangement differences in adding features ($p = .114, .041, .116$, respectively); and racial and education differences in the service environment ($p = .029, .777$, respectively).
SOURCE: Data from National Health and Aging Trends Study.

| Service Environment | | | |
Nursing Home	Assisted/ Independent Living	Retirement/ Sr. Housing	Community
1.1	1.0	3.5	94.4
0.8	1.7	5.7	91.7
1.4	3.0	7.1	88.5
3.9	7.7	7.8	80.6
6.1	13.0	6.7	74.2
13.7	22.3	6.4	57.5
1.5	3.2	5.1	90.3
3.4	5.6	6.2	84.8
2.6	4.8	5.9	86.7
3.7	3.4	5.5	87.5
1.6	3.6	4.9	89.9
8.0	11.3	9.4	71.3
0.0	1.9	5.1	93.0
0.0	0.0	0.7	99.3
0.0	0.8	2.9	96.3
-	4.9	6.6	88.5
-	5.1	5.3	89.6
-	4.3	6.2	89.4
-	4.9	5.4	89.7
-	3.7	5.9	90.4
2.5	4.5	5.7	87.2

TABLE 10-4 Internet Use by U.S. Adults Ages 65 and Older, 2015

		Goes Online for		
	Goes Online	Social Activities	Household Activities	Health Activities
65–69	81.1	76.3	53.7	41.1
70–74	72.9	66.2	44.2	34.4
75–79	56.2	50.3	31.7	25.9
80–84	44.7	39.0	21.1	17.6
85–89	27.7	24.5	13.0	11.0
≥90	18.6	15.9	8.0	6.9
Male	63.7	56.7	41.3	32.2
Female	61.5	57.4	34.7	27.3
White	67.9	62.2	42.4	33.8
Black	40.2	35.9	18.9	13.2
Other	45.4	40.8	22.4	15.5
Alone	53.8	49.5	29.0	22.2
With spouse	75.2	69.4	48.4	39.9
With spouse/others	58.5	52.1	35.1	26.0
With others	42.4	36.8	22.9	13.9
< High school	22.5	18.4	8.1	4.2
High school	51.1	44.7	24.3	16.1
Some college	73.9	68.3	43.9	35.2
College graduate	83.5	77.2	60.2	48.6
> College	90.7	87.2	66.0	57.4
All	62.5	57.1	37.7	29.5

NOTES: Nursing home residents are omitted, $N = 7{,}499$; p-values for F-tests are significant at $p \leq .001$ except for gender differences in going online ($p = .204$), going online for social activities ($p = .678$), and going online for health activities ($p = .004$).
SOURCE: Data from National Health and Aging Trends Study.

TABLE 10-5 Consequences of Activity Limitations for U.S. Adults Ages 65 and Older, 2015

		Unmet Need for Assistance with	
	Participation Restriction	Self-Care or Mobility Activity	Household Activity
65–69	22.5	7.7	6.8
70–74	22.7	7.5	5.3
75–79	26.0	10.7	5.8
80–84	33.2	14.5	6.3
85–89	37.6	17.4	7.2
≥ 90	46.4	26.8	10.9
Male	21.7	7.9	5.2
Female	31.1	13.0	7.3
White	26.0	9.4	5.9
Black	30.9	14.2	7.6
Other	29.7	16.3	8.6
Alone	31.0	11.6	8.5
With spouse	21.8	7.4	4.6
With spouse/others	28.1	10.3	5.1
With others	34.0	19.9	8.7
< High school	33.4	18.5	7.5
High school	28.9	12.0	6.5
Some college	25.3	9.0	6.1
College graduate	24.6	8.1	6.3
> College	20.3	4.8	5.4
All	26.9	10.7	6.4

NOTES: Nursing home residents are omitted, $N = 7{,}499$; p-values for F-tests are significant at $p \leq .001$ except for racial differences for participation restrictions ($p = .004$).
SOURCE: Data from National Health and Aging Trends Study.

TABLE 10-6 An Overview of Disablement Domains by Sex and Race among U.S. Adults Ages 80–89, 2015

	Non-Hispanic White Men	Non-Hispanic White Women	Non-White Men	Non-White Women
Activity Limitations and Accommodations				
Self-Care and Mobility Activities				
Fully able	21.1	9.1	18.5	10.9
Successful accommodation	28.2	31.5	26.9	18.5
Less often	3.4	8.8	7.3	6.7
Difficulty	24.6	18.3	20.8	19.9
Assistance	22.7	32.4	26.5	44.0
Household Activities				
Fully able	50.5	33.7	43.1	23.6
Less often	6.0	9.4	5.7	9.0
Difficulty	13.4	13.3	9.3	13.5
Help for health/functioning reasons	30.1	43.7	42.0	53.9
Capacity				
Low physical capacity	23.9	50.6	46.5	65.7
Poor vision	8.4	11.5	17.4	17.5
Poor hearing	19.0	15.7	20.6	20.8
Probable dementia	15.9	17.9	24.8	26.9
Service Environment				
Nursing home	3.1	6.1	1.6	6.0
Assisted/independent living	8.0	12.7	8.6	3.8
Retirement/senior housing	6.5	8.6	5.2	6.6
Community	82.4	72.6	84.6	83.7
Outcomes				
Participation restrictions	26.9	38.7	34.7	42.8
Unmet need for assistance with self-care or mobility activity	10.7	16.7	14.4	26.4
Unmet need for assistance with household activity	6.2	6.5	3.7	10.7

NOTES: N = 2,564; nursing home residents are omitted for poor vision and hearing and outcomes (N = 2,415); p-values for F-tests are significant at $p \leq .001$ except for poor hearing (p = .079).
SOURCE: Data from National Health and Aging Trends Study.

masks considerable racial and ethnic heterogeneity within this group, and it does not shed light on differences in life expectancy across groups or in life course influences that lead to disparities in late-life health and functioning. Nevertheless, it demonstrates the vast gap between older minority women and other groups on most disablement domains.

Older minority women have about two to three times the risk of non-Hispanic White men of receiving assistance with self-care, mobility, or household activities or of having low physical capacity, poor vision, or probable dementia. They are also much less likely to successfully accommodate with assistive devices to carry out their self-care and mobility activities. Although they live in nursing homes at about the same rate as non-Hispanic White women (6%), they are about one-third as likely as non-Hispanic White women and half as likely as non-Hispanic White men to live in an assisted living or independent living environment (3.8% versus 12.7% and 8.0%, respectively). In terms of outcomes, they have the highest rates of unmet need and participation restrictions.

DISABLEMENT OVER TIME: TRAJECTORIES AND TRENDS

Individual patterns of disablement—including the speed and severity with which decline occurs, the duration of each phase of disablement, and prospects for recovery—unfold over time. At the population level, trends are influenced by the aging of cohorts who have been exposed to distinctive life experiences. Thus, time—whether parameterized as age, period, or cohort—is of fundamental interest when studying individual-level patterns and population-level dynamics.

Disability Trajectories

For many years, studies of disability dynamics focused on the chances of making a transition between discrete states—often between "none" and "any" activity limitations or among levels of activity limitations (Wolf, 2016). The important distinction between catastrophic and progressive disability helped sharpen understanding of the distinction between sudden onset of impairment as the result of an injury, stroke, or other discrete event and the more gradual set of changes often associated with frailty (Ferrucci et al., 1996). Together, such studies emphasized age profiles and identifying higher-risk groups (e.g., females, minorities, individuals with low education levels) as well as modifiable risk factors (see Stuck et al., 1999, for a comprehensive review). Studies have also highlighted the substantial proportion of older adults who regain functioning (Crimmins and Saito, 1993) and factors linked to the chances of recovery (Hardy and Gill, 2004, 2005), such as being cognitively intact and having a history of regular physical activity.

More recently, aided by the availability of data from long-running national panel studies and the release of trajectory estimation procedures in statistical packages, researchers have focused on the implications of risk factors for trajectories, defined as pathways over time rather than simple transitions. Most often, such studies focus on trajectories in activity limitations. Occasionally, studies will emphasize differences in trajectories by indicators of earlier stages of the disablement process—that is, by the presence of a particular health condition (Chiu and Wray, 2011) or functional limitation (Martin et al., 2017). Nevertheless, understanding of how individuals move through the broader disablement process is still limited.

Comparing trajectory study findings is complicated not only by differences in study outcomes but also by choices about modeling approach and depiction of age (Wolf, 2016). There are at least three distinct modeling approaches in use today. Latent growth curve models assume individuals, who are represented by random effects, diverge from a single underlying average pathway (see, for example, Warner and Brown, 2011). Latent class trajectory models assume individuals in an (unobserved) group share a common pathway (see, for example, Taylor and Lynch, 2011). Finally, growth mixture models assume that there are person-level random effects within a set of discrete classes (see, for example, Han et al., 2013). With respect to depiction of time, there are also several different approaches in use. Most often, time is modeled as chronological age. However, in other cases, time from the first survey wave (baseline) is modeled (and age controlled). More recently Wolf et al. (2015) incorporated time until death (along with age) in their analysis of trajectories of activity limitations. Irrespective of modeling approach and depiction of time, researchers typically identify three to five trajectories for activity limitations: for instance, high functioning with no decline, moderate decline, and steep decline.

Disability Trends

A fundamental question in the demography of aging is whether increases in life expectancy at age 65 have been accompanied by more or fewer years lived with limitations. Between 1990 and 2016, life expectancy at age 65 increased by more than 2 years (from 17.2 to 19.4 years); men gained nearly 3 years (from 15.1 to 18.0), and women gained 1.7 years (from 18.9 to 20.6) (National Center for Health Statistics, 2017; Kochanek et al., 2017). The small downturn in life expectancy at birth in 2015 and 2016, which is attributed to the opioid epidemic, is not apparent for life expectancy conditioned on surviving to age 65.

Several competing theories have been proposed to explain how population health changes with population aging. Forty years ago, Gruenberg (1977) suggested that increases in survival of persons with chronic disease and disability would result from medical advances. In contrast, Fries (1980, 1983) asserted that chronic disease would be postponed to later ages and the period of morbidity and disability would be compressed into a shorter time before death. Manton (1982) added a third perspective that recognized that interventions designed to reduce mortality also would have an influence on morbidity, and vice versa. Thus, additional years of life would be gained through postponement of disease onset, slowing of disease progression, and improved clinical management of disease, and the relative amounts of each contribution could not be predetermined.

These theories have guided two broad types of studies. One set has focused on changes over time in disability prevalence—that is, the proportion of the population at a point in time reporting a particular outcome. The other set has focused on active life expectancy, which combines age-specific disability and mortality rates. Several excellent reviews have been published in recent years (Beltrán-Sánchez et al., 2015; Crimmins, 2015; Martin et al., 2010; Wolf, 2016). A brief overview focused on the U.S. experience follows.

Trends in Activity Limitations

Manton and colleagues provided the earliest evidence that a decline in the prevalence of activity limitations may be occurring for older adults in the United States (Manton et al., 1993). Although studies were initially inconsistent (Crimmins et al., 1997a), a systematic review found a convergence of evidence suggesting substantial declines in IADL limitations (Freedman et al., 2002). Notably large were declines from 1984 to 1999 in three IADL activities—managing money, shopping for groceries, and doing laundry (Spillman, 2004). Smaller declines for the 1990s in the use of help and difficulties with ADLs were also found across studies (Freedman et al., 2004). More recent analyses have consistently found that such declines did not continue into the first and second decades of the 21st century, except for those at ages 85 and older, and the share of nonelderly adults reaching late life with limitations in place has been increasing (Freedman et al., 2013; Martin and Schoeni, 2014).

Exploration into reasons for trends has been limited, in part because of data limitations. The most comprehensive investigation of the decline during the 1980s and 1990s revealed that shifting education was the most important factor (Schoeni et al., 2008). Improvements in vision (possibly linked to the diffusion of cataract surgery) and increases in the use of assistive technology to carry out daily activities are also likely to have been responsible in part (Freedman et al., 2006, 2007). Investigations into reasons for the recent pause have pointed to shifts in the obesity profiles and smoking histories of adults now reaching late life (Martin and Schoeni, 2014).

Trends in Active Life Expectancy

Evidence regarding active life expectancy trends in the United States reinforces the notion that neither a compression nor an expansion of late-life disability is an inevitable consequence of mortality declines. Instead, patterns have varied over time periods and for different demographic and socioeconomic groups. For instance, from 1970 to 1980, most of the increase in life expectancy consisted of years lived with activity limitations (Crimmins et al., 1997b). However, during the 1980s and 1990s, the percentage of life expectancy to be lived without limitations increased (Crimmins et al., 2009).

Several long-term studies of active life expectancy have highlighted that not all groups have benefited equally. Looking over the whole life cycle, Crimmins and colleagues (2016) found increases between 1970 and 2010 in life spent "limited in any way in the performance of one's usual or other activities" was greater than the increase in life without such limitations (expansion), but at age 65, changes were consistent with compression for both men and women. Focusing on a different time period and measure (1982–2011 for ADL and IADL limitations), Freedman and colleagues found evidence consistent with a compression for men but not women, and for those reporting their race as White but not those reporting as Black. Older Black women were particularly disadvantaged (Freedman and Spillman, 2016; Freedman et al., 2016).

Although different definitions have been used, studies to date have focused mainly on activity limitations. Yet, as Crimmins (2004) pointed out with respect to prevalence trends, the various domains of disablement will not necessarily change in the same direction, nor are they necessarily consistently related to mortality shifts. Drawing upon the 2011 and 2015 NHATS and published mortality rates for the United States, Table 10-7 provides an overview of years expected to be lived in each stage of the disablement process. Age-specific rates used in the calculations are also provided. Even over this relatively short period, declines are evident in expected years lived fully able to carry out self-care and mobility activities (from 5.7 years in 2011 to 5.3 years in 2015). During the same period, increases were experienced in years expected to be lived successfully accommodating (from 4.7 years in 2011 to 5.3 years in 2015). There were no significant shifts in expected years lived in any of the other categories of activity limitations, nor were there significant changes in years lived with low physical capacity (5.5 versus 5.4 years) or poor vision (1.8 versus 1.9 years). However, years lived with poor hearing did decline (from 3.0 to 2.6 years) because of declines among all age groups except the youngest. With respect to years expected to be lived in residential care, no significant changes were evident, but years to be lived in the community increased from 16.1 to 16.6.

FUTURE RESEARCH ON THE DEMOGRAPHY
OF LATE-LIFE DISABILITY

In the Committee on Population's 1994 volume on the *Demography of Aging*, Manton and Stallard outlined a mathematical "framework for analyzing the relationships among health-related behaviors, genetic predisposition, disease incidence and fatality, population aging, and morbidity and mortality" (National Research Council, 1994, p. 6). The editors noted the value of such models for demonstrating the potential effects of interventions and policies on late-life disability rates. At the time, the language and conceptual models of disablement had not yet been fully developed, panel data were still in their infancy, and statistical algorithms for computing complex models were not yet widely available. The Baby Boom generation was in the prime of its working life (ages 30–48), and concerns about Baby Boomers' retirement, health, and long-term care needs were problems for the distant future.

Since that time, research on late-life disability has benefited enormously from the conceptual advances made by scholars and by the data infrastructure investments in national panel studies, in particular those made by the National Institute on Aging. Statistical advances have also furthered investigations into late-life disability trajectories. The leading edge of the Baby Boom generation began to turn age 65 in 2011 and over the next decade will reach ages 65–82. The personal and societal costs of caring for a large generation of older adults, many of whom are living with disability, is now a more imminent concern (Freedman and Spillman, 2016).

The methods and materials of the demography of aging will continue to be central to addressing issues of late-life disablement and improving the lives of older adults. With respect to understanding how individual trajectories unfold, there is much work yet to be done. As additional rounds of NHATS become available, researchers will be able to refine identification and understanding of signature trajectories, whether "postevent" (such as after an injurious fall or stroke) or in the absence of a discrete event (e.g., cognitive impairment, frailty). Understanding how such trajectories evolve and the factors that influence the speed with which a trajectory unfolds can help clinicians build, tailor, and target interventions to support at-risk groups. Of particular interest is how to promote successful accommodation, including home modification, so that older adults can manage their lives in the least restrictive setting possible for as long as possible.

At the population level, continued tracking of the Baby Boom's experience with respect to disablement is also a priority. This generation has had a unique set of life course experiences (Colby and Ortman, 2014) that will shape its disablement in later life. As a group, the Baby Boom generation is better educated, with more complex families than previous generations,

TABLE 10-7 Age-Specific Percentage with Activity Limitations, Poor Capacity, and Living in Residential Care Environments, 2011 and 2015

	2011						Expected Years Lived
	65–69	70–74	75–79	80–84	85–89	≥90	
Self-Care and Mobility Activities							
Fully able	44.6	39.0	27.4	19.7	10.2	4.0	5.7
Successful accommodation	22.4	24.4	29.2	27.1	21.8	15.2	4.7
Less often	4.9	6.0	6.2	5.3	7.0	4.5	1.1
Difficulty	17.1	17.7	19.1	21.8	19.2	14.6	3.5
Assistance	11.0	12.9	18.1	26.1	41.8	61.7	4.1
Physical Capacity							
Low composite score	11.5	18.0	27.3	37.4	56.0	77.2	5.5
Sensory Capacity							
Poor vision	6.6	5.2	7.9	10.2	17.5	27.2	1.8
Poor hearing	8.8	11.2	15.0	17.8	26.5	36.7	3.0
Cognitive Capacity							
Probable dementia	2.9	4.3	9.5	15.0	25.9	38.5	2.1
Service Environment							
Nursing home	0.4	1.5	2.2	3.8	7.7	16.2	0.6
Assisted/independent	1.2	2.8	3.9	7.0	14.7	23.3	1.1
Retirement/senior housing	5.0	7.3	6.6	7.8	7.1	8.9	1.3
Community	93.5	88.5	87.3	81.3	70.5	51.5	16.1

NOTES: N = 8,077 (2011) and 7,859 (2015); nursing home residents are omitted for poor vision and hearing, N = 7,609 (2011) and N = 7,499 (2015). Test for difference between 2015 and 2011 in expected years lived: * = $p < .10$; ** = $p < .05$; *** = $p < .01$.
SOURCE: Data from National Health and Aging Trends Study.

| 2015 | | | | | | |
65–69	70–74	75–79	80–84	85–89	≥ 90	Expected Years Lived
41.7	36.2	25.5	16.9	9.4	4.2	5.3*
24.0	29.1	32.8	29.1	27.6	16.5	5.3***
5.9	4.8	5.2	7.3	5.8	4.7	1.1
16.2	16.9	19.3	20.6	21.0	15.0	3.5
12.1	13.1	17.2	26.1	36.2	59.7	4.1
12.7	15.1	23.8	38.3	51.2	76.1	5.4
6.5	6.4	8.3	9.1	16.3	23.8	1.8
9.5	8.7	10.1	16.3	20	33.4	2.6**
2.6	3.9	8.0	15.9	23.3	36.3	2.0
1.1	0.8	1.4	3.9	6.1	13.6	0.6
1.0	1.8	3.0	7.7	12.9	22.4	1.0
3.5	5.7	7.1	7.8	6.7	6.4	1.1
94.4	91.7	88.5	80.6	74.2	57.5	16.6***

but also has higher rates of obesity and mobility-related impairments. As members of this generation continue to reach the years of highest risk for long-term-care services and supports, researchers should continue to not only track trends but also explore reasons for such trends. Although restricted in past studies because of data limitations, going forward NHATS offers researchers the unique opportunity to understand the extent to which shifts in activity limitations are related to changes in underlying capacity versus changes in choices about how activities are carried out.

Finally, to guide policy into the future, tying these new frameworks and measures back to the models and projections at the core of formal medical demography is an important priority. Projection models can now be built that recognize not only biological but also environmental and behavioral underpinnings of the disablement process. They can now also recognize the shifting relationships among disease, capacity, accommodations, limitations, and outcomes such as participation restrictions and unmet need. Enhanced modeling of late-life disablement will also facilitate identification of public health interventions that will be most likely to maximize independent functioning and extend quality of life.

REFERENCES

Allen, S.M., and Mor, V. (1997). The prevalence and consequences of unmet need. Contrasts between older and younger adults with disability. *Medical Care, 35,* 1132–1148.

Allen, S.M., Piette, E.R., and Mor, V. (2014). The adverse consequences of unmet need among older persons living in the community: Dual-eligible versus Medicare-only beneficiaries. *Journals of Gerontology: Psychological Sciences and Social Science, 69*(Suppl 1), S51–S58.

Al-rousan, T.M., Rubenstein, L.M., and Wallace, R.B. (2015). Disability levels and correlates among older mobile home dwellers, an NHATS analysis. *Disability and Health Journal, 8,* 363–371.

Beltrán-Sánchez, H., Soneji, S., and Crimmins, E.M. (2015). Past, present, and future of healthy life expectancy. *Cold Spring Harbor Perspectives in Medicine, 5,* ii. doi: 10.1101/cshperspect.a025957.

Chiu, C.J., and Wray, L.A. (2011). Physical disability trajectories in older Americans with and without diabetes: The role of age, gender, race or ethnicity, and education. *Gerontologist, 51,* 51–63. doi: 10.1093/geront/gnq069.

Colby, S.L., and Ortman, J.M. (2014). *The Baby Boom Cohort in the United States: 2012 to 2060* (Current Population Reports P25-1141). Washington, DC: U.S. Census Bureau. Available: https://www.census.gov/prod/2014pubs/p25-1141.pdf [April 2018].

Congressional Budget Office. (2013). *Rising Demand for Long-Term Services and Supports for Elderly People.* Washington, DC: Congressional Budget Office. Available: https://www.cbo.gov/publication/44363 [April 2018].

Cornman, J.C., Freedman, V.A., and Agree, E.M. (2005). Measurement of assistive device use: Implications for estimates of device use and disability in late life. *Gerontologist, 45,* 347–358.

Crimmins, E.M. (2004). Trends in the health of the elderly. *Annual Review of Public Health, 25,* 79–98.

Crimmins, E.M. (2015). Lifespan and healthspan: Past, present, and promise. *Gerontologist, 55*, 901–911. doi: 10.1093/geront/gnv130.

Crimmins, E.M., and Saito, Y. (1993). Getting better and getting worse. *Journal of Aging and Health, 5*, 3–36.

Crimmins, E.M., Saito, Y., and Reynolds, S.L. (1997a). Further evidence on recent trends in the prevalence and incidence of disability among older Americans from two sources: The LSOA and the NHIS. *Journal of Gerontology: Social Sciences, 52*, S59–S71.

Crimmins, E.M., Saito, Y., and Ingegneri, D. (1997b). Trends in disability-free life expectancy in the United States, 1970-1990. *Population and Development Review, 23*, 555–572.

Crimmins, E.M., Hayward, M.D., Hagedorn, A., Saito, Y., and Brouard, N. (2009). Change in disability-free life expectancy for Americans 70-years-old and older. *Demography, 46*, 627–646.

Crimmins, E.M., Zhang, Y., and Saito, Y. (2016). Trends over 4 decades in disability-free life expectancy in the United States. *American Journal of Public Health, 106*, 1287–1293. doi: 10.2105/AJPH.2016.303120.

Erikson, W., Lee, C., and von Schrader, S. (2017). *Disability Statistics from the American Community Survey (ACS)*. Ithaca, NY: Cornell University Yang-Tan Institute (YTI). Available: http://www.disabilitystatistics.org [April 2018].

Ferrucci, L., Guralnik, J.M., Simonsick, E., Salive, M.E., Corti, C., and Langlois, J. (1996). Progressive versus catastrophic disability: A longitudinal view of the disablement process. *Journals of Gerontology: Biological Sciences and Medical Sciences, 51*, M123–M130.

Fragoso, C.A., Gahbauer, E.A., Van Ness, P.H., Concato, J., and Gill, T.M. (2008). Peak expiratory flow as a predictor of subsequent disability and death in community living older persons. *Journal of the American Geriatrics Society, 56*, 1014–1020.

Freedman, V.A. (2009). Adopting the ICF language for studying late-life disability: A field of dreams? *Journals of Gerontology A: Biological Sciences and Medical Sciences, 64*, 1172–1174, doi: 10.1093/gerona/glp095.

Freedman, V.A., and Spillman, B.C. (2014a). The residential continuum from home to nursing home: Size, characteristics and unmet needs of older adults. *Journals of Gerontology: Psychological Sciences and Social Sciences, 69*(Suppl 1), S42–S50. doi: 10.1093/geronb/gbu120.

Freedman, V.A., and Spillman, B.C. (2014b). Disability and care needs among older Americans. *Milbank Quarterly, 92*(3), 509–541. doi: 10.1111/1468-0009.12076.

Freedman, V.A., and Spillman, B.C. (2016). Active life expectancy in the older U.S. population, 1982-2011: Differences between blacks and whites persisted. *Health Affairs (Millwood), 35*, 1351–1358. doi: 10.1377/hlthaff.2015.1247.

Freedman, V.A., Martin, L.G., and Schoeni, R.F. (2002). Recent trends in disability and functioning among older adults in the United States: A systematic review. *Journal of the American Medical Association, 288*, 3137–3146.

Freedman, V.A., Crimmins, E., Schoeni, R.F., Spillman, B.C., Aykan, H., Kramarow, E., Land, K., Lubitz, J., Manton, K., Martin, L.G., et al. (2004). Resolving inconsistencies in trends in old-age disability: Report from a technical working group. *Demography, 41*, 417–441.

Freedman, V.A., Agree, E.M., Martin, L.G., and Cornman, J.C. (2006). Trends in the use of assistive technology and personal care for late-life disability, 1992–2001. *Gerontologist, 46*, 124–127.

Freedman, V.A., Schoeni, R.F., Martin, L.G., and Cornman, J.C. (2007). Chronic conditions and the decline in late-life disability. *Demography, 44*, 459–477.

Freedman, V.A., Kasper, J.D., Cornman, J.C., Agree, E.M., Bandeen-Roche, K., Mor, V., Spillman, B.C., Wallace, R., and Wolf, D.A. (2011). Validation of new measures of disability and functioning in the National Health and Aging Trends Study. *Journals of Gerontology: Biological and Medical Sciences, 66*, 1013–1021. doi: 10.1093/gerona/glr087. Epub June 29.

Freedman V.A., Spillman, B.C., Andreski, P.M., Cornman, J.C., Crimmins, E.M., Kramarow, E., Lubitz, J., Martin, L.G., Merkin, S.S., Schoeni, R.F., et al. (2013). Trends in late-life activity limitations in the United States: An update from five national surveys. *Demography, 50*(2), 661–671. doi: 10.1007/s13524-012-0167-z.

Freedman, V.A., Kasper, J.D., Spillman, B.C., Agree, E.M., Mor, V., Wallace, R.B., and Wolf, D.A. (2014). Behavioral adaptation and late-life disability: A new spectrum for assessing public health impacts. *American Journal of Public Health, 104*, e88–e94. doi: 10.2105/AJPH.2013.301687.

Freedman, V.A., Wolf, D.A., and Spillman, B.C. (2016). Disability-free life expectancy over 30 years: A growing female disadvantage in the U.S. population. *American Journal of Public Health, 106*, 1079–1085. doi: 10.2105/AJPH.2016.303089.

Freedman, V.A., Kasper, J.D., and Spillman, B.C. (2017). Successful aging through successful accommodation with assistive devices. *Journals of Gerontology: Social Sciences, 72*, 300–309. doi: 10.1093/geronb/gbw102.

Fried, L.P., Young, Y., Rubin, G., Bandeen-Roche, K., and the WHAS II Collaborative Research Group. (2001). Self-reported preclinical disability identifies older women with early declines in performance and early disease. *Journal of Clinical Epidemiology, 54*, 889–901.

Fries, J.F. (1980). Aging, natural death and the compression of morbidity. *New England Journal of Medicine, 303*, 130–135.

Fries, J.F. (1983). The compression of morbidity. *Milbank Memorial Fund Quarterly, 61*, 397–419.

GBD 2015 Disease and Injury Incidence and Prevalence Collaborators. (2016). Global, regional, and national incidence, prevalence, and years lived with disability for 310 diseases and injuries, 1990-2015: A systematic analysis for the Global Burden of Disease Study 2015. *Lancet, 388*(10053), 1545–1602. doi: 10.1016/S0140-6736(16)31678-6.

Gill, T.M. (2010). Assessment of function and disability in longitudinal studies. *Journal of the American Geriatric Society, 58*(Suppl 2), S308–S312. doi: 10.1111/j.1532-5415.2010.02914.x.

Gill, T.M, and Williams, C.S. (2017). Evaluating distinctions in the assessment of late-life disability. *Journals of Gerontology: Biological and Medical Sciences, 72*, 1538–1546. doi: 10.1093/gerona/glx022.

Gill, T.M., Robison, J.T., and Tinetti, M.E. (1998). Difficulty and dependence: Two components of the disability continuum among community-living older persons. *Annals of Internal Medicine, 128*, 96–101.

Gitlin, L.N. (2003). Conducting research on home environments: Lessons learned and new directions. *Gerontologist, 43*, 628–637.

Gregory, S.R. (2004). *In Brief: Disability: Federal Survey Definitions, Measurements, and Estimates.* Washington, DC: AARP.

Gruenberg, E.M. (1977). The failures of success. *Milbank Memorial Fund Quarterly, 55*(1), 3–24.

Guralnik, J.M., and Ferrucci, L. (2009). The challenge of understanding the disablement process in older persons: Commentary responding to Jette AM. Toward a common language of disablement. *Journal of Gerontology: Medical Sciences 64A*(11), 1169–1171.

Guralnik, J.M., Branch, L.G., Cummings, S.R., and Curb, J.D. (1989). Physical performance measures in aging research. *Journals of Gerontology: Medical Sciences, 44*, M141–M146.

Guralnik, J.M., Simonsick, E.M., Ferrucci, L., Glynn, R.J., Berkman, L.F., Blazer, D.G., Scherr, P.A., and Wallace, R.B. (1994). A short physical performance battery assessing lower extremity function: Association with self-reported disability and prediction of mortality and nursing home admission. *Journals of Gerontology: Medical Sciences, 49*, M85–M94.

Guralnik, J.M., Ferrucci, L., Simonsick, E.M., Salive, M.E., and Wallace, R.B. (1995). Lower-extremity function in persons over the age of 70 years as a predictor of subsequent disability. *New England Journal of Medicine, 332,* 556–561.

Han, L., Allore, H., Murphy, T., Gill, T., Peduzzi, P., and Lin, H. (2013). Dynamics of functional aging based on latent-class trajectories of activities of daily living. *Annals of Epidemiology, 23,* 87–92.

Hardy, S.E., and Gill, T.M. (2004). Recovery from disability among community-dwelling older persons. *Journal of the American Medical Association, 291,* 1596–1602.

Hardy, S.E., and Gill, T.M. (2005). Factors associated with recovery of independence among newly disabled older persons. *Archive of Internal Medicine, 165,* 106–112.

Iezzoni, L.I., and Freedman, V.A. (2008). Turning the disability tide: The importance of definitions. *Journal of the American Medical Association, 299,* 332–334. doi: 10.1001/jama.299.3.332.

Institute of Medicine. (1991). *Disability in America.* Washington, DC: National Academy Press.

Institute of Medicine. (2007). *The Future of Disability in America.* Washington, DC: National Academy Press.

Jette, M. (2009). Toward a common language of disablement. *Journals of Gerontology: Medical Sciences, 64,* 1165–1168.

Kasper, J.D., and Freedman, V.A. (2014). Findings from the 1st round of the National Health and Aging Trends Study (NHATS): Introduction to a special issue. *Journals of Gerontology Series B: Psychological Sciences and Social Sciences, 69*(Suppl 1), S1–S7. doi:10.1093/geronb/gbu125.

Kasper, J.D., Freedman, V.A., and Niefeld, M.R. (2012). *Construction of Performance-based Summary Measures of Physical Capacity in the National Health and Aging Trends Study* (NHATS Technical Paper No. 4). Baltimore: Johns Hopkins University School of Public Health.

Kasper, J.D., Freedman, V.A., and Spillman, B. (2013). *Classification of Persons by Dementia Status in the National Health and Aging Trends Study* (NHATS Technical Paper No. 5). Baltimore: Johns Hopkins University School of Public Health.

Kasper, J.D., Chan, K.S., and Freedman, V.A. (2017). Measuring physical capacity: An assessment of a composite measure using self-report and performance-based items. *Journal of Aging and Health, 29,* 289–309.

Katz, S., Ford, A.B., Moskowitz, R.W., Jackson, B.A., and Jaffee, M.W. (1963). Studies of illness in the aged. The index of ADL, a standardized measure of biological and psychosocial function. *Journal of the American Medical Association, 185,* 914–919.

Kochanek, K.D., Murphy, S.L., Xu, J.Q., and Arias, E. (2017). *Mortality in the United States, 2016* (NCHS Data Brief No 293). Hyattsville, MD: National Center for Health Statistics.

Land, K.C., and Yang, Y. (2006). Morbidity, disability, and mortality. In R.H. Binstock and L.K. George (Eds.), *Handbook of Aging and the Social Sciences* (pp. 41–58). Amsterdam: Academic Press.

Lawton, M.P. (1986). Environment and human behavior. In M.P. Lawton (Ed.), *Environment and Aging* (2nd ed., pp. 10–19). Albany, NY: Center for the Study of Aging.

Lawton, M.P., and Brody, E.M. (1969). Assessment of older people: Self-maintaining and instrumental activities of daily living. *Gerontologist, 9,* 179–186.

Levine, D.M., Lipsitz, S.M., and Linder, J.A. (2016). Trends in seniors' use of digital health technology in the United States, 2011-2014. *Journal of the American Medical Association, 316,* 538–540. doi: 10.1001/jama.2016.9124.

LIFE Study Investigators. (2006). Effects of a physical activity intervention on measures of physical performance: Results of the Lifestyle Interventions and Independence for Elders Pilot (LIFE-P) Study. *Journal of Gerontology: Biological Sciences and Medical Sciences, 61*, 1157–1165.

Manton, K.G. (1982). Changing concepts of morbidity and mortality in the elderly population. *Milbank Memorial Fund Quarterly: Health and Society, 60*, 183–244.

Manton, K.G., and Gu, X. (2001). Changes in the prevalence of chronic disability in the United States Black and non-Black population above age 65 from 1982 to 1999. *Proceedings of the National Academy of Sciences of the United States of America, 98*, 6354–6359.

Manton, K.G., and Stallard, E. (1994). Medical demography: Interaction of disability dynamics and mortality. In National Research Council, *The Demography of Aging* (Ch. 7, pp. 217–278). L.G. Martin and S.H. Preston (Eds.). Washington, DC: National Academy Press.

Manton, K.G., Corder, L., and Stallard, E. (1993). Estimates of change in chronic disability and institutional incidence and prevalence rates in the U.S. elderly population from the 1982, 1984, and 1989 National Long-Term Care Survey. *Journal of Gerontology: Social Sciences, 48*, S153–S166.

Manton, K.G., Corder, L., and Stallard, E. (1997). Chronic disability trends in elderly United States populations: 1982–1994. *Proceedings of the National Academy of Sciences of the United States of America, 94*, 2593–2598.

Martin, L.G., and Schoeni, R.F. (2014). Trends in disability and related chronic conditions among the forty-and-over population: 1997-2010. *Disability and Health Journal, 7*(1 Suppl), S4–S14. doi: 10.1016/j.dhjo.2013.06.007.

Martin, L.G., Schoeni, R.F., and Andreski, P.M. (2010). Trends in health of older adults in the United States: Past, present, future. *Demography, 47*(Suppl), S17–S40.

Martin, L.G., Zimmer, Z., and Lee, J. (2017). Foundations of activity of daily living trajectories of older Americans. *Journals of Gerontology: Psychological and Social Sciences, 72*, 129–139.

Nagi, S.Z. (1965). Some conceptual issues in disability and rehabilitation. In M.B. Sussman (Ed.), *Sociology and Rehabilitation* (pp. 100–113). Washington, DC: American Sociological Association.

National Center for Health Statistics. (2017). *Health, United States, 2016: With Chartbook on Long-term Trends in Health*. Hyattsville, MD: National Center for Health Statistics. Available: https://www.cdc.gov/nchs/data/hus/2016/015.pdf [April 2018].

National Research Council. (1994). *The Demography of Aging*. L.G. Martin and S.H. Preston (Eds.). Washington, DC: National Academy Press.

National Research Council. (2009). *Improving the Measurement of Late-Life Disability in Population Surveys: Beyond ADLs and IADLs: Summary of a Workshop*. G.S. Wunderlich, rapporteur. Washington, DC: The National Academies Press.

Ostir, G.V., Volpato, S., Fried, L.P., Chaves, P., Guralnik, J.M. and the Women's Health and Aging Study. (2002). Reliability and sensitivity to change assessed for a summary measure of lower body function: Results from the Women's Health and Aging Study. *Journal of Clinical Epidemiology, 55*, 916–921.

Roberts, H.C., Denison, H.J., Martin, H.J., Patel, H.P., Syddall, H., Cooper, C., and Sayer, A.A. (2011). A review of the measurement of grip strength in clinical and epidemiological studies: Towards a standardised approach. *Age Ageing, 40*, 423–429.

Satariano, W.A., Guralnik, J.M., Jackson, R.J., Marottoli, R.A., Phelan, E.A., and Prohaska, T.R. (2012). Mobility and aging: New directions for public health action. *American Journal of Public Health, 102*, 1508–1515. doi: 10.2105/AJPH.2011.300631.

Schoeni, R.F., Martin, L.G., Andreski, P.M., and Freedman, V.A. (2005). Persistent and growing socioeconomic disparities in disability among the elderly: 1982–2002. *American Journal of Public Health, 95*(11), 2065–2070. doi: 10.2105/AJPH.2004.048744.

Schoeni, R.F., Freedman, V.A., and Martin, L.G. (2008). Why is late-life disability declining? *The Milbank Quarterly*, 86(1), 47–89. doi: 10.1111/j.1468-0009.2007.00513.x.

Schoeni, R.F., Freedman, V.A., and Martin, L.G. (2009). Socioeconomic and demographic disparities in trends in old-age disability health at older ages. In D.M. Cutler and D.A. Wise, *The Causes and Consequences of Declining Disability among the Elderly* (pp. 75–102). Chicago: University of Chicago Press.

Simonsick, E.M., Newman, A.E., Nevitt, M.C., Kritchevsky, S.B., Ferrucci, L., Guralnik, J.M., Harris, T., and Health ABC Study Group. (2001). Measuring higher level physical function in well-functioning older adults: Expanding familiar approaches in the Health ABC Study. *Journals of Gerontology: Biological and Medical Sciences, 56*, M644–M649.

Spillman, B.C. (2004). Changes in elderly disability rates and the implications for health care utilization and cost. *Milbank Quarterly, 82*, 157–194.

Stuck, A.E., Walthert, J.M., Nikolaus, T., Büla, C.J., Hohmann, C., and Beck, J.C. (1999). Risk factors for functional status decline in community-living elderly people: A systematic literature review. *Social Science & Medicine, 48*(4), 445–469.

Taylor, M.G., and Lynch, S.M. (2011). Cohort differences and chronic disease profiles of differential disability trajectories. *Journals of Gerontology: Social Sciences, 66*, 729–738.

Verbrugge, L.M., and Jette, A.M. (1994). The disablement process. *Social Science & Medicine, 38*, 1–14.

Warner, D.F., and Brown, T.H. (2011). Understanding how race/ethnicity and gender define age-trajectories of disability: An intersectionality approach. *Social Science & Medicine, 72*, 1236–1248.

Weiss, C.O., Hoenig, H.M., and Fried, L.P. (2007). Compensatory strategies used by older adults facing mobility disability. *Archives of Physical Medicine and Rehabilitation, 88*, 1217–1220.

Wolf, D.A. (2016). Late-life disability trends and trajectories. In L.K. George and K.F. Ferraro (Eds.), *Handbook of Aging and the Social Sciences* (8th ed., Ch. 4). New York: Elsevier.

Wolf, D.A., Freedman, V.A., Ondrich, J.I., Seplaki, C.L., and Spillman, B.C. (2015). Disability trajectories at the end of life: A "countdown" model. *Journals of Gerontology: Psychological Sciences and Social Sciences, 70*, 745–752. doi: 10.1093/geronb/gbu182.

World Health Organization. (2002). *Towards a Common Language for Functioning, Disability, and Health, ICF*. Geneva: World Health Organization.

PART VI

The Demography of Aging
on a Global Scale

11

The Demography of Aging in Low- and Middle-Income Countries: Chronological versus Functional Perspectives

Nikkil Sudharsanan[1] and David E. Bloom[2]

INTRODUCTION

Populations across the world are changing in size and structure, driving prominent social, economic, and health shifts. In some countries, working-age populations are expanding to unprecedented sizes (absolutely and relatively), creating strong potential for economic growth and development (Bloom et al., 2003) along with the threat of greater unemployment and unrest (Easterlin, 1978). In other countries, population aging is creating large older-age populations, increasing older individuals' influence in societies and families (Preston, 1984) while simultaneously stressing health and pension systems (Bongaarts, 2004). Population aging has already had widespread impact, fueling concerns that aging will substantially burden families, communities, and governments. These concerns have prompted increased research[3] and policy making on aging. Indeed, a 2009 survey

[1]David E. Bell Postdoctoral Fellow, Harvard Center for Population and Development Studies, Harvard T.H. Chan School of Public Health, Harvard University, nsudharsanan@hsph.harvard.edu.

[2]Clarence James Gamble Professor of Economics and Demography, Department of Global Health and Population, Harvard T.H. Chan School of Public Health, Harvard University.

We would like to thank Mark Hayward, David Weir, and Rebecca Wong for their valuable feedback. We would also like to thank Malay Majmundar for his guidance, the participants of the National Academies of Sciences Workshop on the Future Directions for the Demography of Aging for their insightful comments, Daniel Cadarette and Alex Khoury for their helpful research assistance, and the Carnegie Corporation of New York for its financial support.

[3]This statement is based on Web of Science citation reports for the terms "population aging" and "population ageing".

309

of 970 population scientists revealed that most experts believe population aging is the most important "population issue" to study over the coming decades (Van Dalen and Henkens, 2012).

The pattern and pace of population aging vary substantially in different settings. Many high-income countries (HICs) already have sizable older-age populations, while many low- and middle-income countries (LMICs) remain relatively young. Looking to the future, population aging is expected to boom in large LMICs such as India and China and slow in the already-aged countries of Western Europe (United Nations Department of Economic and Social Affairs, 2017). Furthermore, causes of aging differ, even among countries with similar rates of aging, with the differences driven by mortality reductions in some settings and by the aging of large cohorts (like the Baby Boomers) in others. These differences have important demographic implications and suggest very different policy responses across countries. Thus, planning for global population aging requires consideration of the historical and future rates of population aging, the forces driving this aging, and their variance across countries and regions. This paper's first major goal is to show how population aging and its causes have differed historically across regions and income groups and how they will evolve in the future.

The challenges of population aging arise because older individuals tend to make smaller economic contributions and have greater needs than younger, working-age people. For example, older individuals are more likely to have functional limitations (Lin et al., 2012), require assistance for everyday tasks (Freedman and Spillman, 2014), and fall sick and suffer from health shocks and hospitalizations (Fry et al., 2005). That older individuals have lower labor income compounds the challenge of these rising age-related needs (Lee, 1994); therefore, families and governments often shoulder the costs (both market and nonmarket) of their needs. In countries with sufficient wealth, the adverse economic consequences of aging can be prevented if health and social security systems can adequately meet the needs of older individuals. However, in LMICs, where aggregate levels of wealth are much lower and welfare systems function poorly or may not exist, the financial burden of aging is more likely to fall on families or the older individuals themselves. This potential for aging without resources to care for older individuals has fueled concerns that LMICs are "growing old before rich." The paper's second main goal is to explore the extent to which current economic and demographic trends support this view.

Most population-aging metrics are based on a chronological conception of age. Researchers, governments, and global policy makers focus on indicators, such as the share of the population above the age of 60 or 70, with the idea that these chronological measures indicate the size of the dependent population. Within this view, 10 percent growth in the share of individuals over 60 is thought to represent 10 percent growth in the dependent population, resulting in a corresponding increase in the resources required to support them. Yet not all individuals above the age of 60 are dependent, and conversely not all individuals younger than 60 are fully independent. Thus, these conventional measures of population aging may inaccurately indicate functional aging, and policies based on these measures may inadequately meet or may exceed the needs of aging populations. A small but influential series of papers has examined the macro-level discrepancies between chronological and functional aging. Lutz et al. (2008) compared chronological measures of population aging with measures based on the population share with a remaining life expectancy of 15 years and found that the magnitude of population aging is smaller when also considering changing patterns of longevity. Similarly, Sanderson and Scherbov (2010) compared chronological measures of aging (the old-age dependency ratio) with similar ratios defined by the population share with a disability in 10 HICs. They concluded that chronological measures greatly overstate the growth in the share of the dependent population (i.e., the share with a disability). The results from these papers suggest that focusing on chronological age may misrepresent actual changes in the share of the population with functional limitations. In the spirit of this work, the final section of this paper will draw on emerging rich microdata from several Health and Retirement Study (HRS) sister studies across the globe to estimate and compare chronological and functional age in three HICs and five LMICs. This section will also explore changes in the relationship between chronological and functional age over time in Mexico and Indonesia.

Our paper proceeds as follows. In the second section, we document sources of chronological population aging for recent historical and future periods by applying decomposition methods to macro-level data from the *United Nations World Population Prospects, The 2017 Revision* (hereafter referred to as *UN WPP*; United Nations Department of Economic and Social Affairs, 2017). In the third section, we discuss the issue of LMIC populations "growing old before rich" and conduct a simple empirical exercise to determine how much support we find for that view. We then shift our perspective away from macro-level chronological measures of aging in the fourth section by using microdata from the Health and Retirement Study sister studies to examine differences in functional aging across five LMICs and three HICs. Together, these distinct analyses provide a robust description of the differences in population aging occurring across income groups and regional settings. In the concluding section, we discuss the implications of our findings for future research and policy on the global demography of aging.

CHRONOLOGICAL AGING

Countries across the globe are aging; however, the rate of population aging varies tremendously across regions and countries at different levels of development. For example, the share of older individuals grew substantially over the past 50 years in HICs and in many countries in Asia. In contrast, countries in sub-Saharan Africa experienced virtually no aging over this same period (United Nations Department of Economic and Social Affairs, 2017). While these trends and patterns of population aging are well established, less is known about the historical and future sources of population aging across countries. To our knowledge, only one paper has examined this issue: Preston and Stokes (2012) used variable-r techniques to decompose the growth rate of the elderly population between 2005 and 2010. They concluded that mortality reductions across cohorts drove aging in more-developed countries, while fertility declines played a larger role in less-developed countries. Our main goal in this section is to expand on Preston and Stokes' work by estimating the historic sources of population aging between 1970 and 2015 and looking forward to 2050 by country-income groups and regions of the world.

Data and Methods

We begin by defining population aging as the change in the population share above the age of 65. Given this definition, four distinct factors drive population aging. First, mortality reductions can result in a rising elder share by allowing a greater fraction of individuals to survive to older ages. Second, fertility reductions can increase the share of older people by reducing the percentage of younger people in the population. Third, the aging of cohorts of individuals into older ages can affect the population distribution if the cohorts entering the 65+ age group are large relative to the rest of the population. While aging cohorts result from past changes in fertility and mortality, quantifying the impact of aging cohorts is relevant for policy makers because cohort influences are thought to exert a strong effect on later-life health and well-being (Finch and Crimmins, 2004). Separate consideration of cohort effects is also useful because they can lead to population aging even if current fertility and mortality are constant. Finally, migration can negatively or positively influence population aging, depending on the age composition of migrants. In this paper we consider only the first three sources of population aging, ignoring the contribution of migration (primarily because data on age-specific migration rates are very difficult to obtain). While migration is likely an important factor in population aging for some countries, we believe that ignoring migration is unlikely to introduce large errors into our estimates when looking at higher levels of aggregation such as regions and country-income groups.

For our analysis, we focus on the historical period between 1970 and 2015 and the future period between 2015 and 2050. We decompose the change in the population share above the age of 65 for both periods using the line-integral decomposition method developed by Horiuchi et al. (2008). We briefly describe the approach here and refer readers to the full paper for more details. We begin by presenting an expression for the share of the population above age 65 as a function of age-specific population counts, age-specific mortality, and age-specific fertility rates. To do this, we express the age-specific population counts in any year as the age-specific counts in a previous year projected forward using the intervening mortality and fertility experiences. Specifically, we take advantage of the 5-year data intervals in *UN WPP* to express the share of the population above the age of 65 at any time t as a function of the population counts at time t–5, the mortality experience between times t–5 and t (estimated based on the 5-year life tables), and the age-specific fertility rates between times t–5 and t. Based on this specification, either changing initial population distributions (the measure of cohorts aging), changing intervening mortality rates, or changing fertility rates must drive any change in the share of the population above age 65 between two time points. Conceptually, any of these components' contribution can then be thought of as the difference between the observed growth in the elderly population and the growth that would result if the population were projected forward while holding the component to be evaluated constant. In practice, this approach would produce a residual interaction term because changes in any of the factors influences the level of the other factors; however, the line-integral method produces estimates without interactions by using numerical integration and assuming a proportionate change in each component over time.

Projected population aging in the future period depends on forecasted trajectories of fertility and mortality. We use several *UN WPP* projection variants to quantify the uncertainty in our decompositions, with the medium variant serving as a point estimate and the high and low variants as bounds. An important point is that the *UN WPP* variants only differ in their projections of future fertility and the resulting changes in population counts. Therefore, we do not test the sensitivity of our results to different assumptions about the magnitude of future mortality decline.

Results

Panel A of Table 11-1 presents the change in the share of adults over the age of 65 between 1970 and 2015 by World Bank country-income groups. We then decompose this change into the contributions of aging cohorts, fertility changes over the period, and mortality changes over the period. Between 1970 and 2015, the magnitude of population aging varied substantially by income level. For example, the share of adults over the age of 65 grew by 7.3 percent in HICs but only by 1.5 percent in lower-middle-income countries and remained virtually unchanged in low-income coun-

TABLE 11-1 Decomposition of Population Aging by Country-Income Group and Region, 1970–2015

	Observed Change	Percentage Attributable to		
		Cohorts	Fertility	Mortality
Panel A: Country-Income Group				
High-income countries	0.073	0.766	0.046	0.188
Upper-middle-income countries	0.047	0.752	0.126	0.122
Lower-middle-income countries	0.015	0.596	0.235	0.169
Low-income countries	0.005	0.218	0.276	0.506
Panel B: Region				
Africa	0.003	−0.091	0.525	0.567
Asia	0.038	0.729	0.133	0.138
Europe	0.072	0.788	0.039	0.173
Latin America	0.036	0.720	0.147	0.133
Northern America	0.051	0.754	0.040	0.205
Oceania	0.048	0.706	0.063	0.231

SOURCE: Data are from the U.N. Department of Economic and Social Affairs (2017).

tries (LICs). For three of the four income groups, the aging of large cohorts was the largest contributor to population aging. However, a strong income gradient remains in the magnitude of this contribution: the aging of large cohorts was most important in HICs (76.6%) and decreased across income groups (75.2% in upper-middle-income countries, 59.6% in lower-middle-income countries, and 21.8% in LICs). Conversely, fertility reductions are most important for LICs (27.6%) and least important for HICs (4.6%). The role of recent mortality declines is fairly consistent across income groups, explaining around 12–19 percent of population aging for the top three income groups. Overall, these findings highlight the substantial influence that large aging cohorts have on population aging. While past histories of fertility and mortality decline determine the size of these cohorts, recent mortality and fertility changes remain important contributors to population aging, especially in LICs.

Panel B of Table 11-1 presents the same set of results, this time for regions rather than income groups. As with income groups, the magnitude of historical population aging differed substantially across regions, with the largest absolute growth in Europe (7.2%) followed by Northern America (5.1%). Africa had the least absolute aging (0.3%), which is perhaps unsurprising because most LICs are within the African continent. In contrast to income groups, the sources of population aging by region differ less strikingly across groups, potentially due to large within-region heterogeneity. Aging cohorts were responsible for 70–80 percent of population aging for all regions except Africa. Fertility declines had the largest influence in Asia and Latin America, explaining about 15 percent of population aging, while mortality improvements were most important in Northern America and Oceania (20.5% for Northern America and 23.1% for Oceania).

To understand sources of future population aging, we conduct the same decomposition exercise for projected population aging between 2015 and 2050 (Table 11-2). The expected future change in the share of individuals

TABLE 11-2 Decomposition of Population Aging by Country-Income Group and Region, 2015–2050

	Projected Change	Percentage Attributable to	
		Cohorts	Mortality
Panel A: Country-Income Group			
High-income countries	0.098 (0.074, 0.126)	0.928 (0.919, 0.946)	0.081 (0.065, 0.105)
Upper-middle-income countries	0.134 (0.112, 0.160)	0.938 (0.934, 0.945)	0.063 (0.055, 0.073)
Lower-middle-income countries	0.062 (0.050, 0.076)	0.919 (0.916, 0.926)	0.055 (0.048, 0.065)
Low-income countries	0.019 (0.015, 0.025)	0.792 (0.775, 0.806)	0.088 (0.072, 0.111)
Panel B: Region			
Africa	0.025 (0.019, 0.031)	0.829 (0.823, 0.835)	0.082 (0.069, 0.101)
Asia	0.101 (0.083, 0.122)	0.937 (0.933, 0.946)	0.052 (0.045, 0.061)
Europe	0.103 (0.077, 0.133)	0.923 (0.916, 0.938)	0.092 (0.073, 0.120)
Latin America	0.116 (0.096, 0.140)	0.947 (0.942, 0.955)	0.043 (0.037, 0.050)
Northern America	0.077 (0.056, 0.102)	0.908 (0.900, 0.926)	0.099 (0.077, 0.132)
Oceania	0.061 (0.045, 0.081)	0.906 (0.898, 0.923)	0.068 (0.053, 0.091)

SOURCE: Data are from the U.N. Department of Economic and Social Affairs (2017). Point estimates are from the medium variant projections, and estimates in parentheses are from the high and low variants.

above age 65 depends on assumptions about the future trajectory of fertility and mortality. Therefore, each cell in Table 11-2 presents three estimates: the point estimate from the medium-variant projections and upper and lower bounds from the high and low variants. Compared with the historical changes in Table 11-1, the patterns of population aging by income group differ substantially looking forward to 2050 (Panel A). While HICs are expected to continue aging (9.8%), upper-middle-income countries are expected to undergo the largest absolute growth in the share of older people (13.4%). Additionally, lower-middle-income countries are expected to see much larger absolute growth in the share of older people (6.2%) than they did in the previous period. The sources of population aging are expected to be far more homogenous over the coming decades. For all but LICs, the continued aging of large cohorts is the dominant source of population aging, contributing more than 90 percent. Fertility reductions have a negligible expected contribution in all but LICs, and mortality reductions are only expected to contribute 5–9 percent.

In Panel B of Table 11-2, we decompose expected future aging by region. The first striking finding is that every region is expected to see greater absolute growth in the share of older individuals between 2015 and 2050, compared with the historical change between 1970 and 2015. Latin America is expected to have the largest absolute growth in older individuals (11.6%) followed closely by Europe and Asia (10.3% and 10.1% respectively). Importantly, even Africa, which underwent virtually no aging between 1970 and 2015, is expected to see 2.5 percent growth by 2050. The aging of large cohorts is, once again, by far the largest contributor to future population aging, accounting for more than 90 percent of aging in every region except Africa, where it still accounts for 83 percent. Mortality reductions are expected to have a much smaller influence, explaining only 4–10 percent of growth in the share of older individuals across regions. Finally, fertility reductions have an essentially negligible effect in every region except Africa (8.9%). While these decompositions are based on assumptions of future fertility change, looking at the high and low variants barely changes our conclusions.

Conclusions

The levels of, changes in, and sources of population aging vary across countries at various income levels and in different global regions. In 1970–2015, richer countries experienced more population aging. The aging of large cohorts, followed by mortality reductions in HICs and fertility reductions in LICs, drove most aging. Looking to 2050, middle-income countries (MICs) and countries in Asia and Latin America are expected to experience the greatest absolute growth in the share of the population above age 65. The continued aging of large cohorts is expected to primarily drive this growth, with mortality declines also playing a small role. Fertility declines are expected to make virtually no contribution to population aging in most settings. Africa and LICs are the primary exceptions to this pattern, as fertility declines are still expected to contribute significantly to future population aging. These findings highlight the long reach of historical trends; for most country-income groups and regions, the aging of large cohorts dwarfs the contribution of recent changes in mortality and fertility.

GROWING OLD BEFORE RICH

Rapid expected population aging in LMICs has spurred concern among academics and policy makers that poor countries may be "growing old before rich." This concern extends to the general public as well, with many news media sources discussing the potential consequences of growing old before rich in large countries such as India and China (Curran, 2017; Gray, 2017). The fear is that LMICs do not yet have the resources or the national systems to meet the financial needs of large, post-employment populations of older people. If this is true, population aging will result in a growing share of older individuals living with poor welfare support. This will in turn strain individuals and families who must provide for older people. This contrasts with the historical experience of HICs, where population aging is generally believed to have occurred more gradually and at higher levels of per capita income. As a result, HICs were able to create national institutions, such as social security and pension programs, to capture a portion of these higher incomes and transfer them to meet the needs of older individuals.

Although this belief is widely held, whether LMICs are indeed growing old before rich has not been empirically examined, as far as we are aware. In this section, we conduct a simple exercise to determine how much support exists for this view. Using historical and projected information on population aging, gross domestic product (GDP) per capita, and national health expenditure per capita, we assess whether aging in LMICs will actually occur at lower overall levels of per capita income and health expenditure relative to the historical experience of HICs.

Data and Methods

For this exercise, we use a chronological measure of population aging, the share of the population above the age of 65 (drawn from the *UN WPP*). We focus on two measures of national income, both drawn from the World Bank's World Development Indicators Database (WB WDI; see

World Bank, 2017). The first indicator is GDP per capita, normalized across countries and time using purchasing power parity adjustments such that all values are expressed in 2017 U.S. dollars (USD). While GDP per capita is an appealing measure of overall national income, it is a rather imprecise indicator of national investments in health. In addition to social security spending, health expenditures are a key input for maintaining the welfare of older individuals. Therefore, we also use data on health expenditures per capita, normalized to 2011 USD (data were not available in 2017 values).

To determine whether LMICs are growing old before rich, we first group countries into three income categories (high-, middle-, and low-income countries) and then plot the relationship between the share of the population above the age of 65 and the wealth indicators for each year from 1990 to 2015. If LMICs are indeed growing old before rich, at any given share of older individuals, we should observe lower levels of wealth in LMICs compared with HICs. However, because LMICs have yet to reach levels of aging comparable to the recent historical experience of HICs, we cannot directly compare across income groups. We must therefore infer what GDP per capita will be in LMICs when they reach levels of population aging comparable to HICs. To do this, we project GDP per capita for LMICs into the future using the prior 10-year average growth rate. In alternative analyses, we projected GDP using growth rates over other time horizons and found no qualitative change to our conclusions.

Results

Figure 11-1 plots GDP per capita (in 2017 USD) against the share of the population above 65 years of age for LICs, MICs, and HICs for the period 1990 to 2040. The solid points represent observed data points, while the crosses represent projected data points based on historic GDP per capita growth rates and expected future shares of older individuals. Because LICs are not expected to reach levels of population aging comparable to MICs and HICs by 2040, the main comparison in the figure is between MICs and HICs. Our findings do not support the view that MICs are growing old before rich when compared with HICs' historical experience. To the contrary, when MICs reach shares of older individuals observed historically in HICs, they are expected to be at higher levels of GDP per capita than observed in HICs. In fact, a 2.9 percent annual growth rate—less than half the annual average growth rate for MICs in recent years—would be sufficient to match the historical income-to-aging ratio of HICs by the time the share of older adults in MICs reaches the HIC 1990 level. These results are robust to using health expenditure per capita, rather than GDP, in conducting the analyses.

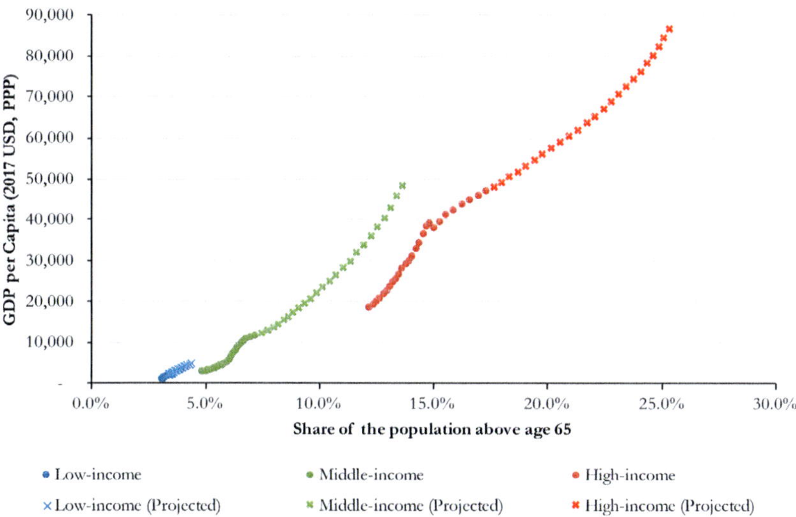

FIGURE 11-1 Share of population above age 65 and GDP per capita in 2017 USD (purchasing power parity adjusted), 1990–2040.
NOTES: Projected points are calculated based on the average GDP per capita growth rate over the past 10 years of observed data and the medium-variant *UN WPP* projections.

Conclusions

Despite the widespread concern that LMICs are growing old before rich, we do not find evidence to support this view. Our results suggest that MICs will actually have higher levels of both GDP per capita and health expenditures per capita when they reach shares of older individuals comparable to the recent experiences of HICs. However, this conclusion is only valid under the assumption that MICs will continue to experience GDP and health expenditure growth at levels suggested by the 10-year historical growth rate. If the growth rate deviates from its historical average, MICs may well reach greater shares of older individuals at lower levels of wealth.

Beyond having sufficient levels of national wealth, MICs' ability to meet the needs of a growing older-age population also depends on having institutions to transfer this wealth to older individuals efficiently. While most MICs nominally have social security and old-age protection schemes (Social Security Administration, 2016, 2017a, 2017b), more research is needed to determine if these programs are sufficiently funded, operate efficiently, and provide coverage to the complete population of older individuals.

FUNCTIONAL AGE AND AGING

The previous analyses in this paper treated age as a purely chronological phenomenon, classifying individuals as old when they reach age 65 and defining population aging as the share of individuals who meet this threshold. Based on these conventional measures, HICs currently have the highest share of older individuals, but MICs are expected to age the most rapidly over the coming decades. The importance of chronological age stems partly from the fact that ability to function independently in society is strongly tied to a person's age (Katz, 1983; Covinsky et al., 2003). However, at any given chronological age, functional ability likely varies significantly both within and across populations. Therefore, chronological measures of aging may mask important heterogeneity in actual functional ability at both individual and population levels.

At the individual level, age is often used as one of the most important proxies for a person's needs. Age is used to determine eligibility for pensions and government benefits such as social security and Medicare (Social Security Administration, 2016, 2017a, 2017b) and to evaluate health and mortality risks (Lloyd-Jones et al., 2004). Both uses of chronological age are not based on some inherent characteristic of age but rather on tight correlations between age and health, ability to work and be independent, and general functional ability. However, if functional ability varies across and within populations at any given chronological age, then these approaches may mischaracterize individual needs and risks. Two individuals at similar ages may have different functional abilities and consequently require different resources. This issue of comparability may be further heightened when comparing individuals of similar ages across countries.

At the population level, chronological measures of age may also understate or overstate the consequences of population aging. This is reflected in popular statements such as "age is just a number" and "60 is the new 50," which seem to imply that functional abilities may be improving over generations. If so, conventional aging measures may overstate the consequences of population aging because more-recent generations of older individuals are expected to have better health and require fewer resources in adulthood (Lutz et al. [2008] and Sanderson and Scherbov [2010] reached this conclusion for HICs). Conversely, if functional abilities are worsening across generations, conventional measures of aging would understate the likely consequences of population aging. This discrepancy between chronological age and functional ability can also affect cross-sectional interpretations of age composition across countries. For example, if two countries have similar shares of the population above age 65 but highly disparate levels of disability, chronological measures would equate the two populations when in reality one has a much larger dependent subpopulation.

The potential discrepancies between functional and chronological age have led to several studies that have sought to reconceptualize and develop alternative measures of aging. For example, Sanderson and Scherbov (2005) developed an alternative measure of aging based on remaining life expectancy. The key insight behind this measure is that an individual's health needs and functional status tend to be closely related to their remaining life expectancy, regardless of their age or their population group's total life expectancy (Riffe et al., 2015). Using this type of indicator, Gietel-Basten et al. (2016) compared traditional old-age dependency ratios to ratios based on remaining life expectancy for several world regions. They ultimately concluded that chronological-based measures substantially overstate the future magnitude of population aging over the coming decades when compared with measures based on remaining life expectancy. While remaining life expectancy–based measures are instructive, they are limited in value because they do not use direct measurements of functional aging such as disability or morbidity status. As an alternative, Sanderson and Scherbov (2017) proposed a new measure, known as "alpha-age," that expresses an individual's age based on the value for that individual of an aging-related indicator relative to a standard age pattern. Because alpha-ages can be estimated for different indicators of aging, this approach allows for a more comprehensive comparison, in an interpretable metric, of aging across multiple dimensions.

In this section, we adapt Sanderson and Scherbov's alpha-age methodology using microdata (the HRS sister studies) from five LMICs and three HICs to compare functional and chronological aging across and within countries over time. We seek to address two broad questions: (1) for any given chronological age, how much variation exists in functional age across countries; and (2) for a given chronological age, is functional age within countries improving over time (e.g., is 60 really the new 50, or is it the new 70)?

Data and Methods

To address our main questions, we must first generate comparable estimates of functional ability across countries. To do this, we take advantage of the HRS sister studies: a group of global aging studies with harmonized data collection procedures and comparable survey questions.[4] Specifically, we use data from the following countries (and datasets): China (China Health and Retirement Longitudinal Survey), Costa Rica (Costa Rican Longevity and Healthy Aging Study), Indonesia (Indonesian Family Life Survey [IFLS]), Mexico (Mexican Health and Aging Study), South

____

[4] See Gateway to Global Aging Data at https://g2aging.org [February 2018].

TABLE 11-3 Data Sources, Waves, and Sample Sizes for HRS Sister Studies

Country	Survey	Wave	Sample Size
Low- and Middle-Income Countries			
China	China Health and Retirement Longitudinal Study (CHARLS)	2013	8,486
Costa Rica	Costa Rica Longevity and Healthy Aging Study (CRELES)	2005	2,826
Indonesia	Indonesian Family Life Survey (IFLS)	2015	3,741
Mexico	Mexican Health and Aging Study (MHAS)	2012	9,881
South Africa	Health and Aging in Africa: A Longitudinal Study of an INDEPTH Community in South Africa (HAALSI)	2014	2,731
High-Income Countries			
The Netherlands	The Survey of Health, Ageing and Retirement in Europe (SHARE)	2013	2,938
Spain	SHARE	2013	4,861
United States	Health and Retirement Study (HRS)	2014	13,885

Africa (Health and Aging in Africa: A Longitudinal Study of an INDEPTH Community in South Africa), Netherlands (Survey of Health, Ageing and Retirement in Europe [SHARE]), Spain (SHARE), and the United States (HRS). For our main analyses, we use data from recent waves of each survey, focusing specifically on adults over the age of 60. Table 11-3 lists more details on the survey waves and sample sizes.

Our primary measure of functional limitation is whether individuals report an activity of daily living (ADL) limitation. ADLs are an extremely common metric of physical functioning (Katz, 1983), measuring individuals' ability to perform essential self-care tasks such as bathing, dressing, and eating independently. ADL limitations are appealing as a measure of functional age because they capture individuals' ability to function independently. In each survey, individuals were asked questions about their ability to perform several different ADLs without difficulty, with difficulty, or not at all (slight variations occurred in the way the question was asked across datasets, but all followed this same structure). To ensure comparability across surveys, we use data on the subset of ADL questions included in every survey (dressing, eating, bathing, getting out of bed, and walking across a room). Individuals are classified as ADL-limited if they reported difficulty or inability to perform any of the five ADLs.

We estimated functional age in each country by comparing the age- and sex-specific prevalence of ADL disability in the country to the age at which that specific prevalence is reached on a "frontier" disability age pattern. For this exercise, the frontier population represents the currently best attainable age pattern of ADL limitations. To construct the frontier age pattern (separately by sex), we first pooled data for 15 SHARE countries and estimated the lowest age- and sex-specific prevalence of disability at every age. We then constructed the frontier age pattern by combining the lowest observed age-specific prevalence of ADL disability across age groups. Because the frontier is made by combining information from multiple countries, the resulting age pattern may be irregular across age. To account for this possibility, we smoothed the observed age pattern with a logistic regression to ensure that prevalence of disability increases monotonically with age.

We then estimated a functional age for each chronological age (in 5-year age groups between 60 and 85) as the age in the frontier population with the same prevalence of disability. For example, if the prevalence of disability reaches 40 percent at age 65 in Indonesia but only does so at age 75 in the frontier population, we would assign Indonesians with a chronological age of 65 a functional age of 75. Finally, to answer our first main question of how much variation exists in functional age across countries, we plot the relationship between chronological and functional age for each country separately by sex.

Our second main question is whether functional age, at any given chronological age, is getting better or worse over time. To answer this question, we would ideally compare functional age across several birth cohorts. Unfortunately, the HRS sister studies are relatively recent, and few have collected data long enough to permit comparisons across multiple birth cohorts. However, Mexico and Indonesia have data separated by roughly a decade (between 2001 and 2012 in Mexico and between 2000 and 2014 in Indonesia). For these two countries, we attempted to identify the degree to which morbidity is expanding or compressing across generations by comparing the difference in functional ability for two periods roughly a decade apart.

While this approach is instructive for comparing cross-country differences in functional ability, it does not account for differential old-age mortality across countries. Because the salience of disability is often thought to arise from how long individuals spend disabled, comparisons of pure age patterns may overstate or understate differences in the average time that older individuals live with a disability. One approach to compare expected years lived with disability across countries is to combine the age- and sex-specific prevalence of disability across countries with the *UN WPP* life tables using the Sullivan method. This approach estimates disabled and disability-free life expectancy under the strong assumption that the prevalence of disability is stable over time. Despite the strength of this assumption, the Sullivan method provides a useful back-of-the-envelope approach to compare the duration of time spent disabled across countries. Using the Sullivan method, we compared cross-country differences in two measures of disability duration: the expected number of years an individual will spend disabled at age 60 and the fraction of remaining life expectancy at age 60 spent disabled.

A major limitation of ADL measures is that they are self-reported. If individuals perceive and answer questions about limitations in a systematically different way, observed differences within and across countries may not represent objective differences in disability status. Anchoring vignettes are commonly used to correct for reporting heterogeneity (King and Wand, 2006). However, vignettes are often only requested for general health status and not for specific domains of health such as functional limitations. ADL-specific vignettes (e.g., asking respondents if they consider an individual who needs to pause three times while walking 100 meters as having trouble with that activity) could greatly help ensure consistent measurement and comparability across responses. In the absence of these data, ADLs can be compared with other measurements of health to better understand whether observed differences in ADLs represent true health differences. If, for example, South African men report very low levels of ADL limitations compared with other countries but are also more obese than individuals in other countries, we might believe that South African men are underreporting ADL limitations. This approach does not solve the issue of reporting heterogeneity, but rather provides a heuristic to qualitatively assess how much confidence one should place in the observed patterns. We adopted this approach and compared the cross-country correlation between measured age-specific body mass index (BMI), the prevalence of poor self-rated health, and the prevalence of ADL limitations. A high correlation between the prevalence of disability and other health indicators may provide some indication that the disability measure is partially capturing an objective measure of health status. A low correlation between the two measures may indicate that reporting differences are driving differences across ages and countries or that the processes that cause disability in these countries are not necessarily related to BMI or poor self-rated health.

Results

Figure 11-2 shows the cross-sectional age-specific prevalence of any ADL disability by country and separately by sex. For all countries, we observe an increasing prevalence of ADL disability with age, with higher levels among women than among men. Beyond these two broad patterns, the initial levels and age gradients of disability vary substantially across

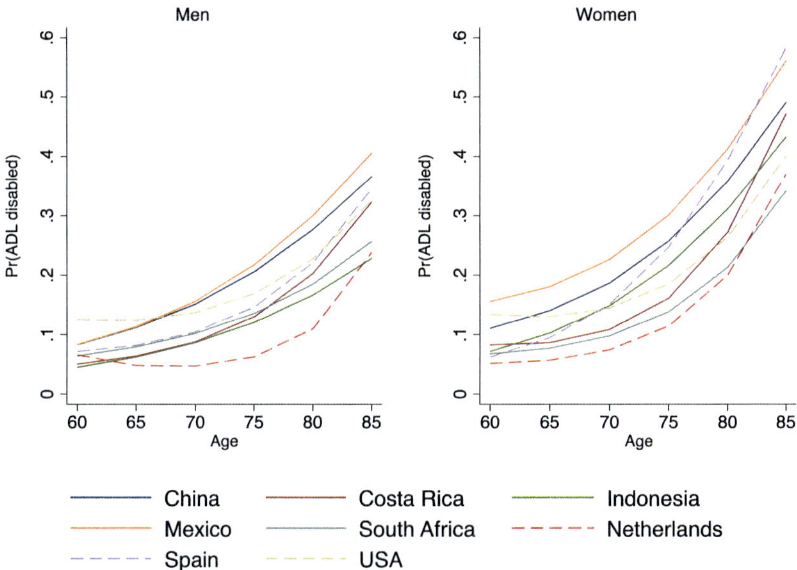

FIGURE 11-2 Age-specific prevalence of any ADL disability across countries separately by sex.
NOTES: Solid lines represent low- and middle-income countries and dashed lines represent high-income countries.
SOURCE: Data are from the HRS sister studies.

countries and by sex. For both men and women, Mexican adults have the highest age-specific prevalence of ADL disability at nearly every age, with a disability prevalence at age 85 of more than 40 percent for men and more than 50 percent for women. Chinese adults follow closely, with similarly high levels of disability, especially at older ages. In contrast, Dutch adults report some of the lowest levels of ADL disability at every age. The differences between these extremes are striking: at age 85, the prevalence of disability in the Netherlands is around 20 percent for men and 35 percent for women—nearly 20 percentage points lower than same-aged Mexican adults. Surprisingly, we do not observe a clear country-income gradient in the prevalence of ADL disability. At any given age, substantial heterogeneity exists across countries, with richer countries such as Spain and the United States often underperforming poorer countries such as Indonesia and South Africa.

Though Figure 11-2 reveals differences in disability across age, sex, and country, interpreting the magnitude of these differences is not straight-

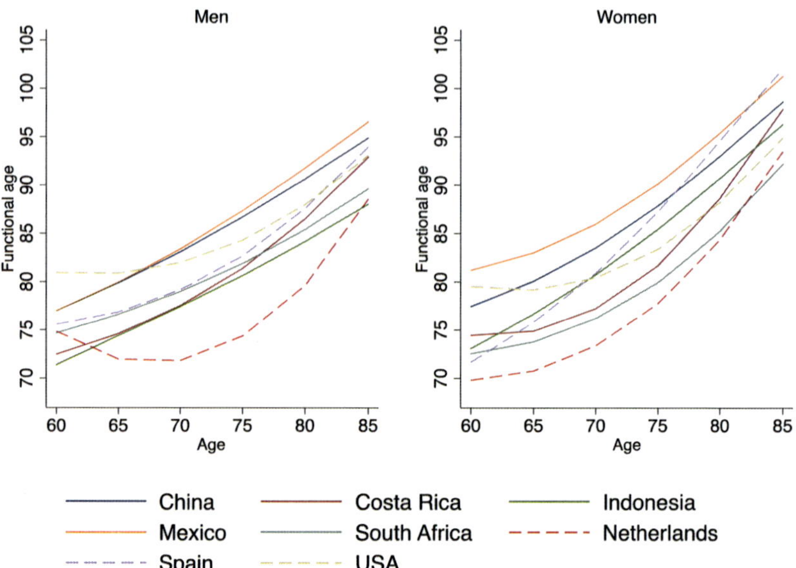

FIGURE 11-3 Functional and chronological age across countries separately by sex. NOTES: Functional age is estimated by benchmarking disability levels to a frontier population. Solid lines represent low- and middle-income countries and dashed lines represent high-income countries.
SOURCE: Data are from the HRS sister studies.

forward. One way to conceptualize the magnitude of these differences is by converting age-specific levels of disability to a functional age by benchmarking each country against a "best-attainable" frontier population. Figure 11-3 compares chronological and functional age for each country separately by sex. These results reveal large differences between chronological and functional age for many countries. The consistent ADL disadvantage we observe for Mexican adults in Figure 11-2 now translates into about a 15-year difference between functional and chronological age for men and a startling 15- to 20-year difference for women. These results imply that older Mexican adults have the functional capacity of much older individuals in the frontier population. We observe similarly large discrepancies for Chinese adults. At the other end of the spectrum, we find much smaller differences between chronological and functional age for individuals in the Netherlands. Overall, these results reveal pronounced and consistent variation in functional age at any given chronological age, with differences between the best- and worst-performing countries ranging from 10 to 20 years across chronological ages.

Our results so far have focused on the cross-sectional differences in functional age across populations, yet the degree to which these findings can translate to conclusions about functional aging at the population level depends on how functional ability is changing over time. Figures 11-4 and 11-5 compare functional ability in Mexico and Indonesia for two time periods roughly a decade apart. We observe a striking increase in the prevalence of disability at nearly every age between 2001 and 2012 in Mexico (Figure 11-4), with a larger absolute increase for men than for women. Figure 11-5 plots a similar comparison of disability prevalence over time in Indonesia. Because the 2000 wave of the IFLS did not ask the full set of ADL questions, we constructed an alternative measure of physical disability based on the set of common indicators between 2000 and 2014. These results for Indonesia show a pattern similar to those for Mexico: at many ages, levels of disability are higher in 2014 than in 2000. These findings bring into question the stability of disability over time in Mexico and Indonesia and suggest a substantial expansion of morbidity, even as life expectancy continues to increase in both countries (United Nations Department of Economic and Social Affairs, 2017).

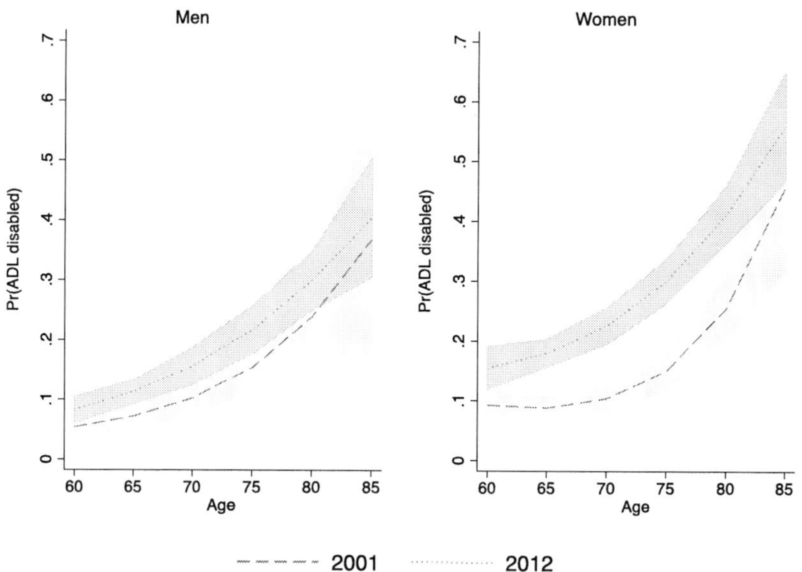

FIGURE 11-4 Change over time in ADL disability separately by sex, Mexico, 2001–2012.
NOTES: Shaded regions represent 95 percent confidence intervals.
SOURCE: Data are from the Mexican Health and Aging Study.

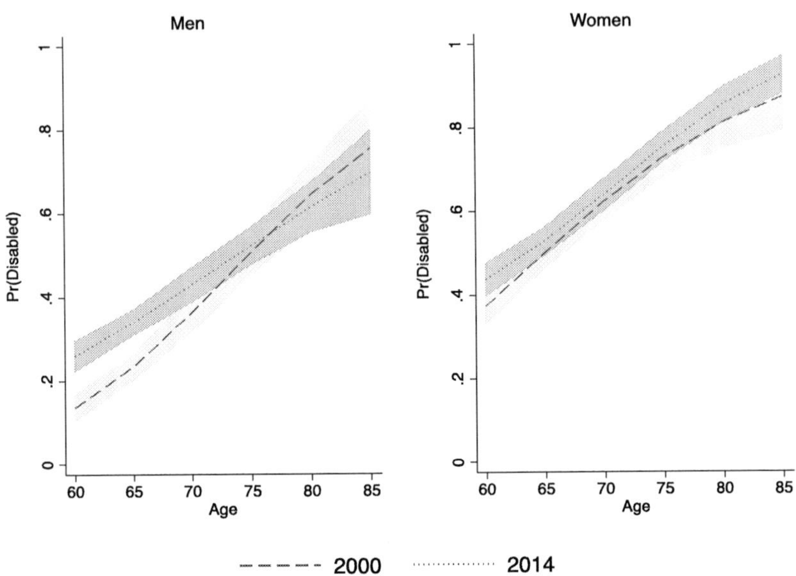

FIGURE 11-5 Change over time in disability separately by sex, Indonesia, 2000–2014.
NOTES: Disability measure used is based on a set of comparable physical disability indicators from the two waves of data. Shaded regions represent 95 percent confidence intervals.
SOURCE: Data are from the Indonesian Family Life Survey.

Finally, we investigated differences in the duration of time spent disabled across countries. Tables 11-4 and 11-5 present the Sullivan method estimates of total, disability-free, and disabled life expectancy for men and women. After accounting for differences in old-age mortality, our conclusions about the relative levels of functional ability across countries remain mostly unchanged. For example, Mexican adults have the highest levels of disability duration, both in absolute numbers of years lived with disability and as a share of overall life expectancy. Our conclusions about the best-performing countries are also consistent across the two methods: we find low levels of years lived with disability and shares of total life expectancy spent disabled for adults in the Netherlands, South Africa, and Indonesia. Beyond the differences across countries, these findings highlight the large sex differences in disability. In nearly every country, women live longer with disability and spend more of their lives disabled relative to men.

One interesting finding that emerges from this analysis is that countries with the highest absolute levels of years lived with disability also tend

TABLE 11-4 Years of Total, Disabled, and Disability-Free Life Expectancy for Men at Age 60 (e_{60}) across Countries

Country	e_{60}	e_{60} Disabled	e_{60} Healthy	Share Disabled	Share Healthy
China	18.5	2.9	15.6	0.16	0.84
Costa Rica	22.2	2.7	19.4	0.12	0.88
Indonesia	15.2	1.2	14.0	0.08	0.92
Mexico	21.6	4.0	17.6	0.19	0.81
South Africa	13.6	1.3	12.3	0.10	0.90
Netherlands	22.0	1.8	20.2	0.08	0.92
Spain	22.7	3.2	19.5	0.14	0.86
USA	21.7	3.7	18.1	0.17	0.83

TABLE 11-5 Years of Total, Disabled, and Disability-Free Life Expectancy for Women at Age 60 (e_{60}) across Countries

Country	e_{60}	e_{60} Disabled	e_{60} Healthy	Share Disabled	Share Healthy
China	20.7	4.4	16.3	0.21	0.79
Costa Rica	25.0	4.6	20.3	0.19	0.81
Indonesia	17.8	2.8	15.0	0.15	0.85
Mexico	23.7	6.8	16.9	0.29	0.71
South Africa	18.6	2.3	16.3	0.12	0.88
Netherlands	25.4	3.4	22.0	0.13	0.87
Spain	27.1	6.7	20.4	0.25	0.75
USA	24.7	4.9	19.7	0.20	0.80

to have the largest shares of overall life expectancy spent disabled. If we assume that countries with lower life expectancies will ultimately resemble the higher life-expectancy countries, our results suggest an almost systematic expansion of morbidity as life expectancy increases. An important caveat is that these analyses are based on cross-sectional estimates of disability; in the presence of morbidity expansion and increasing life expectancy, all the estimates presented here should serve as lower bounds of the true years lived with disability.

Estimates based on self-reported measures of disability may not represent real differences in health across countries if individuals in some areas systematically interpret and answer disability questions differently. To determine whether our measures of self-reported ADL disability are accurately capturing variations in health, we plotted the relationship between the age-specific prevalence of ADL disability and two measures of health (BMI and poor self-rated health) separately for men and women. We find mixed results for BMI, with virtually no relationship for men and a potentially negative correlation between age-specific mean BMI and age-specific disability prevalence for women. By contrast, the correlations between self-reported ADL disability and poor self-rated health are more consistent, with a weak but positive relationship for both men and women. These results do not have a straightforward interpretation but suggest that either individual perceptions of health status do not accurately reflect objective health or the processes that result in poor self-rated health and ADL disabilities are not closely related to those that determine BMI. Testing the correlation of ADL disabilities to other objective biomarker measurements such as blood pressure, cholesterol, and spirometry values could further clarify this relationship.

Conclusions

The evidence suggests that focusing on chronological age masks substantial heterogeneity in physical functioning across countries and over time. Differences in the age-specific prevalence of disability at any given chronological age are stark and do not attenuate at older ages. In particular, Mexican and Chinese adults have much higher levels of disability compared with adults in other countries, a difference that translates to a 10- to 20-year gap in functional age relative to the best-performing countries. These differences remain salient even after accounting for differential old-age mortality across countries. We also do not observe a country-income gradient for functional age, with richer countries such as the United States and Spain performing much worse than LMICs such as South Africa and Indonesia.

Although long-term data were only available for two of the LMICs we considered (Mexico and Indonesia), evidence from both countries suggests that old-age morbidity is getting worse over time. For example, at nearly every age, the prevalence of disability is higher among Mexicans in 2012 than in 2001 (other studies have found similar findings for Mexico; see, e.g., Díaz-Venegas et al., 2015). Understanding why disability is expanding in countries like Mexico and Indonesia should be a first-order priority for future research and policy on aging.

CONCLUSIONS

We find four major stylized facts on the demography of aging in LMICs. First, MICs and countries in Asia and Latin America are expected to experience the largest absolute levels of population aging over the coming decades, driven primarily by the aging of large cohorts and secondarily by continued mortality reductions. The large magnitude of expected population aging in these countries has generated a concern that MICs and countries in Asia and Latin America are growing old before rich. However, we do not find any support for this belief; indeed, our second major finding is that as MICs undergo population aging, they may actually have higher levels of national wealth compared with the historical experience of HICs. Third, large cross-national differences exist in functional ability, with countries such as Mexico and China having a functional age that is consistently 10 to 20 years higher than best-performing countries such as the Netherlands at any given chronological age. Fourth, some evidence suggests that morbidity may be expanding over time in LMICs, with poorer physical functioning in old age among more recent cohorts. These last two findings suggest that chronological measures of aging may mask heterogeneity in functional ability both across countries and within countries over time.

Our findings raise several important future questions for the global demography of aging. In the following section, we conclude by discussing three major areas of future research and some potential short- and long-run policy solutions to promote healthy aging globally.

The Role of Public Policy

Establishing the cost-effectiveness and return on investment of interventions to promote functional independence among older individuals will be essential for crafting public policy over the coming decades. However, in the short run, simple environmental and technological changes do have the potential to provide large welfare improvements for older individuals. These types of changes provide more immediate benefits than interventions to prevent the underlying causes of disability in old age, which may take decades to realize. For example, studies have found that hearing loss is associated with poorer quality of life across multiple measures of well-being (Dalton et al., 2003). Therefore, interventions as simple as providing hearing aids may greatly improve the welfare of older individuals (Chisolm et al., 2007). Similarly, redesigning bedrooms and bathrooms to ease everyday self-care might drastically improve older individuals' ability to be independent (Petersson et al., 2008; Fänge and Iwarsson, 2005). Identifying other simple changes that enable greater independence among older individuals and reduce the burden of caregiving on families will be an important area of future work. Research must also examine the extent to which public policy solutions drawn from HICs will work in LMICs. For example, solutions such as nursing homes or assisted living facilities may see poor usage in countries in which older individuals traditionally live with their children.

Improving the quality of medical care may also provide a cost-effective way of improving functional ability among individuals with noncommunicable diseases (NCDs) such as hypertension or diabetes. Studies from multiple LMICs have found a large burden of disability and mortality due to cardiovascular events such as stroke and diabetes (Kalkonde et al., 2015; Andrade, 2009; Maredza et al., 2015; Tyrovolas et al., 2015; Ferri et al., 2011). Medical and health systems improvements targeting post-stroke care or managing diabetes complications may be effective at reducing these NCDs' disabling consequences. While such potential improvements are promising, many challenges remain in improving the quality of NCD care in LMICs. Future research will have to bring together experts from several fields to address barriers at the health system, physician, and patient levels.

Biology and Epidemiology of Aging: Preventing Functional Dependency

In the long run, preventing physical and economic dependency among future generations in MICs may be more cost-effective than the solutions discussed in the previous section. Addressing this goal will require improving our understanding of the causes of premature morbidity and mortality and identifying whether they are fundamentally different in HICs and LMICs. Related analyses will require a deeper integration of studies of the basic biology of aging with public health, demography, and economics research. Within the field of biology, a large and active community of researchers is already working to identify the biological mechanisms that cause old-age morbidity and mortality. The goal of this work is to promote longevity with the absence of morbidity, or what biologists refer to as "health span." Using animal models and experimental methods, biologists have identified several potential physiological mechanisms that regulate the pace of aging (López-Otín et al., 2013). Drawing from these insights, we believe an exciting area of future research for population scientists will be to determine which biological mechanisms are important for explaining variation in functional ability at the population level.

Research integrating biological insights into population science has become more feasible due to efforts to collect biomarkers in large-scale population surveys, such as the HRS sister studies (Rehkopf et al., 2016). However, because biomarker data have only recently started to be collected in population surveys, current research is limited to short follow-up windows between biomarker measurement and future health outcomes. Comprehension of the most salient causes of premature morbidity and mortality in older age will be strengthened by studying the role of biological conditions earlier in life and dynamic changes over the life course. This later goal will require not only richer measurements and longer follow-up periods but also the adoption and development of new methods to properly deal with dynamic treatment effects, treatment confounder feedback, and other issues that arise with dynamic measurements. Although a rich literature exists in epidemiology and biostatistics to specifically address these methodological challenges, these methods have been slow to move into the social sciences (Robins, 1986; Hernan and Robins, 2018). Better collaborations among researchers across fields will be essential for pushing research on aging and the life course forward.

Economic Consequences of Healthy Aging

Estimating the consequences of healthy aging on various dimensions of economic well-being is important for setting public policy agendas and valuing the full benefits of health interventions. Current valuations are based primarily on data from HICs, yet substantial reasons exist to expect that the value and consequences of health in old age differ in LMICs. Based on time-use data, older individuals in LMICs are on average more engaged in productive activities compared with their counterparts in HICs, spending more time working, contributing to housework, and caring for children (Charmes, 2015). Thus, interventions that promote healthy aging may have greater value in LMICs than patterns of time use in HICs would suggest.

Second, healthy aging may also have indirect intergenerational effects on other household members. Because older individuals in LMICs are far more likely to reside with their children (Bongaarts and Zimmer, 2002), the burden of caring for older individuals may fall on other members of the household, particularly women. Therefore, promoting healthy aging may reduce the burden of care on other household members, enabling them to engage in other productivity activities. Understanding how improvements to older-adult health affect the dynamics of time transfers and labor force participation within households in LMICs remains an important open question.

Both the direct and indirect intergenerational economic effects of healthy aging may aggregate into economic growth at the macro level. However, other household and institutional considerations will determine whether healthy aging leads to growth or is offset by greater expenditure on older individuals. At the household level, postponing morbidity and increasing life expectancy could lead to greater household income through the direct effect of older individuals being more productive and the indirect effects on other members of the household. Yet if older individuals are not engaged in productive activities, their consumption will have to be funded by a combination of household and government transfers. Therefore, healthy aging may not improve growth if the magnitude of spending needed to meet the consumption needs of a longer-lived population outweighs the increase in income being generated. Research is needed to understand how to convert improved functional capacity into productive activity and capture this wealth for future generations of older individuals. Institutional reforms that encourage savings and investment while also strengthening national pension and social security programs may be an important first step to achieving these goals (Mason and Lee, 2006; Gribble and Bremner, 2012).

Data Sources for the Future Study of Aging in LMICs

With the continued emergence of HRS sister studies across the world, the data sources for the study of aging globally are increasing, each with specific benefits and drawbacks. In this section, we briefly summarize the virtues and limitations of the most common global aging datasets. This list is not meant to be exhaustive but rather to highlight three of the most promising sources for the future study of aging globally.

HRS Sister Studies

The HRS sister studies have several important benefits, including a longitudinal study design; rich social, health, and economic information on individuals and households; and harmonization that facilitates cross-country comparisons. The surveys' panel design is extremely well suited for studying aging, allowing researchers to track dynamic changes in aging and use individual-level variation to identify the determinants and consequences of functional changes with age. These data can be used to make cross-sectional comparisons, both within and across countries, and to identify trends and changes over time. The HRS sister surveys also provide one of the few sources of biomarker measurements in LMICs, allowing for objective measurements of health status.

Despite their many benefits, the HRS sister studies have a few important drawbacks. At present, the HRS studies in most LMICs have not been running long enough to study aging over time or across cohorts. Until more waves of data become available, current research using these data will have to rely heavily on cross sections or limited changes observable in short panels. Second, although these studies collect mortality follow-up, whether the surveys can be used to generate accurate mortality estimates remains unclear. Finally, for many of the sister studies, the sample sizes are often not large enough to power subnational or subpopulation analyses of aging.

The inclusion of several additional variables could also enhance the research value of these surveys. Collecting a broader set of biomarker measurements would allow for more robust assessment of health and functional status. For example, incorporating measurements of vitamin D might be useful for evaluating NCD risk, insofar as vitamin D deficiency is particularly prevalent among older adults and is associated with several NCDs (including cardiovascular illness, respiratory problems, cancer, and bone disease) as well as functional decline and increased likelihood of harmful falls among the elderly (Sahota, 2014). Collecting more information on factors that influence cognitive test scores, such as sleep quality and hearing and vision ability, would be useful for improving measurements of cognitive capability and changes over time. Data on indoor and outdoor particulate matter would also be useful for examining the impact of pollution on functional capacity in old age.

National Sample Surveys

Many countries have national administrative and sample survey data sources that are often used for planning and surveillance. Examples of these types of data are the National Sample Survey system in India, the National Household Sample Survey in Brazil, and the Encuesta Nacional de Salud y Nutrición (National Survey of Nutrition and Health) in Mexico. These surveys often have very large sample sizes because they are used to generate national and subnational estimates. The surveys also tend to specialize on specific domains of well-being, focusing, for example, exclusively on health or labor market conditions. Therefore, any single survey often has more detail than the comparable module in the HRS sister surveys. This combination of large sample sizes and detailed information is useful for studies of aging that examine within-country variation across subpopulations or geographic areas, potentially allowing for the identification of health systems and policy effects.

However, these surveys usually do not allow for tracking individuals over time. Furthermore, while specialized surveys have rich information on specific domains of aging, linking information across different domains for individuals is often not possible. Because the data are also not harmonized, data quality can be difficult to evaluate. Finally, most of these surveys do not record incidence of mortality, and as a result they cannot be used to study longevity. Were future surveys to gather the information necessary to link observations across domains and waves and to link mortality incidence, this would greatly expand the analyses that could be conducted with the collected data. Still, noting that these surveys are designed primarily for administrative, rather than research, purposes is important. Thus, analyses that take advantage of both the large sample sizes of the National Sample Surveys and the richer detail of the HRS sister surveys will likely yield more compelling findings.

Demographic and Health Surveys (DHS)

The DHS is one of the longest-running survey programs in LMICs and has several important benefits. The DHS is conducted in many countries with a standardized survey protocol, allowing changes to be examined over time and across countries. The DHS has also started to introduce biomarker measurements in many countries. However, the biggest limitation of the DHS for the study of aging is the age range of participants. Historically, the DHS has focused on children and reproductive-age women, with little to no data on older individuals. Mortality also has to be indirectly estimated and often cannot be linked to individual-level characteristics. Collecting information on sexual behavior, availability of contraception, fertility decisions, and household economic characteristics, all of which are largely absent from these surveys, would be helpful in elucidating the underlying drivers of contextual demographic changes. Finally, the sample sizes in many countries are quite small and individuals are not tracked over time.

Despite the substantial and increasing amount of data sources available for studying aging in LMICs, significant geographic gaps remain in our knowledge of aging. For example, many countries in South America, Africa, and Central Asia do not have HRS-type sister studies. Building and developing new surveys for these regions will be critical for developing a more comprehensive global aging knowledge base. Even in countries with rich data, much potential remains untapped to use and combine existing data sources better. Together, efforts to address these limitations could greatly assist in providing a more complete picture of aging and developing policy suitable for promoting healthy aging and general well-being.

REFERENCES

Andrade, F.C.D. (2009). Measuring the impact of diabetes on life expectancy and disability-free life expectancy among older adults in Mexico. *Journals of Gerontology Series B: Psychological Sciences and Social Sciences, 65*(3), 381–389.

Bloom, D., Canning, D., and Sevilla, J. (2003). *The Demographic Dividend: A New Perspective on the Economic Consequences of Population Change.* Santa Monica, CA: Rand Corporation.

Bongaarts, J. (2004). Population aging and the rising cost of public pensions. *Population and Development Review, 30*(1), 1–23.

Bongaarts, J., and Zimmer. Z. (2002). Living arrangements of older adults in the developing world: An analysis of Demographic and Health Survey household surveys. *Journals of Gerontology Series B: Psychological Sciences and Social Sciences, 57*(3), S145–S157.

Charmes, J. (2015). *Time Use Across the World: Findings of a World Compilation of Time-Use Surveys* (no. 97, September). New York: UNDP Human Development Report Office. Available: http://hdr.undp.org/sites/default/files/charmes_hdr_2015_final.pdf [April 2018].

Chisolm, T.H., Johnson, C.E., Danhauer, J.L., Portz. L.J.P., Abrams, H.B., Lesner, S., McCarthy, P.A., and Newman, C.W. (2007). A systematic review of health-related quality of life and hearing aids: Final report of the American Academy of Audiology Task Force on the Health-Related Quality of Life Benefits of Amplification in Adults. *Journal of the American Academy of Audiology, 18*(2), 151–183.

Covinsky, K.E, Palmer, R.M., Fortinsky, R.H., Counsell, S.R., Stewart, A.L., Kresevic, D., Burant. C.J., and Landefeld, C.S. (2003). Loss of independence in activities of daily living in older adults hospitalized with medical illnesses: Increased vulnerability with age. *Journal of the American Geriatrics Society, 51*(4), 451–458.

Curran, E. (2017). Parts of Asia will grow old before getting rich, IMF warns. *Bloomberg News, May 5, 2017.* Available: https://www.bloomberg.com/news/articles/2017-05-09/parts-of-asia-will-grow-old-before-getting-rich-imf-warns [April 2018].

Dalton, D.S., Cruickshanks, K.J., Klein, B.E.K., Klein, R., Wiley, T.L., and Nondahl, D.M. (2003). The impact of hearing loss on quality of life in older adults. *Gerontologist, 43*(5), 661–668.

Díaz-Venegas, C., De La Vega, S., and Wong, R. (2015). Transitions in activities of daily living in Mexico, 2001–2012. *Salud Pública de México, 57,* s54–s61.

Easterlin, R.A. (1978). What will 1984 be like? Socioeconomic implications of recent twists in age structure. *Demography, 15*(4), 397–432.

Fänge, A., and Iwarsson, S. (2005). Changes in ADL dependence and aspects of usability following housing adaptation—A longitudinal perspective. *American Journal of Occupational Therapy, 59*(3), 296–304.

Ferri, C.P., Schoenborn, C., Kalra, L., Acosta, D., Guerra, M., Huang, Y., Jacob, K.S., Rodriguez, J.J., Salas, A., Sosa, A.L., et al. (2011). Prevalence of stroke and related burden among older people living in Latin America, India and China. *Journal of Neurology, Neurosurgery and Psychiatry, 82*(10), 1074–1082. doi: 10.1136/jnnp.2010.234153.

Finch, C.E., and Crimmins, E.M. (2004). Inflammatory exposure and historical changes in human life-spans. *Science, 305*(5691), 1736–1739.

Freedman, V.A., and Spillman, B.C. (2014). Disability and care needs among older Americans. *Milbank Quarterly, 92*(3), 509–541.

Fry, A.M., Shay, D.K., Holman, R.C., Curns, A.T., and Anderson, L.J. (2005). Trends in hospitalizations for pneumonia among persons aged 65 years or older in the United States, 1988–2002. *Journal of the American Medical Association, 294*(21), 2712–2719.

Gietel-Basten, S., Scherbov, S., and Sanderson, W. (2016). Towards a reconceptualising of population ageing in emerging markets. *Vienna Yearbook of Population Research, 14,* 41–65. doi: 10.1553/populationyearbook2016s041.

Gray, A. (2017). China will grow old before it gets rich. *World Economic Forum, October 6, 2017.* Available: https://www.weforum.org/agenda/2017/10/china-will-grow-old-before-it-gets-rich [April 2018].

Gribble, J.N., and Bremner, J. (2012). Achieving a demographic dividend. *Population Bulletin, 67*(2), 16.

Hernan, M.A., and Robins, J.M. (2018). *Causal Inference.* Boca Raton, FL: Chapman & Hall/CRC.

Horiuchi, S., Wilmoth, J.R., and Pletcher, S.D. (2008). A decomposition method based on a model of continuous change. *Demography, 45*(4), 785–801.

Kalkonde, Y.V., Deshmukh, M.D., Sahane, V., Puthran, J., Kakarmath. S., Agavane, V., and Bang, A. (2015). Stroke is the leading cause of death in rural Gadchiroli, India. *Stroke, 46*(7), 1764–1768.

Katz, S. (1983). Assessing self-maintenance: Activities of daily living, mobility, and instrumental activities of daily living. *Journal of the American Geriatrics Society, 31*(12), 721–727.

King, G., and Wand, J. (2006). Comparing incomparable survey responses: Evaluating and selecting anchoring vignettes. *Political Analysis, 15*(1), 46–66.

Lee, R.D. (1994). The formal demography of population aging, transfers, and the economic life cycle. In National Research Council, *Demography of Aging* (pp. 8–49). Washington, DC: National Academy Press.

Lin, S.-F., Beck, A.N., Finch, B.K., Hummer, R.A., and Master, R.K. (2012). Trends in U.S. older adult disability: Exploring age, period, and cohort effects. *American Journal of Public Health, 102*(11), 2157–2163.

Lloyd-Jones, D.M., Wilson, P.W.F., Larson, M.G., Beiser A., Leip, E.P., D'Agostino, R.B., and Levy, D. (2004). Framingham risk score and prediction of lifetime risk for coronary heart disease. *American Journal of Cardiology, 94*(1), 20–24.

López-Otín, C., Blasco, M.A., Partridge, L., Serrano. M., and Kroemer, G. (2013). The hallmarks of aging. *Cell, 153*(6), 1194-1217. doi: 10.1016/j.cell.2013.05.039.

Lutz, W., Sanderson, W., and Scherbov, S. (2008). The coming acceleration of global population ageing. *Nature, 451*(7179), 716–719. doi: 10.1038/nature06516.

Maredza, M., Bertramm M.Y., and Tollman, S.M. (2015). Disease burden of stroke in rural South Africa: An estimate of incidence, mortality and disability adjusted life years. *BMC Neurology, 15*(1), 54. doi: 10.1186/s12883-015-0311-7.

Mason, A., and Lee, R. (2006). Reform and support systems for the elderly in developing countries: Capturing the second demographic dividend. *Genus, 62*(2), 11–35.

Petersson, I., Liljam, M., Hammel J., and Kottorp, A. (2008). Impact of home modification services on ability in everyday life for people ageing with disabilities. *Journal of Rehabilitation Medicine, 40*(4), 253–260.

Preston, S.H. (1984). Children and the elderly: Divergent paths for America's dependents. *Demography, 21*(4), 435–457.

Preston, S.H, and Stokes, A. (2012). Sources of population aging in more and less developed countries. *Population and Development Review, 38*(2), 221–236.

Rehkopf, D.H, Rosero-Bixby, L., and Dow, W.H. (2016). A cross-national comparison of 12 biomarkers finds no universal biomarkers of aging among individuals aged 60 and older. *Vienna Yearbook of Population Research, 14*, 255–277. doi: 10.1553/populationyearbook2016s255.

Riffe, T., Chung, P.H., Spijker, J., and MacInnes, J. (2015). Time-to-death patterns in markers of age and dependency. *Vienna Yearbook of Population Research, 14*, 229–254.

Robins, J. (1986). A new approach to causal inference in mortality studies with a sustained exposure period—Application to control of the healthy worker survivor effect. *Mathematical Modelling, 7*(9–12), 1393–1512.

Sahota, O. (2014). Understanding vitamin D deficiency. *Age and Ageing, 43*(5), 589.

Sanderson, W.C., and Scherbov, S. (2005). Average remaining lifetimes can increase as human populations age. *Nature, 435*(7043), 811–813.

Sanderson, W.C., and Scherbov, S. (2010). Remeasuring aging. *Science, 329*(5997), 1287–1288.

Sanderson, W.C., and Scherbov, S. (2017). A unifying framework for the study of population aging. *Vienna Yearbook of Population Research, 14*, 7–40. doi: 10.1553/populationyearbook2016s007.

Social Security Administration. (2016). *Social Security Programs throughout the World: The Americas, 2015.* Washington, DC: U.S. Government Printing Office.

Social Security Administration. (2017a). *Social Security Programs throughout the World: Asia and the Pacific, 2016.* Washington, DC: U.S. Government Printing Office.

Social Security Administration. (2017b). *Social Security Programs Throughout the World: Africa, 2017.* Washington, DC: U.S. Government Printing Office.

Tyrovolas, S., Koyanagi, A., Garin, N., Olaya, B., Ayuso-Mateos, J.L., Miret, M., Chatterji, S., Tobiasz-Adamczyk, B., Koskinen, S., Leonardi, M., et al. (2015). Diabetes mellitus and its association with central obesity and disability among older adults: A global perspective. *Experimental Gerontology, 64*, 70–77.

United Nations Department of Economic and Social Affairs. (2017). *World Population Prospects: The 2017 Revision.* New York: United Nations.

Van Dalen, H.P., and Henkens, K. (2012). What is on a demographer's mind? A worldwide survey. *Demographic Research, 26*, 363–408.

World Bank. (2017). *World Development Indicators, 2017.* Washington, DC: World Bank.

12

Health, Economic Status, and Aging in High-Income Countries

Jinkook Lee[1] and James P. Smith[2]

INTRODUCTION

The world is aging at rapid rates and will clearly continue to do so far into the future. With this population aging comes several challenges and opportunities in maintaining decent income flows, good health, and affordable health care into a longer set of retirement years and in doing so within affordable budgets. These goals will certainly require policy adjustments in many countries to provide decent income support and good health during older ages. An important resource for designing these policy adjustments are cross-country panel data that illustrate in principle the consequences of different policies adopted in different countries. Based on significant and ongoing investments over the last few decades, we have such data now in the Health and Retirement Study (HRS) around the world surveys.[3]

In this paper, we use harmonized panel data from high-income countries that are part of the HRS around the world surveys to describe levels and changes in health status and health behaviors for populations across these countries at middle age and older ages. For the high-income countries that are our focus in this paper, population aging due to declining fertility and improving mortality has taken place alongside very different trends across countries and across groups within countries in improved health behaviors, education, and income growth. We document significant varia-

---

[1]University of Southern California and RAND Corporation.
[2]Senior Economist, RAND Corporation.
[3]See https://micda.psc.isr.umich.edu/networks/hrsiss.html [April 2018].

tion in both health outcomes and behaviors across this set of high-income countries. Such variation provides the opportunity to investigate reasons underlying cross-country differences in health outcomes, a continuation of the body of work that started with the England–United States studies in this network (Banks et al., 2006). Part of our discussion is also devoted to suggesting ways in which the underlying data in the HRS network can and should be improved. One focus of that discussion deals with the introduction of biomarker data into the network, a process now under way.

The remainder of this paper is divided into five sections. The second section documents harmonized HRS data that will be used in our research and the operational definition of variables in the analysis. The third summarizes levels and trends in two salient measures of health levels and trends in our set of high-income countries: mortality and disease prevalence. The fourth section summarizes a parallel set of results on health behaviors over time and across countries, while the fifth reports our findings on early-life influences on later-life health in these surveys. The final section highlights our major conclusions.

DATA

In this paper, we use data from high-income countries in the HRS around the world surveys. These surveys represent a set of harmonized, multidisciplinary, longitudinal, and nationally representative aging datasets that have evolved in the last 25 years to document changing health, economic status, and family relations of middle-aged and older populations in many countries. These datasets were explicitly designed in a harmonized way to monitor impacts of new health and retirement policies affecting older cohorts' incentives to continue working or to exit the labor market, to access health care services and/or the related welfare provisions, and to achieve adequate income from retirement savings (Dobrescu and Smith, 2016).

The new set of surveys begins with the HRS in the United States, where the key innovation—adopted subsequently by all other surveys in the network—was to break with the almost universal tradition of other panel surveys on aging, which focused almost entirely on a single life domain—say, economics or health—and were administered mostly by a single academic discipline. But the separation of these life domains was based on the false idea that the domains are independent of each other and that understanding behaviors in one domain can be achieved without knowing much about the others. A major strength of HRS was that it recognized early on that all life domains are interrelated, and it implemented that idea successfully into its modules. HRS is a biennial survey that started in 1992 and includes refresher cohorts every 6 years.

A coherent network of harmonized panel datasets can help study behavioral reactions to changes in public policy (e.g., changes in health care utilization and its implications for health status in the wake of a health care reform; changes in the retirement age and the level of savings preceding a pension reform). In doing so, one can understand not only how individuals respond to their socioeconomic environment (including institutions and policy measures) but also how the aging process unfolds in different cultures, societies, and policy environments over time. The advantage of having this set of international countries with harmonized data is that individual countries have adopted different changes in policies at different times; these differences serve as the backbone for analyzing the central exogenous changes in policies dealing with population aging.

Besides the U.S. HRS, the HRS network of high-income countries includes the English Longitudinal Survey of Ageing (ELSA), conducted in England since 2002; the Survey of Health, Ageing and Retirement in Europe (SHARE) with its coverage of continental European countries conducted since 2004; the Irish Longitudinal Study of Ageing (TILDA) in the Republic of Ireland; the Scottish (Hagis) and Northern Ireland (Nicola) studies in 2016, the Mexican Health and Aging Study (MHAS) in Mexico in 2001: the Korean Longitudinal Study of Aging (KLoSA) in South Korea starting in 2006, and the Japanese Study on Aging and Retirement (JSTAR) in Japan starting in 2007.

Since this paper examines patterns both at a moment in time and in changes over time, we limited ourselves to those high-income country HRS-style surveys that existed in 2006 and that had a 2012 wave, with the exception of JSTAR, which started in 2007 and had a 2013 wave. This dual-year requirement on survey fielding dates meant we could not use surveys from the Republic of Ireland, Northern Ireland, Scotland, and Mexico in this paper. In addition, the specific SHARE countries that are included here had to have a 2006 wave. These SHARE countries are Austria, Belgium, Czech Republic, Denmark, France, Germany, Italy, Netherlands, Spain, Sweden, and Switzerland. Low- and middle-income countries are the subject of another paper in this volume and are not included in our paper.

Our analysis uses the Gateway to Global Aging Data (g2aging.org), a data and information platform developed to facilitate cross-country analyses using the HRS network of surveys. The Gateway has compiled and indexed metadata (i.e., data specifying the content and flow of the questionnaires), as well as other relevant information, such as information about samples, from all available waves of 12 surveys in the HRS network, representing 40 countries. These metadata enable users to quickly attain concordant information across surveys and across waves of individual surveys. The Gateway also provides *harmonized data files* that can be used for analyses across countries and over time. The complexity of survey design and the challenges of longitudinal linkages result in significant costs to construct suitable datasets for international investigations. The harmonized data files have been built to significantly reduce such costs and to eliminate errors.[4]

We use the harmonized measures available from the Gateway to examine cross-country differences in health and health behaviors. The harmonized variables drawn from the study-specific harmonized datasets include several demographic measures. Five doctor-diagnosed diseases as reported by respondents are included as health indicators: diabetes, heart conditions, stroke, hypertension, and cancer. Indicators for several health behaviors are also included: ever smoked, currently smoke, currently drink and amount, exercise, and obesity. Obesity is categorized as having a body mass index (BMI) of 30 or greater, based on height and weight, which are either self-reported or measured, depending on the study. Further details of variable definitions are available from the codebooks of the harmonized data files.

HEALTH STATUS IN THE HRS HIGH-INCOME COUNTRIES

Mortality

Trends in post–World War II mortality, especially at middle and older ages, in high-income industrial countries are well known (Preston et al., 2010). These trends are illustrated in Table 12-1 for selected countries that fall within our focus for the period 1950–2015, as revealed in the Berkeley Mortality Database. More concretely, Table 12-1 shows life expectancy at age 50 by country, starting in 1950–1959, for men and women separately and at selective 10-year intervals in the decades thereafter. The high-income countries in our set of countries that are not shown in this table exhibit similar secular trends. The final three rows for men and for women in the table document changes in life expectancy at age 50 during the 1950–1999 and 1999–2015 decades and during the full 65-year period covered by the table (1950–2015).

Over this 65-year period, secular trends in life expectancy at age 50 are very positive indeed, with a significant expansion in life expectancy in all countries for men and women alike. This increase in life expectancy at age 50 is as high as 12.5 years for Japanese women and as little as 4.5 years for Danish men. Life expectancy growth at age 50 in the United States is clearly

---

[4]For our analysis, we used the harmonized data files built from individual-level data from six HRS-network surveys. This analysis uses data from the RAND HRS Version P, Harmonized MHAS Version A Beta.3, Harmonized ELSA Version D, Harmonized SHARE Version C.2, Harmonized KLoSA Version B, and Harmonized JSTAR Version B. We use harmonized measures available from Gateway to examine cross-country differences in health and health behaviors.

TABLE 12-1 Life Expectancy at Age 50 by Calendar-Year Periods and Country

Year	U.S.	Belgium	Denmark	France	Ireland	Italy	Japan	Netherlands	Spain	UK
Male										
1950–1959	22.9	23.0	25.3	22.6	23.3	23.9	21.9	25.8	23.3	22.4
1990–1999	27.0	26.7	26.0	27.5	25.7	27.7	29.0	27.0	28.0	26.6
2000–2009	28.7	28.6	28.0	29.4	28.7	30.1	30.7	29.0	29.6	29.1
2010–2015	29.9	30.1	29.8	30.9	30.8	31.3	31.7	30.7	31.2	30.9
Δ 1950–1999	4.1	3.7	0.7	4.9	2.4	3.8	7.1	1.2	4.7	4.2
Δ 1999–2015	2.9	3.3	3.8	3.4	5.1	3.6	2.7	3.7	3.2	4.3
Δ 1950–2015	7.0	7.1	4.5	8.3	7.5	7.4	9.8	4.9	7.9	8.5
Female										
1950–1959	27.3	26.6	27.0	27.0	25.5	26.7	25.1	27.6	26.6	26.8
1990–1999	31.6	32.1	30.2	33.8	30.2	33.0	34.5	32.1	33.5	31.0
2000–2009	32.4	33.3	31.6	35.3	32.6	34.8	36.8	33.0	35.1	32.7
2010–2015	33.5	34.3	33.2	36.4	34.1	35.5	37.6	34.1	36.3	34.0
Δ 1950–1999	4.3	5.5	3.2	6.8	5.8	6.3	9.4	4.5	6.9	4.2
Δ 1999–2015	1.9	2.2	3.0	2.6	2.9	2.5	3.1	2.0	2.8	3.0
Δ 1950–2015	6.2	7.7	6.2	9.4	8.7	8.8	12.5	6.5	9.7	7.2

below the average of the other high-income countries, with especially slow improvements so far in the 21st century.

The increase in American male life expectancy at age 50 is about 7 years, with the only two countries in our table below that number being Denmark and the Netherlands. With the exception of the United States and the United Kingdom, secular trends in remaining years of life at age 50 are actually even higher for women than for men. Japan stands out above all the rest of the countries with an increase in life expectancy of 9.8 years for men and 13.5 years for women. But our most important conclusion on mortality is that Americans generally experienced the smallest life expectancy gains among these high-income countries, especially in recent years.

Disease Prevalence in the HRS Surveys

Population aging carries with it many challenges and opportunities. One of the most basic is maintaining and financing good health status into older ages and over calendar time. To highlight the variation across countries and over time, Table 12-2 summarizes separately for women and men self-reports of disease prevalence at any time during life ("ever") for diabetes, cancer, high blood pressure, heart disease, and stroke, for calendar years 2006 and 2012. Two age groups are presented in Table 12-2: the young old, who are ages 55–65, and the older old, who are ages 66+. To conserve space in the table, we have aggregated the SHARE countries into the Central, Eastern, Northern, and Southern Europe groupings defined in the notes to Table 12-2.

Using self-reports of disease as the metric, Table 12-2 shows that American males in both age groups always rank first in highest self-reports of all diseases, in both 2006 and 2012, and American women are mostly number 1 as well (Banks et al., 2006; Avendano et al., 2009). In addition, the very general tendency for all countries is for reported disease prevalence to be higher in calendar year 2012 compared to 2006, with the United States once again tending to lead the way in increases observed over time. Among those ages 55–65, reported disease prevalence tends to be somewhat higher among men compared to women, with the glaring exception of cancer, where the rates are higher among women compared to men.

Table 12-2 also documents substantial variation across countries in reported disease prevalence among our set of high-income countries, both in levels of self-reported disease and in changes over time. Following the United States, the countries in Eastern Europe (Czech Republic) rank a solid second place in reported disease prevalence, with England in third place and Central and Northern Europe performing best in health outcomes. Our two high-income countries in Asia—Korea and Japan—tend to have lower disease prevalence than the United States and the European countries in the table. Age distribution differences within our broad age groups play a very limited role in explaining the differences across countries. Age differences within these age groups are very small and cannot account for prevalence differences across countries or changes over time.[5] Compared to mortality as the health index, America ranks worse when self-reported disease prevalence is our measure. This is because America provides better (albeit more expensive) health care to those who are ill (Banks et al., 2010) and, as we will show below, undiagnosed disease is lower in America compared to the other countries.

In addition to cross-country differences in health status, we are interested in measures of the social gradient in health status within and across these high-income countries. We measure the social gradient using education and wealth as an alternative measure of socioeconomic status (SES). In all countries, education is divided into three groups by an individual's years of schooling: 0–11 years of schooling, 12–15 years of schooling, or 16 or more years of schooling.[6] Household wealth is also divided into three terciles: bottom third, middle third, and upper third. Because our central message does not differ much by gender or by our two age groups, we present in our tables the combined male and female data for the 55–65 age group. Due to space constraints, we also only present tables for the education gradient and discuss the wealth gradient results in the text.

Table 12-3 presents self-reported disease prevalence for three education groups for those ages 55–65, in calendar years 2006 and 2012. For assessing the social gradient in disease, education has the advantage that pathways from health to education are limited to the earlier years of life because schooling is completed by the mid-twenties if not earlier. In contrast, the evidence is that there are strong feedbacks from health shocks to lower wealth (Smith, 2004).

The data in Table 12-3 allow us to compute the education health gradient as the difference in prevalence of lowest education group minus prevalence of highest education group. We prefer to use this absolute

---

[5]The one exception is Japan in the age 66+ group, in which the mean age is less than that in that age group for other countries. This exception is because the Japanese survey is limited to those under age 76. But even in this case, the lower disease prevalence in Japan is not primarily due to this age restriction.

[6]This harmonized measure for educational attainment is based on the 1997 International Standard Classification of Education (ISCED-97) codes. Less than lower-secondary education ranges from no education up to 11 years of education and includes ISCED codes 0 and 1. Upper-secondary and vocational training ranges from 12 to 15 years of education and includes ISCED codes 2, 3, and 4. Tertiary education represents 16 or more years of education and includes ISCED codes 5 and 6. See UNESCO International Standard Classification of Education, ISCED 1997. Available: http://www.uis.unesco.org/Library/Documents/isced97-en.pd [April 2018].

TABLE 12-2 Self-Reported Health Status by Country/Region, Gender, and Age Group, 2006 and 2012

	Diabetes		Cancer		Hypertension		Heart Disease		Stroke	
	2006	2012	2006	2012	2006	2012	2006	2012	2006	2012
Men Ages 55–65										
Central Europe	10.9	13.6	4.2	5.8	34.5	37.4	13.4	12.0	4.1	3.9
Eastern Europe	16.5	19.1	4.0	4.4	46.2	53.8	13.5	14.5	3.4	6.5
Northern Europe	8.8	9.4	6.4	5.5	31.0	35.3	12.8	9.5	4.1	4.0
Southern Europe	12.1	13.8	4.2	5.4	35.5	41.9	10.7	10.0	3.4	3.2
Japan	12.4	15.6	2.9	4.4	28.0	36.8	7.3	8.8	1.8	2.9
Korea	14.3	14.3	2.4	3.2	24.6	28.9	4.6	5.4	3.9	4.3
England	9.4	11.0	4.3	5.0	40.4	38.2	12.7	14.3	3.0	2.5
USA	17.8	20.5	7.5	8.1	47.8	53.1	17.7	18.8	5.4	4.6
Women Ages 55–65										
Central Europe	8.6	9.7	8.6	9.6	35.7	36.0	7.3	6.8	2.7	4.0
Eastern Europe	9.5	14.1	6.6	7.4	41.4	46.7	6.4	8.7	1.9	2.6
Northern Europe	6.1	6.6	9.3	10.3	31.7	31.8	7.7	5.8	2.6	3.0
Southern Europe	10.8	9.8	6.4	6.1	39.0	38.1	6.7	5.4	1.5	1.9
Japan	4.6	7.5	3.7	3.8	25.7	25.7	5.8	6.1	1.9	1.4
Korea	12.1	12.4	3.5	5.5	31.0	31.5	4.8	4.9	3.0	2.9
England	5.3	7.6	8.1	9.2	36.1	33.2	11.4	12.4	1.5	1.7
USA	16.0	18.2	10.3	11.5	45.5	47.0	12.8	14.1	4.0	4.3

Men Ages 66+										
Central Europe	15.9	19.6	10.4	15.0	44.5	51.0	27.4	27.7	9.9	9.8
Eastern Europe	19.1	29.8	5.4	8.7	49.7	64.4	26.6	28.0	9.0	10.9
Northern Europe	14.4	15.7	12.8	14.4	44.3	48.9	29.4	24.4	10.9	11.4
Southern Europe	19.9	24.3	6.0	9.0	50.1	61.0	22.5	26.5	6.7	8.6
Japan	15.7	19.0	5.7	10.0	37.2	48.0	19.7	18.6	8.2	9.2
Korea	15.3	21.3	3.7	7.0	35.5	45.4	7.2	11.1	7.9	9.3
England	14.6	16.2	11.1	14.0	49.9	52.9	27.5	28.9	8.7	8.8
USA	22.8	27.5	21.1	23.6	58.8	67.4	37.0	38.1	11.7	12.7
Women Ages 66+										
Central Europe	16.6	16.3	8.8	13.6	50.7	54.8	20.8	21.7	8.4	9.2
Eastern Europe	21.4	26.5	4.4	9.9	56.6	68.9	20.2	25.2	9.4	11.6
Northern Europe	11.6	11.7	14.5	15.0	45.5	52.1	23.4	19.6	8.6	9.3
Southern Europe	20.3	23.2	6.0	9.2	58.3	66.1	19.3	23.6	5.1	7.3
Japan	9.9	10.3	5.7	5.4	41.6	48.4	14.8	14.2	4.4	5.6
Korea	16.6	22.2	2.2	4.9	42.1	54.7	8.2	12.1	4.5	6.4
England	10.3	13.5	9.5	13.6	54.2	53.2	23.3	26.0	8.0	7.3
USA	18.2	23.5	17.2	19.6	63.0	68.1	26.8	28.6	10.2	10.6

NOTES: Data under 2006 are for calendar 2006 except that Japan data are for calendar 2007. Data under 2012 are calendar 2012 except that Japan data are for calendar 2011.
Central Europe: Austria, Belgium, France, Germany, the Netherlands, Switzerland.
Eastern Europe: Czech Republic.
Northern Europe: Denmark, Sweden.
Southern Europe: Italy, Spain.
SOURCES: Data are from RAND HRS, Harmonized ELSA, Harmonized SHARE, Harmonized JSTAR, Harmonized KLoSA.

TABLE 12-3 Health Status by Country/Region, Education Level, and Age Group, 2006 and 2012

	Diabetes		Cancer		Hypertension		Heart Disease		Stroke	
	2006	2012	2006	2012	2006	2012	2006	2012	2006	2012
0–11 Years of Education, Ages 55–65										
Central Europe	13.1	13.9	5.5	7.3	36.6	38.0	11.4	12.1	3.7	4.5
Eastern Europe	12.9	23.4	4.4	6.5	51.1	53.3	12.0	16.8	2.5	4.6
Northern Europe	9.8	10.7	8.1	8.4	36.6	35.0	12.9	8.8	3.9	3.6
Southern Europe	12.9	13.8	5.3	5.8	39.2	43.9	9.3	8.9	2.4	3.3
Japan	13.1	18.0	2.5	3.4	27.9	44.7	6.6	6.4	3.5	3.9
Korea	14.4	15.0	3.2	4.6	28.3	33.9	5.3	6.2	3.7	4.5
England	9.4	10.9	6.1	7.4	42.0	38.4	12.2	13.6	2.7	3.1
USA	27.6	31.3	7.5	9.0	56.2	60.8	19.1	21.2	7.8	9.4
12–15 Years of Education, Ages 55–65										
Central Europe	7.9	10.7	6.4	7.5	35.1	37.4	9.9	7.6	3.0	3.2
Eastern Europe	13.5	15.1	5.7	6.4	40.7	50.2	8.3	9.7	2.0	4.6
Northern Europe	5.5	7.4	8.1	8.3	27.6	35.0	8.4	6.5	2.8	3.5
Southern Europe	9.3	8.9	6.9	5.9	35.9	32.8	7.5	6.3	2.9	1.3
Japan	9.0	10.2	3.0	4.0	26.9	29.0	7.4	7.5	1.6	1.3
Korea	11.9	11.8	2.3	4.6	27.9	27.1	3.4	4.2	3.8	3.1
England	6.8	9.9	5.7	7.0	37.2	37.4	12.0	14.6	2.4	2.0
USA	16.3	19.2	8.7	10.2	48.1	52.2	16.6	17.5	4.9	4.3

16+ Years of Education, Ages 55–65										
Central Europe	7.0	8.5	8.5	8.8	32.1	32.6	8.6	7.5	3.6	4.2
Eastern Europe	10.5	9.9	6.1	3.4	39.6	42.7	11.8	9.6	5.1	2.3
Northern Europe	5.6	4.4	6.6	6.3	26.0	27.1	6.3	8.0	2.7	3.3
Southern Europe	1.0	5.3	2.1	4.5	22.7	34.4	2.9	3.5	0.0	0.6
Japan	7.4	12.4	4.8	4.9	26.9	31.1	4.9	7.7	0.5	4.0
Korea	8.2	11.9	3.1	2.5	24.2	26.4	3.7	4.1	1.2	2.2
England	5.0	6.6	7.0	6.6	34.2	30.6	10.8	12.1	0.9	1.1
USA	12.5	15.3	10.2	9.6	38.7	42.5	10.4	12.7	2.7	2.9

NOTES: Data under 2006 are for calendar 2006 except that Japan data are for calendar 2007. Data under 2012 are calendar 2012 except that Japan data are for calendar 2011.
Central Europe: Austria, Belgium, France, Germany, the Netherlands, Switzerland.
Eastern Europe: Czech Republic.
Northern Europe: Denmark, Sweden.
Southern Europe: Italy, Spain.
SOURCES: Data are from RAND HRS, Harmonized ELSA, Harmonized SHARE, Harmonized JSTAR, Harmonized KLoSA.

gradient rather than relative gradient (i.e., dividing this difference by the lowest-education group's prevalence) since with relatively low prevalences, relative gradients are quite misleading. If we start again with the United States, we observe a very sharp negative education gradient in all diseases listed in Table 12-3 except for cancer, the equal-opportunity killer. This absolute-disease-difference gradient for other diseases appears to be higher in the United States than in the other sets of countries listed in Table 12-3. To illustrate, the U.S. absolute education gradient is 15.1 percentage points in 2006, whereas only one other region in the table registers a double-digit difference. However, in the other countries, the same pattern of higher disease prevalence among the less educated still prevails, again for all diseases except cancer.

Using wealth terciles as the marker for SES, we observe a very similar pattern to that just discussed for education: a very negative disease prevalence gradient by wealth levels for all countries and for all diseases but cancer, with the United States having the most negative disease social gradient. Again, the absolute difference in diabetes prevalences between the lowest and highest wealth tercile is 15 percentage points in the United States, compared with just single-digit differences in all other high-income countries. The wealth tables are available from the authors on request.

Biomarker Health Measures in the HRS Network

One of the most challenging aspects of the HRS around the world surveys has been to incorporate biomarkers into the surveys, rather than simply relying on self-reports as we have discussed to this point. Even with completely accurate self-reports to the standard type of disease question, "Did a doctor ever diagnose you with x?", self-reports as measures for "ever have had disease x" have several glaring deficiencies. These include the widespread and changing prevalence of undiagnosed disease, the ability to control a diagnosed disease putting someone under the established threshold, and measures of disease severity; all three of these factors vary significantly across and within high-income countries.

We illustrate this point in Table 12-4, which lists relevant components for hypertension for four of the countries in our HRS high-income country network: England, Germany, Ireland, and the United States. We selected hypertension since it is the most common biomarker that is currently often measured in the HRS network. This table provides a two-by-two data stratification of hypertension data by two hypertension measures: measured blood pressure above and below the common diagnosis threshold[7] and

---

[7]Respondent is measured hypertensive if respondent has a measured systolic blood pressure of 140 or greater, or a diastolic blood pressure of 90 or greater.

TABLE 12-4 Proportion of Measured and Self-Reported Hypertension by Country, Age, and Gender, 2012

Measured Blood Pressure	Self-Reported Hypertension	Germany	Ireland	England	USA	Germany	Ireland	England	USA
		Men Ages 55–65				Women Ages 55–65			
Hypertensive	a. Diagnosed	33.4	19.4	16.4	20.8	24.2	14.7	12.2	13.9
	b. Undiagnosed	26.0	29.4	14.9	10.7	22.7	18.6	12.7	8.4
Not Hypertensive	c. Diagnosed	15.2	14.8	21.3	31.8	11.0	18.1	20.3	31.6
	d. Undiagnosed	25.4	36.5	47.3	36.7	42.1	48.6	54.8	46.2
Total diagnosed hypertension (a+c)		48.6	34.2	37.7	52.6	35.2	32.8	32.5	45.5
Total hypertensives (a+b+c)		74.6	63.6	52.7	63.3	57.9	51.4	45.2	53.9
% Undiagnosed among hypertensives		34.8	46.2	28.3	16.9	39.2	36.2	28.1	15.6
% Undiagnosed among total population		26.0	29.4	14.9	10.7	22.7	18.6	12.7	8.4
		Men Ages 66+				Women Ages 66+			
Hypertensive	a. Diagnosed	40.5	27.8	20.2	26.0	46.3	30.9	23.1	24.9
	b. Undiagnosed	25.9	26.4	15.1	8.9	19.9	20.7	14.4	7.9
Not Hypertensive	c. Diagnosed	17.9	18.1	31.5	40.3	20.8	22.0	28.5	42.2
	d. Undiagnosed	15.8	27.7	33.2	24.8	13.1	26.4	34.1	25.0
Total diagnosed hypertension (a+c)		58.4	45.9	51.7	66.3	67.1	52.9	51.5	67.1
Total hypertensives (a+b+c)		84.2	72.3	66.9	75.2	86.9	73.6	66.0	75.0
% Undiagnosed among hypertensives		30.7	36.5	22.6	11.9	22.9	28.1	21.8	10.6
% Undiagnosed among total population		25.9	26.4	15.1	8.9	19.9	20.7	14.4	7.9

self-report of ever having been diagnosed by a doctor as having hypertension. Beneath this two-by-two categorization, we include rows that indicate fraction of the population that has self-reported being hypertensive and the fraction that is hypertensive either by diagnosis or by survey measurement. Finally, we include rows at the bottom of the table documenting the percentage of all hypertensives who are undiagnosed and the fraction of the total population in the relevant age groups who are diagnosed.

Table 12-4 provides separate estimates by two age groups (55–65 and 66+) and by gender. Self-reported hypertension (i.e., positive response to the "ever diagnosed" question) provides an incomplete and often misleading picture. Using men ages 55–65 to illustrate, "ever-diagnosed" hypertension gives U.S. men much higher rates of hypertension than men in the same age group in other countries. Self-reported hypertension in this age group is 53 percent among U.S. men compared to 49 percent among German men and 38 and 34 percent among English men and Irish men. If instead we examine the more complete hypertension rates in this age group that includes the undiagnosed (the "total hypertensives" row in the upper section of Table 12-4), Germany now easily leads the way with 75 percent hypertensive compared to 63 percent in both Ireland and the United States and 53 percent in England.

Undiagnosed hypertension is prevalent in all countries (especially in Germany and Ireland) both as a fraction of all hypertensives and as a fraction of total age group. American men in the 55–65 age group have the lowest fraction of undiagnosed hypertension relative to both the population (11%) and all hypertensives (17%). The flip side is that many people who had previously been diagnosed by a doctor as hypertensive have measured blood pressure levels now below the established diagnosis thresholds, an indication that they are exercising good control of their hypertension. We find similar patterns for women ages 55–65 and for both genders in those 65+.

These concepts, which require both testing for hypertension and self-reports of ever diagnosed, are important in evaluating the health of populations as well as in making comparisons across countries. The extent of undiagnosed disease and the ability to control hypertension after it gets too high are equally important as indicators of the health care system as is the extent of the disease. Most importantly, as we said at the beginning of this section, hypertension is just one example of the need for biomarkers. A set of tables parallel to Table 12-4 could be constructed for all salient diseases of middle and old age including diabetes, cancer, and heart disease.

There is recognition within the HRS high-income countries of a high value of biomarker data to supplement self-reports. There is also the current reality that most of the studies in the high-income HRS network do not now contain such biomarker data available to researchers.[8,9] The reason is the equally recognized high cost of collecting biomarker data in population-based longitudinal surveys at the national level, whether by direct measurement, such as measuring hypertension, or even more costly by collecting and assaying blood through either dry blood spots or venous blood. Compared to self-reports, collecting biomarkers is much more expensive, especially with the eventual necessity of doing repeated measurement. The sensible response to this by the HRS around the world surveys has been to collect biomarkers at a reduced periodicity relative to the normal self-report frequency (for example every other wave), especially for younger respondents in the survey, for whom biomarkers do not change as rapidly over time. Another recent response by the Mexican and Chinese surveys has been to reduce the periodicity of the main survey to achieve sustainable long-term costs. The other surveys in the network are attempting to collect relevant biomarker data, so the situation is about to improve a great deal with respect to having biomarkers in the high-income HRS around the world surveys.

HEALTH BEHAVIORS ACROSS COUNTRY AND YEAR

Before discussing international differences in health behaviors, we first examine long-term changes in these behaviors in the United States. Table 12-5 documents long-term changes in key health behaviors by education over time for non-Hispanic Whites between ages 40 and 64. The behaviors are current smoking, obesity, vigorous exercise, height in inches, and percentage without any health insurance. The first four behaviors are obtained from waves of the National Health and Nutrition Examination Survey (NHANES) and update results obtained by Goldman and Smith (2011), while health insurance data are obtained from the National Health Interview Survey (NHIS). The data are stratified into three education groups: low (0–11 years of schooling), middle (12 years of schooling), and high (13 or more years of schooling).

The best news in health behaviors is the significant long-term decline in smoking, but even for smoking the low-education group did not participate, as their smoking rates have been rising. Moreover, the pace of the American smoking decline has clearly slowed for all education groups since 2002. In contrast, the worst news on the behavior front is a substantial rise in obesity that characterizes all education groups. Obesity has continued to rise unabated in recent decades. The vigorous exercise questions refer to

---

[8]The high-income countries that do not currently measure hypertension are all SHARE countries except Germany, plus Japan and Korea. The countries that do not measure other biomarkers are all SHARE countries, Japan, and Korea.

[9]The large low-income countries in the HRS network of studies are doing a better job collecting biomarker data. Brazil (ELSIE), China (CHARLS), India (LASI), and Indonesia (IFLS) all collect biomarker data.

TABLE 12-5 Health Behaviors by Education and Year, USA Non-Hispanic Whites, Ages 40–64, Education

	Low	Middle	High	All
A. Current Smoking (%)				
Δ 1976–2002	10.9	–4.4	–15.0	–11.4
	4.0	–0.1	1.2	–0.3
Δ 2002–2014	14.9	–4.5	–13.8	–11.7
B. Obesity (% obese)				
Δ 1976–2002	21.4	17.6	15.7	14.8
Δ 2002–2014	2.6	7.6	8.7	7.4
Δ 1976–2002	24.0	25.2	24.4	22.2
C. Vigorous Exercise (%)				
Δ 1976–2002	3.0	11.0	27.8	21.2
Δ 2002–2014	10.8	14.7	–5.6	1.8
Δ 1976–2002	13.8	25.7	22.2	22.9
D. Height (inches)				
Δ 1976–2002	0.5	1.2	0.7	1.2
Δ 2002–2014	0.6	–0.4	–0.4	–0.2
Δ 1976–2002	1.1	0.3	0.3	1.0
E. Without Health Insurance (%)				
Δ 1980–2012	13.9	7.9	0.6	4.1
Δ 2012–2015	–12.7	–6.2	–2.0	–5.6
Δ 1980–2015	1.2	1.7	–1.4	–1.5

SOURCES: Smoking, obesity, exercise, and height data obtained from various waves of NHANES. Health insurance data are from various waves of NHIS.

both recreation and work, and unfortunately the exact question changes somewhat between the surveys. But the general trend, which is documented as well in other studies, is that the groups with more education conduct more vigorous exercise. There has been no real change in height over time for any of the education groups, so the apparent health-protective effect of height is not likely to be a significant factor.

The final factor we examine is the fraction of this age group in the American population without any health insurance. The data show two distinct trends, especially for the less educated. Between 1980 and 2012, the fraction of the population ages 40–64 without health insurance was increasing, especially for the less educated, for whom the fraction without insurance rose by about 14 percentage points. With the passage of the Affordable Care Act, that trend reversed with a significant increase in health insurance in the population—an increase that largely reversed the decline that had taken place in the previous three decades.

Table 12-6 documents well-established salient health behaviors (ever and current smoking, binge drinking, vigorous exercise, and obesity) using our high-income set of HRS around the world surveys. "Smoke Ever" is the percentage answering "yes" to a question of whether the respondent had ever smoked tobacco, while "Smoke Now" is the percentage currently smoking tobacco. The format of Table 12-6 parallels that of Table 12-2 as it highlights prevalence of these behaviors in 2006 and 2012 for men and women in two age groups: 55–65 and 66+.

Though all these surveys aim to measure the same behaviors, it is important to remember that there are some differences in the way the questions were asked. To illustrate, the category of "Smoke Ever" in general indicates whether the respondent ever regularly smoked, but the particular formulation of the question varies somewhat across the surveys.[10] Similarly, the concept of "smoked now" in general indicates if the respondent currently smokes.[11] The questions across the surveys vary in which forms of tobacco are referred to as being smoked, but cigarettes are always included and the meaning of the word "ever" with some surveys allows short periods of smoking in the past to count as a negative response to the category. While these differences certainly do exist and should be kept in mind, we believe that the smoking data can be safely interpreted as evidence for real smoking differences across countries and over time.

Comparing the data for "Smoke Ever" and "Smoke Now" provides an indication of long-term changes in smoking over time. Among men, current smoking ("Smoke Now") rates are lowest in Northern Europe, England, and the United States, where the long-term secular smoking decline is also continuing between the years 2006 and 2012. Current smoking rates for males are at their lowest in America, England, and Northern Europe and are much higher in the two high-income Asian countries, Korea and Japan. Those two countries are characterized by the largest differences in gender

---

[10]SHARE asks if respondent smoked cigarettes, cigars, cigarillos, or a pipe daily for a period of at least 1 year. ELSA asks if respondent ever smoked cigarettes. HRS asks if respondent ever smoked cigarettes (more than 100 in lifetime and does not include pipes or cigars). KLoSA asks if respondent smoked more than 5 packs (100) cigarettes in total. JSTAR asks if respondent regularly smokes or did so in the past.

[11]SHARE asks if the respondent smokes at the present time. ELSA asks if the respondent currently smokes cigarettes at all. HRS asks if the respondent smokes cigarettes now. KLoSA asks if the respondent smokes cigarettes now. JSTAR asks if the respondent regularly smokes or did so in the past.

TABLE 12-6 Health Behaviors by Country Group, Age, and Gender, 2006 and 2012

	Smoke Ever		Smoke Now		Binge Drink		Vigorous Exercise 1+/wk		Obese	
	2006	2012	2006	2012	2006	2012	2006	2012	2006	2012
Men Ages 55–65 (%)										
Central Europe	66.0	64.7	25.6	26.6	10.3	8.4	60.4	61.2	19.2	22.6
Eastern Europe	60.3	60.5	30.1	34.8	10.3	24.0	53.1	53.1	28.5	30.9
Northern Europe	62.5	60.4	21.1	19.0	6.8	11.8	61.1	73.9	15.9	19.3
Southern Europe	64.8	62.1	28.6	26.7	11.4	4.3	46.0	44.6	21.4	18.4
Japan	79.9	79.3	38.5	35.1	4.5	2.8	—	—	2.8	3.5
Korea	62.4	72.8	41.3	42.7	32.6	35.6	43.7	41.6	0.7	0.9
England	69.4	65.3	17.5	16.6	29.4	13.2	35.8	39.0	29.5	33.4
USA	66.8	60.3	21.0	19.5	5.5	6.2	43.9	50.9	33.7	36.3
Women Ages 55–65 (%)										
Central Europe	39.0	47.7	17.0	22.5	5.2	4.4	55.2	55.3	19.1	22.1
Eastern Europe	46.9	46.5	26.7	30.7	6.0	12.4	40.6	37.2	26.9	30.4
Northern Europe	57.9	60.1	25.6	19.7	7.0	6.9	51.7	63.7	15.4	16.3
Southern Europe	30.8	38.1	15.2	18.5	5.9	2.3	42.1	39.5	22.9	17.9
Japan	16.3	21.2	9.6	9.3	1.7	1.8	—	—	1.8	2.5
Korea	3.0	4.0	2.6	2.5	2.4	4.6	39.3	38.0	3.4	2.2
England	58.9	56.7	18.9	16.8	18.9	10.7	30.9	30.0	31.8	36.5
USA	51.6	49.3	17.3	15.2	1.3	1.8	31.4	37.8	37.0	39.7

Men Ages 66+ (%)									
Central Europe	59.4	63.1	12.2	13.4	5.2	4.3	41.5	43.9	15.8	18.4
Eastern Europe	52.5	51.6	12.8	18.9	5.0	14.7	31.5	33.9	20.5	26.7
Northern Europe	61.5	61.5	12.8	13.8	4.5	4.7	45.0	55.0	12.3	13.7
Southern Europe	60.7	58.6	14.5	13.5	9.9	3.8	33.8	31.4	18.5	17.2
Japan	76.8	71.5	23.5	17.6	2.7	3.0	—	—	1.2	2.4
Korea	56.1	62.5	30.2	25.9	23.8	29.0	39.0	41.9	0.9	0.7
England	75.5	75.9	11.1	8.9	13.4	6.9	23.2	26.1	24.4	26.8
USA	71.7	69.1	9.6	10.2	2.2	2.2	33.7	36.8	24.5	28.0
Women Ages 66+ (%)									
Central Europe	19.3	26.7	6.9	8.6	2.3	2.4	31.4	31.5	16.7	19.7
Eastern Europe	21.5	27.7	9.2	12.6	3.5	6.7	23.1	22.3	21.0	27.3
Northern Europe	44.1	47.1	14.1	12.5	2.6	2.9	33.5	45.6	13.3	14.9
Southern Europe	13.8	17.6	5.3	5.4	3.5	1.1	19.5	19.2	21.1	20.9
Japan	11.9	11.6	4.9	4.8	0.2	0.9	—	—	1.1	3.2
Korea	5.2	4.7	4.1	2.7	2.0	3.1	23.1	25.6	2.3	1.7
England	53.6	58.1	10.0	9.1	7.5	3.5	13.8	16.8	30.1	32.0
USA	46.3	48.1	8.5	8.5	0.3	0.5	20.1	27.7	25.1	28.6

NOTES: Data under 2006 are for calendar 2006 except that Japan data are for calendar 2007.
Data under 2012 are calendar 2012 except that Japan data are for calendar 2011.
Central Europe: Austria, Belgium, France, Germany, the Netherlands, Switzerland.
Eastern Europe: Czech Republic.
Northern Europe: Denmark, Sweden.
Southern Europe: Italy, Spain.
SOURCES: Data are from RAND HRS, Harmonized ELSA, Harmonized SHARE, Harmonized JSTAR, Harmonized KLoSA.

smoking because female smoking is almost nonexistent there, whereas male smoking is the highest among the listed high-income countries. Female smoking has risen over time in Southern Europe and the United States. Current smoking rates tend to be significantly lower among those ages 66 and older compared to those ages 55–65, a difference that most likely indicates prior health problems with smoking in the older group.

The second health behavior examined is binge drinking. The definition of "binge drinking" is gender specific; for a man it means five or more drinks at a single occasion, whereas for a woman it means four or more drinks at a single occasion. Those thresholds are applied to the specific questions asked in each survey. Once again, there are operational differences among our surveys on how binge drinking is defined, and these are larger differences than those for smoking.[12]

The two outliers among these high-income countries that make them simply not comparable in drinking to the other countries are England and South Korea. To illustrate, the U.S. HRS question basically asks for the average number of drinks per day on days the respondent drank, whereas the English ELSA question asks for number of drinks on the day you drank the most. Thus, English respondents would appear to drink more, even if they drank the same as U.S. respondents on average. Similarly, by asking for the maximum amount for each type of alcohol consumed, the South Korean question is not directly comparable to the other HRS-network survey questions.

In Table 12-6, the "Vigorous Exercise 1+/wk" column indicates the percentage of respondents who participated in vigorous exercise one or more times per week. Again, there are significant variations among the HRS high-income countries in how "vigorous exercise" is defined. Variation occurs in what activities are included in exercise (only sports, more activities than sports, heavy housework, respondent's job).[13] However, the

---

[12]SHARE asks in last 3 months, on days respondent drank, about how many drinks did respondent have. ELSA asks, during the last 7 days how many measures of spirits/glasses of wine/pints of beer, lager or cider did respondent have, then sums all 3 types and divides by the number days (out of the last 7) respondent had an alcoholic drink. HRS asks in last 3 months on days respondent drank, about how many drinks did respondent have. KLoSA asks how many glasses of soju/beer/makgeolli/whisky and other liquors/wine respondent drank at a time, with each type being asked separately. We used the type with the most drinks in the analysis for this report. JSTAR asks how much respondent drank of beer/sake/distilled spirit/wine/other on average per occasion (sum of 3 types).

[13]SHARE asks about vigorous physical activity, such as sports, heavy housework, or a job that involves physical labor (more than once a week/once a week). ELSA asks about sports or activities that are vigorous (more than once a week/once a week). HRS asks how often respondent takes part in sports or activities that are vigorous, such as running or jogging, swimming, cycling, aerobics or gym workout, tennis, or digging with a spade or shovel (more than once a week/once a week). KLoSA asks how often respondent works out per week (any value of 1 or greater). No vigorous exercise questions are asked in JSTAR.

problems in comparisons of exercise across countries go beyond the specific questions. In a recent paper, Kapteyn et al. (forthcoming) demonstrate using accelerometers that answers to standard exercise questions are very subjective, with the meaning of "vigorous" varying significantly across countries. Thus, standard self-evaluated exercise questions by themselves are not of much use, and this variability becomes instead a call to the surveys to include objective exercise measures.

"Obese" in Table 12-6 is defined in the conventional way as a BMI of 30 or more and thus is the most straightforward of the health behaviors and is comparable across the surveys and across waves. Japan and Korea stand out with very low levels of obesity for both men and women in both 2006 and 2012, compared to all the other sets of countries in Table 12-6. These low obesity levels, especially in older ages, generally get first-level credit for the good health and low levels of mortality in those two countries. Once again, the United States ranks highest in terms of percentages of obesity among both men and women, and U.S. obesity levels have clearly increased over time. U.S. levels of obesity exceed those of England among ages 55–64, but the reverse is true for those ages 66 and older (Banks et al., 2006, 2010). Within continental Europe, the countries of Northern Europe rank best (lowest percentages) in obesity level, followed by the countries of Central and Southern Europe, with the highest levels of obesity occurring in Eastern Europe.

Given the central role of obesity in health outcomes and its variability among countries and over time, Figure 12-1 plots age-adjusted percentages of obese men and women in many high-income countries, for calendar years 1975 and 2012, using World Health Organization data. The United States had by far the highest obesity rate in 2012 but also the largest percentage-point increase in obesity of these countries, with the U.S. obesity rate almost tripling over this period. The United Kingdom stands next in line in obesity levels and increases over time, but it is no match for the United States. Not surprisingly the two Asian countries have very low levels of obesity and also exhibited virtually no increase over time. In the remaining high-income countries, the percentage increase in the population fraction who are obese matches the increase over time in the United States, but since they started at much lower levels in 1975, 40 years later they still are well below U.S. rates.

In addition to obesity, the other central long-term factor that matters for health outcomes is trends in education, with higher education having been shown to be positively associated with improved health (Goldman and Smith, 2011). Figure 12-2 documents cross-national trends by plotting the fraction of those ages 25–34 and the fraction of those ages 55–64 with tertiary education in 2015. Since education is a cohort variable and does not change much after age 25, this graph is essentially plotting education increases by country over a 30-year period. Japan and Korea have the

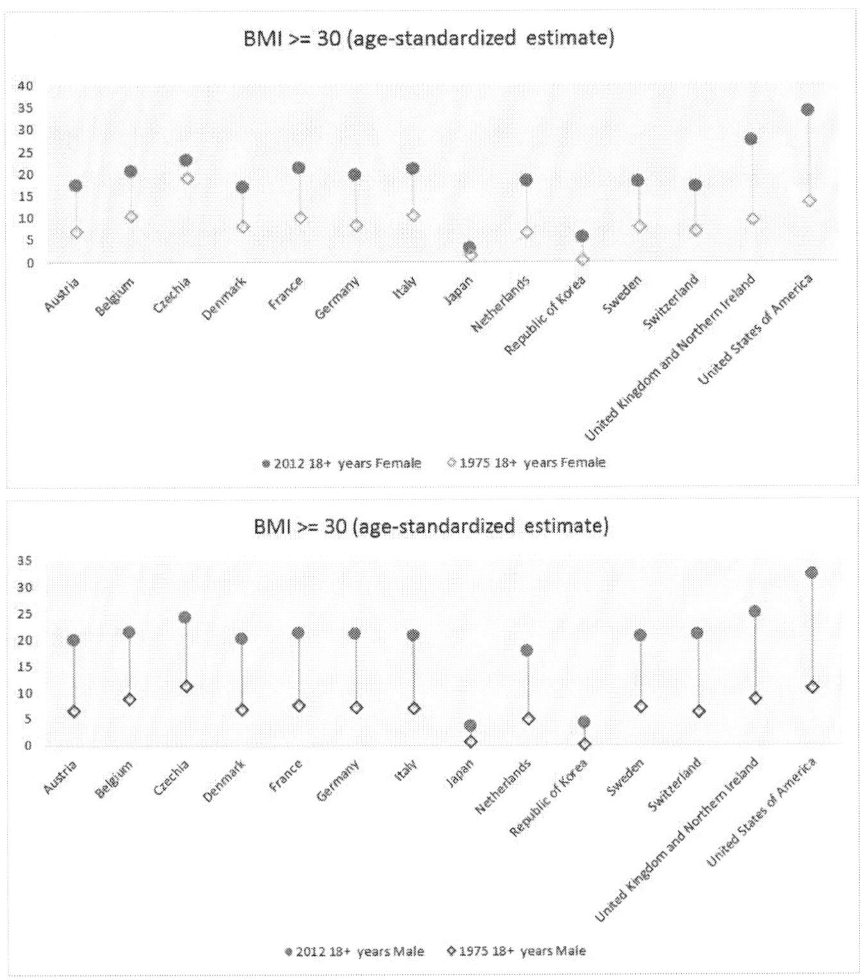

FIGURE 12-1 Long-term changes in obesity by country.
SOURCE: Data are from the World Health Organization.

most impressive time-series experience, and these two countries now rank at the top of this education ladder. In sharp contrast, the United States, which ranked at the top of the education ladder among those ages 55–64, showed very little improvement in education over time and now lies back in the pack among those ages 25–34. Improvements in education over time were also small for Germany, Israel, Estonia, and Finland. The central role that education has played in health improvements over time has important implications for the ranking of countries by their health status.

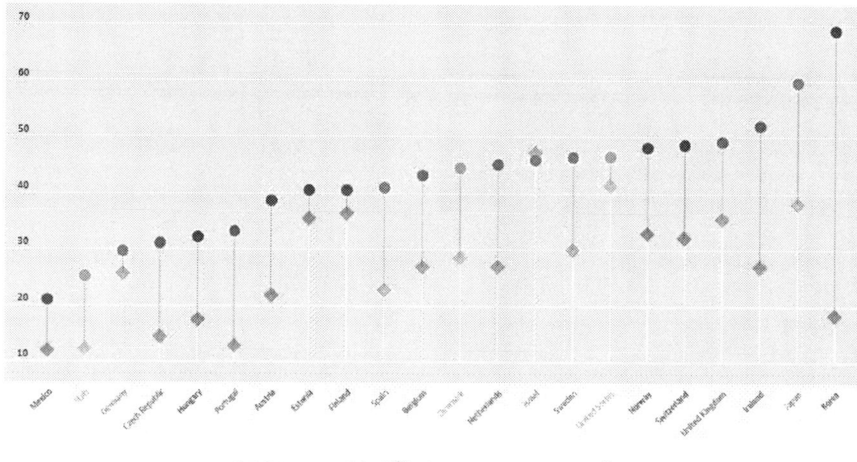

FIGURE 12-2 Population fraction with tertiary education, by country, 2015. SOURCE: Data are from the OECD chart: Population with tertiary education, ages 25–34, percentage in same age group, annual, 2015. Available: https://data.oecd. org/eduatt/population-with-tertiary-education.htm [April 2018].

The lack of comparability in some health behaviors across the set of high-income countries in the HRS network does raise a question of what can and should be done about the current situation. One response is that questions should be made the same, but that creates the problem that the individual studies will no longer be time series consistent in their own question set over time. This would clearly create a lot of problems for within-country analysis. An alternative strategy that should be explored is to add to each survey a common question that allows researchers to create a correspondence between each survey's legacy question(s) and the common question. This correspondence could be used to increase comparability.

To assess the pattern of health behaviors across education groups within countries, Table 12-7 displays three health behaviors—current smoking, binge drinking, and obesity—for our set of high-income countries in 2006 and 2012 among those ages 55–64. In the United States, there are very strong negative gradients with increased education in all three behaviors; smoking, binge drinking, and obesity are all highest among those with 0–11 years of schooling. With the exception of drinking, a similar negative gradient is found in England. We found no such gradients in either of our Asian countries (Korea and Japan) and no smoking gradient in Southern Europe. The negative obesity gradient with education characterizes all the parts of continental Europe displayed in Table 12-7. We found similar patterns

TABLE 12-7 Health Behavior by Country/Region, Education Level, and Age Group, 2006 and 2012

	Smoke Now		Binge Drink		Obese	
	2006	2012	2006	2012	2006	2012
0–11 Years of Education, Ages 55–65 (%)						
Central Europe	19.3	26.1	8.3	6.6	22.9	27.0
Eastern Europe	28.1	42.8	7.8	16.0	32.7	35.9
Northern Europe	27.0	25.1	7.6	11.8	20.4	22.2
Southern Europe	20.4	22.6	8.2	3.7	24.9	21.0
Japan	26.3	29.2	1.6	0.8	1.4	6.0
Korea	19.4	19.3	13.9	16.4	2.7	2.0
England	25.9	21.7	21.4	11.7	37.2	44.0
USA	31.3	28.5	7.2	5.5	41.6	45.4
12–15 Years of Education, Ages 55–65 (%)						
Central Europe	23.0	25.5	7.7	6.4	17.9	20.9
Eastern Europe	31.1	31.6	7.0	18.6	24.5	29.6
Northern Europe	20.4	18.0	6.1	7.4	12.2	16.7
Southern Europe	25.3	23.4	8.0	3.0	16.1	14.0
Japan	28.6	19.5	4.2	2.1	2.5	2.7
Korea	27.4	25.3	24.3	22.8	1.1	1.3
England	15.4	16.9	25.5	12.3	29.9	36.7
USA	20.9	20.6	3.1	4.8	37.7	41.0
16+ Years of Education, Ages 55–65 (%)						
Central Europe	21.7	19.0	6.1	5.5	14.6	15.9
Eastern Europe	19.2	18.9	9.7	15.1	28.2	25.4
Northern Europe	21.1	13.3	7.1	9.0	10.7	11.9
Southern Europe	21.6	20.8	12.0	1.4	11.3	11.0
Japan	29.3	28.7	3.3	3.7	3.6	1.7
Korea	24.8	26.4	23.4	25.3	0.0	0.0
England	8.9	8.2	28.1	10.2	21.1	23.3
USA	9.1	7.7	1.8	2.0	27.7	31.1

NOTES: Data under 2006 are for calendar 2006 except that Japan data are for calendar 2007. Data under 2012 are calendar 2012 except that Japan data are for calendar 2011.
Central Europe: Austria, Belgium, France, Germany, the Netherlands, Switzerland.
Eastern Europe: Czech Republic.
Northern Europe: Denmark, Sweden.
Southern Europe: Italy, Spain.

TABLE 12-7 Continued

Binge drinking is defined according to National Institute on Alcoholism and Alcohol Abuse guidelines: Men having 5+ drinks and women having 4+ drinks at a time. HRS, SHARE, JSTAR binge drinking captures an average number of drinks per occasion, while KLoSA and ELSA capture a maximum number of drinks consumed per occasion.
SOURCES: Data are from RAND HRS, Harmonized ELSA, Harmonized SHARE, Harmonized JSTAR, Harmonized KLoSA.

of health behaviors when wealth terciles are used to define the SES gradient. Among potential reasons for the improvement in secular mortality at age 50, the well-documented reduction in smoking over time is almost always assigned a central role (Preston et al., 2010). The slower pace of mortality gains in Denmark, the Netherlands, and the United States has been attributed to the relative increase in levels of female smoking and, for the first two countries, the nonprovision of medical care to the sick elderly (Glei at al., 2010). Increases in education levels in the population are another factor often pointed to in improving health in general and mortality in particular (Goldman and Smith, 2011). As we demonstrate in this paper, secular increases in education in recent decades have been smaller in the United States than in other high-income countries, consistent with the patterns of mortality increases documented in Table 12-2.

This largely good news concerning sustained long-term positive trends in middle-age life expectancy for the United States received an abrupt shock due to recent papers by Anne Case and Angus Deaton (Case and Deaton, 2015, 2017; Montez and Hayward, 2014). In their papers, Case and Deaton documented that mortality among less-educated middle-aged and younger adult non-Hispanic Whites had actually started to increase, a sharp reversal in U.S. secular trends from prior decades. The exact causes of this abrupt mortality change are not yet fully known, but the general deterioration in economic, social, and family life for these middle-age, less-educated non-Hispanic Whites appears to be the most likely reason.

The question we ask is whether this abrupt Case-Deaton change has affected the attitudes and behaviors of current respondents in the HRS surveys. To do so, we examine answers over time to a regular question in the HRS modules asked of younger HRS respondents about whether they expect to live to age 75.[14] The answers for survey years between 1992 and 2014 for three education groups (0–11 years, 12–15 years, and 16+ years of education) are contained in Table 12-8.

---

[14]In addition to HRS, life expectancy questions are also asked in ELSA, SHARE, KLoSA, and JSTAR. Those other surveys show no such deterioration over time.

TABLE 12-8 Men's Self-Reported Mean Probability of Living to Age 75, by Education Fraction That Expects to Live to Age 75

Respondent Age	1992 Mean	1994 Mean	1996 Mean	1998 Mean	2000 Mean	2002 Mean	2004 Mean	2006 Mean	2008 Mean	2010 Mean	2012 Mean	2014 Mean
0–11 Years of Education												
57–59	56.7	55.9	57.5	56.1	60.8	52.8	52.9	44.4	46.4	48.5	47.8	48.2
60–62	54.7	58.7	56.5	59.0	56.1	52.5	51.1	54.2	53.6	47.5	39.6	37.6
12–15 Years of Education												
57–59	60.1	61.8	63.7	62.6	65.0	60.4	59.5	57.1	59.6	56.9	55.2	56.9
60–62	65.2	62.9	62.7	63.6	66.2	65.4	60.6	57.2	60.0	55.4	58.4	58.3
16+ Years of Education												
57–59	67.5	67.7	69.8	68.5	70.3	71.5	67.3	68.4	70.6	67.9	65.9	66.7
60–62	69.5	69.8	71.7	70.4	70.0	69.2	69.1	68.0	70.5	66.2	66.8	66.3

SOURCE: Data are from RAND HRS.

The data indicate that current less-educated younger respondents in the HRS are now expressing that they expect to live fewer years in the future than their similarly aged counterparts expected when they were the same age, at the time HRS began. To illustrate, in HRS's initial year of 1992, among those ages 57–59 with 0–11 years of schooling, 57 percent expected to live to age 75. The comparable number for the same demographic group in 2014 was 48 percent, a decline that started around the year 2000. If instead we take the highest education group in the table—those with at least a college education—the comparable numbers were 68 percent in 1992 and 67 percent in 2014. The general pattern is easy to summarize: longer life expectancies for the more educated and a growing disparity in life expectancies by education.

The value of such data in the HRS set of surveys is possibly twofold. The first is that we can confirm that the Case-Deaton documentation of mortality trends is now built into the expectations of respondents and should be shaping their future behaviors in savings behavior and wealth decumulation, at a minimum. Improvements in health of these birth cohorts should also then be reflected in these life expectancy questions in future HRS waves. Second, and perhaps more important, we can use HRS-type data to model the changes in remaining years of life, thereby documenting the possible causes of the decline in life expectancy in these groups.

There are certainly legitimate concerns about the use of subjective probability data for this analysis and reasons for caution in its application. For example, these data are known to be characterized by considerable heaping at values of 0, 50, and 100 percent, and there remains some dispute about the precise nature of the mortality trends (Sasson, 2016). However, these subjective probabilities of future life expectancy have been shown to predict future mortality and to also predict future changes in behaviors such as retirement and social security claiming (Hurd, 2009). If the recent subjective probability data in the HRS can be further validated, it would become a valuable tool for analysis of the causes and consequences of these important recent mortality trends.

EARLY LIFE EFFECTS ON LATER LIFE OUTCOMES

A growing literature has demonstrated that there are strong influences of events in childhood and adult life before age 50 on later life paths and levels of health (Caspi et al., 1998; Currie, 2009; Goodman et al., 2011; Hayward and Gorman, 2004; Smith and Smith, 2010). These robust findings highlight a potential limitation of studies, such as the HRS around the world surveys that often begin around age 50. Many of the key determinants of later-life age transitions in health take place at much younger ages.

The existence of specific physical and especially mental health diseases in earlier life needs to be identified alongside a list of events and relationships that are associated with these illnesses. In response to this concern, several of the HRS surveys including ELSA, SHARE, and HRS (in process) have added material on early life. The most extensive surveys consist of life history modules, which have been very important and successful additions. In particular, the life history module in SHARE, which is called SHARE LIFE and was fielded as the third wave of SHARE, documented the interactions of respondents in all SHARE countries with the rich and varied history of the respondent's country at the individual and state levels. These SHARE life histories included impacts of World War II (Kesternich et al., 2014), the political transitions made by many of these European countries, economic recessions and depressions, and changes in the availability of schools and the economic and education status of parents. At the individual level, the histories include information about the circumstances in parental households and in schools. The SHARE surveys are planning on including life histories in their future new countries in SHARE.

Once again, in these early-life diseases the United States leads the way among the HRS-network high-income countries, with higher reported levels of these childhood illnesses than the other countries report. England places a solid second. The general reporting of childhood psychological problems in these surveys indicates that childhood psychological problems have actually been increasing over time and present large challenges to individuals' adult health and economic status throughout their subsequent adult lives. These problems have been particularly severe in the United States but are not confined to the United States (Goodman et al., 2011; Smith and Smith, 2010).

CONCLUSIONS

In this paper, we summarized information available from the high-income countries that are participating in the network of HRS around the world surveys. The data point to several salient facts about the aging process in these countries. First, there is significant variation in health status outcomes among these countries, with the United States ranking poorly both in terms of current health status and in changes in health status over time. Following the United States, countries of Eastern Europe rank second in terms of disease prevalence, England is in third place, and Central and Northern Europe are performing the best in terms of health outcomes. We also find a strong social gradient in health status by our two markers of SES—years of education and terciles of wealth—with apparently stronger gradients in the United States compared to the other high-income countries.

We also examined health behaviors that might underlie these health status differences and changes in health levels over time. Not all the health behavior measures are comparable across these high-income HRS-network surveys. Among those that are comparable, the best news comes from the decline in smoking for all but the least educated group. In the United States, at least, the decline in smoking has slowed considerably in the last decade. With the exception of the Asian countries (Korea and Japan), the worst news is the continuing rise without interruption in levels of obesity in these high-income countries.

There is great variety in trends in these high-income countries in another trait associated with good health: years of education. The increase in education levels over time has continued unabated in many of the high-income countries, especially in Asia, but decidedly not in the United States. The latter condition no doubt contributes to the lack of much improvement in health in the United States. We also find that younger cohorts in the current U.S. HRS datasets are already anticipating shorter remaining years of life, a reflection of the now well-documented Case-Deaton effect. With appropriate new modules, the HRS network of surveys will become an important vehicle for analyses of the reasons for the increase in mortality of less-educated Americans, as well as for predicting and tracking the behavioral adjustments they are making to this new reality.

REFERENCES

Avendano, M., Glymour, M., Banks, J., and Mackenbach, J.P. (2009). Health disadvantage in U.S. adults aged 50 to 74 years: A comparison of the health of rich and poor Americans with that of Europeans. *American Journal of Public Health, 99*(3), 540–548.

Banks, J., Marmot, M., Oldfield, Z., and Smith, J.P. (2006). Disease and disadvantage in the United States and in England. *Journal of the American Medical Association, 295*(17), 2037–2045.

Banks, J., Muriel, A., and Smith, J.P. (2010). Disease prevalence, disease incidence, and mortality in the United States and in England. *Demography, 47*(Suppl), S211–S231.

Case, A., and Deaton, A. (2015). Rising mortality and mortality in midlife among white non-Hispanic Americans in the 21st century. *Proceedings of the National Academy of Sciences of the United States of America, 112*(49), 15078–15083. doi: 10.1073/pnas.1518393112.

Case, A., and Deaton, A. (2017, March 20). *Mortality and Morbidity in the 21st Century.* Brookings Papers on Economic Activity. Available: https://www.brookings.edu/wp-content/uploads/2017/08/casetextsp17bpea.pdf [April 2018].

Caspi, A., Moffitt, T.E., Wright, B.R.E., and Suva, P.A. (1998). Early failure in the labor market: Childhood and adolescent predictors of unemployment in the transition to adulthood. *American Sociological Review, 63*(3), 424–451.

Currie, J. (2009). Healthy, wealthy, and wise? Socioeconomic status, poor health in childhood, and human capital development. *Journal of Economic Literature, 47*(1), 87–122.

Dobrescu, L.I., and Smith, J.P. (2016). The HRS around the world surveys. In J. Piggott and A. Woodword (Eds.), *Economics of Population Ageing Handbook* (vol. B, part V, Ch. 17, pp. 993–1018). Amsterdam, Netherlands: Elsevier.

Glei, D., Mesle, F., and Vallin, J. (2010). Diverging trends in life expectancy at age 50; A look at causes of death. In E. Crimmins, S. Preston, and B. Cohen (Eds.), *International Differences in Mortality at Older Ages—Dimensions and Sources* (pp. 17–67). Washington, DC: The National Academies Press.

Goldman, D., and Smith, J.P. (2011). The increasing value of education to health. *Social Science and Medicine, 72*(10), 1728–1737.

Goodman, A., Joyce, R., and Smith, J.P. (2011). The long shadow cast by childhood physical and mental problems on adult life. *Proceedings of the National Academy of Sciences of the United States of America, 1108*(15), 6032–6037.

Hayward, M.D., and Gorman, B.K. (2004). The long arm of childhood: The influence of early-life social conditions on men's mortality. *Demography, 41*, 87–107.

Hurd, M.D. (2009). Subjective probabilities in household surveys. *Annual Review of Economics, 1*, 543–562. doi: 10.1146/annurev.economics.050708.142955.

Kapteyn, A., Banks, J., Hamer, M., Smith, J.P., Steptoe, A., Van Soest, A., and Saw, H.W. (forthcoming). What they say and what they do: Comparing physical activity across U.S., England, and the Netherlands. *Journal of Epidemiology and Community Health.*

Kesternich, I., Siflinger, B., Smith, J.P., and Winter, J. (2014). The effects of World War II on economic and health outcomes across Europe. *The Review of Economics and Statistics, 96*(1), 103–118.

Montez, J.K., and Hayward, M. (2014). Cumulative childhood adversity, educational attainment, and active life expectancy among U.S. adults. *Demography, 51*(2), 413–435.

Preston, S., Glei, D., Wilmoth, J.R. (2010). Contribution of smoking to international differences in life expectancy. In E. Crimmins, S. Preston, and B. Cohen (Eds.), *International Differences in Mortality at Older Ages—Dimensions and Sources* (pp. 105–131). Washington, DC: The National Academies Press.

Sasson, I. (2016). Diverging trends in cause-specific mortality and life years lost by educational attainment: Evidence from United States Vital Statistics Data, 1990–2010. *PLoS One 11*(10). doi: 10.1371/journal.pone.0163412.

Smith, J.P. (2004). Unraveling the SES–health connection. *Population and Development Review Supplement: Aging, Health and Public Policy, 30*, 108–132.

Smith, J.P., and Smith, G.C. (2010). Long-term economic costs of psychological problems during childhood. *Social Science and Medicine, 71*(1), 110–115.

PART VII

New Approaches in Measurement

13

New Measures and New Designs in Demography of Aging Research

David R. Weir,[1] Linda J. Waite,[2] Rebeca Wong,[3] and Vicki A. Freedman[1]

INTRODUCTION

A volume devoted to the demography of aging does well to recognize the importance of innovative data collection and data sharing. The field has been a leader in developing new designs and measurement approaches, and these studies in turn have shaped and pushed the research frontier for the study of aging. The strong commitment to data sharing with open access to the data for the scientific community—and the resulting high volume of research—has begun to influence other related fields. The National Institute on Aging (NIA), and in particular its branch of Behavioral and Social Research, has been the primary force behind this empirical infrastructure, providing funding, scientific leadership, and encouraging collaboration across the studies it supports and beyond.

The demography of aging is fundamentally about the changes people and societies experience as they age. Thus, virtually all important aging studies are longitudinal, to observe changes with age over time. Design choices arise about which part of that aging process to include directly or to query indirectly. Moreover, individuals are situated in couples, households, families, neighborhoods, schools, workplaces, social networks, and so on. A fully comprehensive study at all levels is infeasible, so studies must choose. The NIA has been successful both at creating studies in pursuit of

---

[1]University of Michigan.
[2]University of Chicago.
[3]University of Texas Medical Branch.

desired goals and at leveraging studies created for other purposes to obtain unique design features.

We begin this chapter with a review of several of the more significant studies with unique design features, both within and outside the United States. The collection of studies showcases how the incorporation of new technologies has greatly improved the measurement of traditional concepts and has provided an expanded toolkit for demographic research. The next section presents an annotated summary of current developments in measurement and design, grouped in large categories of demographic and psychosocial measures, biological and functional measures of health, including cognitive function measures, and other important developments in genetics, administrative and medical record linkages, and mortality ascertainment. After a brief description of data sharing practices, the final section sheds light on what data collection scholars foresee as measurements and designs for the future of the demography of aging, while pointing out possible challenges and ethical issues derived from the vast reach of new data collection technologies that have recently emerged.

STUDY DESIGNS: ADVANTAGES AND CHALLENGES

This section provides a summary of several of the more significant studies, highlighting their unique design features. We begin with three studies, initially conceived for other purposes, that have become important to the study of aging and in particular the influence of early-life conditions on later-life outcomes, before turning to studies designed expressly for aging research (see Table 13-1).

The Wisconsin Longitudinal Study (WLS) is based on a 1-in-3 sample of high school graduates in the state of Wisconsin in 1957, subsequently augmented with a sample of siblings (Herd et al., 2014). Its design is unique

TABLE 13-1 Currently Active U.S.-based Demography of Aging Projects

Year Begun	Project
1957	Wisconsin Longitudinal Study (WLS)
1969	Panel Study of Income Dynamics (PSID)
1992	Health and Retirement Study (HRS)
1995	Midlife in the United States (MIDUS)
2005	National Social Life, Health and Aging Project (NSHAP)
2011	National Health and Aging Trends Study (NHATS)
2017	Add Health Parents Study

in the long-term follow-up and direct observation of late adolescence, including cognitive ability, in a sample now in their 70s. The study has been innovative in the use of biomarkers, including genetic data and, more recently, samples of the microbiome (Hauser and Weir, 2010; Herd et al., 2014). While not national in scope, it captures most of the variation in the non-Hispanic White population of its cohort.

Project Talent is a large, nationally representative study of high school students in 1960 designed by John Flanagan of the American Institutes for Research. A two-day battery of cognitive and personality tests was conducted with 377,000 students in 1,200 schools. The sample had only very limited follow-up until recently. A project aimed at studying twin and sibling pairs is under way (Prescott et al., 2013).

The Panel Study of Income Dynamics (PSID) is the world's longest running national panel study. Begun in 1968 as a nationally representative sample of 5,000 families to study the war on poverty, PSID has expanded its content on health and demographic topics over the past 50 years (McGonagle et al., 2012). With its long-panel design, PSID is well situated to study factors over the life course that influence later-life health and mortality. In addition, because adult children are invited to join the study when they form their own households, the PSID supports studies of health and well-being and transfers across generations. The study's main funders are the National Science Foundation, the NIA, and the Eunice Kennedy Shriver National Institute of Child Health and Development (NICHD).

Midlife in the United States (MIDUS) began in 1995 with funding from the MacArthur Foundation. Its subsequently became a program project and then a cooperative agreement with the NIA. Its sample is derived from a variety of sources, including some sibling and twin pairs (Brim et al., 2004). It combines extensive psychosocial measurement with biomarkers collected in overnight clinic visits (Dienberg Love et al., 2010).

The National Social Life, Health, and Aging Project (NSHAP) began as an NIA-funded project focused on the social relationships of persons 57 and older, including sexual relationships (Suzman, 2009). Its design was initially individual-based but subsequent waves brought spouses and partners into the study. Social relations are queried through innovative survey methods (Cornwell et al., 2009). It has also been innovative in pursuing biomarker acquisition and prescription drug information during in-home interviews.

The National Health and Aging Trends Study (NHATS) was funded by the NIA as a platform for understanding both population-level trends in late-life disability and individual-level dynamics (Kasper and Freedman, 2014). The NHATS sample is drawn from Medicare records and refreshed periodically. Its centerpiece is a validated disability protocol (administered in person annually) that has reengineered traditional measures to capture changes in how activities are carried out by older adults in their daily lives

(Freedman et al., 2011). Detailed information is collected about residential care settings in which older adults live and assistance received. Unpaid and family caregivers are also interviewed periodically as part of the National Study of Caregiving. NHATS also permits analysis of long-term disability trends when used in conjunction with its predecessor survey, the National Long-Term Care Survey (Manton, et al., 1993).

The National Longitudinal Study of Adolescent to Adult Health (Add Health) began in 1994 with funding from the NICHD to study children in grades 7–12, with some information about their parents and families of origin. Rich in biomarker measurement, the study has followed its cohort periodically into middle age (Harris, 2013). Beginning in 2015, the NIA began supporting a study of the parents of Add Health participants, using a reciprocal design that enables studies of parent-child relationships as the parents age.

The Health and Retirement Study (HRS) was created by the NIA explicitly to provide a foundation for research on aging (Juster and Suzman, 1995). It has expanded from a single cohort in 1992 to represent the entire population 51 years and older, with oversamples of minorities and a steady-state sampling design to refresh the study with new cohorts to maintain its age coverage as the cohorts age (Sonnega et al., 2014). It also moved from primarily a telephone survey to a multimode study with biomarkers, administrative linkages, and other enhancements (Weir, 2008). It includes both of the members in coupled households, enabling studies of marital relationships as couples age. Respondents provide information about exchanges with parents and children, but those other family members are not included directly. Administrative linkages to Social Security and Medicare provide information about earnings, employment, health, and health care utilization.

The success of the HRS design has encouraged the development of harmonized sister studies now encompassing more than half of the world's population (Table 13-2). The first was the Mexican Health and Aging Study (Wong et al., 2017), followed by the English Longitudinal Study of Ageing (ELSA; Steptoe et al., 2013), and the multicountry Survey of Health, Ageing and Retirement in Europe (SHARE, Börsch-Supan et al., 2013). A number of studies then developed in Asia (National Research Council, 2012), including the Korean Longitudinal Study of Aging (Park et al., 2007), the adaptation of the ongoing Indonesia Family Life Survey to the HRS model, the Japanese Study of Aging and Retirement, the China Health and Retirement Longitudinal Study (Zhao et al., 2014), and the Longitudinal Aging Study for India (Arokiasamy et al., 2012). The Study of Global Ageing and Adult Health (Kowal et al., 2012) includes Asian and African countries, while South Africa is the location of the Health and Aging in Africa study.

Other recent additions include the Irish Longitudinal Study of Aging (Kearney et al., 2011) in the Republic of Ireland, the Northern Ireland

TABLE 13-2 International Data Projects on the HRS Model

Year Begun	Project
1993	Indonesia Family Life Survey (IFLS)
2001	The Mexican Health and Aging Study (MHAS)
2002	The English Longitudinal Study of Ageing (ELSA)
2004	The Survey of Health and Retirement in Europe (SHARE)
2006	Korean Longitudinal Study of Aging (KLoSA)
2006	Study of Global Ageing and Adult Health (SAGE)
2007	Japanese Study of Aging and Retirement (JSTAR)
2010	The Irish Longitudinal Study of Aging (TILDA)
2011	China Health and Retirement Longitudinal Study (CHARLS)
2015	Health and Aging in Africa (HAALSI)
2016	Northern Ireland Cohort for Longitudinal Study of Aging (NICOLA)
2016	Brazilian Longitudinal Study of Aging and Well-Being (ELSI)
2017	Longitudinal Aging Study in India (LASI)

Cohort for Longitudinal Study of Aging, and the Brazilian Longitudinal Study of Aging and Well-Being (Lima-Costa et al., 2018). Both Irish studies include clinic-based health assessments as part of the core study (Cronin et al., 2013). Another longitudinal aging study with rich clinical health data but less harmonization to the HRS model is the Canadian Longitudinal Study of Aging (Raina et al., 2009). NIA funding has been important to many of the HRS sister studies, particularly for early development, although on average the great majority of funding is from other sources. The encouragement and support to the collaborative network has been essential, including support for data harmonization for analysts through the University of Southern California's Gateway to Global Aging Data.[4]

The ability to collect population-based measures in aging research has accelerated as mentioned, but the pace has varied widely across the globe, in particular in the poorer developing nations. Longitudinal studies with large national cohorts of older adults are just beginning to proliferate in middle- and low-income countries. The approach is costly and requires political and social commitment to data collection that can be difficult to achieve, especially in societies with scarce resources. Often there may be long time gaps between the study follow-up waves, making the data collection efforts more challenging as study subjects move away or die.

---

[4]The Gateway to Global Aging Data website is https://g2aging.org/ [April 2018].

In the case of the Mexican Health and Aging Study, two waves were collected in 2001 and 2003, with a long hiatus thereafter. Nine years later, wave 3 was collected with surprisingly high follow-up response rates. This success was achieved by the fieldwork operations personnel implementing a unique strategy. Approximately 3–4 months prior to the home visits by interviewers, a preliminary "sweep" or visit was conducted to every household in which a follow-up person resided. This preliminary contact resulted in either (a) recontact at the original address, (b) obtaining a new address and recontact at the new address, or (c) notice of death and location of a possible next-of-kin for the final interview. Then, interviewers were sent out to collect their follow-up interviews. After the 9-year gap from the second wave, a successful 88 percent recontact rate was accomplished. Similar strategies can be implemented in other countries, depending on the infrastructure and budget available.

CURRENT MEASUREMENT DEVELOPMENTS

Demographic and Psychosocial Measures

Social Networks

People are connected to others in a variety of ways, from kin relationships to socializing to exchanges. Social networks are created by webs of connections among groups of people, such that the social network of an individual includes that person's connections to others *and* the connections of those other people to each other (Cornwell et al., 2009). There are many ways to define social networks and many ways to measure them. NSHAP pioneered collection of social network data in older adults by focusing on their discussion networks: the people with whom they talk about things that are important to them. The respondent names these people, called "alters," and the relationship of each of them to the respondent (referred to as "ego" in social network research) is ascertained. How are they related? Are they kin? How old are they? Do they live with ego? And does ego talk to them about health? Then the respondent is asked in detail about the connection, if any, between each of the pairs of alters named. Do they know each other? Are they related? How often are they in contact? How close is their relationship? This innovation allows researchers to look closely at the links between all of those in the network, including flows of information and affection (Cornwell et al., 2009).

But social networks are not cast in stone; they change as the situations of the people in them change. The second wave of NSHAP obtained the social network as described 5 years after the first time the social network was measured for respondents. The Wave 2 social network module asked specifically about losses and additions to the network and reasons for them (Cornwell and Laumann, 2013). Network loss over 5 years has been found to be greater for older Blacks and those of low socioeconomic status (Cornwell, 2015). The study of social networks is poised to benefit from recent leaps in social connectivity and the technology that supports it. Facebook and other social media platforms both change people's networks and make them easier to trace. New methods and software are being developed for analyzing these types of data, especially changes in egocentric networks over time. It is critical to distinguish between important contacts on these platforms and those that are casual or fleeting, but this can be difficult to do.

Sexuality

Sexuality is an important component of both individual health and social functioning throughout the life course. A report of the U.S. Surgeon General points to sexuality as essential to well-being, with calls to attend to sexual health (Office of the Surgeon General, 2001). But serious research consideration of sexual behavior and attitudes, especially among older adults, is relatively recent. From the perspective of the demography of aging, sexuality can be conceptualized as a component of well-being, as a social indicator, and as a predictor or consequence of other dimensions of health (Galinsky and Waite, 2014; Waite et al., 2009). Because of the increasing recognition by researchers in the demography of aging of the importance of understanding sexuality, detailed measures of sexual behavior, attitudes, beliefs, functioning, and well-being have been included recently in important national surveys of health, including ELSA and NSHAP, and new measures are appearing in other health surveys, including the National Health and Nutrition Examination Survey (Laumann et al., 2008). The inclusion of both partners in some longitudinal surveys of older adults, together with questions on sexuality asked of each respondent individually, have allowed researchers to study the contribution of each partner to the sexuality of the dyad (Galinsky and Waite, 2014; Kim and Waite, 2014).

The study of sexuality at older ages encompasses multiple dimensions, typically assessed through self-report. These include sexual desire or interest, sexual activity or behavior, sexual functioning, and sexual health (Lee et al., 2016). Especially at older ages, it is important to define sexual activity with a partner quite broadly, as the activities that couples engage in shift away from vaginal intercourse toward touching, cuddling, and kissing (Waite et al., 2009), and sexual inactivity among those with a partner increases with age (Lindau et al., 2007).

Future directions in the research of sexuality among older adults might include in-depth study of health at older ages among lesbian, gay, bisexual, and transgender individuals. New cohorts moving into older ages have very different sexual and relationship histories than earlier cohorts, with implications for their sexuality, partnership, and health at older ages. These younger cohorts were also exposed to different medical practices, including vaccines for human papilloma virus, treatments for HIV/AIDS, and medications to improve sexual function. At the same time, instability in relationships, the obesity epidemic and concomitant rise in the prevalence of diabetes, and increases in death rates for middle-aged men (Case and Deaton, 2015) all make the landscape of sexuality at older ages different than it was several decades ago.

Time Use and Experienced Well-Being

At all stages of the life course, time is arguably among the most fundamental of human currencies. Either time can be spent for some immediate purpose (work, household tasks, family care, leisure) or it can be invested for some later benefit (e.g., learning or physical activity to improve health). Participation in valued activities constitutes an important domain in the disablement process (National Research Council, 2009; also see the chapter by V. Freedman on late-life disability in this volume). Time use influences demographic processes such as marriage, fertility, and survival, and it is in turn influenced by demographic and health processes.

How individuals allocate time to the activities and experiences of daily life also shapes enjoyment and other emotions experienced through the day. Conceptually, this notion of "experienced well-being" is distinct from evaluations of life as a whole (National Research Council, 2013). Evaluations of well-being, such as reports of life satisfaction, typically require an individual to appraise their situation, often relative to an unspecified standard. Evaluative well-being often is thought to be more strongly related to more enduring aspects of quality of life such as one's health, job, partner, family, and so on. By contrast, experienced well-being reflects how one is feeling in the moment and is therefore more responsive to immediate circumstances.

As with many of the measurement innovations in aging studies, time use had been traditionally measured in separate surveys before ongoing national panel studies such as HRS, PSID, NHATS, and the National Study of Caregiving supplement to NHATS, among others, began to incorporate time-use measures and in some cases associated measures of experienced well-being. The three most common forms of time assessment are experiential sampling methods (Csikszentmihalyi and Larson, 1987), time diary methods (Juster and Stafford, 1991), and stylized reports (Juster and Stafford, 1985). The three approaches differ in the type of data they produce, in their cognitive demands, and in accuracy (Juster et al., 2003).

Experiential sampling methods typically involve contacting respondents randomly multiple times per day. They have the highest accuracy of the three approaches because reports are provided in real time. In time-diary measures, respondents are asked a chronology of events, typically for the previous day, with follow-up descriptors similar to those used in experiential sampling. Diaries have good accuracy for respondents at older ages but can take 20–25 minutes to administer with descriptors (Freedman et al., 2013). Moreover, there is variability across days in how individuals spend their time (Kalton, 1985), making longitudinal comparison more difficult. In stylized reports, a respondent (or informant) aggregates time use over a specified reference period (e.g., a week or month) and reports typical amounts of time devoted to a particular class of activities, such as working for pay or housework (Juster and Stafford, 1985; Juster et al., 2003). The stylized reports are brief, have good reliability, and can be reported by knowledgeable proxies.

The time-use measurement methods also differ in their ability to incorporate measures of experienced well-being. Experiential sampling and time diaries, but not stylized time-use questions, can be used to reinstantiate memories of the day prior to asking about emotional experiences. Use of time diaries with follow-up questions that ask about emotion is also referred to as the Day Reconstruction Method (Kahneman et al., 2004). Briefer instruments that review activities the day before the interview in less detail before asking about emotions have also been developed, and preliminary evidence suggests that the measurement properties for the resulting experienced well-being measures are similar to the full Day Reconstruction Method (Lucas et al., 2018).

Biological and Functional Measures of Health

Biomeasures are objective measures of health, reflecting aspects of physiology that may not be known to a survey respondent. They provide information on biological aging prior to the development of age-related disease and physical dysfunction, as well as the progression of disease processes and functioning of multiple organ systems in the aging population. Although some aging studies do incorporate clinic visits, most surveys use biomeasures, obtained by trained interviewers in the home, that have been modified from and validated against clinical measures (O'Doherty et al., 2014). A review by McClintock et al. (2016) contains an extensive list, by dimension of health, of survey items and biomeasures, together with specification of their coding and validation against other national data.

Anthropometric measures generally include height, weight, waist circumference, and sometimes hip circumference, which is correlated with waist circumference. Height and weight can be measured objectively or by respondent report. While self-reports are generally accurate, small biases among older persons toward overstating height and understating weight can lead to significant shifts in the distribution of BMI categories (Weir, 2008).

Cardiovascular Function

Blood pressure (systolic and diastolic), pulse, and heart rate variability are basic health indicators obtained in virtually every medical encounter. They are also safe and easy for field interviewers to collect using automated cuff machines with digital readouts. This makes them standard for virtually any biomeasure panel in a survey that claims to measure health.

Physical Function and Performance

Physical functioning is the hallmark of successful aging: someone who cannot walk across a room, whose balance is poor, who is weak and tired a good deal of the time cannot be considered to be in good health. Many studies now routinely include both self-reported and performance-based measures of physical function, and international comparisons are now possible (Payne et al., 2017; Capistrant et al., 2014). Because such measures have been included repeatedly, researchers have been able to examine trajectories (Pettee et al., 2017). Researchers have also studied the consequences of poor physical functioning for subsequent disability onset, trajectories, and well-being (Martin et al., 2017; Freedman et al., 2017). Details on advances in conceptualization and measurement of physical function and its role in the broader disablement process are provided in the chapter by V. Freedman in this volume.

Many studies, including NSHAP, NHATS, and HRS, collect all or part of the Short Physical Performance Battery, which includes measures of mobility, balance, and lower body strength (Guralnik et al., 1994). Measures of physical functioning in surveys have often been designed to allow for the assessment of frailty, a condition rather than a disease, which signals increased vulnerability to dysregulation of organ systems, leading to hospitalization, disability, and death. Frailty is typically measured in surveys as an accumulation of health deficits such as poor balance, weakness or exhaustion, unintentional weight loss, slow walking speed, poor grip strength, low physical activity, limited lung capacity, and poor leg strength (Fried et al., 2001; Huisingh-Scheetz et al., 2014). Some frailty indexes include more and different measures, but evidence to date suggests that the association of these various indexes with poor health outcomes is robust to the differences in frailty (Searle et al., 2008). Measures of physical performance are key to measuring frailty and have predictive value on their own. Those most often used in surveys include timed walk, chair stands, balance, grip strength, and most recently, physical activity (Huisingh-Scheetz et al.,

2014). These can be combined with self-reported exhaustion, unintentional weight loss, falls, activities of daily living, instrumental activities of daily living (IADLs), depressive symptoms, and other survey measures to create a variety of frailty indexes (Searle et al., 2008).

Actigraphy

The development and popularity of activity tracking devices, which are worn on the wrist, ankle, or hip and are often used by individuals to track their daily exercise, have made it possible to measure characteristics of sleep and daytime activity for survey respondents (Lauderdale et al., 2014). These *actigraph* devices measure and record movement using an accelerometer, which enables the identification of periods of sleep, awakenings during periods of sleep, sleep latency (measured as time to fall asleep), and other characteristics of sleep (Lauderdale et al., 2014). The actigraph measures of sleep can be used in conjunction with self-reports of sleep and sleep problems. Comparison of self-reported sleep with that measured by actigraph suggests fairly low correspondence between the two (Chen et al., 2015). Recent research has used actigraph measures of activity during nonsleep periods to identify sedentary behavior, a characteristic of frail older adults, as well as periods of moderate and vigorous activity (Huisingh-Scheetz et al., 2017).

Sensory Function

A more recent development is the direct measurement of sensory function, which is increasingly recognized as essential to physical and social functioning and as a possible early indicator of neurodegeneration (Correia et al., 2016; Welge-Lüssen, 2009). Deficits in sensory function become common with age and predict disability, cognitive decline (Adams et al., 2017), and mortality (Genther et al., 2014).

The first nationally representative survey to include measures of the five classical senses—vision, taste, touch, smell, and hearing—was NSHAP, which measured all but hearing (assessed by self-report) (McClintock et al., 2016). Hearing has now been successfully measured in ELSA and in HRS.

Blood Spots

Advances in field methods for use in countries that are less developed have been translated successfully to social surveys (Williams and McDade, 2009). The most prominent of these is dried blood spots, which can be collected by field interviewers; dried, stored, and mailed without much difficulty; then assayed for various blood-borne markers of biological function. New assays of dried blood spots continue to come into use, but the most common include hemoglobin, hemoglobin A1c, C-reactive protein, and Epstein-Barr virus, which are markers of blood iron, glucose metabolism, systemic inflammation, and immune function, respectively. Recently, cholesterol and high-density lipoprotein (HDL) have been assayed from dried bloods spots, and genotyping has been successfully accomplished. One substantial drawback of biomarkers collected through dried blood spots is the cost of the assays, which can run to $25 per assay per person, which adds up quickly given the number of markers to be assayed and the number of respondents. Another drawback is the variability across laboratories and between venous blood and dried blood assays of identical samples (Crimmins et al., 2014). Wave 2 of NSHAP collected a microtainer of blood at the same time as the dried blood spots, which permitted assay of a much wider range of biomeasures (O'Doherty et al., 2014). Outside the United States, in developing countries, intravenous blood collection is also common, with a phlebotomist or equivalent personnel conducting the sample collection at home. The experience is positive in general, as health personnel tend to be well received in home visits, which tends to raise the response rates in household surveys on aging (see, for example, Arokiasamy et al., 2012, for India; Zhao et al., 2014, for China; Wong et al., 2017, for Mexico).

Saliva Samples

Easy to collect, with high rates of completion by respondents, saliva samples allow endocrine and cortisol assessment (Kozloski et al., 2014). HRS and WLS have established their genetic repositories based on saliva samples collected via Oragene kits. Such kits stabilize DNA but thereby make samples unusable for other analytes.

Cognitive Function

Cognitive function is among the most important abilities to measure in studies of aging—and the most challenging. It varies across individuals from at least four major sources of variation: innate ability; the impact of formal education and life experience; decline due to "normal" aging; and pathological changes in the brain due to Alzheimer's disease, vascular disease, or other dementing conditions. Some would add *plasticity* to this list: the ability to recover brain function.

Cognition is multidimensional, and age-related changes affect different domains of function differently in different people. In aging studies, the focus has often been on the emergence of dementia because of the magnitude of its impact on individuals, families, and society. Recent estimates suggest nearly half of 65-year-olds will develop dementia in their lifetime, with the other half dying younger due to other conditions. The disease costs about $200 billion per year, about half of which is for paid formal health care and half is the estimated burden on families for unpaid care (Hurd et al., 2013). But dementia is not the only reason to measure cognitive function. Early stages of decline, long before dementia would be diagnosed, can impair judgment and lead to problems managing finances or health care.

The measurement of cognitive abilities comes from two very different scientific disciplines: the clinical neurological approach, which seeks to identify organic brain disease in vivo through performance testing and other observations, and the psychometric approach, which sees cognitive ability measurement as an extension of intelligence measurement. Surveys have tended to draw more on the former, reflecting both the importance attached to dementia and the development of short scales for clinical use.

One of the earliest studies to include a measure of cognition was the National Long Term Care Survey, which used the Pfeiffer short portable mental status questionnaire (Pfeiffer, 1975) and later the Mini-Mental State Examination (MMSE; Folstein et al., 1975). The MMSE has been widely used, but aggressive copyright practices in recent years have made it less appealing to large surveys. The HRS faced a particular challenge in that its design called for a mix of telephone and in-person surveys, requiring it to identify measures that could be administered comparably in both modes. The basis for the HRS measures is the Telephone Interview for Cognitive Status (TICS; Brandt et al., 1988), augmented by a version of the CERAD[5] immediate and delayed word recall tasks.

Most of the longitudinal studies of aging are harmonized with the HRS. The international family of HRS studies has adapted the HRS measures in a variety of ways that, with caution, allow integrated analysis (e.g., Rohwedder and Willis, 2010). WLS is unique in having good measures of cognitive ability in high school paired with harmonized measures at older ages. MIDUS relies primarily on the Brief Test of Adult Cognition by Telephone (Tun and Lachman, 2006), which has similar measures of orientation, word recall, category fluency, and fluid intelligence, along with a measure of processing speed. NHATS uses TICS and word recall measures, with an additional test of executive function that requires in-person administration. NSHAP is the least harmonized of the major NIA-supported studies, relying most on the Montreal Cognitive Assessment, a public-use screening tool for mild cognitive impairment (Nasreddine et al., 2005). In addition to the direct measurement of cognitive abilities, most studies assess difficulty with IADLs, which are tasks affected by cognitive decline.

---

[5]The acronym "CERAD" derives from the Consortium to Establish a Registry for Alzheimer's Disease.

Another critical issue for longitudinal studies of aging is how to maintain participation of persons experiencing cognitive decline. These studies are cognitively demanding. HRS and a number of other studies allow for interviews with proxy respondents when a participant is unwilling. This eliminates what would otherwise be a substantially lower participation rate by the cognitively impaired (Weir et al., 2011). However, it poses a different challenge for the measurement of cognitive status and comparability with direct assessment. HRS relies mainly on proxy-reported IADL difficulties and the IQCODE[6] instrument designed for informant reporting of cognitive status (Jorm, 1994). NHATS uses the AD8, an informant dementia screen that asks about changes in behaviors (Galvin et al., 2005). PSID recently added the AD8 to identify families with an older adult with memory-related behavior issues. Various approaches have been used to combine proxy reports with direct assessments (Crimmins et al., 2011).

Large studies representative of national populations can also serve as sampling frames for more in-depth studies of cognition. HRS did this with its substudy, the Aging, Demographics, and Memory Study (ADAMS; Langa et al., 2005; Plassman et al., 2007). More recently, HRS in conjunction with most of its international sister studies developed a new assessment termed the Harmonized Cognitive Assessment Protocol, a flexible structure harmonized to ADAMS and other major U.S. studies but also to the assessment used in developing countries in the 10/66 studies (Prince et al., 2011) and adaptable to many different national populations.

Other Important Developments in Measurement and Study Design

Genetics

An important area of recent development is genetics, fueled by the improving technology and falling cost of generating statistical data from DNA samples (genotyping). The social sciences were somewhat slow to respond to these opportunities, due in part to the bad reputation of the so-called "eugenics" movement of the early 20th century, which linked most genetic study to the study of racial differences (and the justification of differential treatment and outcomes). Modern human genetics mostly avoids examining differences between races and is highly concerned with eliminating the influence of ethnic (ancestral) differences (population stratification) from inferences about genetic influences (Pritchard and Rosenberg, 1999). Eugenics and related strands of scientific racism derive from a particularly naïve deterministic view about the role of genes. Both biomedical and

---

[6] "IQCODE" stands for Informant Questionnaire on Cognitive Decline in the Elderly (Jorm, 1994).

behavioral scientists have at times been lured by the prospect of single-gene or other simple determinants of complex outcomes; they have been inevitably disappointed by evidence to the contrary. In fact, complex organisms, and human beings in particular, are highly adaptable in the course of an individual life to respond to opportunities and challenges in their environments, including social environments. DNA plays a part in this as well, with some genes regulating the expression of other genes (Boyle et al., 2017). As a result, the genetic associations with outcomes of interest are complex and extremely difficult to infer from even relatively large samples. From stale debates over "nature versus nurture," the field has moved toward increasingly sophisticated models of gene-environment interactions.

The large aging studies have an extremely valuable role to play in the development of good genetic research. Large samples are important, as are good observations on outcomes and on environments that might modify outcomes or the relationship between genetics and outcomes (Boardman et al., 2013). ELSA began providing data on *candidate genes*: a small number of polymorphisms identified in prior research as related to outcomes of interests. In part because early findings often proved spurious in replication and in part because of the complex interactions created by the regulation of gene expression, the field moved toward genome-wide approaches covering millions of polymorphisms (e.g., genome-wide association studies). HRS was the first of the large aging studies to build a large database of genomic data, using saliva samples and a dedicated consent that those samples would be used for genetic research (Weir, 2008). ELSA and WLS followed soon after, using harmonized technology to maximize the potential for joint work. Most studies collect DNA through either saliva samples or blood draws, although dried blood spots have also been used.

A particularly promising approach for bringing genomic science to bear on social and health questions is the use of polygenic scores (Belsky et al., 2013). These involve applying genetic relationships estimated in large, pooled studies to the genetic data on individuals to produce a quantitative estimate of relative risk for an outcome of interest. As these scores depend on the state of scientific knowledge about genetic relationships, they require frequent updating. HRS, ELSA, and WLS have worked together to construct similar polygenic scores. Such scores are particularly useful for studying the interactions of genes and environments because they greatly reduce the dimensionality of the genetic side of the interactions.

Record Linkages

Surveys rely on participants to report on the entire range of objective conditions and subjective perceptions. Aging surveys often also seek retrospective information on life experiences before recruitment. Administrative records can provide valuable supplementary information to augment the scope of survey coverage, improve the accuracy of information, and reduce the burden on respondents and interviewers. Linkages to administrative records can either be direct linkage at the individual level, which generally requires consent of the individual, or indirect linkage through geographic location or some other characteristic. Indirect linkages through geographic areas are a valuable source of information on the social and physical environments in which people live. Both types have implications for the confidentiality of participants, and these implications require careful attention to data security throughout the process of consent, linkage, and data distribution.

For studies of aging and health, the records of the Medicare program are a rich source of individual information on health care use, health conditions and events, and cost. The Centers for Medicare & Medicaid Services (CMS) has an extensive system for managing the research uses of its data. The NIA has supported the development of a private third-party organization to facilitate linkage of data from its surveys to Medicare data. HRS has obtained high rates of consent for linkage to Medicare and high research use of the linked data. The NHATS sample is generated from a Medicare list, greatly facilitating linkage. PSID has also linked to Medicare records. Valuable as they are, Medicare records are not a gold standard that should always override self-reported information (Sakshaug et al., 2014; Wolinsky et al., 2014; St. Clair et al., 2017). A further significant limitation of Medicare records is that managed care systems, which currently cover 20 percent or more of Medicare beneficiaries, do not report individual information comparable to that generated by fee-for-service billing. At present there is also no comparable linkage resource for the population under age 65, and no standardized system of electronic medical records that would permit the study of health and not just health care billing.

The other major federal record system for older populations is the Social Security Administration (SSA). Unlike the CMS, the SSA is not configured for general support of outside research linkages and must determine a specific value and purpose to justify record sharing. This has been done for HRS. The linkage provides information on employment and earnings over the full life course, as well as applications for, and receipt of benefits for, retirement, disability, and supplemental security income. Consent for linkage to SSA is more variable than that for Medicare (Sakshaug et al., 2012). Repeated requests for consent are valuable in improving the overall linkage rate.

Mortality Ascertainment

Mortality ascertainment is critically important to longitudinal studies of aging. Mortality is itself a crucial outcome to assess for evaluating determinants of health and disparities in health. Moreover, failure to accurately capture deaths makes it difficult to properly define the surviving study population at risk for any outcome, including mortality, leading to potentially biased findings. Longitudinal studies have two primary sources for ascertaining vital status: the study's own efforts to recontact respondents (tracking) and linkage or search of vital registration records. The latter, when successful at reasonable cost, can extend the life of a study past its active interviewing phase to follow survival and study mortality differentials long after, as has been done for several studies managed by the National Center for Health Statistics (NCHS)(Office of Analysis and Epidemiology, 2017) . The NCHS also manages the National Death Index (NDI), the only national source of mortality registration. NDI combines death certificate information on dates and causes of death obtained from state vital registration offices, and regulates research access to them.

Weir (2016) evaluated mortality ascertainment in HRS. Mortality rates were statistically identical to national life table rates, for periods and for cohorts. The only exception was the early years of the oldest-old cohorts, who were initially sampled from the community-dwelling population, excluding the higher-mortality nursing home residents. Study tracking and NDI linkage agreed in almost all cases. For continuing panel members, study tracking found slightly more deaths missing in the linkage than vice versa. For study dropouts, linkage is the only source of vital status information after the last contact. Thus, the higher the rate of study attrition, the more important linkage becomes to maintain complete ascertainment.

Outside the United States, opportunities for linkage vary widely. In the United Kingdom, ELSA is linked to the National Health Service Central Register of mortality records. China and Mexico do not have national registration systems that would support a linkage. Europe has a diverse array of record systems and legal restrictions. To date, only Denmark has created a linkage to SHARE participants. Thus, for many studies, imputation of missing vital status will be important. Simple reliance on those with known vital status to do imputation implies assumptions about missing-at-random data that are almost certain to be violated, even with extensive covariate controls. Conversely, using national life table rates as constraints on the overall imputation could add valuable information.

DATA SHARING

The commitment to measurement innovation in the demography of aging has been matched by the commitment to public sharing of data. This runs throughout the range of studies, from HRS, which was designed for the express purpose of creating data for the research community, through to MIDUS and NSHAP, which have had extensive analytic aims as part of their core. Many studies manage their own web-based distribution systems while some use data archives, such as that managed by the Inter-University Consortium for Political and Social Research. All studies must strictly protect respondent confidentiality, which typically involves multiple levels of data release from public access up to restricted access. HRS has recently pioneered the use of remote access through secure encrypted dual-authenticated channels to both protect data on its own servers and expand access to more researchers.

MEASUREMENT ISSUES AND DESIGNS FOR THE FUTURE

As mentioned previously, the future of data collection for demography of aging research is expected to be driven largely by information technology, which implies that this future is highly uncertain. Nevertheless, current developments in approaches allow a glance into the future. Mixed-mode collections are bound to provide the most comprehensive assessments and will continue to be pursued. In the short-to-medium run, the likely mode will be a combination of survey data, data from administrative/medical records, and monitoring data from mobile device applications, to provide a picture more complete than researchers have ever been able to collect from just one or even two of these modes. Survey data will provide individual self-reports, administrative and medical records will provide objective historical measures on individuals, and mobile devices will provide monitoring of individuals' functionality and activities. The personalized medicine movement has emphasized the use of medical records and monitoring devices, combined with genetic and other biomarkers of disease, in order to support the design and implementation of large clinical trials. Data-driven science systems are currently aiming to develop ways to extract insights from data in several forms, similar to data mining. These approaches are supported, again, by technological innovations likely to become more and more common, and the data collection for demographic aging research will benefit in parallel.

The nature of clinical encounters and clinical assessments will drastically change through advances in technology, including mobile sensors, smart voice technology, smart homes, the collection of ambulatory data from the real environment, and the incorporation of these data streams into individuals' electronic medical records. Further, technology will make it easier for older adults to reconnect to resources such as friends, family, caregivers, health care providers, and information that they often struggle to reach due to physical limitations.

There is a long-standing call in the research community for wider coverage of the large cohort studies, expanding their samples to include diverse, minority groups in the population. Future directions in the research of racial/ethnic groups among older adults might include in-depth study of health at older ages among lesbian, gay, bisexual, and transgender individuals. But this may only be possible with the expansion of coverage of the large national studies. The personalized medicine movement is looking to include diverse groups; hence the ability to expand demographic research on aging to these groups will be positioned to benefit as well.

The study of social networks for older adults is bound to benefit from technology developments supporting social media platforms. In this regard, as more data are collected through social media, it will be critical to distinguish between important contacts on these platforms and those that are occasional or irrelevant, which may be difficult to do. Advances in graphical user interfaces can help respondents in identifying and describing their networks. These approaches enable faster, complete data collection and facilitate the measurement of network change. Mobile devices such as cell phones will increasingly provide the opportunity for passive collection of network data and for tracking the movement of respondents. Internet panels such as NORC's AmeriSpeak could be used to collect network data for mapping exchanges across networks, changes in network membership, and different types of networks. Furthermore, new methods and software are being developed for analyzing these types of data, especially changes in egocentric networks over time. These changes will increase the value of network data in panel studies.

Cellular phones, wearable devices with sensors, and cloud clusters will increasingly enhance the ability to gather data, as service providers can leverage the technology and offer users a service such as health monitoring and corresponding health alerts sent to the individual when certain markers reach critical levels. In exchange, there would be consent to continuous data gathering on individuals (Topol, 2010; Schatz, 2016). Participants' health markers (such as heart rate and rhythm, lung function), health activities (such as steps taken, gait speed, swimming laps), locations where activities are conducted in daily life (such as supermarkets, restaurants, pharmacies, and others), and details on networks' size and frequency of contacts are only the beginning of the spectrum of data that can be collected (Van Remoortel et al., 2012). In the future, it will be possible to measure stress and other common markers (Ertin et al., 2011), and mobile devices combined with online applications will be able to apply certain questionnaires periodically to obtain longitudinal assessments of self-reports as well. It will be important to assess the quality of the data gathered, as well as the likelihood that studies using these approaches can represent the overall population, sick and healthy, active and sedentary, and can represent disadvantaged groups and persons who are either unable to, or prefer not to, use these mobile electronic devices.

As a tool for data collection for national populations, telephones seem to offer the current advantage over wearable devices and Internet surveys, as many adults in the developed and developing worlds carry a phone and the simpler phones will soon have the current capabilities of smartphones. While the advantages of collecting massive amounts of data appear to be obvious and the need to monitor their health may be the most compelling reason for individuals to agree and consent to data being collected, the essence of the scheme is monitoring or continuous observation. Data generated by social media, commercial interactions, and other activity not designed for research, which are possible to obtain even now, will only increase as a potential for research use in the future. These modes of data collection bring up the thorny issues of personal privacy and data confidentiality, which will need to be addressed as new information technologies continue to be developed and applied.

There are many foreseeable ways in which the current momentum of progress in data science can directly benefit research in the demography of aging, and the coming decades may see leaps in progress in this regard. Large data analytics will be another future challenge for the scientific community. The previous generation of studies, with the features of data sharing and collaborative multidisciplinary teams, served to prepare the stage for the challenges to come.

REFERENCES

Adams, D.R., Kern, D.W., Wroblewski, K.E., McClintock, M.K., Dale, W., and Pinto, J.M. (2017). Olfactory dysfunction predicts subsequent dementia in older U.S. adults. *Journal of the American Geriatrics Society*. Published online Sept 2017. doi: 10.1111/jgs.15048.

Arokiasamy, P., Bloom, D., Lee, J., Feeney, K., and Ozolins, M. (2012). Longitudinal aging study in India: Vision, design, implementation, and preliminary findings. In National Research Council, *Aging in Asia: Findings from New and Emerging Data Initiatives*. J. Smith and M. Majmundar (Eds.). Washington, DC: The National Academies Press.

Belsky, D.W., Moffitt, T.E., and Caspi, A. (2013). Genetics in population health science: Strategies and opportunities. *American Journal of Public Health, 103*, S73–S83.

Boardman, J.D., Daw, J., and Freese, J. (2013). Defining the environment in gene–environment research: Lessons from social epidemiology. *American Journal of Public Health, 103*, S64–S72.

Börsch-Supan, A., Brandt, M., Hunkler, C., Kneip, T., Korbmacher, J., Malter, F., Schaan, B., Stuck, S., Zuber, S., and the SHARE Central Coordination Team. (2013). Data resource profile: The Survey of Health, Ageing and Retirement in Europe (SHARE). *International Journal of Epidemiology, 42*(4), 992–1001.

Boyle, E.A., Li, Y.I., and Pritchard, J.K. (2017). An expanded view of complex traits: From polygenic to omnigenic. *Cell, 169*, 1177–1186.

Brandt, J., Spencer, M., and Folstein, M. (1988). The telephone interview for cognitive status. *Neuropsychiatry, Neuopsychology, and Behavioral Neurology, 1*, 111–117.

Brim, O.G., Ryff, C.D., and Kessler, R.C. (Eds.). (2004). *How Healthy Are We? A National Study of Well-Being at Midlife*. Chicago, IL: University of Chicago Press.

Capistrant, B.D., Glymour, M.M., and Berkman, L.F. (2014). Assessing mobility difficulties for cross-national comparisons: Results from the World Health Organization Study on Global Ageing and Adult Health. *Journal of the American Geriatric Society, 62*(2), 329–335. doi: 10.1111/jgs.12633.

Case, A., and Deaton, A. (2015). Rising morbidity and mortality in midlife among White non-Hispanic Americans in the 21st century. *Proceedings of the National Academy of Sciences of the United States of America, 112*(49), 15078–15083. doi: 10.1073/pnas.1522239113.

Chen, J.-H., Waite, L., Kurina, L.M., Thisted, R.A., McClintock, M.K., and Lauderdale, D.S. (2015). Insomnia symptoms and actigraph-estimated sleep characteristics in a nationally representative sample of older adults. *Journals of Gerontology, Series A: Biological Sciences and Medical Sciences, 70*(2), 185–192. doi: 10.1093/gerona/glu144.

Cornwell, B. (2015). Social disadvantage and network turnover. *Journals of Gerontology, Series B: Psychological Sciences and Social Sciences, 70*, 132–142. PMCID: PMC4342724.

Cornwell, B., and Laumann, E.O. (2015). The health benefits of network growth: New evidence from a national survey of older adults. *Social Science & Medicine, 125*, 94–106. doi: 10.1016/j.socscimed.2013.09.011.

Cornwell, B., Schumm, L.P., Laumann, E.O., and Graber, J. (2009). Social networks in the NSHAP study: Rationale, measurement, and preliminary findings. *Journals of Gerontology, Series B: Psychological Sciences and Social Sciences, 64B*(Suppl 1), i47–i55. doi: 10.1093/geronb/gbp042.

Correia, C., Lopez, K.J., Wroblewski, K.E., Huisingh-Scheetz, M., Kern, D.W., Chen, R.C., Schumm, L.P., Dale, W., McClintock, M.K., and Pinto, J.M. (2016). Global sensory impairment in older adults in the United States. *Journal of the American Geriatrics Society, 64*(2), 306–313. doi: 10.1111/jgs.139955.

Crimmins, E.M., Kim, J.K., Langa, K.M., and Weir, D.R. (2011). Assessment of cognition using surveys and neuropsychological assessment: The Health and Retirement Study and the Aging, Demographics, and Memory Study. *Journals of Gerontology, Series B: Psychological Sciences and Social Sciences, 66*(Suppl 1), i162–i171. doi: 10.1093/geronb/gbr048.

Crimmins, E., Kim, J.K., McCreath, H., Faul, J., Weir, D., and Seeman, T. (2014). Validation of blood-based assays using dried blood spots for use in large population studies. *Biodemography and Social Biology, 60*(1), 38–48. doi: 10.1080/19485565.2014.901885.

Cronin, H., O'Regan, C., Finucane, C., Kearney, P., and Kenny, R.A. (2013). Health and aging: Development of the Irish Longitudinal Study on Ageing health assessment. *Journal of the American Geriatrics Society, 61*(Suppl 2), S269–S278.

Csikszentmihalyi, M., and Larson, R.W. (1987). Validity and reliability of the experience-sampling method. *Journal of Nervous and Mental Disease, 175*, 526–536.

Dienberg Love, G., Seeman, T.E., Weinstein, M., and Ryff, C.D. (2010). Bioindicators in the MIDUS national study: Protocol, measures, sample, and comparative context. *Journal of Aging and Health, 22*(8), 1059–1080.

Ertin, E., Stohs, N., Kumar, S., Raij, A., Al'Absi, M., Shah, S., Mitra, S., Kwon, T., and Jeong, J.W. (2011). AutoSense: Unobtrusively wearable sensor suite for inferencing of onset, causality, and consequences of stress in the field. *Proceedings of the 9th ACM Conference on Embedded Networked Sensor Systems, SenSys 2011*, 274–287.

Folstein, M.F., Folstein, S.E., and McHugh, P.R. (1975). "Mini mental state": A practical method for grading the cognitive state of patients for the clinician. *Journal of Psychiatric Research, 12*, 189–198.

Freedman, V.A., Kasper, J.D., Cornman, J.C., Agree, E.M., Bandeen-Roche, K., Mor, V., Spillman, B.C., Wallace, R., and Wolf, D.A. (2011). Validation of new measures of disability and functioning in the National Health and Aging Trends Study. *Journals of Gerontology, Series A: Biological Sciences and Medical Sciences, 66A*(9), 1013–1021.

Freedman, V.A., Stafford, F., Schwarz, N., and Conrad, F. (2013). Measuring time use of older couples: Lessons from the Panel Study of Income Dynamics. *Field Methods, 25*(4), 405–422. doi: 10.1177/1525822X12467142.

Freedman, V.A., Carr, D., Cornman, J.C., and Lucas R.E. (2017). Aging, mobility impairments and subjective wellbeing. *Disability and Health Journal, 10*(4), 525–531. doi: 10.1016/j.dhjo.2017.03.011. Epub March, 22, 2017.

Fried, L.P., Tangen, C.M., Walston, J., Newman, A.B., Hirsch, C., Gottdiener, J., Seeman, T., Tracy, R., Kopm, W.J., Burke, G., et al. (2001). Frailty in older adults: Evidence for a phenotype. *Journals of Gerontology, Series A: Biological Sciences and Medical Sciences, 56*(3), M146–M157. doi: 1093/gerona/56.3.M146.

Galinsky, A., and Waite, L.J. (2014). Sexual activity and psychological health as mediators of the relationship between physical health and marital quality. *Journals of Gerontology, Series B: Psychological Sciences and Social Sciences, 69*, 482–492. doi: 10.1093/geronb/gbt165.

Galvin, J.E., Roe, C.M., Powlishta, K.K., Coats, M.A., Muich, S.J., Miller, J.P., Storandt, M., and Morris, J.C. (2005). The AD8: A brief informant interview to detect dementia. *Neurology, 65*(4), 559–564.

Genther, D.J., Betz, J., Pratt, S., Kritchevsky, S.B., Martin, K.R., Harris, T.B., Helzner, E., Satterfield, S., Xue. Q.L., Simonsickm E.M., and Lin, F.R. (2014). Association of hearing impairment and mortality in older adults. *Journals of Gerontology, Series A: Biological Sciences and Medical Sciences, 70*(1), 85–90. doi: 10.1093/Gerona/glu094.

Guralnik, J.M., Simonsick, E.M., Ferrucci L., Glynn, R.J., Berkman, L.F., Blazer, D.G., Sherr, P.A., and Wallace, R.B. (1994). A short physical performance battery assessing lower extremity function: Association with self-reported disability and prediction of mortality and nursing home admission. *Journal of Gerontology: Medical Sciences, 49*, M85–M94.

Harris, K.M. (2013). *The Add Health Study: Design and Accomplishments.* Unpublished manuscript. Chapel Hill, NC: University of North Carolina. Available: http://www.cpc.unc.edu/projects/addhealth/documentation/guides/DesignPaperWIIV.pdf [March 2018].

Hauser, R.M., and Weir, D.R. (2010). Recent developments in longitudinal studies of aging. *Demography, 47*(Suppl), S111–S130.

Herd, P., Carr, D., and Roan, C. (2014). Cohort Profile: Wisconsin Longitudinal Study (WLS). *International Journal of Epidemiology, 43*(1), 34–41.

Huisingh-Scheetz, M., Kocherginsky, M., Schumm, P.L., Engelman, M., McClintock, M.K., Dale, W., Magett, E., Rush, P., and Waite, L. (2014). Geriatric syndromes and functional status in NSHAP: Rationale, measurement, and preliminary findings. *Journals of Gerontology, Series B: Psychological Sciences and Social Sciences, 69*(Suppl 2), S177–S190.

Huisingh-Scheetz, M., Wroblewski, K., Kocherginsky, M., Huang, E., William, D., Waite, L., and Schumm, L.P. (2017). Physical activity and frailty among older adults in the U.S. based on hourly accelerometry data. *Journals of Gerontology, Series A: Biological Sciences and Medical Sciences.* Epub ahead of print, November 2, 2017. doi: 10.1093/Gerona/glx208.

Hurd, M.D., Martorell, P., Delavande, A., Mullen, K.J., and Langa, K.M. (2013). Monetary costs of dementia in the United States. *New England Journal of Medicine, 386*(14), 1326–1334. doi: 10.1056/NEJMsa1204629.

Jorm, A.F. (1994). A short form of the Informant Questionnaire on Cognitive Decline in the Elderly (IQCODE): Development and cross-validation. *Psychological Medicine, 24*, 145–153.

Juster, F.T., and Stafford, F.P. (Eds.). (1985). *Time, Goods, and Well-Being.* Ann Arbor: Institute for Social Research, University of Michigan.

Juster, F.T., and Stafford, F.P. (1991). The allocation of time: Empirical findings, behavioral models, and problems of measurement. *Journal of Economic Literature, 29*, 471–522.

Juster, F.T., and Suzman, R. (1995). An overview of the Health and Retirement Study. *Journal of Human Resources, 30*(Suppl), S7–S56.

Juster, F.T., Ono, H., and Stafford, F.P. (2003). An assessment of alternative measures of time use. *Sociological Methodology, 33*, 19–54.

Kahneman, D., Krueger, A.B., Schkade, D.A., Schwarz, N., and Stone, A.A. (2004). A Survey method for characterizing daily life experience: The Day Reconstruction Method. *Science, 306*, 1776–1780.

Kalton, G. (1985). Sample design issues in time diary studies. In F.T. Juster and F.P. Stafford (Eds.), *Time, Goods, and Well-Being* (pp. 93–112). Ann Arbor: Institute for Social Research, University of Michigan.

Kasper, J.D., and Freedman, V.A. (2014). Findings from the 1st round of the National Health and Aging Trends Study (NHATS): Introduction to a special issue. *Journals of Gerontology, Series B: Psychological Sciences and Social Sciences, 69*(Suppl 1), S1–S7.

Kearney, P.M., Cronin, H., O'regan, C., Kamiya, Y., Savva, G.M., Whelan, B., and Kenny, R. (2011). Cohort profile: The Irish Longitudinal Study on Ageing. *International Journal of Epidemiology, 40*(4), 877–884.

Kim, J., and Waite, L.J. (2014). Relationship quality and shared activity in marital and cohabiting dyads in the National Social Life, Health and Aging Project, wave 2. *Journals of Gerontology, Series B: Psychological Sciences and Social Sciences, 69*(Suppl 2), S64–S74. doi: 10.1093/geronb/gbu038.

Kowal, P., Chatterji, S., Naidoo, N., Biritwum, R., Fan, W., Lopez Ridaura, R., Maximova, T., Arokiasamy, P., Phaswana-Mafuya, N., Williams, S., et al. (2012). Data resource profile: The World Health Organization Study on Global AGEing and Adult Health (SAGE). *International Journal of Epidemiology, 41*(6), 1639–1649.

Kozloski, M., Schumm, L.P., and McClintock, M.K. (2014). The utility and dynamics of salivary sex hormone measurements in the National Social Life, Health, and Aging Project, wave 2. *Journals of Gerontology, Series B: Psychological Sciences and Social Sciences, 69*(Suppl 2), S215–S228. doi: 10.1093/geronb/gbu123.

Langa, K.M., Plassman, B.L., Wallace, R.B., Herzog, A.R., Heeringa, S.G., Ofstedal, M.B., Burke, J.R., Fisher, G.G., Fultz, N.H., Hurd, M.D., et al. (2005). The Aging, Demographics and Memory Study: Study design and methods. *Neuroepidemiology, 25*, 181–191.

Lauderdale, D.S., Schumm, L.P., Kurina, L.M., McClintock, M.K., Thisted, R.A., Chen, J.-H., and Waite, L. (2014). Assessment of sleep in the National Social Life, Health and Aging Project. *Journals of Gerontology, Series B: Psychological Sciences and Social Sciences, 69*(Suppl. 2), S125–S133. doi: 10.1093/geronb/gbu092.

Laumann, E.O., Waite, L.J., and Das, A. (2008). Sexual dysfunction among older adults: Prevalence and risk factors from a nationally representative U.S. probability sample of men and women 57 to 85 years of age. *Journal of Sexual Medicine, 5*(10), 2300–2312.

Lee, D.M., Vanhoutte, B., Nazroo, J., and Pendleton, N. (2016). Sexual health and positive subjective well-being in partnered older men and women. *Journals of Gerontology, Series B: Psychological Sciences and Social Sciences, 71*(4), 698–710. doi: 10.1093/geronb/gbw018.

Lima-Costa, M.F., de Andrade, F.B., de Souza, P.R.B., Neri, A.L., de Oliveira Duarte, Y.A., Castro-Costa, E., and de Oliveira, C. (2018). The Brazilian Longitudinal Study of Aging (ELSI-BRAZIL): Objectives and design. *American Journal of Epidemiology*. In press, January 31, 2018. doi: 10.1093/aje/kwx387.

Lindau, S.T., Schumm, P., Laumann, E.O., Levinson, W., O'Muircheartaigh, C.A., and Waite, L.J. (2007). A national study of sexuality and health among older adults in the U.S. *New England Journal of Medicine, 357*(8), 762–774.

Lucas, R.E., Freedman, V.A., and Carr, D. (2018). *Measuring Experiential Well-Being among Older Adults.* Unpublished manuscript. Available: Open Science Framework, https://osf. io/x9rek/ [March 2018].

Manton, K.G., Corder, L.S., and Stallard, E. (1993). Estimates of change in chronic disability and institutional incidence and prevalence rates in the U.S elderly population from the 1982, 1984, and 1989 National Long Term Care Survey, *Journal of Gerontology, 48*(4), S153–S166. doi: org/10.1093/geronj/48.4.S153.

Martin, L.G., Zimmer, Z., and Lee, J. (2017). Foundations of activity of daily living trajectories of older Americans. *Journals of Gerontology, Series B: Psychological Sciences and Social Sciences, 72*(1), 129–139.

McClintock, M., Dale, W., Laumann, E.O., and Waite, L.J. (2016). Empirical redefinition of comprehensive health and well-being in the older adults in the U.S. *Proceedings of the National Academy of Sciences of the United States of America, 113*(22), E3071–E3080. doi: 10.1073/pnas.1514968113.

McGonagle, K.A., Schoeni, R.F., Sastry, N., and Freedman, V.A. (2012). The Panel Study of Income Dynamics: Overview, recent innovations, and potential for life course research. *Longitudinal and Life Course Studies, 3*(2), 188.

Nasreddine, Z.S., Phillips, N.A., Bedirian, V., Charbonneau, S., Whitehead, V., Collin, I., Cummings, J.L., and Chertkow, H. (2005). The Montreal Cognitive Assessment, MoCA: A brief screening tool for mild cognitive impairment. *Journal of the American Geriatrics Society, 53*, 695–699. doi: 10.1111/j.1532-5415.2005.53221.x.

National Research Council. (2009). *Improving the Measurement of Late-Life Disability in Population Surveys: Beyond ADLs and IADLS: Summary of a Workshop.* Washington, DC: The National Academies Press.

National Research Council. (2012). *Aging in Asia: Findings from New and Emerging Data Initiatives.* J. Smith and M. Majmundar, Eds. Washington, DC: The National Academies Press.

National Research Council. (2013). *Subjective Well-Being: Measuring Happiness, Suffering, and Other Dimensions of Experience.* Washington, DC: The National Academies Press. doi: 10.17226/18548.

O'Doherty, K., Jaszczak, A., Hoffmann, J.N., You, H.M., Kern, D.W., McPhillips, J., Schumm, L.P., Dale, W., Huang, E.S., and McClintock, M.K. (2014). Survey field methods for expanded biospecimen and biomeasure collection in NSHAP wave 2. *Journals of Gerontology, Series B: Psychological Sciences and Social Sciences, 69*(Suppl. 2), S27–S37. doi: 10.1093/geronb/gbu045.

Office of Analysis and Epidemiology. (2017). *The Link age of National Center for Health Statistics Survey Data to the National Death Index—2015 Linked Mortality File (LMF): Methodology Overview and Analytic Considerations* (November 2017). Hyattsville, MD: National Center for Health Statistics. Available: https://www.cdc.gov/nchs/data-linkage/ mortality-methods.htm [April 2018].

Office of the Surgeon General. (2001). *The Surgeon General's Call to Action to Promote Sexual Health and Responsible Sexual Behavior.* Rockville, MD: Office of the Surgeon General.

Park, J.H., Lim, S., Lim, J., Kim, K., Han, M., Yoon, I.Y., Kim, J., Chang, Y., Chang, C.B., Chin, H.J., et al. (2007). An overview of the Korean Longitudinal Study on Health and Aging. *Psychiatry Investigation, 4*(2), 84–95.

Payne, C.F., Gómez-Olivé, F.X., Kahn, K., and Berkman, L. (2017). Physical function in an aging population in rural South Africa: Findings from HAALSI and cross-national comparisons with HRS sister studies. *Journals of Gerontology, Series B: Psychological Sciences and Social Sciences, 72*(4), 665–679. doi: 10.1093/geronb/gbx030.

Pettee Gabriel, K., Sternfeld, B., Colvin, A., Stewart, A., Strotmeyer, E.S., Cauley, J.A., Dugan, S., and Karvonen-Gutierrez, C. (2017). Physical activity trajectories during midlife and subsequent risk of physical functioning decline in late mid-life: The Study of Women's Health Across the Nation (SWAN). *Preventive Medicine, 105*, 287–294. doi: 10.1016/j.ypmed.2017.10.005.

Pfeiffer, E. (1975). A short portable mental status questionnaire for the assessment of organic brain deficit in elderly patients. *Journal of the American Geriatrics Society, 23*(10), 433–441.

Plassman, B., Langa, K., Fisher, G., Heeringa, S., Weir, D., Ofstedal, M.B., Burke, J., Hurd, M., Potter, G., Rodgers, W., et al. (2007). The prevalence of dementia in the United States: The Aging, Demographics, and Memory Study. *Neuroepidemiology, 29*, 125–232.

Prescott, C.A., Achorn, D.L., Kaiser, A., Mitchell, L., McArdle, J.J., and Lapham, S.J. (2013). The Project Talent twin and sibling study. *Twin Research and Human Genetics, 16*(1), 437–448.

Prince, M., Acosta, D., Ferri, C.P., Guerra, M., Huang, Y., Jacob, K.S., Llibre Rodriguez, J.J., Salas, A., Sosa, A.L., Williams, J.D., et al. (2011). A brief dementia screener suitable for use by non-specialists in resource poor settings—The cross-cultural derivation and validation of the brief Community Screening Instrument for Dementia. *International Journal of Geriatric Psychiatry, 26*, 899–907. doi: 10.1002/gps.2622.

Pritchard, J.K., and Rosenberg, N.A. (1999). Use of unlinked genetic markers to detect population stratification in association studies. *American Journal of Human Genetics, 65*, 220–228.

Raina, P.S., Wolfson, C., Kirkland, S.A., Griffith, L.E., Oremus, M., Patterson, C., Tuokko, H., Penning, M., Balion, C.M., Hogan, D., et al. (2009). The Canadian Longitudinal Study on Aging (CLSA). *Canadian Journal on Aging, 28*(3), 221–229.

Rohwedder, S., and Willis R.J. (2010). Mental retirement. *Journal of Economic Perspectives, 24*(1), 119–138.

Sakshaug, J.W., Couper, M.P., Ofstedal, M.B., and Weir, D.R. (2012). Linking survey and administrative records: Mechanisms of consent. *Sociological Methods & Research, 41*(4), 535–569. doi: 10.1177/0049124112460381.

Sakshaug, J.W., Weir, D.R., and Nicholas, L.H. (2014). Identifying diabetics in Medicare claims and survey data: Implications for health services research. *BMC Health Services Research, 14*(1), 1–11.

Schatz, B.R. (2016). National surveys of population health: Big data analytics for mobile health monitors. *Big Data, 3*(4), 219–229. doi: 10.1089/big.2015.0021.

Searle, S.D., Mitnitski, A., Gahbauer, E.A., Gill, T.M., and Rockwood, K. (2008). A standard procedure for creating a frailty index. *BMC Geriatrics, 8*, 24. doi: 10.1186/1471-2318-8-24.

Sonnega, A., Faul, J.D., Ofstedal, M.B., Langa, K.M., Phillips, J.W.R., and Weir, D.R. (2014). Cohort profile: The Health and Retirement Study (HRS). *International Journal of Epidemiology, 43*(2), 576–585. doi: 10.1093/ije/dyu067.

St. Clair, P.A., Gaudette, É., Zhao, H., Tysinger, B., Seyedin, R., and Goldman, D. (2017). Using self-reports or claims to assess disease prevalence: It's complicated. *Medical Care, 55*(8), 782–788.

Steptoe, A., Breeze, E., Banks, J., and Nazroo, J. (2013). Cohort profile: The English Longitudinal Study of Ageing. *International Journal of Epidemiology, 42*(6), 1640–1648.

Suzman, R. (2009). The National Social Life, Health, and Aging Project: An introduction, *Journals of Gerontology, Series B: Psychological Sciences and Social Sciences, 64B*(Suppl. 1), i5–i11. doi: /10.1093/geronb/gbp078.

Topol, E. (2010) Transforming medicine via digital innovation. *Science Translational Medicine, 2*(16), 16cm4. doi: 10.1126/scitranslmed.3000484.

Tun, P.A., and Lachman, M.E. (2006). Telephone assessment of cognitive function in adulthood: The Brief Test of Adult Cognition by Telephone. *Age and Ageing, 35,* 629–632.

Van Remoortel, H., Raste, Y., Louvaris, Z., Giavedoni, S., Burtin, C., Langer, D., Wilson, F., Rabinovich, R., Vogiatzis, I., Hopkinson, N.S., et al. (2012) Validity of six activity monitors in chronic obstructive pulmonary disease: A comparison with indirect calorimetry. *PLoS One, 7*(6), e39198. doi: 10.1371/journal.pone.0039198.

Waite, L.J., Laumann, E.O., Das, A., and Schumm, L.P. (2009). Sexuality: Measures of partnerships, practices, attitudes, and problems in the National Social Life, Health and Aging Study. *Journals of Gerontology, Series B: Psychological Sciences and Social Sciences, 64B*(S1), i56–i66.

Weir, D.R. (2008). Elastic powers: The integration of biomarkers into the Health and Retirement Study. In National Research Council, *Biosocial Surveys: Current Insight and Future Promise* (pp. 78–95). M. Weinstein, J.W. Vaupel, and K Wachter, Eds. Washington, DC: The National Academies Press.

Weir, D.R. (2016). *Validating Mortality Ascertainment in the Health and Retirement Study.* Ann Arbor: Survey Research Center, Institute for Social Research, University of Michigan.

Weir, D.R., Faul, J.D., and Langa, K.M. (2011). Proxy interviews and bias in cognition measures due to non-response in longitudinal studies: A comparison of HRS and ELSA. *Longitudinal and Life Course Studies, 2*(2), 170–184. doi: 10.14301/llcs.v2i2.116.

Welge-Lüssen, A. (2009). Ageing, neurodegeneration, and olfactory and gustatory loss. *B-ENT, 5*(Suppl 13), 129–132.

Williams, S.R., and McDade, T.W. (2009). The use of dried blood spot sampling in the National Social Life, Health, and Aging Project. *Journals of Gerontology, Series B: Psychological Sciences and Social Sciences, 64B*(Suppl 1), i131–i136. doi: 10.1093/geronb/gbn022. .

Wolinsky, F.D., Jones, M.P., Ullrich, F., Lou, Y., and Wehby, G.L. (2014). The concordance of survey reports and Medicare claims in a nationally representative longitudinal cohort of older adults. *Medical Care, 52*(5), 462–468.

Wong, R., Michaels-Obregon, A., and Palloni, A. (2017). Cohort profile: The Mexican Health and Aging Study (MHAS). *International Journal of Epidemiology, 46*(2), e2.

Zhao, Y., Hu, Y., Smith, J.P., Strauss, J., and Yang, G. (2014). Cohort profile: The China Health and Retirement Longitudinal Study (CHARLS). *International Journal of Epidemiology, 43*(1), 61–68.